mylabschool
Where the classroom comes to life!

From watching actual classroom video footage of teachers and students interacting to building standards-based lessons and web-based portfolios . . . from a robust resource library of the "What Every Teacher Should Know About" series to complete instruction on writing an effective research paper . . . **MyLabSchool** brings together an amazing collection of resources for future teachers. This website gives you a wealth of videos, print and simulated cases, career advice, and much more.

Use **MyLabSchool** with this Allyn and Bacon Education text, and you will have everything you need to succeed in your course. Assignment IDs have also been incorporated into many Allyn and Bacon Education texts to link to the online material in **MyLabSchool** . . . connecting the teachers of tomorrow to the information they need today.

 PEARSON

VISIT www.mylabschool.com **to learn more about this invaluable resource and Take a Tour!**

Here's what you'll find in mylabschool
Where the classroom comes to life!

VideoLab ►

Access hundreds of video clips of actual classroom situations from a variety of grade levels and school settings. These 3- to 5-minute closed-captioned video clips illustrate real teacher–student interaction, and are organized both topically *and* by discipline. Students can test their knowledge of classroom concepts with integrated observation questions.

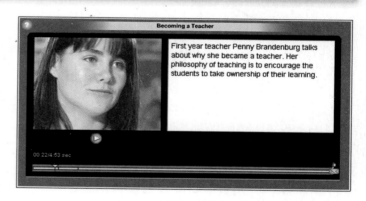

Becoming a Teacher

First year teacher Penny Brandenburg talks about why she became a teacher. Her philosophy of teaching is to encourage the students to take ownership of their learning.

00 22/4.63 sec

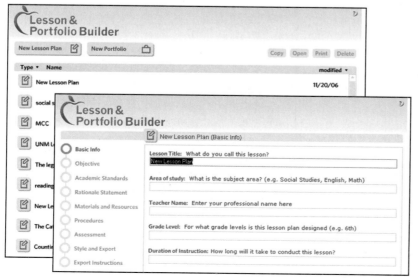

◄ Lesson & Portfolio Builder

This feature enables students to create, maintain, update, and share online portfolios and standards-based lesson plans. The Lesson Planner walks students, step-by-step, through the process of creating a complete lesson plan, including verifiable objectives, assessments, and related state standards. Upon completion, the lesson plan can be printed, saved, e-mailed, or uploaded to a website.

Here's what you'll find in mylabschool

Where the classroom comes to life!

Simulations ▶

This area of MyLabSchool contains interactive tools designed to better prepare future teachers to provide an appropriate education to students with special needs. To achieve this goal, the IRIS (IDEA and Research for Inclusive Settings) Center at Vanderbilt University has created course enhancement materials. These resources include online interactive modules, case study units, information briefs, student activities, an online dictionary, and a searchable directory of disability-related web sites.

◀ Resource Library

MyLabSchool includes a collection of PDF files on crucial and timely topics within education. Each topic is applicable to any education class, and these documents are ideal resources to prepare students for the challenges they will face in the classroom. This resource can be used to reinforce a central topic of the course, or to enhance coverage of a topic you need to explore in more depth.

Research Navigator ▶

This comprehensive research tool gives users access to four exclusive databases of authoritative and reliable source material. It offers a comprehensive, step-by-step walk-through of the research process. In addition, students can view sample research papers and consult guidelines on how to prepare endnotes and bibliographies. The latest release also features a new bibliography-maker program—AutoCite.

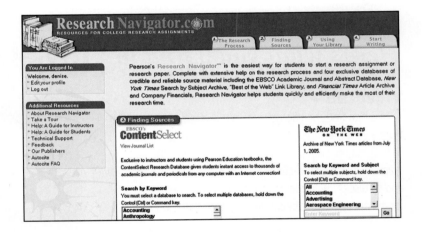

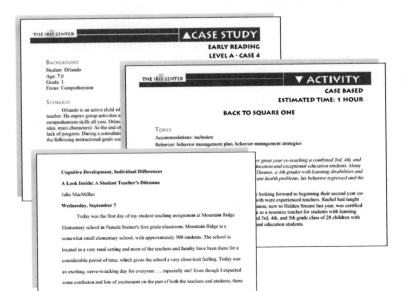

◀ Case Archive

This collection of print and simulated cases can be easily accessed by topic and subject area, and can be integrated into your course. The cases are drawn from Allyn & Bacon's best-selling books, and represent the complete range of disciplines and student ages. It's an ideal way to consider and react to real classroom scenarios. The possibilities for using these high-quality cases within the course are endless.

THIRD EDITION

Teaching and Learning with Technology

Judy Lever-Duffy, Ed.D.
Miami Dade College

Jean B. McDonald, Ed.D.
Lambuth University

Contributing Authors

Ana A. Ciereszko, Ed.D.
Miami Dade College

Al P. Mizell, Ed.D.
Nova Southeastern University

PEARSON

Boston   New York   San Francisco
Mexico City   Montreal   Toronto   London   Madrid   Munich   Paris
Hong Kong   Singapore   Tokyo   Sydney

Senior Editor: Arnis E. Burvikovs
Editorial Assistant: Erin Reilly
Development Editor: Shannon Steed
Marketing Manager: Erica DeLuca
Production Editor: Gregory Erb
Editorial Production Service: Nesbitt Graphics, Inc.
Composition Buyer: Linda Cox
Manufacturing Buyer: Megan Cochran
Electronic Composition: Nesbitt Graphics, Inc.
Interior Design: Carol Somberg
Photo Researcher: PoYee Oster
Cover Designer: Joel Gendron

For related titles and support materials, visit our online catalog at www.ablongman.com.

Between the time web site information is gathered and then published, it is not unusual for
some sites to have closed. Also, the transcription of URLs can result in typographical errors.
The publisher would appreciate notification where these errors occur so that they may be corrected in subsequent editions.

Library of Congress Cataloging-in-Publication Data

Lever-Duffy, Judy.
  Teaching and learning with technology / Judy Lever-Duffy, Jean B.
McDonald. -- 3rd ed.
    p. cm.
  Includes bibliographical references and index.
  ISBN 0-205-51191-0
  1. Educational technology. 2. Computer-assisted instruction. 3. Computer
network resources. 4. Audio-visual materials. I. McDonald, Jean B. II. Title.

LB1028.3.L49 2008
371.33'4--dc22
                                        2007000075

Printed in the United States of America
10 9 8 7 6 5 4 3 2 1   RRD-OH   11   10   09   08   07

Credits appear on page 485, which constitutes an extension of the copyright page.

About the Authors

Dr. Judy Lever-Duffy, Professor of Computer Science and Education at Miami Dade College, Miami, Florida, teaches computer and education courses on campus and in MDC's Virtual College. She holds a B.A. degree in Education from Florida Atlantic University, Boca Raton, Florida, and an M.S. in Computer Studies and Ed.D. in School Management and Instructional Leadership from Nova Southeastern University, Ft. Lauderdale, Florida. Dr. Lever-Duffy enjoys teaching, writing, traveling, and living in the Florida Keys.

Dr. Jean B. McDonald, Associate Professor of Education at Lambuth University, Jackson, Tennessee, teaches educational technology and methods courses for middle school and high school pre-service teachers. She holds a B.S. degree in English and an M.A. in English from Bradley University, Peoria, Illinois, and an Ed.D. from the University of Memphis, Memphis, Tennessee. Dr. McDonald enjoys international travel, reading, and classical music.

BRIEF CONTENTS

CONTENTS

PART TWO   Applying Technologies for Effective Instruction   87

chapter 3
Computers in the Learning Environment   88

chapter 4
Digital Technologies in the Classroom   132

chapter 5
Administrative Software   164

chapter 6
Academic Software   206

chapter 7
The Internet and the World Wide Web   246

chapter 8
Using the Web for Teaching and Learning   280

chapter 9
Audiovisual Technologies
314

PART THREE Technology in Schools: Changing Teaching and Learning   359

chapter 10
Distance Education: Using Technology to Redefine the Classroom   360

chapter 11
Issues in Implementing Technology in Schools   396

chapter 12
Technology, Teaching, and You   432

WEB Resources

PODCAST

Administrative Tools   195

VIDEO

Tools for Tracking Students   168
Using PowerPoint   189
Classroom Management Software   194
Digital Portfolios   197

chapter 6: Academic Software   206

E-Learning

ON THE WEB

www.mylabschool.com

SKILLS BUILDER

PODCAST

Selecting Software   239

VIDEO

chapter 7: The Internet and the World Wide Web   246

E-Learning

ON THE WEB

www.mylabschool.com

SKILLS BUILDER

PODCAST

The Web and the Classroom   270

chapter 8: Using the Web for Teaching and Learning   280

E-Learning

chapter 9: Audiovisual Technologies   314

E-Learning

chapter 10: Distance Education: Using Technology to Redefine the Classroom   360

E-Learning

chapter 11: Issues in Implementing Technology in Schools   396

E-Learning

ON THE WEB

www.mylabschool.com

PODCAST

VIDEO

chapter 12: Technology, Teaching, and You   432

E-Learning

ON THE WEB

www.mylabschool.com

PODCAST

VIDEO

PREFACE

Introduction

Educational technology can enrich and enhance instructional experiences for both the teacher and the learner. *Teaching and Learning with Technology* explains, on many levels, how educational technology can provide resources for teachers and students and open the door to more comprehensive learning as well as extend the learning process.

The power of the Internet can put the world body of knowledge quite literally at one's fingertips. A computer in a classroom can be an endlessly patient and positive tutor. An audio recording of a children's story can encourage the development of good listening skills and meet the needs of auditory learners, and a nature video can bring the most remote corner of the world into the classroom. These technologies, from traditional audiovisual technologies to the newest digital technologies, provide powerful tools for creative teachers and support diverse learners.

However, educational technology remains underutilized in many classrooms. Too often teachers have not learned how to work effectively with educational technologies in teaching and learning. Current and future teachers need exposure to and experience with the many and growing number of technologies that exist in schools and that schools are likely to acquire. Teachers also need a basic understanding of the technologies themselves—they need hands-on practice with them, and they need to explore how the technologies fit into the teaching and learning process.

In response to these needs, courses in educational technology are becoming a critical part of teacher preparation programs across the country. Some are computer courses adapted for educators. Others are focused on the historical and theoretical aspects of educational technology. Each approach has merit, but perhaps the most effective and pragmatic solution is a balance that includes components of both. To find the points at which these approaches intersect has been challenging. This text is a result of that challenge.

Organization of This Text

Teaching and Learning with Technology was designed to combine theoretical, technical, and experiential components into a single pragmatic approach suitable for current and future teachers using educational technology in the classroom.

In creating the text, we followed three basic principles:

1. Ground the study of educational technologies in effective teaching and learning and in the real-world classroom;
2. Explore all technologies likely to be found in the classroom; and
3. Offer pragmatic tools and activities throughout the text that prepare students to effectively use educational technology.

We present technology throughout this text within the framework of education and from a classroom perspective. We follow our principles in three parts. **Part One** provides an overview of learning theories and instructional design, maintaining a focus on teaching and learning as the force that drives the selection and implementation of technology.

In **Part Two,** we thoroughly study the major categories of educational technologies likely to be found in schools, from traditional audiovisual technologies to the current and emerging digital technologies. These technologies are examined both as objects of instruction to be mastered by technology-literate educators and, more importantly, as tools within the broader framework of teaching and learning.

As an outgrowth of this technological exploration, we then present distance learning as an instructional model in **Part Three.** We examine these approaches both as professional development tools and as delivery systems that have the potential to redefine the classroom. This part also offers an in-depth consideration of the issues associated with implementing technologies in education, including the teacher's role in strategic planning for technology and the ethical, legal, and social issues resulting from its implementation. The final chapter focuses on the role of technology in the education profession, from its incorporation into standards to its impact on training. Together these topics converge to provide a powerful and complete experience for those who must soon face the challenges of the effective application of technology to their own classrooms and in their schools.

Features of the Text

In this third edition, chapter features have been enhanced, expanded, and revised. Some of our new, enhanced features reinforce and expand the content, while others offer hands-on problem solving both on a computer and in cooperative learning groups.

Real People, Real Stories, at the beginning of each chapter, initiates the discussion of the educational technology addressed in the chapter with an exemplary case, interview, or personal story by an in-service teacher. ▶

◀ **In the Classroom** stories throughout the text demonstrate real-world implementation of various technologies in a variety of content areas by highlighting particular teachers and their lessons.

Cool Tools highlights particularly useful technology tools for educators. ▶

◀ **You Decide!** offers a deeper examination of critical issues related to using or implementing technology. This feature presents contrasting opinions on important technological issues in education.

Topical notations in the margin reference key points in adjacent paragraphs to assist students in recognizing and finding significant content.

E-Learning Icons in the margin direct students to the companion web site and MyLabSchool, where text content is expanded in online activities that deepen understanding of the concepts presented through individual and group discovery and exploration of related web sites.

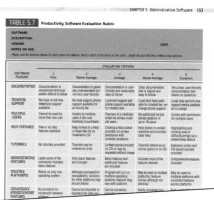

◀ **Rubrics** offer students pragmatic tools and myriad opportunities to evaluate and study technologies throughout the text. They are also available for download from the companion web site.

(continued)

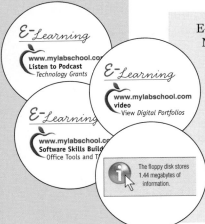

E-Learning icons also direct students to view videos and listen to podcasts on MyLabSchool. Additionally, E-Learning icons point students to Software Skills Builders exercises included on MyLabSchool (www.mylabschool.com). These activities include step-by-step, hands-on exercises for Microsoft Office basic skills in Word, Excel, Access, Publisher, and Explorer; for Inspiration and Kidspiration; and for HyperStudio. Many of these Software Skills Builders are offered in both PC and Macintosh versions. Icons direct students to a collection of Hardware Skills Builder. These multimedia activities teach hardware basics such as going inside a PC, using a digital camera, and using optical discs. Hardware Skills Builders activities culminate in a hardware review assessment activity.

Information icons draw student's attention to key points that are discussed in detail in the adjacent text.

Student Activities at the end of every chapter offer various exercises, from chapter review questions to group activities to discussion topics.

Illustrations include screen grabs, figures, flow and process charts, and both historic and up-to-date photographs of equipment and classroom uses of technology. These illustrations present content visually to assist students in achieving competencies.

Interchapters focus on special topics in educational technology that expand on the content in the chapters they follow. Interchapters can be found following every chapter and include topics such as the evolution of technology in instruction, writing grants to fund technology purchases, creating a class web site, copyright and fair use, and strategic planning for technology. ▼

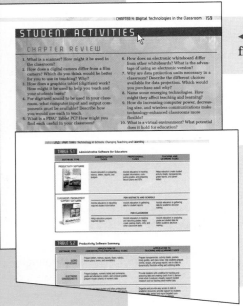

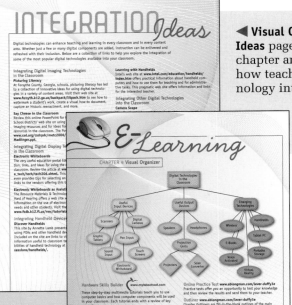

Visual Organizer and Integration Ideas pages near the end of every chapter are presented to explore how teachers can integrate technology into their classrooms and to provide a visual summary of key chapter concepts.

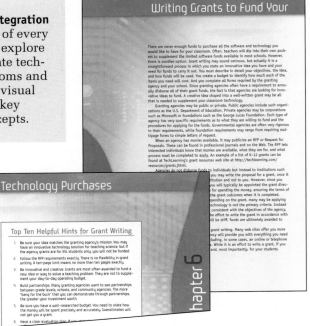

Using a Pragmatic Approach

A constant aspect of our pragmatic approach in *Teaching and Learning with Technology* is the reader-friendly style of the text. In order to maintain interest and readability in a content area that tends toward jargon and technical detail, we deliberately engage students with a conversational tone and easy-to-use definitions and tools. Together, these elements present the complexities of educational technology in the most readable and engaging format possible.

Teaching and Learning with Technology provides current and future educators with a pragmatic survey of educational technology and an exploration of the applications and issues related to its use. This approach and style present key technological content while remaining well grounded in the theoretical foundations of teaching and learning.

 # Supplements for Students

Skills Builders on MyLabSchool

Available free with every new text are Skills Builders on MyLabSchool (www.mylabschool.com) that include fully illustrated step-by-step, hands-on exercises that develop proficiency with Microsoft Office and hardware basics. Software Skills Builders are included for Word, Excel, Access, Publisher, Explorer, Inspiration and Kidspiration, and HyperStudio, many in both PC and Macintosh versions. Hardware Skills Builders are multimedia activities that teach basics such as going inside a PC, using a digital camera, and using optical discs.

Companion Web Site

Students using this text can take advantage of a robust, interactive companion web site that expands the learning opportunities beyond the printed text. Visit www.ablongman.com/lever-duffy3e. This student site includes:

- **Chapter Outliners** to help students organize their reading and aid in studying chapter content.
- **Online Practice Tests** to reinforce chapter content.
- **Chapter Downloads** that let students download preformatted files and all chapter rubrics to help them with lesson planning and other chapter activities.
- **Power Practice Reviews,** created using Microsoft PowerPoint™, to further exercise content knowledge as well as to demonstrate educational applications of the software.
- **Links of Interest** that provide students with suggestions for further resources and readings on chapter topics.
- **On the Web!** activities, mentioned in the margin of the textbook, offer indepth experiences in the topics and content presented.
- **Downloadable Templates and Rubrics** including planning forms and rubric tables to use when creating lessons and evaluating technology.
- **Integration Ideas** annotated links to articles and innovative technology integration ideas across content areas.
- **Virtual Suggestion Box** to communicate student feedback on the text, resource materials, and web site so that they can be more closely adapted to student needs.

Learning Guide

The Learning Guide allows students hands-on practice and practical application of what they have learned in the text through a mix of activities ranging from puzzles to projects. The Learning Guide contains the following sections for every chapter: project activities, video review guides, puzzles, and reflection questions. Field work projects, problem-based learning projects, and a course pre-test and post-test are included as well.

mylabschool
Where the classroom comes to life!

Discover where the classroom comes to life! *Teaching and Learning with Technology* includes access to a text-specific version of Allyn & Bacon's MyLabSchool, a collection of online tools designed to help prepare students for success in this course, in licensure exams, as well as in their teaching careers. Visit www.mylabschool.com to access the following:

- An **E-book** of *Teaching and Learning with Technology* with integrated chapter pre- and post-tests that generate individualized study plans to identify areas of weakness and strength and thus help students focus their attention and efforts where they're needed most.
- **Podcasts** address key educational technology topics that expand on the text content in an audio format. Podcasts cover a broad range of current topics including, "How to Buy a Computer," "Using Technology to Meet Student Needs," and "Grant Writing." Podcasts range from 15–30 minutes and can be downloaded to computers or iPods.
- **Skills Builders** exercises develop proficiency with Microsoft Office and hardware basics. Software Skills Builders are included for Word, Excel, Access, Publisher, Explorer, Inspiration and Kidspiration, and HyperStudio, many in both PC and Macintosh versions. Hardware Skills Builders are multimedia activities that teach basics such as going inside a PC, using a digital camera, and using optical discs.
- **Video footage** of real-life classrooms, with opportunities for students to reflect on the videos and offer their own thoughts and suggestions for applying theory to practice. More than seven hours of new video illustrating the use of technology in the K-16 classroom has been added and integrated into this text.
- **Video Review Guides** provide questions to accompany the chapter videos and help tie the video clips to the topics discussed in the text.
- Help with research papers using **Research Navigator™**, which provides access to four exclusive databases of credible and reliable source material, including EBSCO's ContentSelect academic journal database, the *New York Times* On The Web subject archive, the "Best of the Web" Link Library, and FT.com business archive.
- An extensive archive of **text and multimedia cases** that provide valuable perspectives on real classrooms and real teaching challenges.
- **Careers** offers resources for Praxis exams and licensure preparation, professional portfolio development, job searches, and interview techniques.

Supplements for Faculty

Instructor's CD-ROM

The CD-ROM includes:

- **PowerPoint™ Presentations** for each chapter that present key chapter points.
- **Classroom Activities Ideas** for each chapter to help in presenting chapter content.
- **Evaluation Suggestions** that provide alternative evaluation strategies for determining mastery of chapter concepts.
- **Supplemental Readings** on content areas presented in each chapter should faculty desire to further explore the content presented.
- **Figures and Graphics** of key illustrations in the chapter that can be downloaded and used in the preparation of custom teaching materials.
- **Additional Research** in the form of annotated references presenting current research related to each chapter's content.
- **Audiovisual Supports,** a list of audiovisual materials that can enhance presentation of the chapter topics, and the sources from which they can be ordered.
- **Downloadable Files,** offered in Microsoft Word format, so that resources available on CD and on the student site can be downloaded and customized to your course.
- **Web Sites of Interest,** annotated URLs of web sites that may be useful in teaching chapter topics.

- **Test Bank** with over 1,000 multiple choice, short answer, and matching questions.
- **Answer Keys to Chapter Review Questions,** to assist in responding to student questions.
- **Answer Keys to Chapter Puzzlers** to assist students in solving chapter crosswords and word searches.
- **Answer Keys** to Video Reviews, Pre/Post Tests in the Learning Guide.
- **PBL Scenario Solutions,** which include key points for assessment and evaluation of student resolution of scenarios.
- **Links to Student Resources** to facilitate exploring the components of the student web site that you may wish to include in your course.
- A **Virtual Suggestion Box** to communicate your feedback on the text, resource materials, and web site so that they can be more closely adapted to your needs.

Instructor's Resource Manual and Test Bank

The Instructor's Resource Manual offers a printed selection from the Instructor's CD and includes a wealth of interesting ideas and activities designed to help instructors teach the course. Each chapter includes chapter objectives, classroom activities, evaluation suggestions, supplemental readings, additional research, audiovisual resources, web sites, answer keys to chapter review questions, and answer keys to chapter puzzlers. There is also a test bank for each chapter. (Available for download from the Instructor Resource Center at www.ablongman.com/irc.)

Computerized Test Bank

The printed Test Bank is also available electronically through the Allyn & Bacon computerized testing system, TestGenEQ. Instructors can use TestGenEQ to create exams in just minutes by selecting from the existing database of questions, editing questions, and/or writing original questions. (Please request this item from your local Allyn & Bacon sales representative; also available for download from the Instructor Resource Center at www.ablongman.com/irc.)

PowerPoint™ Presentations

Ideal for lecture presentations or student handouts, the PowerPoint™ Presentation created for this text provides dozens of ready-to-use graphics and text images. (Available for download from the Instructor Resource Center at www.ablongman.com/irc.)

The authors of this text empathize with and understand the challenge of teaching and learning about how best to use our ever-changing technology resources to help people learn. With so many technological resources changing so quickly and so many diverse pressures affecting teachers and schools, it is difficult to determine what needs to be included in a first course in educational technology. In preparing this text for your use, we have used as our barometer the ongoing question, "What do teachers really need to know about this technology to help them use it effectively in teaching and learning?" The result of our continuous response to this question is this text, which we hope will offer you an inclusive, focused, and practical survey of educational technology.

With this third edition, we have tried to streamline content while updating the text to reflect the latest technologies currently available and on the horizon. With support from the resources in MyLabSchool, the Learning Guide, and with a robust instructor CD-ROM and student companion web site, we hope we have provided both faculty and students with an abundance of useful and practical tools with which to teach and learn about technologies for education. With the electronic Instructor's Resource Manual, test-generator software, and PowerPoint™ Presentation, we hope we have offered to our colleagues the full array of tools they might require when teaching this course. However, we know we can always do more for both the faculty and students using this text. We encourage both faculty adopting this text and students using it to share with us your thoughts about whatever further might be done to make this text, MyLabSchool, and our web site more useful to you. We look forward to hearing from you!

Acknowledgments

When we created the first edition of our text, we discovered how essential the help, encouragement, and support of those with whom we live and with whom we work are. It was a critical component of our very successful first edition, and we continue to be very grateful to all. As we prepared this third, greatly improved edition, we found the support of our families and colleagues to be critical once again. First, we would like to thank our families for their continued encouragement and for their patience and tolerance of the time spent away from them during the creation of this edition. Special thanks to Judy's son, Jonathan Lever; mom, Ena Schwartz; and late husband, Mike Duffy, for the continued confidence and encouraging words that helped keep her going through another edition; and to Jean's sons and daughters-in-law, Mike and Mary and Tom and Jenny; to her daughter, Melany; and to her son, Mark, and his friend, Lori; as well as to Jean's grandchildren.

And at Allyn and Bacon, we gratefully acknowledge the patience, hard work, creativity, and support of all those known and unknown to us who made our third edition a reality. Special thanks to Arnie Burvikovs, senior editor, for his tireless encouragement, support, and advice and for championing our cause time and again, which ultimately added many new features; to Shannon Steed, development editor, who shepherded this edition to completion with infinite care and patience to our production team. We thank Greg Erb, production editor; Carol Somberg, text designer; and PoYee Oster, photo researcher, who together made this edition better than we had hoped; to Barbara Strickland for a tremendous job coordinating the many supplemental materials that enrich this text, and to the Allyn and Bacon Media Production staff for their fantastic work on the web site. We also thank Nesbitt Graphics including Jude Bucci and especially Susan McNally whose patience and artful requests made the process flow.

We also gratefully acknowledge the many reviewers of this edition including Sandra Leslie, Belmont Abbey College; Cynthia Rich, Eastern Illinois University; Donna Kitchens, University of Wisconsin, Stevens Point; Rick Richards, St. Petersburg College; Denis Hlynka, University of Manitoba; Temba Bassoppo-Moyo, Illinois State University; Tanaka Gaines, San Francisco State University; Locord D. Wilson, Jackson State University; and Craig Kami, Western Michigan University. Their suggestions and comments helped us to improve and refine this text and make it a more meaningful instructional support.

And finally, thanks to our many colleagues who offered up suggestions, advice, and support. At Miami-Dade College, we offer special thanks to Judy's Homestead Campus colleagues, all of whom offered continuous encouragement and support; to Judy's technowizard nephew, Rob Schwartz, who made our web site, Skills Builders, and Podcasts a reality; to Al Mizell and Ana Ciereszko for their valuable contributions and unwavering support; and to Shawn Bingham who has offered up valuable additions even when asked too late to do too much.

At Lambuth University, a sincere expression of gratitude to Charles Young, Manager of Computer Support; Sammy Chapman, Assistant Professor of Library Science and Reference Librarian; and Jan Kelley, Administrative Assistant for the Education Department, for the advice and assistance they unfailingly and competently have given Jean.

Thank you all. Surely, this new, very improved edition could not have come into existence without you!

Judy Lever-Duffy
(judy.leverduffy@mdc.edu)
Jean B. McDonald
(mcdonald@lambuth.edu)

PART ONE

Technologies for Teaching and Learning

All too often, those who begin the study of educational technology expect to spend all their time learning how to use a computer and perhaps some of the other equipment available in a typical classroom. After all, isn't a course on educational technology (and its textbook) supposed to focus on the technology—the audiovisual and electronic equipment—that helps teachers teach and students learn?

The equipment is a primary concern, of course. However, equipment is simply a tool. It extends the reach of the teacher and of the learner. We can do more, and we can do it better, by using these tools—if we use them at the right time, in the right way, and for the right purpose. You can expect this text to help you explore, with great enthusiasm, the many kinds of materials and equipment that can be used to support teaching and learning. But you can also expect this text to encourage you to conduct this exploration from the perspective of, and with emphasis on, the educational processes these technologies serve.

Educators who want to understand how to use technology effectively in instruction must do so within the context of sound educational theory and practice. What is the point of knowing what a technology can do if you aren't sure where and how to use it to help teach a lesson or support a learner?

The chapters in Part One review the teaching and learning process itself, from its theory to its application. In Chapter 1, you will explore learning and the factors that help or hinder communication between teacher and learner. In Chapter 2, you will explore the process of designing effective instruction and the development and implementation of an instructional planning system that you can use when teaching. These chapters will help you build the educational framework you need as you begin your exploration of educational technologies. Without this framework, you would be learning only about how a variety of equipment works. With this framework, you will understand when, where, and why to use this equipment to help you teach and your students learn. This broader understanding is the goal of this text and the purpose for taking a course in educational technology.

chapter 1
Theoretical foundations

This chapter addresses these ISTE *National Educational Technology Standards* for Teachers:

II. PLANNING AND DESIGNING LEARNING ENVIRONMENTS AND EXPERIENCES

Teachers plan and design effective learning environments and experiences supported by technology. Teachers

A. design developmentally appropriate learning opportunities that apply technology-enhanced instructional strategies to support the diverse needs of learners.

B. apply current research on teaching and learning with technology when planning learning environments and experiences.

C. identify and locate technology resources and evaluate them for accuracy and suitability.

D. plan for the management of technology resources within the context of learning activities.

E. plan strategies to manage student learning in a technology-enhanced environment.

III. TEACHING, LEARNING, AND THE CURRICULUM

Teachers implement curriculum plans that include methods and strategies for applying technology to maximize student learning. Teachers

A. facilitate technology-enhanced experiences that address content standards and student technology standards.

B. use technology to support learner-centered strategies that address the diverse needs of students.

C. apply technology to develop students' higher-order skills and creativity.

D. manage student learning activities in a technology-enhanced environment.

To understand the role of educational technology in the teaching and learning process, it's best to begin with a solid understanding of what teaching and learning really are. To be effectively used, educational technology should not be segregated from the teaching and learning that it supports. It is therefore critical to begin our examination of educational technology with a closer look at the teaching and learning process and technology's role in that process.

This chapter will help you develop the conceptual groundwork for the remaining chapters in this text. In Chapter 1, you will

- Examine differing views of educational technology
- Explore learning within the framework of communication
- Review key learning theories
- Examine the learner characteristics that affect learning
- Investigate teaching styles and their impact on learning
- Explore teaching, learning, and technology from a holistic view
- Briefly review educational technology within a historical perspective
- Synthesize your own view of the relationships among teaching, learning, and technology

CHAPTER OUTLINE

- Real People, Real Stories
- What Is Educational Technology?
- Why Study Educational Technology?
- Teaching and Learning: A Closer Look at the Instructional Event
- Perspectives on Learning
- A View of the Learner
- A View of the Teacher
- Toward a Holistic View of Teaching, Learning, and Technology
- Teaching, Learning, and Educational Technology: A Personal Synthesis

Real People
Real Stories

Meet Sandra Burvikovs. A growing challenge in education is to find a way to meet the needs of a wide variety of youngsters in overcrowded schools with limited resources and expertise. Teachers have heard that they need to find ways to reach students with differing ways of cognitive processing, including different learning and cognitive styles and multiple intelligences.

We all share in this challenge in large or small ways. It is of concern to all of us. In all classrooms, the same challenges exist—too many students with too many different learning needs for the teacher to address without help. *Without help:* that is the key part of the challenge. But technology can help.

The purpose of this text is to share that insight with you and to help you find ways to use technology to solve the problems you do or will face. To assist in this process, we have asked practicing educators to share some of their experiences with you.

We are pleased to introduce Sandra Burvikovs, a teacher of gifted students in a crowded elementary school in Illinois. Sandra tells about the challenges of meeting the diverse needs of her students and how she used technology to help her succeed.

I teach a gifted education pilot program for grades 3–5 replacement classes. My school, May Whitney Elementary, is located in the center of Lake Zurich, Illinois; it is one of the oldest elementary schools in the district and has a very diverse student population. The school has approximately 500 students, significantly over its capacity. I taught my groups in the hallway for three months and then was moved to the stage in the gym because there were no other locations available. The district was in the process of building a new elementary school to accommodate the increased enrollment. Regardless of the overcrowding while we waited for our new school, the staff and administration at the school were very dedicated, innovative, and committed to providing students with a positive learning experience

About 7 percent of the students in the Lake Zurich Elementary School District take part in the district's gifted education programs. As the teacher of the gifted pullout program, I met with my students for two hours per week, with classes varying in size from seven to eighteen students. These students displayed a wide range of strengths, weaknesses, and individual learning styles. I met with my groups on the gym stage; my classroom equipment consisted of two large tables, chairs, a metal storage cabinet, an old TV and VCR, and a filmstrip projector. This is not what the parents expected from the program. I knew that I had to find a way to accommodate the large variety of learning styles and still meet all of the learning objectives for these students in spite of the teaching location or the difficulties involved in finding ways to meet their unique needs.

The district had just purchased a computer cart with laptop computers and wireless Internet connections. One of the curricular goals for this group of students was to complete a long-term project. I knew that, no matter where I taught, my students' parents had very high expectations about the quality of the long-term project. All the projects were to be displayed at a district-wide fair. I knew I had to find a way to use technology to change my teaching and to better meet students' individual learning needs.

I believed I could use technology to meet my students' individual learning needs and thus better help them meet their learning objectives. Therefore, I asked about the availability of the district's laptop computers. I found that after a simple sign-up procedure, the computers were mine for a few hours each day.

Even though there were only eight computers and my largest class had eighteen students, I felt the addition of the computers would help me meet student needs. But to use the computers, I needed both power and Internet connections, and I didn't have these on the gym stage. I discovered that if I placed the carts near the stage door, I had access to the Internet connection in the gym office. Once connected, my students could start working on their projects.

I know that an essential aspect of working with gifted students is addressing their social and emotional needs. As part of our curriculum, students work to identify their strengths and weaknesses and even address their passions. To accommodate these individual differences, the long-term project was developed with both required elements and multiple options.

The students decided what elements they wanted to include with their technology component of the project, in addition to the computers. To accommodate different learning styles, students were given options that included videotaping their construction of models, conducting interviews, building models, designing booths in which to display their products, and recording informational audiotapes about their topics.

I developed technology goals for each grade level. Most of my second-grade students had a great deal of difficulty using a keyboard, so they were required to type only part of the information that would be displayed on their posters. The third-grade students, who were ready to explore additional programs, used Inspiration, TimeLiner, and Kidspiration to help them display their information. I felt that the fourth- and fifth-grade students were capable of a more challenging project. My fourth-grade students loved seeing pictures of themselves, so I borrowed a digital camera from the library media center and had the students take pictures of each other. The students then copied the images to Microsoft Word and, using Word-Art, added thought bubbles to express the most important thing that they had learned while researching. Because this was one of my larger groups, the use of the digital camera allowed the class to work on different segments of the project at the same time and decreased the wait time for the computers.

I knew that my greatest challenge was going to be my largest group, the fifth graders. I had the students work in small groups to develop PowerPoint presentations to share their research results. The final projects were well received by the parents; some were amazed at the creativity and level of proficiency that the students displayed in the projects.

Overall, the technology that I was able to use last year and have begun using again this year has enabled my students to advance at a more appropriate pace for their intellectual development and to find greater interest in their schoolwork, because the use of technology gave me a greater number of options, enabling me to match the students' learning activities with their individual learning styles.

For further information, contact Sandra Burvikovs at:

May Whitney Elementary School
120 Church Street
Lake Zurich, IL 60047
Email: sburvikovs@lz95.org

SOURCE: Online interview with Sandra Burvikovs conducted by Al P. Mizell.

 ## What Is Educational Technology?

The definition of educational technology often varies depending on whether the term is used by educators or by technologists. Many educators use the term **educational technology** very broadly. Educational technology for those educators includes any **media** that can be used in instruction. From their perspective, educational technology might include printed media, models, projected and nonprojected visuals, as well as audio, video, and digital media. Other, more computer-oriented educators take a narrower view. Those individuals confine educational technology primarily to computers, computer peripherals, and related software used in teaching and learning. For **technologists,** those whose primary responsibilities relate to the management of equipment, educational technology is often defined in terms of the hardware available that might be used in the classroom. This would include both audiovisual equipment and computers. As you can see, the body of knowledge broadly defined as educational technology is not yet exact, even in its definition.

The field, like our society in general, is in a state of rapid change under the influences of the Information Age. Therefore, to begin our exploration of educational technology, we must first define its scope. For the purposes of this text, our definition of technology is based on the definition provided by the **Association for Educational Communications and Technology (AECT).** The AECT has been prominent in the area of design and implementation of educational technology for seventy-five years. As described in its 1994 publication, *Instructional Technology: The Definition and Domains of the Field,* "Educational technology is the theory and practice of design, development, utilization, management, and evaluation of processes and resources for learning." This definition takes the broadest view possible and allows us to explore the full range of media that a teacher might use to enhance his or her instruction and augment student learning. Our definition of educational technology, then, is *any technology used by educators in support of the teaching and learning process* (see Figure 1.1 on page 6).

Media refers to different means of communication.

A technologist manages and implements materials, tools, and equipment to improve or enhance operations.

E-Learning
ON THE WEB! 1.1
Educational Technology Organizations

 ## Why Study Educational Technology?

The **International Society for Technology in Education (ISTE)** has led a federally funded initiative to develop standards for technology for both teachers and students. This initiative is helping to define what you need to

1

FIGURE 1.1

Educational Technology: What Is Your Definition?

What do you think of when you think of educational technology? Check all that you think apply to educational technology in this figure. How many did you choose? In fact, educational technology can include all of these and much more! Anything used to help you teach or your students to learn can be considered an educational technology.

Computers   Slides   Print materials/Books   Posters

Instructional television   Photographs   Videotapes   Email

Models   Overhead projectors   Bulletin boards   CDs and DVDs

Audiotapes   Dioramas   The Internet   Teleconferencing

know about educational technology. ISTE's project is called the National Educational Technology Standards for Teachers (NETS•T) Project. It is part of the Preparing Tomorrow's Teachers to Use Technology (PT3) grant program sponsored by the U.S. Department of Education. The NETS•T Project states, "The world is different. Kids are different . . . learning is different . . . and teaching must be different too. Today's classroom teachers must be prepared to provide technology-supported learning opportunities for their students" (NETS•T, 2002). NETS•T describes a performance profile of a technology-literate teacher and twenty-one key competencies that such a teacher should have. These competencies are listed in Figure 1.3 on pages 8–9. Clearly, the national expectation for educators is to have a sound foundation in the technologies you need to teach and your students will need to learn.

Like ISTE, AECT has also developed standards to guide current and future teachers in their educational technology competencies. AECT's domains and subdomains of standards are summarized in Figure 1.2. AECT's approach to defining necessary competencies, like its definition of educational technology, takes a broad approach that incorporates design and

FIGURE 1.2
AECT Standards Domains and Subdomains
SOURCE: www.aect.org/standards/initstand.html.

AECT STANDARDS DOMAINS AND SUBDOMAINS

DESIGN	DEVELOPMENT	UTILIZATION	MANAGEMENT	EVALUATION
Instructional Systems Design Message Design Instructional Strategies Learner Characteristics	Print Technologies Audiovisual Technologies Computer-Based Technologies Integrated Technologies	Media Utilization Diffusion of Innovations Implementation and Institutionalization Policies and Regulations	Project Management Resource Management Delivery System Management Information Management	Problem Analysis Criterion-Referenced Measurement Formative Evaluation Summative Evaluation

development as well as the areas of utilization, management, and evaluation typically included in most standards.

The AECT and ISTE standards contribute to and have been folded into the professional preparation requirements for all teachers as defined by the National Council for Accreditation of Teacher Education (NCATE). These requirements and their impact on current and future educators are more fully explored in Chapter 12. However, within the framework of student educational technology, it is clear that competence in educational technology and its application in education are now considered a national mandate.

But beyond professional standards, the need to be able to use educational technologies effectively is intuitive. Think about the last time you sat in a classroom taking a course. Chances are that your teacher presented information to you primarily by talking to you about the course content. This familiar teaching **method,** called lecture or presentation, is one of several available to your instructor. Like most methods of teaching, it can be enhanced through the use of educational technology. Let's consider how technology might improve this common teaching strategy.

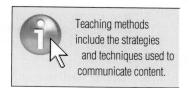

Teaching methods include the strategies and techniques used to communicate content.

Lecture or oral presentation, when used alone, can be challenging for many students. If a teacher using this method did not occasionally stop to write a key word on the board or perhaps show a graphic using an overhead or digital projector, most people would find it fairly difficult to follow the presentation, much less take adequate notes on what was said. We intuitively understand that common technologies, such as a whiteboard, a chalkboard, and a projector, can enhance a lecture substantially and significantly improve communication. Beyond the familiar and obvious media, many different types of strategies and technologies can contribute substantially to the teaching and learning process. The NETS•T Project (see Figure 1.2) reminds us that educators must acquire a broad range of methods and skills to enhance teaching and support learning with technology effectively.

FIGURE 1.3

ISTE Professional Preparation Performance Profile

ISTE National Educational Technology Standards for Teachers (NETS•T) summarize what teachers should know about and be able to do with technology.

SOURCE: Reprinted with permission from *National Educational Technology Standards for Teachers—Preparing Teachers to Use Technology*. Copyright © 2002, ISTE (International Society for Technology in Education), 800.336.5191 (U.S. & Canada) or 541.302.3777 (Int'l), **iste@iste.org.** All rights reserved. Permission does not constitute an endorsement by ISTE. For more information about the NETS Project, contact Lajeane Thomas, Director, NETS Project, 318.257.3292, lthomas@latech.edu.

Profile for Technology–Literate Teachers
FIRST-YEAR TEACHING PERFORMANCE PROFILE

Upon completion of the first year of teaching, teachers

1. assess the availability of technology resources at the school site, plan activities that integrate available resources, and develop a method for obtaining the additional necessary software and hardware to support the specific learning needs of students in the classroom. (I, II, IV)

2. make appropriate choices about technology systems, resources, and services that are aligned with district and state standards. (I, II)

3. arrange equitable access to appropriate technology resources that enable students to engage successfully in learning activities across subject/content areas and grade levels. (II, III, VI)

4. engage in ongoing planning of lesson sequences that effectively integrate technology resources and are consistent with current best practices for integrating the learning of subject matter and student technology standards (as defined in the ISTE National Educational Technology Standards for Students). (II, III)

5. plan and implement technology-based learning activities that promote student engagement in analysis, synthesis, interpretation, and creation of original products. (II, III)

6. plan for, implement, and evaluate the management of student use of technology resources as part of classroom operations and in specialized instructional situations. (I, II, III, IV)

7. implement a variety of instructional technology strategies and grouping strategies (e.g., whole-group, collaborative, individualized, and learner-centered) that include appropriate embedded assessment for meeting the diverse needs of learners. (III, IV)

8. facilitate student access to school and community resources that provide technological and discipline-specific expertise. (III)

9. teach students methods and strategies to assess the validity and reliability of information gathered through technological means. (II, IV)

10. recognize students' talents in the use of technology and provide them with opportunities to share their expertise with their teachers, peers, and others. (II, III, V)

11. guide students in applying self- and peer-assessment tools to critique student-created technology products and the process used to create those products. (IV)

12. facilitate students' use of technology that addressess their social needs and cultural identity and promotes their interaction with the global community. (III, VI)

13. use results from assessment measures (e.g., learner profiles, computer-based testing, electronic portfolios) to improve instructional planning, management, and implemenatation of learning strategies. (II, IV)

14. use technology tools to collect, analyze, interpret, represent, and communicate data (student performance and other information) for the purposes of instructional planning and school improvement. (IV)

15. use technology resources to facilitate communications with parents or guardians of students. (V)

16. identify capabilities and limitations of current and emerging technology resources and assess the potential of these systems and services to address personal, lifelong learning, and workplace needs. (I, IV, V)

17. participate in technology-based collaboration as part of continual and comprehensive professional growth to stay abreast of new and emerging technology resources that support enhanced learning for PK–12 students. (V)

18. demonstrate and advocate for legal and ethical behaviors among students, colleagues, and community members regarding the use of technology and information. (V, VI)

19. enforce classroom procedures that guide students' safe and healthy use of technology and that comply with legal and professional responsibilities for students needing assistive technologies. (VI)

20. advocate for equal access to technology for all students in their schools, communities, and homes. (VI)

21. implement procedures consistent with district and school policies that protect the privacy and security of student data and information. (VI)

FIGURE 1.3 (continued)

ISTE NATIONAL EDUCATIONAL TECHNOLOGY STANDARDS (NETS) AND PERFORMANCE INDICATORS FOR TEACHERS

All classroom teachers should be prepared to meet the following standards and performance indicators.

I. TECHNOLOGY OPERATIONS AND CONCEPTS

Teachers demonstrate a sound understanding of technology operations and concepts. Teachers

A. demonstrate introductory knowledge, skills, and understanding of concepts related to technology (as described in the ISTE *National Educational Technology Standards for Students*).

B. demonstrate continual growth in technology knowledge and skills to stay abreast of current and emerging technologies.

II. PLANNING AND DESIGNING LEARNING ENVIRONMENTS AND EXPERIENCES

Teachers plan and design effective learning environments and experiences supported by technology. Teachers

A. design developmentally appropriate learning opportunities that apply technology-enhanced instructional strategies to support the diverse needs of learners.

B. apply current research on teaching and learning with technology when planning learning environments and experiences.

C. identify and locate technology resources and evaluate them for accuracy and suitability.

D. plan for the management of technology resources within the context of learning activities.

E. plan strategies to manage student learning in a technology-enhanced environment.

III. TEACHING, LEARNING, AND THE CURRICULUM

Teachers implement curriculum plans that include methods and strategies for applying technology to maximize student learning. Teachers

A. facilitate technology-enhanced experiences that address content standards and student technology standards.

B. use technology to support learner-centered strategies that address the diverse needs of students.

C. apply technology to develop students' higher order skills and creativity.

D. manage student learning activities in a technology-enhanced environment.

IV. ASSESSMENT AND EVALUATION

Teachers apply technology to facilitate a variety of effective assessment and evaluation strategies. Teachers

A. apply technology in assessing student learning of subject matter using a variety of assessment techniques.

B. use technology resources to collect and analyze data, interpret results, and communicate findings to improve instructional practice and maximize student learning.

C. apply multiple methods of evaluation to determine students' appropriate use of technology resources for learning, communication, and productivity.

V. PRODUCTIVITY AND PROFESSIONAL PRACTICE

Teachers use technology to enhance their productivity and professional practice. Teachers

A. use technology resources to engage in ongoing professional development and lifelong learning.

B. continually evaluate and reflect on professional practice to make informed decisions regarding the use of technology in support of student learning.

C. use technology to communicate and collaborate with peers, parents, and the larger community in order to nurture student learning.

VI. SOCIAL, ETHICAL, LEGAL, AND HUMAN ISSUES

Teachers understand the social, ethical, legal, and human issues surrounding the use of technology in PK–12 schools and apply that understanding in practice. Teachers

A. model and teach legal and ethical practice related to technology use.

B. apply technology resources to enable and empower learners with diverse backgrounds, characteristics, and abilities.

C. identify and use technology resources that affirm diversity.

D. promote safe and healthy use of technology resources.

E. facilitate equitable access to technology resources for all students.

For those who want to teach, it is therefore essential to first have a thorough working knowledge of the many kinds of educational technologies available that might assist in teaching and in enhancing learning. Educational technologies become the tools that a teacher might use to create an effective instructional event. This text will assist you in discovering the tools that are now available and those on the technological horizon. You will learn how to use these tools and explore their application to the teaching and learning process to make it as effective and meaningful as possible.

Teaching and Learning: A Closer Look at the Instructional Event

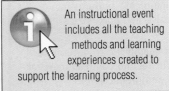

An instructional event includes all the teaching methods and learning experiences created to support the learning process.

To understand how technology fits into instruction, you must first have a very clear picture of the nature of teaching and learning. Teachers construct **instructional events** to transfer knowledge and skills to their students. Technology is a key tool in this construction. For a teacher, this conceptual framework of teaching, learning, and the role of technology is important. A clear and precise grasp of key teaching and learning theories provides a solid base for development of this framework and is therefore a logical place to begin your exploration of technology in teaching and learning.

What Is Learning?

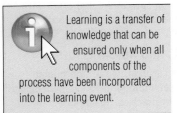

Learning is a transfer of knowledge that can be ensured only when all components of the process have been incorporated into the learning event.

We teach so that our students will learn the concepts or skills we have identified as critical. Teachers want to transfer the knowledge and skills they currently possess to their students so that they too can embrace, enjoy, and use that knowledge academically, personally, and professionally. It is imperative that teachers begin the transfer process with a full understanding of learning so that they can plan and implement appropriate instruction that will result in learning success. Just as an architect must understand the properties of wood, steel, and glass and the purpose of a building before designing it, so too must a teacher understand the essential components of the teaching and learning process (see Figure 1.4).

How Do We Learn?

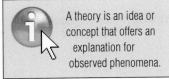

A theory is an idea or concept that offers an explanation for observed phenomena.

The human mechanism of incorporating new knowledge, behaviors, and skills into an individual personal repertoire broadly defines learning. For a deeper understanding of how learning occurs, you must first examine the underlying psychological views of human behaviors. Psychologists are not unanimous in these views. There are, in fact, a variety of **theories** to explain how and why people do what they do. Most of these theories, however, fall within a few prevailing schools of thought. Each school has its

Plan the design → Use materials and tools to create the building → The outcome: a building

Constructing a Building

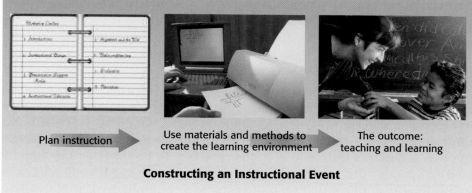

Plan instruction → Use materials and methods to create the learning environment → The outcome: teaching and learning

Constructing an Instructional Event

FIGURE 1.4
Building the Learning Environment
Constructing a learning environment is like constructing a building.

own perspective on human behavior. To understand learning, then, you must examine the prevailing views and the learning theories that result from each.

As an educator, awareness of these differing views helps you understand the options you have in approaching the design of an instructional event and, indeed, the entire learning environment. Examining these sometimes opposing views of learning will help you determine the position with which you personally most agree. In turn, this will help you design instruction that is consistent with your own view of the teaching-learning process and its principles.

Understanding learning is even more critical when a teacher integrates technology into an instructional event. Technology is best viewed as a robust set of instructional tools that help you accomplish the objectives of the teaching-learning process. Technology is a means to an instructional end, not an end in itself. To use technology effectively, the teacher must have a clear understanding of learning and the teaching strategies that will result in the intended knowledge transfer. The teaching strategies you select will then determine the appropriate types of technological tools necessary to carry them out.

E-Learning

www.mylabschool.com
video
View *Strategies for Teaching Diverse Learners*

 Perspectives on Learning

Different people can look at the same thing and see it in very different ways. This describes the concept of **perspective**. Learning is a complex activity that can be explained differently depending on one's perspective on how and why people do what they do. Each of the different schools of psychology has its own view or perspective of learning.

In the next few sections, you will be introduced to differing, sometimes contrary views of learning. Each is correct from the perspective of the theorists presenting it. As you read about each of these perspectives on learning, consider which most closely coincides with your views on learning. As you consider these different viewpoints, you might find that you agree with one of the following theories part of the time and prefer a different theory at other times or for different learners. If that is the case, you have an eclectic approach that takes key ideas from multiple theories.

**Focus on Communications
Theory**

Learning as Communication

One of the earliest approaches to understanding learning was to examine the phenomenon as a communication process. The teacher was the sender of a message, and the student was the receiver of the message. Within this framework, learning was considered to have occurred when the information was accurately transmitted to the receiver. To be sure that this had indeed happened, the sender checked returning messages (**feedback**) from the receiver to confirm that accurate communication had taken place. This **communications cycle** is diagrammed in Figure 1.5.

FIGURE 1.5
The Communications Cycle
An analysis of the components of the communication process.

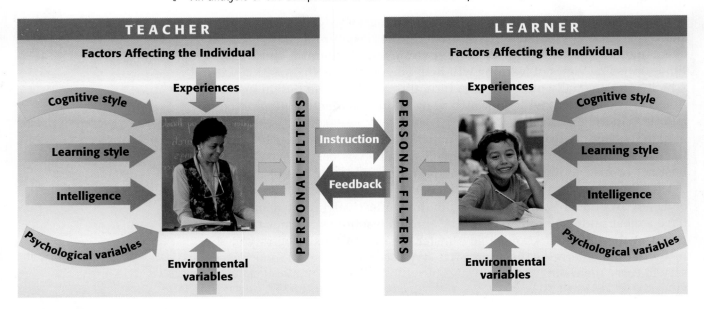

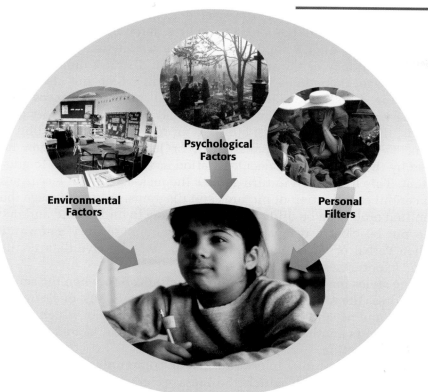

FIGURE 1.6

Variables Affecting Learning
Environmental factors, psychological factors, and personal filters are among the many variables that affect learning.

As you know from your own personal experiences, clear and precise communication does not always occur. There are three general types of variables that can interfere with the communication of ideas: (1) environmental factors, (2) psychological factors, and (3) personal filters (see Figure 1.6). It is important for those trying to communicate to have an awareness of the nature and impact of each of these.

Environmental factors that may interfere with the communication process include environmental conditions that cause the message to be distorted or even blocked. In a classroom, as the teacher (sender) engages in the communication process, loud, incessant noise from outside the classroom may interrupt communication or cause environmental static that interferes with the clarity of the message the student receives. Dim lighting, excessive movement, and uncomfortable temperatures inside the classroom are among other physical distractions that can cause the participants to lose focus and thus add a different but equally disruptive static to the process. Any factors emanating from the environment that cause a learner to lose focus and disengage from active participation in the communication process may be included in environmental factors. Some environmental factors affect some learners but not others. This can be the result of those environmental factors interacting with individual psychological factors.

Psychological factors are the unique individual psychological differences that define and affect the reception of a communicated message.

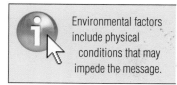

Environmental factors include physical conditions that may impede the message.

Psychological factors are the internal psychological conditions that affect communication.

Learning styles are the sensory preferences that impact learning.

Personal filters include values, cultural heritage, and beliefs.

Psychological factors can include the receiver's emotional state at the time the message is transmitted. For a receiver who entered the communication process immediately after a highly emotional or traumatic event, internal emotional turmoil may be the source of static that distracts the individual from the message. Sometimes, it is the manner in which the message is transmitted that causes the static. Individuals all have preferences as to how they best receive information. Each of us has a preferred sensory gateway, that is, the sense that is most effective for receiving and decoding information. This collection of preferences, or **learning style,** when not addressed by the sender, can cause frustration as the learner tries to grasp the content. This frustration in turn garbles the message. If one learns best through careful examination of pictures and diagrams, then a message that is transmitted orally can be difficult and frustrating to understand and may therefore not be clearly received. If one's dominant sensory gateway is touch, then verbal or visual communication is less effective than tactile-kinesthetic experiences.

Learning styles may act as a barrier to communication when the sender does not address the receiver's preferred learning style. Thus, one's unique physiological and psychological predisposition to the way in which a message is delivered is another example of the psychological factors that may disrupt communication.

The final factor that may interfere with the communication process is the **personal filter** through which the message must pass. Both sender and receiver have a number of personal filters. These include the individual's personal values, cultural heritage, and social belief system. The pure message, that is, the objective set of data that is to be transferred, may be distorted by the belief system held by the sender or the receiver. For example, if the sender or the receiver comes to the process with a predisposition toward the message content, that predisposition may distort the message itself. A negative attitude toward the message or toward the participants in the communication process may cause the intended message to be distorted on delivery. This type of filter may be referred to as having a closed mind with reference to the message. Cultural beliefs can also act as filters by distorting the message content. If one holds a belief that is directly opposed to the content of the message, then the information may be distorted to be more consistent with the belief or rejected because it is in conflict with the belief. In teaching, awareness of potential filters, both your own and those of the receiver, will help you overcome the potential for distortion.

Review now the communications model diagrammed in Figure 1.5. Note each of the unique elements that affect communication, from the message itself to the filters through which it must pass. Together, these components interact to determine the success of the teaching-learning process.

Whether the message was the original content sent from sender to receiver or the feedback from receiver to sender, you can see that many factors can help or hinder communications. With an understanding of the nature of communication as a foundation, you can begin to see the complexity of successful teaching. The teaching-learning process embraces the entire component of the communication process but then continues a step further. Understanding the teaching-learning process also

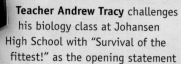
in the Classroom

IN SECONDARY SCIENCE

Teacher Andrew Tracy challenges his biology class at Johansen High School with "Survival of the fittest!" as the opening statement in his lecture to introduce the unit on Darwin's theory of evolution. When teaching this unit, he realizes that the course content will be filtered differently by his students. Robert Jones, an active member of a church that advocates intelligent design, will be predisposed to reject evolution. Mr. Tracy is aware that Robert is firmly in agreement with his church's teaching that evolution is insufficient to explain humanity's appearance on Earth. Robert instead subscribes to a belief that God is the intelligence behind the design for life on this planet. Robert's religious beliefs will act as a filter when listening to Mr. Tracy's lecture on evolution. He may not hear or accept the message or scientific evidence presented by Mr. Tracy.

Another student, Lucy Leaky, whose father is an anthropology professor at the local college, has a much different filter. As a result of being raised in a home where science as a profession dominates, Lucy's filter mirrors her father's. She is likely to openly accept and fully hear the instructional message relating to the theory of evolution being presented by Mr. Tracy.

Filters have an impact on the instructional message. But to teach, it is important to open the lines of communication to the maximum possible. What might Mr. Tracy do to present the content with minimal distortion by his student's personal filters?

requires understanding what happens once the message has been correctly transmitted. Is receipt of the message learning, or is there more to it? What are the differences among hearing, understanding, and learning? To answer these questions, we must delve deeper into theories about how we learn. Thus far, we have examined teaching and learning from a macro view, that is, from the larger perspective of communication. Now it is time to consider the process from a micro view, the narrower perspective of the internal processes that determine how one learns.

The Behaviorist Perspective

Behaviorists, that is, those who see learning from a behaviorist perspective, view all behavior as a response to external stimuli. A stimulus is the initial action directed to the organism, and a response is the organism's reaction to that action. According to behaviorists, the learner acquires behaviors, skills, and knowledge in response to the rewards, punishments, or withheld responses associated with them. A reward includes all positive, negative, or neutral reinforcement to a behavior. Rewards determine the likelihood that the behavior will be repeated. Such reinforcing responses can include rewards (positive reinforcement), punishments (negative reinforcement), or withheld responses (no reinforcement). For behaviorists, learning is essentially a passive process, that is, one learns as a response to the environment, not necessarily because of any specific mental activity. Key theorists in this perspective include **Ivan Pavlov, John Watson,** and **B. F. Skinner.** To learn more about these behaviorists and their theories, explore On the Web! Activity 1.3.

Focus on Behaviorists

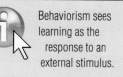
Behaviorism sees learning as the response to an external stimulus.

B. F. Skinner

B. F. Skinner (1904–1990) was born and raised in Susquehanna, Pennsylvania. He attended Hamilton College in Clinton, New York,

intending to become a writer. However, his discovery of John B. Watson's seminal book *Behaviorism* inspired him to pursue graduate studies in psychology at Harvard University. Toward the end of 1929, he began work on the Skinner box, from which he derived his theory of operant conditioning. In 1938, he published *The Behavior of Organisms: An Experimental Analysis,* a book that would have a far-reaching effect on such diverse areas as teaching machines, programmed instruction, treatment for juvenile delinquents, industrial safety, assistive training for the disabled, and even frequent-flyer programs. To simplify child care by means of a controlled environment, Skinner invented the

aircrib, or baby box. His daughter Deborah spent her first two years in this box. Skinner became chairman of the Department of Psychology at Indiana University in 1945 and in 1948 published *Walden Two,* a utopian novel, in an effort to persuade Americans to live simply by utilizing operant conditioning. He returned to Harvard in 1948 as a professor of psychology. In *The Technology of Teaching* (1968), he propounded the value of the teaching machine he had invented. His most controversial book, *Beyond Freedom and Dignity* (1972), stated his thesis that in behavioral engineering, not individual freedom, lies the key to the survival of the human race.

Focus on Cognitivists

The Cognitivist Perspective

In contrast to the behaviorist view, **cognitivists** focus on learning as a mental operation that takes place when information enters through the senses, undergoes mental manipulation, is stored, and is finally used. Unlike behaviorism, with its exclusive focus on external, measurable behaviors, this theory makes mental activity (cognition) the primary source of study. Although behavior is still considered critical, it is viewed as an indicator of cognitive processes rather than just an outcome of a **stimulus-response** cycle. Cognitive theorists attempt to explain learning in terms of how one thinks. Cognitivists believe that learning is more complex than a simplistic behaviorist view. Learning and problem solving, according to cognitivists, represent mental processes that are undetectable by mere observation. Key theorists in this perspective include **Jerome Bruner** and **David Ausubel.** The early works of constructivist **Jean Piaget** also significantly contributed to the cognitivist perspective. Each brings a unique perspective to the view of learning as a function of thinking. You can learn more about these theorists in On the Web! Activity 1.4.

The Constructivist Perspective

Cognitivists and constructivists both recognize learning as a mental process.

For **constructivists,** knowledge is a constructed element resulting from the learning process. Further, knowledge is unique to the individual who constructs it. Mahoney (1994) places constructivism on the cognitive family tree because it relies on the cognitive concepts of inquiry-based learning and social interaction. However, it differs from the cognitivist view in that learning is not seen as just the product of mental processes; it is an entirely

Jean Piaget

SPOTLIGHT ON

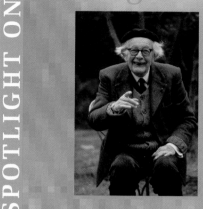

When applying his theory to teaching, Jean Piaget wrote, "The new methods [of teaching] are those that take account of the child's own peculiar nature and make their appeal to the laws of the individual's psychological constitution and those of his development." As a developmentalist, Piaget was interested primarily in intelligence and inferred that at specific calendar ages, a child is capable of performing specific mental functions, endeavoring to gain equilibrium with the environment through assimilation and accommodation. Piaget described four major stages of development: *sensorimotor* from birth to 18–24 months, *preoperational* from 18–24 months to 7 years, *concrete operations* from 7 years to 12 years, and *formal operations* from 12 years on. These progressive stages allow the child to survive and prosper. Learning becomes responsive to the environment in ways that are not all measurable and observable.

As a constructivist, Piaget theorized that children build cognitive structures during all developmental stages. When children are exposed to something new that easily fits into prior experiences, they *assimilate* it. However, when children encounter new knowledge for which they do not have a previous cognitive map, they *accommodate* it. This process of assimilation and accommodation continually modifies their cognitive structures, and thus knowledge is continually under construction.

unique product for each individual based on the experiences within which those mental processes occurred. Constructivism is at present the most influential force in shaping contemporary education.

Perhaps the most notable early constructivist was Jean Piaget. Piaget theorized that children construct mental maps as they encounter information. New knowledge is either assimilated (fitted into existing maps) or accommodated (existing maps are adjusted to accommodate the new information). Thus, children maintain a type of mental equilibrium (see Spotlight on Jean Piaget). In the area of educational technology, **Seymour Papert** adapted

YOU Decide!

Learning theories attempt to explain how we learn. Each explanation focuses on different attributes, conditions, and outcomes. Sometimes the theories seem to contradict each other; at other times they may resonate with us and help us to grasp how we can best help our students learn. Is becoming familiar with learning theories useful to current and future teachers?

YES! Learning is very difficult to understand. Is it physical? Is it psychological? How does it really happen? Theories help you create your own mental model of learning. You consider alternative theories; and, whether you agree with them or not, becoming familiar with them helps you to come to your own conclusion about what learning is and how best you can promote it in your own classroom.

NO! A theory is just a hypothesis or guess about reality. Learning theories are just someone's idea of what learning actually is. Spending time becoming familiar with guesses, even by famous educators and scientists, does not help you to decide anything concrete enough to use in the classroom. The different and sometimes conflicting views of learning too often confuse the issue and offer no practical solutions for teachers.

Which view on learning theories do you agree with? YOU DECIDE!

Piaget's perspective and applied it to children engaged in using technology. Papert's application of this approach resulted in the development of Logo, a graphical programming language that, when used by children, effectively transferred complex mathematical skills. Papert, a founding faculty member of MIT's Media Lab, continues to develop constructivist educational software and to research learning.

Within the constructivist school of learning, two views dominate. The first is a cognitive-constructivist view championed by **Robert Gagné.** In this perspective, learning is a result of an individual's cognitive efforts to construct his or her personal knowledge. The other view, that of social constructivism, was well articulated by **Lev Vygotsky** and **Albert Bandura.** In this view, learning is considered a result of the collaboration of a group of learners in an effort to construct a common core of knowledge. Cognitive constructivism is an outgrowth of the cognitivist view of learning. However, it differs in that the emphasis is placed on the constructs that the individual creates as a result of his or her own cognitive processes. Table 1.1 compares several important constructivists. To learn more about each of these constructivists and his theories, try On the Web! Activity 1.5.

Focus on Constructivists

Toward an Integrated View of Learning

All of the theoretical perspectives described in this section attempt to explain the complex process called learning. Depending on the psychological framework that you believe best explains why people behave the way they do, you may find one of these perspectives more attractive than the others. Still, it is best to think of all of them together as the range of possible explanations of learning and to think of each individual approach as a unique and special addition to your collection (see Figure 1.7 on page 20). Then, as an eclectic instructor, you can choose to implement those parts of the theories that best match your learners' needs and the characteristics of a particular lesson's specific objectives.

Which theory is correct? If you decided to research the answer to a question of interest to you, you would probably read a variety of resources and surf a number of web sites to get an idea of the possibilities. After reviewing these possibilities, you would ultimately form your own personal answer. Perhaps that, too, is the best approach to learning theory. To create the best possible **learning environment** for your students, you need to have an understanding of how a student learns. To do that, you need a working knowledge of learning theory. Then, once this knowledge base is in place, it is wise for you to develop your own, possibly eclectic, view of various learning theories. You may choose to use some parts of each theory or accept a learning theory in its entirety. At this point, you should examine all the options and let your own mental model of learning develop.

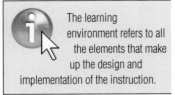

The learning environment refers to all the elements that make up the design and implementation of the instruction.

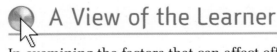

A View of the Learner

Cognitive style, learning style, and intelligence are key characteristics unique to each learner.

In examining the factors that can affect effective communication and theories related to the learning process, it becomes critical to carefully examine the unique nature of the learner who is participating in the process.

TABLE 1.1   Key Theorists and Their Differences

THEORIST	DEFINING CHARACTERISTICS	TEACHER ROLE
JEAN PIAGET (developmental theorist)	Identified key developmental stages that may affect learning; children either assimilate or accommodate knowledge based on existing schemas.	Be aware of child's developmental stage when presenting content; help child construct schemas.
ROBERT GAGNÉ (bridge theorist between (behaviorism and cognitivism)	Controlled, external, sequential instructional events with eight conditions for learning determined by developmental stage of learner and by subject matter.	Create systematic design to address student's needs; individualize instructional events.
LEV VYGOTSKY (social learning theorist)	Zone of proximal development recognizes student's readiness to bond with the community; speech and language are keys to intelligence.	Arrange for tutoring by skilled and learned adults as a means of student enculturation.
ALBERT BANDURA (social learning theorist)	Concern with the way people acquire socially appropriate behavior; builds on Skinner to form social learning theory; agrees with Gagné that subject matter is central to learning stages.	Outcome expectancies (prediction of results of a behavior) motivate students to imitate the behavior, "modeling."
SEYMOUR PAPERT (mathematician and educational technologist)	Technology should help children experience knowledge and construct meanings; developed Logo and constructivist software based on this perspective.	Provide opportunities for children to develop constructs through experience; use technology to support experiences.
HOWARD GARDNER (multiple-intelligences theorist)	Nine innate capabilities (with more under study): linguistic, spatial, bodily-kinesthetic, logical-mathematical, and others; every child is smart in his or her own way and possesses combined intelligences that should be encouraged to develop.	Gear curricula and instructional approaches to individual intelligences and their dominant ways of knowing, for the successful pursuit of knowledge, both vocational and avocational, by all.
B. F. SKINNER (stimulus-response)	Described learning as a response to events or stimuli and the result of the reinforcement of the response.	Responses should be reinforced with immediate and appropriate feedback.
JEROME BRUNER (constuctivist theorist)	Finds learning to be an active process in which learners build new ideas or concepts based on their current/past knowledge.	Try to encourage students to discover knowledge with instruction organized in a spiral manner so students continually build on what they have already learned.
DAVID AUSUBEL (subsumption theorist)	Suggests that learning is based on cognitive processes that occur during the reception of information.	General information should be presented first; use preorganizers to best prepare for information integration.

SOURCE: Theory into Practice (TIP) Database. Retrieved 12/15/05 from http://tip.psychology.org/.

Understanding learning is just the first step a teacher must take in planning effective instruction. Learning theory tells us how learning might occur. The next area for consideration is to examine characteristics that might have an impact on an individual's attempt to learn.

Each learner in a classroom is likely to have a unique cognitive style, a unique learning style, and some parameters related to intelligence.

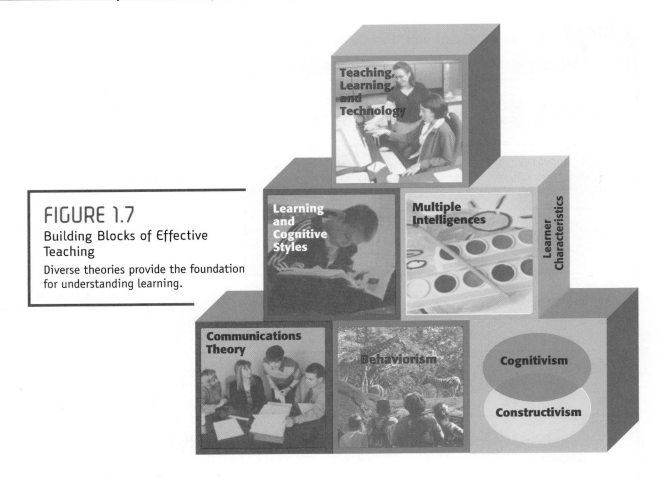

FIGURE 1.7

Building Blocks of Effective Teaching

Diverse theories provide the foundation for understanding learning.

This section will help you understand how each of these relates to the teaching-learning process.

Cognitive Styles

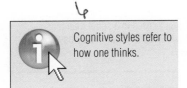

Cognitive styles refer to how one thinks.

Cognitive style refers to how one thinks. Each person has his or her own tendencies and preferences when it comes to cognition (thinking). Such preferences can even be measured. One of the most widely used cognitive style instruments to determine one's own patterns of thinking is the Myers-Briggs Type Indicator (MBTI). The Myers-Briggs instrument is based primarily on a constructivist view of learning. In it, a learner answers a series of questions about his or her own preferences. The responses are then totaled and categorized. The clustering of responses points to one of four sets of opposing cognitive preferences: extrovert (E) or introvert (I), sensing (S) or intuitive (N), thinking (T) or feeling (F), and judging (J) or perceiving (P). Everyone has a preference in each of these pairs of opposites. Thus, a person's cognitive type may turn out to be the ENFP type (Extrovert, Intuitive, Feeling, Perceiving). Such an individual would be likely to be excited by and involved in new ideas and possibilities. He or she would join in enthusiastically and energetically while maintaining a deep concern for the world and others (Martin, 2002). Everyone has preferences in each of these four pairs of opposites, and each combination of types results in a noticeably different cognitive style.

Myers and Briggs

SPOTLIGHT ON

Katherine Briggs wanted to become a novelist. In searching for ways to develop characterization, she explored Carl Jung's theory of personality types, from which a major field of literary criticism—archetypal criticism—is derived.

During World War II, her daughter, **Isabel Briggs Myers,** extended the use of the personality typing that her mother had studied to aid in the war effort by attempting to ascertain which workers were best suited to which wartime jobs. Decisions were based on their responses to an inventory she devised. She also added two more functions of personality, judging and perceiving.

The Myers-Briggs Type Indicator (MBTI) is a personality inventory developed by Isabel Briggs Myers and her husband, Peter B. Myers. It is widely used not only in education, but also in counseling, business, industry, and the armed forces. Unlike the personality inventories found in the popular media, the MBTI can be administered only by psychologists. Particularly important for education is an adaptation of the MBTI for children ages 6–12, the Murphy-Meisgeier Type Indicator for Children (MMTIC).

SOURCE: A. M. Fairhurst & L. L. Fairhurst. 1995. *Effective teaching, effective learning.* Palo Alto, CA: Davies-Black Publishing.

These cognitive characteristics are also likely to influence how the individual might successfully learn. Awareness and understanding of students' cognitive preferences can help a teacher design instruction that is consistent with these preferences and therefore more palatable to those students. Figure 1.8 gives you a sense of the cognitive types that the MBTI identifies.

EXTROVERT
More interested in outer world of persons and events

INTROVERT
More interested in inner world of concepts and ideas

SENSING
Perception based on real objects and solid facts

INTUITIVE
Perception based on possibilities and personal meaning

THINKING
Decides on the basis of objectively analyzing facts

FEELING
Decides on the basis of subjective values and views

JUDGING
Lives in a planned, organized way, prefers control

PERCEIVING
Prefers a more flexible and spontaneous way of life

FIGURE 1.8
Summary of Myers-Briggs Types
Cognitive types as measured by the MBTI.

Learning Styles

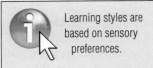

Learning styles are based on sensory preferences.

Learning style is another factor influencing how an individual learns. Unlike the broader concept of cognitive style—that is, how we think—learning style refers to those conditions under which we best learn. Most learning style theorists identify three primary modalities for learning: auditory, visual, and kinesthetic. Some individuals learn best by listening; thus, they may be said to have a predominantly auditory learning

CHECK YOUR LEARNING STYLE

A number of learning style instruments are available online. The Index of Learning Styles (ILS), developed by Richard M. Felder and Linda K. Silverman of North Carolina State University, assesses preferences on four dimensions based on a learning styles model they developed. Here is a sampling of the forty-four questions included in the ILS. To read more about learning styles and to try the instrument yourself, go to Dr. Felder's web site at **www.ncsu.edu/felder-public/ILSpage.html.**

ILS Sample Questions

When I start a homework problem, I am more likely to
(a) try to fully understand the problem first.
(b) start working on the solution immediately.

I understand something better after I
(a) try it out.
(b) think it through.

When I think about what I did yesterday, I am most likely to get
(a) a picture.
(b) words.

When I am learning something new, it helps me to
(a) talk about it.
(b) think about it.

I prefer to get new information in
(a) pictures, diagrams, graphs, or maps.
(b) written directions or verbal information.

Once I understand
(a) all the parts, I understand the whole thing.
(b) the whole thing, I see how the parts fit.

In a book with lots of pictures and charts, I am likely to
(a) look over the pictures and charts carefully.
(b) focus on the written text.

Learning style instruments such as this one include questions that help students identify various aspects of their personal learning styles. Try the ILS and other online instruments to determine your own learning style and to see if the results you get from various instruments provide you with a reasonably consistent and accurate description of your personal style.

SOURCE: Reprinted with permission from the Index of Learning Styles by B. A. Soloman and R. M. Felder, www.ncsu.edu/felder-public/ILSpage.html.

style. Others may learn best by seeing, thus having a visual learning style. Yet others learn best by doing, which suggests a kinesthetic learning style. Although everyone can learn using each of these modalities, learning style theorists suggest that each person has a preference, a dominant sensory gateway. It is easiest for the individual to learn when information is presented in a manner consistent with her or his personal learning modality preference. Learning styles are therefore of considerable importance to those who are constructing the learning environment.

Learning style is consequently another individual factor that affects learning regardless of the psychological perspective with which you agree. Understanding the dominant learning styles of the students you are trying to teach and then designing the components of the instructional event to be consistent with their styles will make instruction significantly more effective for those learners.

Intelligence

A final factor affecting learning is **intelligence,** or the inherent capability of the learner to understand and learn. Intelligence quotient (**IQ**), a quantitative measure of intelligence, was once thought to be a definitive way to measure this capability within a specified range. Extensive research was done to develop an instrument that would provide a snapshot of a person's intelligence without regard to cultural or other bias. Bias is any tendency or prejudice that might distort a view. An example of cultural bias in intelligence testing would be the inclusion of questions that rely on a framework that is outside the test taker's cultural experience, thus potentially distorting the results.

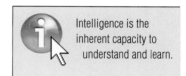
Intelligence is the inherent capacity to understand and learn.

One of the most commonly used IQ tests is the Stanford-Binet. Alfred Binet, a French psychologist, initially developed the test in 1905 for the French Ministry of Education to help predict which students would succeed in school. Binet's test was later adapted for the United States by Louis Terman of Stanford University. The Stanford-Binet or a similar test is typically given to students several times during their academic careers. Teachers can easily get an idea of their students' potential by reviewing student records—or can they? Increasingly, this traditional means of measuring intelligence based on verbal and mathematical abilities has come under attack. In fact, the very definition of intelligence is being debated.

E-Learning ON THE WEB! 1.6
Intelligence Tests

How to measure intelligence and the value system we attach to it are variables that are being given scholarly consideration. McLuhan (1998) asserts, "It is in our IQ testing that we have produced the greatest flood of misbegotten standards. Unaware of our typographic cultural bias, our testers assume that uniform and continuous habits are a sign of intelligence, thus eliminating the ear man and the eye man." As a result of the inadequacies of traditional intelligence testing, extensive research is being done to develop instruments that will provide a more accurate result.

Tech Tips *for* TEACHERS

Many web sites offer online cognitive style, learning style, and multiple intelligence tests that you can have your students take to get an idea of their styles. While not as accurate as the validated and tested instruments developed by Dunn and Dunn, Myers-Briggs, and Howard Gardner, these brief online tests can give a busy teacher some indication as to their students' styles. Often, these instruments will score the tests and provide results instantaneously. And there are instruments available for almost any grade level. For an example of this type of online style resource, visit the Learning Disabilities Pride web site at **www.ldpride.net/learningstyles.MI.htm.**

E-Learning
ON THE WEB! 1.7

Howard Gardner

Gardner theorizes that
multiple intelligences
exist.

Howard Gardner provided a new view of intelligence, the **theory of multiple intelligences.** He theorized that there is more to intelligence than what was historically measured by IQ tests. Gardner suggested that these objective tests did not go far enough in representing intelligence. He suggested instead that each individual has multiple types of intelligences, only a few of which can be measured by IQ tests. In Gardner's theory of multiple intelligences, he describes nine different aspects or types of intelligences that every person possesses (see Figure 1.9). These intelligences (or talents) include the following:

- Linguistic intelligence (verbal skills and talents related to sound, meanings, and rhythms)
- Logical-mathematical intelligence (conceptual and logical thinking skills)
- Musical intelligence (talents and abilities related to sound, rhythm, and pitch)
- Spatial intelligence (skill in thinking in pictures and visioning abstractly)
- Bodily-kinesthetic intelligence (skill in controlling body movements)
- Interpersonal intelligence (responsiveness to others)
- Intrapersonal intelligence (high degree of self-awareness and insight)
- Naturalist intelligence (skills in recognizing, categorizing, and interacting with the natural world)
- Existential intelligence (ability to consider and deal with questions of human existence)

According to Gardner's theory, every individual possesses some degree of each of the intelligences he details but one or more of the intelligences dominates. If any one of the intelligences is of significant capacity, the result is a prodigy in that area. Gardner's view equally recognizes the unique abilities of Mozart (musical intelligence), Frank Lloyd Wright (spatial intelligence), and Babe Ruth (bodily-kinesthetic intelligence), whereas standard IQ tests might recognize only Albert Einstein (logical-mathematical

Howard Gardner

SPOTLIGHT ON

Howard Gardner earned his undergraduate and graduate degrees from Harvard University and received a post-doctoral fellowship from the Harvard Medical School. He is now a professor of education at Harvard and directs Project Zero, a project for the study of cognition and creativity.

His own multiple intelligences are evident from his skill as a pianist, accordionist, writer, scientist, educator, philosopher, and administrator. Gardner's devotion to the arts, including a postdoctoral study of the neurological aftereffects of strokes on artists and musicians and his own performance skills, is carried on by his children: One plays the piano, another plays the double bass, one is a photographer, and another is an arts administrator.

Gardner's books and articles are numerous. His 1983 book *Frames of Mind: The Theory of Multiple Intelligences* is the source book for subsequent publications and studies of multiple intelligences. He has eleven other books and more than two dozen articles to his credit, as well as many coauthored writings. He has recently undertaken the study of ethics in an effort to deal with misinterpretations of his concepts. Gardner continues his ardent pursuit of diverse knowledge.

SOURCE: H. Gardner. 1999. A multiplicity of intelligences [About the author]. *Scientific American* 9(4): 23.

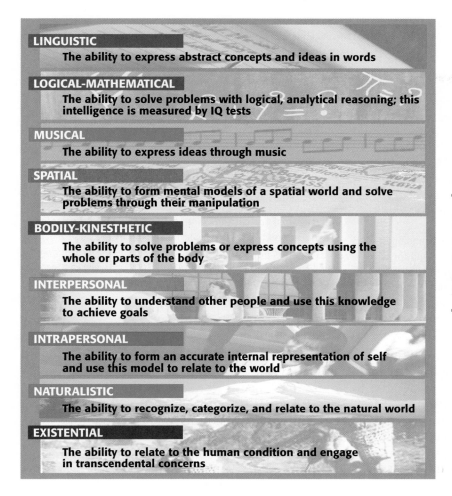

LINGUISTIC
The ability to express abstract concepts and ideas in words

LOGICAL-MATHEMATICAL
The ability to solve problems with logical, analytical reasoning; this intelligence is measured by IQ tests

MUSICAL
The ability to express ideas through music

SPATIAL
The ability to form mental models of a spatial world and solve problems through their manipulation

BODILY-KINESTHETIC
The ability to solve problems or express concepts using the whole or parts of the body

INTERPERSONAL
The ability to understand other people and use this knowledge to achieve goals

INTRAPERSONAL
The ability to form an accurate internal representation of self and use this model to relate to the world

NATURALISTIC
The ability to recognize, categorize, and relate to the natural world

EXISTENTIAL
The ability to relate to the human condition and engage in transcendental concerns

FIGURE 1.9
Howard Gardner's Theory of Multiple Intelligences
Multiple forms of intelligence as theorized by Howard Gardner.

intelligence) and William Shakespeare (linguistic intelligence). This broader view of individual capacities changes the assumptions a teacher might make about a student's potential and capacities. Such reevaluation, in turn, should change that teacher's plan for instruction. If one adopts the multiple-intelligences approach, then learning will be affected by the dominance of one or more of the intelligences in each individual student. Teaching then would have to accommodate these various propensities to maximize student learning.

E-Learning

www.mylabschool.com
video
View *Multiple Intelligences*

A View of the Teacher

Teaching is a systematic, planned sequence of events that facilitates the communication of an idea, concept, or skill to a learner. The act of teaching requires an understanding of learning and an understanding of the individual and environmental factors that affect the learner. It also requires an understanding of yourself and the individual and environmental factors that affect you. Every teacher has his or her own learning style, cognitive style, and dominant intelligence. Given these variables, teachers also differ in their styles of teaching. **Teaching style** is typically a function of one's personal preferences. Research has shown that we teach in

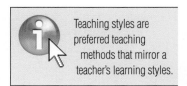

Teaching styles are preferred teaching methods that mirror a teacher's learning styles.

TECHNOLOGY SOLUTIONS *for All Learners*

The idea of student diversity initially brings to mind ethnic, racial, and cultural differences. But students are diverse in many ways. As you have seen in this chapter, students can have differing learning and cognitive styles and multiple intelligences. They might also have differing physical needs if they are physically challenged in some way. How might a teacher address so many very different students with so many different preferences and needs?

One way is through the application of the many technologies available for teachers and students. Students who are auditory learners can be assisted by using books on tape and software that pronounces words for them. Students who have a strong interpersonal cognitive style may deepen learning through Internet communication with other students. A student with dominant musical intelligence may embrace history by using technology to listen to the changes in the lyrics and melodies characteristic of different periods. Students with learning disabilities may use software to help them practice strategies they can implement to help them overcome their unique learning problems.

What technology might you use to help you to assist a student who:

- Is physically impaired and has limited movement?
- Demonstrates dominance of linguistic/verbal intelligence?
- Is sight impaired?

You may want to visit the Center for Applied Special Technology via the Internet to read the online version of the book *Teaching Every Student in the Digital Age: Universal Design for Learning* by David H. Rose and Anne Meyer (ASCD, 2002) at **www.cast.org/teachingeverystudent/ideas/tes/** for more ideas on using technology to address student diversity.

---

the way we like to learn, think, or do. Although that is unavoidable and often positive, a teacher must have an awareness of his or her own teaching style to be able to adjust it to meet the needs of the learners. Have you ever had instructors who were difficult to learn from? Did they lecture too much, or were they too unorganized for you? Did you notice that some of your peers did not seem to have difficulty with those instructors' teaching styles? This is the result of a conflict between components of the teaching-learning process. Some may be consistent with components and the environment (teaching style) and how others in the process prefer to interact (learning style).

A well-developed and well-articulated teaching style can be a positive trait that separates the master teacher from the average teacher. Yet one must always maintain awareness of how effective one's style is with reference to the goal of teaching: learning. The same understanding of learning theory, cognitive styles, learning styles, and intelligence will serve you well in understanding and improving your own teaching style.

Toward a Holistic View of Teaching, Learning, and Technology

Teaching, learning, and technology work together to achieve the ultimate goal of effective knowledge transfer. When you consider the process of teaching and learning as a holistic system, you can begin to sense how all of the elements of the process, from the learning environment to teaching strategies, to learning activities, to support technologies, interact in support of the learner. (These relationships are diagrammed in Figure 1.10.) When you take the time to carefully examine each component and its interaction with other components, you are better able to design an effective process that will help you teach and help your students learn. Using such a

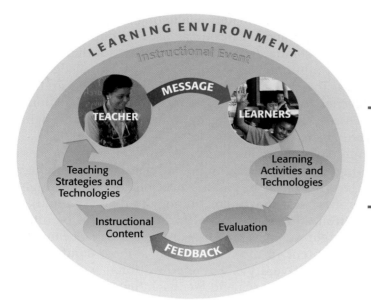

FIGURE 1.10
A Holistic View of Teaching, Learning, and Technology

holistic **systems approach** helps to give you the perspective needed to effectively apply each aspect of instruction to the creation of a meaningful teaching and learning process.

Once the teaching-learning process is defined, it is much simpler to see the role technology plays in it. Technology supports teaching, and it supports learning. However, educational technologies cannot be selected or implemented until the teaching and learning process they support has been planned and detailed by an educator.

At this point, you have already explored many theoretical foundations of the teaching and learning process. The next step is to consider how technology fits into the instructional system we have created.

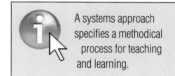

A systems approach specifies a methodical process for teaching and learning.

Why Use Technology?

You have explored communication. You have examined learning theories. You have reviewed cognitive and learning styles. You have explored another way of looking at intelligence. You have been encouraged to find out how your students process information. You have applied these concepts to yourself to begin to understand the personal characteristics that will define your teaching style. You have viewed the whole of the teaching-learning process as a system. But what does all this have to do with the focus of this text, educational technology?

To see the relationship, it is appropriate to review the definitions and standards offered by the AECT and ISTE. The AECT definition of educational technology was offered earlier in this chapter: "Educational technology is the theory and practice of design, development, utilization, management, and evaluation of processes and resources for learning." This definition suggests that the concept of educational technology is more than a certain type of computer or a specific brand of camera. It is, instead, a wide variety of theories and practices associated with designing,

Technology is an Information Age teaching tool.

developing, using, managing, and ultimately evaluating both the teaching-learning process and the technological resources used to implement that process. The ISTE NETS•T standards and AECT standards articulate domains of competency and minimum levels of technology knowledge and performance for teachers. Together, these two national organizations reflect the need for every teacher to have a solid command of the educational technology skills necessary for integrating appropriate and meaningful technologies into teaching and learning.

Educational technology can include any resource and any process that facilitates learning. A teacher might use educational technology to enhance the quality and clarity of communication. A teacher might employ a particular process or a specific technology to increase the likelihood that a presentation addresses a specific learning style or intelligence. Or a learner might select a process or technology because it organizes and presents content in the manner that is most comfortable for his or her personal cognitive style. Some educational technologies can be employed to ensure the rewards and feedback that are critical to a behaviorist approach. Other technologies help a learner construct and test the mental models suggested by cognitivists. Still others encourage and support social exchange to construct new knowledge through social interaction. Educational technologies can be used to enhance and support the teaching-learning process at any number of points in the process. Educational technology is a support for teaching and learning that both teacher and learner can call on to help ensure the opportunity for optimum performance.

TEACHING WITH TECHNOLOGY

Problem-Based Learning

Imagine that you have been selected to mentor a new teacher, Ms. Adkins, at your school. Ms. Adkins, like most new teachers, is eager to learn about teaching from her experienced and talented fellow teachers. You want to help her to see teaching and learning holistically and to understand how to effectively integrate the technology available to her. When you first asked her how she would use technology, she immediately mentioned showing videos on Friday and using computer game time as a reward. Ms. Adkins appears to be a very creative teacher, but she also seems to have very limited experience with technology in instruction. You feel certain that if you can orient her toward a more holistic view of teaching and learning with technology, she will see many more effective applications to help her teach and help her students learn.

Using Figure 1.10 as your visual aid, decide what you need to share about each component of the diagram to help her understand the role of technology in instruction. Develop a one-page handout for her that (1) explains each component, (2) summarizes the relationship of each component to the others, and (3) gives an example for a class lesson.

Technology serves both learners and teachers in a variety of settings.

This holistic approach to educational technology has not always been the accepted model. For many years, educational technology had a very narrow, technical definition. The evolution from an equipment-based view of educational technology to a teaching-and-learning-based view may cause confusion for those who are new to education. A brief review of this evolution may help clarify the changes (see Interchapter 1) and will help you follow the influences of technology on instruction.

Educational Technology: The Past

For many, the term *educational technology* conjures up images of audiovisual equipment such as a tape recorder or videocassette player. Indeed, audiovisual equipment is so prevalent in education that it is worth exploring how this came to be and why it continues to have an impact. The audiovisual movement as we define the term today came into existence in the early 1900s with the advent of the first form of motion media: early movies. So strong was the belief in this new educational technology that Thomas Alva Edison (1913) suggested, albeit incorrectly, that "Books will soon be obsolete in schools." Although books have not become obsolete even today, motion media have indeed made their influence felt in schools, as they have in society in general. It was soon discovered that films incorporating sound and images could be used to teach as well as to entertain. Thus, the movie projector became an important addition to a teacher's arsenal of teaching tools. Thomas Edison also predicted that the movie projector would replace teachers. As far-fetched as this might sound, it was a widely believed and sometimes feared idea. By now, we have learned that predictions suggesting that any particular technology will replace professional educators or be the ultimate answer to improving teaching are not realistic.

During the 1920s and 1930s, both audio and visual educational technology evolved steadily. Technological advances in slides, radio, and sound

Teachers have historically sought technology to support instruction.

The advent of instructional television (ITV) changed the role of TV in schools.

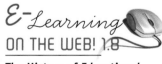
The History of Educational Technology

recordings and continuing improvement in the quality of motion pictures all contributed to this evolution. With World War II and the use of audiovisual instruction by the military, a surge in the development of audiovisual equipment occurred. To the array of technologies used in training and instruction, the military added the overhead projector, slide projector, simulator, and audio equipment for teaching foreign languages.

After World War II, research on the use of audiovisual tools supporting instruction was begun so that the training successes that evidently resulted from audiovisual-intensive military training could be better understood. This was followed in the 1950s by a greater articulation of the theories and models of communication and an exploration of how audiovisual technologies fit in with them.

The audiovisual movement gained further momentum with the spread of television in the 1950s. Many people assumed that instructional television would revolutionize education. Although the Federal Communications Commission (FCC) set aside television channels for educational purposes and the Ford Foundation and other organizations made serious investments in educational programming, instructional television (ITV) had slid into decline by the mid-1960s. The factors that led to this decline included teacher reluctance to use television programming in the classroom, the high cost of production of good-quality programming, and the passive nature of television viewing, which did not adequately meet student learning needs.

Although not the revolutionary technology it was expected to be, broadcast television and its counterpart, videotapes, have indeed changed the face of education. Further, ITV did not disappear from the education scene. Dollars from various sources continued to flow into the Public Broadcasting System, and much fine-quality educational programming emanated from it. Much of this programming, in videotape form, is still a mainstay of school video libraries.

Educational Technology: A Modern View

The 1960s saw a change in the concept of audiovisual instruction as a model closer to our current views of educational technology began to evolve. Although audiovisual equipment remained a component of the educational technology concept, the technology was no longer limited to just equipment—audio, visual, or otherwise. By the 1970s, AECT's broader view dominated. Instructional technology came to be seen as all types of learning resources and the systems necessary to place them in service to teaching and learning.

The first broadly implemented educational technology appeared in the mid-1950s as an outgrowth of the popularity of B. F. Skinner's work and behaviorist views of learning.[10] **Programmed instruction** was an instructional system in which material was presented in a series of small steps. Each step required an active learner response, to which there was immediate feedback as to the correctness of the response. Programmed instruction emphasized individualized learning materials that would require students to interact with the information presented. In keeping with Skinner's behaviorist approach, immediate feedback to student responses was a key feature. Additional features of programmed instruction included self-paced, self-selected sequencing of the materials resulting from the learner's responses. Although popular at its inception, programmed instruction faded quickly. By the late 1960s, interest in this technology had declined. Research on programmed instruction indicated that it did not significantly improve learning. This finding, combined with negative feedback from students and teachers who found the format unstimulating, moved programmed instruction to the background of the educational landscape.

However, during its short term as an educational innovation, the programmed instruction movement did manage to have a lasting impact on educational technology. It has, in fact, turned out to be the grandfather of subsequent approaches. Its methodical approach to the analysis of instruction, its rigorous statement of observable learning objectives, and its use of a systematic development process made it a forerunner to current systems approaches to designing instruction and selecting educational technologies. Programmed instruction empirically analyzed the data related to content and learner, identified strengths and weaknesses, adjusted the system accordingly, evaluated the resulting learning, and revised the system in accordance with the evaluation data. The logic and organized approach embodied in these steps ultimately gave rise to other individualized educational technology systems.

It was not until the advent of the microcomputer in the late 1970s that the concept of interactive individualized instruction introduced by programmed instruction could be fully realized. Because computers could be programmed to be interactive, to provide immediate feedback, and to allow students to navigate the material according to their own learning inclinations, educational technology entered a new era.

Computer-assisted instruction (CAI) broadly refers to the body of computer software that is the digital equivalent of the programmed instructional packages of the 1950s and 1960s. Early CAI was primarily text-based, drill-and-practice software; but as computing power expanded, so too did the capabilities of CAI. Today's CAI typically contains colorful graphics, easy navigation, and many instructional management features. Overall, however, the basic concepts of a systematic, organized, and responsive instructional system remain intact.

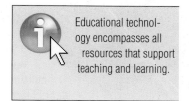

Educational technology encompasses all resources that support teaching and learning.

The Skinner teaching machine was the precursor to the programmed instruction materials popular in the 1960s.

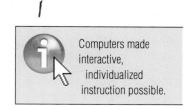

Computers made interactive, individualized instruction possible.

COOL TOOLS

Multimedia Software

Early computer-assisted instruction (CAI) has given way to engaging and exciting multimedia software that helps students learn in fun and novel ways.

With computer hardware becoming more powerful and programs more sophisticated, CAI has evolved into a very cool teaching and learning tool.

One popular example is Riverdeep, an online and CD-based learning system that offers innovative interactive programming aligned with state curriculum standards. The software includes interactive courseware in the content areas of math, science, language arts,

critical thinking, social studies, early learning, and special needs. Designed for use in all grade levels, this software is today's evolutionary end point for CAI.

You can experience this cool tool by going to Riverdeep's web site at **www .riverdeep.com** and registering for a demonstration and 30-day free download of its courseware.

With the advent of powerful and inexpensive computers, early CAI programs have long since evolved into the powerful, multimedia programs available today that entice students to learn and support teachers' instructional efforts. Although still based on the theoretical foundations you have been introduced to in this chapter, today's educational technologies offer teachers an amazing array of teaching and learning support media from which to choose. This text is designed to introduce you to the full array of

CAI software can provide interactive learning experiences.

technologies you might select to help you teach and to help your students learn. How you choose to use these many and varied technologies will be your personal and professional decision.

Teaching, Learning, and Educational Technology: A Personal Synthesis

To understand educational technology, you need to understand its role in support of the teaching-learning process. To understand the teaching-learning process, you need to understand teaching. To understand teaching, you need to understand communication and the participants in the communications cycle. To understand the participants, you need to understand the learner. To understand the learner, you need to understand learning theory and the factors that affect individual learning. This chapter has presented information related to each of these layers of understanding to help you lay a solid foundation on which to build your own personal framework for using educational technologies.

You must now synthesize the knowledge you have gained from this chapter into your own personal view of the teaching and learning process. You must decide how technology will fit into your teaching-learning model. You must consider what you have learned thus far and synthesize the following:

- Your own view of how students learn and how you should best communicate with them
- How best to assess the learning characteristics of your students
- How best to adapt your teaching style to your students' needs
- What you need to know to develop systematic and effective instruction
- How educational technology fits into your synthesized view of teaching and learning

Thinking about how you will apply these concepts is the first step toward really understanding what you need to do to be an effective educator.

Chapter 2 takes this process to its logical conclusion. Once you have developed your personal synthesized view of teaching, learning, and technology, you will be ready to explore the techniques that can make the job of designing effective instruction easier. Chapter 2 teaches you how to design effective instruction to focus your instructional efforts on making your teaching as meaningful as possible for your students. Further, the instructional design principles and skills that you will explore will enable you to incorporate educational technology in a manner that will be appropriate and effective for the learners you serve.

HANDS-ON LEARNING

After examining the role of technology in teaching and learning and after reviewing the foundational concepts presented in this chapter, you should be able to synthesize your own view of technology integration. It is a much discussed and explored topic. Some of the best educational minds in the nation have carefully articulated and defended sometimes contradictory positions. Reviewing some of their views will help you better clarify your own thinking.

Using online or library resources, research the role of technology in teaching and learning. Examine articles by those who agree with your personal view on using technology in your classroom as well as articles by those who hold opposing views. Summarize what you find on both positions and include the appropriate references. Conclude with your own position and explain what impact your reading had on it.

KEY TERMS

Association for Educational Communications and Technology (AECT) 5
behaviorists 15
cognitive style 20
cognitivists 16
communications cycle 12
computer-assisted instruction (CAI) 31
constructivists 16
educational technology 5
environmental factor 13

feedback 12
instructional events 10
intelligence 23
International Society for Technology in Education (ISTE) 5
IQ 23
learning environment 18
learning style 14
media 5
method 7

personal filter 14
perspective 12
programmed instruction 31
psychological factors 13
stimulus-response 16
systems approach 27
teaching style 26
technologists 5
theories 10
theory of multiple intelligences 24

KEY LEARNING THEORISTS

David Ausubel 16

Albert Bandura 18

Katherine Briggs 21

Jerome Bruner 16

Robert Gagné 18

Howard Gardner 24

Isabel Briggs Myers 21

Seymour Papert 17

Ivan Pavlov 15

Jean Piaget 16

B. F. Skinner 15

Lev Vygotsky 18

John Watson 15

STUDENT ACTIVITIES

CHAPTER REVIEW

1. What is educational technology? How is it different when perceived by educators versus technologists?
2. What is the relationship between the teaching-learning process and educational technology?
3. What factors can affect effective communication? Explain how each can interfere with the sender's message.
4. Contrast the three perspectives on learning. How are they the same? How are they different? With which do you most agree?
5. Explain the difference between cognitive styles and learning styles. How might each affect learning?

6. Describe the theory of multiple intelligences. How might this theory affect teaching?
7. What is a holistic approach to education? How might educational technology be viewed as a system?
8. How does the current view of educational technology differ from earlier views?
9. What is programmed instruction? What has been its impact on the current approach to educational technology?
10. Describe your synthesized view of teaching, learning, and technology.

WHAT DO YOU THINK?

1. Imagine that you are going to teach a unit on Christopher Columbus to the grade level of your choice. What immediately comes to mind as you consider how you might teach this unit? Is there any relationship between how you might want to teach this unit and your own learning or cognitive style? Describe how you think your own personal style might affect your teaching style.

2. Cultural filters can make a difference as to whether your message is communicated clearly. Considering the potential diversity of the students you will teach, imagine teaching a unit on how the U.S. president is elected. Analyze the possible cultural filters that you need to address to ensure that the lesson is communicated accurately. List these filters and suggest how you would overcome each.

3. You have learned about a variety of learning theories in this chapter. Which one of the theoretical frameworks are you most comfortable with? Explain why the theory you selected is most appealing to you.

4. For this course, the study of educational technology begins with a very close look at the teaching-learning process. Why do you think this is an important place to start?

5. In our Information Age, some educators believe that having computers in the classroom is just another educational fad, like the emphasis in the 1950s and 1960s on television in the classroom. Do you agree or disagree? Defend your answer.

LEARNING TOGETHER!

The following activities should be done in small groups.

1. Describe to your peers the teachers you have had that seem to fit into the theoretical frameworks described in this chapter. After each member of the group shares her or his experiences, select a single teacher from your collective experiences who best represents each learning theory. Summarize the teachers and the reasons they were selected. Be prepared to share your group's views with the class.

2. Select a single theorist to study in greater depth. In your group, explore the theorist's life, work, and theories. Prepare a summary of key points of interest to share in a group oral report to the rest of the class.

3. Visit a school classroom and media center to observe the technologies that are available in these areas. Considering the historical trends in technology described in this chapter, where would you place the school in terms of its level of technological innovation? Share your observations with your group and together build a snapshot of the state of technology in the average school today.

E-Learning

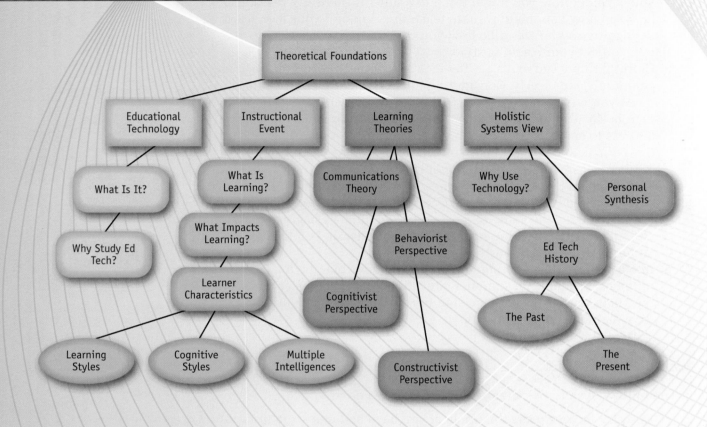

Podcasts www.mylabschool.com

Listen to a podcast relating to the use of technology in teaching and learning. Download the audio discussion to your iPod, computer, or MP3 player.

Video Lab www.mylabschool.com

On the **mylabschool** web site, you will find several video vignettes that offer you a look at addressing learning needs via technology. Learning guides for all videos can be found in the text's Learning Guide Supplement.

On the Web! Activities www.ablongman.com/lever-duffy3e
Noted in the margins of the chapter, these activities offer you in-depth experiences in the topics and content presented in the chapter.

Online Practice Test www.ablongman.com/lever-duffy3e
Practice tests offer you an opportunity to test your knowledge and then review the results and send them to your teacher.

Outliner www.ablongman.com/lever-duffy3e
Chapter Outliners are fill-in-the-blank outlines of the main ideas presented in the chapter. Download the outliner and fill it in for an effective chapter study guide.

Power Practices www.ablongman.com/lever-duffy3e
Power Practices are animated tutorials made using Microsoft's presentation software, PowerPoint. This flash card tutorial will help you practice key concepts in the chapter.

Puzzler www.ablongman.com/lever-duffy3e
Puzzlers include content in crossword, word search, and other puzzle formats to help you master chapter content.

Useful Links www.ablongman.com/lever-duffy3e
These links offer you suggestions for expanded online research in the topics presented in the chapter.

INTEGRATION *Ideas*

The foundational knowledge you have mastered in Chapter 1 helps you to understand how technology fits into the learning environment and how it can be useful in meeting the needs of your diverse learners. Regardless of which learning theory you subscribe to, technology can provide a powerful tool to engage learners and reinforce instruction. The Integration Ideas summaries below offer you a more in-depth look at some ideas shared by educators across the nation. Read these abstracts and follow the references to the full text articles to connect this chapter's content to the grade level and/or subject you will teach.

The Learning Environment in the Primary Classroom

In *Reorganizing Primary Classroom Learning*, Nigel Hastings and Karen Chantrey Wood address classroom organization in primary education. They explore existing environments and suggest new ways of arranging classrooms that offer flexible and strategic approaches to the organization of learning. These environments create a better match between working contexts and tasks. To review their comments, suggestions, and resources to help teachers plan and evaluate ways of using their classrooms more effectively to support learning, visit **www.eric.ed.gov/ERICDocs/**.

Effects of Using Instructional Technology in Elementary and Secondary Schools

James Kulick conducted a review of 8 meta analyses on the effect of instructional technology in elementary and secondary schools. In this review he exams how the use and effectiveness of technology integration has changed since earlier studies in the 1990s. Within his review he addresses critical questions including how technology impacts academic performance, what affect it has on higher order thinking, and what strategies result in effective technology application. To learn more of the fascinating study, go to the following location on the ISTE website to access it. **http://caret.iste.org/index.cfm?fuseaction=studySummary&studyid=1044.**

Standards in the Elementary Classroom

In *The Goal Is Excellence*, Luana Ellison describes how she successfully creates an engaging learning environment that remains focused on the standards her students must achieve. Far from teaching to the test, Ms. Ellison has found innovative ways to "weave student's interests and learning style needs with larger themes surrounding the individual standards." For more on teaching to standards without sacrificing innovation, visit **www.newhorizons.org/strategies/assess/ellison.htm.**

Multiple Intelligence in the Classroom

In this article, elementary teacher Bruce Campbell describes how he sets up learning centers in his classroom so that each center supports one of Gardner's identified intelligences. Using this approach, each day every student has an opportunity to work within the framework of his or her dominant intelligence. For specifics on how this innovative strategy was achieved, visit **www.newhorizons.org/strategies/mi/campbell3.htm.**

Addressing Diversity in Math and Science Education

In "*An Interview with Sheila Tobias on Re-Thinking Teaching Math*," *Science Education World* interviews author and educator Sheila Tobias as she explores how best to teach math and science to diverse students. Ms. Tobias discusses a broad range of topics from teaching math and science to diverse learning to handling math phobia. For more on these educational concerns, visit **www.educationworld.com/a_curr/profdev026.shtml.**

Learning Styles

In *Your Students: No Two Are Alike,* middle school math teacher Brenda Dyck discusses how she helps her students discover their own learning strengths while developing a learner profile she can refer to. She provides links to online styles instruments that teachers can use to better target instruction to their student's learning needs. For more, visit **www.educationworld.com/a_curr/voice/voice061.shtml.**

Multiple Intelligences

Tapping into Multiple Intelligence is a free online teacher workshop, one of several offered by Concepts to Classrooms, that provides visitors with eight multimedia pages exploring multiple intelligence theory and its application to the classroom. To take the workshop and discover more about multiple intelligence, visit **www.thirteen.org/edonline/concept2class/mi/index.html.**

History of Educational Technology

The Association for Educational Communications and Technology offers an interactive history of educational technology in the twentieth century. Review each period of educational technology evolution and see historical photos of each. Exploring these web pages will add depth to your understanding of how educational technology has evolved and become a vital component of instruction. To learn more, visit **www.aect.org/About/History/.**

For these and many more *Integration Ideas* for understanding the role of technology in learning, visit the text web site at **www.ablongman.com/lever-duffy3e.**

1901
Manipulatives
Maria Montessori's kinesthetic approach offered a variety of manipulatives from which students could learn.

1600s
Quill Pens and Slates
Early one-room schoolhouses in the 1700s and 1800s used these materials to teach students how to write and cipher.

1826
Wall Charts
To save the cost of individual books, passages were sometimes printed in large letters and hung for all to see in Lancastrian schools.

1855
Models
With the introduction of kindergarten in Wisconsin, models and materials were given to students to manipulate and to learn from.

1700s
Primers
The New England Primer remained the basic school text for 100 years after its publication.

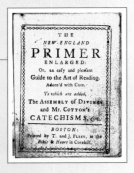

1904
Educational Museums
The visual-education movement resulted in educational museums with abundant visual displays.

interchapter 1

SOURCES: A Hypertext History of Instructional Design. Retrieved October 3, 2003, from **www.coe.uh.edu/courses/cuin6373/idhistory/idex.html**; P. Saettler. 1968. A history of instructional technology. New York: McGraw-Hill.

1923
AECT
The Association for Educational Communications and Technology was created to help improve instruction through technology.

1940–1945
Instructional Technologists
With the role of technology in learning increasing, the need for expertise in both education and technology grew, and professional instructional technologists emerged.

1914
Behaviorism Theory
John Watson helped establish behaviorism, which became one of the theoretical foundations for learning.

1929
Radio
The Ohio "School of the Air" broadcast instruction to homes.

1945
Multiple Media Used by Military Armed Forces
Training used films, sound, graphics, models, and print to help prepare recruits for war.

1910
Films
Edison declared after inventing motion pictures that books would soon be obsolete. Public schools in New York City implemented films for instruction for the first time.

Education as a Science
Edward Thorndike helped establish education as a science.

1933
Objectives in Education
Ralph Tyler at Ohio State University developed and refined procedures for writing objectives.

Continues on next page ▶

1956
Bloom's Taxonomy
A team led by Benjamin Bloom identified
and articulated levels of cognition.

1967
PBS and NER
The Public Broadcasting
Act established the
Public Broadcasting
Service and National
Educational Radio.

1965
Instructional Design System
Robert Gagné introduced a model for a
systems approach to designing
instruction.

1970
Cognitive Approach
Cognitivists including
Ausubel, Bruner, Gagné,
and others dominated
thinking about
learning.

1957
Programmed Instruction
Programmed instruction materials based on
Skinner's behaviorism were used at the
Mystic School in Winchester,
Massachusetts.

1953
ITV
The University of
Houston launches KUHT,
the first noncommercial
education station.

1977
Personal Computers
The first microcomputer, the Apple, was created by Steve Wozniak and Steve Jobs.

2008 and beyond
Online Life
The Internet expands to include "live" audio and video, leading to instruction anytime, anywhere.

The Grid
Using distributed computing technology, the Grid will make it possible to dynamically pool and share computer resources, making unprecedented computing power available to everyone on the Grid.

1991
World Wide Web
The Internet became accessible to all with the creation of the Web by Tim Berners-Lee.

1980s
CAI
Computer-assisted instruction on personal computers reached its peak of popularity.

2003
Mobile Devices
Cell phones, hybrids, PDAs, and tablet PCs joined with wireless networking to make mobile computing commonplace everywhere, including in the classroom.

1990s
Constructivist Approach
The influence of Dewey, Piaget, Vygotsky, and others led to the emergence of the constructivist view of learning.

Computer-Based Technologies
Video discs, CD-ROMs, multimedia, digital presentations, interactive video, teleconferencing, compressed video, and the Internet combined to greatly increase the technologies available to enhance teaching and learning.

Virtual Reality
Digital representations of a given reality let teacher and student "experience" it; e.g., the inside of a volcano erupting.

Digital Assistants
Intelligent agents help you interact with your equipment and cyberspace.

chapter 2

Designing and Planning Technology-Enhanced Instruction

This chapter addresses these ISTE *National Educational Technology Standards* for Teachers:

II. PLANNING AND DESIGNING LEARNING ENVIRONMENTS AND EXPERIENCES
Teachers plan and design effective learning environments and experiences supported by technology. Teachers
A. design developmentally appropriate learning opportunities that apply technology-enhanced instructional strategies to support the diverse needs of learners.
B. apply current research on teaching and learning with technology when planning learning environments and experiences.
C. identify and locate technology resources and evaluate them for accuracy and suitability.
D. plan for the management of technology resources within the context of learning activities.
E. plan strategies to manage student learning in a technology-enhanced environment.

III. TEACHING, LEARNING, AND THE CURRICULUM
Teachers implement curriculum plans that include methods and strategies for applying technology to maximize student learning. Teachers
A. facilitate technology-enhanced experiences that address content standards and student technology standards.
B. use technology to support learner-centered strategies that address the diverse needs of students.
C. apply technology to develop students' higher-order skills and creativity.
D. manage student learning activities in a technology-enhanced environment.

IV. ASSESSMENT AND EVALUATION
Teachers apply technology in a variety of effective assessment and evaluation strategies. Teachers
A. apply technology in assessing student learning of subject matter using a variety of assessment techniques.
B. use technology resources to collect and analyze data, interpret results, and communicate findings to improve instructional practice and maximize student learning.
C. apply multiple methods of evaluation to determine students' appropriate use of technology resources for learning, communication, and productivity.

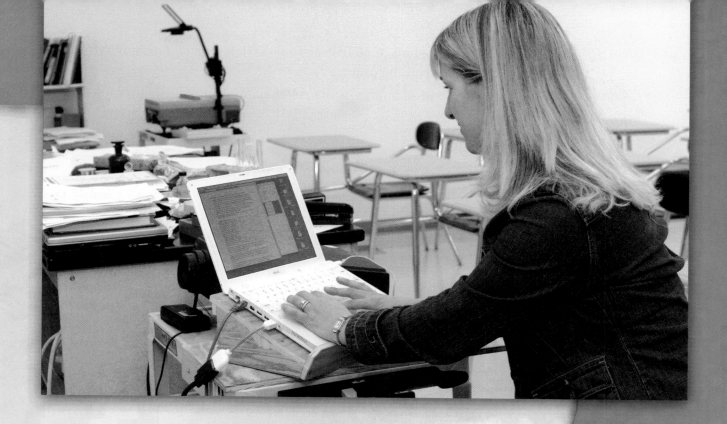

n Chapter 2, you will begin your exploration of the way in which effective teachers design and plan instruction enhanced and supported by technology. In Chapter 1, you learned a great deal about the teaching and learning process. Chapter 2 will help you discover how to apply what you have learned as you plan and carry out effective instruction.

In this chapter, you will examine learning environments, beginning with the physical aspects of the environment such as classroom layout and facilities. You will then have the opportunity to explore the less tangible, more critical aspects of the environment: the instructional design that drives instruction and the teaching strategies that might be incorporated in the design. You will then explore the planning of day-to-day lessons for use in your classroom. Finally, you will learn to create an instructional action plan to help ensure that your lessons are implemented just as you planned them.

In Chapter 2, you will

- Examine classroom facilities and their impact on the teaching and learning process

- Explore instructional design and how design affects instruction

- Examine performance objectives and their role in targeting learning outcomes

- Review the instructional design process and the pedagogical cycle incorporated therein

- Examine the process of lesson planning

- Review the components of an instructional action plan and examine its role in the teaching and learning process
- Explore the role of planning in the selection and implementation of instructional technology

Real People Real Stories

Meet Liz Brennan and Stacy Still. To build an effective learning environment requires planning. While planning may not be as exciting as delivering the instruction, careful and systematic planning is what makes effective teaching and learning. When Liz Brennan and Stacy Still recognized the problems their teachers were experiencing incorporating technology into their plans, they sat down with them and met the challenge together.

University School of Nova Southeastern University is a campus-based, independent college preparatory day school located in Fort Lauderdale, Florida. I am Liz Brennan, Associate Head of the University School of Nova Southeastern University. I would estimate that at least 75 percent of the "work" I do each day involves curriculum design and development. Whenever we think of curriculum, we are also thinking *planning*; and, one cannot think planning without thinking *learning*. On a daily basis working with my faculty, I can see that issues with student learning can, many times, be connected to breakdowns in classroom curriculum design—planning.

My name is Stacy Still. I am the Technology Facilitator at the Lower School. There are many aspects to my job as Technology Facilitator, but one of the most important functions is to assist faculty in the planning of lessons that tie technology into the learning process.

Our problem involves a condition where, despite the knowledge and skills for generic lesson planning, the teacher is unable to effectively or consistently "fit" appropriate uses of computer-based learning experiences into a previously developed lesson plan. In addition, either she may lack the personal technical skills to feel comfortable with available hardware or she lacks an understanding of software options available either within the school or via the Internet.

Liz: To get the most from a planning experience, Stacy often sits with an individual teacher, and together they plan the lesson in a collaborative mode. Stacy, with her expertise in technology, is able to guide the teacher and help her gain certain technical skills; the teacher, with her expertise in pedagogy, is able to assess the design of the plan as they study it together and make decisions as to how and where to use technology effectively. This empowers the teacher to determine if the technological ideas that Stacy suggests, or the ones that they find together, are appropriate for the lesson, connect to the outcome objectives, address various learning styles of their students, and match the students' current performance levels. During their collaborative planning process, teachers can practice the lesson with the selected technology to simulate how it will work in their classrooms. This preinstructional step helps the teacher feel more comfortable and confident in the quality of the plan and in his or her use of technology.

Stacy: I worked with one of our teachers in planning a lesson. Through our discussion, the teacher determined that her plan was sound in most of the steps of the planning process. We identified and listed the areas of strength: clearly stated objectives, an appropriately established learning environment, and a well-targeted summative evaluation. However, given the large number of students for whom the lesson was intended, it was difficult for her not only to identify but to manage the learning styles and specific learning needs of all of these students. We decided to strengthen several areas: knowing the learner, identifying teaching and learning strategies, and identifying and selecting technologies to be used to enhance and extend the lesson to be meaningful to more students.

Our first planning collaboration was to go online and find instructional plans that effectively integrated technology. The first time, the teacher searched while I assisted and guided her through the general search to locate the most appropriate lesson plan sites. We started with a simple search using www.google.com. We found hundreds of sites that included well-planned technology-enhanced lesson plans. I suggested that we try to use a kid's search engine, such as www.yahooligans.com, sunsite.berkeley.edu/KidsClick!/, or www.ajkids.com to look for other resources and lesson plan sites that would be more limited or controlled by age level and content. She was able to incorporate both audio and video experiences from sites such as

www.rainforesteducation.com/FunNGames/canuseethem.htm
www.exploratorium.edu/frogs/rainforest/
www.christiananswers.net/kid/vidclips.html

The next step was to determine how to incorporate these links and the other information into a PowerPoint presentation. Having me there as a guide enabled her to learn, in a hands-on mode, how to do these things, yet she was not "afraid" of the task or the technology. The final step in the plan then was to determine the best way to display this presentation. We decided to use a portable smart board to deliver the instruction and present the PowerPoint project.

This was a tremendous experience for both of us. The teacher gained confidence in herself, as a professional, and in her own ability to use the technology effectively, and I was able to see the lesson plan implemented and use its outcome as a reference later with other teachers.

For further information, you may contact the writers at the following:

Dr. Elizabeth C. Brennan's email: brennan@nova.edu
    phone: 954-262-4500
Stacy Still's email: stacy@nova.edu
    phone: 954-262-4500

Planning for Effective Instruction

The foundation in learning theory and educational technology you gained from Chapter 1 can now be used to build an approach for the creation of effective instruction. Instruction can be broadly defined to include all of the components of teaching and learning from the instructional environment to the actions taken by both teacher and students to evaluating instructional success. To be effective in creating effective instruction, a teacher must carefully consider everything that needs to occur in the classroom and during the lesson. Questions that need to be answered through reflection and planning include

Planning for Quality Teaching

- What are my students like, and what special needs do they have that should be addressed via instruction?
- What exactly should my students to be able to do when I am done with the instruction?
- What do I need to do in my classroom to get everything ready for instruction?
- What strategies am I going to use to teach the content?
- What should I have my students do to learn the target skills and content?
- What technologies do I need to support instruction?
- How will I know if instruction was successful, and what is the process for changing it if it was not?

These questions offer a framework for the systematic process that will lead to the creation of effective instruction. These questions are the core of the planning process engaged in by every effective teacher. Initially, a carefully articulated planning process seems long and cumbersome. But ultimately and with years of practice, it becomes inherent in the way a teacher approaches instruction. The essential skill of instructional planning eventually becomes a way of thinking in the classroom. This chapter introduces you to systematic instructional planning, while subsequent chapters provide you with the technology tools to enhance your plans. This approach allows instruction to drive technology selection and implementation, which in turn keeps the focus on teaching and learning.

Using an Instructional Planning System

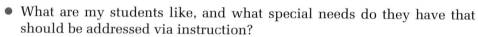

Effective instruction is instruction that has been thoroughly thought out and articulated by a skillful and creative educator. To ensure that every moment of a learner's educational time is productive, an educator must envision all aspects of instruction, from what will be covered in an instructional unit to what needs to be done each day. The notion of a carefully planned, step-by-step process to design, create, evaluate, and revise instruction is called a **systems approach** to instruction. In this chapter, you will explore a comprehensive three-part system that will help you maximize the quality of your teaching. The system, called the **design-plan-act! (D-P-A) system,** includes the following three planning processes (see Figure 2.1):

1. Design: Designing the instructional unit
2. Plan: Articulating specific daily lesson plans within the unit
3. Act: Developing an instructional action plan for each day of instruction

Together, these three system elements will help you effectively plan and implement all aspects of effective instruction.

The Design Phase

At this most comprehensive and strategic level of the instructional planning system, the educator envisions the delivery of the targeted curriculum in its entirety. The content is typically an instructional unit that includes a clearly identified series of competencies. This is the design phase of the system. All aspects of instruction are considered, and decisions are made with regard to each step of the teaching and learning process. Although specific daily details might not yet be determined, the instructional design articulates all of the broad steps that must be taken to ensure that the intended instruction occurs as conceived. Typically, an **instructional design model,** a fully articulated design template, is used to help educators in the first phase of the planning system to envision their planned instruction holistically, as an entire unit. Using such a model as a foundation, you will ultimately be able to develop an effective daily lesson plan and a subsequent instructional action plan.

The instructional design model must be flexible and adaptable to accommodate the continual changes in strategies that are supported and enhanced by technology. To that end, on the following pages, the **dynamic instructional design (DID) model** is presented. It will serve as the basis for designing technology-rich instruction and as a practical guide as you conceptualize how you will create an effective instructional unit. The DID

Design-Plan-Act! is a systematic approach to effective instruction.

Design identifies overall goals and the steps to achieve them.

FIGURE 2.1

The Design-Plan-Act! (D-P-A) System

D-P-A's three system components work together to create effective instruction.

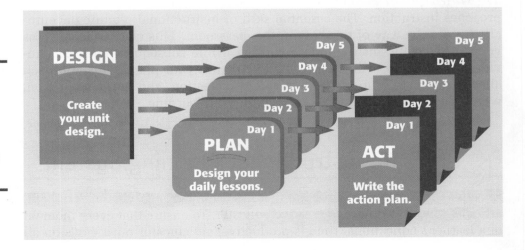

model will serve as the foundation for the creation of two additional tools, a lesson planner and instructional action planner, that you can use to help you plan to teach components of the unit effectively and successfully each day.

The Plan Phase

The second phase of the D-P-A system is the planning phase. During this phase, the unit design is broken down into daily lesson plans. The design developed the instructional approach broadly during the entire unit, while the planning phase details what needs to be done each day to achieve the design goals. During this phase, the teacher considers which components of the design should be presented during each day of instruction and describes precisely how the lesson will unfold. For many experienced teachers who have already learned to think about instruction using a systematic approach, it is this phase that is typically noted in lesson plan books.

The Act Phase

Once daily lesson plans are articulated, a teacher needs to remember many small but critical details in order to prepare for instruction. The teacher may need to requisition supplies or reserve a video from the media center. These many details need to be planned and acted on so that instruction can move forward smoothly and without incident. This is the action phase of planning. For an experienced teacher, this phase may be as informal as jotting down a to-do list. When planning an instructional unit, however, this phase needs to be articulated to be sure no critical element is forgotten.

In a systematic instructional design process, then, the teacher considers instruction as a series of steps from the broadest components of the sequence to the most detailed. The unit may cover several weeks, so the design model takes into account all aspects of instruction for the entire unit. On a day-to-day basis, the intermediate step of planning daily lessons for each of the days the unit will be taught offers the teacher a guideline as to what must be completed each day to meet unit goals. In the final planning step, the action plan, each detail needed for successful daily instruction to occur is articulated. Together, reflecting on and planning each phase result in smoothly executed, comprehensive, and effective instruction.

 ## The Dynamic Instructional Design Model

The DID model includes all of the critical elements necessary to design effective instruction. Every step of the model is crucial to the process and must be considered carefully. Just as the architectural process must begin with an understanding of the qualities of the land on which a building will be built and must proceed through discussions of the purpose and use of the building before any plans are made, so too must educators think broadly and strategically about their intended instruction.

A number of instructional design systems models are available for educators to follow. The most pervasive and influential of these is the systems model originally developed by **Robert Gagné**. Known for the application of

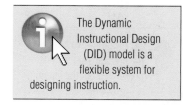

The Dynamic Instructional Design (DID) model is a flexible system for designing instruction.

Spotlight on Robert Gagné

Feedback is the return of information regarding the success of each step.

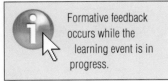

Formative feedback occurs while the learning event is in progress.

10

Summative feedback occurs at the conclusion of the learning event.

systems thinking to instructional design, Gagné is perhaps the leading figure in instructional design systems. He was the first to promote and develop a comprehensive systems view of instructional design, that is, a system of steps that provide a logical systematic foundation for designing instruction. His definitive work is the foundation for many subsequent models.

Gagné's model and the others that were developed as a result are the foundation for today's instructional design systems. The DID model, which builds on these definitive systems models, differs primarily in its emphasis on a dynamic design, which is necessary to represent the capability for continuous adjustment and change. The instructional design must be flexible enough to embrace and use data provided by ongoing feedback from learners. The DID model is specifically designed to ensure that responsiveness while maintaining the logical sequencing of the design process.

The DID model is therefore built around a continuous internal and external **feedback loop** to ensure that each step of the process is functioning at its maximum effectiveness. Internal feedback loops occur within each step of the process. External loops are built between all steps of the process. Continual self-examination, feedback, and correction are built into the model to emphasize its flexibility while maintaining its system integrity. Although each step of the process includes the classic elements articulated initially by Gagné, the DID model is designed to help educators envision instruction as a changing and dynamic process.

Teachers who embrace a systems approach such as the D-P-A system better understand and are better able to envision the instructional big picture. They start with a conception of all the instructional elements necessary for effective teaching and learning and of the relationship of these elements to each other. From this strategic beginning, they can then narrow and refocus their efforts on lesson planning, through which they can specify the instructional events on a day-to-day basis. Finally, they reach the pragmatic stage, during which they articulate an instructional action plan or to-do list for making the instructional events flow flawlessly. The DID model is the first step in this process: the design step.

As you review the DID model illustrated in Figure 2.2, note that a formative feedback process is a component of each step. **Formative feedback occurs during an event or process.** Formative feedback ensures a way to facilitate the continuous flow of information as a system is implemented so that corrections and adjustments can be made while the process unfolds. The DID model includes a formative feedback loop during every step of the process so that feedback can be gathered and midcourse corrections can be made. In implementation of the model, this would mean that the design includes strategies to respond quickly to feedback during implementation. Thus, each step is dynamic and flexible; that is, each step remains a work in process throughout and after the design phase.

Additionally, summative feedback is built into the DID model. **Summative feedback** is returned at the end of a process. In the DID model, the summative feedback loop can return information to help revise each step of the process once the entire process is completed. Because formative feedback is continuous throughout all steps of the process, the summative feedback loop serves as a final check once all steps are completed.

The feedback loops of the DID model encourage you to create a dynamic instructional process that remains responsive even as you are actively

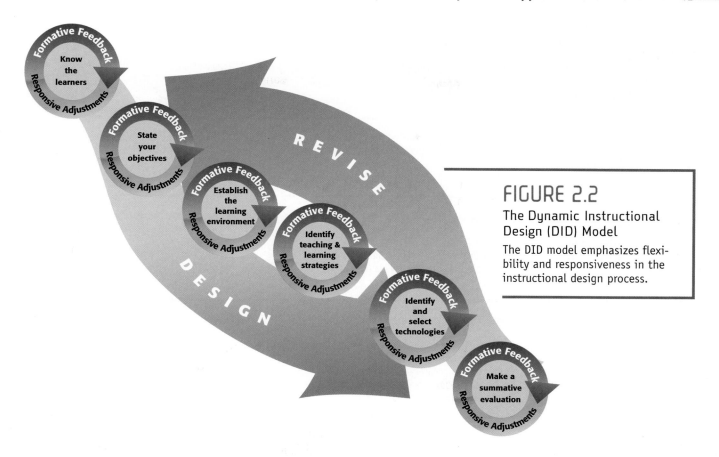

FIGURE 2.2

The Dynamic Instructional Design (DID) Model

The DID model emphasizes flexibility and responsiveness in the instructional design process.

engaged in planning and implementing the instruction. In this model, you are encouraged to think about how you intend to continuously correct and improve each step. Rather than simply completing a step and going on to the next, this model incorporates an internal process for continuous improvement. Such a continuous improvement process is at the core of high-quality instruction. Table 2.1 on page 50 shows how formative feedback and summative feedback are used at each step in the DID model.

Let's examine how each step contributes to the design phase. Typically, these steps are initially taken in the sequence presented, but as any new information comes to light as a result of ongoing feedback, it may be necessary to step out of the sequence to respond and adjust. The DID model is designed to encourage this flexibility.

Step 1: Know the Learners

To begin the process of designing instruction, you must first have a clear picture of those for whom the instruction is being created. As much as possible, instruction must be adjusted to ensure that it is the most appropriate sequence of events for those who stand to benefit from experiencing those events. To successfully focus instruction in this way, you must begin by carefully reviewing the characteristics of your learners. To do so, you will need to ask yourself a number of questions about your learners. You may also have additional questions based on the instructional setting in which

TABLE 2.1   DID Formative and Summative Feedback Loops

DID STEP	FORMATIVE FEEDBACK QUESTIONS Questions to Ask during the Design Process	SUMMATIVE FEEDBACK QUESTIONS Questions to Ask at the End of the Design Process
1. KNOW THE LEARNERS.	• Am I responding to all learning styles? • Am I accurately depicting the students' developmental stages? • Am I correctly assessing student skill levels?	Did the design successfully meet the needs of the learners?
2. STATE YOUR OBJECTIVES.	• Are my objectives targeting the performances I intended? • Are my objectives stated in a format that makes it possible to accurately measure performance? • Do my objectives include multiple levels of critical thinking?	Did my objectives accurately capture, in performance terms, the essence of the content the students needed to learn?
3. ESTABLISH THE LEARNING ENVIRONMENT.	• Does the physical space I am planning offer sufficient diversity to meet learner needs? • Is the environment nurturing and secure for all students? • Does the class management system promote positive and productive interaction? • Am I planning student and teacher exchanges that support and enhance learning?	Was the learning environment that I established effective in promoting learning?
4. IDENTIFY TEACHING AND LEARNING STRATEGIES.	• Am I addressing all of the steps of the pedagogical cycle? • Does each step make sense in terms of the cycle and the student learning it is intended to promote? • Am I including sufficiently varied teaching strategies and learning activities to meet the needs of my diverse students?	Are the teaching and learning strategies sufficient for and effective in meeting the objectives I identified?
5. IDENTIFY AND SELECT TECHNOLOGIES.	• Are the technologies I have selected appropriate to the content and pedagogy? • Am I selecting a variety of technologies that will meet the diversity of learning styles? • Are the technologies and support materials readily available?	Were the technologies I selected successful in supporting the targeted teaching and learning?
6. PERFORM A SUMMATIVE EVALUATION.	• Am I identifying a method of assessment that will measure achievement of objectives? • Is the data to be gathered from the assessment useful to determine necessary revisions? • Are the evaluation techniques valid and reliable with reference to the design?	Does the summative evaluation provide the data I need to determine whether the objectives were achieved? Was the data sufficient for effective revision?

you are teaching. A few of the most common questions that lead to careful examination of your learners are:

- What are their developmental stages, both physically and cognitively?
- What in their cultural or language backgrounds may affect how instruction is received?

- What are their incoming skills and knowledge base relative to the intended instruction?
- What are their individual characteristics, such as learning styles, cognitive styles, and types of intelligence?
- As a group, how are the learners the same, and how are they different?
- How might these similarities or differences affect the design of the intended instruction?

Each of these questions must be answered to establish a clear picture of the learners for whom you are designing instruction. The more accurate your examination and assessment of your learners, the more likely that the instruction will be appropriate and successful. Your answers may be informal, that is, based simply on your observations of your students or discussions with them, or your answers may be formal, that is, derived from objective data. Such data may be from student records kept by your school or gathered by you using assessment tools such as the learning style inventories you learned about in Chapter 1. The more information you gather, whether formal or informal, the more likely it is that your instruction will be targeted correctly to meet the needs of your students.

Use formal and informal methods to profile students.

Remember that at any time during or after completing this first step, you must be ready to adjust your conclusions. As the design process continues, new information may come to light, or, through feedback, you may discover that some of your conclusions about your learners need adjustment. Staying flexible and ready to alter each of the components of the process is a key element in maximizing your instruction's potential for success.

Step 2: State Your Objectives

Objectives are statements of what will be achieved as a result of the instruction you are designing. **Performance objectives** are objectives that specify what the learner will be able to do when the instructional event concludes.

Performance objectives detail expected competencies.

To teach effectively, you must know and address the diverse characteristics of your students.

HANDS-ON LEARNING

Instructional planning is required at every level of education from kindergarten through college level. Many tools and templates have been developed to help teachers plan. Whether a formal instructional design model is required or a more concise daily lesson plan is used, every teacher can find a template that makes sense to him or her.

Investigate your options by completing a Google search with the key words *lesson plan template*. From the results of your search, explore at least three different types of templates. Compare the steps of each of the templates you review to the D-P-A templates. Describe how they differ and how they are the same. What did you like best about each?

To keep your instructional design focused on helping the learner achieve competencies or skills, it is critical that you take the time to state your instructional objectives in terms of student performance. This step will keep all subsequent steps tightly targeted on student outcomes.

Performance objectives typically include a stem plus three key components: targeted student performance, a description of the method for assessing the intended performance, and a criterion for measuring success. Let's examine a performance objective for a grammar unit in a middle school language arts class:

Objective: The student will be able to identify, with 95 percent accuracy, the subject and the verb in sentences contributed by peers and written on the board.

- *Stem:* The student will be able to
- *Target performance:* identify the subject and verb
- *Measurement conditions:* in sentences contributed by peers and written on the board
- *Criterion for success:* with 95 percent accuracy.

Notice that in this objective, the critical factor is the performance expected of the *student* as a result of the anticipated instruction, not the performance of the teacher. In our example, the student is going to be able to perform a measurable action, that is, *identify* targeted knowledge. In this case, the targeted knowledge is the concept of subject and verb. Furthermore, the objective indicates the method that will be used to assess performance. Again in our example, success in identifying the target concepts will be measured by the student's correctly identifying the subject and verb

YOU Decide!

Planning can be a cumbersome process. It takes time to think through exactly what you want your students to be able to do when you are done teaching. It takes a great deal of thought to consider all aspects of content that you want to include in the unit. It takes time to research what other teachers have done to see if you are including the most innovative ideas and the best technology available. It takes creativity to consider how the content can be best delivered in a manner that meets the needs of all of your learners. Is it worth the time and effort to create comprehensive plans?

YES! Teaching isn't an easy profession. It takes time, effort, and dedication to create lessons that really work. Everyone has been in a class where the teacher seemed to be unprepared. The instruction came off disjointed and confusing. It wasted everyone's time. But when a teacher comes to class with a clear idea of what he or she wants to accomplish, a good plan as to how to teach the content, and activities that help students to learn the content, that teacher makes instructional time worthwhile. It may be hard, but planning is essential.

NO! Teaching just has too many requirements to make it possible to write out detailed lesson plans. Between all of the administrative tasks, the paperwork, and grading, planning just can't be done at the level everyone seems to expect. Something has to give. Thinking about what you want to do for a lesson and jotting down brief notes in a lesson plan book is enough. Writing down objectives, strategies, and assessments and relating it all to standards just isn't a reasonable expectation.

Which view of planning do you agree with? YOU DECIDE!

in sentences contributed by peers and written on the board. Finally, the criterion that indicates success in achieving that objective, that is, per-forming the action cor-

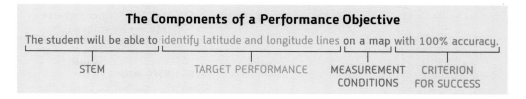

The Components of a Performance Objective

The student will be able to identify latitude and longitude lines on a map with 100% accuracy.

| STEM | TARGET PERFORMANCE | MEASUREMENT CONDITIONS | CRITERION FOR SUCCESS |

rectly 95 percent of the time, is articulated. Thus, in our example, a student who mistakes the subject and verb 5 percent of the time would still be considered to have sufficiently mastered the target knowledge. Objectives written in this format leave no doubt about what performance is expected of the student. This, in turn, leaves no doubt about what the teacher needs to teach for the designated outcomes to occur.

This focus on student outcomes is the purpose of fully articulated performance objectives. These objectives not only detail precisely what the student is supposed to learn and how such learning is to be mea-sured, they also require that teachers stay centered on outcomes in their teaching. Generic objectives such as "The student will have an under-standing of grammar" do little to assist the teacher in deciding what and how to teach. Furthermore, it is difficult to accurately measure some-thing as broad as "understanding." Such overly broad objectives help neither teacher nor student to engage in a meaningful exchange. They do not assist either party in focusing on the task at hand. Indeed, they con-fuse what needs to happen in the learning environment and in the teach-ing-learning process.

Use action verbs to describe expected performance.

Another role of performance objectives is to ensure that the teaching and learning experience includes a full range of cognitive levels, from sim-ple recall of facts to higher-end critical thinking. Writing down perfor-mance objectives identifies exactly which skills and related cognition the teacher is targeting. If all objectives are recall objectives, that is, their out-come is the memorization of facts, it is clear before instruction begins that critical thinking and higher cognitive skills are being ignored. This is a sig-nificant loss in terms of student growth, although it is admittedly some-times easier for a teacher to plan when the goal is to achieve lower-level objectives. Designing instruction that targets higher-order thinking skills is a much more complex task than asking your students to recall facts. However, the benefit to learners of engaging in such tasks far outweighs the instructional costs involved in creating them.

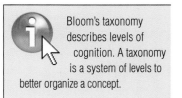

E-Learning
ON THE WEB! 2.3

Examples of Performance Objectives

Several theorists have developed methods for categorizing differences in thinking skills. One of the most prominent was developed in 1956 by a group of researchers led by **Benjamin Bloom.** The categories of cognition that resulted from their efforts have come to be called **Bloom's taxonomy.** Bloom's taxonomy (Bloom, 1956) provides a very useful delineation of the levels of thinking that should be included in creating objectives. These lev-els do not interfere with the knowledge outcomes of the objectives. Instead, they help you identify the level of thinking desired from the learner with regard to that knowledge.

Bloom's taxonomy describes levels of cognition. A taxonomy is a system of levels to better organize a concept.

Bloom's taxonomy includes six levels of cognition ranging from recall of knowledge to evaluation of knowledge (see Figure 2.3 on page 54). Each of these levels is described in the following list, along with action verbs that might be used in objectives that are aimed at that level of thinking:

FIGURE 2.3

Bloom's Taxonomy and Action Verbs

Use Bloom's taxonomy to step up to higher levels of thinking.

SOURCE: Loosely adapted from Bloom's wheel at www.vacadsci.org/teaching/bwheel.htm.

EVALUATION *Action Verbs*
Assess, weigh, critique, consider, judge, recommend

SYNTHESIS *Action Verbs*
Combine, hypothesize, design, develop, originate, formulate, invent, produce

ANALYSIS *Action Verbs*
Analyze, examine, contrast, infer, subdivide, compare, research, construct

APPLICATION *Action Verbs*
Apply, solve, interpret, classify, discover, model, show, sketch, report, modify

COMPREHENSION *Action Verbs*
Explain, match, illustrate, compare, relate, restate, express, defend, distinguish

KNOWLEDGE *Action Verbs*
Identify, name, define, describe, state, label, recite, select, recognize, list

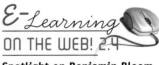

E-Learning ON THE WEB! 2.4

Spotlight on Benjamin Bloom

- *Knowledge:* This level of cognition includes memorizing, recognizing, or recalling factual information. Objectives at the knowledge level would include verbs such as *list, identify, name, recite, state,* and *define* with reference to the material.

- *Comprehension:* At this level of cognition, the emphasis is on organizing, describing, and interpreting concepts. Verbs used in objectives at the comprehension level might include *explain, illustrate, summarize, restate, paraphrase,* and *defend* concepts or information. You can see that the thinking required at this level extends beyond rote learning.

- *Application:* The application level of cognition requires that the student apply the information presented, solve problems with it, and find new ways of using it. Objective verbs that would represent outcomes at this level of thinking would include *apply, classify, demonstrate, discover, predict, show, solve,* and *utilize.*

- *Analysis:* This level of the taxonomy requires higher-level thinking skills such as finding underlying structures, separating the whole into its components, identifying motives, and recognizing hidden meanings. Verbs used in objectives at this level might include *analyze, ascertain, diagram, differentiate, discriminate, examine, determine, investigate, construct,* and *contrast.*

- *Synthesis:* The synthesis level raises desired outcomes to significantly higher levels of cognition. At this level, the student is expected to create an original product based on the knowledge acquired, combine the ideas presented into a new whole, or relate knowledge from several areas into a consistent concept. Action verbs in objectives at the synthesis level would include *combine, compile, create, design, develop, expand, integrate, extend, originate, synthesize,* and *formulate.*

- *Evaluation:* The highest level of cognition in Bloom's taxonomy is the evaluation level. At this level, the learner is expected to make thoughtful value decisions with reference to the knowledge; resolve differences and controversy; and develop personal opinions, judgments, and decisions. Objective verbs at this level would include *assess, critique, judge, appraise, evaluate, weigh,* and *recommend.*

As you can see from the taxonomy, each level ratchets up the cognition required for successful achievement of the objective. Outcomes at the highest levels require significant levels of critical thinking. At the lowest level, knowledge, simple memorization is all that is required. However, after examining Table 2.2, you will see that the lower levels are a necessary prerequisite as you move up the taxonomy. For example, one must know the facts to comprehend, apply, analyze, synthesize, or evaluate them. Although some performance objectives may reasonably target the lowest levels, too often a majority of objectives aim only at these levels. Awareness and application of Bloom's taxonomy in writing performance objectives will help you to create instruction that encourages and emphasizes a broad range of thinking skills for your students.

Clearly and concisely articulating the performance objectives is the second step of the DID model. Because the model emphasizes the dynamic nature of instructional design, you must remain flexible and ready

TABLE 2.2 Bloom's Taxonomy and Performance Objectives

LEVEL	DESCRIPTION	PERFORMANCE OBJECTIVE
KNOWLEDGE	Student recalls or recognizes information, ideas, and principles in the approximate form in which they are learned.	On an unlabeled diagram, the student will be able to label the parts of the human eye with 85 percent accuracy.
COMPREHENSION	Student translates or comprehends information based on prior learning.	In an oral presentation, the student will be able to summarize the plot of *The Lion, the Witch, and the Wardrobe* mentioning at least five of the seven major events with 85 percent accuracy.
APPLICATION	Student selects, transfers, and uses data and principles to complete a problem or task with a minimum of direction.	On a test, the student will be able to solve word problems with two variables with 90 percent accuracy.
ANALYSIS	Student differentiates or examines the assumptions, hypotheses, evidence, or structure of a statement or question.	The student will be able to contrast the causes of the Korean War and the Vietnam War in an oral report with 80 percent accuracy.
SYNTHESIS	Student originates, integrates, and combines ideas into a product, plan, or proposal that is new to him or her.	The student will be able to design a science experiment that includes each step of the scientific method in a written activity with 90 percent accuracy.
EVALUATION	Student appraises, assesses, or critiques a work or works using specific standards or other criteria.	Using a rubric created by the students, the student will be able to critique sample media on the basis of five criteria with 90 percent accuracy.

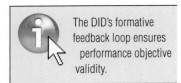

The DID's formative feedback loop ensures performance objective validity.

Creating a Learning Environment

Alternative instructional spaces within a classroom meet diverse learner needs.

to adjust your objectives if you find that they do not keep you sufficiently focused on the target skills, concepts, or levels of cognition you intended. Furthermore, if the method or criterion for measuring success that you included in an objective does not ultimately provide an accurate indicator of student success, it is crucial to alter the objective itself even while the process is continuing. Monitoring the effectiveness of the objectives you have written is an important internal formative feedback mechanism in the DID model. Because your objectives provide the foundation for all subsequent design decisions, their accuracy and validity are critical.

Step 3: Establish the Learning Environment

As you learned in Chapter 1, a **learning environment** includes all conditions, circumstances, and influences that affect the learner's development. Every aspect of the milieu in which teaching and learning take place is an element in the learning environment, from the physical surroundings to the instructional events that occur within those surroundings. So let us begin our exploration of the learning environment with an examination of how physical space affects learning.

The learning environment includes the space and facilities in which instruction occurs. The classroom or learning space itself, the student furniture and its arrangement in the instructional space, and the teaching facilities built into the classroom are all essential elements of the learning environment. Each can have a significant impact on the teaching-learning process. By adjusting these elements to be consistent with the students' learning styles and the educator's teaching style, the effectiveness of the instructional space can be maximized.

Rita and Kenneth Dunn have done extensive research on matching the physical environment to individual learning styles (Dunn and Dunn, 1992). Their learning styles research indicates that changes in lighting, seating, and other physical accommodations in the classroom can reduce distractions to the learning process by providing a sensory environment that accommodates individual preferences. They suggest that a teacher can readily improve the learning environment for students by making simple physical adjustments to the classroom. Such adjustments might include creating well-lit reading areas, arranging for areas of the classroom to be warmer or cooler than normal, establishing classroom sections in which students can work with a peer or a group, providing informal seating such as beanbags or a couch, and setting up quiet or screened study areas for individuals or pairs. These adjustments can be accomplished through creative use of the floor space and traditional furniture found in most classrooms.

To be effective in establishing the learning environment, you should first take inventory of the physical space in which learning occurs. Table 2.3 on page 58 provides a rubric for assessing the learning space. It is important to provide, whenever possible, alternatives in terms of learners' sensory preferences. For example, alternative seating arrangements and lighting intensities should be made available. Rigid one-size-fits-all physical facilities will not meet the needs of many learners and may impede their learn-

Dunn and Dunn

SPOTLIGHT ON

Rita Dunn, professor of administrative and instructional leadership and director of the Center for the Study of Learning and Teaching Styles at St. John's University, Jamaica, New York, has written, "Prize-winning research has made it clear that most children can master the curriculum when they're taught with strategies, methods or resources that complement how they learn" (1999). To identify students' learning style strengths, **Rita** and **Kenneth Dunn** created a chart to represent the five different elements that either stimulate or inhibit learning and constitute each individual's particular learning style. To capitalize on their learning styles, students must become aware of the following:

- Their reaction to the classroom environment—learning with sound or in silence, bright versus soft lighting, warm versus cool temperatures, and formal versus informal seating
- Their own emotionality—motivation, persistence and responsibility levels, and preference for structure versus options
- Their sociological preferences for learning—either alone, with peers, with a collegial or authoritative adult, and/or in a variety of ways as opposed to patterns or routines
- Their physiological characteristics—perceptual strengths (auditory, visual, tactual, and/or kinesthetic modalities), time-of-day energy highs and lows, intake (snacking or sipping while concentrating), and/or mobility needs
- Their global versus analytic processing, as determined through correlations among sound, light, design, persistence, sociological preference, and intake

ing. It might not be feasible to make all the adjustments you desire, but if you make every possible effort to become aware of and adjust your teaching and learning space, you will help to optimize the conditions for your students' learning. As always, the dynamic nature of the DID model requires that you remain vigilant in assessing the effectiveness of your arrangement of the physical space. Observation of the impact of the space on students as they engage in learning activities and on student performance is an important feedback tool that will help you continually monitor and adjust the learning environment.

Nonphysical aspects of the learning environment include the general academic climate of the classroom, the dominant attitudes of learners and the instructor, and the quality of instructional organization provided by effective planning. The general climate of the classroom refers to the tone of the psychological environment in which the teaching and learning process occurs. For effective instruction, learners need a safe, nurturing environment that offers opportunities to engage in learning and to excel. Friendly competition and gentle but persistent attainable challenges are valuable motivators for learners. Too often, the classroom climate is passive and nonengaging. Some students remain unchallenged, while others may feel overwhelmed. Awareness of the nature of the classroom climate will help you continually monitor and adjust it to maximize its support of teaching and learning.

Research has demonstrated that the attitudes of learners and of the teacher directly affect student performance (Dunn, 1999). Therefore, a component of designing instruction must be a deliberate effort to ensure

The learning environment includes all aspects of the environment that affect the learner.

TABLE 2.3 Learning Environment Rubric

Using the criteria below, evaluate the effectiveness of the learning environment across each dimension. Highlight the box that best reflects the learning space with reference to the evaluation dimension. Effective learning environments are those that score 4 or higher in most dimensions.

DIMENSION	1 Poor	2 Below Average	3 Average	4 Above Average	5 Excellent
PHYSICAL SPACE	Space is not arranged in an orderly manner and does not promote active learning and positive interaction.	Space is arranged neatly and safely but does not address individual learner needs.	Space is adjusted to the learning style of some but not all learners. Space arrangement promotes safety and some interaction.	Space meets the needs of most learners. Arrangement clearly promotes safety and positive interaction.	Space has been maximally adjusted to meet learner diversity. Space arrangement promotes interactivity, active learning, and positive interaction.
CLASSROOM CLIMATE	Climate is not flexible and responsive to learners. Climate promotes strong competitiveness and does not sufficiently foster cooperation or active learning.	Climate is somewhat flexible to learners. Learner is somewhat nurtured. Competitiveness exceeds cooperation. Active learning is insufficiently emphasized.	Climate is sufficiently flexible. Learner is nurtured to a moderate degree. Competitiveness is equaled by cooperation. Active learning is present.	Climate is flexible and meets most learners' needs. Minimal competitiveness is in evidence. Active learning is supported.	Classroom climate is flexible and meets diverse learners' needs. Cooperation is emphasized without loss of healthy competition. Active learning is emphasized.
ATTITUDES	Teacher attitude is usually cold and tends toward criticism and negativity. Learners typically demonstrate lack of self-confidence and self-criticism.	Teacher attitude is inconsistent and is often negative. Learners demonstrate inconsistency and ambivalence about their capability and self-worth.	Teacher attitude includes both positive and negative components. Learners demonstrate some confidence and self-worth.	Teacher attitude is mostly positive, friendly, and nurturing. Students appear confident and are usually risk takers.	Teacher attitude is consistently positive and encouraging. Teacher is always friendly and nurturing. Students demonstrate confidence and are clearly willing to be risk takers.

This and other downloadable forms and templates can be found on the companion web site at www.ablongman.com/lever-duffy3e.

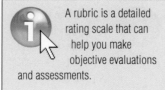 A rubric is a detailed rating scale that can help you make objective evaluations and assessments.

that the learning environment fosters positive, confident attitudes on the part of the learner. Furthermore, it is important to ensure that the teacher's words and actions reflect a positive, caring attitude. However, with the pressures of school life, it is all too easy to shift emphasis away from this affective aspect of instruction and to focus instead on completing the planned lesson. To create an effective learning environment, it is important to stay aware of the steps you are taking to encourage attitudes that nurture learning rather than hinder it. The learning environment rubric will assist you in maintaining the level of awareness necessary to implement this step of the DID process with maximum benefit to the learner.

The final aspect of the nonphysical learning environment relates to the organization of the learning process itself. Well-conceived and clearly articulated instructional plans will create an organized, cohesive environment that fosters learning. Although this might seem to be common sense, all too often the pressures of time and tasks cause teachers to skip steps that are necessary for instructional success. Teachers who do not apply instructional design principles and who do not carry these through to sound lesson plans often find the learning environment turning chaotic and frustrating to both learner and teacher. Just as you would plan a house before you begin building, you must plan instruction before implementing it. Taking the time and energy to carefully plan instruction will make the teaching-learning process smooth and effective.

Well-designed lesson plans improve teaching and learning.

Step 4: Identify Teaching and Learning Strategies

At this point in the process, you have a high degree of awareness of your learners and their needs, your instructional objectives are clear and stated in terms of the desired student outcomes, and the learning environment has been established. Now it is time to decide on your teaching strategies. **Teaching strategies** are the methods you will use to assist your students in achieving the objectives. As you learned in Chapter 1, both teacher and learner are involved in this process, so it is important to consider both the teaching strategies and the learning strategies you intend to employ. **Learning strategies** are the techniques and activities that you will require your students to engage in to master the content.

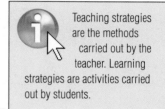

Teaching strategies are the methods carried out by the teacher. Learning strategies are activities carried out by students.

The combination and implementation of planned teaching and learning strategies is sometimes referred to as pedagogy. **Pedagogy** can be defined as the principles and methods of instruction. A series of events that are pedagogically sound are those that are appropriate to the learning environment and that result in the students' successful achievement of the stated objectives. One way of thinking about teaching and learning strategies is to consider them components of a **pedagogical cycle** that is played out again and again as instruction is implemented. The pedagogical cycle is a sequence of specific methods that promote and support effective

YOUR NEW CLASSROOM

Problem-Based Learning

Imagine that you have been assigned a new classroom and you have just reported to your school for your three before-school planning days. You have set tomorrow aside to arrange your classroom. You need to sketch out a design for your room. You have thirty-two student desk/chair combinations, four long worktables, and twelve individual student chairs. Your school has some furniture available, including a tall and a short bookcase, two beanbag seats, two student study carrels with chairs, and a portable whiteboard that flips over to be a bulletin board. You also have your teacher desk, chair, and a four-drawer file cabinet. The technology support team will be coming in to install four student computers, a printer, your teacher's computer with printer, and a pull-down ceiling screen as soon as you have finished arranging your room. The sooner you submit your sketch indicating your room design showing where the technology will go, the sooner the tech team will set up your computers.

Prepare a room sketch showing how you would arrange your new classroom to make it the best learning environment possible. Use the Learning Environment rubric to help you evaluate your plan.

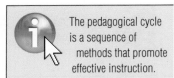

The pedagogical cycle is a sequence of methods that promote effective instruction.

instruction. Teachers engage in each of these methods as they introduce new skills and concepts in their classroom. Each methodology becomes a unique step within the cycle. These in turn incorporate the teaching and learning strategies to be implemented. This cycle and its eight steps are described in Figure 2.4.

The quantity of information provided in a lesson must be subdivided into manageable chunks before the information is introduced to students. Otherwise, the learners may be overcome by the sheer quantity of knowledge and may shut down or suffer confusion. Each information chunk may need to be handled in a distinct way to be effectively communicated to students. One cycle is required for the introduction of each chunk. Once the learners have absorbed it, the next chunk is introduced. Thus the cycle is repeated again and again in the classroom. Planning what to do at each step of the cycle is the way you determine the teaching and learning strategies you intend to use. Examine carefully the pedagogical cycle illustrated in Figure 2.4 to help you complete the fourth step of the DID model.

When identifying teaching strategies, it is important to clearly understand the difference between methods and the media that support them. **Methods** are the actions and activities that a teacher uses to communicate a concept. The methods you select should address the needs and learning styles of your students. They should offer alternative ways of explaining

FIGURE 2.4
The Pedagogical Cycle
Each step in the cycle contributes to successful student learning.

The Pedagogical Cycle

Culminating Review

Reinforce content through verbal, visual, and auditory review of the materials presented.

Provide a Preorganizer

To focus students' attention, use displays or explanations to let students know in advance what they are responsible for learning.

Use Motivators

Use objects or activities or the beginning of the lesson to ensure students are focused and engaged.

Provide Practice Experiences

Shift to learning strategies to provide students with opportunities to work with and practice content.

Build Bridges to Prior Knowledge

Scaffold or connect the concepts to be introduced to content or experiences students already have acquired.

Reinforce Knowledge

Use demonstrations, modeling, formative feedback, and examples to reinforce content acquisition.

Introduce New Knowledge

Use the methods and media you have selected to present new content.

Share Objectives

Explain the objectives of the lesson to your students so they understand what is expected of them when the lesson concludes.

and exploring the information presented. The methods you select should keep your learners active and engaged in learning. Concepts should be carefully matched with the most appropriate methods for communicating them. Selecting the right teaching method for the knowledge is one of the most creative activities in which a teacher engages. The right method or combination of methods is one of the keys to achieving the lesson objectives.

Media are the technologies that are used to facilitate the method (see Table 2.4). For example, lecture may be the method, but the overhead transparencies used by the teacher are the media used to support and enhance the teaching method selected. Various technologies and media are simply tools to enhance and facilitate instructional delivery. The teaching method that a creative teacher chooses is at the core of the teaching process. Instructional media and technologies play a supporting role, not a starring one. It is unfortunate that method and media are sometimes confused. This can lead to a teacher's use of a technology just because it is interesting or fun to use even when it does not directly support the teaching method. This inappropriate use of technology can shift focus from the knowledge itself and the instructional task at hand. The appropriate use of technology can add excitement and interest to many methods, but the key to its use is its role as a support to teaching methodology. This differentiation is the reason that the identification of teaching and learning strategies and the selection of instructional media are two distinct steps in the DID model.

Media are the technologies that support methods.

TABLE 2.4   Methods Versus Media

Methods are . . .
The strategies you use to achieve the lesson objective(s).

Methods include . . .
Teacher-Centered Strategies:
- Presentation
- Lecture
- Demonstration
- Class discussion

Student-Centered Strategies:
- Research projects
- Oral reports
- Cooperative learning groups
- Simulations
- Role playing
- Games

Media are . . .
All audio, visual, video or digital resources you use to carry out your methods.

Media include . . .

- Nonprojected visual media (posters, charts, bulletin boards, models, dioramas)
- Projected visuals (overhead transparencies, slides, computer displays)
- Audio media (tapes, CDs, audio broadcasts, and webcasts)
- Video media (videocassettes, DVDs, broadcasts, webcasts)
- Digital media (anything generated via computer technologies)

Materials and media differ in that materials are any supplies you or your students use during a lesson.

We select media and materials that support our methods to achieve our objectives.

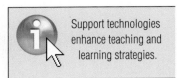

E-Learning
ON THE WEB! 2.6
Connecting Theory to Practice

Support technologies enhance teaching and learning strategies.

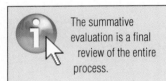

The summative evaluation is a final review of the entire process.

Step 5: Identify and Select Technologies

Instructional technologies are the tools used to enhance and support the teaching and learning strategies planned by the teacher. Once strategies have been mapped out, the tools needed to build the experience become evident. In this step of the instructional design process, you will identify the types of technological tools you need and select from those available to you.

As you will learn throughout this text, different technological tools have different uses, advantages, and disadvantages. Knowing what a technology can do in support of instruction, how to use it, and when it is appropriately used are the focus of this course. At this point, it is sufficient to differentiate between teaching and learning strategies and instructional technologies and to understand that technology's primary role is in support of the strategies you select for yourself and your students. The remainder of this text will familiarize you with the many technologies available to support teaching and learning, some of which are listed in Table 2.5.

Step 6: Summative Evaluation and Revision Plan

No design is ever perfect. However, a systematic process for continuous improvement will maximize quality. Therefore, it is important to end your instructional design with a plan to evaluate its effectiveness and to make appropriate revisions. The results from this summative evaluation can then be used to improve the design. Building this final evaluative step into the process ensures that a continuous improvement process will be in place and that the design will undergo positive revision with each use. Ultimately, through multiple implementations, evaluations, and revisions, your instructional design will come ever closer to your ideal.

Instructional design evaluation can take many forms. You can develop a success rubric (evaluation matrix) that can help you quantitatively self-evaluate the effectiveness of your lesson, or you may ask students to complete student feedback forms that you create to determine their perception of the effectiveness of the various components of the design. Regardless of the method you use for the specific evaluation of the design components, the ultimate evaluation is in the students' performance. Your instructional objectives identify very specific criteria and methods for measuring student success. Your students' achievement of your instructional objectives, then, is the most significant evaluation of your design. Student achievement com-

TABLE 2.5 Sampler of Support Technologies

AUDIO	VISUAL	DIGITAL
Cassette tapes	Videotapes	Computer hardware
Radio	Video discs	Productivity software
Music CD-ROMs	Overhead projector	Educational software
Talking books	Slide projector	Presentation software
Multimedia CDs	Other projection devices	Streaming audio
Recordings: Rhymes and reading	Models, real objects	Streaming video
Recordings: Musical instruments	Boards (bulletin, white, chalk, etc.)	Webcasts
	Digital-analog converter	Internet resources
	Cartoons and drawings	Electronic whiteboards
	Document camera	

in the Classroom

THE KINDERGARTEN LEARNING ENVIRONMENT

Lynn McDonald, kindergarten teacher at Hillside Elementary School, Roswell, Georgia, arranges the physical environment in her classroom to meet the developmental stage of the children by providing distinct, easily identifiable spaces for the varied activities and instructional components of her curriculum. When the children enter the room, they find a row of cubbies to the right on which are placed three little baskets—one for work and two "lunch boxes." Hillside Elementary stresses a free-choice approach to education, so the room arrangement Lynn has designed reinforces this concept in every section of the classroom. There is a check-in poster by the cubbies where the children can pull their name cards and a lunch card to show their choice of lunch for the day. The cards have a picture of what is for lunch, say meat loaf, and the words *meat loaf* written on the card. There is also a card that says "Lunch from Home." The students select the card they want and place it in either the menu choice basket or the no-choice basket because they have brought their lunch. Over the cubbies is a bulletin board that is divided in half: One side is for parent information, including photos of the children and a showcase of projects they have competed, as well as upcoming events and other information of interest to parents. The other half of the bulletin board displays student work.

Lynn's room has two kidney-shaped tables, and her desk is opposite the door so that she can keep an eye on the entire classroom when she is at her desk. Her assistant's desk is located across the room from Lynn's desk. The room has a chalkboard and a whiteboard, neither of which are used as writing surfaces. The whiteboard shows the Calendar Math program, which has many features such as counting money and a clock. Lynn refers to the whiteboard frequently during the school day. The chalkboard has the class schedule affixed on 4" × 6" index cards attached with Velcro so that they can be changed. There are also pocket cardholders on the job chart from which the children choose jobs to do.

The room is arranged into organizational centers. The children find their names posted above cubbies located on the other side of the door. Names are listed under the days of the week. A child who finds his or her name under Wednesday, for example, then gets to choose from one of the twelve literacy centers, which are color coded, or a regular learning center. The areas are identified by a color-coded card hanging from the ceiling. There is even a teacher center where the children get to be the teacher and use the pointer, generally for the Calendar Math program.

The room is divided with the noisy activity areas in the middle and the quiet areas around the perimeter. The room has two shelving units located at the back of the carpeted area. Here the children find manipulatives and baskets of supplies to use in the regular centers. This area also has a table that backs up to the shelving units and two additional tables pushed together to make a square. A section of the room, divided by a half-wall, contains on one side the computer area and, on the other side, the sand table and a sink. Next to this section is a corner with a red couch and floor cushions for a reading center.

Although the room is not overly large, the way Lynn has planned the physical arrangement allows for a free-flowing, free-choice learning environment where the children can work together, separately, or as a whole class. They have room to move easily from one part of the room to another, and they have the opportunity to make decisions as to the activities they wish to engage in as a result of Lynn's use of cards accessible and understandable to children by means of pictures, words, and colors. There are comfortable places in the room and many interesting things to do, not the least of which is the Greeting Card Center placed in the housekeeping area. When children select this center, they clip a card to their shirts identifying this center. They find materials with which to make greeting cards to give someone. There are laminated strips that spell out "Dear . . . ," "From . . . ," and various brief messages for them to copy.

Finally, in keeping with state requirements, Lynn has two long charts posted with the Georgia professional standards for kindergarten listed on them. She uses a paper clip to point to the standards that are being addressed on that day. Any observer who enters the class can immediately see what the standard-based instruction for the day covers.

SOURCE: Interview with Lynn McDonald, kindergarten teacher, Hillside Elementary School, Roswell, Georgia 30076, February 12, 2006.

---

bined with results from other summative feedback efforts will give you the information you need to make future improvements to your design.

If you find that your design did not work as effectively as you intended, this step of the design can suggest remedial follow-up strategies. While summative feedback will ultimately cause you to revise the design for the next time it is used, you must also consider what you can do for the

Instructional designs that include a variety of educational technologies engage students in active learning.

students currently being taught using this design. Remediation strategies that could follow design implementation might include additional review activities, small group instruction, or technology support. When articulating this step, while the design is fresh in your mind, it is appropriate to note possible remediation strategies should you need them.

Using the DID Model to Plan Instruction

Now that you have reviewed all of the steps of the DID model, you can begin to see how they create a blueprint for the teaching-learning process. The model helps you ask yourself the critical questions that will improve the quality of the instructional experience for both you and your students. Using the model is an important first step before the instructional event and a skill that needs to be acquired through practice. Table 2.6 summarizes each step of the DID model and provides a template with a series of prompts to help you build your own design.

TABLE 2.6   DID Model Template with Examples for a Unit on Money and Banking

STEP 1: KNOW THE LEARNERS	EXAMPLE ANALYSIS OF LEARNERS
Summarize the characteristics of the learners for whom you are creating the lesson. • What are the personal demographics (ethnicity, socioeconomic level, cultural background) that might affect learning? • What is the developmental stage of the student relative to the content? • What is the cognitive/learning style of each student? • What are the student's strengths in terms of multiple intelligences? • What group dynamics might help or hinder the teaching-learning process? • What are the student's entry skills with reference to the content?	The students are seventh-grade middle-class students with an ethnic mix of 43 percent white non-Hispanic, 26 percent Hispanic, and 31 percent black. Five students are ESL students with a good command of English but who occasionally need an assist with spelling. Twenty-three students are predominantly kinesthetic learners, six show some preference for visual learning, and two show a preference for auditory learning. The two auditory learners need a quiet area in which to work. The kinesthetic learners need multiple spaces in which to move and experience the content. The visual learners need screened areas for studying. One student has strong musical intelligence, ten have strong logical intelligence, and all have good verbal intelligence. The students are generally friendly, noncompetitive, and cooperative. Working in teams is a preferred strategy for all but three students. Entry skills for this unit include only a limited understanding of money and banking.

STEP 2: ARTICULATE OBJECTIVES	SAMPLE OBJECTIVES
State the behaviors that you expect your students to be able to demonstrate at the conclusion of the unit. • What performance will result from the unit? • What criteria for success are necessary to ensure mastery? • How will you assess the performance? • Have you included all the levels of Bloom's taxonomy that are appropriate for the content?	On a written test, the student will be able to explain the difference between a checking and a savings account with 90 percent accuracy. The student will be able to define interest with 95 percent accuracy on a written test. Given a matching exercise, the student will be able to distinguish between credit cards, debit cards, and ATM cards with 90 percent accuracy. The student will be able to contrast, with 85 percent accuracy, cash spending and credit spending on a written test.

Continues on next page ▶

Table 2.6 continued

STEP 2: ARTICULATE OBJECTIVES	SAMPLE OBJECTIVES (cont.)
	In a simulated checking account, the student will be able to deposit money, write checks, and balance the account with 95 percent accuracy.

STEP 3: ESTABLISH THE LEARNING ENVIRONMENT	EXAMPLES
Clarify what you plan to do to create an environment for this unit conducive to learning. • What changes need to be made to the classroom space? • What reinforcers are needed for this unit to motivate and build learning success? • How can learning be made active? • How should students be grouped for positive interaction?	For the duration of this unit, a corner of the classroom will become a banking center in which all transactions will take place. As closely as possible, the center will be arranged to emulate the lobby of a bank. A screened quiet corner with additional lighting will be set up adjacent to the banking center. Students will be rewarded with classroom currency for sound banking practices and for maintaining a balanced checkbook. Practices and checkbook will be evaluated weekly. Interim spot checks will be rewarded with game center time. Audit teams will be used to check each other's progress and to assist students who need peer support to complete the unit.

STEP 4: IDENTIFY TEACHING AND LEARNING STRATEGIES	SAMPLE PEDAGOGY FOR OBJECTIVE 1
Given the objectives, describe the pedagogical cycle of teaching and learning strategies that need to be implemented to meet the objectives. • What preorganizers are you planning? • What prior knowledge do you need to connect to as a prerequisite for the lesson? • How will you introduce the new information? • What media, materials, or technologies will support the content? • What teaching and learning strategies will support active learning? • How will you reinforce the new knowledge? • What practice will be necessary to ensure mastery of the content? • How will you perform a culminating review?	*Preorganizer:* Display bank forms. *Bridge to prior knowledge:* Review types of money. *Share objective:* Write objective on the board and ask why it is important to know this content. *Introduce new knowledge:* Share and discuss a chart of bank processes and have students act out a customer–teller interaction; invite a local banker as guest speaker; show a bank web site; add checking and savings accounts to the bank center and open each for all students. *Reinforce knowledge:* Give examples and nonexamples of transactions to class and ask students to identify and/or correct them. *Provide practice:* Give students 100 hypothetical dollars to deposit in accounts at the bank center. *Culminating review:* Check students' accounts and individually reinforce or correct banking activity.

STEP 5: IDENTIFY AND SELECT TECHNOLOGIES	EXAMPLES
Given the strategies selected, identify the technologies that will be needed to support those strategies. • What technologies and related materials are needed for this unit? • Which technologies are required for each strategy?	*Strategies for Objective 1 of this unit will require the use of:* Scanner, printer, and copier to create bank center forms Overhead projector for guest speaker Computer connected to the Web LCD display for large-group projection of computer image

STEP 6: MAKE A SUMMATIVE EVALUATION	EXAMPLES
Describe the summative feedback process you will use to evaluate the design and how the results of the evaluation will be used to revise it. • How will you know whether the design is effective? • What assessment instruments are needed to measure effectiveness? • What is the revision process once you have the results from your evaluation?	The design will be evaluated on the basis of student achievement of outcomes and student satisfaction. Evaluation will be completed through objective measures (tests and quizzes) and through performance assessment (observation of the performance of each student in the bank center). A summative student feedback form will assess student satisfaction with the unit and provide self-evaluation of mastery of the content.

This and other downloadable forms and templates can be found on the companion web site at www.ablongman.com/lever-duffy3e.

Creating Lesson Plans from the DID Model

The DID model helps you to see the instructional big picture. With it, you can build an effective instructional experience that carefully details each step of the instructional process. However, you might wonder how busy teachers manage to use instructional design models on a day-to-day basis. Essentially, even busy teachers know that, to teach effectively, they must have formulated an instructional design, either fully articulated on paper or, at the very least, jotted down in brief notes to themselves. Just as artists plan the elements of their artwork or architects create blueprints for their building, teachers use instructional design to create their personal overview of the instructional events in which they and their students will engage. Over time and with experience, such planning becomes intuitive. Very experienced teachers can create complex designs with just a few notes on each of the steps, just as an experienced and talented artist paints a powerful picture with just a few brushstrokes. Beginning teachers need to practice their instructional design technique until it becomes a skill that is second nature to them. Whether you are a new teacher who must fully articulate the design or an experienced teacher who needs only a list of summary ideas, the systematic planning of instruction remains the foundation of effective teaching and learning.

DID Designer Template

But, from a day-to-day perspective, the instructional outline provided by the design may be too broad. For daily lesson planning, you must narrow the focus to more specific topics. An instructional design frequently includes content that will take several days of instruction to complete. The lesson plan focuses on what must be done each day in each class to implement the instructional activities outlined in the design. The relationship of the DID model to lesson plans is illustrated in Figure 2.5.

Lesson Planning

While the instructional design provides the overview of the planned unit of instruction, it is the lesson plan that provides a day-to-day snapshot of what will happen in the classroom. The design is the foundation for the daily lesson plans that will emerge from it. For that reason, the lesson plan follows the same general organization as the instructional design. Let's look now at the essential components of the lesson plan.

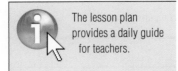

The lesson plan provides a daily guide for teachers.

Readying the Learners

In the instructional design, you have already carefully analyzed the characteristics of your learners and their specific needs. When beginning the lesson plan, you should review learner characteristics and update any information about your students that has changed. Once you feel confident that you have a clear picture of those you will teach, it is then necessary to evaluate their current level of skills, called entry skills, with respect to the targeted lesson. Such evaluation can be done formally through a pretest or informally through select verbal questions. The complexity of the content and the diversity of the learners will help you determine the best way to assess their entry skills. In the lesson plan, you should articulate how you plan to assess these skills.

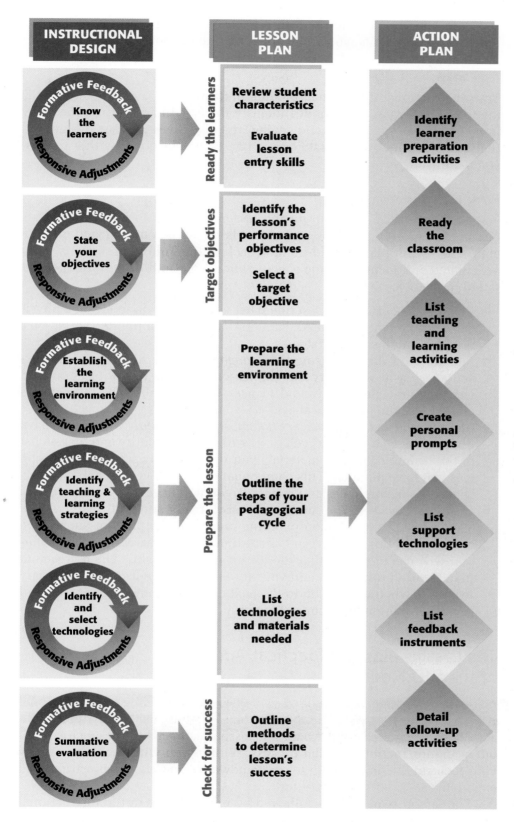

INSTRUCTIONAL DESIGN	LESSON PLAN	ACTION PLAN

Ready the learners

Formative Feedback — Know the learners — Responsive Adjustments
- Review student characteristics
- Evaluate lesson entry skills
- Identify learner preparation activities

Target objectives

Formative Feedback — State your objectives — Responsive Adjustments
- Identify the lesson's performance objectives
- Select a target objective
- Ready the classroom

Prepare the lesson

Formative Feedback — Establish the learning environment — Responsive Adjustments
- Prepare the learning environment
- List teaching and learning activities
- Create personal prompts

Formative Feedback — Identify teaching & learning strategies — Responsive Adjustments
- Outline the steps of your pedagogical cycle
- List support technologies

Formative Feedback — Identify and select technologies — Responsive Adjustments
- List technologies and materials needed
- List feedback instruments

Check for success

Formative Feedback — Summative evaluation — Responsive Adjustments
- Outline methods to determine lesson's success
- Detail follow-up activities

FIGURE 2.5

Relationship of Design-Plan-Act! Elements

All phases of the D-P-A system work together to create and implement quality instruction.

Once you are clear on the learners' needs and on how you will determine their entry skills, you are ready to plan the lesson itself.

Targeting Specific Objectives

Your instructional design may include multiple objectives from your DID model. Your lesson plan should identify the specific objectives the daily lesson is targeting. You should review the objectives in your design and then select, review, and restate one or two target objectives within the lesson plan itself.

Preparing the Lesson

You are now ready to write out the lesson you plan to implement. This component closely parallels and expands on its parent instructional design. The lesson plan should include each of the following sections, fully articulated and focused on the specific knowledge and/or performance detailed in the objective:

Lesson Planning Ideas

- *Prepare the classroom:* Describe what you need to do to create a physical environment that meets learners' needs and supports the lesson's teaching and learning strategies.
- *Summarize your plan using the pedagogical cycle steps:* Articulate exactly how you will carry out the lesson in terms of the teaching and learning strategies you intend to use. To ensure that all steps are included, use the pedagogical cycle as your guide.
- *Identify and list required technologies and materials:* Once you have planned each step in the cycle, you will need to identify and make a list of the technologies and materials you will need to carry out the strategies you have planned. This component of the lesson plan helps you organize the technologies and materials you will need.
- *Check for success:* You have your lesson ready and well planned out. The last step in the lesson planning process is the plan for summative feedback. In this section, you should identify the assessment strategies you will use to ensure that the lesson was successful. The assessment plan should provide you and your students with the feedback necessary to decide whether to go on to the next chunk of knowledge or stop and review or reinforce the current lesson.

www.mylabschool.com
video
View *Learning the Rules for Computer Use*

The Lesson Planner: Practical Application of the DID Model

Lesson Planner Template

Just as the DID template provided you an assist in building an instructional design, the sample **lesson planner** (Table 2.7 on page 70) will help you create a fully articulated lesson plan. The lesson planner is the pragmatic product of the instructional design process. With it, you will be able to narrow your focus of the daily lesson to create powerful and effective instructional experiences.

The lesson plan itself is followed by one last step in the instructional planning process. Although less formal than the previous steps in the process, this last step—action planning—is a necessary culmination to the process.

COOL TOOLS

While many web sites offer a library of lesson plans, the Lesson Architect located at www.ibinder.uwf.edu/steps/welcome.cfm offers a tool that helps you to build an instructional unit, plan lessons, and align your lesson to appropriate standards. This online tool was designed for Florida teachers and therefore uses the Florida standards, but the planning tool is useful for all teachers.

The Lesson Architect has been integrated with a lesson planning tutorial called STEPS that can help you learn to plan while creating your own plan. This site also provides a feature called ANDIE that guides you through each step of a lesson plan and provides you with questions you may not have considered. While not identical to the steps in the D-P-A system, like all systematic planners, the Lesson Architect is similar in its approach. Try it to experience online planning, to gain access to its database of plans, and to try aligning lessons to standards.

Instructional Action Planning

Instructional action planning helps you articulate your lesson's to-do list. It is the detailing of all of the preparations that need to be made to successfully carry out your lesson plan. The **instructional action plan (IAP)** includes the following steps:

- *Identifying learner preparation activities:* This component describes the preparations that are necessary to assess and prepare the learners before the lesson. It should list the materials, props, and assessment instruments you will need.
- *Getting the classroom ready:* When action planning for the physical space, you should describe the steps you have to take in the classroom to prepare it for the lesson implementation. Be sure to list any changes to the classroom furniture or fixtures that need to be made before the lesson.
- *Listing teaching-learning activities:* In this component of the IAP, you should list the materials that need to be created, gathered, copied, or assembled for the teaching and learning strategies you have identified. Be specific about these needs so that your list can serve as a last-minute checklist before the lesson. You might also include in this section of the IAP alternative activities that could be used if unexpected circumstances interfere with the lesson plan's scheduled activities.
- *Creating personal prompts:* Personal prompts are reminders of the things you want to do and/or say as you implement the lesson. They are personal cues to remind you in case you forget to include something you had planned to do. Listing them in the IAP gives you a single point of review that you can use just before the lesson.
- *Listing support technologies:* This section of the IAP provides you with an opportunity to identify the technologies you will need and any associated materials that are required. Here you should list the technolo-

TABLE 2.7   The Lesson Planner Template with Examples for Money and Banking Unit

STEP 1: READY THE LEARNERS	EXAMPLES
Describe how you will prepare the students for the lesson. ● Have any of the characteristics previously recognized changed? ● Do any assumptions about learners need to be corrected? ● What techniques will you use to gauge entry skills?	**Unit on Money and Banking** Most student characteristics have not changed; however, an ESE (exceptional student education) student has now been mainstreamed into this class. This student will need additional support, so a copy of all work relating to this lesson must be given to the ESE team. A money and banking pretest will be created and administered at the start of the lesson. The same test will be given as a posttest to measure progress.

STEP 2: TARGET SPECIFIC OBJECTIVES	EXAMPLE
State the instructional design objective that will be addressed by this lesson. ● To which of the design's objectives does this lesson relate? ● How, if at all, does this lesson relate to the other design objectives?	This lesson targets design Objective 1: On a written test, the student will be able to explain the difference between a checking and a savings account with 90 percent accuracy.

STEP 3: PREPARE THE LESSON	EXAMPLES
Describe what you need to do to prepare for the lesson. ● What needs to be done in the classroom to get it ready? ● What must be accomplished for each step of the pedagogical cycle? How will it be accomplished? ● What materials, media, and technologies are needed, and how will they be used? ● What needs to be done to implement the intended assessments?	**Classroom Preparation** The banking center will consist of a refrigerator box with a cutout as the teller window and a small table behind it with a desk organizer for managing forms and transactions. The rolling bookcase will serve as a forms counter. A table on the other side of the bookcase with a study carrel next to it will provide quiet space. **Lesson Preparation** *Preorganizer:* Gather bank forms from a local bank, cover identifying numbers, enlarge and laminate the forms, and hang them on the front board. *Bridge to prior knowledge:* Use transparencies to compare paper and coin equivalence.

Continues on next page

gies, what you need to do to get them into your classroom, and what preparation or practice sessions you need to successfully use the technologies you selected.

● *Listing feedback instruments:* Formative and summative feedback are a part of your lesson plan and your design. In the IAP, you should list any instruments or techniques that you need to develop or use to accomplish the feedback you have planned. You should also indicate what you need to do to use the feedback from the instruments. This list will serve as a feedback checklist to use before you implement your lesson.

● *Detailing follow-up activities:* Once you have collected formative and summative feedback, the data that result will prompt you to go on to the next lesson or to review and reinforce the current lesson. In this section of the IAP, you should detail what you need to do as a followup to a less successful lesson, what you might want to do to rein-

Table 2.7 continued

STEP 3: PREPARE THE LESSON (cont.)	EXAMPLES (cont.)
	Introduce new knowledge: Show students a bank process poster. Give a blank version to students to fill in as the information is presented.
	1. Present and explain each banking form to students, filling out an enlarged version while they complete their paper versions.
	2. Prepare a checklist of the steps in a customer–teller interaction for depositing, withdrawing, and checking balances to review with students. Give some example transactions and have students role-play the key steps.
	Reinforce knowledge: Open a class checking and savings account for the teacher, perform a series of correct and incorrect transactions, and let class decide whether the teacher is doing it right or wrong.
	Provide practice: Have students open a checking and savings account and give them $100 in class "dollars." Have them deposit half in each of their accounts at the bank center, filling in the correct forms for the transactions. Then ask them to write a check for $10 to move this amount from checking to savings, filling in the correct forms.
	Culminating review: Have each student request a bank statement at the end of the activity. Review each for accuracy. When done correctly, give each student a personal bankbook to store transactions and documents.
	Technology/Media Preparation
	Scan, print, and make copies of bank center forms. Enlarge one of each and laminate them.
	Prepare money equivalence transparencies.
	Create a chart of bank processes on a computer, print out, enlarge, and laminate.
	Locate a suitable bank web site to share.
	Assessment Preparation
	Prepare and administer a quiz asking students to fill in each type of form and to compute their account balances.

This and other downloadable forms and templates can be found on the companion web site at www.ablongman.com/lever-duffy3e.

force a successful lesson, and/or what you need to do to improve the lesson.

The Instructional Action Planner: Getting Ready to Teach

Action Planner Template

To help you create a useful instructional action plan, a template, similar to the previously presented lesson planner, is provided in Table 2.8. on page 72. The instructional action planner provides a format in which you are prompted to list your lesson requirements and to detail what you will need for successful implementation. The action planner is your last step in the planning process. With its completion, you are finally ready to teach and to help your students learn.

TABLE 2.8 The Action Planner Template with Examples for Money and Banking Unit

TO-DO #1: IDENTIFY LEARNER PREPARATION ACTIVITIES

EXAMPLES

Describe what action needs to be taken to prepare the learners.
- What steps need to be taken to prepare the learners?
- What props are needed?

Learner Checklist
____ Contact ESE teacher and review unit plan for inclusion student.
____ Review prerequisite vocabulary with ESL students.
____ Obtain bank forms, bankbook covers, bank signs, and customer "goodies" from local bank.

TO-DO #2: READY THE CLASSROOM

EXAMPLES

Describe what you need to do to get the classroom ready for the lesson.
- What furniture needs to be acquired or moved?
- What additional materials are needed?
- Whom do you need to contact to assist in making the intended adjustments?

Classroom Checklist
____ Stop by an appliance store for refrigerator box.
____ Borrow a rolling bookcase from the library.
____ Move the reading center temporarily to make room for the bank center.
____ Purchase or borrow three desk organizers for the teller.

TO-DO #3: LIST TEACHING AND LEARNING ACTIVITIES

EXAMPLES

List the materials you need to prepare and/or tasks that need to be done for the intended activities
- What materials are needed by teacher and students?
- What tasks need to be completed for these activities?

Materials Checklist
____ Money equivalence transparency
____ Laminated poster
____ Deposit/withdrawal forms for checking accounts
____ Deposit/withdrawal forms for savings accounts
____ Poster-size laminates of each form
____ Blank bank statement forms for reconciliation
____ Blank bankbooks

Task Checklist
____ Contact a potential guest speaker to discuss lesson requirements.
____ Scan and print copies of forms if necessary.
____ Bookmark bank web sites.

Activity Backup Plan
Locate a banking video, preview it, and prepare a related activity in case the guest speaker cancels or web access is unavailable.

Continues on next page ➤

Linking Planning, Teaching, Learning, and Technology

As you learned in Chapter 1, teaching and learning are, at their core, processes of effective and successful communication. Just as you would carefully plan and rehearse an important speech before giving it, so too must you carefully plan and rehearse the important communication process that takes place between teacher and learner. This chapter has reviewed the many components of this planning process and has provided specific planning tools for effective teaching and learning. Each step of the systematic instructional process is a critical one, and each of-

E-Learning

www.mylabschool.com
Listen to Podcast
Meeting Student Needs

Table 2.8 continued

TO-DO #4: CREATE PERSONAL PROMPTS	SAMPLE PROMPTS FOR OBJECTIVE 1
List the prompts you want to remember to use to cover all points of the lesson. ● What specifics do you want to remember to do? ● What specifics do you want to remember to say?	***Talking Points*** ● Why do we save? ● What is a budget? ● Advantages and disadvantages of checks versus cash. ● How banks make their money. ***Don't Forget To*** ● Close the teller window at the end of the class session ● Monitor the location of the class cash supply.

TO-DO #5: LIST SUPPORT TECHNOLOGIES	EXAMPLE
Describe the things you need to do to ensure that the technologies you have selected are available and working. ● What technologies and related materials need to be acquired for another source? From where? ● What hardware or software adjustments need to be made? ● Which technologies need to be checked to be sure they are functioning?	***Technology Checklist*** ____ Make sure the scanner is working. ____ Check the printer cartridge. ____ Get colored paper from the art room. ____ Get ink-jet transparency film from the office. ____ Install a software upgrade. ____ Print the home pages of web sites on which to make notes. ____ Check the LCD display for all cables and to be sure it is working.

TO-DO #6: LIST FEEDBACK INSTRUMENTS	EXAMPLE
Describe the feedback instruments you need to have ready for this lesson. ● What do you need for formative feedback? ● What do you need for summative feedback?	***Feedback Checklist*** ____ Rubric for assessing performance while at the bank center. ____ Quiz on filling in forms and determining balances. ____ Lesson objective test on terms and concepts. ____ Student satisfaction questionnaire.

TO-DO #7: DETAIL FOLLOW-UP ACTIVITIES	EXAMPLE
Given the feedback, describe the follow-up activities. ● If the lesson was not successful, what remediation is planned? ● If the lesson was successful, what reinforcement is planned?	*Remediation:* PowerPoint self-paced review of key terms followed by a quiz on key points; direct tutoring or peer mentoring if mastery is not demonstrated on quiz. *Reinforcement:* Continued use of the bank center for a token-economy reward system.

This and other downloadable forms and templates can be found on the companion web site at www.ablongman.com/lever-duffy3e.

fers a unique contribution to the process. Now that you are aware of all of the planning components, let's take a moment to see how they fit together to help you effectively plan your teaching and your students' learning experiences.

Design

Instructional design is the component of the process that helps you think strategically about the teaching and learning experience. It offers you, through the DID model, a way to plan for and articulate every essential ingredient in the instructional unit you are planning. Instructional design paints the big-picture version of instruction that results in a complete and precise blueprint of what should happen and how.

Teachers must plan for, select, and effectively use the best technologies to support teaching and learning.

Plan

The lesson plan brings the instructional design down to Earth. It moves the planning process from a systems model to a mainstream, day-to-day lesson plan. While never deviating from the elements of the instructional design model, the lesson plans that result from it narrow the focus of planning to a specific objective and knowledge segment. Using the lesson planner template, you are able to clarify precisely what you need to do to successfully complete each day's lesson.

Act

Design-Plan-Act!
completes the
instructional systems
cycle.

Action planning is the final step in the three-part planning process. The action plan specifies everything you need to do to make learning happen in the classroom. Through the action planning step, you review the lesson plan and stop to create your lesson plan to-do list. By completing the instructional action planner, you culminate the planning phase of instruction and are ready to begin implementation.

Planning for Technology in Teaching and Learning

All aspects of instruction benefit from careful planning, but for using technology in instruction, planning is especially critical. Technology-enhanced teaching and learning must be well thought out, with appropriate technologies identified and justified within the framework of the instructional event. Adding a technology to your instruction just because it is available can detract from the instruction and even hamper the teaching-learning process. Technology should be employed only when instructional planning has been completed and it is clear that a technology in support of instruction is called for. A general rule of thumb suggests that a technology included in a lesson should make it possible for something that was done before to be done better or make it possible for something that couldn't have been done before to happen. A fully implemented plan, with its emphasis on carefully thought-out instructional events, helps to ensure such appropriate selection and utilization of technology.

When the instructional plan does call for technological support, the planning process helps to identify the technologies that are appropriate for a targeted instructional event. It also articulates the preparations necessary to use the technologies effectively and describes the specific activities in which they will be used. The planning process helps to ensure that identified technologies are implemented within the learning environment in a manner appropriate to stated objectives. The planning process also serves to remind you what you need to do, from acquisition to preparation, to use the technologies effectively.

As you proceed through this text, you will have the opportunity to learn about a wide variety of technologies that will assist you in effective teaching. Although each of these technologies will serve you well as a tool with which you can build a sound learning environment for your students, none should be used until you have fully planned the intended instruction. The old axiom in carpentry, "Measure twice, cut once," suggests that we should be careful to take the time to plan before taking action in order to avoid irreversible, costly mistakes. The instructional mistakes of teachers affect the students who are in our charge. No mistakes can be more costly than those that affect our students. Careful instructional planning helps us avoid instructional errors and maximize the effectiveness of our teaching time and our students' learning time. So when time pressures cause you to consider shortcutting the planning component of the teaching-learning process, remember this modified axiom: "Plan well, teach well."

E-Learning

www.mylabschool.com
video
View *Using Technology to Meet Objectives*

A well-designed learning event ensures that the appropriate technology is used.

KEY TERMS

Bloom's taxonomy 53
design-plan-act (D-P-A) system 46
dynamic instructional design
   (DID) model 46
feedback loop 48
formative feedback 48
instructional action plan (IAP) 69

instructional design model 46
learning environment 56
learning strategies 59
lesson planner 68
media 61
methods 60

pedagogical cycle 59
pedagogy 59
performance objectives 51
summative feedback 48
systems approach 46
teaching strategies 59

STUDENT ACTIVITIES

CHAPTER REVIEW

1. What is an instructional planning system? What are the components of the D-P-A system?
2. How can an instructional design model help you develop your instructional plan? Identify the steps of the DID model and briefly explain each.
3. What is the difference between formative feedback and summative feedback?
4. What is a performance objective? How does it differ from more generic objectives?
5. Name and briefly describe the six levels of Bloom's taxonomy.
6. What components constitute a learning environment?
7. Name and briefly describe each step of the pedagogical cycle.
8. What role do educational technologies play in teaching and learning?
9. What is the difference between an instructional design and a lesson plan?
10. What is an instructional action plan? How does it help a teacher prepare for the instructional event?

WHAT DO YOU THINK?

1. Assume that you have been asked to assist a fellow teacher in writing objectives in performance terms. He shares with you the following objective for his sixth-grade science class: "*When I complete my instruction, my students will understand and appreciate the ecology of the rainforest.*" What would you say to your colleague to explain why his objective as written would not help him decide what to teach and what his students should learn? Help him rewrite this objective in performance terms.
2. Many teachers write objectives and focus their instruction at the three lowest levels of Bloom's taxonomy. Why do you think this happens? Do you believe it is an appropriate emphasis? How might it help or hurt the learners?
3. You are about to teach a lesson on the importance of the Nile in ancient Egypt at the grade level you would prefer to teach. Describe the steps you would take to effectively prepare for teaching this instructional unit.
4. Observe a teacher presenting a lesson and note which of the steps of the pedagogical cycle he or she includes. Critique the lesson in terms of the cycle. Be sure to include how the lesson might have been improved through application of the pedagogical cycle's components.
5. Assume that the teacher in the next classroom is a computer enthusiast. He creates most of his lessons around the use of machines and software he has available in his classroom. Do you believe this is an appropriate approach to instruction? Why or why not?

LEARNING TOGETHER!

The following activities are designed for groups of three to five students:

1. Lay out an ideal classroom space that would meet the needs of a variety of learners. Include the number and placement of desks, tables, teacher's desk, file cabinets, bookcases, bulletin boards, chalkboards or whiteboards, and any less traditional fixtures and furniture you would like to include. Draw your group's ideal classroom to share with your class.

2. Select a teaching unit of your choice at the grade level you would like to teach. Together, write ten performance objectives related to the unit, with at least one at each of the levels of Bloom's taxonomy. Be prepared to share your objectives with the class.

3. Use all three components of the D-P-A system to complete a hypothetical instructional unit plan. Use as the instructional-unit content a topic appropriate to the grade level you would like to teach.

E-Learning

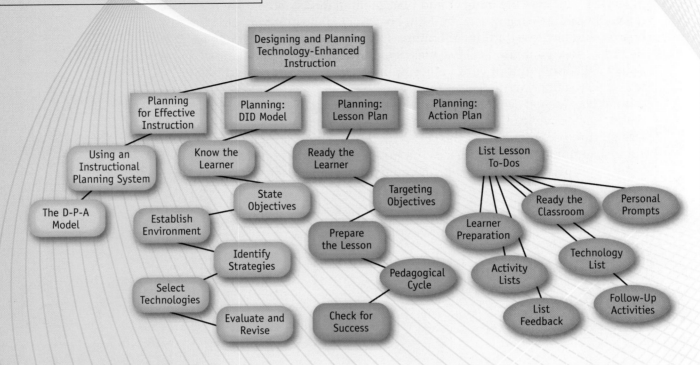

Podcasts www.mylabschool.com

Listen to an audio discussion on planning to effectively use technology in instruction. Download the audio discussion to your IPod, computer, or MP3 player.

Video Lab www.mylabschool.com

Accessible through the **mylabschool** web site, *Instructional Planning* video vignettes offer you a look at planning and technology. Learning guides for all videos can be found in the text's Learning Guide Supplement.

On the Web! Activities www.ablongman.com/lever-duffy3e
Noted in the margins of the chapter, these activities offer you in-depth experiences in the topics and content presented in the chapter.

Online Practice Test www.ablongman.com/lever-duffy3e
Practice tests offer you an opportunity to test your knowledge and then review the results and send them to your teacher.

Outliner www.ablongman.com/lever-duffy3e
Chapter Outliners are fill-in-the-blank outlines of the main ideas presented in the chapter. Download the outliner and fill it in for an effective chapter study guide.

Power Practices www.ablongman.com/lever-duffy3e
Power Practices are animated tutorials made using Microsoft's presentation software, PowerPoint. This flash card tutorial will help you practice key concepts in the chapter.

Puzzler www.ablongman.com/lever-duffy3e
Puzzlers include content in crossword, word search, and other puzzle formats to help you master chapter content. Puzzlers can also be found in the text's Learning Guide supplement.

Useful Links www.ablongman.com/lever-duffy3e
These links offer you suggestions for expanded online research in the topics presented in the chapter.

INTEGRATION *Ideas*

Abundant resources are available for planning. Online you can find sample plans for every grade level and every content area. You will also find national standards for all content areas. These standards are typically adopted by states and districts and used to align curriculum. Formats for planning may vary from the D-P-A system presented in this text, but most adopt a similar systematic approach. You will ultimately need to plan in accordance with the requirements of your school and district, but becoming familiar with standards and reviewing online plans aligned to them can help you discover new and innovative strategies that you can incorporate into your lessons. Connect to plans and standards in your content area by reviewing the resources below.

All Grade Level Lesson Plans

Apple Learning Interchange, sponsored by Apple Computers, provides a powerful and innovative Web-based collection of lesson plans that use Apple computers. This site provides in-depth plans aligned to standards. **http://ali.apple.com/ali_sites/ali/**.

Discovery Schools offers a Lesson Plan Library featuring original lesson plans, written by teachers for teachers. The web site offers a searchable data base with pull-down menus so teachers can browse plans by subject, grade, or both. Most content areas and grade levels are included. Review this site for innovative plans. **http://school.discovery.com/lessonplans/k-5.html**.

Education World is a highly popular resource for teachers. Its lesson planning center provides teachers with field-tested teacher-contributed plans at every grade level and for every content area. Review this site frequently, as new plans are added daily. **www.educationworld.com/a_lesson/**.

The Educator's Reference Desk offers numerous resources, including a teacher's guide to writing lesson plans as well as their Lesson Plan Collection. Resources at this site include more than 2,000 lesson plans, 3,000 links to online education information, and more than 200 question archived responses to educator's questions. Review this site at **www.eduref.org/Virtual/Lessons/index.shtml**.

Smithsonian Education is the education web site of the Smithsonian Museum in Washington, D.C. This list of science, technology, history, and cultural lessons offer high-quality, fully articulated plans and activities on a variety of unusual topics. Visit this unique collection at **www.smithsonianeducation.org/educators/index.html**.

Teachers Net offers their Lesson Plan Bank to all teachers in all content areas and grade levels. This web site encourages teachers to submit plans as well as browse an extensive data base of curriculum ideas. There is even a lesson plan request board so teachers can communicate their unique curriculum needs to other teachers. **http://teachers.net/lessons/**.

English/Language Arts Lesson Plans and Standards

The **National Council of Teachers of English** web site provides standards for K–12 English and language arts curricula as well as lesson plans for all areas within the discipline. The Read/Write/Think link provides quality plans aligned to standards that integrate Internet resources into meaningful instruction. **www.ncte.org/**.

Math Lesson Plans and Standards

The **National Council for Teachers of Mathematics** offers their national standards for PreK through grade 12 at this site. E-Examples are provided for each standard to give teachers ideas for activities to meet each standard. The Illuminations link offers innovative math lesson plans for all grade levels aligned with standards. **http://standards.nctm.org/document/chapter3/index.htm**.

Science Lesson Plans and Standards

The **National Science Teachers Association** web site provides standards for teaching science at all grade levels. In addition, it offers a compendium of science educator web sites that covers science topics at every grade level, including numerous lesson plan sites. Visit the web site to become familiar with science standards and resources. **www.nsta.org/standards**.

Social Studies Lesson Plans and Standards

The **Library of Congress** offers powerful and innovative lesson plans that use the original resources stored in the library as their source. Lessons are organized by theme, topic, discipline, or era, with grade level indicators for each lesson. Visit the Library of Congress for this resource at **http://memory.loc.gov/learn/lessons/index.html**.

The **National Council for the Social Studies** web site includes a list of standards and lesson plans aligned with those standards for use in the social studies curriculum. **www.socialstudies.org/standards/**.

For these and many more *Integration Ideas* for planning for instruction visit the text web site at **www.ablongman.com/lever-duffy3e**.

The DID Designer

Vowels Unit

STEP 1 Know the Learner

The class consists of kindergarten students. The class has eighteen students, ten girls and eight boys. There are seven Caucasians, five Hispanics, five African Americans, and one Asian American.

The learning styles of the students include seven visual learners, nine auditory learners, and two kinesthetic learners. The seven visual learners need materials to assist them in learning. The nine auditory learners need lessons to be discussed verbally as well as a quiet place to study. The two kinesthetic learners need hands on activities and an open space to learn.

The multiple intelligences of these students consist of musical, linguistic, spatial, intrapersonal, interpersonal, and logical.

The entry skills of this unit are very limited. Some students may know the letters of the alphabet, but overall students do not know what vowels are.

STEP 2 Articulate Objectives

The student will be able to differentiate vowels from consonants orally with 100 percent accuracy.

The student will be able to identify letters that are vowels by creating a poster board with 100 percent accuracy.

The student will be able to critique other student's vowel posters on a rubric with 100 percent accuracy.

STEP 3 Establish the Learning Environment

The consonants on the alphabet chart that is posted in front of the room need to be covered, leaving only the vowel letters to be displayed. Also, the PowerPoint presentation needs to be saved onto each computer. The computers all need headphones attached to them.

A flash card game will be placed at the manipulative center, a cassette will be placed at the listening center, a handout will be placed at the writing center, and books on vowels will be placed at the reading center.

Also, magnetic boards and cloth boards need to be placed at each group table with letter magnets and cloth letters.

Students will be encouraged to work together with about four to five students per group, including a variety of multiple intelligences in each group. Within the groups, students will be encouraged to help their partners.

Students will be rewarded with stickers and smiley faces and by having a vowel celebration.

STEP 4 Identify Teaching and Learning Strategies

Preorganizer

The consonants on the alphabet chart will be covered. The students will be asked to note that some letters of the alphabet are special. The students will read each vowel from the chart and the teacher will write each on the board as the students say it.

Bridge to Prior Knowledge

As a class, students will be asked to recite the alphabet. The teacher will ask a student to read the letters that are written on the board. Students will be asked to think about how these letters are the same as each other but different from the rest of the alphabet.

SOURCE: Adapted from a unit developed by Elizabeth Polo, Miami Dade College and Nova Southeastern University Education Major.

interchapter 2

Share Objective

The objectives of the unit will be explained, and the teacher will discuss why it is important to know these special letters called vowels.

Introduce New Knowledge

- Ask a student to read the letters that are posted on the board. Then six students will be asked to come up to the board to write the vowels again. Students will be told how these letters are different from the rest of the letters. The importance of vowels in making words will be discussed. The class will read together the vowels that are displayed on the alphabet chart. Following that, students will write the six vowel letters in their journal.
- The teacher will show a vowel PowerPoint presentation to the class. After viewing the slide show, the students will again say all the vowels and a word that begins with each vowel.

Reinforce Knowledge

- As a class, students will sing a vowel song. The song will be repeated multiple times. Then students will be divided into groups, and each group will come up to the front of the room to sing the song. As groups of students are singing the song, the remaining students will follow along with the vowels they wrote in their journals.
- Students will draw on a blank sheet of paper a vowel that is in their first or last name. For instance, John will draw the letter O on a paper as well as write his name in pencil, but color the vowel in green. The students will write their name on construction paper and color the vowel a different color or decorate it in some way to differentiate it from the consonants.

Provide Practice

- As a class, we will read the section covering vowels in the language arts text. Following the reading, students will have time to play with the magnetic boards or cloth boards that are placed at each group table. Students will be encouraged to create words with vowels and help their partners to do so. The teacher will be visiting each group and asking students about their words and the different vowels used. Also, a worksheet will be given to the students to be done as part of their home learning weekly packet.
- Students will visit the different learning centers. Students will rotate among all the centers in intervals of ten minutes. After the students are done at each center, they will return to their desk to begin illustrating their poster.

Culminating Review

- Students will work independently composing a vowel poster. The poster must illustrate all six vowels with pictures that begin with that vowel. Pictures can be drawn or cut out of magazines. The pictures must be labeled. When students are done making their poster, they will present it to the class. All posters will be hung in the classroom after presentations are completed.
- While the posters are being presented and displayed, students will fill out an easy rubric evaluating each other's work. Students will evaluate the presenter on categories such as speech, listing of all vowels, and pictures drawn with labels.

STEP 5   Identify and Select Support Technologies

Technologies and materials needed include:

Magnetic boards, cloth boards, flash cards, poster boards, art supplies, alphabet chart, books on vowels, cassette player and talking books, rubric and worksheets, computer, LCD display, PowerPoint presentation.

Continues on next page ➤

STEP 6 Evaluate and Revise the Design

Students will be graded upon the outcome of the vowel in the name drawing, the home learning worksheet, and the vowel poster.

If more than three students score less than 100 percent on the vowel in the name drawing, then this assignment will be assigned as a home learning activity.

If more than three students score less than 100 percent on the home learning worksheet, the worksheet will be completed together in class.

If more than three students score less than 100 percent on the vowel poster, then a second poster will be assigned as a group activity.

Changes to the design will be made if two of four evaluations are lower than anticipated per the unit objectives.

The Lesson Planner

Vowel Unit Day One

STEP 1 Ready the Learner

Students will be asked to observe that the alphabet chart has only a few letters showing. Students will be asked to share why the vowels displayed may be different from the other letters.

STEP 2 Target Specific Objectives

The student will be able to differentiate vowels from consonants orally with 100 percent accuracy.

STEP 3 Prepare the Lesson

Classroom Preparation

- The alphabet chart needs to display only the vowels. A handout will be shared with all students. Magnetic boards with magnetic letters and cloth boards with cloth letters need to be placed at each group table.

Lesson Preparation

Preorganizer

- Cover consonants on the alphabet chart and post each vowel on the board. Also, post words that begin with the vowel on the board.

Bridge to Prior Knowledge

- Recite the alphabet as a class. Then have one student read the letters posted on the board.

Introduce New Knowledge

- Ask students why there are only six letters posted on the board and why the rest of the alphabet chart is covered.
- The teacher will explain to students why these letters are vowels and how they are different from the rest of the letters.
- A PowerPoint presentation will be shown to the class. We will discuss the slide show and the students will practice writing vowels in their journals.

Reinforce Knowledge

- As a class, the students will sing a vowel song. The class will sing the song at least two times. Then a few students will lead the rest of the class singing the vowel song for the third time.

Provide Practice

- Students will use alphabet manipulatives and flash cards in groups at the class centers to find vowels and create words using vowels.

Technology/Media Used

- PowerPoint presentation
- Flash cards and alphabet manipulatives
- Magnetic boards with magnets and cloth board with cloth letters

Check for Success

- Review journal pages of vowels and observe students using manipulatives and flash cards to ensure that students can distinguish vowels and consonants.

Continues on next page ➤

STEP 1 Ready the Learner

As a brief review, students will be asked to write the vowels on a sheet of paper and recite them aloud together in class. Students will sing the vowel song practiced in the previous lesson.

STEP 2 Target Specific Objectives

The student will be able to identify letters that are vowels by creating a poster board with 100 percent accuracy.

STEP 3 Prepare the Lesson

Classroom Preparation
- The alphabet chart in the classroom will have all letters uncovered.
- Art supplies and poster materials will be placed at each group table.

Lesson Preparation

Preorganizer
- Ask students to review the alphabet chart. Ask volunteers to come to the board to write one letter from the chart they think is a vowel.

Bridge to Prior Knowledge
- Recite the alphabet as a class. Ask students to identify which of the letters written on the board are in fact vowels. Ask students to think of a word that begins with each vowel.

Introduce New Knowledge
- Explain that the remaining letters of the alphabet are known as consonants.
- Write short words on the board and circle vowels. Write additional words on the board and ask students to come to the board and circle vowels and underline consonants.

Reinforce Knowledge
- Students will draw on a blank sheet of paper a vowel that is in their first or last name. For instance, John will draw the letter O on a paper as well as write his name in pencil, but color the vowel in green. The students will write their name on construction paper and color the vowel a different color or decorate it in some way to differentiate it from the consonants.

Provide Practice
- Students will be encouraged to create words with vowels and help their partners to do so. The teacher will be visiting each group and asking students about their words and the different vowels used.

Culminating Review
- Students will work independently composing a vowel poster. The poster must illustrate all six vowels with pictures that begin with that vowel. Pictures can be drawn or cut out of magazines. The pictures must be labeled. When students are done making their poster, they will present it to the class. All posters will be hung in the classroom after presentations are completed.

Technology/Media Used
- Art materials, poster board

Check for Success
- Student names will be checked for accuracy in identifying vowels. Vowel posters will be reviewed for accuracy.

interchapter 2

Vowel Unit Day Three

STEP 1 Ready the Learner

Student characteristics remain constant. The vowel song will be sung in preparation for the final day of the unit.

STEP 2 Target Specific Objectives

The student will be able to critique students' vowel posters on a rubric with 100 percent accuracy.

STEP 3 Prepare the Lesson

Classroom Preparation
- Student vowel posters will be displayed around the classroom.
- Rubrics will be provided to all students with extras at group tables.

Lesson Preparation

Preorganizer
- Rubric will be reviewed. The criteria for a correct poster will be discussed.

Bridge to Prior Knowledge
- Students will be asked to recite the vowels. Students will then be asked to recite consonants. The class alphabet chart may be used in the recitation.

Introduce New Knowledge
- Steps in rubric assessment will be presented. The concept of fairness and accuracy in evaluation will be discussed.

Reinforce Knowledge
- The PowerPoint presentation will be shown to the class. The slide show will be discussed and since the song correlates with the presentation, it will be sung again.

Provide Practice
- A sample poster prepared by the teacher that includes errors will be shared with the class. Students will be asked to evaluate it to see if they correctly detect errors and fairly evaluate the poster. After students finish the assessment, the teacher will demonstrate appropriate application of the rubric by assessing the sample poster.

Culminating Review
- Posters on display in the classroom will be assessed by peers. Students will fill out the rubric and turn it in for a grade. The rubric will evaluate posters based on categories such as speech, listing of all vowels, and pictures drawn with labels.

Technology/Media Used
- Assessment rubrics

Check for Success
- Rubric evaluations of peer posters will be reviewed and should demonstrate understanding of vowels.

Continues on next page ➤

The Instructional Action Planner

Vowel Unit

TO-DO #1 Prepare for the Learners
_____ Prepare PowerPoint.
_____ Make copies of handouts and rubrics.

TO-DO #2 Ready the Classroom
_____ Cover the consonants on the alphabet chart.
_____ Set up materials at all centers.
_____ Place magnetic boards with letters and cloth boards with cloth numbers at each group table.

TO-DO #3 Teaching and Learning Activities
_____ Get poster boards and art supplies.
_____ Test talking books, cassette players, and headphones at listening center.
_____ Secure flash cards and alphabet manipulatives for group tables.
_____ Review and select pages from language arts text for practice.
_____ Set up magnetic boards with magnetic letters and felt letters for cloth boards.

Activity Backup Plan
Vowel and consonant word game: Students can draw a vowel or consonant on a piece of paper, which will be taped to the front of their shirt. Students can then arrange themselves in words for reward points.

TO-DO #4 Personal Prompts
Talking Points
- Why are there vowels?
- Which letters are consonants?
- What how many vowels are there?
- Name some words that begin with a vowel.

Don't Forget to:
- Monitor students at the different learning centers.
- Close all applications on the computer.
- Lock your computer.
- Uncover consonants on Day 3.

TO-DO #5 Support Technologies
Technology Checklist
_____ Make sure the listening center equipment works.
_____ Make sure the computer, display, and PowerPoint presentation work.
_____ Make sure manipulatives, flash cards, and magnetic and cloth letters are full sets.

TO-DO #6 Feedback
_____ Prepare and distribute rubrics for assessing poster presentation.

TO-DO #7 Follow-Up
_____ Set up student computer with the PowerPoint presentation for continued practice and review.

PART TWO

Applying Technologies for Effective Instruction

Every classroom has its own personality, which is usually defined by a teacher's teaching style. Some have desks arranged in tidy rows; others have pods of desks arranged in circles. Some classrooms have an abundance of technology to help a teacher teach and students learn; others have only a few types of technology present.

Part Two examines the many kinds of technology available, how they work, and how they might best be used to help you teach and your students learn. Chapters 3 through 6 explore the most talked-about classroom technology: the personal computer. The U.S. Census Bureau in its 2000–2001 report estimated that the total number of computers in schools has reached just over 12 million—one for every four students. This number will no doubt continue to grow. Although the distribution across classrooms nationwide may vary, most educators want to see more computers, preferably connected to the Internet, in their classrooms. Chapter 3 introduces the personal computer as a classroom tool. Chapter 4 examines how various computers and their components can support teaching and learning. Chapters

5 and 6 explore the wide variety of administrative and academic software tools available to help accomplish the many tasks involved in teaching and learning. Chapters 7 and 8 explore the Internet and the World Wide Web, and their role in education. These chapters will give you a chance to take a closer look at all aspects of the personal computer and related digital technologies as educational tools and see why so many teachers want computers in their classroom.

Chapter 9 examines audio, visual, and video technologies. It explores the role of traditional visuals such as posters, bulletin boards, and models as well as computer software tools such as projected visuals, slides, and overhead transparencies. It further explores digital and analog video technologies and how motion media materials and equipment can aid in instruction.

Together, these chapters will help you build the knowledge base and skills you need to evaluate and select the most appropriate technology for your instructional design. Furthermore, these chapters will help you learn how to teach with and effectively implement the technologies you will find in schools.

chapter 3

Computers in the Learning Environment

This chapter addresses these ISTE *National Educational Technology Standards* for Teachers:

I. **TECHNOLOGY OPERATIONS AND CONCEPTS**
   Teachers demonstrate a sound understanding of technology operations and concepts. Teachers
   A. demonstrate introductory knowledge, skills, and understanding of concepts related to technology (as described in the ISTE *National Education Technology Standards* for Students).
   B. demonstrate continual growth in technology knowledge and skills to stay abreast of current and emerging technologies.

III. **TEACHING, LEARNING, AND THE CURRICULUM**
   Teachers implement curriculum plans that include methods and strategies for applying technology to maximize student learning. Teachers
   A. facilitate technology-enhanced experiences that address content standards and student technology standards.
   B. use technology to support learner-centered strategies that address the diverse needs of students.
   C. apply technology to develop students' higher-order skills and creativity.
   D. manage student learning activities in a technology-enhanced environment.

imagine that you enter a time machine and travel back fifty years. When you arrive, you decide to find out how things have changed from the past to the present. You select a few places to visit. Close by, you see a hospital and decide that it would be a good place to start. You go in and are amazed at the changes. There are beds, patients, doctors, and nurses; but you wonder what happened to all of the equipment you are so used to seeing in a hospital. Where are the many monitors that keep tabs on every patient's status? Where are the many diagnostic machines that pinpoint illness? Where are the constant audio messages paging one doctor or another? Where are the sophisticated life-support systems in the operating room? It is immediately clear that the medical technologies of the twenty-first century are as abundant as they are sophisticated when compared with those available fifty years ago.

Your time-travel investigation continues as you decide to visit a school. As you walk into the school of fifty years ago, you see teachers, students, and administrators in familiar classroom and office settings. When you peek into a classroom, you see a teacher at the front of the room, chalk in hand, writing on the board while lecturing on a topic. You see maps and charts on the walls and a globe and other models around the room. Sets of books are available on classroom bookshelves. The teacher may be preparing to show a filmstrip or movie. Students are sitting in rows of desks taking notes on what the teacher is saying. Sound familiar? Unlike medicine, a field in which technology has transformed the way doctors and other medical personnel work, education has changed relatively little, despite technological advances. With the exception of the addition of a VCR and monitor and perhaps one or two personal computers in the typical classroom today, very little has really changed in the last fifty years. (Adapted from the metaphor described by Seymour Papert, 1992.)

Yet the same computer revolution that dramatically altered medicine could and should have altered education. There are many reasons why this has not occurred; one of the key reasons is that teachers simply don't know why and how to use much of the audio, video, and digital equipment that is available, even if it is accessible. Until only recently, courses like the one you are taking in educational technology were not emphasized in teacher preparation. Now, with the investment schools are making in technology and the need to prepare students for life in the twenty-first century, teacher technology skills have become a critical element in teacher training. This chapter introduces you to computer technologies and their role in education and helps you build the skills you need to be an effective educational user of this technology.

This chapter will help prepare you to use personal computers in your classroom for administrative tasks, classroom management, and instruction. In Chapter 3, you will

- Discover and identify the components of a computer system
- Examine the role of input devices and explore the most common types
- Explore the roles and most common types of output devices
- Investigate the relationship and functions of the central processing unit, memory, and storage
- Explore the roles and most common types of storage devices
- Relate the components and functions of a computer system to teaching and learning tasks

Real People Real Stories

Meet Amy Gates and Sherri Lewis. Knowing how to plan instruction is important for effective teaching. However, to be able to plan for the use of personal computers in the learning environment requires knowledgeable teachers. Let's see how two educators helped plan and carry out the training of new and experienced teachers in their district so they could make effective use of computers in their teaching.

Amy Gates and Sherri Lewis work for a suburban school district located in the Midwest. Amy is the supervisor for instructional technology and has over sixteen years experience in education with a concentration in elementary and middle school. Sherri Lewis has eighteen years of experience in the secondary environment and has worked out of the office of professional development as a facilitator for the Beginning Teacher Assistance Program and Mentor Program.

Their district, the Lee's Summit District, is made up of 16,000 students with sixteen elementary schools, three middle schools, and three high schools. The district has a technology plan in place that provides each certified classroom teacher with a laptop to use as an instructional tool in the classroom.

Our first-year teachers were starting their careers with a diverse set of technological skills and were often able to use technology on a personal basis but not able to effectively use it as a tool for instruction. It was time for the trainers and educational leaders to catch up to the Millennials—the children of digital age.

The Millennial Generation includes those born between 1980 and 2000. That makes Millennials not only the young teachers who are just getting started in the teaching profession but also the students that educators currently have in the classroom. Technology has always been a part of the young Millennial teacher's life. Cell phones, instant messaging, and email are a daily routine for many; however, that does not mean that these teachers know how to effectively use technology to have an impact on student learning.

The goal of the Professional Development Department is to provide educators with the tools necessary to increase student achievement. Helping these teachers learn to use their computers to improve student learning is a critical element in our teacher preparation.

The district developed a comprehensive school improvement plan that provides each classroom teacher with a wireless laptop and two full days of technology integration training using it. Under the guidance of district mentor teachers and instructional technology specialists, new classroom teachers begin to incorporate this technology into their lessons. The instructional technology specialist and mentor teacher provide a no-fail support system for new teachers as they plan their use of computers in the classroom.

Following a new teacher in-service, teachers use what they have learned in various ways. Here are several examples of the uses of computer technology resulting from this technology initiative:

- A middle school math teacher shared how students created PowerPoint presentations to teach lessons to peers using textbook interactive links.

- Another teacher decided to go back to her classroom and restructure a poetry unit because a colleague demonstrated how poetry sites could be used to change a typical poetry reading into a "Poemapalooza" extravaganza including refreshments and readings of original student poetry.

- Hooking the laptop to a Classroom Performance System (CPS) allowed one teacher to receive immediate feedback on students' understanding of the material she presented in her folktale unit. The teacher was immediately able to differentiate her lesson based on the feedback.

- Another teacher was able to differentiate her instruction through the web page she has published on the district server. This web page contains links to the classroom objectives that the teacher uses to reinforce or extend student learning.

- One teacher integrates the laptop technology into his classroom using the district's United Streaming subscription (www.unitedstreaming.com/) to introduce the day's objective. The short video segments provide a lead-in to the content. Students are then asked to do a short writing assignment.

- Here in the Midwest, it is not feasible to take a traditional field trip to Mount Vernon, the home of George Washington. However, one teacher used her laptop hooked to a data projector and took students on a virtual field trip to this famous landmark at www.mountvernon.org/.

- One health teacher has been successfully using the Millionaire and Jeopardy game templates found at the district site (http://its.leesummit.k12.mo.us/gametemplates.htm) to review body systems content that students must master. The PowerPoint games are easy to download and edit. The teacher then hooks up to a data projector and begins the review.

The convergence of instructional technology and the teacher induction program is grounded in the philosophy that instructors teach as they have been taught. The goal for the Lee's Summit R7 school district's new teachers is to receive immediate exposure to technology and instructional design early in the first year of teaching. Systematic planning for the use of computers and other technology has increased as a result of this initiative.

For more information about this program, please contact

Amy Gates, Supervisor of Instructional Technology, Lee's Summit School District, amy.gates@leesummit.k12.mu.us.

Sherri Lewis, District Mentor, Lee's Summit School District–University of Missouri, sherri.lewis@leesummit.k12.mo.us.

Computers, Teaching, and You

You might be one of the many future or current educators wondering how you are going to use computers in your classroom. Or you might wonder whether their use will undermine your role as a teacher. Or, like many educators who are happy to use a personal computer to create a test or an assignment, you might see their value in classroom management but wonder whether they are worth the expense and extra effort when it comes to teaching and learning.

Educators sometimes feel a degree of concern when they are faced with the idea of using personal computer technology in their classrooms. This is not surprising because most teachers teach in the manner they were taught. They are comfortable using the tried-and-true strategies from which they learned. There is no doubt that these strategies continue to be valuable, but new technological tools make many enhancements to these strategies possible.

E-Learning

www.mylabschool.com
video
View *Managing Technology in the Classroom*

To overcome any possible reluctance to using a computer, it is best to begin by becoming more familiar with computers. This process starts by developing an understanding of how computers work and how they can be used for administrative and academic tasks. During this process of familiarization, it is also important to develop hands-on skills with the hardware and software that educators frequently use. Let's begin by getting to know what a computer is and how it works.

Computer Basics

Computers are machines made of metal, plastic, chips, and wire. These machines, unlike other small appliances, have no predetermined purpose built in. Instead, they are designed to be versatile, able to do a variety of tasks depending on the instructions (programs) they are given. Understanding how this unique digital technology works will help you to judge when a computer's capabilities will be useful in your classroom and how you can use computing capability to enhance your planned instruction. It will also help you to be able to recognize and correct minor computing problems or to know when you need to call for technical support.

A personal computer is a device that takes in data (input) from you, processes it according to your instructions, and then sends out the finished information product (output) to you. Because the quantity of data you input might be large and the size and complexity of the processing you want done can sometimes be great, computers have both short-term memory and long-term storage capabilities. These are used to help in completing the larger and more complex processing jobs you require. Computer **memory** is a temporary electronic storage space used by the computer to do short-term tasks or to complete a task that is too complex to do all at once. Longer-term **storage** is a more permanent electronic storage space in which the computer can store instructions and data for use at a later time. The use of a combination of temporary memory and long-term storage makes it possible for the computer to work on complex jobs a little at a time until the entire task is completed.

Together, these steps of taking in data, processing the data, storing it as necessary, and outputting the results to you, the end user, make up the **computing cycle.** This computing cycle and the components of a computer system are diagrammed in Figure 3.1. Regardless of the complexity of the task the computer is asked to perform, this basic computing cycle is always the same. With an understanding of this basic operational framework, you can more easily understand the interrelationship of the various components of a computer system.

The computing cycle takes place in and with the help of computer hardware and computer software. Computer **hardware** includes all of the computer components that are physical, touchable pieces of equipment. Together this collection of hardware is known as the **computer system.** Computer **software** is the term for **programs,** or sets of computer instructions, written in special computer languages that tell a computer how to accomplish a given task. You, as the end user of the hardware and software, really need to know relatively little about the details of how the computer components work together electronically or how a program is written. What you do need to know is which pieces of hardware and software you might

E-Learning
ON THE WEB! 3.1
Teachers Using Computers

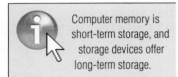

Computer memory is short-term storage, and storage devices offer long-term storage.

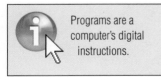

Programs are a computer's digital instructions.

E-Learning

www.mylabschool.com
Hardware Skills Builder
Setting Up a PC

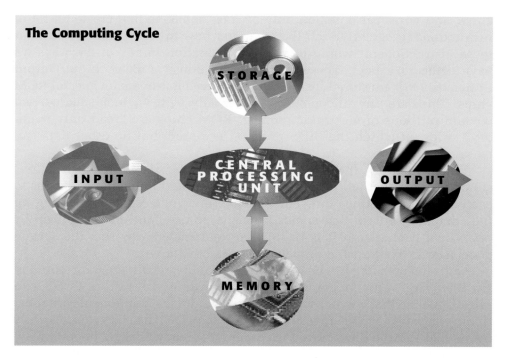

The Computing Cycle

The Computer System

STORAGE
DVD Drive
CD-RW Drive
Floppy Drive

Monitor
OUTPUT DEVICES
Printer

System unit containing the CPU and RAM

Mouse   INPUT DEVICES   Keyboard

FIGURE 3.1

The Computer

All computers use the same computing cycle to operate. The computer system consists of the computer and all related peripheral hardware.

need to accomplish the classroom management or instructional tasks you want done and how to use these computer components effectively for teaching and learning.

 # What Educators Need to Know about Software

As incredible as computers are, they lack the ability to accomplish much of anything unless someone tells them precisely what to do and how to do it. When we turn the computer's power on, the collection of metal, plastic, chips, and wires can function only because someone first created a set of instructions (program) to tell the computer how to start itself up. Without these instructions, it would be unable to function in any of the ways we have come to expect. These initial instructions, or Basic Input/Output System (BIOS), are stored inside the computer's hardware on special ROM **chips.** Chips are tiny silicon slices—often only $1/4$ to $1/2$ inch square—that contain millions of electronic circuits. **ROM** chips are "read only memory" chips on which the BIOS program is stored, but no other data can be saved.

"Booting up" the computer means starting it.

When you turn the power on, the computer reads the instructions stored in ROM that tell it how to start itself up and immediately begins to carry these instructions out. This is sometimes referred to as **booting up** the computer, a term that comes from the phrase "pulling oneself up by one's own bootstraps." It is in this very automated way that the system boots (starts) itself up and prepares to interact with you.

Once the machine has booted up, it runs a diagnostic program stored in the BIOS chip. This program, called the power-on self-test, or **POST,** is a self-diagnostic that ensures that all of the computer's components are functioning as expected (see Figure 3.2). Once the POST has been successfully completed and the BIOS runs, the computer is ready to begin operations. If the computer finds an internal problem during the POST, it will display an error message on the screen describing the problem that it found and suggesting what you need to do to resolve it. The results of the POST will help you determine whether your machine needs any technical intervention before you try to use it for the task at hand.

Let's assume that the POST was completed successfully and the BIOS loads. Even though the computer is now ready to operate, before it can begin to function like the computing device you have become familiar with, it must first be given instructions on how to operate as a computer. It must be told how to respond to and perform the many little interactive

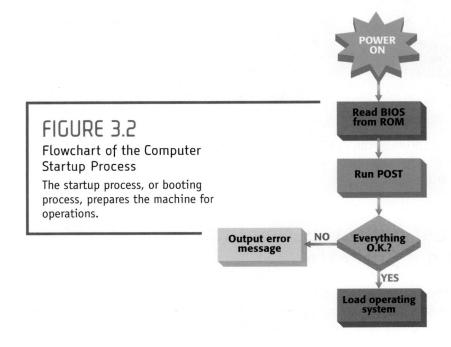

FIGURE 3.2

Flowchart of the Computer Startup Process

The startup process, or booting process, prepares the machine for operations.

tasks you expect, such as how to save data on a disk and what to do when you click a mouse button. The machine requires an additional program that provides specific instructions on how to act like a computer. That is done by a special set of programs called the operating system. Every computer must have an **operating system,** a collection of programs that tells it how to function and how to manage its own operation. The operating system also creates an interface between you and the machine. An **interface** is the component of the operating system that establishes the methods of interaction (via menus, text, or graphics) between the user and the machine. The operating system is thus the first external (not built-in) piece of software the machine needs to be able to know how to run in order to communicate with you. The operating system must therefore start before you can begin your personal tasks. Learning to use the operating system on your computer is a prerequisite skill for using your computer to do the management and instructional tasks you need it to do.

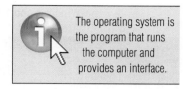

The operating system is the program that runs the computer and provides an interface.

Today's most popular operating systems are Windows for personal computers and Macintosh OS for the Apple Macintosh computer. Both of these operating systems use an interface that is a combination of typed-in (text) commands, choices from preset menus, and selected icons that appear on the opening screen, called the desktop. A **menu** is a listing of command options that appears across the top of the program window. Usually, after the user selects one of these menu choices, additional options will appear in a submenu that drops down from it. An **icon** is a small graphic that represents one of the system's options. Typically, **commands** can be issued in multiple ways: by typing a series of keystrokes, selecting a menu option, or clicking on the appropriate icon. There is no one right way to issue most operating system commands but, instead, there are a variety of ways to use the operating system. Both **Windows** and Macintosh OS present command options to users via windows, or boxed collections of icons and text. The user can then choose commands by clicking on an icon. This style of interaction between user and machine that depends so heavily on graphics and visuals instead of text is referred to as a graphic user interface, or **GUI** (pronounced "gooey"). Every effort has been made to make it friendly and convenient for users. An example of the Windows and Macintosh interfaces appears in Figure 3.3 on page 96. As a technology-using educator, you should make it a priority to master Windows or Macintosh OS, whichever is used in the school in which you teach. Although some operating system basics are presented in this chapter, practicing with an operating system is the only way to gain the skills you need.

E-Learning

www.mylabschool.com
Software Skills Builder
Windows Skills

You can tell the machine what you want it to do by selecting a menu option, entering a text command, or pointing to an icon with an arrow that you control through manipulation of a mouse. A **mouse** is a "work-alike" pointing device that rolls about on your desk, usually on a special pad. It is called a work-alike device because it moves the pointing arrow on the computer screen in the same direction in which you move the mouse on your desk. Although using a mouse or other pointing device might at first take some practice, most people find it very intuitive and are comfortable with only a little bit of use.

The operating system controls and interacts with both the hardware components of the computer and any software you choose to use. It also provides common ways for you to select options and to issue commands

FIGURE 3.3
GUI Interfaces
Windows and Macintosh OS operating systems allow users to interact by pointing and clicking.

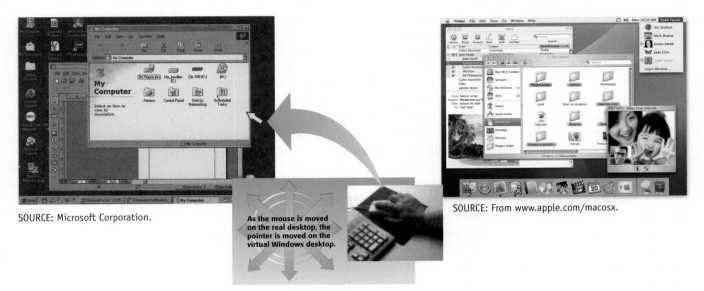

SOURCE: Microsoft Corporation.

As the mouse is moved on the real desktop, the pointer is moved on the virtual Windows desktop.

SOURCE: From www.apple.com/macosx.

E-Learning
ON THE WEB! 3.2
Operating Systems

Different software applications are needed to do specific tasks.

E-Learning
ON THE WEB! 3.3
What Software Applications Are Most Useful?

across a wide range of programs. You control the operating system through the menu or icon choices you make, and they, in turn, control the rest of the computer's functions for you.

Once the operating system is loaded and running, the computer is ready to address your task. However, the computer still needs a more specific program to enable it to perform the particular task you have in mind. The operating system enables the computer to use software, but to understand how it must perform for you, the computer has to have instructions installed and running. These task-specific instructions are provided by an application program. An **application program** is a set of instructions that tell the computer how to complete a unique task such as word processing, database management, or drawing. Applications range from **utility programs** that improve or monitor computer operations, to administrative applications (e.g., word-processing and gradebook programs), to academic applications (e.g., tutorials and electronic encyclopedias). Every application is a specific computer program written to accomplish a single task or a group of interrelated tasks. For example, if you want to use your computer to type up a test, you need a word-processing application. If you want to use an electronic spreadsheet to keep your gradebook, you need a spreadsheet application. The advantage of this versatility is that a single bundle of hardware—the personal computer system—can do many different jobs. The disadvantage is that you need as many pieces of application software as you have tasks to perform. Table 3.1 lists some of the most frequently used types of application software.

Because software manufacturers are aware of the need for multiple types of programs to perform common tasks, they often bundle their most popular applications into a related collection (suite) of applications. One

TABLE 3.1   Popular Microcomputer Software

COMMON SOFTWARE	FUNCTION
OPERATING SYSTEM	The operating system provides the interface for the user and controls the computer operations.
WORD PROCESSING	Word processing gives the user an environment for entering text and other data and manipulating its format prior to printing it out.
ELECTRONIC SPREADSHEETS	Spreadsheets manipulate, format, and calculate numerical data and arrange them in a display called a worksheet.
DATABASE MANAGEMENT	Database software provides an environment in which large quantities of data can be entered, stored, manipulated, queried, and reported.
PRESENTATION SOFTWARE	Presentation software enables the user to create electronic slide shows with special effects, including sound and animation.
DESKTOP PUBLISHING	Publishing software combines word-processing capability with desktop layout capability for easy-to-use layout and design of complex publication formats.
GRAPHICS PROGRAMS	Graphics programs provide an environment in which the user can draw pictures, create diagrams, or manipulate digital photos for inclusion in other programs or to print out.
COMMUNICATIONS SOFTWARE	This category of software includes the software to connect a computer to one or more other computers via phone lines and the browsers that let users examine the sites on the World Wide Web.
UTILITIES	Utilities include all of the various types of software that help users maintain their computers in good working order.

of the most popular suites available today is Microsoft's Office Suite, which includes a word processor (Word), a spreadsheet (Excel), a database management system (Access), and a presentation package (PowerPoint). Together, the programs in this suite, like those in its competitor products, can enable you to accomplish almost any administrative task.

Another approach, one that reduces the number of application programs needed, is to integrate the main features of a collection of popular applications into a single comprehensive application, called an **integrated software package.** Such a package has the capability to perform many, but not all, of the functions of the full-blown versions of the software. Microsoft Works and ClarisWorks are examples of integrated software packages. They contain most of the same types of software as does Office, but each component piece is a little less powerful than its Office counterpart, having fewer features and capabilities.

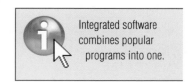

Integrated software combines popular programs into one.

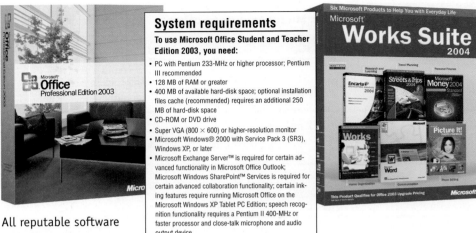

All reputable software includes equipment specifications to help you decide whether it will work on your computer.

Most integrated and/or bundled software products usually include the most popular types of applications—typically word processing, a graphics program, a spreadsheet program, a database management program, a communications program, and a presentation program. An advantage of both bundled and integrated packages is that all the software offered in this manner uses similar commands and looks familiar on the screen. This common "look and feel" can make it easier to learn and use each of the applications. Also, an integrated package usually takes up less space on the computer's hard disk. A disadvantage of an integrated software package is that each of its components might not contain as many functions as similar software sold in separate application packages.

It should be remembered that every piece of software is written with specific hardware in mind. Typically, software specifications identify the minimum levels of hardware necessary to use a given piece of software. It is important that you be sufficiently familiar with your hardware to be able to select appropriate software. Information about the technical aspects of hardware can be found in the documentation that accompanies the hardware when it is purchased. The hardware specifications required for determining whether software will run typically include the speed of the machine, the amount of available memory, the capability of the monitor, and the space required on the hard drive. These details are included on the side of every commercial software box. You should take a moment to jot down the specifications of the machine on which you plan to install the software and have these specifications available whenever you shop for software.

What Do I Need to Know When Buying Software?

What Educators Need to Know about Hardware

Although it is not necessary to understand the intricacies of how hardware works at the level of its electronics, it is important to understand what different hardware components do. This baseline knowledge will help you to identify the components you need to get the job done in your classroom. The remainder of this chapter will introduce you to these components.

Input Devices

To make the computer look for, load, and run application software, you, the user, must first tell the computer to do so. To issue this type of command and to later add your personal data, you need some way to communicate your wishes to the computer. This is done through the use of an input device. An **input device** includes any computer peripheral that you might use to enter data into the computer. A peripheral is any device that can be connected to a computer. The keyboard and the mouse are the most often used types of input devices. Let's take a closer look at each of these devices to determine its respective role in accomplishing your tasks.

The typical computer **keyboard** is laid out much like the keys on a typewriter. However, the computer keyboard has several additional keys not typically found on a typewriter, which are used to control the computer or give software commands. Typing commands or data into the machine is usually referred to as keyboarding. Because of the prevalence of computer technology in schools and in society in general, many schools now require their students to have keyboarding competencies before they leave elementary school.

The other most prevalent input device is the mouse. The mouse is one of several types of pointing devices that allow you to move the selection arrow on the screen. Pointing devices include any input device that enables users to point to the commands or icons they wish to use. The selection arrow, sometimes called a pointer, is an icon shaped like an arrow used to point to the command icons or menu items that you want to choose. Other common types of pointing devices include a trackball, a joystick, and a

E-Learning

www.mylabschool.com
video
View: *An Adaptive Keyboard*

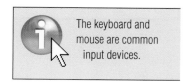

The keyboard and mouse are common input devices.

TECHNOLOGY SOLUTIONS *for All Learners*

If you wanted to use a computer but had a physical disability that interfered with operating your keyboard or mouse, you might feel that using computers was beyond you. Fortunately, that is not the case. Assistive devices are special technologies that help students with special needs. Assistive input devices, in particular, are widely available for students with limited mobility and for those who are sight impaired.

Some children cannot use the keyboard as typically configured. Alternative keyboards that have larger or smaller keys and others that are designed for use with one hand are options for these students. For those whose hand movement is severely limited, there are wands and sticks that can be worn, held, or strapped to the head to press keys.

If the mouse is the problem, various assistive devices are available in lieu of the standard mouse. These include devices

that can control the cursor without use of the hands via eye movements; sip-and-puff systems that use the breath; and joysticks that can be manipulated by feet, chin, or hand. Touch screens, which do not require a keyboard or mouse for input, offer another option.

For sight-impaired students, Braille embossers create refreshable Braille displays to provide students with a display that uses mechanically lifted rounded pins to form Braille characters representing information on a computer screen. The student can type his or her input and then read the Braille representation to review what has been written. Another option is to use a screen reader that will "speak" whatever is written on the screen. A screen reader will turn menus, icons, and text into an audio equivalent.

These and many more assistive devices are available to meet the unique technological needs of any child with disabilities. Teachers wanting to learn more about the technologies to help their special needs students should visit the North Regional Educational Laboratory at **www.ncrel.org/sdrs/areas/issues/ methods/technlgy/te7assist.htm.**

The keyboard is configured like a typewriter keyboard with some additional keys. It is used primarily to enter data, but it also includes cursor keys to move the pointer.

A mouse is used to give commands, make selections, and move objects on a GUI interface. It is used by rolling it around on the desktop and clicking its buttons.

The trackball is really an upside-down mouse. It is used by rolling the ball on the top with your fingers to move the pointer on the screen. It too has buttons you can click or double click.

A touch pad is a flat, pressure-sensitive panel. To move the pointer, you just press lightly and move your fingertip around on the surface of the panel. It too has buttons for clicking.

FIGURE 3.4

Input Devices: The Keyboard and Various Pointing Devices

A variety of input devices are available for inputting data or commands.

touch pad. As you can see in Figure 3.4, each of these devices has a slightly different configuration, but all control the movement of the selection arrow, allow you to issue commands, and make it possible to move (drag and drop) items on the desktop.

Each of these devices also includes one, two, or, in some cases, three or more buttons. Once the pointing device is used to position the pointer arrow on the icon or menu item desired, the appropriate button is clicked to select the menu item or to execute an action represented by an icon. When a mouse has two or more buttons, the leftmost mouse button is typically preset by the software to work in a specific way, and those settings are fairly consistent across all pieces of software. The other one or more mouse buttons either control scrolling (moving up and down the screen) or are programmable by the software; that is, different types of software use those buttons in different ways, or you can assign special functions to them. You should read through the documentation that accompanies the software you want to use to see what convenient features may be available through the use of these other buttons.

Tech Tips for TEACHERS

Mouse buttons are typically set up for right-handed students, but this can be modified. If your students are left-handed, you can switch the button's function. All operating systems provide this option. In Windows, click on the Control Panel, found via the Start button, and select Mouse to change the mouse from a right-handed to a left-handed orientation. The Macintosh OS uses similar commands. Using the same Mouse menu, you can also make the pointer larger and add additional visual representations of mouse movement (pointer trails) for students who have sight impairments.

Although the keyboard and mouse are the two most often used input devices, there are, in fact, several others. Each of these other input devices has unique properties that make it very useful in an innovative teaching and learning environment. These other input devices are more fully described in Chapter 4, "Digital Technologies in the Classroom." For now, it is sufficient that you understand the function of input devices in general and the mouse and keyboard in particular. This will serve as a basis for contrast with the hardware necessary at the other end of the computer cycle: output devices.

Output Devices

If input devices are used to put data into the computer, then **output devices** are the pieces of hardware that move information (data that has been processed) out of the computer. The two primary output devices for most computer systems are the monitor and the printer. The monitor displays information in **soft copy** (electronic form), and the printer turns that information into **hard copy** (printed form).

Hard copy is printed output; soft copy is displayed on the monitor.

A **monitor** displays computer information on its screen. The screen works much like a television screen, but it typically has much higher resolution. **Resolution** refers to the clarity and crispness of the images on the monitor screen. Resolution can be measured by the number of pixels the screen displays. A **pixel,** or picture element, is a single colored dot on the monitor screen that, when combined with other pixels, forms an image. Resolution measurements are provided both vertically and horizontally (see Figure 3.5). You have probably seen this type of measurement indicated in relation to computers. A screen resolution may be 800 × 600. This measurement

A monitor's resolution is determined by the vertical number of pixels (picture elements) and the horizontal number of pixels. Monitors also vary in terms of the number of colors they can display. The greater the resolution and the number of colors, the more realistic the picture.

Flat-screen LCD monitors, like their bulkier CRT counterparts, vary in resolution and screen size. While they take up less desk space, they may be more easily damaged in a busy classroom.

A monitor's screen size is measured diagonally in inches.

The viewing screen on a notebook computer is really a high-resolution color liquid crystal display (LCD) screen. It is based on the same technology that is used in digital clocks and wristwatches, only much more sophisticated. This same technology is used for flat-screen monitors.

FIGURE 3.5

Output Devices—Monitors
Different monitors and screens provide different levels of display.

Tech Tips
for TEACHERS

You can create transparencies for an overhead projector on your printer. Using a variety of standard software packages, you can create a document that includes text, clip art, and photos to teach your target concept. Then you can print the document on special printer transparency film instead of paper. Once printed, it is ready to use on your overhead.

If you have an ink jet printer, you will need to use transparency film made especially for it. Ink jet printers work by squirting small droplets of ink onto the printing surface. Using an ink jet with standard transparency film will result in the ink running off and smearing. Ink jet transparency film has been specially prepared so that one side of the plastic has a rough, porous surface. Printing on the porous side of the film will allow the ink to adhere and dry. Ink jet printing of transparencies lets you create full-color transparencies for use in instruction.

If you have a laser printer, be sure to use laser transparency film instead. Laser printers transfer images by heating toner. Laser transparency film is thick enough to be unaffected by the heat needed to transfer the image. Any other type of film may at best buckle and at worst melt inside the printer. The limitation of laser-printed transparencies is that most laser printers print in black only.

To avoid costly mistakes and wasted transparency film, you should carefully read the transparency film boxes to be sure you are purchasing the appropriate material for your printer.

means the screen image is made up of 800 vertical columns of pixels in each of 600 horizontal lines of pixels. The higher the numbers the denser but smaller the image becomes. Another measure of a monitor is screen size. Screen size refers to the number of inches measured diagonally across the screen. The most common monitor sizes are 14", 15", 17", 19", and 21". Larger sizes are needed for exacting work such as digital graphics and computer-aided design.

The resolution on most monitors is adjustable to accommodate different software. It is important to check the software's hardware specifications to ensure that the program's output can be displayed with the monitor you are using and to ensure you have your resolution set correctly.

A popular alternative to the more traditional computer monitor is the **LCD** (liquid crystal display) screen that has been used on notebook (small portable) computers for several years. Although the LCD screens on notebooks have had some viewing limitations, new, full-size, high-resolution LCD screens do not. These LCD screens have the advantage of being much thinner and lighter than traditional monitors, making them easier to position on a desk or in the classroom. LCD monitors also consume less energy. They are still somewhat more expensive than traditional monitors of the same screen size but may be worth the additional cost.

Monitors of all types display soft copy, that is, data that is still in electronic form within the computer. Soft copy is volatile (temporary). It will disappear when power to the machine is cut off. To output the same data to a more permanent form, a printer is used. There are many types of printers, each with its own advantage. The most common types of printers and their respective advantages and disadvantages are summarized in Figure 3.6.

Like monitors, printers vary in their resolution. The higher the resolution, the crisper and clearer the text and graphics that are produced. With printers, resolution is measured in **dpi** (dots per inch). Like images on a monitor, printed text and graphics are really just a series of tiny dots, in this case printed on a page. The more dots there are in an inch of print, the crisper the text or graphic appears and the more intense its color seems.

If you wish to make copies of a printout for your class, the greater the clarity of the original, the better the copies will look. For this reason, it is wise to make at least one original hard copy at the highest possible resolution. Most printers offer you the opportunity to print out in various modes, from draft to normal to high quality. Draft mode saves printer ink and usually prints more quickly. Normal is good for most documents. However, you should select high quality for your copier masters.

E-Learning

www.mylabschool.com
Hardware Skills Builder
Printers

E-Learning
ON THE WEB! 3.5

Which Printer Is Best for My Classroom?

LASER PRINTER

This printer uses a laser beam, toner, and heat to transfer letters to paper, similar to copy machine technology. It offers the best resolution, fastest print speeds, and highest quality.

INK JET PRINTERS

Ink jet printers squirt a small puff of ink onto paper to create the image. They include both black and color ink. These usually inexpensive printers are slower than laser printers but offer good resolution.

MULTIFUNCTION DEVICES

These combination fax/copier/printers actually use ink jet, thermal, or laser printing technology to print images from a fax, a computer, or another sheet of paper.

FIGURE 3.6

Output Devices—Printers and Their Print Resolutions

Printers vary in technology, speed, and quality of display.

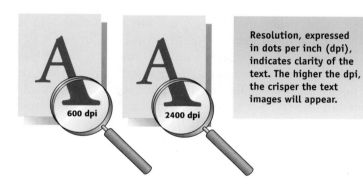

600 dpi   2400 dpi

Resolution, expressed in dots per inch (dpi), indicates clarity of the text. The higher the dpi, the crisper the text images will appear.

Printers not only produce their output on paper, they can also be used to produce their output on transparencies for use with an overhead projector. Specific types of transparency film are available for different types of printers. In addition to transparency film, many other specialty papers are available for both ink jet and laser printers. Using your classroom printer and selected specialty paper, you can print T-shirt transfers, custom stickers, CD labels, magnets, glossy digital photos, and a variety of other unique printouts. To do so, you must buy the paper appropriate to your printer, whether ink jet or laser. These specialty papers can add interest and customized activities to any classroom.

 Printers can create overhead transparencies and more.

E-Learning
ON THE WEB! 3.6

How Are Printers Useful in the Classroom?

A variety of transparency film and specialty papers are available for use with ink jet and laser printers.

The number and variety of output devices that can be added to a computer system offer many possibilities for innovative application to teaching and learning. These devices will be explored more fully in Chapter 4.

The System Unit

Each component of a computer system is assigned a different part of the total information-processing job. However, at the core of every computer is the system unit, the box that holds the computer's circuit board (motherboard) with the chips and circuits that make processing on the computer possible. Input, output, and storage devices enable the movement of data into and out of the system unit. But within the system unit, it is the central processing unit, or **CPU,** a powerful microprocessor chip, that is responsible for controlling almost all operations of the computer and processing data as instructed by the user. All computer components are ultimately interconnected through and coordinated by the CPU. Within the CPU chip, calculations are performed; flow of information among input, output, and memory is coordinated; and program instructions are transmitted at a speed measured in billionths of a second (nanoseconds). Current CPU chips, such as Intel's Pentium series, can carry out billions of instructions per second. Such speeds, typically measured in gigahertz (megahertz in older machines), are necessary, especially for complex software, to minimize the time the user has to wait for processing to complete. The faster the CPU, the more responsive the machine will be. For that reason, computer users want the fastest microprocessor chips with the highest number of gigahertz they can acquire.

When you issue a command to begin a computing task, the CPU must find the instructions for how to do what you want done and then accept the data you input to perform the processes on it that you have requested. The CPU typically seeks its instructions in one or more of the storage devices attached to the machine and in the instructions it received from you via an input device.

Once the CPU has located the appropriate set of instructions or program (such as a word processor), it will load the program into the computer's memory called random-access memory (RAM). **RAM** is the temporary memory space located on a set of chips that the CPU uses while it is carrying out its processing. The CPU reads the program from its permanent storage location (a disk) and then places a copy into RAM to make it readily accessible. The CPU then uses RAM to store the input you enter so that it can be processed in accordance with the program's instructions. When you are finished with your processing tasks, at your command, the CPU will save the processed data it has stored in RAM on a storage device so you can use it again later. Because data in RAM is volatile, it will be lost when power is lost. It is therefore critical to frequently give the Save command, which moves data in RAM to a more permanent location on a disk. When you complete your task and close the application, the CPU empties RAM of both program and data so that it is clear and available for your next task. Throughout every task you ask the computer to complete, the CPU controls the job and automatically uses RAM as necessary to assist in getting your processing task done.

E-Learning

www.mylabschool.com
Hardware Skills Builder
Inside the PC

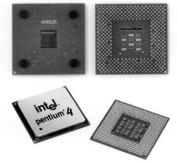

Microprocessor chips are the "brains" of a computer system.

Storage

Because we generally do not want to have to reenter data every time we want to use that same data, we need to store it in a more permanent location. Furthermore, we need to be able to store programs that we want available when we need to complete a specific type of job. Permanently storing data and programs is the function of the storage devices included in a computer system. All computers have a hard disk drive to store programs and data. However, there are many possible additional configurations for storage devices in a computer. You may select any combination of a floppy disk drive, CD drives, and a DVD drive. How a machine is configured in terms of storage is determined by your needs.

Hard Disks

Each type of storage device uses its own media. Figure 3.7 and Table 3.2 summarize and compare the most common types of disk storage media. Because of its large storage capacity, the **hard disk** drive is the most commonly used mass storage device for a computer. Inside the hard disk drive are a series of stacked metal platters (hard disks) on which data is stored. These disks comprise the storage area in which the operating system, applications programs, and most personal data are stored.

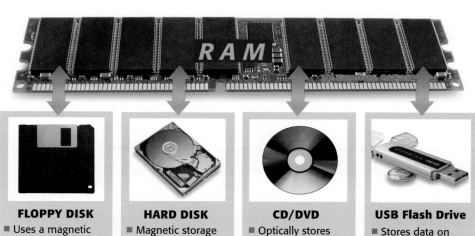

FLOPPY DISK
- Uses a magnetic storage system on a "floppy" Mylar disk
- Stores up to 1.44 megabytes (millions of bytes of data)
- Useful to move data between machines
- Disk is inserted into the A drive

HARD DISK
- Magnetic storage on stacked "hard" metal platters
- Size varies by machine—holds billions of bytes of data as measured in gigabytes
- Permanently mounted inside the machine
- Usually called the C drive

CD/DVD
- Optically stores data on a thin platter that is read by a laser beam
- CD stores up to 650 megabytes (millions of bytes of data)
- DVDs store up to 17 gigabytes (billions of bytes)
- Can be read only or recordable

USB Flash Drive
- Stores data on flash memory chip
- Stores gigabytes (billions of bytes of data)
- Recognized as if it were a physical disk
- Can be retrieved or saved just as on a disk

FIGURE 3.7
From Storage to Virtual Desktop

Data and programs are moved into RAM whenever the user needs to start an application or use information stored on one of the available storage devices. Once in RAM, the program or data is active and available to use.

TABLE 3.2   Comparison of Storage Media

STORAGE MEDIA	CHARACTERISTICS
FLOPPY DISK	• Disk of Mylar inside rigid plastic shell • Magnetic film on both sides of Mylar stores data • Up to 1,444,000 bytes (1.44 megabytes) of data can be stored on a high-density 3.5" disk • Disks must be prepared to accept data (formatted) before using • Previously the most popular portable storage medium, may become obsolete • Some computers no longer include floppy disk drives but have replaced them with optical media
HARD DISK	• Stack of metal platters (disks) permanently mounted inside the computer box • Platters are coated with magnetic material on both top and bottom of disk • Sensitive to contaminants, so the disk and drives are permanently encased and mounted in the system unit • Storage capacity ranges but is typically multiple gigabytes (billions of bytes) of data • Usually designated the C drive, it is the primary mass storage area for both programs and data
PORTABLE MEDIA	• A portable hard disk is a self-contained disk and drive that plugs into one of the USB ports in the system unit • Portable hard disks can have hundreds of gigabytes in capacity • Flash drives can hold multiple gigabytes of storage • Like portable hard disks, jump drives connect via the USB port • Both types of media are convenient for transporting large files
CD-ROM, CD-R, CD-RW	• Optical discs of plastic on which microscopic pits have been burned using a laser • Holes and flat areas are read by a laser mounted in a CD drive • CD-ROMs are read only, making them a one-way storage media, unlike disks • CD-Rs are special-purpose CDs that can be written on once and read multiple times; they require a recordable drive to create them but can be read by any CD drive • CD-RWs are specially constructed CDs that are rewritable; CD-RW drives are necessary to store and erase data on CD-RWs; CD-RWs can be read by most CD drives • CDs can store up to 650 megabytes of data • Often used for multimedia storage because of their large capacity for storing audio, video, and text data
DVD-ROM, DVD-R, DVD+RW, DVD-RW	• DVDs are optical media that can store up to 17 gigabytes of data depending on the format of the DVD • DVD-ROMs are read only; after initial recording, data cannot be stored on them • DVD-Rs are recordable but require a DVD writer • Three competing formats are available: DVD+R/W and DVD-RW are competing formats with similar features; DVD-RAM offers additional features but is incompatible with some players • DVD-Rs and DVD+RWs can record approximately 2 hours of quality video

For most machines, the hard disk drive is designated with the drive letter C. The disks, or platters, built into the hard disk drive can hold **gigabytes,** or billions of bytes, of data, with some disks now capable of storing terabytes (trillions). A **byte** of data is roughly equal to one alphabetic (A) or numeric (1) character of information (see Table 3.3). Thus, a typical hard disk can hold billions of letters or numbers (alphanumeric characters) as stored data. In the physical world, the hard disk might be analogous to a

TABLE 3.3 Relative Sizes of Stored Data

SIZE	CHARACTER EQUIVALENT	EXAMPLE
1 BYTE	1 alphanumeric character	The letter A or number 5
1 KILOBYTE	Approximately 1,000 characters	Slightly less than 1 page of typed, double-spaced text
1 MEGABYTE	Approximately 1 million characters	1,000 pages of typed, double-spaced text
1 GIGABYTE	Approximately 1 billion characters	1 million pages of typed, double-spaced text
1 TERABYTE	Approximately 1 trillion characters	1 billion pages of text

roomful of very large multiple-drawer file cabinets. The surfaces of hard disks are so sensitive that ordinary airborne contaminants such as dust or a strand of hair can interrupt the flow of information if caught between the drive head and the disk itself. Hard disks are therefore usually fixed inside the computer's case and encased in their own protective housing. Because they are permanently fixed inside the computer, hard disks are also sometimes called fixed disks.

Permanently fixing the hard disk inside the computer does not make it immune to problems. Problems can and do affect the data you store on a disk. Because any electronic or mechanical device can break, it is important to remember to **back up** your data, that is, make a duplicate or backup copy of your files. Usually, when a disk crashes (loses its storage ability), all of the information that was stored on that disk is lost. If you suffer a hard or floppy disk crash, your data may be irretrievable unless you have a backup copy. For teachers with lesson plans, tests, activity sheets, and student grades stored on a hard drive, such a loss can be devastating to your work. Backup files are usually made on removable storage media (floppy disks, external hard drives, or CD- or DVD+RWs) that can be stored away from the machine. It is not necessary to back up your application programs, because they can always be reinstalled. However, it is a good idea to keep the original media and their documentation in a safe place and available for reinstallation if it becomes necessary.

Most of the time when you are working on the computer, you will be using the hard disk drive for storage. If you need to use more than one machine, perhaps one at home or in the faculty workroom as well as one in your classroom, you will need a way to move your data from one machine to the other. This is one of the reasons for the

How Is Disk Storage Useful?

Today's hard disk drives offer storage space for billions of pages of text, millions of graphics, and thousands of audio and video clips.

COOL TOOLS

Portable Hard Drive

Maxtor 300-Gigabyte
Portable Hard Drive

Backing up your files is a necessary task. However, large files or just many smaller files quickly overwhelm the storage capacity of floppy disks and recordable CDs. Even with larger capacity DVDs, while you may have enough space to back up your My Documents folder, you do not have enough space to back up your software. You would therefore not be able to use your DVD in place of your hard drive if it crashes. So how best can a teacher back up his or her computer system?

A portable external hard drive can be used to create a backup of your computer's internal hard drive. This backup includes all the software and files stored on your computer system. The portable unit typically plugs into the USB port of any machine and can move from computer to computer. You can even take your portable drive home over your summer break should you want to work on preparation for the next school year. Once connected, you can launch software and retrieve files from your portable hard disk, just as you did with your classroom computer's internal hard drive. And, if your internal drive fails, it can be used to restore software and files when you get the damaged hard drive replaced.

Portable drives are often packaged with software to make the backup process a simple one-click procedure. For under $300, this device offers busy teachers a very reasonable data "insurance policy."

---

popularity of removable storage media. Although being phased out on many newer computers, one of the most common types of removable storage media has been the floppy disk.

Floppy Disks

The floppy disk stores 1.44 megabytes of information.

Although floppy disks are an aging technology, many classrooms still have computers with floppy disk drives. The floppy disk drive is an electromechanical device that is usually mounted inside the computer. It is able to read and write magnetic pulses from and to the surface of a **floppy disk.** Although the floppy disk is encased in a hard plastic protective case, it is not considered a type of "hard" disk. Inside the floppy's hard casing, the disk itself is made of flexible (floppy) Mylar-type material coated with a magnetically sensitive coating. Like its bigger cousin, the hard drive, it is sensitive to many environmental factors. The standard floppy disk can contain 1.44 megabytes (millions of bytes) of data, compared to the gigabyte (billions of bytes) capacity of today's hard disks. It can hold many files and many folders, but it has a limited capacity. This small capacity is because information is packed less densely on the floppy disk, lowering its sensitivity to contaminants. Thus, it can be removed and exposed to the environment with a low probability of data loss. The floppy disk's increased durability makes it a viable and inexpensive medium for use in schools with other computers.

Whether on a floppy or hard disk, the organizational units for storing data are known as files and folders, as illustrated in Figure 3.8. An electronic **file** is a collection of related data, usually a product of a single task. A file is typically created through the use of a single application program. An electronic **folder** is a digital organizer that you create to hold related

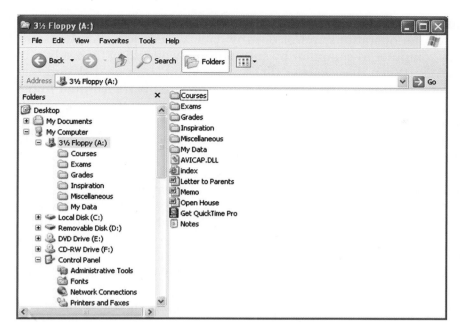

FIGURE 3.8

Windows Explorer and Its Organizational System

Windows organizes your data using a file and folder system. When a folder is expanded, in the left pane of Explorer you will see icons representing the contents of the folder.

Microsoft Windows Explorer® is a registered trademark of Microsoft Corporation.

files on a disk. In the physical world, a file would be equivalent to one or more printed sheets of information that resulted from the completion of a task. A folder, like its paper counterpart, the file folder, would be used to hold related documents (files).

Copying files onto floppy disks or other portable media also allows you to transport them from one computer to another. Just copy the file to the media and copy the data from it into the new computer. Of course, it is necessary that the application software that created the file also be available in the second computer. Copying a file copies the data only; it does not copy the application program that made and initially saved the file.

Floppy disks have proven their usefulness in classroom settings. Students who are creating their own personal files for an activity need a place to store them. If the files are saved on the hard disk drive, other students in the class can potentially have access to them. Furthermore, if you are teaching in a secondary school with a student load of more than 150 students per day, the available space on your hard drive is rapidly consumed. Instead, to ensure privacy and to save hard disk space, it is easier to give each student his or her own floppy disk(s) to use throughout the term or the project. Students can then be responsible for their own data for the duration of the project. At the end of the term or year, the disks can all be erased and reused by the next group of students. While the floppy disk remains the most inexpensive and reliable media for student files, the USB flash drive is quickly gaining dominance.

One disadvantage of using student floppy disks is the possibility of a computer virus entering your system through a

Although an older media, floppy disks remain a versatile and popular storage format.

student's disk. A computer **virus** is a program written specifically to disrupt computer operations and/or destroy data. Viruses are often transmitted from computer to computer by surreptitiously attaching themselves to normal files. When these carrier files are saved on a floppy disk and that disk is later used in a virus-free computer, the virus is transmitted to the "healthy" computer's hard disk drive (Figure 3.9). Once there, it executes its damaging program either immediately or at a later time. If designed to do so, the virus may infect other floppy disks used in the once-healthy computer, thus further spreading the problem.

Viruses can be a challenge for computer-using teachers. Clearly, student floppy disks are effective for ensuring student file privacy and for keeping the classroom computer's hard disk space available. However, students often exchange games and information if they have home computers, or they download files from the Internet that may be infected. Once a virus infects a student's home machine, a disk carried back and forth to school for a class assignment can result in that same virus infecting and destroying data on the classroom machine.

To protect the classroom computers, teachers and technology-support personnel often install **antivirus programs.** Antivirus programs detect and destroy computer viruses. They scan the hard drive and floppy disks used in the machine and warn if any possible virus is detected. Every classroom computer should have an antivirus program installed. It is also important to subscribe to

Computer viruses, damaging computer programs that can erase files or destroy computer operations, can infect a healthy machine via contaminated disks or downloads.

FIGURE 3.9
Computer Viruses
Schools need to be on the alert for computer viruses.

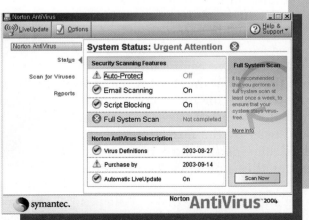

Antivirus software is a must to keep your computer healthy. You should set it to check your hard drive and disks frequently, but you also need to remember to update the database of viruses frequently. Unfortunately, new viruses are being created every day.

continuous updates of the installed antivirus programs. Unfortunately, as fast as viruses are recognized and neutralized, new virus programs are written by malicious programmers and let loose on unsuspecting computer users. The typical classroom computer should therefore have its antivirus program updated at least monthly. A frequent update will ensure that the antivirus program has the latest list of new viruses and virus countermeasures.

Portable Media

Some hard disk drives are designed to be used as removable hard disks. This portable version of a hard disk offers the transportability and convenience of a floppy disk while providing much greater storage capacity and the durability of a firm, hard disk. Portable hard disks are external drives with storage capacities in the hundreds of gigabytes. They are typically plugged into the computer's USB port.

Portable hard disks have become very popular, now that many programs incorporate graphics, animation, and sound files. These types of **multimedia** files—files that include multiple types of media (text, graphics, sound, video, and animation)—are often too large to fit on a floppy disk. To transport them, a portable disk is ideal.

For the classroom, portable hard disks are especially useful. A single portable hard disk can serve as a backup medium for an entire class's individual personal files, or it can store all multimedia files related to a specific content area for easy access. Further, for older machines originally designed with smaller hard drives the addition of a portable hard disk can make the computer more usable by increasing its storage capacity.

CD-ROMs

A **CD-ROM** (compact disc–read-only memory) is also removable. However, this is a read-only medium, so you can get information from it but you cannot store any information on a typical CD-ROM. Most computers today are equipped with a drive that will read CD-ROMs. Such a drive reads the information from CD-ROMs that contain programs, files, or other data. It is also capable of reading and, given the right software and speakers, playing musical CDs as well.

Unlike magnetically recorded floppy and hard disks, CD-ROMs are recorded by a laser beam that burns pits into the tracks on the disc's surface. Then another laser reads those pits and the remaining flat surface of the disc as data. Because CDs use light to store and read data, they are known as optical drives. Approximately 650 megabytes of data (text, sound, graphics, animation, or video) can be stored on a single CD. This is equivalent to the storage capacity of approximately 400 floppy disks.

HANDS-ON LEARNING

Examples of the creative use of computers to further instruction by K–12 teachers are everywhere. Many teachers have found technology to be a remarkably versatile and powerful means to the end of making learning both fun and effective in their classrooms. Here is one example.

Having one's work published is the ultimate reward for writing. In the fourth-grade class at the Orchard School in South Burlington, Vermont, Dylan Novelli, Shannon Edmunds, and Deb Gurwicz have found a way to ensure that their students get the most visibility for their writing projects. These teachers place their students' writing on the computers' screen savers in their classroom. Mr. Novelli, Ms. Edmunds, and Ms. Gurwicz tell us, "Kids love to see their work pop up on the computer screen and enjoy reading one another's writing."

Explore journal and online resources to discover how other creative teachers are using computer symtems to enhance instruction. Summarize the most innovative application you find to share with your peers.

SOURCES: D. Novelli, S. Edmunds, & D. Gurwicz. Screen-saver stories. *Instructor* (May/June 2001) 110 (8), 74.

Removable disks are particularly useful for storing large multimedia files

CD Storage

COMPUTERS AND NCLB GOALS

Problem-Based Learning

No Child Left Behind mandated standards for technology literacy. It states, "every student is technologically literate by the time the student finishes the eighth grade, regardless of the student's race, ethnicity, gender, family income, geographic location, or disability" (U.S. Department of Education, 2001). Imagine that you are a classroom teacher and your principal has asked each grade-level team to brainstorm ways to use the classroom computers to address this standard. As an example, the principal described how one of the teachers on the second-grade team added labels to each component of the computer systems in his class to help students learn computer terminology. Another teacher in kindergarten has the children practicing mouse and math skills together by playing a flash card game. As part of the fifth-grade team, what would you suggest might be done to help your students become computer literate? How could you integrate this technology literacy concept while learning social studies, language arts, or science?

E-Learning

www.mylabschool.com
Hardware Skills Builder
Optical Media

Because of their storage capacity, CD-ROMs are used to store and transport large programs and graphic files that should not be altered. These programs are usually full-featured applications designed to be installed on your computer. Installing a program means moving essential components of a program from a transport medium (floppy disk or CD-ROM) to the hard drive so that it can be accessed and run whenever it is requested. CDs may also store self-contained multimedia programs that are too large to install on most computer systems, such as educational games.

Programs are designed to either install themselves on the hard drive or run from the CD drive. Installed software can take up sizable amounts of space on the hard drive. However, programs that are run from the hard drive are quicker to access and run. If the programs are left on the CD-ROM drive, you will keep your hard drive space available for other uses, but the CD-ROM-based program may run more slowly. Furthermore, you must keep the CD available in the drive at all times to use the program. For data files (usually graphics files and clip art libraries), you must keep the CD available in the drive until you are done with the files stored on it. Many teachers prefer to install programs to classroom hard drives even though they are large programs. Doing so allows the teacher to store the original CD in a safe place and avoids costly and inconvenient loss.

CD-Rs and CD-RWs

A **CD-R** (compact disc–recordable) is a unique type of CD on which you can record (write) data. You must have an optical drive, CD-R recording

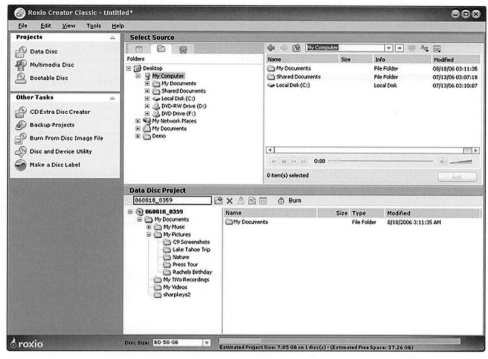

CD/DVD recording software such as Roxio's Creator helps you to select and organize the files you want burned on your recordable optical media.

software, and blank CD-Rs to use for this process. Any data that you can create with any application (text, graphics, sound, video) can be stored permanently on a CD-R. Once recorded, a CD-R is not changeable. It becomes read-only. Once created, a CD-R can be read by any optical drive.

Because of their permanence and large storage capacity, CDs are particularly useful for archiving information (such as student portfolios) and storing teacher- or student-created multimedia files.

A **CD-RW** (compact disc–rewritable) takes the concept of reusable CDs one step further. These drives and the special disks that are designed for use in them allow you not only to record but also to change stored data. Because a CD-RW holds approximately the same amount of data as other CDs, it offers the same advantage of large storage capacity. However, its usefulness has been somewhat limited by the fact that the CD produced by a CD-RW drive might not be readable by the optical drives in the older machines.

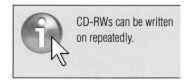

CD-RWs can be written on repeatedly.

DVDs

DVD-ROM (digital versatile discs) are another type of optical medium. A DVD drive will read both DVDs and CDs, thus allowing DVD-equipped computers to use older CD-ROM technology as well (a phenomenon called backwards compatibility). The advantage of a DVD is its ability to store considerably more data than a CD. DVDs can store data on both sides (unlike the one-sided CD) and on up to two layers per side. A DVD can store 4.7 gigabytes of data in the same physical space (one side, one layer), a

TABLE 3.4 Optical Media Comparison

OPTICAL MEDIA	CHARACTERISTICS	CLASSROOM APPLICATION
CD-ROM	• Holds 650 megabytes of data • Read-only • Stores data or music	Used to deliver commercial software or music to end user
CD-R (CD-Recordable)	• Holds 650 megabytes of data • May be recorded on once by an optical drive (CD or DVD) that can record (burn) a CD • Once recorded, cannot be erased	• Most inexpensive recordable optical media that can be used to store teacher- or student-made files • Can be used to duplicate CDs
CD-RW (CD-Rewritable)	• Holds 650 megabytes of data • May be recorded and erased by an optical drive (CD or DVD) that can record (burn) and erase a CD	• More expensive recordable optical media for storage • Can be used to duplicate CDs • Most useful to store files that need continual updates
DVD (Digital Versatile Disc)	• Holds up to 4.7 gigabytes on one-layer, one-sided disc or 17 gigabytes on two layers for two-sided discs • Cannot be recorded on or erased	• Used for video recordings
DVD±R (DVD-Recordable)	• Holds up to 4.7 gigabytes on one-layer, one sided disc or 17 gigabytes on two layers for two-sided discs • Can be recorded once with DVD drive that can record; cannot be erased • DVD-R drives can also burn CD-Rs	• Most inexpensive recordable DVD that can be used to store very large teacher- or student-made files • Can be used to duplicate DVDs
DVD±RW (DVD Rewritable)	• Holds up to 4.7 gigabytes on one-layer, one-sided disc or 17 gigabytes on two layers for two-sided discs • May be recorded and erased by a DVD drive that can record (burn) and erase a DVD • Can also burn CD-Rs and burn/erase CD-RWs	• Most flexible but expensive recordable DVD; can be used to store very large teacher- or student-made files • Can be used to duplicate DVDs • Most useful to store very large files that need continual updates

great advantage compared to the 650 megabytes of data that can be stored on a CD-ROM. When both sides and both layers are used, the DVD can store up to 17 gigabytes of data, enough to hold a full-length, full-screen movie. (See Table 3.4.)

For education, DVDs hold the promise of a high-quality, very durable video medium. Unlike videotape, which can wear out or break relatively easily, a DVD will last through years of classroom use without degrading—that is, losing any of its audio or video quality. Some DVDs even offer special options, such as displaying subtitles with the video or zooming in on an image.

Recordable DVD drives are the most common optical storage technology found on newer computers. This technology allows users to record data on a DVD just as you can record on a CD-R or CD-RW. This medium makes it possible to store and update large files, teacher- or student-made videos, audios, and computer-based multimedia data all on a single disc.

Recordable DVDs are currently available in several formats. It is important for teachers to be aware of the type of DVD used by their classroom computers so that they buy the appropriate type of DVD.

For a teacher interested in a recordable DVD, it is also important to first decide whether a recordable DVD is necessary for the storage task at hand. Recordable CDs are typically a more economical choice. If the extensive DVD storage capacity is not required, CDs may be a better option.

Regardless of the type of DVD player or recorder a computer is equipped with, one advantage of a DVD in a classroom computer is that it can be configured to take the place of a VCR and monitor. If the classroom is equipped with a projector capable of displaying computer images, then it can be used to display a DVD image as well. Using a computer display and the computer's DVD player, you can easily display a video recorded on DVD so that that the entire class can view it. This type of configuration thus can serve two purposes and may make a VCR and monitor combination redundant.

E-Learning

www.mylabschool.com
Listen to Podcast
Buying a Computer

Networking Computers

One of the most cost effective and powerful ways to configure school computer hardware is to **network** it. Networks offer schools a way to communicate information and share resources. Individual computers connected to a network are usually called network **workstations.** In a network, workstations and sharable peripherals (such as printers) are connected together to a single, more powerful computer called a server. A server provides services to all the machines on the network. A network's server contains the networking software that manages network-wide communication. The server includes one or more very large hard disk drives on which it stores the network management software, common files, and programs that the workstations can share. Together, the server, the workstations and peripherals, and the wiring that connects them constitute a network.

Networks are configured, or arranged, in many different ways to suit the facilities and the number of workstations that need to connect to that particular network. Configurations vary, but all networks have some common elements and terminology. Every workstation must connect in some way to the server. This is accomplished through a special piece of equipment, called a **switch,** that offers a series of centralized connections. Any workstation or peripheral that is connected to the network becomes a **node** on the network, with all nodes ultimately connected back, through one or more switches, to their server. Individual workstations, peripherals, and switches are connected to the server through some type of wiring or, in some cases, through a wireless communication channel. This relationship is illustrated in Figure 3.10 on page 116.

A network connects a group of computers to a server to share resources and files.

E-Learning

www.mylabschool.com
Hardware Skills Builder
Networks

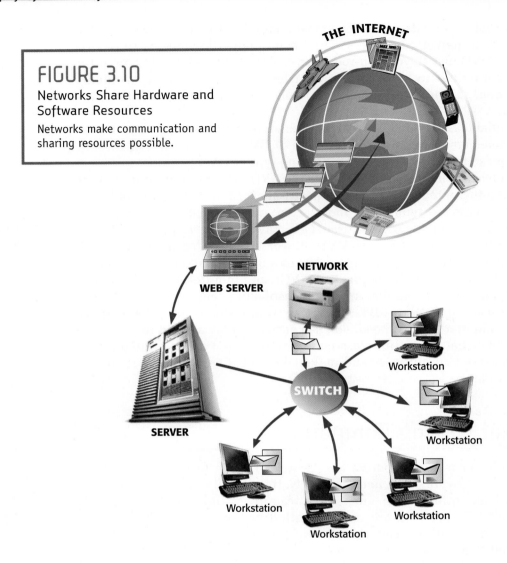

FIGURE 3.10
Networks Share Hardware and
Software Resources
Networks make communication and
sharing resources possible.

THE INTERNET

WEB SERVER

NETWORK

SERVER

SWITCH

Workstation

Workstation

Workstation

Workstation

Workstation

    In a typical school, workstations and a **server** are usually wired together
by using a type of cable similar to telephone wire. The wiring is strung from
the server, often above ceilings, to each classroom, where a single network
wire must be dropped for every computer in the room. Each network wire, in
turn, connects to a network card that must be installed in each computer that
is to be connected to the network.

    Often, when schools are retrofitted for a network, because of the cost
of pulling network wire through existing ceilings and walls, only one or
two drops are made to a classroom. In such cases, one drop is often designed to connect a teacher workstation to the school network. A second
drop in a classroom would provide for one other workstation to be connected for student use. Deciding how to use available network connections and arranging classroom space around them can be a challenge. As
you learned in previous chapters, it is important to create a physical classroom environment that meets diverse learner needs. The addition of networked workstations can add further complexity to the classroom
arrangement. You will need to look for the network connection point(s) in

the classroom in which you will be teaching and plan your teaching and learning space accordingly.

One alternative to wiring schools and classrooms that is rapidly gaining popularity is wireless networking technology. In a **wireless network,** information is transmitted via wireless technology rather than across wires. In a school, a wireless network may require that transmitter hubs be strategically placed in rooms and across the campus to receive and transmit data from computers. This approach to networking has several advantages for schools. First, wireless networking eliminates much of the retrofitting cost. Although some retrofitting may still be required, it is less work than what is necessary for wired networks. The cost saving may enable the purchase of additional computers for classroom use. Second, a wireless network makes it easier to create a flexible learning environment that fully integrates networked resources. Classrooms no longer have to set up workstations according to where network connections are available. Additionally, with the use of notebook and handheld computers that are equipped for wireless networking, a classroom could conceivably have a bank of computers available for students to take to their desks for individual or group research. The downside of wireless networks is the cost of the technology itself and also some security issues typical of wireless networks. As the cost falls, however, and network technology improves, wireless networking may well become the strategy of choice for more schools.

Regardless of the networking technology selected, individual classrooms with multiple computers can be networked, computer labs can be networked, schools can be networked, and entire districts can share resources across a network. Smaller networks that connect machines in local areas, such as a classroom or school, are called **local area networks (LANs).** Networks that connect machines across a wide area, such as all of the schools in a district or all of the districts in a state, are called **wide area networks (WANs).** The interconnectivity of the workstations on both types of networks and the potential for connecting these networks to each other are what make possible our modern-day ability to communicate instantly.

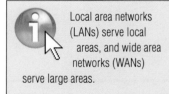

Local area networks (LANs) serve local areas, and wide area networks (WANs) serve large areas.

Using a School Network

Networks have promise as powerful teaching and learning tools, but to use networks for teaching and learning, some challenges must be addressed and overcome. Although it is usually not a teacher's responsibility to respond to these challenges alone, it is useful to understand how they affect this technology.

Many different sizes of files of information are sent across a network. Large text files are measured in thousands of bytes or kilobytes. But other files, such as graphic, photo, video, and audio files, can be made up of multiple megabytes (millions of bytes) of data each. To better understand the impact of file sizes in networking, imagine a network wire as a roadway. On that electronic roadway, some files are of a size analogous to subcompact cars, while others are more like tractor-trailer trucks. Furthermore, some types of wiring offer a roadway the size of an alley, while others offer a roadway the size of a ten-lane superhighway. The challenge for communication occurs when you try to fit a large "tractor-trailer truck" of data through an "alley"-sized network wire. It can be done, but the going is alarmingly slow. Servers manage such feats by breaking the data into small units, or **packets,** and sending it through one packet at a time. The network software then reassembles the data at the other end into its original form. This transmission process can take considerable time with large, complex files.

In network terms, the carrying capacity (size of the roadway) of the transmission media for sending information is called its **bandwidth.** (See Figure 3.11.) The speed at which the network can transmit data is measured in the number of bits that can be sent per second. The larger the bandwidth and greater the speed of the transmission media, the faster the data flows across it, even if the data includes large files. As a network-using educator, you need to be aware of the capabilities of the network you are going to use so that you can plan appropriately. If you want to share the digital or scanned photographs your class took on their last field trip with a class at

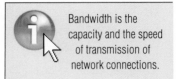

Bandwidth is the capacity and the speed of transmission of network connections.

FIGURE 3.11

Bandwidth

Different transmission media offer different speed and capacity for data transmission, just as physical highways provide different capacities for automobile traffic.

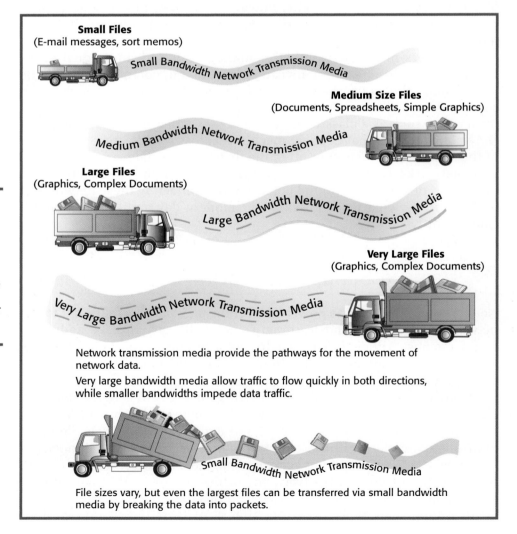

Small Files
(E-mail messages, sort memos)

Small Bandwidth Network Transmission Media

Medium Size Files
(Documents, Spreadsheets, Simple Graphics)

Medium Bandwidth Network Transmission Media

Large Files
(Graphics, Complex Documents)

Large Bandwidth Network Transmission Media

Very Large Files
(Graphics, Complex Documents)

Very Large Bandwidth Network Transmission Media

Network transmission media provide the pathways for the movement of network data.

Very large bandwidth media allow traffic to flow quickly in both directions, while smaller bandwidths impede data traffic.

Small Bandwidth Network Transmission Media

File sizes vary, but even the largest files can be transferred via small bandwidth media by breaking the data into packets.

another school, you need to discover how long that process will take before scheduling it into a lesson. If you want to add audio components to a PowerPoint presentation for use in all sixth-grade classes via the network, you need to be aware of a potential delay caused by the transmission of large audio files. Although you, as an educator, do not need to be able to create a network, it is important to be a well-versed consumer with regard to the network you use.

Another challenge when using a network for teaching and learning is the question of data privacy and security. For educators, ensuring that students do their own work and that their efforts are private is essential. If networks allow users to share files and resources, how can a teacher ensure the security of each student's work? Furthermore, how can a teacher's files be securely segregated from student files? This challenge is addressed by the network software and the network support staff through the use of security measures inherent in the system. User security on a network is provided through a system of user names (also called log-in names) and **passwords.** Even though all of the computers in any given room may be physically capable of providing access to the network, such access is granted only when the network recognizes that an authorized user is at a computer.

Log-in names and passwords are features that help ensure network security.

Every network user is given access to some or all of the files and programs stored on the server's hard drive(s), as shown in Figure 3.12. This assigned ability to access specific files and resources is called the user's rights or privileges. When creating user accounts, the network administrator issues specific rights to every account, thus ensuring that no account

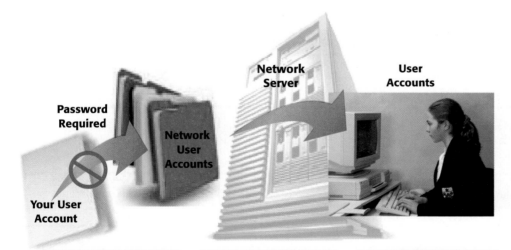

Password Required

Your User Account

Network User Accounts

Network Server

User Accounts

To open and access your network account, a unique personal password must be entered.

Every network user has a personal account "folder" with a user profile and storage space on a server hard disc drive.

Every account has a user profile that includes log-in name, password, and the rights that the individual user has to access files and move about the network.

FIGURE 3.12

Individual User Accounts on a Network

Every account includes a user profile that contains a log-in name, password, and the rights that individual user has to access files and move about the network.

has access to resources or files that are inappropriate for that user. Student network users therefore can access only files and resources for which they have been given rights. These restricted rights typically allow them only to use particular software and to access the files that they created themselves or that were created for them by their teacher. This system of user names, passwords, and assigned rights ensures a high degree of security for most users. Of course, people with advanced computer skills can sometimes break through the security and hack into a network. But cautious network administrators can implement and monitor various levels of roadblocks, called **firewalls,** to keep hackers out of their networks and keep your data safe.

Firewalls prevent unauthorized access to data and files from outside the network.

Sharing and Communicating via a Network

Networks enable and support communication and the sharing of resources in many ways. Communications are enhanced through a variety of tools, including the most familiar of them, electronic mail. Hardware and software resources on the server and across the network can be shared via the coordination offered by the network software. For teachers looking to maximize their computing capabilities while minimizing costs, networks offer many advantages. These are summarized in Table 3.5 and are described in more detail in the following sections.

TABLE 3.5 Network Features and Applications

NETWORK FEATURE	USE	CLASSROOM APPLICATION
SHARED HARDWARE	Costly hardware can be shared by many workstations.	One printer, scanner, or other peripheral can be shared by all computers in the classroom.
SHARED SOFTWARE	Programs can reside on the server or be pushed to individual machines to save space, maintenance, and technical-support time.	Classroom software is simple and quick to install, upgrade, or maintain in a single process via the server.
DATA SHARING	Files and folders can be made accessible to all network users or can be tagged for use by specific users.	Class handouts and other content files can be made available to all or some students for copying or printing.
NETWORK TOOLS	Groupware offers common organizing tools and calendars across the network. Network monitoring and tracking methods ensure appropriate use of technology.	Class calendar and address book are simple to maintain and access from anywhere in school; teacher can monitor all students' activity while they are logged in to the network.
COMMUNICATIONS	Electronic mail provides all users the ability to communicate with each other or groups and to send attachment files along with messages.	Students can communicate with peers and their teacher; electronic pen pal (e-pal) projects can be initiated.

Shared Programs

Programs can be installed on the server and made available via the network to all workstations. This process can save the time and labor that would otherwise have been necessary to install identical programs on every machine. In such situations, the programs reside on the server's hard disk, and the workstations run the software from there through the network. This leaves the local workstation's drives available for file storage or for nonnetwork software. Other network scenarios use workstation hard drives to store some or all elements of common network software. In such cases, the network can be used to "push" (copy) the software from the server to the workstations' hard drives to update or maintain it. In either scenario, sharing programs makes their update and maintenance easier and more efficient.

Another advantage of shared networked software resources is that such an arrangement may save software acquisition dollars as well as worker resources. Many software vendors provide discounts for network versions of software that can be used on all machines in the network. Such network **site licenses** allow the use of a program on any machine on the network at a defined site, usually at a substantial savings over the purchase of multiple copies of the same software for use on individual computers. When you work in a networked environment and you are considering acquisition of software that may benefit others at your school, you should explore the costs of a networked version of the program you desire. You may find that, for close to the purchase price of a few individual copies, you can buy a site license for everyone at your school.

 Site licenses offer discounts across a school.

A final advantage for sharing programs via a network relates to the support that all software eventually needs. With a network, when software upgrades become available, the support staff need only upgrade the software on the server to make the upgrade available to each workstation, rather than having to visit and upgrade every individual machine at a school. Similarly, if problems arise with any software, they are resolved at the more centralized server level, a much faster support process. For a busy teacher, waiting for a "house call" from the support staff to fix a problem with a single computer's unique software is likely to take much longer than reporting to the network administrator a network problem that can be simultaneously corrected for all workstations via the server.

Although server-based software has these support advantages, there are some disadvantages. Because workstations rely on the server's software, should any problems occur with software on the server or with the server itself, all workstations will be unable to use the programs. For that reason, many networks have redundant systems such as backup servers in place to ensure that there is no interruption of service. Other networks keep redundant backup disks of all server programs and data so that the administrator can quickly reinstall files and restore services if a problem occurs. Still other networks may store backup copies of critical software programs on the hard drives of the individual workstations as a redundancy. In a classroom that has integrated network resources into instruction, it is important to be aware of your network's backup system and to develop your own backup plan in case the network or a shared program is not accessible when you need it. Although such situations are rare, it is a good idea to anticipate them and discuss the options with the network administrator at your school.

Shared Data

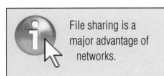

File sharing is a major advantage of networks.

Using programs across a network is just one of the ways networked workstations can share resources. Of equal importance is the ability to share data and other files. Network servers are usually configured with ample storage that can be used in several different ways depending on the needs of the users of that network system. Typically, each user is given a small network storage area associated with his or her user name and on which he or she can store personal data. Such user storage areas are private to the extent that they can be accessed only by using both the user name and password of the individual user. The advantage of user storage areas on a network is that the user can go to any workstation, regardless of its location, and still be able to access the files in his or her user space stored on the server. For teachers, this can mean that they can access their class files from their networked classroom computer, from a workstation in a networked computer lab, or from a networked workstation in the faculty workroom. For students, this means that they can work on an interdisciplinary assignment while in the media center or in different subject-area classrooms. This ease of accessibility to files is a major advantage of user storage on a network server. The disadvantage is the quantity of hard disk storage that the network server needs to give each user. Nevertheless, the relatively low cost of expanding disk storage space and the significant benefit of easy access usually make this option worth the investment.

Shared Administrative Tools

E-Learning
ON THE WEB! 3.9

Using Groupware

Most network software provides a series of **administrative tools** that are shared by all network users. Such **groupware,** as it is sometimes called, usually provides, at minimum, a common calendar, address book, and facilities reservation list, as well as electronic mail. Using this type of shared tool, a busy educator who wishes to set up a meeting with other teachers on the network can have the server automatically poll all the teachers' electronic calendars to find a free common meeting time. If a teacher wishes to reserve a special classroom space for his or her class, the common facilities reservation list on the network can be automatically checked for open dates for that space. Although these time-saving tools vary with the network system installed, most network software provides abundant groupware options. You should explore your school's network to see which is available for your use.

Network software may also offer teachers a way to monitor activity on, and take control of, student workstations in the classroom or media center. This type of software allows the teacher to observe student progress by "tuning in" to an individual workstation and monitoring the activity on the screen. It also allows the teacher to take over one or more workstations

in the Classroom

NETWORKS IN THE SECONDARY CLASSROOM

Coming up with the best of both worlds, the Frederick County Public Schools in Virginia have a school network, sometimes called an intranet, that has links to the Internet. Rod Carnill points out that the two "nets" complement each other. The intranet is especially helpful to teachers because students' work and identifiable photographs, special projects, and events at school can be shown without having to obtain permission in the form of releases. The intranet, he relates, "uses a collection of HTML files in a single folder on the school's web server" and is, at the same time, "a self-created portal for Internet use." The portal provides guided access to the Internet for students to use in completing research and other coursework and also permits in-house file sharing.

Progressive schools like Tampa Catholic High School in the Diocese of St. Petersburg, Tampa, Florida, have found many ways to make their schools' intranets perform services for the teachers and administrators alike. Kevin Yarnell, the technology director, wrote in *School Executive* of some of these methods that simplify and improve the overall operating infrastructure of the school. When scheduling tests, teachers can check to see what other testing is being done on the same day. Student data—birthdays, clubs, athletics, and honors—and other information can be stored in a database on the intranet. Announcements and even personal communications to and from school personnel can be posted. School records and reports can be archived in a database for that purpose. Student work, if electronic, can also be kept on the site. The limited access to the intranet makes it invaluable to schools, whether it is a small site affecting only one or a few classrooms or a large site that connects an entire school district, for many school-related communications are confidential legally and ethically.

SOURCES: Integration via a browser-based intranet. 2002. Retrieved June 11, 2003, from **www.nps.k12.va.us/infodiv/it/techconf/ integbrw.htm;** K. Yarnell. 2002. Intranets: Repositories of school data. *School Executive* (September/October), 39 (1), 28.

to provide a demonstration or instruction. Finally, it allows the teacher to broadcast the images on any one workstation's monitor to all other workstations to share a student's work. Although often used in computer lab settings, this software is also useful in classrooms and media centers with multiple student workstations.

Shared Hardware

Software sharing is not the only type of resource sharing made possible by a network. Hardware sharing is another advantage of school networking. In a classroom or media center that is configured only with stand-alone computers, each machine needs its own printer plugged into its parallel port to be able to print. In a networked scenario, a single printer can be used by all workstations in the vicinity. This can be done either by attaching a networkable printer as an independent network node or by attaching a printer to one of the workstations on the network. In either configuration, the printer hardware is then available to be shared by all local network workstations. Using this arrangement makes it possible to maximize the use of printer resources.

Networks enable sharing of hardware resources.

TABLE 3.6   Hardware Evaluation Rubric

HARDWARE:

DESCRIPTION:

VENDOR: **COST:**

NOTES ON USE:

Please rate the features below for each hardware component. Next to each of the items in the rubric, mark the box that best reflects your opinion.

HARDWARE FEATURE	EVALUATION CRITERIA				
	1 Poor	2 Below Average	3 Average	4 Above Average	5 Excellent
CPU	Speed below school standard; insufficient to run class software	Speed below standard but sufficient to run most class software	Speed at standard; will support current class software	Speed at or above standard; will support newer software	Speed above standard; likely to support next-generation software
RAM	Capacity below school standard; insufficient to run class software	Capacity below school standard but sufficient to run most class software	Capacity at standard; will support current class software	Capacity at or above standard; will support newer software	Capacity above standard; likely to support next-generation software
INPUT DEVICES	Keyboard flimsy with limited features; mechanical mouse; no scroll wheel	Keyboard flimsy but with some extra features; mechanical mouse with scroll wheel	Keyboard includes features (wrist guard, etc.); optical mouse with scroll wheel	Multimedia keyboard; optical mouse with scroll and program-mable buttons	Multimedia keyboard; laser mouse with scroll/tilt wheel and programmable buttons.
MONITOR	Low resolution; slow scan rate minimum color depth; insuffi-cient for newer software	Low resolution; acceptable scan rate and color depth; may be insufficient for some software	Resolution, scan rate, color depth meet school standards; will display most software	Resolution, scan rate, color depth meet or exceed school standards; will display newer software	Resolution, scan rate , color depth meet or exceed school standards; will display next-generation software
HARD DRIVE	Capacity below school standard; insufficient to run class software	Capacity below school standard but sufficient to run most class software	Capacity at standard; will support current class software	Capacity at or above standard; will support newer software	Capacity above standard; likely to support next-generation software
PORTABLE MEDIA DRIVES	No removable media drive; no expansion capacity	Limited to 1 floppy disk drive; limited expansion capacity	1 or more floppy disk drives; expandable	Floppy disk and 1 other removable media drive; expandable	Multiple removable media drives; capacity to expand
OPTICAL DRIVES	No optical drive	CD-ROM only	1 optical drive (CD-R or CD-RW)	Multiple optical drives (CD-RW and CD-ROM)	Multiple optical drives (CD-RW and DVD or DVD-R)
SOUND SYSTEM	Minimal sound card; nonpowered speakers	Minimal sound card; powered speakers	Adequate sound card; powered speakers	Upgraded sound card; amplified speakers	Upgraded sound card; amplified speakers with woofer
PORTS	Minimal ports; no USB ports	Adequate ports; 1 USB port	All standard ports; 2–4 USB ports	All standard ports; 4 or more USB ports	All standard ports; 4 or more USB ports, front-accessible and/or Firewire
WARRANTY SUPPORT	No warranty; no free phone support	Less than 1-year warranty; no free phone support	1-year warranty; free phone support for less than 1 year	1-year warranty; free phone support for 1 year	1-year warranty; free phone support; on-site support

Total the score for each hardware component. Compare the scores. The component with the highest score is your best choice.

Educational Computing

Computers and networks are tools that can help you build the kind of learning environment you might once only have imagined. Using a computer, your students can publish their own class newsletter with digital images from their recent field trip. They can create interactive stories that their peers can explore. They can connect to online resources that place the world's knowledge base literally at their fingertips. Using a network, they can share data and resources across a school or district. But having such powerful tools available means little if you don't know how to use them. Mastery of the computer basics presented in this chapter is an excellent first step.

As you increase your understanding of and skills with computers, you will find your own personal applications for this unique digital technology. Computers have changed our society and have ushered in the Information Age. There is little doubt that they will ultimately have the same impact throughout education. Your own personal mastery of this revolutionary digital tool will serve both you and your students well. And, as with all educational technologies, it is important to carefully evaluate computers before selecting them for your classroom. An evaluation rubric (Table 3.6) can be a powerful tool when reviewing and evaluating computer hardware.

Of course, digital technologies include more than just a computer system. As an outgrowth of computers, a true digital revolution has begun. Many of today's cameras use digital methods of capturing and storing images instead of film. Audiotapes and vinyl records are being replaced by CDs and DVDs. What does all this mean to educators?

As you will see in the next three chapters, it means that more and more tools are becoming available to individualize instruction, meet learner needs, and help you teach and manage your classroom. It means that a more diverse and robust learning environment can be constructed for your students. All you need to do to use current and emerging digital innovations is, first, be aware that they exist and, second, be willing to learn to use them. Increasing your digital awareness and helping you learn to use digital technologies are the purposes of the rest of this unit.

KEY TERMS

administrative tools 122
antivirus programs 110
application program 96
back up 107
bandwidth 118
booting up 94
byte 106
CD-R 112
CD-ROM 111
CD-RW 113

chips 94
commands 95
computer system 92
computing cycle 92
CPU 104
dpi 102
DVD-ROM 113
file 108
firewall 120
floppy disk 108

folder 108
gigabytes 106
groupware 122
GUI 95
hard copy 101
hard disk 105
hardware 92
icon 95
input device 99
integrated software package 97

STUDENT ACTIVITIES

CHAPTER REVIEW

1. Describe each of the four major components of the computing cycle.
2. What is the difference between hardware and software? Give an example of each.
3. What is the difference between memory and storage in a computer system? Why are both necessary?
4. Describe the role of the operating system. How does it help you interact with a computer?
5. What are the three different classes of application software? What different types of tasks does each perform?
6. What is the CPU, and what is its role in the computer system?
7. Describe the difference between input and output devices. Give two examples of each.
8. What do you need to know about monitor resolution before purchasing a monitor? About printer resolution before buying a printer?

9. What is a computer virus and how is it transmitted? What can you do to protect your classroom?
10. How do the following storage devices differ: hard disk, floppy disk, removable disk, CD-ROM, CD-R, CD-RW, DVD, DVD±RW?
11. What is a network? What is the relationship between a server and workstations?
12. How are typical classrooms wired? What impact does this have on the learning environment?
13. How do bandwidth and transmission speed affect network communications?
14. Describe the techniques used in networking to protect the privacy of an individual's data and the security of the network.
15. Why is it advantageous for educators to share resources and programs on a network? What concerns are associated with program sharing?

WHAT DO YOU THINK?

1. Interview three of your fellow students to see how they think computers affect their learning and the teaching they have been exposed to in their academic careers. On the basis of the interviews and your own views, what can you conclude about the role of computers in instruction?

2. Interview a network administrator to discover the issues he or she is most concerned with relating to network security. Be sure to ask what other issues are of concern with regard to helping users. Summarize the interview questions and responses. Explain how the network issues may affect the way in which you use this technology in your classroom.

3. Interview one of the technical-support staff members at your school and ask what types of storage devices he or she would recommend in a computer system. Be sure to ask whether the person prefers CD-RW or DVD drives and ask what size permanent and portable hard drives he or she recommends and why. What can you conclude about how to configure a computer for your classroom?

LEARNING TOGETHER!

The following activities are designed for learning groups of two or three students.

1. Select three different computer systems and compare them using the hardware evaluation rubric (Table 3.6). After discussing the options with your group, describe which system you would buy and explain why. Be prepared to share your preference and your reasons with the class.

2. Each member of your group should interview a teacher who uses a computer in his or her classroom. Ask the teacher how the computer is used for academic and for administrative tasks. Compare your interviews with those of the other members of your group and list the uses you discover.

3. Brainstorm how computers have changed society in general and education in particular. Identify and list all of the ways in which computers have had an impact. Then determine five ways in which they are likely to change society and education in the future. Be prepared to share your group's outcomes with your peers.

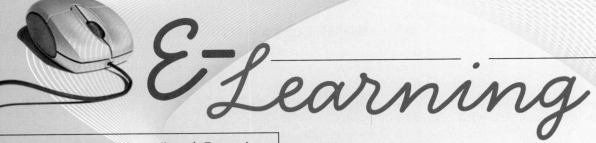

E-Learning

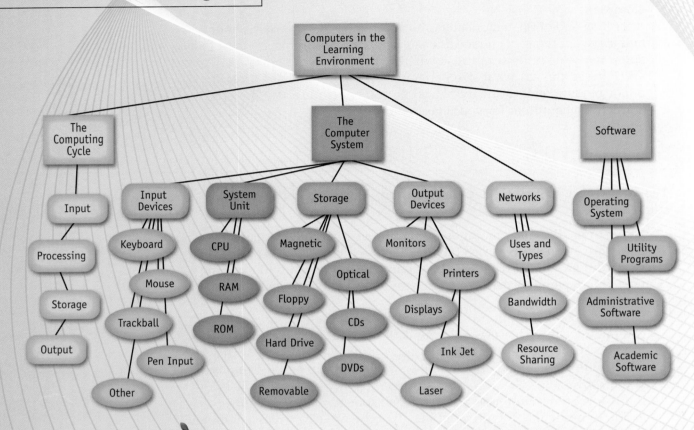

Hardware Skills Builder www.mylabschool.com

These step-by-step multimedia tutorials, accessible through **mylabschool.com**, teach you to use computer basics and how computer components will be used in your classroom. Each tutorial ends with a review of key concepts.

Podcasts www.mylabschool.com

Listen to an audio discussion on what a teacher should know when buying a computer. Download the audio discussion to your iPod, computer, or MP3 player.

Video Lab www.mylabschool.com

Video clips on computers in the classroom are accessible through the **mylabschool** web site. Learning guides for all videos can be found in the text's Learning Guide Supplement.

On the Web! Activities www.ablongman.com/lever-duffy3e
Noted in the margins of the chapter, these activities offer you

in-depth experiences in the topics and content presented in the chapter.

Online Practice Test www.ablongman.com/lever-duffy3e
Practice tests offer you an opportunity to test your knowledge and then review the results and send them to your teacher.

Outliner www.ablongman.com/lever-duffy3e
Chapter Outliners are fill-in-the-blank outlines of the main ideas presented in the chapter. Download the outliner and fill it in for an effective chapter study guide.

Power Practices www.ablongman.com/lever-duffy3e
Power Practices are animated tutorials made using Microsoft's presentation software, PowerPoint. This flash card tutorial will help you practice key concepts in the chapter.

Puzzler www.ablongman.com/lever-duffy3e
Puzzlers include content in crossword, word search, and other puzzle formats to help you master chapter content.

Useful Links www.ablongman.com/lever-duffy3e
These links offer you suggestions for expanded online research in the topics presented in the chapter.

INTEGRATION *Ideas*

Ideas for the use of computers in every content area and at every grade level are abundant in print and on the Internet. Creative technology-using educators have found innumerable ways to integrate technology into their classrooms. Below are a few ideas for integration into core content areas at a variety of grade levels. Explore these to begin your discovery of how you might include technology in your classroom.

Integrating Technology into English/Language Arts

Writing and Grammar Help
Purdue's **Online Writing Lab**, OWL, at **http://owl.english .purdue.edu/** has earned a reputation for excellence in helping secondary and postsecondary students in reviewing and practicing grammar, citations, types of writing styles, and the writing process. This online lab offers an example of the seamless integration of technology and teaching writing skills. This is an excellent support resource for any writing assignment.

National Council of Teachers of English sponsors ACE, the **Assembly on Computers in English.** This group offers a workshop at the annual NCTE conference and online. The workshop provides an online journal and recommended links and resources to integrate technology into language arts at **http:// aceworkshop.org/**

Integrating Technology into Math

Virtual Manipulatives
Using manipulatives to reinforce abstract math topics has become a common practice in math education. For teachers who do not have an abundance of manipulatives for their classrooms, another option is to put the classroom computer to work to present students with "virtual manipulatives." Not only are a large variety of manipulatives instantly available, their flexibility exceeds their real-world counterparts. To explore virtual manipulatives, visit **Educational Java Programs** at **www.arcytech.org/java/** or the **National Library of Virtual Manipulatives** at **http://nlvm.usu.edu/en/nav/vlibrary.html** and try the manipulatives available through this site.

Spreadsheets
Spreadsheet software can be used to organize data, test formulas, or graph information. Students can use an electronic spreadsheet to test their hypotheses and perform what-if analysis. **The National Council of Teachers of Mathematics** offers **Illuminations,** a series of lesson plans and activities that demonstrate a vision for math in schools. This resource at **http://illuminations.nctm.org/** offers unique lessons using spreadsheets as well as links to mathematics standards.

Integrating Technology into Science

Science Exhibits
At the **Exploratorium (www.exploratorium.edu/exhibits/ f_exhibits.html)** your students can view and interact with an assortment of science exhibits for an in-class science field trip. Access the Exploratorium directly or link to it via the **Science Learning Network (www.sln.org/resources/index.html)** for other computer-based science resources.

Science Experiments
Bring science to your students so they can take it home with them at **http://pbskids.org/zoom/games/kitchenchemistry/, PBS's Kitchen Chemistry** web site. Virtual experiments are presented in an online kitchen, and their home counterparts are outlined for students to try. Kids get rewards for participating. Use this site to help students individually participate in science experiments, even in the most crowded classroom.

Integrating Technology into Social Studies

History Museum
Visit the **Constitution Center** at **www.constitutioncenter.org/ timeline/** to explore an interactive multimedia timeline of our history. History topics come alive with images and audio of key events in U.S. history. This site also offers an interactive Constitution; Abraham Lincoln Crossroads, an online social studies game; and numerous other resources. Bring history to your classroom when you bring your students to this museum.

Government Resources
Go to the **National Archives** at **www.archives.gov/education/ index.html,** where you can have your students print out and sign the Declaration of Independence, view the Emancipation Proclamation in Lincoln's own hand, or view an online photo album of the last century. Just one of many government resources available to teachers, this site brings historical documents into your classroom.

For these and many more *Integration Ideas* for using computers in teaching and learning visit the text web site at **www .ablongman.com/lever-duffy3e.**

Before selecting a personal computer system and periperals for your classroom, complete the decision matrix below to help you determine whether the equipment is right for you.

PLACE CHECKS IN
THE COLUMNS THAT
MATCH YOUR ANSWERS.

COMPONENT	QUESTIONS TO ASK ABOUT THIS COMPONENT	YES	NO	N/A
SYSTEM UNIT				
RAM / CPU	Is the CPU chip a name brand? Is the chip speed faster than required by the majority of the software you want to use? Can the chip be upgraded if necessary?			
Bays	Does the amount of RAM exceed the requirements of the software you want to use? Can you add more RAM if needed?			
Ports	Is there room in the system unit to add more internal drives if you want to?			
Hard Drive	Are there multiple USB ports available? Are some of the USB ports available on the front of the machine?			
STORAGE				
Floppy Drive / CD Drive(s)	Is this drive the largest size possible for your budget? Is this a high-speed drive?			
	Is a CD-RW drive included in this computer? Is the CD-RW drive high-speed (more than 40x)? Does CD recording software come installed? Is there more than one CD (or DVD) drive included to facilitate copying student CDs?			
DVD Drive	Is a floppy disk drive included in this machine?			
	Is a DVD drive included? Is a DVD-recordable drive included?			
USB Drive	Does the drive provide sufficient storage space for your largest collection of files? Does the shape of the drive allow it to be easily plugged into accessible USB ports? Do any necessary software drivers come with the drive? Does the drive come with a lanyard or key chain?			
OUTPUT DEVICES				
Monitor	Is the monitor resolution sufficient for your highest-output program? Is the monitor size appropriate to your viewing and space needs? Does the monitor have an adjustment control in front so it is easy to access?			
Printer	Is the page per minute (ppm) speed sufficient to print in a timely manner? If ink jet, is each color inkwell separate so colors can be replaced independently when they run out? If laser, is the cost of replacement toner cartridges reasonably within your budget?			

interchapter3

Computers and Peripherals

PLACE CHECKS IN
THE COLUMNS THAT
MATCH YOUR ANSWERS.

YES	NO	N/A	QUESTIONS TO ASK ABOUT THIS COMPONENT	COMPONENT
			Is the paper tray large enough so you don't have to continuously load paper? Can the printer print two sides automtically? Are speakers included?	
			Is a headphone jack easily accessible? Are the speakers powered with a separate plug? Are the speakers and amplifier (if included) small enough for classroom space requirements?	Speakers
			Is the brightness (in lumens) sufficient so that it will display with classroom lights on? Can the device display both video and digital data? Does it have built-in speakers? Does it have a remote control? Does it have sufficient adjustment controls (focus, align, zoom, etc.)? Are all necessary cables provided?	Digital Projector

INPUT DEVICES

YES	NO	N/A		
			Are the keys sufficiently tactile (not spongy to the touch)? Does the keyboard include a wrist rest? Are there additional easy-access multimedia keys or buttons? Does the keyboard have a built in USB hub?	Keyboard
			Is the mouse an optical rather than a ball mouse? Is a scroll wheel included on the mouse? Is a mouse pad provided?	Mouse
			Is a microphone included? Is its cord sufficiently long to be used comfortably? Is a holder provided to store the microphone when not in use?	
			Is the resolution sufficient for the type of scanning you want to do? Is the scanner software easy to use? Is the software OCR-capable? Will the scanner scan larger documents? Does the scanner have a feeder for multiple pages?	Microphone
			Is this camera's image quality (in megapixels) sufficient for the types of photos you wish to take and print? Is extra storage capacity available at a reasonable cost? Is the battery type rechargeable? Are extra batteries available at a reasonable cost? Can the camera zoom sufficiently for your needs? Is there an LCD display to preview pictures? Is there an easy-to-use download system to move images to your computer? Are the setting adjustments easy to use? Is a strap provided for easy carrying? Is a camera case provided?	Scanner Digital Camera

MAKE YOUR DECISION!

YES	NO	N/A		
TOTALS				
			Add the number of checks in each column. The higher the number of *Yes* checks, the more likely the computer system is appropriate for your classroom.	

chapter 4

Digital Technologies in the Classroom

This chapter addresses these ISTE *National Educational Technology Standards* for Teachers:

I. TECHNOLOGY OPERATIONS AND CONCEPTS

Teachers demonstrate a sound understanding of technology operations and concepts. Teachers

A. demonstrate introductory knowledge, skills, and understanding of concepts related to technology (as described in the ISTE *National Education Technology Standards* for Students).

B. demonstrate continual growth in technology knowledge and skills to stay abreast of current and emerging technologies.

II. PLANNING AND DESIGNING LEARNING ENVIRONMENTS AND EXPERIENCES

Teachers plan and design effective learning environments and experiences supported by technology. Teachers

A. design developmentally appropriate learning opportunities that apply technology-enhanced instructional strategies to support the diverse needs of learners.

B. apply current research on teaching and learning with technology when planning learning environments and experiences.

C. identify and locate technology resources and evaluate them for accuracy and suitability.

D. plan for the management of technology resources within the context of learning activities.

E. plan strategies to manage student learning in a technology-enhanced environment.

III. TEACHING, LEARNING, AND THE CURRICULUM

Teachers implement curriculum plans that include methods and strategies for applying technology to maximize student learning. Teachers

A. facilitate technology-enhanced experiences that address content standards and student technology standards.

B. use technology to support learner-centered strategies that address the diverse needs of students.

C. apply technology to develop students' higher-order skills and creativity.

D. manage student learning activities in a technology-enhanced environment.

Computers have changed our world, both inside and outside the classroom. It is not just the computer itself, with all of its capabilities, that has caused this change. Indeed, the computer has proven itself to be just the forerunner of a much greater digital revolution. As a result of the advances in personal computers, many other digital devices have evolved. These devices can serve teaching and learning in dramatic and innovative ways.

Consider for a moment the process teachers once used to duplicate materials for their students. Have you ever heard the term *dittos* applied to teacher-prepared worksheets? Have you ever wondered where this term comes from? Before personal computers began to be mass produced, teachers had to go through a laborious process to prepare student worksheets. Two technologies were available to them: the spirit duplicator, which used blue-backed transfer paper to run a limited number of duplicate copies, and the dittograph machine, which used a waxed paper that was cut (like a stencil) by typewriter keys or by a special sharp stylus. The duplicator used an alcohol-based chemical to transfer the blue ink from the master to plain paper. The dittograph ran ink through the temporary stencil the teacher created and transferred that ink to paper. Both technologies were very messy and could reproduce a very limited number of copies before the masters deteriorated. Also, teachers had to be very careful not to make mistakes when creating those masters. No "delete" keys were available on typewriters or when creating a master by hand! Mistakes were transferred along with correct content. And, of course, these types of technology could not change the size or style of the font, add graphics, or make transparencies.

With the first personal computer came the first word processor. This combination made it possible for teachers to see the finished product on the screen, correct all mistakes, adjust fonts, and even add graphics before transferring the document to paper. Furthermore, as printers became more sophisticated and cheaper, it became easy to print out high-quality transparencies and worksheets that incorporated color and graphics.

The computer was just the beginning. The digital tools that have resulted from it are even more amazing. The change from laborious duplication to quick word processing and printing is just one example of the digital revolution computers began. Just as this necessary teaching task was simplified and enhanced by digital technologies, so too have countless more teaching and learning tasks been improved through the application of digital equipment.

This chapter will help you explore the many digital technologies that have evolved out of the digital revolution led by the personal computer. In Chapter 4, you will

- Explore how digital input technologies can be used in teaching and learning
- Examine how digital output technologies can be used in teaching and learning
- Review the issues and concerns associated with using these diverse technologies in the classroom
- Explore emerging digital technologies that may be useful to teachers and learners in the future

Real People Real Stories

Meet Deborah Lacek, Lisa Palonka, and Troy Robinson. Using digital technologies in the classroom to "support learner-centered strategies that address the diverse needs of students" is an important skill for teachers in today's schools, as specified in the ISTE technology standards for teachers. Teachers must use the ubiquitous computer and other digital technologies to address content standards and maximize student achievement. The three elementary school teachers you are about to meet have demonstrated how a comprehensive curriculum package, LCD projector, and wireless laptop computers can make it possible to address their diverse learners' needs.

Deborah Lacek, Media Specialist; Lisa Palonka, Technology Specialist; and Dr. Troy Robinson, Reading Specialist, work for a Title I school in Broward County, Florida, the nation's sixth-largest school district. The district has 138 elementary schools serving 120,000 students in PK–5, representing 168 countries and 55 languages. Their school, Lloyd Estates Elementary, serves a diverse student body of 560 students with 45 percent ESOL and 86 percent nonwhite minorities.

Like all schools in Florida, Lloyd Estates Elementary administers the Florida Comprehensive Assessment Test (FCAT). It is administered to students in Grades 3–5 to measure achievement of the skills and content described in the Sunshine State Standards (SSS). Promotion criteria are based on FCAT proficiency level. Level 1 students, who are identified as possible retainees, are provided regular instruction (whole-group and differentiated), ongoing assessment, and immediate intensive instruction. This year, the school initiated a curriculum map and instructional focus calendar targeting specific SSS benchmarks with a weekly assessment. Results are entered in a schoolwide database.

From this intensive analysis of students, it was recognized that classroom instruction and computer-assisted instruction must be tailored to meet the identified needs of each student. Differentiated instruction within the classroom was facilitated efficiently through the instructional focus calendar, as teachers provided specialized practice in centers and small groups. After differentiation of instruction in the classroom, it became apparent that some children needed an additional, alternative approach. Outdated software prevented teachers from utilizing newly acquired wireless laptop computers to address the individual needs of struggling readers in immediate intensive instruction.

The solution to meeting the needs of the students became clear when the school upgraded to a comprehensive learning system. The Compass Learning Odyssey computer program provided a new strategy with SSS curriculum correlations. As the school's technology leadership team, Ms. Lacek, Mrs. Palonka, and Dr. Robinson attended training for the new learning system and immediately realized this program was the perfect solution for individualized computer-assisted instruction.

Fourth graders who scored Level 1 in reading on the previous year's FCAT were targeted for immediate intensive intervention with Ms. Lacek. The team devised a plan to address the needs of Level 1 students in Grades 4 and 5 using the wireless laptops and the new program. Using the LCD projector, the team introduced the computer program to students who were spread out across the media center, one or two students at each wireless computer. Students were also taught the proper care of the computers and charging cart and how to access their own progress reports.

Assignments were made in Compass Learning Odyssey tailored to each student's needs, as revealed in weekly benchmark assessments and the program's pretest. The program provides an automatic learning path, which Ms. Lacek further individualized by assigning appropriate phonics lessons and lower-level lessons. Students were thus provided personalized practice sessions on the computer several times a week.

Students are able to self-monitor their progress through the program's unique "My Portfolio" feature. The Student Score Report displays the activity name, date/time, duration, score, and mastery status. Ms. Lacek confers regularly with classroom teachers to share a progress report for each student.

As a result of this technology intervention, students have assumed responsibility for their own progress. As weekly benchmark assessments are examined, students know they will receive additional instruction and will be expected to show progress and mastery on subsequent assessments. Struggling readers are identified early before they experience failure on the state's high-stakes test. Deficiencies are identified early so that prescribed activities can provide remediation.

Reluctant readers have accepted the challenge and demonstrated a renewed enthusiasm for reading by focusing on individual reading goals. Students ask to use the program during the school's before- and after-school programs. Students report they love using the wireless laptop computers, rather than only using the networked lab computers, because of the flexibility. Consequently, students are reading more and practicing specific skills without feeling as if they are "working."

The school's plan has been in effect less than a year; therefore, specific data about percentage of benchmarks passed are not yet available. The progress of each student is slow and steady, but positive results are expected from using Compass Learning Odyssey and wireless computers to individualize instruction. Other teachers have seen the success of the program, which has provided an opportunity for the team to mentor other teachers in the use of digital technologies in the classroom to individualize instruction and enhance student achievement.

For more information about this initiative, contact

Deborah Lacek
Lisa Palonka
Dr. Troy Robinson
Lloyd Estates Elementary
750 NW 41 Street
Oakland Park, FL 33309
(754) 322-6800
deborah.lacek@browardschools.com
lpalonka@browardschools.com
t.robinson@browardschools.com

Digital Technologies in the Classroom

Once you have computer systems in the classroom, the possibilities for expanding their capabilities by the addition of digital peripherals are enormous. You can add input devices that let you scan photos from your field trip; that let students operate a computer by touching a display projected onto the classroom whiteboard; or that let you dictate input via voice instead of a keyboard. Or you can add output devices that enable you to share what you see on your monitor with the whole class, that can turn segments of a videotape into digital pictures, or that can read sections of the textbook to your auditory learners. Whatever your academic or administrative needs, you can usually find and add hardware and software to your computer to get the job done. The subsequent sections of this chapter will examine some of the most useful and innovative digital technologies for classroom use.

Input Devices for Teaching and Learning

The keyboard and the mouse are the two most commonly used devices for inputting data into a computer. However, there are many other devices that enable you and your students to enter data as well. These include scanners; digital cameras; digital tablets; sound input, pen input, and touch screen devices; devices that let you input via voice; and electronic whiteboards. Each of these input devices is uniquely valuable in the classroom. In the following sections, you will be introduced to each.

Using Scanners

If you want to modify a question on a previously typed test or add an instructional notation to a photographic image that you plan to use in teaching a lesson, you can use a scanner to easily and quickly accomplish your task. Scanners are input devices that capture and then translate printed copy or images into digital data. When you scan a page, the scanning software that is packaged with the scanner hardware turns the image or text on the page into its digital equivalent. The scanner is connected to the computer; as it scans, it inputs a digital version of the scanned object into the computer. This image is then stored in RAM or on a disk. Once the image is in this digital format, you can use image-editing software, such as a draw, paint, or photo-styling program, to enhance or modify the image or add text to it. The modified image can then be printed out in black and white or in color on paper, transparency film, or photographic paper. This same image can also be incorporated into other programs, such as a publishing program to create class newsletters or a presentation program to create effective lecture support visuals.

Scanners can also turn printed pages of text into a digital document that can be altered with word-processing software. This type of scanning requires that you use optical character recognition (OCR) software. OCR software is usually bundled with a scanner or incorporated into the scanning software. **OCR software** recognizes printed characters when they are scanned and then turns them into their electronic word-processing equivalent so they can be easily edited.

The most common type of scanner is the **flat-bed scanner** (Figure 4.1). It works something like a small personal copier. A scanner makes a digital

E-Learning
ON THE WEB! 4.1

What Scanner Is Right for My Classroom?

FIGURE 4.1

Scanners and Their Uses

Flat-bed scanners are the most versatile scanners, able to scan various sizes of bound or loose pages or graphics. Most flat-bed scanner software can save the scans as both graphic and OCR files.

duplicate of whatever is placed facedown on the bed. Once the page, photograph, or other item is scanned, the resulting digital image is saved to the computer's storage areas for further enhancement or eventually to be printed out. Any type and most sizes of paper (and even other material, such as cloth) can be placed on the bed of a flat-bed scanner. Thickness or type of material will not interfere with the process. However, flat-bed scanners do vary in the maximum image resolution they can produce.

In terms of resolution, it is important to note the dots per inch (dpi) the scanner is able to produce. This number is related to the number of sensors built into the scanner, which determines its ability to capture clear and crisp images. The higher the dpi, the higher the quality of the captured image.

Scanners may also vary in the way in which they connect to a computer. Since scanned files are quite large, high-speed connections are necessary. In the past, scanners connected through the parallel port. **Ports** are points of connection between a computer system and its peripherals. Today scanners connect through high-speed USB (universal serial bus) ports found on newer computers. Either connection will be effective; however, it is important for a teacher who wants to acquire a scanner to check which type of port is available on the computer the scanner will be connected to. If you purchase a USB scanner but your computer has no available USB ports, you will have to purchase additional hardware (e.g., a USB expansion hub) to make the connection.

These and the features of the software that is packaged with a flat-bed scanner cause price differences in scanners. Careful identification of your needs and examination of the hardware and software capabilities will help you select the scanner that is best suited for your budget and purposes.

E-Learning

www.mylabschool.com
Hardware Skills Builder
Digital Imaging

Tech Tips *for* TEACHERS

Scanners offer you a variety of resolution settings up to the maximum resolution the scanner is capable of. When scanning images, files may end up being quite large depending on the resolution you select. It is important to decide ahead of time how you will use the image so that you can choose the best resolution setting. If you plan to reproduce the image in its original size, the lowest-resolution setting that appears reasonable to your eyes may be best. But if you plan to enlarge the image or edit it, it is best to select the highest resolution the scanner offers so that there is no loss of detail in the image. However, you may have to plan to use a high-capacity storage device for a high-resolution image. A single image may be more than a few megabytes in size, making it impossible to save on a floppy disk. Whatever your purpose, it is best to purchase a scanner capable of the highest resolution your budget will allow so that when you want this feature, it will be there for you.

COOL TOOLS

The Scantron

Optical Mark Recognition (OMR) technology for scanners is the basis for a cool tool that helps you grade tests and analyze results. The Scantron, one of the most popular OMR scanners used in schools, lets your students respond to test questions by filling in bubbles on preprinted answer sheets. The Scantron scanner will then compare their marks on the answer sheet with your key and grade all of the tests for you. Results can then be automatically imported into grading software to be posted to your computer-based grade book and even analyzed to give you a graphical picture of class and individual results. This dedicated scanner can save busy teachers time when grading and tracking student progress. For more information about Scantrons, visit the company web site at **www.scantron.com.**

SOURCE: Photo from **www.scantron.com.**

Digital cameras capture pictures in digital form with varying resolutions.

E-Learning

www.mylabschool.com
video
View *Integrating Digital Cameras*

Using Digital Cameras

As you have learned, if you want to digitally capture a group picture of your class for use in the school newsletter, you can scan a photograph and incorporate it into your publishing program. The process requires that you first take a picture, have the film developed, and then complete the scanning process. Wouldn't it be easier just to capture the image digitally in the first place? That is exactly what can be done with a digital camera (see Figure 4.2).

A **digital camera** works like a traditional camera except that it does not use light-sensitive film. Instead, photos are stored in the camera's memory card or on CD as digital data. The capacity of storage media in digital cameras varies. The higher the desired resolution of your photos, the more memory space you will need. If, however, you are planning to take numerous high-resolution photos, you can always purchase multiple memory cards for your camera.

FIGURE 4.2

Comparison of Digital Cameras and Their Features

Digital cameras are made by a number of manufacturers. Each type of digital camera has features that affect its price. Most have an LCD display that lets you preview your pictures as soon as you take them.

COMPARISON OF DIGITAL CAMERAS AND THEIR FEATURES

DIGITAL CAMERAS store photographs either on reusable storage cards, disks, or miniature hard drives.

• Storage cards come in various capacities and you can buy more than one if you need to be able to store large quantities of pictures. Photos can then be downloaded via cable or card reader to the computer for editing and printing.
• CD recordable disk storage uses mini compact disks for easy portability to the computer.
• Microdrives are miniature hard drives that store many gigabytes of high-resolution photos.

The memory card a camera uses varies in type as well as size. Current popular types of cards include SmartMedia, CompactFlash, and Memory Stick. Every camera manufacturer selects the type it will use for its cameras. It is therefore important to note the type of memory card used by the camera you have available so you can purchase additional cards if you need to.

One of the most recent additions to storage media for digital cameras is the Microdrive. This miniature hard disk drive is capable of storing multiple gigabytes of information. For digital camera users, this technology will make it possible to store hundreds of images before having to download them to a computer. To use Microdrive storage, the camera must have been designed with a storage card slot that is compatible with this technology.

When the camera's storage media is full, the images can then be transferred to a computer for more permanent storage. This is done by connecting the camera to the computer with a special cable that comes bundled with the camera or by means of a camera cradle that connects to the computer. Some newer cameras are available with wireless link capability as well. Once copied to the computer's hard drive, the images can be enhanced with a photo-styling program or used in other software applications. Ultimately, digital photographs can be printed out on photographic or regular paper with a color printer. After transfer to the hard drive, the images can then be deleted from the camera's memory so that space is again available for new pictures.

Digital cameras allow you to input photographic images directly without having to scan them, but the scanner may be a more versatile addition because it enables you to digitize text and printed graphics as well. Compared to traditional photographic equipment, digital cameras have many unique features. In addition to letting you directly manipulate the photos with computer software, digital cameras allow you to preview photos as you take them. Digital cameras are equipped with small LCD screens on the back that let you preview pictures you have taken before saving them or view the photos you have already taken and saved. This feature saves you the time and expense of taking film to a developer only to find that your photos did not turn out as you expected. It also allows you to use your available photo storage space wisely by deleting shots you don't like and retaking a photo whenever you choose.

When determining a camera's potential for high-resolution images, manufacturers specify how many megapixels the camera is capable of producing. A pixel (or picture element) is a single dot in the image captured by the camera. Millions of dots make up a single image. The higher the number of dots captured, the clearer the image will be. Thus, a digital camera's capacity is indicated by the number of megapixels (millions of dots) it can capture. The Tech Tip for Teachers feature summarizes the relationship of a camera's megapixel capacity and the types and

Tech Tips *for* TEACHERS

Selecting the right digital camera for your classroom is a challenge. One of the most significant features to consider is the possible image quality or resolution that you need. The megapixel number for a camera identifies how many millions of pixels (picture elements) the camera is capable of. The table below will give you an idea of how many megapixels you want to do the job.

Camera's Megapixels	Image Quality and Size
2–3 megapixels	Good, detailed screen images; excellent 4 × 6 and very good 5 × 7 prints; some cameras may produce reasonable 8 × 10 prints
4–5 megapixels	Equal to 35-mm photos; able to print high-quality 8 × 10 images
6 or more megapixels	Allow you to crop and blow up portions of photos without losing clarity; able to produce high-quality images greater than 8 × 10

in the Classroom

ELEMENTARY AND MIDDLE SCHOOL ART

Linda Holbrook chose the Sony Mavica for her students "to take digital pictures, download into a document, scan a baby picture into a document, and then write a story about themselves using the pictures as their guide." For these three procedures, taking the pictures, downloading them onto a document, and scanning the baby pictures into the document, the children who already know how to use a digital camera, along with Ms. Holbrook, show the class how to operate the camera. Then they all take pictures of each other for the autobiographies they will write. The children are shown how to download the pictures and insert them into a computer document and save the files. The children then write their autobiographies and, in so doing, learn how to work with text and pictures. Baby pictures are then scanned and inserted as well. After the autobiographies are complete, they are proofread and printed out. Ms. Holbrook notes that this is an excellent project that integrates digital camera, scanner, and computer skills into a language arts lesson.

Connie Ferguson, a middle school art teacher at Monroe Middle School, Monroe, Wisconsin, uses the digital camera to teach claymation; she covers how to storyboard, how to use the digital camera, and how to make movies with Microsoft's Movie Maker. Students work in teams and base their work on themes derived from content in the core (science, insects; social studies, world cultures; language, Greek myths; math, careers) and encore (famous artists, musicians, athletes, chefs, fashion designers, architects, and authors). The characters that will appear in the movies are made of plasticine. Sets are constructed, and, using a digital camera, the animation is filmed by taking approximately 30 photos to present the theme. The video clips are downloaded, and the moviemaking begins. Voice-overs and music are added. Ms. Ferguson said that when the claymation videos were presented to the school board, "They loved it! They have spent a lot of money on technology, so they were very pleased that someone was using it for something besides PowerPoint."

SOURCES: Ferguson, C. Claymation—Art Technology. Retrieved July 21, 2005, from **www.princetonol.com/groups/lessons/middle/Clay-Connie.htm.**
Holbrook, L. Autobiography. Retrieved July 18, 2005, from **www.lessonplanspage.com/printables/PLACIWriteAutobiographyPlusDigitalCameras24.htm.**

E-Learning ON THE WEB! 4.2

Which Digital Camera Should I Buy?

Monitor-top cameras can be used to share digital still and video images via the Web.

quality of images it can produce. When requesting or purchasing a digital camera for your classroom, its capacity for the type of image you want to create is likely to be your most important consideration.

Digital cameras vary in terms of many optional features as well. Some cameras record brief video and audio clips as well as still pictures. Although the digital video clip files are of relatively low resolution, if the ability to capture a brief video is important, the inclusion of this feature may be a buying consideration. Further, cameras vary in their ability to zoom in on an object. If close images of a student's work or an object of instruction is a consideration, then zoom capabilities must be taken into account. These features and others, as well as a camera's megapixel capacity, are the reasons for the dramatic variation in the prices of digital cameras. For you as a teacher, it is best to first determine what you want to use the digital camera for and then select one within your school budget that gives you the capabilities you desire.

One other type of digital camera that is useful for the classroom is the monitor-top camera, sometimes called a webcam. This type of digital camera is mounted on the computer's monitor and connected via cable to a computer USB port. It often has a built-in microphone as well as still and video capabilities. The monitor-top camera can be used to capture still and video images for communication via the Internet. It can be used for teleconferencing across the Internet, that is, conducting a live conference via the Internet that includes still images, video, and audio as well as text communication. Or it can be used simply for sharing still or video images via the Net. This adaptation of the digital camera has some of the same resolution parameters as a still camera, but because it is attached to the computer, it does not need to have independent storage capability.

As you can see, digital cameras of all types and designs are available to classroom teachers. Applications of this technology in the classroom range from capturing a field trip to taking digital photos of children's work, to displaying work on classroom web sites, to customizing a class newsletter, to documenting a science experiment. The applications are as diverse as the talents and creativity of the teachers who use these versatile input devices.

Using Graphics Tablets

A **graphics tablet** lets you use a stylus with an electronic pad to draw diagrams or create artwork. A stylus is a pen-shaped device that is designed to press against the pressure-sensitive surface of a graphics tablet. Graphics tablets are also sometimes called **digitizers** or digital tablets, because they convert the lines sketched on the tablet into their digital equivalents on the screen. As the stylus presses down on the plastic-covered surface of the pad, contacts are made and electrical circuits are completed. The resulting signals are translated by the software and hardware into digital images that can be seen on the monitor, printed out, or saved for use in other documents.

Graphics tablets are useful for drawing or annotating displays.

Architects, designers, and artists are the most frequent users of graphics tablets, because the stylus gives the user more precise control when drawing than a mouse or other pointing device can. However, digitizer technology can easily be adapted for educational use by teachers and learners. Using this type of tablet, teachers can place a word-processed or graphics document on the computer screen. With a digitizer, they can add their own comments to these images and mark them up as they are displayed on the computer screen. For example, when reviewing material with a small group of students, a teacher might annotate and circle key features on a computer-generated map displayed on the classroom computer's display. In combination with appropriate software, the teacher can mark up the diagram using various colors, lines of various types, and predetermined shapes. The computer image with annotation can then be saved and printed out or used in another document.

With a digital tablet, the teacher can create complex images, emphasize points, or fully annotate graphics.

Art students can use a more typical digitizer to draw original images, enhance computer-generated images or photographs, or annotate scanned images. Digitizers that are designed primarily for this type of art function usually add color, brush, and other art command options on the tablet, making it easier for the artist to use these features. Such customized tablets are often designed to be compatible with specific art software. Once again, it is important to balance your potential uses to determine the type of equipment that will work best in your classroom.

HANDS-
ON
LEARNING

Multimedia helps to address the diverse learning styles of your students. Input and output devices let you create and use multimedia by capturing text, audio, still images, and video clips that might be just the added extra to help that unique student learn. Consider a topic you will be teaching at the grade level or in the content area of your choice. Using the available multimedia capture technology available to you, including scanners, digital cameras, graphics tablets, and microphones, create images and audio and video elements that you feel could enhance a lesson on that topic. Share the multimedia elements with your peers and explain how you would use each in your lesson.

Once that decision has been made, it is important to remember to examine both software and hardware specifications to ensure compatibility.

Using Microphones

Computers today, especially those found in schools, are typically multimedia machines. These types of machines are equipped with the hardware and software necessary to play back and record sound and show video clips as well as display text and graphics. To play back the sound files and clips that come with multimedia software, the machines are equipped with a set of small speakers. To record audio, such machines are also usually equipped with a personal-sized microphone. Both speakers and microphone plug into ports located on the back of the machine. These ports are connected to the sound card, the computer component designed to input and output sound.

Through the microphone, music, sounds, and the spoken word can be input, digitized (turned into digital data), and stored. The digitized sound can then be played back by using a sound program, or it can be included in a multimedia program. In the classroom, the teacher might record a brief comment or an instruction to be included in a teacher-made computer tutorial, or a student might add recorded sounds from a field trip to his or her presentation of the field trip experience. Digitized sound can also be edited and enhanced by using sound-editing software. Sounds can be clarified, have special effects added to them, or be speeded up or slowed down. The edited or enhanced versions of sound recordings can be a valuable part of a computer-based lesson.

With the use of a simple, inexpensive microphone, sound can be added to round out computer-based materials and help address the needs of auditory learners. It should be noted, however, that sound files tend to be very large, requiring a lot of storage space. Programs are available to compress sound files for easier storage. These programs compress and convert audio into common formats such as mp3 or AAC for iPods. Classroom applications using sound without compression need to be saved on high-capacity storage media such as a hard drive or a removable hard drive or stored on a CD.

E-Learning
ON THE WEB! 4.3

How Can Digital Sound Capabilities Help Learners?

Using Pen Input Devices

Pen input devices use a stylus to input handwritten information, to select commands, and to make predetermined written symbols, called gestures, that represent computer commands. Pen input is typically used with a **personal digital assistant (PDA)** or a **tablet PC.** A PDA is a portable computing device that can recognize handwritten notes and translate them into a word-processed document through the use of the PDA's handwriting recognition software. These written-to-word-processed documents are then usually transferred to a desktop computer for storage or further use. PDAs also typically offer simplified office management tools, such as an appoint-

Personal digital assistants combine a handheld computer and organizer.

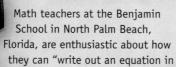

in the Classroom

TABLET PCS FOR TEACHING AND LEARNING

Math teachers at the Benjamin School in North Palm Beach, Florida, are enthusiastic about how they can "write out an equation in a shared workspace that is displayed on the classroom's whiteboard, and students seated at their desks can use their tablet pens to take turns adding steps to it." Students there are equally keen about tablet PCs. Shohan Shetty, a rising ninth grader, said, "It writes just like a pen and paper. It's fast." William Fraser, another ninth grader at the Benjamin School, called attention to the importance of "having Internet access at his desk for fast research," and, for students not used to keyboarding, he pointed out the ease of using the pen for writing and for all students drawing diagrams. The tablet PCs, in conjunction with a program from Smart Technologies, SynchronEyes, make it possible for teachers to "poll students anonymously to determine if the subject matter is being understood," as well as "view the students' screens to catch instant messaging or to administer electronic testing."

Tim Kilbride, AST in ICT at Ninestiles, Birmingham, England, says he "believes [the Tablet PC] bolstered his own efficiency and quality of teaching." He cites the ease and quickness with which he can access teaching resources and keep records of his students' work. He adds, "I can wander round the classroom, jotting down assessment notes while observing a pupil's ability. Entering data is fast and more natural with a pen—compared to a mouse—and I like being able to scribble emails!"

Sheela Gutteridge, AAL (Anytime Anywhere Learning) Coordinator at Ninestiles, praised the tablets by alerting teachers to the ways they are being applied: "Increasingly, these PCs are being used in place of electronic whiteboards, simply because they're so portable and versatile." The advantage for pupils of being able "to write directly on the screen" without standing in front of a board helps overcome student shyness in presenting their work and removes the handicap younger children have of not being able to reach the board.

Kathryn Broadhurst, head teacher at Green Lane Infant School, inner-city Leicester, England, has observed that the tablets allow students to experience learning through different learning styles: "With the right software, tablet PCs offer an extremely powerful multisensory learning experience, stimulating different parts of the brain. Pupils can see, hear, and touch their work as it progresses, becoming completely absorbed and fascinated in the results of their own actions."

Jackie Aspinall, ICT Teaching and Learning Support Manager for East Manchester Education Action Zone, assigned Year 4 students at St. Barnabas in East Manchester, England, to write a story using the Toshiba Protégé 3500. She observed, "They enjoyed seeing their handwriting on the screen and found the use of the pen very natural. They then converted their handwritten words into text using Microsoft Word, which revealed any incorrectly formed letters, words, or sentences. Pupils could then consider and rectify their mistakes, creating a piece of work they were proud of. One pupil even exclaimed she didn't like writing normally, but could write all day on this!"

SOURCES: Fitzgerald, T. J. (2004, September 9). The tablet PC takes its place in the classroom. Retrieved June 16, 2005, from **http://tech2.nytimes.com/mem/technology/techreview.html.** Keynote Speakers. (2005). Sir Dexter Hutt, Head Teacher, Ninestiles School, Birmingham, England. Retrieved August 10, 2005, from **www.novemberlearning.com/Default.aspx?tabid=1948:2400 PM.** Primary & secondary schools: Tablet PC—the ultimate teaching and learning tool. Retrieved June 26, 2005, from **http://uk.computers.toshiba-europe.com/cgi-bin/ToshibaCSG/ case_studies.jps?service=UK.**

ment book, a calendar, and a phone book (see Figure 4.3 on page 144). Pocket-PC types of PDAs may also include scaled-down versions of familiar computer software such as a word processor or electronic spreadsheet.

Make PDA technology considerably larger and more powerful, and you have tablet PCs. A tablet PC is approximately the size of a traditional writing pad (although substantially thicker), and you use it much as you would paper. You write on the surface of the tablet with your stylus, and the software converts written text into a word-processing file or a drawing you create into a graphics file. You can also use the stylus as you would a pointer controlled by a mouse, to give commands and make selections. The tablet

E-Learning
ON THE WEB! 4.4

Tablet Devices

FIGURE 4.3

Pen Input Devices
Go to School

PDAs and tablet PCs are versatile pen devices in the classroom. Using a stylus, these computers can be used to take notes, organize data, create drawings, and when connected to display devices, present information.

is essentially an LCD screen mounted over a motherboard with a hard disk drive, making this portable device a convenient and relatively lightweight pen input device.

PDAs and tablet PCs can be very useful classroom management tools that allow the teacher to make notes on lessons and activities, record and annotate student behavior, and track appointments. The data written into a PDA can be stored for later use, so the information can be easily transferred into computerized gradebooks, lesson plans, and student files. Essentially, PDAs act like digital memo pads, the pages of which can be transferred to a computer disk for safekeeping and easy retrieval. In the case of pocket PCs, they can also serve as very portable "palmtop" computers with many of the same capabilities of a desktop machine.

In the classroom, tablet PCs offer teachers and students some unique opportunities. Teachers can download students' word-processed essays and grade them via the tablet PC. The word-processed document is displayed on the tablet screen, and the teacher can add comments via the stylus. The graded document can be saved and returned to the student electronically for review. Connected to a classroom display device, the tablet PC can also be used for sharing digital images without the physical barrier of computer and monitor between teacher and class. And, while displaying digital presentations via tablet PC, teachers can easily add annotations with the stylus to emphasize or annotate key points.

The tablet PC presents distinct options for students as well. Using this device, students can take notes and organize them into clear word-processed documents without typing. They can easily integrate multimedia and web resources into their work and create documents for activities that include a full range of resources. They can also use the tablet PC to download and read the pages of electronic books and magazines, thereby bringing the library into the classroom.

Using Touch Screens

A **touch screen** is a computer monitor screen that responds to human touch. Touch screen software usually displays a series of graphics or icons. Instead of using a mouse and pointer to select an icon or command, you touch the icon itself as it is displayed on the touch screen, and the computer responds. The screen is touch sensitive and the touch screen software interpolates your finger's location on the screen as a command to select the icon or option that is displayed on that spot. On computers equipped with a touch screen, a keyboard and/or mouse might not even be available.

Touch screens are quick and easy to use. If large amounts of data need to be entered or many choices need to be made from complex sets of options, touch screens are an inappropriate choice of input device. They work best with simple, straightforward displays. Touch screens are often used in information kiosks at hotels and airports and with medical or other complex equipment that requires quick setting changes. They can also be useful in the classroom for young children who are preliterate, cannot type, or have difficulty controlling a mouse owing to physical impairment.

Touch screens can be used in the classroom by prereaders or as an assistive device for students with special needs.

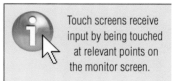

Touch screens receive input by being touched at relevant points on the monitor screen.

TECHNOLOGY SOLUTIONS
for All Learners

Touch Screen for Special Needs Students

Touch screen monitors and related software that enable a traditional monitor to emulate a touch screen are powerful tools for students with disabilities. Touch screens may display graphics that the user can touch to enter commands and make software selections. Special software can display the image of a computer keyboard on the screen so that keys or commands can be pointed to and clicked on. Whether hardware- or software-based, touch screen technologies can improve the life of a student with disabilities.

The Alliance for Technology Access (**http://ataccess.org/**) is a network of resources that provides information and support services to children and adults with disabilities including information about assistive devices. Its web site includes many success stories. Two such stories demonstrate the power of touch screen technology.

United Cerebral Palsy of Idaho shared the story of Melissa. Melissa, a 4-year-old with cerebral palsy, had difficulty holding her head up and moving her arms. In her school's computer lab, a TouchWindow was installed so she could play math games. In addition to practicing math concepts, Melissa was able to strengthen her right arm by reaching out to touch the screen. She was also able to strengthen her neck as she worked to keep her head up to see the monitor and work with the software. This adaptive technology not only assisted in teaching skills, it helped improve the learner's muscle tone.

Technology Assistance for Special Consumers in Huntsville, Alabama, shared the story of Steven, who had a stroke at age 16 that left him a quadriplegic. He had partial paralysis of all extremities and was unable to speak. After the stroke, he could move only his head, but that was enough, with the help of a combination of assistive technologies that included a keyboard display on a screen. Steven learned to use a computer by scanning. Scanning is a system in which a keyboard is displayed on a screen with keys highlighted one after another. Simply by pressing a single switch button when the highlight appeared on the right key, Steven was able to communicate via computer. Today, having gained more movement in his arms, he can use a similar keyboard display that allows him to point to and click on the keys he desires with a glide pad.

SOURCE: Retrieved April 20, 2002, from **http://etacess.org/community/successes/successes.html.**

Using Electronic Whiteboards

Every classroom is equipped with display surfaces on which teachers can write and illustrate concepts as they teach. Some classrooms may still have blackboards and chalk. Most now use whiteboards with erasable color markers. These media offer the advantage of spontaneous explanation during the teaching and learning process. Once these display surfaces are filled with explanations, to continue, the teacher must begin to erase what has been previously written. For students who were absent on a particular day, for students who were not able to copy the information down quickly enough, or for the teacher who would like to refer back to previously erased material, the blackboard or whiteboard offers little support.

Electronic whiteboards convert whiteboard images and text into computer files.

What if it were possible to write on a whiteboard and, just before erasing the information, print it out or save it to a computer file? That is precisely what an **electronic whiteboard** does. As you write on an electronic whiteboard, a built-in scanner records the drawings or text in the colors you are using. The recorded digital image is then displayed on a monitor. Furthermore, the recorded image can be saved, edited, or printed out. The image can then be erased from the electronic whiteboard, and a new computer file can be opened to capture and record new images. Once saved, whiteboard information can be included in other documents or placed in an electronic archive for you or your students to access for review.

If desired, some whiteboards in different locations can be connected over a phone line so that the writing in one location shows up in the other locations at the same time. This can be especially useful in bringing a distant guest speaker into your class or in delivering instruction to a homebound student.

Electronic whiteboard technology is available in many different types, including whiteboards that are touch sensitive and rear-projection whiteboards. Each of these has its own unique features and advantages although still somewhat expensive for the average classroom. A newer technology turns your own classroom whiteboard into its electronic counterpart. This type of whiteboard technology uses a projection unit that attaches to the corner of your traditional whiteboard and a series of electronic sleeves for your markers. Once connected to your computer, the projection device captures anything written on the whiteboard with the marker in its sleeve and saves it as a digital file. This type of system can do most of the tasks of its more expensive dedicated electronic whiteboard counterpart but typically at much less cost. Additionally, this system does not require any extra wall

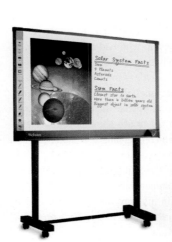

Stand-alone electronic whiteboards (left) and electronic conversion kits for a traditional whiteboard (right) allow you to work interactively with your classroom's displays and save or print for future reference.

in the Classroom

ELECTRONIC WHITEBOARDS IN ELEMENTARY AND SECONDARY CLASSROOMS

Carrie Rigney, a fourth-grade teacher in the Maplewood–Richmond Heights School District, Maplewood, Missouri, praises her rear-projection SMART Board by telling us, "I can be completely ready for that lesson. . . . I have everything typed up. I have graphics for everything. The lesson goes a lot smoother, which gives us more time to get things accomplished." Having it all ready to go on the interactive board helps teachers who find the constant pressure of transitioning from one lesson to another during actual class time to be a frustrating experience that teachers at any level have because presenting materials and information for the next lesson often results at best in restlessness on the part of unoccupied students and at worst in downright disruptive behavior.

Ms. Rigney continues that she uses the SMART Board software to create her lessons. She "downloads text and images from the Internet and saves them for later application on the board. She can show videos on the board and even 'write' over the top of them."

Enid Smith-Becker's middle and high school students have art at their fingertips in her art and French classes at the International School in Bellevue, Washington. "It's an incredible teaching tool," Ms. Smith Becker remarked about the interactive whiteboard where she has her art students "draw on the 4 × 5-foot board in a wide range of colors, and even do it with a fingertip." She also is enthusiastic about how the board supports instruction in advanced French lessons that she has written on the board and stored on her laptop computer to be "projected again for a later class, eliminating the tedious task of erasing the board for an intervening beginners' class and rewriting the material for another advanced section later in the day."

SOURCES: Roberts, G. (2004, September 21). Interactive whiteboards save all kinds of schoolwork, and time. Retrieved September 21, 2004, from **http://seattlepe.nwsource.com/printer2/index.asp?ploc=t&refer.** Starkman, N. (2004, November 19). To the rear—project! Retrieved November 19, 2004, from **www.thejournal.com/thefocus/ featureprintversion.cfm?newsid=45.**

or floor space, since it uses your existing whiteboard. For these reasons, this input device is becoming a popular electronic whiteboard alternative for K–12 classrooms.

Output Devices for Teaching and Learning

Using Data Projection

One of the challenges of using a computer in a classroom is that the computer's monitor is too small for display to a large group. To meet this challenge, a variety of computer data projection units are available. **Data projectors** plug into the computer's monitor port and display the signals that are also sent to the monitor. Each type of data projection unit has unique features and capabilities (see Figure 4.4 on page 149) with a corresponding difference in prices.

Computer screen images can be projected using data projectors.

Data Projectors

The **data projector** is a projection unit that combines an LCD display and a light source into a single, relatively lightweight box. These units can typically

COOL TOOLS

Bluetooth Whiteboard Tablets

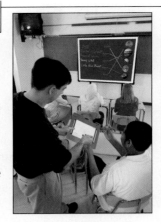

An adaptation of the digital tablet, this innovative device uses Bluetooth technology (the ability to wirelessly connect unlike devices) to connect multiple tablets to a computer and/or an electronic whiteboard. The teacher can use the tablet to freely move around the room while adding annotations to the whiteboard or computer display. The tablet can be used to control the computer or change from one image to another. Students can use their tablets from their desk to make real-time additions or comments on the teacher's presentation, fill in answers to questions displayed on the whiteboard, or create their own presentation to the class via the classroom whiteboard from the tablet at their desk. These classroom tablets use a stylus to issue commands, capture written comments, or make annotations to whatever is displayed to the class. When added to your classroom, digital presentations become entirely interactive, with both teacher and students able to operate the computer from anywhere in the room.

E-Learning

www.mylabschool.com
Hardware Skills Builder
Data Projector

project both images from a computer system and video from a video source in a display that is large enough and bright enough to be seen across a classroom. For the brightest, clearest, and best results, these images should be displayed on a projection screen. Projection to a wall will not offer the same level of clarity and brightness; projection to a whiteboard will often be difficult to view, owing to the high reflectivity and resultant glare of the whiteboard surface.

Different data projectors offer different levels of resolution and brightness (measured in lumens). As the resolution and brightness of data projectors increase, there is a corresponding increase in price. It is best to purchase a projector that exceeds the capabilities of your current computer in terms of resolution. In terms of brightness, it is best to select a projector with the maximum brightness your budget will allow. If you select a less costly projector that may be of insufficient brightness, you might find that you have to turn all the lights off in the classroom and/or cover the windows to be able to see the computer display clearly.

Other features that are typically available on data projectors include built-in speakers, multiple computer input capability, software storage capability, and remote control. Many projectors are designed to accept a variety of video inputs, making them an effective replacement for the large TV monitor so often seen in today's classrooms. Thus, the same projector that can display your computer image can also display a videotape, a TV program from the school's cable connection, or the images from your digital camera. Although these units cost more than large CRT monitors, they are less expensive than newer, large screen plasma or LCD monitors making them the most cost effective means for classroom display.

E-Learning
ON THE WEB! 4.5

How Can I Share My Computer Image?

Scan Converters

One of the most inexpensive methods for displaying a computer image to an entire class is to use a digital (computer signal) to analog (video

LCD projectors are compact LCD display units with their own built-in light source. The typically brighter picture, enabling displays that are clear even with room and outside light, and its compact, lightweight size are key features for the classroom.

LCD PROJECTOR

Scan converters connect the computer and video monitor through a converter box that alters the computer signal so that it can be displayed on the video monitor. These very inexpensive devices are the most reasonable method for sharing and projecting computer images. The disadvantage is the reduced resolution when compared with a digital display.

SCAN CONVERTER

FIGURE 4.4
Digital Display Technologies and Their Characteristics
Teachers have several options for displaying computer images.

signal) converter, or **scan converter.** This device converts a computer's image into one that can be displayed through analog (video) technology. To use it, one end of the converter's cable is plugged into the computer's monitor port and the other into the video input port on the back of a large classroom television monitor; the computer image is then visible on the monitor.

These converters are well within the budget of most schools, making it possible to share computer displays across the classroom. The disadvantage of this type of display, however, is in the quality and size of the image. Television monitors are not designed with the same resolution as computer monitors. Although graphics may look fine, text may appear choppy and difficult to read when displayed through a converter and on a television monitor. Additionally, even the largest television monitors can be difficult to see from the back of a large classroom. Thus, the details of the computer image may be lost to those in the back when it is displayed on the classroom television monitor.

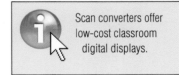

Scan converters offer low-cost classroom digital displays.

Using Speakers and Headphones

Computer systems today are sold with varying levels of sound capabilities. **Speakers** are a common component included with every system. Some systems have built-in speakers; others have external speakers. Although sound is not critical for many administrative applications, such as word

YOU Decide!

Every teacher needs to be able to communicate visually with the entire class during instruction. As you have learned, there are many technologies available to do so. But is it worth the time and trouble to invest in and use high-tech displays and whiteboards?

YES! Teachers need to use every possible tool available to meet student needs. Older technologies like a black- or whiteboard or an overhead projector may work, but they don't offer a teacher a way to use all of the possible resources when they teach. Also, these older technologies are very static and don't offer the excitement and interactivity of a digital display or electronic whiteboard. You may have to invest a bit of time to learn how to use them, but the effort is worth it for your students. Why use a teaching and learning support that is less effective when something better is available?

NO! New digital technologies are complicated. They take time to learn and use. They take up space in the classroom and may even break down in the middle of a lesson. Why go through all that trouble? Besides, it is the teacher who is the heart of every lesson. The support technologies are just there to help the teacher teach. Fancy new technologies don't guarantee that a lesson will be any better than one presented via a whiteboard and markers. We don't need all of this new equipment to teach. Students learn from teachers, not from technology.

Which view do you agree with? YOU DECIDE!

Speakers and headphones help meet the needs of auditory learners.

Headphones can allow students to hear computer audio output without disturbing others.

processing, it is an integral part of much of the academic software that is available today. To address multiple learning styles, most learning software is designed with a rich auditory component. To take advantage of this aspect of the software, an audio output device is necessary.

Just as is the case with home audio systems, computer speakers vary significantly in capability. Some are designed for a single user working on his or her home computer. These speakers, even at maximum volume, are often incapable of playing back sound at a level and clarity that would be useful for a small group of students. It is important to consider how audio-rich computer software will be used to determine what type of sound output hardware is necessary.

If there is a single computer in the classroom and it is used for a large-group display, good speakers are essential so that all students can hear as well as see the program. Of course, if the display unit used is multimedia capable, that is, it includes both visual and audio capability, additional speakers might not be necessary at all. If the computer display is through a multimedia-capable data projector, the projector itself contains sufficiently large speakers for all to hear. Alternatively, if you use a converter, the speakers in the television monitor will carry the audio component of the software.

However, if the instructional intent is to use academic software as learning support for one student at a time, speakers might not be the preferred type of audio output. When a single student is working with software to master a targeted skill, the audio component of the software can be distracting to those around him or her. In that case, instead of speakers as audio output, you might want to select headphones. **Headphones** allow individual students to listen to audio without disturbing anyone else. Multimedia computers include both headphone ports and speaker ports.

TECHNOLOGY SOLUTIONS
for All Learners

The Second "R" and the Special Needs Student

Writing, the active, creative verbal skill, poses many challenges for teachers of regular classrooms and, especially, for those of inclusion classrooms where the physical act of writing creates an added hurdle to be dealt with. Assistive technology, however, provides a pathway of access to writing for the diverse range of student learning styles, intelligences, and physical limitations found in these classrooms. David Davis, a technology consultant serving nine Florida public school districts, describes four types of technologies that perform well as aids for students needing help in the physical writing process: portable writing devices, alternative keyboards, voice recognition systems, and universal access stations.

Portable writing devices assist students who can't grasp a writing instrument. This computer-writing equipment has a keyboard like a computer or laptop with alternative keyboards that accommodate the physically challenged student. These al-

ternative keyboards work well for students with visual, physical, or cognitive limitations, making it possible for them to write by means of menu commands. The keyboards can be affixed to computers so teachers can modify the standard keyboard. Voice recognition systems are software programs that offer "speech-to-text, document navigation and page navigation" and, with verbal commands, make any computer-based information source accessible for reading and organizing. Universal access stations comprise multimedia computers, scanners, optical character recognition (OCR) software, alternative keyboards, text-to-speech software, and other assistive devices for special populations. Mr. Davis explains the access these technologies give to students with special needs: "With the Universal Access Station available, students can scan in pages from a magazine or book, and have the computer read the text out loud. This is a great strategy for students with limited reading skills as well as students who use English as a second language. Text-to-speech software can also be used to translate web pages to spoken text. Students with limited vision can take notes using a talking word processor with the screen set to high contrast. Word prediction software provides further assistance in taking notes."

SOURCE: D. Davis. 2002. Using assistive technology to help students write. *Media & Methods* (September/October) 39 (1), 14.

Sample Assistive Devices

Many types of assistive devices, such as BrailleLite and VoicePal, have been developed to support special needs students.

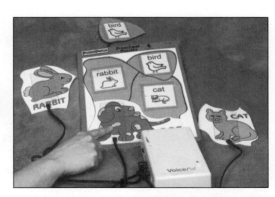

You might even be able to use the headphones that are available for other audio devices. Occasionally, a headphone plug may look different and will not fit into the jack (port) on the computer. It is, however, very possible that the headphones can still be used. Local electronics stores often stock a good selection of converter plugs. These are typically very inexpensive and easy to find.

Emerging Digital Technologies for the Classroom

At this point, you have learned much about computers and the peripheral digital technologies that you might use in your classroom. Computer technology, however, is in a constant state of flux, and new digital equipment is constantly emerging. As these new technologies evolve and become part of our world, many will be adapted for use in teaching and learning. Some of the most fascinating types of hardware that are likely to be adapted for use in schools are described next.

Using Wireless Devices

Wireless connections for computers and other digital equipment are quickly becoming as commonplace as cell phones. Today most cellular phones offer incoming voice calls, text messages, and Internet access. Wireless hot spots through which you can access your email and the Internet are now available at coffee shops, malls, airports, and hotels. Similar access at schools is not far behind.

Classroom wireless technologies can take several different forms. Classroom wireless often uses radio frequency (RF) technology to connect classroom workstations to a network server. Access points, or points at which connection is made to the wired backbone, are strategically placed throughout the school building. Adapters are used in workstations to connect to the access points. Since no wires tether computers to the wall, computers with adapters can be moved as needed, as long as they stay in range of an access point.

One of the fastest-growing wireless technologies is called WiFi (wireless fidelity). It too uses radio frequency to connect WiFi-enabled computers and other digital devices to networks at very fast speeds. Base

E-Learning

www.mylabschool.com
video
View *Teaching with Wireless Devices*

COOL TOOLS

Clickers in the Classroom

Wireless response systems, also called clickers, can be used to get instantaneous feedback from your students. Students are provided a remote device (clicker) that is connected via infrared, radio-frequency, or WiFi technology to the teacher's workstation. A teacher can then ask for responses throughout the lesson, and students simply click a button to send their answer. Everyone's response is instantly received and tallied. Results can be displayed for everyone to see in the form of data or charts or the teacher can simply view the responses privately on the teacher workstation to see if everyone is following the lesson.

With instantaneous feedback available, a teacher can modify a lesson, add additional information or practice sets, or just use student opinion data as a jumping-off point for further discussion or research. And since the student responses are anonymous from the point of view of others in the classroom, even the shyest student feels free to respond and express his or her views. This emerging classroom technology may make raising hands and counting them a thing of the past.

stations serve as access points, and these can be placed anywhere, inside or outside of buildings. A WiFi-enabled building, campus, or other area allows individuals to access the local network and the Internet while moving anywhere in the area. Schools use WiFi to connect buildings, auditoriums, and outside areas. Some business districts even provide WiFi capability to shops, restaurants, and offices within the WiFi zone. This technology is likely to continue to grow and to expand wireless connectivity significantly. Indeed, some metropolitan areas are already attempting to create WiFi access across their entire cities. Purchasing WiFi-enabled mobile technologies may therefore be a good investment for the future.

For educators, **wireless devices** have the potential to solve several challenges. Wireless technologies allow you to sever the wire tether necessary in the wired classroom. Using a portable wireless computer, students can research an interesting insect they discover while they are still on a field trip rather than wait until the next day when they return to their classrooms. The teachable moment when students inquire and are ready to learn does not have to be postponed until wired connections are available. Furthermore, teachers can access online resources or their stored instructional files from anywhere, whether they are in or out of the classroom. What you need to teach remains at your fingertips wherever you may be. The advent of wireless devices also means that computer-enhanced classrooms do not need to be physically arranged according to where network connections are available on walls. Instead, computers can be easily moved to locations that are best for student interaction and communication.

Emerging hardware holds promise for teachers and learners.

Wireless communications and the emerging smaller and more powerful digital devices that are supported by this type of interaction are quickly evolving and coming into wide use. Wireless technology offers greater flexibility in terms of physical location and logistical arrangement. The devices using this technology will most likely become as commonplace as cell phones. Creative educators will no doubt develop many innovative applications for wireless devices in teaching and learning.

Using Handheld Computers

Handheld computers already offer all of the capabilities of personal information management (calendar, phone list, notes, to-do list, address book, and the like) with abbreviated versions of the most popular types of software (word processing, spreadsheets, games, and music recording and playback, to name an available few). As these devices continue to evolve, their size and weight continue to decrease while their capabilities increase. More and more software is being adapted for use on a handheld. Digital cameras, audio and video players, and cell phones are now being integrated into handhelds. Add to that a browser for access to the Internet, and the handheld easily becomes a powerful, fully functional, and truly portable computer.

E-Learning

www.mylabschool.com
Hardware Skills Builder
Handheld Computers

For teachers and students alike, handheld computing can make note taking, using educational software, or using the Internet as easy and convenient as taking out a pen and pad. Today handheld computers are used in as many diverse ways as there are student and teacher needs. For students,

PDAs let teachers move about the class while taking advantage of computer support.

E-Learning

www.mylabschool.com
video
View *Using Handhelds in the Classroom*

handhelds can be used to track and store weather information for science, word process an essay, create diagrams while on a field trip, prepare a group presentation, conduct science experiments (by the attachment of sensors to a handheld), replace graphing calculators, create a spreadsheet, and, with appropriate software, view tutorials for many subjects. For teachers, handhelds can be used to store grades, make impromptu annotations for a student file, connect to and display digital instructional files, organize a calendar and parent contact list, create a word document, and, in fact, do almost every task a full-size computer can do. And for handhelds connected to wireless school networks, the possibilities expand exponentially. The application of handheld technology to schools has even given rise to web sites dedicated to handheld technology in education. As this technology continues to evolve, handhelds will become even more powerful; and as prices decline, they will become more accessible to educators and their students.

Using E-books

Electronic books, also known as **e-books,** are electronic versions of books for PDAs and other portable computers. A single device can store and display many digital books along with related instructional and reference materials. E-book software typically has the capacity to allow you to take digital notes on segments as you read them, and some can play sound and audio enhancements or read text to students.

The educational applications for this emerging mobile technology are many. Rather than having to carry multiple textbooks and notebooks, students and teachers will need only a single, lightweight device into which several texts can be downloaded. New versions of texts are quickly and easily updated without the time and expense of printing new editions.

The potential of imbedding audio and visual enhancements in text makes it possible to address diverse learning styles from within the text itself. Note taking on text content is convenient and is done in a digital form that allows it to be edited and reorganized for studying. The potential for this technology in education is clear and is likely to change the future definition of a book.

Using Voice-Activated Devices

PDAs have expanded input capabilities to include keyboard input or both keyboard and pen input. The next technology that will revolutionize how we input data into computers is voice technology. Already available for assistive devices and for business and home computing, **voice technology** enables a computer to accept voice commands and dictation of data. As voice input technology improves, more and more digital devices will be adapted to accept voice commands. Already, some cellular phones have been adapted so that callers can simply speak the name of the person to be called, and the cell phone will dial the correct number.

Voice activation makes it easier for learners who are physically disabled or who have limited keyboarding skills to fully use the capabilities of a computer. For educators, it enables you to start up and conduct an Internet-search demonstration without having to leave a part of the classroom that needs your attention. Rather than having to return to your desk to issue commands via keyboard and mouse, you can simply speak to your computer from across the room. This technology, too, has great potential for improving the convenience of using computers in the classroom.

Using Portable Storage

Portable data storage has been revolutionized by the USB drive. This drive, also called a key chain drive, jump drive, or flash drive, is small and lightweight enough to attach to a key chain. The USB drive is approximately the size and shape of a mini highlighting pen, but it can store up to gigabytes of information or more than 100 CD-ROMs. The inner working of this drive is similar to a memory card like that found in digital cameras. Although the term *drive* is used, it is not an electromechanical device like a hard disk or floppy drive that records and plays back data from different types of disks. Instead, the USB drive is plugged into a computer's USB port, and the operating system recognizes it as an external drive, albeit based on memory-card technology. Data can be saved to the USB drive, and then the device is unplugged from the USB port. Later, the device can be plugged into a different machine's USB port, and that machine too will recognize it as an external drive. Thus, data is easily transported on a large-capacity storage device that can fit on a key chain.

For teachers and students, this inexpensive device can offer massive storage relatively inexpensively. Teachers using USB drives do not have to be concerned about finding the right disk or securing sensitive files. Data stored on the USB drive can be easily and safely carried with the teacher anywhere in the classroom, school, or even back and forth to home. Large multimedia files or presentations can be easily transported from machine to machine.

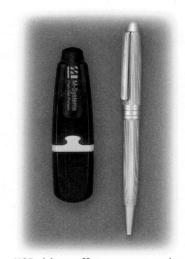

USB drives offer a way to make large files easy to move between computers equipped with a USB port.

When selecting a USB drive, teachers should be aware of two possible issues. First, older machines may have few or no readily available USB ports, making the use of these devices problematic. Even if USB drives are available, they may be inconveniently located at the back of a computer in an awkward location. If that is the case, extension USB ports may be necessary to easily use this technology. Second, USB drives are changing as their popularity rises. Newer 2.0-type USB drives, while backward compatible, will work much more slowly when used in 1.0 ports. The original USB 1.1 type may not offer the additional features and capacity you desire. USB drives are powerful portable storage devices that can serve a busy classroom teacher well.

Using Virtual Environments

As personal computer system capacity increases, more complex programs can be created. **Virtual reality** (VR) is a combination of hardware and software that together create a digital environment with which you can interact.

Virtual reality implementations range from the very sophisticated, requiring specialized hardware, to the relatively simple process of stitching together successive images to create a three-dimensional space. The extremely high-tech versions are typically found at universities and research institutions. The simpler process can be found and used in any classroom.

Using virtual reality hardware, which typically includes a headpiece and glove, you can see and interact with a three-dimensional digital world. VR environments let you take realistic virtual field trips using digital images of real and imaginary places. Some VR worlds are constructed from images of real places such as the Amazon or the Arctic. Still others are constructed from microworlds at a molecular or atomic level. Others are constructed from images gathered from NASA space probes. Using the headgear, you see these worlds before you. Using the special interactive glove that adjusts the VR world to the movement of your hand, you can reach out, touch, and grab a planet, a molecule, or a plant in the virtual Amazon. Virtual reality spaces that are created via software offer students a chance to interact with a simulated world created by and presented via

Virtual reality hardware and software let you feel as if you are participating in a virtual world.

computer. One of the most popular software packages for this purpose is Apple Computers' QuickTime VR. By using an artist's rendering or a collection of photos, images are joined into a single seamless world that students can explore through movement of the mouse. Students can move an object in the VR world around to see it from every angle, or they can zoom in, out, and around the virtual space. Students can easily create and share their own virtual world using this software. Class projects using this VR software might include school or classroom tours, virtual field trips, creating a virtual museum, or displaying specimens or exhibits that other students can manipulate. The limit is the teacher and student's imagination.

VR worlds are already in place. As you will see in later chapters, many exist on the Internet. Other, more complex environments exist only in research labs. Still others are beginning to appear in video arcades. These VR environments are a precursor to what is possible. As VR evolves, it will give students unlimited opportunities to interact with places they may never visit, with environments too dangerous to visit, or with realities too small for humans to interact with directly. The potential for educational applications and experiential learning in VR environments is enormous.

E-Learning
ON THE WEB! 4.6

Is Virtual Reality Worth the Visit?

 ## From Hardware to Software

The abundant hardware resources explored in this chapter are only the beginning of the potential for computer enhancement of the teaching and learning process. A broad range of administrative and academic **software** related to almost every aspect of education is also available for you to use in your classroom. Administrative software programs support you in almost every area of classroom administration, from helping you to track and average student grades, to helping you create a class newsletter, to helping you make custom, lesson-specific crossword puzzles. Academic software packages that help you teach range from a variety of multimedia encyclopedias, to content-area drill-and-practice programs, to software that provides a simulation that promotes discovery learning. All of these programs are designed to enhance and support what you do in the classroom.

The next two chapters focus on the software resources available to you and explore how they might be effectively used to teach and to learn. Of course, hardware and software are entirely interrelated, so the understanding of hardware you have achieved in this chapter should serve you well as you select the devices you might want for your classroom and as you consider the software you might want to use. As you begin considering these various tools, it is helpful to have a way to determine the usefulness of any particular piece of hardware. Clearly, not only do you need to be aware of many types of computer hardware and how each might be applied in your classroom, you also need to know how to evaluate them effectively. To assist you in determining the value of the hardware you are considering, a classroom equipment evaluation rubric is included in Table 4.1 on page 158. Similar evaluation tools are available in Chapter 5 for software evaluations.

Software enables computers to support instructional and administrative tasks.

E-Learning

www.mylabschool.com
Listen to Podcast
Technology Grants

TABLE 4.1 Classroom Equipment Evaluation Rubric

EQUIPMENT:

DESCRIPTION:

VENDOR: **COST:**

NOTES ON USE:

Please rate the features below for each piece of hardware. Next to each of the items in the rubric, mark the box that best reflects your opinion.

HARDWARE FEATURE	EVALUATION CRITERIA				
	1 Poor	2 Below Average	3 Average	4 Above Average	5 Excellent
EASE OF SETUP	No or minimal setup instructions; poor or missing summary list of hardware components	Instructions poorly written and somewhat difficult to follow; minimal description of equipment components	Instructions complete and adequately user-friendly; necessary equipment descriptions included	Clear and complete instructions; parts identified by letter or code to correspond to instructions	Pictorial or video guide showing step-by-step assembly with clear, easy-to-follow instructions; equipment goes together easily and smoothly
EASE OF USE	Equipment complex and difficult for students to use alone; time consuming and complex for teachers	Students can use with minimal support by teacher; teachers can use with some difficulty	Students can use without support after initial orientation; teachers can use with minimal practice	Students can use with brief orientation; teachers can use with little or no practice	Students can use without orientation or supports; teachers can use with no practice
SPACE	Space required may exceed maximum available	Space required somewhat large, but available room could be adjusted to accommodate equipment	Space required by equipment is appropriate to available space with current room configuration	Space requirement is appropriate and equipment will fit comfortably in the room	Space requirement is equal to or less than the space available; equipment adds to the look and usefulness of the room without crowding
TUTORIALS/ TRAINING AVAILABLE	No tutorials packaged with equipment; no online or other training available	Minimal tutorials packaged with equipment; few free or inexpensive optional tutorials or training available	Brief tutorial provided on CD-ROM with equipment; some additional tutorials or training available at minimal cost	CD and online tutorials readily available for free or minimal cost; some in-house training available for a reasonable fee	CD and online tutorials and training materials available without charge; in-house training provided for free or minimal cost
OTHER CRITERIA (List your own topic and criteria)					

Total the score for each piece of hardware. Compare the scores. The piece of hardware with the highest score is your best choice.

KEY TERMS

STUDENT ACTIVITIES

CHAPTER REVIEW

1. What is a scanner? How might it be used in the classroom?
2. How does a digital camera differ from a film camera? Which do you think would be better for you to use in teaching? Why?
3. How does a graphics tablet (digitizer) work? How might it be used to help you teach and your students learn?
4. For digitized sound to be used in your classroom, what computer input and output components must be available? Describe how you would use each to teach.
5. What is a PDA? Tablet PC? How might you find each useful in your classroom?
6. How does an electronic whiteboard differ from other whiteboards? What is the advantage of using an electronic version?
7. Why are data projection units necessary in a classroom? Describe the different choices available for data projection. Which would you purchase and why?
8. Name some emerging technologies. How might they affect teaching and learning?
9. How do increasing computer power, decreasing size, and wireless communications make technology-enhanced classrooms more flexible?
10. What is a virtual environment? What potential does it hold for education?

WHAT DO YOU THINK?

1. After considering the various types of digital technologies presented in this chapter, what three pieces of equipment do you think you would most want for your future or current classroom? Explain why you selected these three and how you would use them for teaching and learning.
2. Some teachers believe that too much emphasis is placed on computers in the classroom. Considering the computer technology you have learned about in this chapter, do you agree or disagree? Defend your view.

LEARNING TOGETHER!

The following activities are designed for learning groups of two or three students.

1. Imagine that your grade-level team or department has been given a $20,000 grant for adding technology to your classrooms. How would you spend the money to best equip your classrooms for teaching and for learning? Include a budget showing how the money would be spent.
2. Visit a technology-rich classroom and interview the teacher about how he or she uses the technology in place. Compare your interviews with those of the other members of your group and develop your group's ideal classroom. Describe the technologies you would include and how you would plan to use them.
3. Select three different computer systems and compare them using the classroom equipment evaluation rubric in Table 4.1. After discussing the options with your group, describe which system you would buy and explain why. Be prepared to share your preference and your reasons with the class.

E-Learning

CHAPTER 4 Visual Organizer

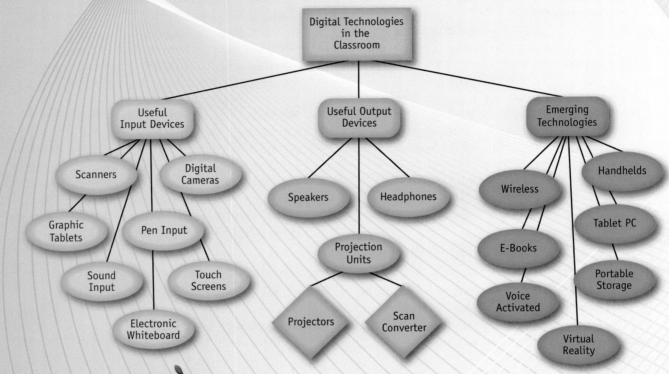

Digital Technologies in the Classroom

- **Useful Input Devices**
  - Scanners
  - Digital Cameras
  - Graphic Tablets
  - Pen Input
  - Sound Input
  - Touch Screens
  - Electronic Whiteboard
- **Useful Output Devices**
  - Speakers
  - Headphones
  - Projection Units
    - Projectors
    - Scan Converter
- **Emerging Technologies**
  - Wireless
  - Handhelds
  - E-Books
  - Tablet PC
  - Voice Activated
  - Portable Storage
  - Virtual Reality

Hardware Skills Builder   www.mylabschool.com

These step-by-step multimedia tutorials teach you to use computer basics and how computer components will be used in your classroom. Each tutorial ends with a review of key concepts.

Podcasts   www.mylabschool.com

Listen to a discussion of some of the best technological cool tools available for teaching and learning. Download the audio discussion to your iPod, computer, or MP3 player.

Software Skills Builder   www.mylabschool.com

These step-by-step illustrated tutorials teach you to use Microsoft Windows and Office on both PC and Mac by preparing documents that will be useful in your classroom.

Video Lab   www.mylabschool.com

Video clips showing how digital technologies can be used in the classroom are available through the **mylabschool** web site. Learning guides for all videos can be found in the text's Learning Guide Supplement.

On the Web! Activities www.ablongman.com/lever-duffy3e

Noted in the margins of the chapter, these activities offer you in-depth experiences in the topics and content presented in the chapter.

Online Practice Test www.ablongman.com/lever-duffy3e

Practice tests offer you an opportunity to test your knowledge and then review the results and send them to your teacher.

Outliner www.ablongman.com/lever-duffy3e

Chapter Outliners are fill-in-the-blank outlines of the main ideas presented in the chapter. Download the outliner and fill it in for an effective chapter study guide.

Power Practices www.ablongman.com/lever-duffy3e

Power Practices are animated tutorials made using Microsoft's presentation software, PowerPoint. This flash card tutorial will help you practice key concepts in the chapter.

Puzzler www.ablongman.com/lever-duffy3e

Puzzlers include content in crossword, word search, and other puzzle formats to help you master chapter content.

Useful Links www.ablongman.com/lever-duffy3e

These links offer you suggestions for expanded online research in the topics presented in the chapter.

INTEGRATION *Ideas*

Digital technologies can enhance teaching and learning in every classroom and in every content area. Whether just a few or many digital components are added, instruction can be enlivened and refreshed with their inclusion. Below are a collection of links to help you explore the integration of some of the most popular digital technologies available into your classroom.

Integrating Digital Imaging Technologies in the Classroom

Picturing Literacy
At Forsythe County, Georgia, schools, picturing literacy has led to a collection of innovative ideas for using digital technologies in a variety of content areas. Visit their web site at **www.forsyth.k12.ga.us/backpack/litpack.htm** to see how to watermark a student's work, create a visual how-to document, capture an historic reenactment, and more.

Say Cheese in the Classroom
Review this online PowerPoint for tips from the Cooperating School Districts' web site on using digital cameras and other imaging resources and for ideas for the creative use of digital resources in the classroom. The PowerPoint can be viewed at **www.csd.org/csdrpdc/metc2006/handouts/Say_Cheese_Madlinger.ppt.**

Integrating Digital Display Technologies in the Classroom

Electronic Whiteboards
The very useful education portal Education World offers information, links, and ideas for using the electronic whiteboard in the classroom. Review the article at **www.education-world.com/a_tech/tech/tech206.shtml.** This comprehensive resource even provides tips for selecting an electronic whiteboard and links to the vendors offering this technology.

Electronic Whiteboards as Assistive Devices
The Resource Materials & Technology Center for the Deaf and Hard of Hearing offers a web site with ideas, suggestions, and information on the use of electronic whiteboards for special needs and other students. Visit the Center's web site at **www.fsdb.k12.fl.us/rmc/tutorials/whiteboards.html.**

Integrating Handheld Devices into the Classroom

Discover Handhelds
This site by Annette Lamb presents the basics of and ideas for using PDAs and other handheld devices in the classroom. Included on the site are links to videos, research, lessons, and information useful to classroom teachers. Explore the possibilities of handheld technology at **http://eduscapes.com/sessions/handhelds/.**

Learning with Handhelds
Intel's web site at **www.intel.com/education/handhelds/index.htm** offers practical information about handheld computers and how to use them for teaching and for administrative tasks. This pragmatic web site offers information and links for the interested teacher.

Integrating Other Digital Technologies into the Classroom

Camera Scope
Visualization tools can help students observe events that are too small, too fast, or too slow to see otherwise. CameraScope is a free software product developed by the Thinking Spaces Tools Initiative for use with digital microscopes and digital cameras. In addition to capturing images, the software lets you collect and transfer data for analysis into an electronic spreadsheet. For more information and to download the beta version go to **http://teacherlink.org/tools/.**

Digital Tablet
The Wacom drawing tablet site presents K–12 lesson ideas for using a digital tablet in the classroom. Visit **www.wacom.com/education/** to view these innovative uses of this versatile device.

Images and Sound
Apple iPhoto, iMovie, and iTunes software can be used to bring social studies, math, language arts, and science to life. To examine innovative lesson plans using Apple's products visit the iLife web site at **http://ali.apple.com/ali_sites/ali/ilife.html.**

Integrating Digital Technologies for Special Needs Students

For an overview of a variety of assistive technologies, the Learning Disabilities Online web site at **www.ldonline.org/article/6380** offers an article entitled *Tech Tools for Students with Learning Disabilities: Infusion into Inclusive Classrooms* featuring links, descriptions, and graphics to help you become familiar with assistive devices.

For these and many more *Integration Ideas* for using digital technology in teaching and learning visit the text web site at **www.ablongman.com/lever-duffy3e.**

The Technology-Rich Classroom

What exactly would the ideal technology-rich classroom look like? Take a look in the table below at one teacher's description of the technology that she would like to have in a middle school classroom. Which of the technologies do you feel are must-have technologies for you? Which would you do without? Are there any that make little difference to you? Enter a checkmark next to each item to develop a profile of your ideal technology-rich classroom.

Check which you prefer.

MY TECHNOLOGY-RICH CLASSROOM SPECIFICATIONS AND RATIONALE	MUST HAVE	DON'T WANT	NO PREFERENCE

Teacher's Computer System:

3-gigahertz CPU: This is enough speed for editing video and graphics, and more than enough for common office tasks. ○ ○ ○

1-GB RAM: I'll need the RAM for multitasking and for graphics and video applications. ○ ○ ○

250-GB hard drive: I'll need a lot of space for multimedia applications, video, and pictures of my classroom activities. ○ ○ ○

DVD+/-RW drive: For reading and backup with any type of optical media, and to create my own instructional DVDs. ○ ○ ○

19" flat-panel monitor: Takes up less desk space, and I need that much viewable space for graphics and video editing programs, which tend to have cluttered interfaces. ○ ○ ○

Six or more USB 2.0 ports: Almost everything connects to USB ports these days. I'll need a lot of them to keep all my high-tech gear connected! ○ ○ ○

Upgraded speaker system: I'll need a relatively loud speaker system so that when I'm using a CD-ROM or DVD for classroom instruction, all the students can hear. ○ ○ ○

Bluetooth connectivity: This new wireless standard for computers will be used for many of my high-tech devices. ○ ○ ○

IEEE-1394 connection (or "Firewire"): I'll need this connection for high-speed access to my digital camcorder. ○ ○ ○

Approximate cost: $900–$1,200

5 Student Computer Systems

3-gigahertz CPU: Going slower here probably wouldn't save me much money, so I wouldn't sacrifice the speed. It would be expensive to update later. ○ ○ ○

512-MB RAM: This is really inexpensive and easy to upgrade later; I'll wait until it looks as though I'll need more. ○ ○ ○

80-GB hard drive: Also easy and inexpensive to upgrade later. There are some good external options that students could share when working on multimedia or video projects. ○ ○ ○

DVD+/-RW drive: This will make sure students can write to whatever media they bring in from home. ○ ○ ○

17" flat-panel monitor: Less expensive than 19" monitor. I'd go to a CRT before going to something smaller than 17" since so many programs require higher resolution than a 15" LCD can display. ○ ○ ○

Check which you prefer.

	MUST HAVE	DON'T WANT	NO PREFERENCE
Six or more USB 2.0 ports: Same as teacher station.	◯	◯	◯
Headphones: This helps keep the noise down when students are working with multimedia applications.	◯	◯	◯
IEEE-1394 Connection (or "Firewire"): They'll need this connection for high-speed access to the digital camcorder for video reports.	◯	◯	◯

Approximate cost: $600–$1,000 each

Printer

Laser printer: I would probably go with an inexpensive laser printer that connects to the network. This is *much* less expensive in the long run than an ink-jet printer, and the whole class can use just one printer. ◯ ◯ ◯

Approximate cost: $400

Video/Data Projector

Ceiling mount data projector: This is one of the most important parts of the whole. It makes my teacher computer a teaching tool rather than administrative. I can download free educational videos, show DVDs, demonstrate how to use software, or share a web site with the whole class. With a VCR attached, I can view TV or our in-school broadcasts. I can also let students present their multimedia projects to the class. ◯ ◯ ◯

Approximate cost: $700

Digital Camera

Five megapixel camera: They're so inexpensive, I would want at least three to capture images of student projects, record short video clips, and to make great decorations with my students for the bulletin board! Make sure they're at least five megapixels for decent prints, and record video with sound if I don't also get a digital camcorder. ◯ ◯ ◯

Approximate cost: $130 each

Scanner

Combination scanner/copier/printer: Another inexpensive way to get student projects and drawings imported to make rich multimedia lessons. Also great for getting images from trips or books to display on my LCD projector. In a pinch I can even use it to make a few copies or as a backup printer. ◯ ◯ ◯

Approximate cost: $150

Handheld Tablet

Bluetooth Tablet: A wireless Bluetooth tablet would let me roam the entire classroom but give me all the functions of an interactive whiteboard. It's great being able to teach "from the board" when I'm in the back of the classroom! It's a whiteboard, remote control mouse, and graphics tablet all in one. ◯ ◯ ◯

Approximate cost: $500

interchapter 4

chapter 5

Administrative Software

This chapter addresses these ISTE *National Educational Technology Standards* for Teachers:

I. TECHNOLOGY OPERATIONS AND CONCEPTS
Teachers demonstrate a sound understanding of technology operations and concepts. Teachers
- **A.** demonstrate introductory knowledge, skills, and understanding of concepts related to technology (as described in the ISTE *National Education Technology Standards* for Students).
- **B.** demonstrate continual growth in technology knowledge and skills to stay abreast of current and emerging technologies.

V. PRODUCTIVITY AND PROFESSIONAL PRACTICE
Teachers use technology to enhance their productivity and professional practice. Teachers
- **A.** use technology resources to engage in ongoing professional development and lifelong learning.
- **B.** continually evaluate and reflect on professional practice to make informed decisions regarding the use of technology in support of student learning.
- **C.** apply technology to increase productivity.
- **D.** use technology to communicate and collaborate with peers, parents, and the larger community in order to nurture student learning.

Imagine that your school district has decided to conduct a districtwide upgrade of technology in the coming year. As a result of this initiative, you have just been given five new computer systems for use in your classroom. The computer-support department tells you that the district will make a variety of administrative software packages available to you. Will you know how to use them? Will you know how to apply them to improve the teaching and learning environment in your classroom?

As you can see, the understanding of computer hardware that you gained from Chapters 3 and 4 is only half the challenge for a computer-using educator. You must be just as competent when it comes to understanding and selecting the software programs that will run on that hardware. This chapter will lead you through an exploration of administrative software and how its types of programs can assist you in your professional responsibilities, from managing your classroom to helping your students learn. It will also help you gain the skills you need to effectively evaluate and select the software that will help you do your job and benefit your students.

In Chapter 5, you will

- Explore the differences between administrative and academic software

- Identify how various types of administrative software can help you be more effective and efficient in carrying out your professional responsibilities

- Examine how the major types of administrative software can be used to enhance the learning environment
- Explore key theoretical frameworks relating to the use of software in teaching and learning
- Investigate and use methods for reviewing and evaluating software so that your technology acquisitions will meet your needs

Real People Real Stories

Meet Brian Moore. Brian is in his first year at his school. He teaches a regular algebra class in addition to his two honors sections. He came in at midyear to replace the former teacher who became an assistant principal. Taking over math classes at midyear meant Brian had an immediate need for organization. He solved this with the use of administrative software.

I teach honors Algebra II in one of five public high schools in our district in Tennessee. Most of my honors students aim for college, and they prefer differentiated instruction. Our school uses block scheduling with four ninety-minute classes per day and the teachers have one of these blocks for their planning time. The school is a Title I school and enrolls over a thousand students in grades 9–12. The area is mostly agricultural, and the parents like to get involved with the school. We have an excellent principal, and the teachers have high morale.

When I took over the classes, I found that the previous teacher kept all of his records on paper, and there was just too much paperwork for me to continue in the same way. I knew that technology could make life simpler if I used the right programs. My first concern was with keeping accurate track of student grades. The problem I encountered was that the electronic gradebook provided for me by the school had limitations. I wanted to be able to have access to it at any time; I needed to be able to modify the layout, size, formulas, and so on; and the provided gradebook's fields were locked, preventing my ability to modify it. Since it was on a network, there were times when it was not available to me.

I also needed to organize my data on my students, that is, names, addresses, phone numbers, contact information, and the like. Information in their files was often dated and had been changed since it was originally entered. I wanted to have current and accurate information that I could easily pull up right when I needed it. We also had to send out attendance logs when students had more than six absences; these students would not receive credit. Two parents to whom I sent out information did not receive it because the addresses in the files were not current. So, if I had my own data, after six absences, I could send the information to the parents and know that it was going to the right address. The problem was that I did not have a database program like Access to use. However, I did have Excel, a spreadsheet program.

In resolving the first problem, the need for a better gradebook, I decided that since I had the MS Excel spreadsheet program available to me, I would design and create my own gradebook. I was able to create fields for my students' names, nicknames, and dates for each item graded, so I could insert their number grade below each date; and I used a formula to add the scores together to provide a column with their mean grades. The second problem was the need for a database for current information on my students. In seeking a way to create a database without having an actual database program available, I hit upon the idea of using my Excel spreadsheet as a substitute database. I set up a new spreadsheet with columns for the students' names, addresses, phone numbers, contact information, date warning letters were sent out, and a column for comments. To be sure that the information was secure, I took two steps. The first was that I saved the information on a floppy disk that I kept with me. In addition, when I got home, I saved a copy to my own hard disk.

When I was working on setting up my Excel gradebook, a colleague helped me adjust the formula so that the lowest grade would automatically be dropped before the mean (the "average") was calculated. I was then able to copy the formula from that cell into the cells for the other students so the same process would be used with all of my students. Then I went on to use Excel to help with my data organization problem. Using the spreadsheet as a database worked well for me. I was able to pull out any contact information that I needed. I could also show the dates I had sent warning letters and the like to parents if a question arose. Using the comments column, I was able to include background information on students, so I had notes about home situations and special requests or needs of students. This was especially helpful in keeping up with special situations.

Teachers always have administrative tasks to perform as a part of their jobs. This one software package, Excel, helped me easily manage two essential tasks, making my professional life easier. It was well worth the time and effort to learn and use this software.

For further information, you may contact Brian at: bmooremath @hotmail.com.

Understanding Software

The knowledge that you gained from Chapters 3 and 4 relating to the use of computer hardware is the first step in a two-step process leading to the computer competencies an educator needs. The second step is to be able to identify, evaluate, and apply computer software to the direct and indirect tasks associated with teaching and learning.

Whether an educator needs to use software as a tool to create a letter to send home to parents or to turn a computer into a tireless student tutor, being able to select and use the best software package for the task is a skill every educator needs. The ability to evaluate software is especially valuable when you are selecting software specifically designed to assist educators. It is the educator's expertise in teaching and in learning that ensures that the programs acquired by a school address the specific, targeted competencies that have been articulated through the instructional design process. Educators must be sufficiently software literate to be able to recommend software that can help their students learn and then be able to serve as guides through the software acquisition and implementation process.

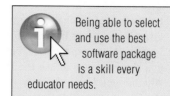

Being able to select and use the best software package is a skill every educator needs.

Educational computer software can be divided into two major categories. The first category is **administrative software,** that is, software that assists an educator in accomplishing the administrative, professional, and management tasks associated with the profession. The second category is **academic software,** or software that assists both educators and learners in the teaching and learning process itself. Both types of software are important tools for educators in helping them work efficiently and effectively as classroom managers and educational professionals. This chapter focuses on the use of administrative software for teacher productivity and for classroom application. Chapter 6 more fully explores academic software.

The vital role of software in education is consistent with the role of software in many other aspects of contemporary life. Few businesses could do without the use of software. Word processing has become as critical a skill as typing once was. Spreadsheets are essential for accounting, budgeting, and other financial tasks. The use of the Internet and its support software for information, sales, and communication is as commonplace as the use of a library or telephone. For teachers, the role of software is no less important for their administrative and academic tasks. Standards, today's measure for effectiveness in education, have even been developed to specifically address the use of software by educators. ISTE's NETS (Appendix 1) emphasize the importance of being able to use software appropriately for teaching, learning, and productivity.

Given the recognized importance of software in education, it becomes necessary for every educator to develop sufficient software literacy, that is, the ability to effectively identify and use appropriate software. To do so, an educator must be able to locate and review software options to select the software package that will accomplish the desired task. Then, you must be able to objectively evaluate the software to see whether it indeed fills your need. Resources for the acquisition of educational technology are typically very limited, and careful purchases will make those limited resources go much further. Once the software has been acquired, you might even need

YOU Decide!

ISTE's NETS-T standard on Productivity and Professional Practice (V) suggests that it is a teacher's responsibility to use technology to enhance his or her productivity. Administrative software is one of the primary tools to accomplish this standard. Most districts use and make available to teachers a suite of productivity tools including a word processor, spreadsheet, database, and presentation tool as well as communications tools such as an email program. Should teachers be required to be knowledgeable in each productivity tool in the suite available to them?

YES! As the NETS-T standard indicates, it is part of a teacher's professional responsibility to be productive and effective, not just in teaching tasks, but also in the administrative tasks expected of him or her. To be productive, you have to learn to use the tools the district provides. Whether you learn the software on your own time or take the in-service training classes the district provides, it is every teacher's job to be familiar with and use the tools available.

NO! A teacher's job is to teach. While everyone has to do administrative tasks, there is no reason these need to be done using technology. Teachers have barely enough time to get lessons together, grade papers, and do the extras the students need to help them learn. There just isn't time to bother with learning other types of software packages that aren't directly related to teaching. Teachers can be just as productive using their own ways of handling administrative tasks. Technology shouldn't be a requirement.

Which view do you agree with? YOU DECIDE!

Administrative software includes productivity and classroom management support software.

E-Learning

www.mylabschool.com
video
View *Tools for Tracking Students*

to install it on the hardware you have available to you. Finally, so that you and your students can get the most out of the software, you will need to become familiar with how it works. If this sounds like a somewhat time-consuming process, that is because software evaluation, acquisition, installation, and training are indeed extensive tasks. The up-front investment of time and energy in this process, however, will make the difference between the acquisition of valuable educational tools and the purchase of software that looked good on first inspection but ended up gathering dust in a storage closet.

To begin the exploration of software, we will first examine administrative software, the programs you might use in accomplishing tasks associated with your teaching and professional responsibilities as well as classroom management. Administrative software can be divided into two general software types (see Table 5.1). These are productivity software and school and/or classroom management software. **Productivity software** is typically generic business-application software that educators can use and adapt for the administrative and professional tasks they must address. Word processing, spreadsheet, and database management software are all examples of productivity software. In contrast, **classroom management software** is usually customized software written for educators to help them manage school and classroom tasks, including the creation and maintenance of seating charts, class rolls, student records, or school budgets.

All these administrative software tools help educators do their jobs more effectively and productively. Because a fairly significant time investment is involved in finding, installing, and learning software, you should be cautious

TABLE 5.1   Administrative Software for Educators

SOFTWARE TYPE	ADMINISTRATIVE TASKS	PROFESSIONAL TASKS	TEACHING AND LEARNING TASKS
PRODUCTIVITY SOFTWARE	Assists educators in preparing memos, letters, reports, and budgets	Assists educators in tracking student information, computing grades, and preparing lesson plans and IEPs	Helps educators create student activity sheets, transparencies, grade reports, and parent letters
CLASSROOM MANAGEMENT SOFTWARE	*FOR DISTRICTS AND SCHOOLS*		
	Assists educators in reporting required student information	Assists educators in gathering data for student reports	Assists educators in gathering data for academic decision making
	FOR CLASSROOM		
	Helps educators prepare required reports	Assists educators in tracking and reporting grades; helps create seating charts, rolls, and other classroom tasks	Assists educators in analyzing grade and student data for better academic decision making

in your selections. That is the reason software evaluation skills are so important for computer-using educators. This chapter includes evaluation rubrics to assist you in this critical process.

Administrative software can be purchased as an off-the-shelf commercial package or as a custom-made program, or it can be acquired as freeware or shareware. **Freeware** is software that is offered to users without charge; **shareware** is software that is offered to users for a small fee or for a limited time and is sometimes paid for on the honor system after you have had a chance to try out the software and determine whether it is useful for you. Freeware and shareware present a great temptation for educators on a very constricted budget. Even though many fine administrative software tools are offered as freeware or shareware, they too must be carefully evaluated. Low-cost or no-cost software still costs you the time and effort it takes to install and learn the software. When making software decisions, it is useful to complete a rubric like those included later in this chapter (Tables 5.7 and 5.8) comparing products to determine the features and value of each program you plan to purchase. Rubrics help you to objectively determine the effectiveness of the software. Freeware and shareware can be found on many education sites on the Internet, often along with some annotation or review of the software's quality.

Freely distributed software can be either freeware or shareware.

Evaluating and Using Productivity Software

www.mylabschool.com
Software Skills Builder
Office Tools and Tips

> Most productivity software packages include a word processor, electronic spreadsheet, database management system, and presentation software.

Much of an educator's time is consumed in completing the many administrative tasks necessary to prepare and maintain an effective learning environment and to meet the record-keeping demands of the typical school system. The office productivity software that has facilitated business operations can frequently serve educators equally well for their administrative educational tasks. Such software is typically designed for ease of use, with each application performing a specific function for the user. And, although created for different purposes, productivity software programs often have a similar look and feel so that it is easy to learn one type of software and then apply the same skills to learning another software package produced by the same vendor. At mylabschool.com, you may want to try the *Office Tools and Tips* Skill Builder activity to experience the format and skills associated with one of the most common types of productivity software groups, Microsoft Office.

The four major types of productivity software found in most business environments are word processors, electronic spreadsheets, database management systems, and presentation software. These types of software can be purchased in individual packages or in application suites and are designed to run on either a PC or Macintosh platform. Often, a school system will equip the administrative component of its operation with productivity software, which teachers can adapt to address educational tasks. The district will often purchase a **site license,** that is, a license that allows the use of a software package on all machines at locations within one organization. The acquisition by district or school computing departments of a site license for productivity software for administrative purposes can benefit the educational staff as well. Although individual educators may have little choice in what productivity software is available to them, with a bit of creativity that software can be applied to myriad teaching and professional tasks. Office productivity software, used in the classroom or other academic spaces such as the media center or faculty workroom, can be a great asset to busy educators. The computer-using educator's job is to learn to use the software and apply it to the many nonteaching tasks for which he or she is responsible. Let's look at the characteristics of the "big four" applications (word processing, spreadsheets, database management, and presentation software) that are included in office software suites and explore how educators can use each of them (see Table 5.2).

Word Processors

Word-processing software is the most commonly used computer application. Computers loaded with word-processing software have all but replaced typewriters for text-oriented tasks, although the typewriter still has a niche in the completion of noncomputerized forms. Today's word processors, however, are capable of doing far more than even the most advanced electronic typewriter. In addition to creating, editing, and printing documents, these software packages are capable of desktop publishing, creating

TABLE 5.2 Productivity Software Summary

SOFTWARE TYPE	APPLICATION TO ADMINISTRATIVE/PROFESSIONAL TASKS	APPLICATION TO TEACHING AND LEARNING TASKS
WORD PROCESSING	Prepare letters, memos, reports, flyers, rubrics, lesson plans, forms, and newsletters	Prepare transparencies, activity sheets, posters, study guides, and class notes; help students prepare stories, essays, and group reports; use in class to dynamically illustrate writing and outlining skills
ELECTRONIC SPREADSHEETS	Prepare budgets, numeric tables and summaries, and grade and attendance rosters; compute grades; prepare visuals (charts) of numeric data	Provide students with a method for tracking and analyzing data and creating charts from it; demonstrate what-if analyses visually; support student research such as tracking stock market data
DATABASE MANAGEMENT SYSTEMS	Organize and track student and other professional data; prepare inventories, mailing lists, and reports	Organize and provide easy access to lists of academic resources; provide support for students' tracking data; extract and report targeted summaries of content or resources to address student needs
PRESENTATION SOFTWARE	Create presentations for workshops, conferences, and meetings	Create class lecture support that features text, audio, and visual elements with special effects; produce transparency masters; create student worksheets to accompany class lectures

and editing graphics, and developing web pages. Combined with a relatively inexpensive color ink jet printer, word-processing software packages are also powerful tools for creating full-color transparencies, classroom signs and posters, customized certificates and awards, and even personalized stickers and buttons (see Figure 5.1). Of course, they are also essential tools for creating tests, student worksheets, and memos.

Unlike most typewriters, word-processing programs maintain large amounts of data in an electronic format until it is ready to print out. This allows educators to store and easily update or modify the many documents they use in the daily administrative tasks that are a part of every educator's job. Word processing offers educators a way to easily file and access electronic documents and then to modify and update them with little effort. Furthermore, word processors typically include a built-in capacity to check grammar and spelling and an interactive thesaurus, all of which make this software application a valuable tool for every educator.

Most word-processing packages share several significant and useful features. These can be broadly grouped in terms of the word-processing functions they enhance. These functions include document preparation and editing, desktop publishing, and archiving and printing.

At mylabschool.com, each of these functions is explored. As you try each of the word-processing exercises, you will experience and practice the unique and powerful functions built into one of today's most popular word processors, Microsoft Word.

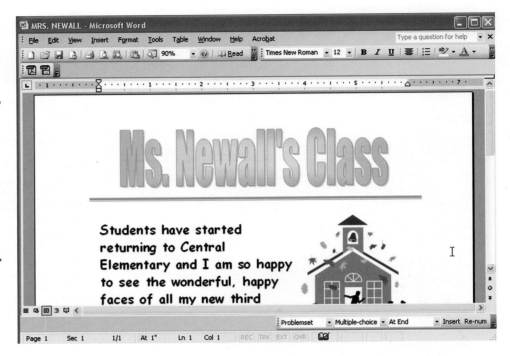

FIGURE 5.1

Word Processing in the Classroom

Word processors can create flyers and transparency masters in addition to text documents.

Microsoft Word® is a registered trademark of Microsoft Corporation.

E-Learning

www.mylabschool.com
Software Skills Builder
Word Skills–Bake Sale Flyer

Document Preparation and Editing

Document preparation is the most common use of word-processing software. This function enables the user to type data into the software and then edit the data while they are still in the electronic format. Error correction, adjustments to the document's text, and experimentation with different fonts and formats can be completed before the document is printed on paper (that is, in a hard copy). Editing features may vary with the complexity of the word-processing software, but all word processors include the following key features. You will practice using many of them when you try the Word Skills Builder, *Bake Sale Flyer* activity accessible through mylabschool.com.

- *Insertion and Deletion of Text.* The cursor, or insertion point, that is displayed on the word-processing screen indicates the point at which text will be entered. As a document is created, the cursor typically stays at the end of the data and moves along as additional text is entered. By using the computer's mouse or arrow keys, the user can move the cursor back or forward to any point in the body of the document. By positioning the cursor at a targeted spot in the document, you can either insert additional text by typing it in at the cursor position or remove unwanted text by pressing the Backspace or Delete key on the computer keyboard.

- *Text Selection and Enhancement.* Once a document has been entered, specific letters, words, paragraphs, lines, or whole pages can be selected. Text selection is accomplished by using the mouse to point to the desired text and then dragging the cursor across it. The selected material will be highlighted in reverse color. Once text is selected, the word processor is ready to apply subsequent commands to that portion of the text only. Enhancement commands include changing the type size or font used or adding visual augmentation, such as changing normal text

TECHNOLOGY SOLUTIONS *for All Learners*

Productivity Software Features for Special Needs Students

Microsoft Word and Windows XP have several built-in features that can be useful as assistive devices for special needs learners. When preparing a document for your learners, it is a good idea to be sure to make the document as flexible and accessible as possible. There are many techniques for doing so, including using settings like high contrast and the Microsoft Magnifier for sight–impaired students, altering pointer and mouse controls for physically impaired students, and using sound control options including the Text-to-Speech option described below for hearing-impaired students.

A document you create for your students can be read to them as well as displayed using the Text-to-Speech option. To use this option, after creating the document, click on Tools from the menu bar and select the Speech option. Using the computer voice style and reading speed you can select via the Speech icon in the control panel, your students can listen as well as see the information you present in your Word document. You can also record, store, and play back voice annotations in Word documents if you want to add audio information to your text.

For more information and tutorials in making Word and other Office products accessible for special needs students, visit Microsoft's Accessibility web site at **www.microsoft.com/enable/products/windowsxp/default.aspx**.

---

to bold, italics, or underlined text. After selecting text, enhancing it is typically a matter of pointing and clicking on the software button representing the enhancement desired or using a keyboard command.

- *Word Wrap and Formatting.* When you type on a traditional typewriter, it is necessary to move the paper carriage back to its start position and down one line after completing each line of type. Word processors eliminate this step with their word wrap feature. With word wrap, when the text reaches the end of the line, the software automatically moves down to the beginning of the next line in preparation for additional input. If a word does not quite fit on a line, the software will recognize this and move it down to become the first word on the next line. This feature is especially useful when you decide to insert additional text. The software makes room for the inserted text by wrapping all subsequent lines down the page. Page formatting features allow you to change the look of the page, such as changing margins, adding headers and footers, or altering line spacing on all or part of the document. Such page changes may cause the text in any given line to move. The word wrap feature will once again automatically adjust the text and line length to accommodate such formatting changes.

- *Spelling and Grammar Tools.* The most popular of the common word-processing features include built-in spell-checker, grammar checker, and thesaurus. The spell-checker will check spelling word by word against a built-in dictionary of thousands of words and suggest alternatives to words it does not recognize. This same dictionary can be used as a thesaurus to provide both synonyms and antonyms of selected words. Finally, the software is created with recognition of proper grammar and sentence construction. The software can check a document and find sentences that are questionable grammatically and make suggestions for alternative sentence construction.

- *Copy, Cut, Paste, Drag, and Undo.* Editing functions in word processors provide the user with the ability to select letters, words, or blocks of text and then remove them from the document or move them to a different

COOL TOOLS

Clip Art

Microsoft Word in-cludes a large library of clip art images for use in illustrating documents for your students. But beyond the images that come with Word, you can tap into an expansive and ever-changing library online. Microsoft's online clip art and media web site at **http://office.microsoft.com/clipart** offers you clip art, animation, and photos that you can download for free. It also provides templates for specialty docu-ments such as banners and greeting cards for special occasions as well as tips on how to use and edit im-ages. Teachers are always looking for the right image to illustrate the concept they are teaching or to com-municate an idea. Word's clip art library offers thou-sands of useful images. Microsoft's clip art and media web site adds many thousands more. The only diffi-culty in using this cool tool is picking the image you like the best.

location within the document. The *copy* feature creates a duplicate ver-sion of the selected text, which can be *pasted* elsewhere. The *cut* feature removes a block of text from its original location permanently. The ma-terial can then be pasted into another location. Some word processors have combined a cut-and-paste function into a single feature called *drag and drop.* This feature allows you to select text anywhere in the docu-ment and, using the mouse, drag and drop it anywhere else in the docu-ment. Finally, the *undo* feature provides a safety net against mistakes. It allows the user to back up and undo the last several actions.

Desktop Publishing

Most word processors include the ability to manipulate the look of a page. By using this feature, an attractive arrangement of graphics and text on a page can be created and manipulated with a few clicks of the mouse button. Although word processors can perform some desktop publishing tasks, they cannot perform the extensive adjustments to page displays that dedicated desktop publishing software can make. The basic desktop publishing capa-bilities included in most word processors are summarized here:

- *WYSIWYG Displays.* Word processors are able to display a document on the screen in a "what you see is what you get" **(WYSIWYG)** format. This feature allows the user to preview a document and see exactly what it will look like before it is printed out.
- *Graphics and Clip Art.* Most word processors today include rudimen-tary graphics capabilities that allow you to add and position a drawing on a document page. The creation of a complex or custom graphic is typically done with dedicated graphics programs, but most word processors include a library of clip art (ready-made artwork) that can be inserted into a document. Additional clip art can usually be added to the word-processing clip art library. The size and position of this art-work can then be changed, thus adding interest to an all-text document.
- *Tables and Columns.* Text data can easily be arranged into multiple columns of data per page or into a table or grid. These word-processing

E-Learning

www.mylabschool.com
Software Skills Builder
Word Skills–Behavior Tracker

features give the user the ability to organize data, with just a few clicks of the mouse, into something other than a narrative. Once the data is in table or column form, all of the typical text enhancements can be applied.

- *Autoformats.* Tables, columns, and documents can be formatted in many different ways. Borders can be added, titles can be enhanced, and graphics can be placed in any type of document. For users who do not have the time or experience to experiment with formats, many word processors include an autoformat feature. This feature lets you preview the look of various styles that can be applied to a document and then select the one you like best to use with your document. Once selected, the format is automatically applied to the entire document under construction.

- *Word Art.* A fairly recent addition to word processors' publishing features is the ability to create fancy, colorful titles. This word art feature offers you the ability to add color, shapes, and styles to a document's title or to make sections of your document stand out.

Today's word-processing packages can create and edit documents, complete desktop publishing tasks, and develop web pages.

Archiving and Printing

Once a document is completed, word processors provide the ability to save the document in numerous formats and to print it out in black and white or color, depending on the available printers. Archiving or storing a document to a removable drive or hard disk stores the text you typed, along with all of its related formatting commands, in a single word-processor file.

The final feature shared by all word processors is the ability to print documents. One of the sets of word-processing codes saved with every document is information about the type of printer to be used to print the document out. Because a number of types of printers are available, the printer that is set up as the default printer for the word processor will be used automatically unless you instruct the program to do otherwise. Some formatting features may change when printer defaults change, thus unexpectedly changing the way your document looks. It is therefore important to save your document with the appropriate printer settings to avoid such conflicts. Of course, as you learned in Chapter 3, printers can just as easily output crisp laser copies as they can colorful transparencies, depending on the specific capabilities of the hardware.

Tech Tips for TEACHERS

When you save a word document you are creating, the file will include the text you type in as well as formatting codes. Every word processor saves these unique codes within the file so that when you open the file at a later date, it looks exactly like the one you saved. However, these codes can become a problem when you open a document using a word processing software package different from the word processor originally used to create the document. When trying to open the file, you may find the document unreadable or containing many extraneous characters.

Word includes a translator feature that will automatically translate document codes from most other word processors so that they may be opened by Word. However, not all word processors do. If you are unsure of the software that will be used to open a document you are creating in Word, it is a good idea to save the document in a more universal format. When saving the document, select Save As, and in the dialog box that appears, note that you can save a file as various types including text and rich text formats. These formats can be opened by any word processing software and may therefore be the best choice for documents you create for use outside of your classroom.

Ready-Made Word-Processing Tools

Because word processors are such commonly used tools in education, educators have developed many documents, templates, and macros. **Templates**

in the Classroom

WORD PROCESSING IN MIDDLE SCHOOL

IN ENGLISH CLASS

Pamela D. Laurenzi, an English teacher at Houston Middle School in Germantown, Tennessee, has her students who are learning about poetry use word-processing software to create a poetry anthology that gives definitions of common poetic terms. The poems selected by the students are copied and pasted from the Internet into the document, along with poems they have written. Each poem is accompanied by a word-processed paragraph that tells why the particular poem was selected. The poems are illustrated using the Paint program. With the Draw program, the students complete the publishing cycle by creating a folded minibook.

IN MATH CLASS

Charlotte Moore, a Booneville (Mississippi) Middle School math teacher, combined word processing with Microsoft Publisher to teach a cross-disciplinary activity to "research and organize data about the Civil War." After finishing web-based research, the students created a calendar depicting events that took place during one month. Ms. Moore describes the activity for teachers to emulate if they wish:

They will list each event by month, day, and year on a one-month calendar of their own creation. The students work in small groups of two to four based on class size and the number of computers available for use. Calendar listings will be color coded so that the reader will have visual cues related to the sequence of events during the war. After their one-month calendars have been completed, each group will give a presentation of their findings to the class.

Ms. Moore prepared four handouts to guide students through each step. The procedures are given for the teacher's responsibilities and for the activities the students will carry out. These instructions are listed numerically; for example, on the list of tasks, the students will

5. Develop math word problems based on the data they encounter as they search for important events. Record the problems on Handout 3: Math Word Problems Related to the Civil War. Each student should create one problem that relates to the data for the month.

Laurenzi, P. D. (2000, March 2). The power of poetry. Retrieved June 12, 2004, from **www.teachers.net/ lessons/posts/1607.html.**

Moore, C. (2004). Calendar creations about the Civil War. Retrieved October 11, 2004, from **www.create.cett .msstate.edu/Create/classroom/lplan_printer. asp?articleID=14.**

E-Learning

www.mylabschool.com
Software Skills Builder
Word Skills–Rubrics

are documents that are preformatted for a specific use but contain no data. An example of a template might be a meeting announcement flyer. To use it, you would open the template with your word processor to find a fully laid-out flyer. With this premade document open, you would only need to type in your organization's name and the date and time of your meeting. You can also create templates for your own future use. When you complete the Word Skills Builder, *Rubric Template*, you will be creating a template you can use in your classroom.

You can also modify a template further if you want to. A word-processing **macro** is a prerecorded set of commands for your word processor that automates a complex task such as formatting output to fit on labels. Macros are stored in files that can be retrieved and activated with a few keystrokes. An example of a macro might be a file that automatically sets up the official school letterhead using the school's logo and name. Very often, such predesigned templates and macros are freely shared among educators across the Internet.

A final tool built into most word processors is a **wizard.** A wizard is a mini-program that creates a customized template for you. It asks a series of questions about the format you desire for your document and then creates a custom template as you respond to each question. Wizards will help you create sophisticated documents without having to know how to issue complex formatting commands.

Templates, macros, and wizards can facilitate complex word-processing tasks.

Word Processors in the Classroom

Word processors offer great promise as a teaching tool as well as a productivity tool for busy educators. The same features that facilitate the creation of memos and tests can be creatively applied to teaching and learning. The application of these features to teaching and learning is summarized in Table 5.3. There are numerous examples of the creative ways in which teachers have applied the same word-processing software they use for productivity tasks to teaching and learning as well. Teachers use word processors to make calendars, publish class books of poetry, create newsletters, prepare flyers, make class stationery, and even author classroom web sites. The In the Classroom feature on page 176 features just a few innovative teacher-developed applications of this common productivity software. Many more can be found in an exploration of the Web and through On the Web! Activity 5.1.

E-Learning
ON THE WEB! 5.1

How Can Teachers Use Word Processing for Teaching and Learning?

TABLE 5.3	Word Processing in Teaching and Learning	
WORD-PROCESSING FEATURE	APPLICATION TO ADMINISTRATIVE/PROFESSIONAL TASKS	APPLICATION TO TEACHING AND LEARNING TASKS
DOCUMENT PREPARATION	Provides capabilities to • Enter documents • Edit documents • Format documents • Correct grammar and spelling • Enhance with graphics • Print color and black and white	Allows students to • Create organized documents • Edit errors easily • Add graphics and enhanced text elements • Print draft copies for review and proofreading • Finalize, correct, and print final copies
DESKTOP PUBLISHING	Provides or lets you create formats for • Forms • Flyers • Invitations • Newsletters	Provides students with a tool for preparing • Creative presentation of text • Alternative report formats (newsletter, comics, minibooks) • Supports for oral reports
FORMATTING	Lets you adjust documents for • Professional appearance • Emphasis on key points • Consistency of appearance • Letterhead and memo styles	Students can • Experiment with formats for best presentation Teachers can • Create appealing documents for their students • Alter documents to meet specific learning needs

continued ➤

GRAMMAR CHECKING	Helps to ensure that documents are grammatically correct	Assists students in • Proofreading and correcting their work • Practicing the application of grammatical rules Assists teachers in • Demonstrating grammar corrections in real time • Helping students find and correct grammatical errors
SPELL-CHECKING	Helps to ensure that documents are free from spelling errors	Assists students in • Proofreading and correcting their work • Practicing correct spelling Assists teachers in • Demonstrating spelling corrections in real time • Helping students find and correct spelling errors
MAIL MERGE	Provides an easy way to make form letters personal	Can be used by teachers to individualize reports to students and letters to parents
TABLES	Provides tools to present information professionally, concisely, and clearly in an organized format	Assist students in • Organizing data • Presenting data clearly • Summarizing key data Assist teachers in • Creating clear summaries for study guides • Displaying organized data in support of presentation • Teaching interpretation of data
WEB FORMAT	Converts files from documents to web format so that they can be easily added to web sites	Allows students and teachers to create documents and save them in Web format for display on a class web site without knowing any HTML
ARCHIVING	Provides an inexpensive and easy-to-access archive system for documents	• Saved teacher data files are easy to access and update to keep lessons current and available • Students can save files for later work or find and reprint lost hard copies • Archived files can easily be added to electronic portfolios

Electronic Spreadsheets

Electronic spreadsheet software is to numeric data what word-processing software is to text. With an **electronic spreadsheet,** you can organize, input, edit, and chart data, and produce accurate professional reports for any administrative task that deals extensively with numbers. Spreadsheet software not only allows you to organize numeric information but also has built-in mathematical and statistical formulas that can be applied to the data with just a few clicks of the mouse button. With a spreadsheet, budgets can be easily developed and modified, grades can be tracked and averaged, and class statistical information can be extracted. Furthermore, most spreadsheets include built-in graphing capabilities that can turn numeric data into colorful, three-dimensional charts that will visually illustrate numeric relationships.

One of the key advantages of electronic spreadsheets over their manual counterparts is in their accuracy. Given accurate data, a spreadsheet will always produce accurate results. A second advantage is the fact that spreadsheets can be modified easily. Consider as an example the grade-level media budget pictured in Figure 5.2. If it had been done manually and the cost of printer cartridges turned out to be $10 instead of the budgeted $8, you would have to erase and recalculate a number of different entries on the spreadsheet. With an electronic spreadsheet, however, you would need to type in only the new value, and all the other entries associated with that value would be automatically recalculated. This time-saving feature makes electronic spreadsheets easier to use, less time consuming, and far more accurate than doing the calculations manually.

Several software vendors produce electronic spreadsheet programs. Some of these, such as Microsoft Excel, are powerful, business-oriented software packages that have numerous features. Others are for home or general consumer use, such as the spreadsheet component of AppleWorks, ClarisWorks, or Microsoft Works. Regardless of the capabilities of any given spreadsheet package, they all have a full range of common features.

At mylabschool.com, there is material that demonstrates and provides you practice with Excel, one of the most common of all electronic spreadsheets. When you try the Excel Skills Builders, you will have an opportunity to see firsthand how the features of this useful tool can be applied in your classroom for both administrative and academic tasks.

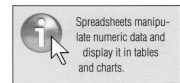
Spreadsheets manipulate numeric data and display it in tables and charts.

Spreadsheet Organization

Electronic spreadsheets, like their paper counterparts, organize data into vertical columns and horizontal rows. The user then types in alphabetic or numeric data in the appropriate locations. This organizational structure provides the framework for lining up and clearly labeling numeric information.

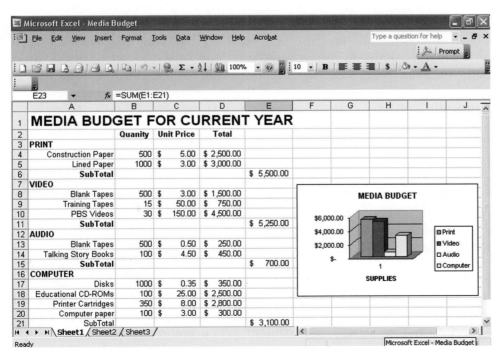

FIGURE 5.2

Electronic Spreadsheet Application

Spreadsheet software is a useful tool in maintaining school budgets.

Microsoft Excel® is a registered trademark of Microsoft Corporation.

E-Learning

www.mylabschool.com
Software Skills Builder
Excel Skills–Club Budget

The intersections of spreadsheet rows and columns are called cells. It is in the nature and use of these cells that electronic spreadsheets have great advantage over their manual counterparts. Each cell of a spreadsheet can contain text, values, or a formula. This variety of cell content can be seen in Figure 5.2. The cells in column A all contain text labels, and the cells in column B all contain data representing budget amounts. The cells in columns C through E contain labels, values, subtotals, or totals. Column D's cells do not contain totals calculated by hand and then typed in. Instead, they contain instructions to the spreadsheet software directing it to perform a mathematical calculation—in this case, multiplying the data entered in columns B and C.

This independent data-handling capability of each spreadsheet cell makes it a quick and easy task to alter or correct the data entered. Furthermore, once a single cell's data have been changed, that change will be reflected in all cells that use those data for a calculation. Thus, if the budget amount for lined paper in Figure 5.2 is changed, the print media subtotal will also be changed, as will all other related totals. This automatic recalculation feature is one of the key reasons why spreadsheets have become as popular a tool for handling numbers as word-processing software has become for handling text.

Formulas and Functions

As in all math, formulas are used in a spreadsheet to indicate the types of calculations that should be performed to achieve a specific outcome. The cells that contain instructions that tell the software to perform specific mathematical activities may, in fact, contain detailed formulas that the user has typed in. In addition to user-entered formulas, most spreadsheets contain hundreds of stored, premade formulas that the user can easily place into a cell. These range from formulas appropriate to finance and statistics to those necessary for trigonometry. These built-in formulas make it particularly easy to direct the spreadsheet software to perform complex mathematical tasks without the user having to remember the specific syntax of mathematical expressions. You will practice using formulas and functions in the Excel Skills Builder activity, *Club Budget,* at mylabschool.com. Once you are comfortable with the software, you will find electronic spreadsheets to be powerful and useful tools.

What-If Analysis

Spreadsheets offer a what-if feature for decision making.

Perhaps the most intriguing feature of an electronic spreadsheet is its ability to perform **what-if analysis.** Because some cells contain the mathematical results of the data in other cells, changes to those data can be immediately reflected in the product. For example, a teacher who is using a spreadsheet to compute grades will have entered not only student grade data but also the formula needed to reflect how those grades will be averaged or weighted. So if a student wanted to know what his or her average would be if the score on the next test were 100 percent, the teacher could enter the hypothetical 100 percent into the spreadsheet, and the student could see the result in terms of a final grade computation. This is a what-if analysis; that is, what if the student gets a grade of 100 percent—how will that affect the outcome? This is a valuable tool for both business and education. Some educators have students keep spreadsheets of their own grades to motivate their achievement and to stay aware of their grade in a course.

Charts and Graphs

Another useful feature of almost all spreadsheet software is the ability to turn the data that have been entered into rows and columns into its graphic counterpart. The graphing (also called charting) function allows the user to select specific cells, and the software will automatically turn the data in those cells into an accurate graph in any number of formats from line, to bar, to pie charts. Some spreadsheet software even adds the ability to graph in color and three-dimensional shapes. For professional-looking displays and to assist visual learners, this spreadsheet tool is extremely useful. The *Student Measurement* Skills Builder activity at mylabschool.com will demonstrate the instructional power of this feature.

www.mylabschool.com
Software Skills Builder
Excel Skills–Student Measurement Activity

Templates and Macros

Like word-processing software, spreadsheet software makes use of templates and macros, allowing the user to create and reuse useful spreadsheet formats and commands. Spreadsheet templates and macros can also be found as shareware or freeware at numerous educational web sites. You can also create your own spreadsheet templates. Try the Excel Skills Builder activity *Grade Keeper*, at mylabschool.com, to experience this feature.

www.mylabschool.com
Software Skills Builder
Excel Skills–Grade Keeper

Electronic Spreadsheets in the Classroom

Table 5.4 shows how many of a spreadsheet's key features can be used both administratively and in teaching and learning. Just as word-processing software can be repurposed for academic projects, so too can spreadsheet software. Whether a teacher uses a spreadsheet to track grades or a student uses a spreadsheet to collect and record data from an experiment, this software provides a wealth of possibilities to the creative teacher. See the In the Classroom feature on page 183 for just a few of the many creative activities that educators around the country have developed for using this software. Many more ideas are shared on the Web. Try On the Web! Activity 5.2 to discover even more creative adaptations of spreadsheet software.

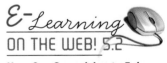

How Can Spreadsheets Enhance Teaching and Learning?

Database Management Software

Every educator's job includes the cumbersome tasks of organizing, maintaining, and retrieving many types of data. Whether it is a student's home phone number or a school district's targeted language arts objectives for the sixth grade, educators must be able to easily and quickly gain access to and extract the information they need. The productivity software that accomplishes this type of task electronically is called a database management system.

TABLE 5.4 Electronic Spreadsheets in Teaching and Learning

SPREADSHEET FEATURE	APPLICATION TO ADMINISTRATIVE/PROFESSIONAL TASKS	APPLICATION TO TEACHING AND LEARNING TASKS
SPREADSHEETS AND WORKBOOKS	Allow for the preparation and display of clearly organized numerical data on individual spreadsheets and in workbooks or related spreadsheets	Assist students in • Organizing numerical data • Creating and testing formulas • Formatting data to produce clear and concise reports Assist teachers in • Organizing and reporting numerical data • Creating customized gradebooks • Tracking student data • Presenting clear reports
AUTO FORMATTING	Provides premade formats to give a spreadsheet a distinct professional appearance	Teachers and students can create appealing, professional-looking spreadsheet reports
CHARTING	Provides easy-to-use tools for visual displays of numeric data	Provides students with • A tool for visual presentation in student reports • A tool to view saved data visually for better understanding • A way to visually explore alterations of the numeric data stored in the spreadsheet Provides teachers with • A tool for preparing visual reports of abstract mathematical relationships • A presentation tool to demonstrate numeric data visually
FORMULAS AND FUNCTIONS	Assist in preparing accurate calculations that will automatically adjust to changes in data	Help students • Create and test formulas • See changes in mathematical relationships as data changes Help teachers • Demonstrate mathematical concepts in action • Test and use appropriate grading formulas • Demonstrate to students how final grades are calculated
WHAT-IF ANALYSIS	Allows for the real-time demonstration of the impact of changes in data; e.g., budgeted amounts can be tested for different results	Assists students in • Seeing the impact of data changes on outcomes in mathematical scenarios • Testing relationships and outcomes by manipulating data Assists teachers in • Demonstrating changes and their impact on the results • Explaining how different test grades will affect a student's final grade
ARCHIVING	Provides an inexpensive and easy way to store and access worksheets for budgets and other numeric files	Saved data files are easy to access and update to keep records current; students using spreadsheets for math practice can retrieve as needed

in the Classroom

SPREADSHEETS

IN THE SECONDARY BUSINESS CLASS

David Messina, business teacher at Reagan High School in Houston, Texas, introduces a lesson on Microsoft Excel's spreadsheet software:

Some of you will go to college, others will go straight into the workforce, and some will enter the military. It is important to see what opportunities will await you. The following assignment will provide you with the opportunity to see how much money you will potentially earn and how much it will cost you to live in various cities. You will find that you pay different taxes in different states. You will discover how the cost of living can vary.

He narrows the focus by telling them that working in groups they will have access to information to be placed into a spreadsheet. To begin, they are directed to the Occupational Outlook web site where they will find the entry-level salary in a career of their choice. Given a list of 16 cities, the students select five to compare the cost of living with that in Houston. Moving to the third section of the assignment, the students determine the tax rate for the states; and going to the Paycheck City web site, they estimate their net pay for each city. With all the data before them, Mr. Messina informs them:

In your groups, discuss and decide on a format that incorporates all the information you have gathered into a spreadsheet. You must create column headings for salary,

gross salary, the different taxes, cost of living, and other important information you have found. Your spreadsheet must contain at least three formulas. Use the information you have found to create possible formulas.

Finally, they write up an analysis of their findings by comparing and contrasting "different costs of living and tax rates from different states."

IN THE ELEMENTARY CLASS

Gayle Ryan, an elementary school teacher in the Chicago public schools, has shown that even the students in her K–2 classes can work with spreadsheets. They learn to use Microsoft Excel "to chart individual math totals," she explains. They measure their heights in inches and write the numbers on paper. Next, they "type the height in inches by their name on an Excel chart." She shows them "how to highlight the data and click the Chart Icon." Each student then receives a copy of the chart to take home. The chart allows them to visualize the range of heights in their class. Ms. Ryan assigns a follow-up activity for the students to "measure different objects in the classroom and around the school building and chart the heights on Excel." For homework, they "measure" objects at home and "bring the data in inches to school to chart on Excel."

Messina, D. (2003, January 24). Building your future. Retrieved August 12, 2004, from **www.teachers.net/ lessons/posts/2800.html.**

Ryan, G. Charting heights on Excel. Retrieved July 18, 2005, from **www.cps.k12.il.us.**

Database management software offers educators an easy-to-use system for creating customized records to contain data, retrieving targeted records, updating and editing the information in those records, and then organizing clear and accurate reports from the data (see Figure 5.3). Furthermore, database software allows you to sort all your data automatically at the touch of a key or to query the database for a match to any single word or phrase. Considering the amount of information an educator must deal with, database management software offers many advantages over manual filing systems.

An electronic card catalog in a media center library is one example of the advantage of database management systems over manual systems. Consider for a moment the complexity of cataloging or locating a book using a manual system. In manual cataloging, a book must be cross-referenced on at least three different index cards under title, author, and subject. All of

 Database management software can organize, sort, retrieve, and report data.

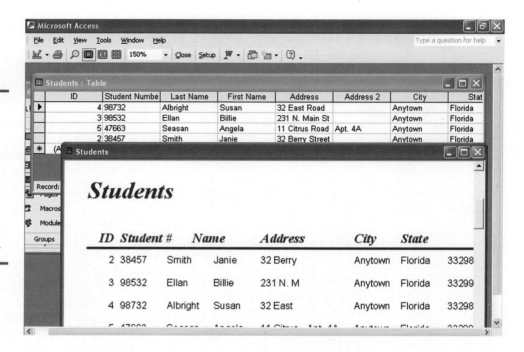

FIGURE 5.3

Using a Database Management System for Student Data

Database management software helps teachers organize student information.

Microsoft Access® is a registered trademark of Microsoft Corporation.

E-Learning

www.mylabschool.com
Software Skills Builder
Access Skills–Department Inventory

these must be typed out and manually sorted and filed. To find the book, the card catalog user must look through drawers full of cards until just the right card is located. For both the media specialist and the library patron, the process can be laborious. With an electronic card catalog that is a dedicated database management system of the library collections, the process is much simplified.

All database management software contains key features to make the organization and manipulation of data easy. These key features are summarized in Table 5.5. Of course database management software packages vary significantly in the extent to which they can perform these functions, and powerful business database systems offer many additional features.

At mylabschool.com, you will find activities that demonstrate and provide you practice with Access, Microsoft's popular and powerful database management software. When you try the Access Skills Builders, you will have an opportunity to experience how the features of this powerful business tool can also be creatively applied in your classroom to your administrative and academic tasks.

Database Organization

In database management systems, a field is the electronic storage location in which a specific type of data is stored. In our library example, a field might contain an author's last name in a Last Name field. A record is a collection of all related fields, such as a record that contains all the information about a specific book. A file is a collection of all related records, such as a file containing records representing all the books in a library. This organizational structure provides the facility with the ability to organize and manipulate data at both the macro and micro levels and to easily update and accurately maintain information.

TABLE 5.5 Database Management Software in Teaching and Learning

DATABASE FEATURE	APPLICATION TO ADMINISTRATIVE/PROFESSIONAL TASKS	APPLICATION TO TEACHING AND LEARNING TASKS
DATABASES	• Allow for the definition of customized database formats • Provide for inputting and storing large amounts of complex and/or cumbersome data	Assist students in • Thinking through and creating logical data organizations • Easily entering data for subsequent organization and reporting Assist teachers in • Creating customized data organization that suits their specific needs • Managing student and content data
FORMS	Provide a format for support staff and aides to input data	Teachers can create easy-to-use and familiar input screens for students to use
REPORTS	Professional-looking output created by tools and wizards	Assists students in • Presenting project data in a variety of attractive formats Assists teachers in • Customizing output for each student, class, or lesson
SORTING	Provides multiple levels of sorts to make data easy to comprehend	Assists students in • Practicing alphabetizing skills • Thinking abstractly to determine appropriate sorts • Presenting data clearly Assists teachers in • Presenting data to students in an easy-to-use format • Demonstrating critical-thinking and alphabetizing skills • Preparing logical reports
QUERIES	Provide for customized output through the selection of specific records based on predefined criteria	Assist students in • Practicing logical and critical-thinking skills • Finding and reporting targeted data • Identifying key criteria to look for Assist teachers in • Finding and working with only those records needed • Demonstrating concepts in equality and Boolean logic • Presenting real-time demonstrations of critical thinking
ARCHIVING	Provides an inexpensive and easy way to store and access data	Saved database files are easy means to use to • Query data • Access data • Update information • Sort data • Make reports

In our library example, the media specialist can simply type in the data representing a new acquisition in a new record in the media center's database file. The database software automatically stores the new record. From that point on, the user can access that new record according to the data stored in any of the information fields on the record. By typing in a key word or phrase, the user can retrieve the desired record from the database. This electronic process is a fast and accurate data input and retrieval system.

Sorting

Once entered, records can be sorted according to the data in any one or in multiple fields. Sorting arranges all records in a database into ascending or descending order based on the alphabetic or numeric characters stored in any field. In our library example, with this sort function, no matter how many additions or deletions to the library's collection of books may occur, the database of holdings is always in alphabetical order and ready to use. And because all the data are stored electronically and automatically sorted, a record cannot be as easily removed or misfiled as is possible in a manual system.

Querying

One of the most significant features of database management is the ability to find one single item of data from the potentially thousands of items in a database. When querying a database, the user instructs the software to look for and match targeted criteria. In our library example, to find a specific author's name, you would, in a query operation, instruct the software to look in the Last Name fields of all records to find that targeted last name. Once it is found, the software returns the record in which the matching name resides. Despite the size of the database, any single item of information can be quickly and easily accessed. The *PTA Membership* Skills Builder at mylabschool.com will demonstrate an Access query and give you practice using this feature.

Reports

Whether you need to print a written summary of all of the records in the database or only those resulting from a query, most database management software packages contain report formats that ensure a professional and polished look. Reports are essentially templates built into the software to create output that is attractive and easy to read. Although it is possible to print the entire database, including all fields of all records, if the database is large, this can result in an overwhelming and difficult-to-read quantity of data. Using a report instead allows you to use the results of a database query to report only those records you want and then to identify and display only the desired fields within the records. In our library example, we can easily query the database to find any new additions to the library and then create a New Acquisitions Report that includes only the most pertinent information about each book. Your *Science Database* Skills Builder activity at mylabschool.com will help you master effective reports as well as the other essential features of this versatile software.

Database Management in the Classroom

Like word-processing and spreadsheet software, database management software, when creatively applied by educators, can be more than a productivity tool. It can become a creative teaching and learning tool when used to categorize, store, access, and retrieve large amounts of data or to demonstrate logic when creating a query. More ideas are available in On the Web! Activity 5.3.

E-Learning

www.mylabschool.com
Software Skills Builder
Access Skills–PTA
Membership

The query feature selects and displays data that match specific criteria.

E-Learning

www.mylabschool.com
Software Skills Builder
Access Skills–Science
Database

E-Learning
ON THE WEB! 5.3

Using Database Management Software to Enhance Teaching and Learning

Presentation Software

Whether for teacher-led presentations or student-led class reports, presentation software can help to organize and enhance the delivery of content. **Presentation software** includes programs that are designed to create digital support materials for oral presentations. From a software perspective, presentations are a prearranged group of electronic slides that present one idea or theme after another. Completed presentations sequence and display these slides on a computer monitor, large-screen video monitor, or projection screen (see Figure 5.4). Presentations typically proceed through all slides in a linear sequence but the software has the capabilities needed for nonlinear, hyperlink-driven sequencing. These programs, originally designed for use in business as a sales and presentation tool, have been adapted by educators to assist the communication process by providing electronic visual displays that enhance verbal delivery.

Presentation software includes a wide range of capabilities in one typically very easy-to-use package. The presentation software Skills Builders at mylabschool.com provide both demonstration and practice in the use of these features. The most common features of presentation software are summarized here.

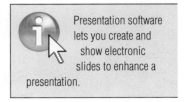

Presentation software lets you create and show electronic slides to enhance a presentation.

E-Learning

www.mylabschool.com
Software Skills Builder
PowerPoint Skills–Class Rules

Multimedia Elements

The individual slides in a presentation slide show can contain a number of multimedia elements including text, graphics, animation, sound, and video clips. The software can thus create a presentation appealing to the variety of learning modalities found in a typical audience of learners. The slide show as a whole may also contain multimedia elements that tie the slides together, adding interest and excitement to the presentation. Each

FIGURE 5.4

Using Presentation Software

With presentation software, you can construct slides and view the results in a slide show presentation.

Microsoft PowerPoint® is a registered trademark of Microsoft Corporation.

in the Classroom

DATABASE MANAGEMENT

IN THE MIDDLE SCHOOL SCIENCE CLASS

Doug Saulter, eighth-grade science teacher at Portsmouth Middle School, Portland, Oregon, designed a Community Tree Project—Friends of Trees & Mapping Trees in the Portsmouth Neighborhood—for his students to practice compiling and using databases. They inventory street trees and analyze the data to be presented as "poster displays and PowerPoint presentations at different venues." The Friends of Trees program serves the community by showing where trees should be planted and helps with the planting. To see more about this project, go to the Institute of Portland Metropolitan Studies web site, ArcView GIS 3.2.

IN HIGH SCHOOL SCIENCE CLASS

Dr. Peter Auger, a science teacher at Barnstable (Massachusetts) High School, used HOBOs, data-logging devices that are battery-powered and can display the data gathered on a computer graph, to save diamondback turtles on Cape Cod with his students under his direction. Together they sought to find out if where and when female diamondback turtles lay their eggs affected the survival rate of the eggs. The data they gathered will become a database that can be used to stimulate investigations into how to modify the survival rate of those turtles that spend so much time looking for a nesting place that their eggs do not hatch because of the lateness of the season. "The kids are tracking turtles, identifying nests, burying HOBOs, and swatting horseflies. . . . The students put a logger where the old nest was and where the new nest is to see how closely they can match nesting conditions," Dr. Auger reported.

Auger, P. HOBOs help students save diamondback turtles on Cape Cod. Retrieved October 12, 2003, from **www.iscienceproject.com/stories/ 6416_diamondbackturtles.html.**

Saulter, D. Community tree project—friends of trees & mapping trees in the Portsmouth neighborhood. Retrieved July 17, 2005, from **http://159.191.14.139/ .docs/master/print/_uri/teachers.pps.k12or.us/ teachers/Portsmouth_treespro . . .**

---

multimedia element included in a presentation can be constructed from scratch or copied from other sources and easily pasted into slides.

Wizards and Templates

Although multimedia presentations of this complexity may seem difficult to create, most presentation software programs include built-in wizards that help even a novice computer user to create very professional and attractive presentations. In addition, the software includes a variety of slide templates with designer formats already created and ready to fill in. For busy teachers who use these templates, the design tasks are already done, and only the content needs to be added.

Resource Libraries

Although art, photos, and animation can be created or scanned for inclusion in a customized presentation, presentation software also offers useful libraries of multimedia from which to choose. Electronic clip art, animation, sound, and video libraries are typically included on the presentation software CD-ROM. These resources and built-in help features assist any user in creating professional-looking slides. With minimal training, educators and students alike can create and display complex and high-quality slide show presentations using just the software's library resources.

Hyperlinks

Many presentation software programs include hypermedia features that make them seem more like multimedia authoring software than presentation tools adapted from business. Such programs include hyperlink capability via buttons to hyperjump (move directly to a target slide) to out-of-sequence slides, other slide shows, or even other software. Adding a hyperlink to a word, image, or button is as simple as clicking on a toolbar button and typing in the slide number or Internet address you wish to jump to.

Animation

Many presentation software packages also come with built-in options for dramatic special effects that can be applied to the moment of transition between slides or to the way bulleted items appear on a slide. Such animation schemes add visual interest and excitement to the concepts presented in text on the screen. Sound effects may also be included with animation to add auditory interest.

Printing

In addition to displaying the presentation itself, presentation software typically includes a variety of printing options for the presenter. Once the presentation is created, a hard copy can be printed and copied for distribution to the viewers. A presentation can be printed out as an outline, as a speaker's note pages, or as customized audience handouts displaying anywhere from one to six slides per page. In addition, with a color printer and transparency film, each slide of the presentation can be printed out as a transparency for use on an overhead projector.

E-Learning

www.mylabschool.com
Software Skills Builder
PowerPoint Skills–Creating an Outline

Display Options

In addition to a presenter-controlled display, presentation software provides alternative display options. A presentation can be set to display itself as a timed, self-playing slide show that will run without assistance by either the presenter or the viewer. This is a particularly useful feature to use for a self-guided display in a classroom center or in a library to guide students as they begin a group or individual task.

Presentation Software in the Classroom

One of the most successful applications of presentation software takes presentation preparation beyond helping an educator prepare an effective lecture. Presentation software is especially valuable when used by students to create support materials for their own presentations. The software can help students organize their thoughts into manageable and logical chunks as a result of the automatic limitation of information displayable on any given slide. Further, discrimination and critical thinking are applied as the students review the quantity of material they have found in their research and then pare it down and identify key elements. Finally, as a by-product of using presentation software in this way, students gain valuable experience with multimedia-type software and with basic computer and software skills. Students enjoy and can be highly motivated by the software component of their report project, which in turn leads to improved retention and learning.

E-Learning

www.mylabschool.com
video
View *Using Power Point*

With the inclusion of the multimedia elements of text, sound, graphics, animation, special effects, and audio and video clips, these high-end presentation programs become essentially hybrid authoring systems. You will find that these packages are useful for anything from creating a transparency to developing multimedia tutorials (see Table 5.6). At mylabschool.com, you will be able to see and try activities that use the many features of presentation software. These activities feature Microsoft PowerPoint, one of the leading presentation software packages available today.

If "a picture is worth a thousand words," as the saying goes, the popularity of presentation software integrated into the curriculum is well justi-

TABLE 5.6 Presentation Software in Teaching and Learning

PRESENTATION SOFTWARE FEATURE	APPLICATION TO ADMINISTRATIVE/PROFESSIONAL TASKS	APPLICATION TO TEACHING AND LEARNING TASKS
SLIDES	• Allow for the creation of a sequence of screens that present content and information • Individual screens can be printed on transparency film for use with an overhead projector	Assist students in • Thinking through and organizing logical reports • Preparing support materials for oral reports Assist teachers in • Creating customized presentation of content • Creating transparencies • Presenting professional reports to colleagues
GRAPHICS	Allow for the addition of graphics, charts, and photos to illustrate content	Assist teachers and students in presenting visually rich content
MULTIMEDIA	Provide tools to include audio and video files as a component of individual slides	Assist students in • Adding multimedia to the presentation of content Assist teachers in • Adding elements to presentations to address diverse learning styles
HYPERLINKS	Provide tools for nonsequential linking of individual slides to allow for individualized exploration of content	Assist students in • Critical thinking, organizing, and planning content • Creating individualized study tools and reports • Presenting data clearly Assists teachers in • Preparing tutorials and electronic flash cards • Individualizing instruction
PRINTING OPTIONS	Provide for customized output options	Assist students in • Preparing class handouts to support oral reports Assist teachers in • Creating speaker's notes to assist in presentation • Preparing class handouts and activity worksheets • Preparing content outlines
PRINTING OPTIONS	Provide easy-to-use tools to add professional-looking layouts and exciting special effects to slide presentations	Assist teachers and students in presenting professional-looking and stimulating presentations and reports

 in the **Classroom**

POWERPOINT

IN THE HIGH SCHOOL COMPUTER CLASSROOM

Lorrie Jackson, a computer teacher at the Lausanne Collegiate School in Memphis, Tennessee, knows that time management is a problem for most people, and students taking tests are no exception. She shows teachers "how to make a countdown clock to help students stay on task during timed activities." She points out how it used to be "movie reels started with a 10, 9, 8 . . . countdown." Today we associate countdowns with launches of space missions and easily see how they help us focus on the passage of time. To aid students in keeping track of how much time they have to complete timed assignments, she suggests teachers create their own countdown clocks, consisting of a series of PowerPoint slides, in a three-step procedure that is both quick and easy. After the slides are created, the timing is set to add the slide transitions, and a sound file can be added as the final step if the teacher wishes to do so. The instructions Ms. Jackson has written are found on the Education World web site. She also notes that additional information about classroom uses for PowerPoint can be found on the Instructional Resources pages found at Microsoft Education **(www.microsoft.com/Education/HowTo.mspx).**

IN THE MIDDLE SCHOOL SOCIAL STUDIES CLASS

Yaminoh Childress, who teaches sixth-grade social studies at South Delta Middle School in Auguilla, Mississippi, asks her students how a trip to the Caribbean sounds. That's probably a rhetorical question for most of them, but she takes them there regularly and, well, virtually, of course. She writes that the trip will introduce the students to the island cultures, give them an in-depth look at one of the Caribbean countries, and show them how to "create photo albums using the photo album template in Microsoft PowerPoint." The albums "will be presented to the class and put on display for all students to review."

In preparation for the "trip," on each computer Ms. Childress downloads and installs the photo album template from Microsoft's web site if Office XP is not installed on the computers. (The template is built into the Office XP version of this software.) The template can be downloaded for use with Office 2000 from Microsoft's online template gallery at **http://office.microsoft.com/downloads/2000/album .aspx.**

She also bookmarks web sites for the students to use in their research, along with five handouts that have links, for the students to access for information to include on the PowerPoint slides as they travel the warm, sunny seas of the Caribbean.

Childress, Y. (2004). A trip to the Caribbean. Retrieved October 12, 2004, from **www.create.cett.misstate.edu/ create/classroom/lplan_printer.asp?articleID=198.**

Jackson, L. (2004, October 6). Make a PowerPoint countdown clock. Retrieved January 31, 2005, from **www .educationworld.com/a_tech/techtorial022.shtml.**

fied. A cursory look at a few actual classroom projects in the In the Classroom feature reveals a wide range of possibilities for taking presentation software beyond its role as a productivity tool and using it as the means to an invigorating revitalization of instruction. Many more ideas can be found by completing On the Web! Activity 5.4.

E-Learning ON THE WEB! 5.4

How Can Teaching and Learning Be Enhanced with Electronic Presentations?

Integrated Productivity Packages

As you have learned, productivity software is often packaged in application suites of programs that share a similar look and feel. Office productivity software bundles, such as Microsoft Office, are examples of this distribution format. Occasionally, however, software vendors integrate three distinct software applications (word processing, spreadsheets, and database management) into a single comprehensive blended application. These combined programs are called **integrated productivity packages.** Individual software components of integrated packages include many but not all of the capabilities of the stand-alone application packages. Typically, an integrated package contains the most popular and widely used components of each major type of productivity tool (see Figure 5.5). These are combined together in a single easy-to-use software program. Many schools opt for an integrated package for classroom use because many of the advanced features of office software are used only occasionally by educators, and combined packages are easier to learn and use than separate programs. Typically, integrated productivity software is a more economical purchase for a school. Its reduced cost is reflected not only in the initial price of the software, but also in the time it takes to train people to use it. One of the chief advantages of an integrated productivity package is that you have to learn only one comprehensive software package rather than having to learn three individual packages. Furthermore, little of the functionality that the average educator needs is sacrificed in these streamlined applications.

Whether using a productivity suite or an integrated package, it is important to carefully review and evaluate software before purchasing it. The Productivity Software Evaluation Rubric (Table 5.7) will help you make a considered decision before selecting productivity software.

Using Productivity Software

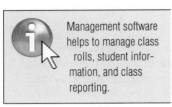

Management software helps to manage class rolls, student information, and class reporting.

Evaluating and Using School and Classroom Management Software

The second major category of administrative software is **school and classroom management software.** This type of software assists educators in accomplishing the many tasks associated with the day-to-day management of their classrooms or their schools. Whether the task is keeping an

FIGURE 5.5

Integrating Productivity Software

Several productivity applications may be merged together to form an integrated package.

Microsoft Works® is a registered trademark of Microsoft Corporation.

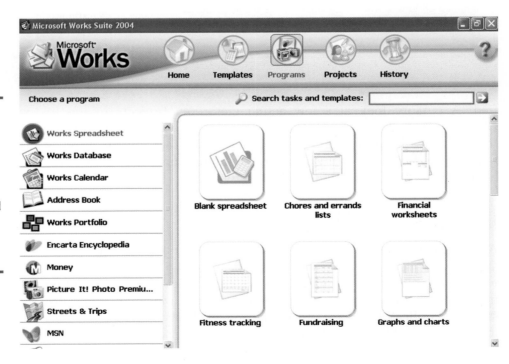

TABLE 5.7 Productivity Software Evaluation Rubric

SOFTWARE:

DESCRIPTION:

VENDOR: COST:

NOTES ON USE:

Please rate the features below for each piece of software. Next to each of the items in the rubric, check the box that best reflects your opinion.

SOFTWARE FEATURE	EVALUATION CRITERIA				
	1 Poor	2 Below Average	3 Average	4 Above Average	5 Excellent
DOCUMENTATION	Documentation is excessively technical and/or difficult to follow	Documentation is generally understandable but not very user-friendly	Documentation is user-friendly and reasonably easy to follow	Clear documentation that is logical and easy to follow	Very clear, user-friendly documentation that leaves no questions
TECHNICAL SUPPORT	No local or toll-free telephone support available	No local support; phone support available for an hourly fee	Local tech support and phone support available for modest fees	Local tech help available for modest fee; no-charge phone support	Local help and toll-free support readily available at no charge
MULTIPLE USERS	Cannot be used by more than one user	Usable by multiple users if per-user licensing is purchased	Payment of a relatively small fee allows multiple users	No additional fee but allows addition of up to 10 users	Comes with permission for multiple users
HELP FEATURES	Few or no help features available	Help limited to a Help or Read-Me file on installation CD	Clicking a Help button provides on-screen assistance with common problems	Help button is context sensitive and provides clear help	Highlighting and clicking area of difficulty brings up a related Help feature
TUTORIALS	No tutorials provided	Tutorials may be ordered for a fee	Limited tutorial provided on CD or may be requested without charge	Tutorials offered as an online option or on CD	Extensive online and CD-based tutorials provided
ADMINISTRATIVE FEATURES	Lacks some of the commonly included basic features	Only basic features are included	Basic features and additional features are included	Includes most of the features desired	Comprehensive features included
MULTIPLE PLATFORMS	Works on only one operating system	Although purchased for one platform, versions for other platforms may be purchased	Program will run on multiple operating systems; features may vary with platform	May be used on multiple platforms; features similar although not identical	May be used on multiple platforms with consistent features across platforms
CONVERSION/ IMPORT/EXPORT FEATURES	No provision for conversion between software	Cannot be imported or exported into other programs but can be converted into a few of the more popular formats	Can be converted, imported, or exported into programs by major vendors	Easily converted into common formats; maintains most of format features	Fully compatible via conversion, import, and export with all vendors
ALL NEEDED APPLICATIONS (IF A SUITE OR INTEGRATED SOFTWARE)	Missing many applications that are needed	Some needed applications missing from package	Most of the expected applications are included and compatible with each other	All basic applications included and fully integrated	Includes applications beyond those needed; full integration within suite and compatible with other vendor software
HARDWARE COMPATIBILITY	Requires upgrades for some hardware to work on all machines	Requires limited upgrades to some machines	Will work on most machines without upgrades	Works acceptably on all machines without upgrades	Maximum performance with no hardware upgrades required on any machines
COST	Expensive when compared to other vendors	Cost is relatively high when compared to other vendors	Average cost	Reasonably priced; includes some discounts	Special pricing for educational users

Total the score for each piece of software. Compare the scores. The piece of software with the highest score is your best choice.

alphabetized grade roll, taking attendance, or creating an up-to-date seating chart, management software is available to make the task easier.

Management software is written for use at the district and school levels and by the individual classroom teacher (see Figure 5.6). Implemented at the district level, management software can offer many advantages. Software implemented by the district and offered to all schools and classrooms via networks can provide a standardized platform for entering and tracking student data. Furthermore, such software often has the option of interfacing with the Web. Web-enhanced districtwide management software can make student grades stored in a teacher's electronic gradebook accessible to the students' parents by means of a password. District-level software can also track attendance for school, districtwide, and state reporting purposes. When implemented districtwide, management software expands the capabilities of similar software used in individual classrooms.

School-level management software includes customized software that helps the district track districtwide enrollment, manage finances and budgets, and report on its operations both internally and externally. For example, schools designed with a computerized attendance system may have the teacher workstation in the classroom configured so that the teacher can report attendance by entering it into the school management software on the networked computer. The attendance data are then collected with that from other schools across a district and tallied daily. This type of districtwide application allows every school to maintain and gain access to up-to-date and accurate information on enrollment, expenditures, and attendance.

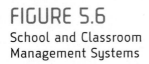
FIGURE 5.6
School and Classroom Management Systems

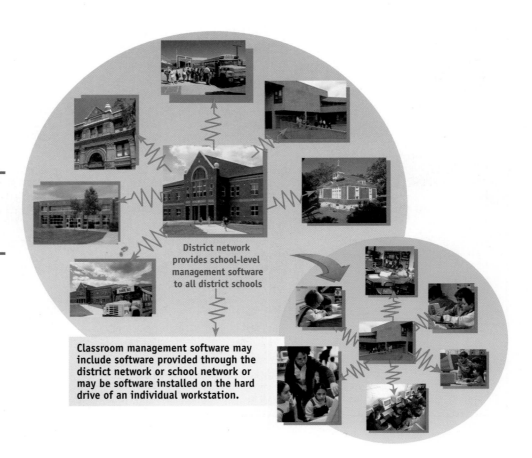

District network provides school-level management software to all district schools

Classroom management software may include software provided through the district network or school network or may be software installed on the hard drive of an individual workstation.

At the classroom level, management support software makes managing class rolls, student information, and class reporting easier. Such software often includes a variety of tools packaged together that have the same look and feel. It is also often able to transfer data seamlessly between components. These packages contain programs that help the teacher create student rolls (often with a wide range of built-in grading functions), assist in making and maintaining seating charts, help in attendance tracking and reporting, and provide a statistical and graphing component for assessment feedback (see Figure 5.7). Teachers using one of these software tools might begin the term by entering their students' names into the class roll component of the program and then generating an alphabetical class seating chart, a daily attendance report, and summary reports of both grades and attendance whenever interim reporting is necessary. Some packages even interface with district computers so that teachers can simply download their student rolls directly from the district computers rather than having to enter the initial data by hand. Management support packages are also often customizable so that all teachers using these tools can work with a format that is comfortable for them.

E-Learning
ON THE WEB! 5.6
Management Software

E-Learning

www.mylabschool.com
Listen to Podcast
Administrative Tools

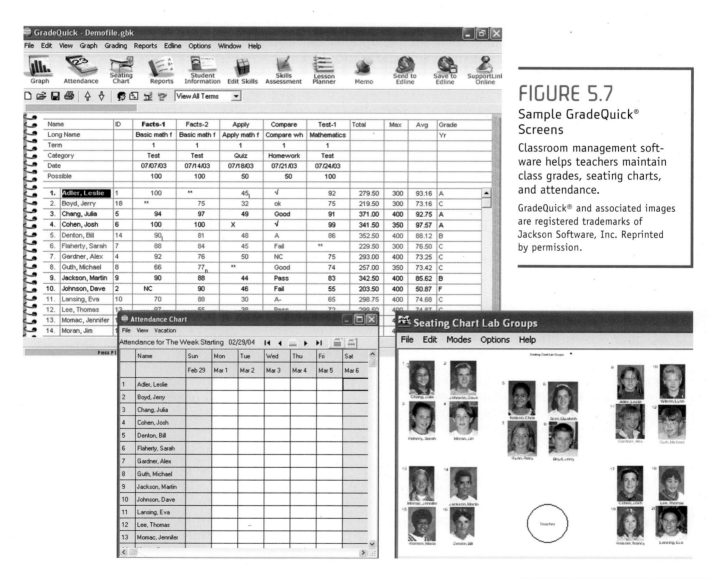

FIGURE 5.7

Sample GradeQuick® Screens

Classroom management software helps teachers maintain class grades, seating charts, and attendance.

GradeQuick® and associated images are registered trademarks of Jackson Software, Inc. Reprinted by permission.

Portfolio Assessment Software

For teachers who regularly use portfolio assessment, an alternative type of assessment for tracking student progress, classroom management tools often provide useful assistance in the many and sometimes complex tracking tasks required. Portfolio assessment is a type of performance assessment that enables the teacher to assess competencies on the basis of a collection of student work rather than by using test scores. Portfolio assessment software provides the teacher with the tools necessary to document student achievement. Typically, these tools include portfolio formats and checklists and the ability to add comments and create custom reports. Some portfolio software tools also offer the teacher and student the option of maintaining portfolios in an electronic format with the capacity to electronically "snapshot," view, and collect student work to share with parents. For special education teachers, alternative assessment software tools include those that generate, track, and produce reports for required individual education plans (IEPs) for special needs students.

Whether portfolio software is designed for hard copy or digital output, the powerful features of this type of management software offer support for the authentic assessment of student achievement. Although each vendor adds some unique options, electronic portfolio software will typically include the key features listed below.

Organization by Standards and Competencies

The goal of a portfolio is to create a collection of student work, teacher commentary, and other files that evidence student progress and achievement. Portfolio assessment software packages offer a variety of ways to organize and store examples of student work as well as your assessment of it. The software usually offers teachers a way to define specific content areas or other academic categories and then identify related standards and competencies. Copies of student work and its evaluation can then be organized according to the competencies it evidences. Over time, organizing and storing longitudinal records in this manner offers a cumulative view of student achievement over the course of an academic year or from year to year.

Observations

Portfolio assessment software often includes a way to record observations of student behaviors and notations on academic progress. Using either standard or teacher-defined commentary, observation entries offer teachers an opportunity to record student evaluations and comments related to them.

Multimedia Samples

Many portfolio assessment software packages include the ability to record images and audio and video samplings of student works. Audio-clip recordings of students reading standard passages or a sample of a student-created PowerPoint presentation offers multimedia evidence of current student progress.

E-Learning

www.mylabschool.com
Software Skills Builder
Using Word to Create an Electronic Portfolio

HANDS-
ON
LEARNING

Electronic portfolios enable you to capture and present student work for a more authentic and holistic assessment of progress and achievement. Visit at least three electronic portfolio web sites, including an e-portfolio software vendor web site, a publication about electronic portfolios in the classroom, and a web site presenting samples of student portfolios in K–12 classrooms. After visiting the sites and becoming more familiar with the use of electronic portfolios, create an e-portfolio template using the administrative software of your choice. The template should be designed to assist you in presenting and sharing your future students' work. Be prepared to demonstrate and share your template with your peers.

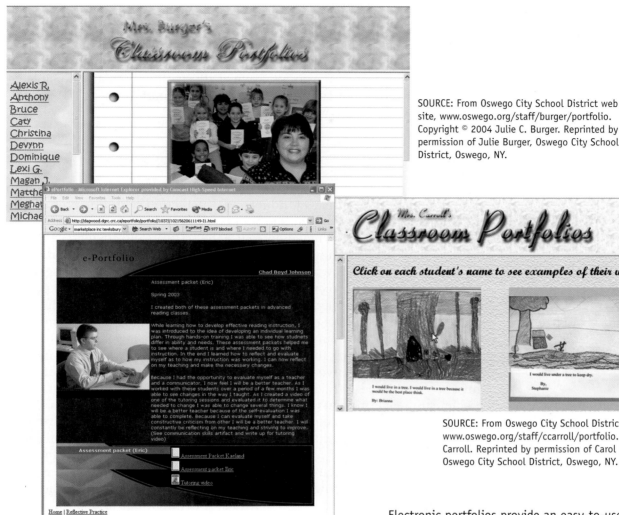

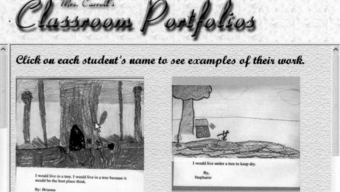

SOURCE: From Oswego City School District web site, www.oswego.org/staff/burger/portfolio. Copyright © 2004 Julie C. Burger. Reprinted by permission of Julie Burger, Oswego City School District, Oswego, NY.

SOURCE: From Oswego City School District web site, www.oswego.org/staff/ccarroll/portfolio. © 2004 Carol Carroll. Reprinted by permission of Carol Carroll, Oswego City School District, Oswego, NY.

Electronic portfolios provide an easy-to-use and efficient way to digitally record, store, organize, and display student work.

SOURCE: From http://www.chalkandwire.com/eportfolio/overview/ Makespreso.html.

Customization

Because every school district has its own standards and assessment guidelines, most portfolio assessment software is customizable to address specific standards and to assess student work using the district's criteria. Legends identifying standards and assessment methods are often definable by teachers so that their grading and assessment notes match the requirements of their school or district.

Hyperlinks

Some portfolio assessment software provides the capability of creating links that can be used to navigate the electronic portfolio of a student's work. Often related to standards, benchmarks, or competencies, these links offer an accurate and holistic picture of a student's achievement relative to target achievement. Hyperlinks also offer an intuitive and easy-to-use method for examining a portfolio's contents.

E-Learning

www.mylabschool.com
video
View *Digital Portfolios*

Electronic Portfolios

Electronic portfolio assessment software may be dedicated software designed specifically to create e-portfolios, or it may be multipurpose software adapted to creating portfolios. Several popular multimedia and authoring software packages can easily be adapted to portfolio generation. For more precise and complete e-portfolios, such as those directly related to targeted standards or those that conform to district guidelines (such as IEPs), dedicated portfolio software may be required.

Evaluating and Selecting Management Software

School or districtwide management software may be custom tailored to meet the needs of the district. Educators' interaction with this type of districtwide software may be limited to attending the necessary training sessions to ensure that they know how to use the software effectively. Classroom management software, however, requires careful review and evaluation on the part of the teachers who will be using it. Some classroom management systems are offered as freeware or shareware from the Internet or other software sources. Others may be inexpensive packages available to educators who are using a vendor's other software titles. Still others may be substantial but expensive comprehensive classroom management solutions. Although it is tempting to decide quickly to select freeware or shareware rather than the expensive software, there is a longer-term investment that must be considered. Whichever software is selected, educators must spend precious time learning to use it and entering data into it. In addition to this initial time investment, once student records are stored in a particular software format, the format may be difficult to change. If, after the initial selection of management software, an educator decides that the program does not have all of the desired components, changing to another software package may require reentering a great deal of data. Thus, even more time is invested. As with all software acquisitions, it is important to make a careful and thoughtful selection at the onset. The Classroom Management Software Evaluation Rubric (Table 5.8) will help you evaluate and choose the most appropriate classroom management software.

Software, Teaching, and Learning: A Practical Approach

To end this discussion of administrative software, let us return to the hypothetical situation presented in the chapter preview. Imagine that your school district has decided to make a major technology initiative for the twenty-first century. As a result, you have just been given five new computer systems for use in your classroom. The computer-support department tells you that you have a software budget with which you can augment the collection of district productivity software from which you can choose. Will you know what to do? Will you know which types of software will best accomplish the tasks you need to do? Will you know what to select to improve your productivity and make the administrative tasks associated with your job easier? Perhaps now you are better able to tackle these questions.

TABLE 5.8 — Classroom Management Software Evaluation Rubric

SOFTWARE:

DESCRIPTION:

VENDOR: **COST:**

NOTES ON USE:

To help you determine the value of a piece of classroom management software that you want to evaluate, please rate the features listed below. Next to each of the items in the rubric, check the box that best reflects your opinion.

SOFTWARE FEATURE	EVALUATION CRITERIA				
	1 Poor	2 Below Average	3 Average	4 Above Average	5 Excellent
INSTALLATION INSTRUCTIONS	Minimal or missing installation instructions	Instructions poorly written and somewhat difficult to follow	Instructions fairly clear and complete	Clear and user-friendly written instructions	Step-by-step installation instructions appear when the CD is inserted
SITE LICENSING PROVISIONS	No licensing available	Somewhat expensive and/or limited site licensing	Site licensing available at reasonable cost	Low licensing rates for educators	Multiple educators may use without paying a fee
TECHNICAL SUPPORT	No local or toll-free telephone support available	No local support; phone support available for an hourly fee	Local support and phone support available for modest fees	Local tech help available for modest fee; no-charge phone support	Local help and toll-fee support readily available at no charge
EASE OF UPDATES	No provisions for updates	Must purchase new versions; most data will transfer to new version	Updates for less than cost of new versions; data transferrable	Minimal fee for up-updates; data fully compatible	Free updates available online; seamless transfer of data
TUTORIALS	No tutorials provided	Tutorials may be ordered for a fee	Limited tutorial provided on CD or may be requested without charge	Tutorials offered as an online option or on CD	Extensive online and CD-based tutorials provided
MULTIPLE PLATFORMS	Works on only one operating system	Although purchased for one platform, versions for other platforms may be purchased	Program will run on multiple operating systems; features may vary with platform	May be used on multiple platforms; features similar although not identical	May be used on multiple platforms with consistent features across platforms
STUDENT REPORT CAPABILITIES	Can record and report out data only in form it was entered	Reports can be modified so only the data is eported out	Using templates, reports can be generated; minor modifications can be made	Customizable reports and forms can be easily created and printed	Data may be reported out in any format desired
NOTATION CAPABILITIES	No provision for notations	Can attach brief notes on problems but can't add action taken at a later time	Notes can be entered and added to later	Data entry forms include provision for unlimited comments on the problem and the actions taken	Call up record by name; click on problem type; appropriate report form appears automatically
SPECIAL NEEDS REPORT CAPABILITIES	No capability for notes or reports	Notes limited to 10 words; may be reported out on templates provided	Notes may be made up to 50 words and printed out; supplied templates may be modified by user	Limit of 100 words; both templates and instructor-designed forms may be used for reports	Unlimited notes may be made, and desired reports can be designed and printed out
NONACADEMIC INFORMATION CAPABILITIES	Cannot record or report any nonacademic data	Limited provision to record and report nonacademic data in the same form it was entered	Numerical and text data, up to 50 characters, can be entered and then selectively printed out	Numerical and text data may be entered; multiple field sizes available; various templates for reporting	Unlimited data entry capabilities; customizable reports can be printed as desired

Total the score for each piece of software. Compare the scores. The piece of software with the highest score is your best choice.

Still, even armed with an understanding of the role of administrative software in teaching and learning, with so many types of software packages available, a busy educator is faced with a significant demand of time and energy just to explore and decide on software for his or her classroom. Indeed, the tasks of researching, evaluating, and mastering the features of even the most appropriate software packages might seem daunting, but they are entirely necessary. Technology resources are limited in most school districts. Wise use of these limited funds is a skill every computer-using educator must master. This problem is no different from many others faced by educators dedicated to executing their professional responsibilities effectively and efficiently and to making the learning experiences of their students as complete and exciting as possible. From the discussion of software on the preceding pages, it is clear that administrative software can facilitate a wide variety of teaching tasks in the classroom, in your school, and across the district. It is up to you to become adequately familiar with this type of software to make the time you devote to administrative tasks as productive as possible.

In the next chapter, you will explore the other major category of software used by educators: academic software. There you will learn about the wide variety of academic software possibilities that you can integrate into teaching and into learning. For computer-using educators, knowledge of administrative and academic software packages and the hardware necessary to run them is the foundation for the effective use of computers in teaching and learning. You are well on your way toward establishing the firm foundation you will need when you teach.

KEY TERMS

academic software 167
administrative software 167
classroom management software 168
database management software 183
electronic spreadsheet 178
freeware 169
integrated productivity packages 192

macro 176
presentation software 187
productivity software 168
school and classroom management software 192
shareware 169
site license 170

templates 175
what-if analysis 180
wizard 177
word-processing software 170
WYSIWYG 174

STUDENT ACTIVITIES

CHAPTER REVIEW

1. How do academic and administrative software differ?
2. What is productivity software? How can it be adapted to benefit teaching and learning? Give specific examples.
3. Name three types of software that might be included in classroom management support software. Describe an application for each.

4. What is desktop publishing? How does it differ from word processing? How is it the same?
5. What are the key features of word-processing software? How might you use each in completing administrative tasks?
6. What are the advantages and features of electronic spreadsheets? How do you see them as a benefit in an educational environment?

7. Define database management software and describe how you might use it to help you in your teaching responsibilities. How might you construct a learning assignment for your students that uses this productivity tool?

8. What is presentation software?
9. Describe the difference between an integrated productivity package and a productivity suite.
10. Why is it important to take the time to fully evaluate administrative software before buying it?

WHAT DO YOU THINK?

1. List the top ten things you think you need to know about administrative software to be an effective computer-using educator. Why is each of these things critical in your technology decision making?
2. For most productivity software, many see the ability to save data in electronic format as a significant advantage over hard copy. Do you agree that this characteristic of productivity software is of value in education? Explain why or why not.
3. There is some concern over the use of database software for private student records. How might using a database management system make it easier to violate the privacy of student information? Do you think the benefits of such systems outweigh the risks? Explain your position.
4. Some educators think that it is too much trouble to learn the administrative software packages that might assist them in completing their required paperwork. Others believe that the benefits in productivity and editability of records outweigh the effort it takes to master the programs. What do you think?

LEARNING TOGETHER!

The following activities are designed for learning groups of three to five students.

1. Assume that you and your learning group make up the technology committee for your school. The committee has been assigned the task of deciding whether to upgrade or change the productivity software application suite your school has used over the past two years. Create a list of all of the issues that must be considered before making this decision. Then itemize the list and weigh each item in terms of its priority in importance to teaching and learning. Finally, describe the process you would go through to use the list and make your software decision.
2. Have each member of your learning group interview a teacher who uses any of the four major types of productivity software. Ask the teacher how he or she uses the software to help perform teacher management tasks and how he or she uses it to help children learn. Compare the interview responses with those of the other members of your group. Be prepared to share what you have learned with your peers.
3. You and your group members are team-teaching a science unit on climate to the grade level of your choice. Describe how you might integrate each of the four main types of productivity software into your unit. Create an instructional design, using the dynamic instructional design model you learned in Chapter 2, that articulates your unit.

E-Learning

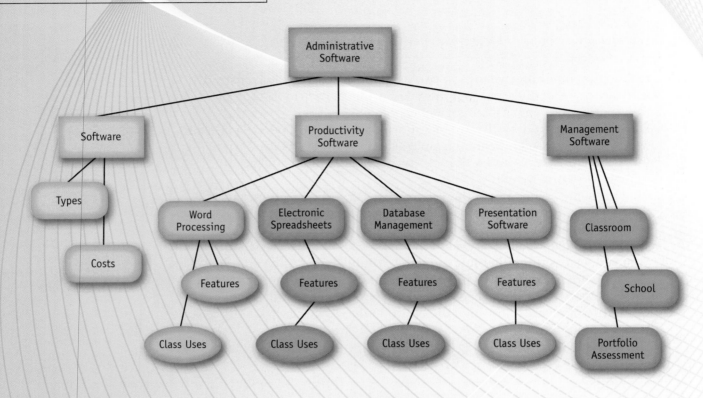

Administrative Software

Software — Types — Costs

Productivity Software
- Word Processing — Features — Class Uses
- Electronic Spreadsheets — Features — Class Uses
- Database Management — Features — Class Uses
- Presentation Software — Features — Class Uses

Management Software
- Classroom
- School
- Portfolio Assessment

Podcasts www.mylabschool.com

Listen to a podcast relating to the use of administrative software in teaching and learning. Download the audio discussion to your iPod, computer, or MP3 player.

Software Skills Builder www.mylabschool.com

These step-by-step illustrated tutorials teach you to use Microsoft Windows and Office on both PC and Mac by preparing documents that will be useful in your classroom.

Video Lab www.mylabschool.com

Accessible through the **mylabschool** we bsite, you will find several video vignettes that offer you a look at software in teaching and learning. Learning guides for all videos can be found in the text's Student Activity Supplement.

On the Web! Activities www.ablongman.com/lever-duffy3e

Noted in the margins of the chapter, these activities offer you in-depth experiences in the topics and content presented in the chapter.

Online Practice Test www.ablongman.com/lever-duffy3e

Practice tests offer you an opportunity to test your knowledge and then review the results and send them to your teacher.

Outliner www.ablongman.com/lever-duffy3e

Chapter Outliners are fill-in-the-blank outlines of the main ideas presented in the chapter. Download the outliner and fill it in for an effective chapter study guide.

Power Practices www.ablongman.com/lever-duffy3e

Power Practices are animated tutorials made using Microsoft's presentation software, PowerPoint. This flash card tutorial will help you practice key concepts in the chapter.

Puzzler www.ablongman.com/lever-duffy3e

Puzzlers include content in crossword, word search, and other puzzle formats to help you master chapter content.

Useful Links www.ablongman.com/lever-duffy3e

These links offer you suggestions for expanded online research in the topics presented in the chapter.

INTEGRATION *Ideas*

Integrating administrative software into content areas is one of the easiest applications of technology. Many colleges and universities require knowledge of administrative applications as a graduation requirement. Knowing how to use this software is the first step; the next step is finding out how to use it to teach in the content areas. Here are some ways teachers in the major content areas have enriched their lessons by calling on administrative software to help out.

Integrating Word Processing into Social Studies

Combining a keypals lesson (e-mail) with word processing works three ways in "Cultural Exchange through Internet Keypals." The students word process the e-mails to counterparts living in different cultural settings, keep a weekly word-processed journal about what they learn from the direct communication with others, and write a final word-processed paper summing up what they have learned from this lesson. Visit this site at **www.eduref.org/Virtual/Lessons/ Social_Studies/World_History/WRH0008.html.**

Integrating Spreadsheets into Language Arts

Education World's Techtorials provide many lesson plans that show how administrative software tools can be woven into lessons in any content area, not just math, to make for an effective learning experience. Lorrie Jackson in "Create an Adlib Story with Excel" details how to make Excel work in the English/Language Arts classroom. Using this Techtorial as a starting point, creative teachers can design many variations on the theme for a variety of lessons. The Techtorials include the NETS.T. Review them at **www.educationworld.com.**

Integrating Database Software into Science

"The Wave of Spring" is a science lesson that guides students in creating a database that reports on their observations of when tulips bloom at locations around the world. This is a year-long project that involves students from Palo Alto, California, in communicating with fellow students in Europe and middle Tennessee. From this data, they track the arrival of spring around the world. Visit **www97.intel.com/odyssey/Story.aspx?storyid=268.**

Integrating Presentation Software into Math

"The Stock Market" is a lesson plan that gives each group of students $1,000 to spend on the market but in a competitive setting. Each group competes with the other groups to determine who will gain the most from their investments. Whether they win by making the most money or lose, each group prepares a PowerPoint presentation to represent their buying and selling strategies. Go to **www.lessonplanspage.com/ printables/PMathSSLACITheStockMarketGame6.htm.**

For these and many more Integration Ideas for using administrative software in teaching and learning visit the text web site at **www.ablongman.com/lever-duffy3e.**

Administrative Software Summary

In addition to the traditional productivity software suites such as Microsoft Office, many dedicated administrative software packages have been created to help teachers manage their classrooms and districts manage their schools. Numerous web sites offer summaries and reviews of these software packages. The list of software below demonstrates the diversity and capability of some of the many unique types of administrative software you might find available in your classroom and in your school. This is just a small sample of the kinds of software you can find to help you with your administrative tasks. Many alternative software packages exist in each category of use, and it can therefore be difficult to decide which one to buy. When selecting administrative software, it is a good idea to use an evaluation tool such as the rubric presented in this chapter.

USE	NAME	VENDOR	DESCRIPTION
• Assessment	Teacher's Workbench	Campus Online Inc.	Teacher's Workbench allows teachers to print their own answer sheets on any laser or ink jet printer. Once these are created, grading can be done using any scanner or high-end copy machine. The software analyzes the results and is available for view in an Internet Explorer window.
• Classroom Management	NetOp School	Cross Tec Corp.	NetOp School allows a teacher using a classroom network to broadcast his or her screen, multimedia files, or any student's screen to everyone on the network; it allows teachers to record and play back instructional screen sessions for later review, mark up or magnify a portion of the featured screen to highlight a lesson, monitor students as they work, restrict the use of applications and web sites, and interact with students as a group or one-on-one. The software gives teachers total management of their classroom network.
• Curriculum Management	Curriculum Mapper	WestJam Enterprises	This software enables teachers and administrators to identify standards, analyze when standards are being addressed, and show exactly what is being covered and when. It also provides a venue for teacher collaboration and identification of resource needs and parental communication.

USE	NAME	VENDOR	DESCRIPTION
District Management	Active Classroom	School Management Solutions	This web-based system allows teachers to align with state standards and implement their lesson plans and deliver them to students online. Both parents and students have access to the lessons. Capabilities include developing lessons, uploading files, posting homework and calendars, corresponding with students and parents, managing grades, and creating forums for open discussion.
Grading	Easy Grade Pro	Orbis	This gradebook software lets you record all of your classes' work, create your own custom grading system, create seating and assignment charts, record attendance, print out reports in multiple formats, and import and export data to the school network. It also provides summaries of student results to help a teacher analyze lesson effectiveness.
School Management	Infosnap Online School Forms	Infosnap Inc.	This software will change any school form to an online form and then enable the data entered to be exported to database management software for easy use.
Worksheet Creation	Essential Teacher Tools	Tom Snyder Productions	This multipurpose worksheet software helps teachers to create a variety of worksheets, puzzles, flash cards, and tests. A teacher enters the content once, and it can be used to create many types of worksheets.

Adapted from Educational Technology Information Center's review forums at www.edtechinfocenter.com.

chapter 6

Academic Software

This chapter addresses these ISTE *National Educational Technology Standards* for Teachers:

II. PLANNING AND DESIGNING LEARNING ENVIRONMENTS AND EXPERIENCES

Teachers plan and design effective learning environments and experiences supported by technology. Teachers

A. design developmentally appropriate learning opportunities that apply technology-enhanced instructional strategies to support the diverse needs of learners.

B. apply current research on teaching and learning with technology when planning learning environments and experiences.

C. identify and locate technology resources and evaluate them for accuracy and suitability.

D. plan for the management of technology resources within the context of learning activities.

E. plan strategies to manage student learning in a technology-enhanced environment.

III. TEACHING, LEARNING, AND THE CURRICULUM

Teachers implement curriculum plans that include methods and strategies for applying technology to maximize student learning. Teachers

A. facilitate technology-enhanced experiences that address content standards and student technology standards.

B. use technology to support learner-centered strategies that address the diverse needs of students.

C. apply technology to develop students' higher-order skills and creativity.

D. manage student learning activities in a technology-enhanced environment.

IV. ASSESSMENT AND EVALUATION

Teachers apply technology in a variety of effective assessment and evaluation strategies. Teachers

A. apply technology in assessing student learning of subject matter using a variety of assessment techniques.

B. use technology resources to collect and analyze data, interpret results, and communicate findings to improve instructional practice and maximize student learning.

C. apply multiple methods of evaluation to determine students' appropriate use of technology resources for learning, communication, and productivity.

I n Chapter 5, you explored the advantages of using administrative software as a tool to make you more productive as a teacher. This chapter presents the other category of software available to educators: academic software. Academic software enriches the teaching and learning process. Carefully selected by the teacher, academic software can significantly enhance a lesson and address the needs of learners.

As you learned in Chapter 2, when you design instruction, you must articulate your objectives carefully and then select the appropriate methods and media to support those objectives. Even in a one-computer classroom, the many types of academic software that are available to educators today offer a broad array of new and exciting media choices. You might decide to have students research a topic using a multimedia encyclopedia that appeals to a wide variety of learning styles. Or you might have cooperative learning groups experience discovery learning through a simulation on CD-ROM. Or you might simply give a child who needs additional practice with the content an opportunity for computer center time with math practice software that lets the child shoot down aliens bearing the correct answers to math problems on their ships. The choices are broad and appealing and can add visual, auditory, and kinesthetic interest to many lessons.

To be able to select the best academic software from the thousands of such packages, you need first to be aware of the choices available to you. In this chapter, you will explore the principal types of academic software and review a sampling of their application in the teaching and learning process.

In Chapter 6, you will

- Explore the major categories of academic software and their application in teaching and learning

- Review a sampling of how academic software is used in different classrooms

- Investigate and use methods for reviewing and evaluating software so that your technology acquisitions will appropriately meet your needs

Real People Real Stories

Meet Carol S. Holzberg, PhD, Christine Morin, and Chris Wings. Carol S. Holzberg is the Technology Coordinator, Christine Morin is the Technology Integration Specialist, and Chris Wings is the fourth-grade classroom teacher at Swift River School in New Salem, Massachusetts. Swift River School is a dynamic and educationally vibrant elementary school serving about 155 preschool and elementary age children in New Salem, a remote rural setting in the hill-town region of western Massachusetts.

When Chris Wings received a Model Technology Integration Grant from the Massachusetts Department of Education to enrich her standards-driven science and English language arts curriculum with technology tools and supports, she faced a challenge. She met that challenge with a technology team (Chris, Christine, and Carol). Together they developed a project, *On the "Write" Path to Literacy: Field Guides by Kids for Kids,* that incorporated advanced technology to improve the students' learning in the content of the district's curriculum guidelines and the Massachusetts Curriculum Frameworks.

In the project, Chris required my fourth-grade students to use technology to create a crafted and illustrated local geology field guide. The problem was finding software that would help the students in their research and in producing the field guide with improved writing skills as a by-product. We reviewed various software programs to find which software would work best with this project.

Some of the technology that was involved in this project included word processing, Internet research, scanning, digital cameras, and AlphaSmart keyboards. In addition, the fourth graders conducted Internet research and used a ProScope digital microscope to examine rock samples that they gathered in the field. The administrative software that we ended up using included Microsoft Word, Inspiration, Co:Writer, and Adobe Photoshop.

Technology tools made it easier to customize learning solutions and customize instruction to accommodate individuals with different learning styles and abilities. Visual learners who struggled with organizational issues benefited from Inspiration, a concept mapping application. This software helped them depict key relationships with symbols, colors, and words to create meaning, clarify thinking, connect ideas, brainstorm, and visualize difficult concepts. Learners who experienced difficulties with fine-motor coordination, spelling, note taking, or handwriting appreciated how Microsoft Word and AlphaSmart word-processing tools and spell-checkers helped with writing and editing. Struggling or emergent writers who had difficulty with vocabulary recall relied on Don Johnston's Co:Writer (a word predictor) to give them voice.

Adobe Photoshop (an image editor), scanners, and digital cameras enabled students to produce high-quality digital guidebook photographs and illustrations. Internet browsers (such as Internet Explorer and Safari) and web-based search engines (such as Google) facilitated online research. A color laser printer produced high-quality project output. Finally, Macromedia Dreamweaver enabled the technology coordinator to post student projects on the Web.

As a result of this project, Swift River fourth graders developed a deeper appreciation of real science and improved their writing skills. In addition, they posted their work on the school's Internet web site. The result was a beautiful field guide that exceeded our expectations. (You can download an Acrobat Reader PDF copy of the student Geology Field Guide from the Swift River web site at www.swiftriver.k14.mass.edu/write_path/ GeologyGuideFullsm.pdf).

We evaluated learner facility with technology by noting comfort levels, the questions asked during lab time, the amount of prompting students required to use hardware and software independently, and how many times we needed to review basic procedures. Analyzing this behavior helped us identify problem areas and alerted us to tech skills that the students needed to revisit.

With embedded instructional technology, students exhibited great enthusiasm and task engagement. They were invested in their work, partly because the tools are fun to use. Individualized electronic supports (for example, spelling and grammar checkers, thesaurus, and dictionary) lent a hand when needed. All students appreciated being able to generate great-looking final products enhanced with pictures and illustrations.

The use of AlphaSmart keyboards and Microsoft Word facilitated writing for most of the youngsters, especially those with fine-motor difficulties. They drafted longer, neater sentences with fewer spelling and grammatical errors. It was easier for them to proofread and edit their own work. They could easily elaborate and organize their text.

The technology that the team integrated into the unit helped the students organize their ideas and write, revise, and gather scientific data. It also boosted their confidence, understanding, and performance. Pre- and postproject assessments confirmed that writing skills improved across the learning spectrum from mainstream students to the challenged and gifted.

For further information, you may contact:

Carol S. Holzberg, PhD (carolh@anthro.umass.edu), Technology Coordinator

Christine Morin (christinemorin1@netscape.net), Technology Integration Specialist

Chris Wings (cwings@crocker.com), fourth-grade classroom teacher

Academic Software

Academic software includes the wide variety of software packages that can be used to enrich the teaching and learning environment for both teachers and students. Academic software may include packages that help the teacher teach and those designed to help the learner acquire targeted competencies. A teacher needs to be aware of the many common categories of academic software to be able to select the best software to achieve his or her objectives. Table 6.1 lists the most common categories of academic software and their uses. Within each of these categories, there are literally hundreds of commercial, freeware, and shareware programs available to educators. As with administrative software, although the initial costs vary, the need to invest time in mastering, using, and supporting a software program does not. Educators need to be careful in selecting the software to which they commit themselves and their students.

In the remainder of this chapter, you will be introduced to and have the opportunity to explore fully the many types of academic software that will be available to you for use in your classroom. As you can see from the list in Table 6.1, the options are many. Taking the time now to explore what each type of academic software can do to help you teach and help your students learn will save you time, effort, and your classroom budget when you teach.

Authoring Systems

As you learned in Chapter 2, the first step in effective instruction is to analyze your learners carefully so that you can adjust instruction to their needs. Although educators may teach the same grade level or the same course content, good instruction is bound to vary in response to the learners being addressed. Many educators are somewhat reluctant to use commercially produced instructional software simply because it does not fit well enough with their particular students or with their lesson plans and objectives. Teachers may therefore want to create their own instructional software. To do so, you may select to use a category of academic software known as **authoring systems.**

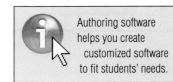

Authoring software helps you create customized software to fit students' needs.

TABLE 6.1   Academic Software Summary

SOFTWARE TYPE	APPLICATION TO TEACHING AND LEARNING
AUTHORING SYSTEMS 	Hypermedia and web authoring systems enable teachers to create their own hypermedia tutorials and web pages to support their curriculum.
DESKTOP PUBLISHING 	Another communication tool for educators, desktop publishing software enables teachers to create professional-looking newsletters, flyers, transparencies, and other printed media.
GRAPHICS	Graphics software enables teachers and students to support teaching and learning through visuals created or enhanced electronically.
REFERENCE 	Reference software, usually on CD-ROMs, includes visual- and sound-enhanced, hyperlinked electronic resources, such as dictionaries, encyclopedias, and atlases.
TUTORIALS AND DRILL-AND-PRACTICE	Tutorials and drill-and-practice software give students one-on-one, usually interactive reviews of target concepts.

continued ▶

EDUCATIONAL GAMES 	Games present content in a format that engages the learner while providing practice.
SIMULATIONS 	Simulations provide students an opportunity to interact with model environments that promote discovery learning.
SPECIAL NEEDS 	Software for students with special needs assists them in multiple ways, from reading screens to enlarging pointers, in order to help them function effectively in school.
INTEGRATED LEARNING SYSTEMS 	Combining classroom management tools with tutorial software designed to reinforce target objectives, ILS software provides an integrated package of resources.

Authoring systems include programs that create computer-based customized multimedia lessons and those that create lessons for presentation online. Both types use a **hypermedia** format. They create and present multimedia via a series of jumps or links so that students can move through the learning experience in their own unique way. Authoring systems range from easy-to-use software to robust but more complex software that can create commercial-looking programs. Regardless of the software you select, authoring systems can help you or your students organize and present lessons, projects, or reports to the class.

One of the earliest types of hypermedia authoring systems available was Hypercard for the Macintosh. This software, designed for computer-based presentation, created a series of cards each with multimedia elements, similar to multimedia flash cards. Together these cards formed a "stack" to represent all of the concepts in the lesson. Once created, the stack could be saved so it could be played back on most computers or

E-Learning

www.mylabschool.com
video
View *Using Authoring Software*

presented to the entire class via LCD display or large-screen monitor. While Apple recently discontinued this software, many playable educational stacks are still in use in schools and available on the Web.

As a result of the popularity of Hypercard, several products were developed for the Windows environments. HyperStudio is one of the more widely used programs for Windows computers (Figure 6.1). It works much like Hypercard did in that it creates a series of linked cards each of which may contain text, audio, graphics, animation, or video (Figure 6.2). It is relatively easy to use by both teachers and students. A Software Skills Builder that creates a sample lesson using HyperStudio is available at mylabschool.com.

PowerPoint has more recently become the most popular software for creating hypermedia lessons. While most PowerPoint shows are designed to be linear or shown in a fixed sequence, the software does contain the features necessary to emulate hypermedia software. Using PowerPoint, you can include multimedia elements on every slide, and you can provide buttons on each slide to link to other slides in nonlinear sequences. PowerPoint can thus easily be repurposed to be used as an authoring system. At mylabschool.com, you will find a Software Skills Builders activity that uses PowerPoint's features to link nonsequential slides to create flash cards, a very simple hypermedia example.

Each of these authoring systems is primarily designed to create in-class presentations. While most lessons created with these software packages can also be adjusted and saved in a format that can be used for presentation online, some authoring systems are designed specifically to create lessons for presentation online. This class of software, known as web authoring systems, can assist you in creating multimedia web pages that can be linked to other pages within the lesson or to support sites elsewhere on the web.

E-Learning

www.mylabschool.com
Software Skills Builder
HyperStudio—About Me

E-Learning
ON THE WEB! 6.1

Bridging Theory and Practice

FIGURE 6.1

HyperStudio for Multimedia Authoring

HyperStudio and similar multimedia authoring software enable teachers and students to create their own tutorials.

Screen captures of HyperStudio for Multimedia Authoring. Reprinted by permission of Vivendi Universal Games, Inc.

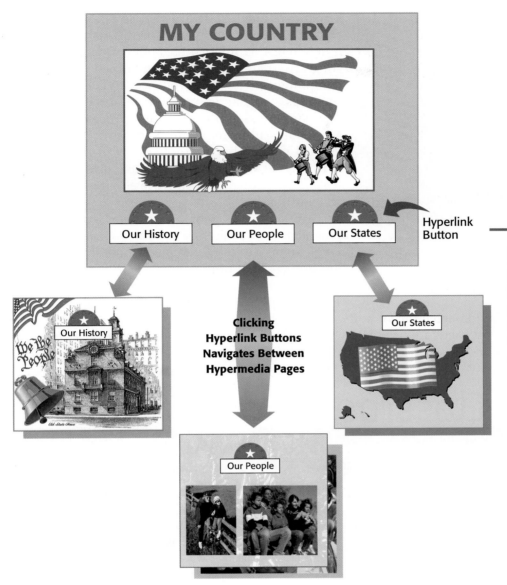

Our History · Our People · Our States

Hyperlink Button

Clicking Hyperlink Buttons Navigates Between Hypermedia Pages

Our History

Our States

Our People

FIGURE 6.2
Hyperlinks for Navigating Hypermedia
Hyperlinks let students jump to different cards at the click of the mouse.

Internet authoring software shares many of the tools and features of hypermedia authoring software. Programs designed for creating Internet-based displays (web pages) generate hypermedia that is saved in a format called Hypertext Markup Language (HTML). HTML is the computer language that has been agreed on for use on the Internet's World Wide Web sites. Internet browsers, that is, special programs designed to translate HTML data into computer displays, are then used to view and navigate these types of hypermedia pages.

The demand for software to assist in the creation of web pages by educators and their students has created increasing pressure on software vendors. For this reason, in addition to software that was specifically created to produce web pages, many software companies are adding an HTML conversion feature to their other types of software. Most word processors and desktop publishing software include the ability to turn a word-processed page into an HTML page with just a click on a button or

E-Learning
ON THE WEB! 6.3
Hypermedia in Instruction

Web authoring systems translate input into HTML for presentation on the web.

Authoring systems allow teachers to create multimedia lessons to fully engage learners by addressing diverse learning styles through interactive experiences.

a menu choice. Software that is specifically designed to create web page documents is typically much more sophisticated and full-featured than software that simply has an added conversion component. The material at mylabschool.com includes two hands-on activities that will guide you step-by-step through the process of using Microsoft Publisher's and Microsoft Word's Web Wizard web authoring tool. You will no doubt be surprised at how simple and easy it is to create a web page—indeed an entire web site—using this web authoring tool.

Web authoring tools range from extremely sophisticated to relatively simple to use and from very expensive to free. Indeed, some Internet hosting services that offer web space to the public also provide free and easy-to-use web authoring tools. The web pages that can be developed with this wide selection of software vary just as significantly. High-end authoring packages are used to develop sophisticated commercial web sites; freeware

in the Classroom

HYPERMEDIA IN THE LANGUAGE CLASSROOM

Hablamos español! Increasingly, American schools are accepting the responsibility of teaching languages other than English. Jerie Milici, a high school Spanish teacher from Greenwich, Connecticut, found a way to make not only learning the language but becoming familiar with the culture of Hispanic countries both fun and effective. Her innovative approach to this dual challenge, designing a contest for her students, employed the students' fascination with technology and their love of competition.

In this innovative activity, Ms. Milici gave students placed in groups the choice of a country in which Spanish is the native tongue. Their initial assignment was to create "a HyperStudio program on their particular country using information they downloaded from the Internet or scanned from other sources" which she shared with recipients of the Etools-weekly email list from the National Education Association. To present their programs, students were required to have "at least five cards plus sound and visuals" in their program and to be "responsible for submitting ten questions that could be answered by their presentation." In addition, a different

computer was designated for each country, and the students were required to decorate the computers to be representative of the countries. For example, "Mexico wore a sombrero and Spain had a bull close by." Each group also wrote ten questions about the country that were to be answered as their presentation was viewed.

When groups had created their programs, the contest phase of the assignment began. Each group "visited" a country (computer station) they had not originally been assigned. Referring to the list of ten questions at that station, the students were challenged to come up with the right answers. Each group strove to be first to complete the hunt and receive a prize. In case students visiting the computer stations didn't know how to work the HyperStudio program, a student was placed at each of the stations to walk the contestants through the process. With this unique combination of student-made hypermedia software and kinesthetic activity, students were taught not only a language but also the culture that gave it life.

SOURCE: J. Milici. (2003). Foreign studies. Retrieved October 23, 2003, from **http://www.nea.org**.

or shareware authoring packages can create very attractive personal home pages or whole web sites. Educators need to carefully review and evaluate their options before investing time in learning a web authoring tool and developing a web site.

Using Authoring Systems

Regardless of the authoring tool that is selected, with training, both you and your students can use this software to create customized, targeted lessons. Teacher-made lessons allow you to create learning software that meets the specific lesson objectives identified in your instructional design. Such lessons can be used in large- or small-group presentations to present and demonstrate key content points. They can also be used with individual students for additional review and reinforcement of content or to study a missed lesson after an absence. Teacher-made lessons can be specifically designed to present material that is consistent with identified student learning modalities and at content levels that are appropriate to those observed in any given class of students.

While authoring software will support a teacher in developing customized academic lessons, another type of software, desktop publishing software, will assist teachers who want to create customized handouts, transparencies, class newsletters, or flyers. Desktop publishing software provides tools for creating professional-looking hard copies as well as authoring web pages.

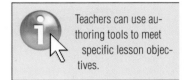

Teachers can use authoring tools to meet specific lesson objectives.

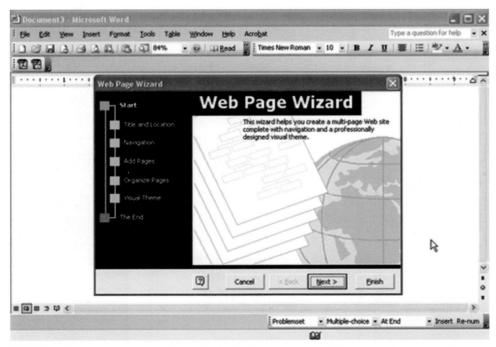

Web Wizards support the creation of a web site using a familiar program such as MS Word and then converting your document.

Microsoft Word® is a registered trademark of Microsoft Corporation.

Desktop publishing (DTP) software produces professional-looking hard-copy output.

E-Learning

www.mylabschool.com
Software Skills Builder
Publisher Skills–Classroom Sign

 Desktop Publishing Software

Originally written to make the work of manual layout and design in the publishing business easier, **desktop publishing (DTP) software** has brought to the average computer-using educator the ability to create professional-looking printed or electronic pages. Sophisticated documents can be created that include text, graphics, digital pictures, stylized headlines, and professionally prepared design elements. These elements can then be arranged and manipulated on a page until the best possible page layout is achieved (see Figure 6.3).

At mylabschool.com, you will find three hands-on activities to assist you in becoming familiar with this very useful software. Trying all three activities will give you the skills you need to effectively use the software for creating handouts, flyers, transparencies, and even a classroom web site.

Desktop publishing software is a versatile tool for educators. With it, an educator can easily design and print

- Customized transparency masters to illustrate a critical concept
- Customized student worksheets with clip art or digital pictures
- Posters and signs for the classroom, media center, or school
- Class or school newsletters
- Customized booklets for reading, coloring, or reinforcing concepts
- Customized award certificates
- Flash cards and sight-word cards
- Custom instructional packets for review of targeted competencies

In students hands, desktop publishing software can be used to

- Create cards and letters to give to parents
- Produce hard-copy enhancements to group projects

FIGURE 6.3

An Example of Desktop Publishing Software

Microsoft Publisher is an easy-to-use DTP program that creates professional-looking publications.

Microsoft Publisher® is a registered trademark of Microsoft Corporation.

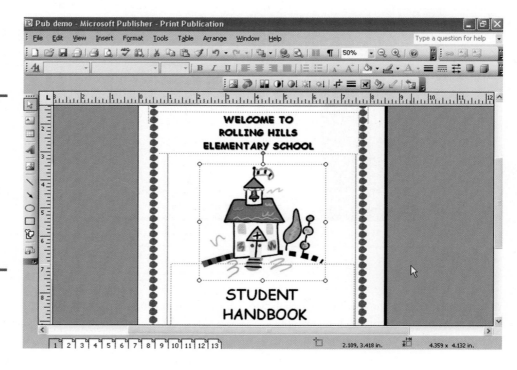

- Write up a field trip report
- Make classroom or school banners
- Create homework calendars and assignment tracking sheets
- Lay out school yearbooks

Many popular desktop publishing software packages also include a web site authoring component. With this feature, web pages can be laid out using the same tools and skills that it takes to create a print document. Then, with a built-in conversion component, the software automatically converts the elements of the laid-out page into one that can be viewed on the World Wide Web with any suitable browser. Thus, teachers or their students can very easily create and maintain a very sophisticated, attractive web site.

As you can see, desktop publishing software can be used to create a wide range of instructional materials, and neither teacher nor students need to be computer experts to create attractive and useful materials. To maximize effectiveness, materials created with desktop publishing software should follow some general design suggestions. Elements of effective visuals will be more extensively explored in Chapter 9, but for the purposes of desktop publishing, educators should stay mindful of the design principles demonstrated in Figure 6.4.

At mylabschool.com, you will find hands-on Microsoft Publisher activities that demonstrate good visual design as well as the features of desktop publishing software. Try these activities to gain skill in using this useful educational software tool.

E-Learning

www.mylabschool.com
Software Skills Builder
Publisher Skills–Overhead Transparency Master

Graphics Software

Digital visual images, whether drawings, photos, or graphs, are typically referred to as graphics. **Graphics software,** then, is the broad category of software that can be used to create, edit, or enhance digital images. Different types of graphics software perform different functions and have different capabilities, as you will see next, but all help you add digital visuals to clarify and enhance instruction.

Graphics software also includes packaged collections of prepared graphics that are usually organized into libraries of images. Such collections may include drawings, photos, and even animated graphics. The images included in these graphics libraries are organized so that you can easily preview the images, copy them, and then paste them into other applications. You may choose to paste them directly into a document you create with desktop publishing software, or you can paste them into other graphics software to further edit the images before using them. In either case, these collections offer a valuable alternative to creating visual images from scratch.

Clip Art Libraries

Most software that uses graphic elements includes a library of prepared drawings and digital pictures. These libraries are called clip art libraries, a term that is carried over from the days of manual page layout when layout artists literally clipped artwork with scissors and then pasted it onto pages.

FIGURE 6.4

Design Principles in Desktop Publishing

Whether publishing web pages or creating flyers, always follow the principles of good design. Contrast the balanced design of the web page on the left with the poor design of the flyer on the right. Which is more likely to effectively communicate information?

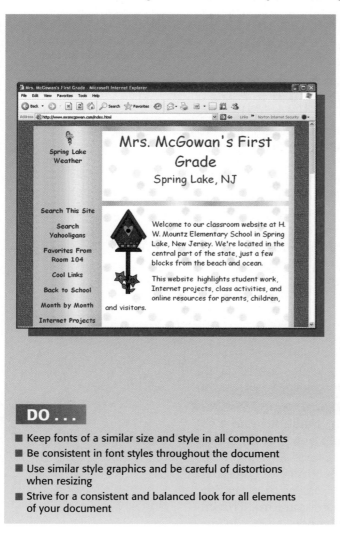

DO . . .

- Keep fonts of a similar size and style in all components
- Be consistent in font styles throughout the document
- Use similar style graphics and be careful of distortions when resizing
- Strive for a consistent and balanced look for all elements of your document

DON'T . . .

- Use many different font types and enhancements
- Mix number of columns on a single page
- Distort graphics when sizing or use too many diverse types of graphics
- Change line spacing or font sizes on a single page

Clip art images offer educators ready-made artwork that can easily be added to word-processed documents, presentations, or desktop-published pages. Typically, all of these types of software packages include extensive clip art libraries with thousands of prepared images. Supplemental clip art libraries are also available and may include tens of thousands of rendered or photographic images, in color or black and white. Most clip art image libraries are sold with each image preformatted in the many different digital formats that are needed for inclusion in word-processing, presentation, desktop publishing, or authoring software. Other clip art images are available via the Internet, often offered free without any copyright restrictions. For educators, this wealth of ready-made images can be used to easily enhance

COOL TOOLS

Online Clip Art Libraries

Microsoft Office provides an extensive library of clip art images that are shared by all applications within the suite. But beyond that, Microsoft also offers an online library of thousands of free clip art images available for download. The available images include graphics, animation, and photos. As a link on the Clip Art Library site, Microsoft also provides Clip Art and Media Assistance to help you maximize the use of the images. There you will find helpful hints on how to search for the clip art you want, edit it once it is down-loaded, and add images to a file. There are even online demonstrations with animation and audio to show you how to use the clip art library. Visuals are an important addition to any lesson. With this cool tool it is simple for any teacher to find the perfect images to illustrate the content being taught.

printed or displayed instructional materials. With just a few clicks of the mouse, visual richness can be added to text materials.

However, clip art is limited in that a ready-made image might or might not be exactly what is needed to illustrate a point. It is occasionally necessary to create or customize images to better represent a concept. For this purpose, programs that enable you to create graphics can be used. These programs include three distinct categories based on functions. The first, illustration software, gives you the electronic tools to create and edit digital images. The second, imaging software, creates images from nonelectronic sources. The third, editing software, provides the capabilities to alter, enhance, or add special effects to digital images. All of these software packages offer you the capabilities of working with graphics, but each has its own set of tools and functions to perform its unique tasks. All add to an educator's ability to add powerful visual imagery to instructional materials.

E-Learning
ON THE WEB! 6.4
Clip Art Online

Illustration Software

Software that provides you with the tools to create new images from scratch includes paint programs and draw programs. Each of these makes it possible to create new artwork or customize existing artwork. However, they operate somewhat differently, and each has a specialized set of tools.

Paint Programs

Paint programs allow you to create and manipulate digital pictures in a manner very similar to the way one paints a picture in the real world. Like real-world painting, paint software provides electronic pen and brush tools to draw straight, curved, and free-form lines; to color in objects; or to erase them in whole or part. Paint programs also offer a variety of brush and pen sizes and shapes and even a spray-paint tool for different visual effects. Additionally, these programs provide a selection tool that lets you identify and select distinct pieces of the artwork so that specific identified components of an image can be copied into another document or printed out.

Paint programs simulate traditional painting with electronic painting tools.

Paint programs range from the extremely sophisticated software used to create the high-end digital artwork featured in magazine displays or movie backgrounds to simple-to-use software included as a free accessory program with Windows and Macintosh operating systems. Regardless of the sophistication level selected, educators and students can use paint programs to create digital images for inclusion in presentations, multimedia files, desktop-published documents, or word processing. These programs can also be used to adjust and customize existing clip art or digital photographs to better meet the objectives of an instructional event. Paint programs are powerful software tools that the teacher or students can easily use to enhance instructional materials or delivery.

Draw Programs

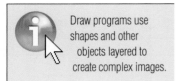

Draw programs use shapes and other objects layered to create complex images.

Draw programs can also create and customize digital images. However, draw programs, sometimes called object-oriented or vector graphic programs, work differently from paint programs. Drawing tools do not include the familiar brushes, paint cans, pencils, or erasers you can find in paint programs. Rather than creating individual pixel elements such as lines by using an electronic pencil, draw programs create objects that can be manipulated to create images. Like paint programs, draw programs have a variety of tools to customize or create graphics. These tools are designed to define and manipulate a series of geometric objects such as squares, curves, and circles that can be arranged to create a picture. With draw programs, graphics are created by layering objects on top of one another, as illustrated in Figure 6.5.

FIGURE 6.5

A Comparison of Draw and Paint Programs

Paint programs use virtual pens, pencils, and brushes, while draw programs create images by layering shapes.

Paint® and Windows Draw® are registered trademarks of Microsoft Corporation.

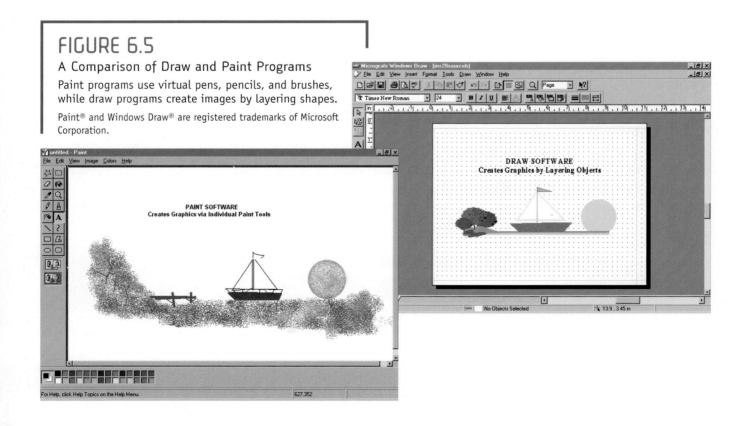

Both types of software packages are useful to teachers and their students in creating visual support for instructional content. Teachers can easily create colorful and meaningful transparencies or graphic elements for presentation with a draw program even if they do not have extensive art skills. For those who are artists, paint programs provide the electronic means to create editable artwork for inclusion in materials. For students, drawing software provides them limitless tools to create or edit just the right picture for their oral report, an electronic card to send to their parents, or a page for their class web site.

Further, both types of software are capable of editing existing clip art or graphics, although with different sets of tools. Using such software, teachers can enhance a digital image by highlighting targeted areas for emphasis or adding text annotation to a graphic's components. Students can create a collage of selected clip art to add interest and dimension to their work. Draw and paint programs can range widely in price and capabilities, but even the easiest and most inexpensive of these software packages can add significant visual enhancement to all types of instructional materials.

Imaging Software

Imaging software generally refers to the family of software packages that are used with scanners to convert hard-copy images to digital images. Typically, scanners are bundled with imaging software that is compatible with their hardware. All imaging software is capable of converting a hard-copy page of text or graphics to a digital graphic. This graphic can then be treated like any other digital image. A photograph of a flower could be

Imaging Resources

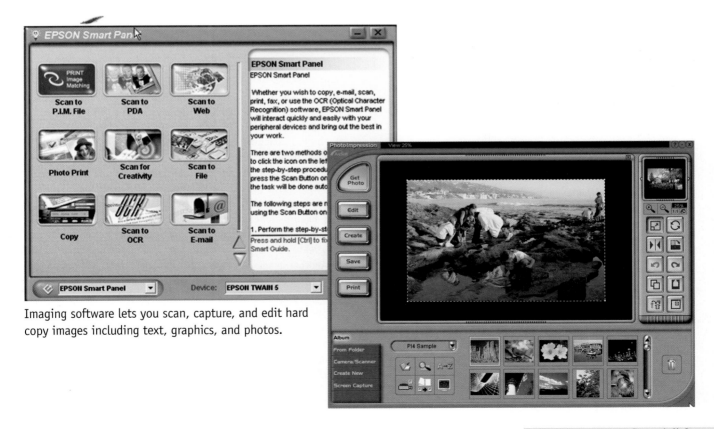

Imaging software lets you scan, capture, and edit hard copy images including text, graphics, and photos.

scanned with imaging software and saved as a digital graphic; it could then be opened in a drawing program so that arrows and text enhancements could be added to label the image. In this way you can add instructional elements to any image.

Some imaging software is capable of not only converting hard copy into graphic elements but also converting pages of text into pages of electronic text that can be manipulated by a word processor. Hard-copy versions of worksheets or tests can be digitized and saved as word-processed documents. They can then be updated, edited, or entirely repurposed for other instructional activities. This added feature found in some imaging software packages can add a valuable tool for busy educators while adding very little additional cost to the software.

Editing Software

Editing, the third category of graphics software that works with digital images, provides the tools to alter and enhance images. Whether the images are digital photographs, clip art, scanned images, or images you have created, **editing software** allows you to change the image.

Some draw and paint software packages include an import feature that allows you to bring in an image created or saved outside of that package. The image may be a digital photo, a scanned image, clip art, or even something saved from the Internet. Once imported, the software may then let you alter the image using the same tools that are available to alter images you create. The ability to import software for further editing is a useful feature to look for when selecting draw and paint software.

TECHNOLOGY SOLUTIONS
for All Learners

Using Imaging to Assist Special Needs Learners

Imaging software translates hard-copy pages into their equivalent digital image or text files. While this resource can be used effectively to supplement lessons for sighted students, those who are sight impaired need more than images or text. A unique type of imaging software, called Optical Braille Recognition (OBR) software, serves these students and their teachers by using a scanner to translate Braille. OBR software enables the teacher to scan a Braille page and translate it into text for the teacher and for sighted students. Further, the text file can be saved, stored, and later used with a Braille printer to recreate the original Braille document. This imaging software makes it possible for non-Braille readers to read documents used by sight-impaired students, to archive Braille books, and to reprint Braille pages when needed.

For learning-disabled students, another scanner and software serves to help those with reading disorders. The reading pen is a scanner built into a pen-shaped device that contains a small screen display and speaker. The student can move the pen across a word or line of text, much like a highlighter, and the built-in imaging software recognizes the words and finds them in its internal dictionary. The student can then select to have the word or passage pronounced aloud or have the screen display present the word's meaning from the dictionary, synonyms from the thesaurus, or the syllabication of the words. This small handheld imaging device makes it possible for reading-challenged students to get immediate support as they read.

Another imaging software package scans printed pages and reads them aloud to sight-impaired and learning-disabled students. Any text from the printed page, the Web, or an electronic file may be scanned and read aloud to the student. Further, the software visually highlights the text as it is read. This type of imaging product can also help students take tests by first scanning them, then reading them to the student who needs this additional support.

Imaging software more typically offers the capability of in-depth editing of digital images, whether acquired through scanning or digital photography. This type of imaging/editing software usually includes a variety of photo-styling and special effects software packages that range in price and capability from those used at home to the powerful packages that are used to create the dramatic digital special effects seen on television and in films. Many medium-priced programs allow you to edit images in unusual ways, ranging from blending one image into another to creating animations that can be included in presentation and multimedia files. These effects add significant interest and appeal but may require a substantial investment in time.

For educators, imaging and editing software adds an element of control over the quality of images produced by digital photography or via scanning. Photo-styling software can typically alter the lighting, contrast, color intensity, and cropping of a digital image (see Figure 6.6). Many can also add corrections to an image, such as correcting "red-eye" in pictures of animals and people. Still others offer some special effects capabilities such as blurring parts of the image or making it into a mosaic display.

For those who need advanced special effects features to add artistic elements, special effects software packages are available that enable all types of enhancements, from morphing, in which one image appears to melt into another, to altering images to appear as if they were created through a variety of different camera lenses. These more advanced styling features are particularly dramatic in multimedia displays, as they add interest to the multisensory elements included in that type of presentation.

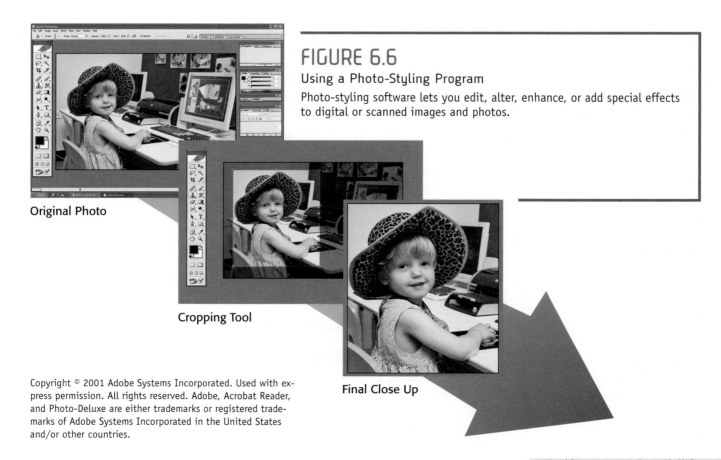

Original Photo

Cropping Tool

Final Close Up

FIGURE 6.6
Using a Photo-Styling Program
Photo-styling software lets you edit, alter, enhance, or add special effects to digital or scanned images and photos.

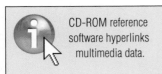

CD-ROM reference software hyperlinks multimedia data.

E-Learning
ON THE WEB! 6.6
Reference Software

Reference Software

Reference software, digital versions of volumes of reference materials, can now be easily stored on a single compact disc. This capacity has revolutionized the way in which, and speed at which, great stores of reference materials can be used. Using CD-based reference software, students can jump to any points of information recorded on the CD. With a simple point and click on an interactive link, a student or teacher can follow an idea and questions that emerge from exploring that idea in whatever order he or she chooses. In addition, because it is just as simple to store digital images, sounds, and video as it is to store text, reference material that was once confined to text with only an occasional static illustration can become dazzling and informative multimedia information. The potential of these additional types of digital information for learners of different modalities is clear.

These types of digital enhancements, combined with the compact and easy-to-use storage media offered by CD-ROMs, have led to the creation of a variety of new educational reference software tools. These broad categories of CD-ROM-based reference programs and their applications are summarized in Table 6.2.

The wide variety of software manufacturers that produce reference CDs leads to great variability in the features in any one piece of software. Some have extensive multimedia components; in others, text is dominant. Some include facilities for printing the text and graphics elements; others may not. Because of the variety in this type of software, it is important for educators to carefully review and evaluate the capabilities of this type of software before investing in it. The academic software evaluation rubric (Table 6.3) can be a valuable tool for effective software decision making. This rubric or one like it should be used before making any academic software purchases.

Tutorials and Drill-and-Practice Software

Software designed to teach new content or reinforce a lesson can assist an educator in addressing learner needs, particularly when time demands or the teacher–student ratio limits the teacher's ability to provide sufficient one-to-one interaction. This category of academic software can offer students opportunities to learn new content or provide additional practice to reinforce concepts already presented.

Tutorials

Tutorial software presents new material, usually in a carefully orchestrated instructional sequence with frequent opportunities for practice and review. These software packages are often self-contained lessons designed and planned according to the principles of instructional design. Tutorial software programs can either be linear or use a hypermedia approach. Linear tutorials take the learner step-by-step through each phase of the instructional process for each objective. For example, a student using a linear

TABLE 6.2   Reference Software Summary

SOFTWARE TYPE	FEATURES	APPLICATION TO TEACHING AND LEARNING TASKS
ENCYCLOPEDIAS	• Easy-to-use hypermedia connections to browse cross-referenced items • Can include text, graphics, animation, and audio and video clips to support information • Some support note taking on content	• Enables teacher and student research in all content areas • Interactive format promotes discovery learning • Presentation can help meet multiple learning styles
ATLASES	• Hypermedia connections allow user to move between countries and features by pointing and clicking • Often includes satellite images from NASA to present topographical features • Can include text, graphics, animation, and audio and video clips to support information • Some support note taking on content	• Enables teacher and student examination of global geography • Interactive format promotes discovery learning • Presentation can help meet multiple learning styles
GRAMMAR TOOLS	• Can include a thesaurus and grammar checker • Provides suggestions for alternative words or grammatical structures from which the writer can choose	• Provides students support for editing their work • Interactive format promotes discovery learning • Presentation can help meet multiple learning styles
DICTIONARIES	• Provides quick search for target words • Can include text, graphics, animation, and audio and video clips to support definitions	• Provides students support for vocabulary • Interactive format promotes discovery learning • Presentation can help meet multiple learning styles

tutorial will typically be presented with content, then evaluated to see whether the competencies have been achieved. Finally, this type of software will provide feedback to the learner as to his or her attainment of objectives along with suggestions to return to the sections that have not yet been mastered before going on to the next competency.

By contrast, tutorials that use a hypermedia approach allow students to explore more freely the various content pathways available in the program. Using hyperlinks, students can move through the materials in accordance

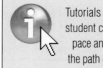

Tutorials can give the student control of the pace and, sometimes, the path of interaction.

TABLE 6.3　Academic Software Evaluation Rubric

SOFTWARE:

DESCRIPTION:

VENDOR:　　　　　　　　　　　　　　　　　　　　　　**COST:**

NOTES ON USE:

Please rate the featues below for each piece of software. Next to each of the items in the rubric, check the box that best reflects your opinion.

SOFTWARE FEATURE	EVALUATION CRITERIA				
	1 Poor	2 Below Average	3 Average	4 Above Average	5 Excellent
DOCUMENTATION	Documentation is excessively technical and/or difficult to follow	Documentation is generally understandable but not very user-friendly	Documentation is easy to follow and understand; includes all necessary components	Clear documentation that is logical and easy to follow	Very clear, easy-to-read, logical, and complete documentation
SITE LICENSE	No licensing available	Site licenses are available but limited or expensive options	Site licensing available at reasonable cost	Special, low site licensing pricing for education	Educators may use for free without a site license
INSTALLATION	Complex to install; poor installation instructions	Installation somewhat difficult; instructions minimal	Installation process typical; instructions fairly clear and complete	Easy to install; clear, easy-to-understand instructions	Self-installing; step-by-step installation included
TECHNICAL SUPPORT	No toll-free telephone support available	No local support; phone support available for an hourly fee	Local support and phone support available for modest fee	Local tech help available for modest fee; no-charge phone support	Local help and toll-free support readily available at no charge
HELP FEATURES	No online or text-based help available	A Read-Me text file is included; no online help	Both online and text help available on CD	Online help is context-sensitive and provides clear assistance; text included	Automatic online help available for every feature; supplementary text help included
GRADE LEVEL	Not suitable for intended grade level	Some features unsuitable for intended grade level	Majority of features suitable for intended grade level	Most features appropriate and suitable for intended grade level	All features both suitable and appropriate for grade level
STANDARDS	Does not address target standards	Few standards addressed; many ignored	A majority of the standards are addressed	Most of the desired standards are addressed	All of the target standards and others are addressed
ACTIVE LEARNING	Interaction is passive; no active learning encouraged	Interaction mostly passive; a few active learning opportunities included	Interaction offers average active learning opportunities; some activities too passive	Good active interaction provided through a majority of the software	Students are actively engaged during all components of software
SAVE FEATURES	Students cannot interrupt and save work	Student work can be saved on an external disk, but it cannot be reused	Students may save their work to continue working on it in the future	Automatically saves the student's work when the program is closed	Both automatically and manually, student's work can be saved and restarted at the same point later
HARDWARE COMPATIBILITY	Works on relatively few available computers; requires additional hardware	Works on several machines; requires upgrades to some available computers	Will work on most machines with minimal or no hardware upgrades or additions	Works on most available machines without hardware upgrades or additions	Works on all machines available without hardware upgrades or additions
COST	High cost relative to features	Somewhat expensive relative to features	Average cost for features offered	Reasonably priced with numerous features for the cost	Special low pricing for educational users for abundant features

Total the score for each piece of software. Compare the scores. The piece of software with the highest score is your best choice.

with their personal preferences and interests. Of course, these hypermedia-style tutorials also include evaluation and feedback components.

Tutorials of both types may be primarily text or a combination of text and multimedia components, including graphics, animation, and audio and video clips. Some may have built-in classroom management support components that track, record, and report individual student progress on each included lesson. All are interactive, in that the student must respond and interact for the tutorial to progress.

Tutorials give the student control of the pace and, in the case of hypermedia tutorials, the path of instruction. Tutorials are limited by their ability to respond to stu-

Tutorial software presents and pratices new concepts in a format that maintains learners' interest throughout the process.

dents' questions or concerns outside their programming. Even the best-designed tutorial software may not be able to respond to the divergent thinking of many learners. For many users, tutorials are viewed as limiting and potentially boring because of their rigidity in the presentation of topics. Still, a well-written tutorial that is programmed with multimedia components in the presentation of materials can be very useful for support or review of material or even as an additional strategy in the communication of content.

Drill-and-Practice Software

Whereas tutorials may present new material, **drill-and-practice software** is designed to reinforce previously presented content. Drill-and-practice software is used to question learners on key content points, giving them the opportunity to practice content by responding to specific questions. This type of software provides instant feedback as to the correctness of a response. Some drill-and-practice software packages track correct answers and move the level of questioning to more complex content as the students' responses indicate increased mastery.

Drill-and-practice software, like tutorials, ranges from fairly simple text-based, flash-card-type software to complex and sophisticated multimedia software. Drill-and-practice software allows the student to control the pace of the interaction, but users typically cannot alter the path of the review until they have mastered each level. Unlike answering review questions or taking a pop quiz for content practice, using drill-and-practice software provides instant feedback, and it may respond with additional drills targeting diagnosed weaknesses.

Critics of this type of software refer to it as "drill-and-kill" software, expressing the notion that it can be a boring and passive learning experience. Indeed, some drill-and-practice software lacks quality and interest.

E-Learning

www.mylabschool.com
video
View *Drill and Practice*

Furthermore, if used for overly long periods of time or for too many review sessions, it does not stimulate learning or promote interest in the content practiced. However, well-constructed, multimedia-rich drill-and-practice software can provide valuable supplemental experiences and targeted feedback for learners. It can also provide excellent practice before formal evaluations and can be used as a diagnostic for teachers who are fine-tuning their classroom instruction. As with all software, it is critical that educators carefully evaluate the academic value of drill-and-practice software before acquiring it and using it in the classroom.

Drill-and-practice software lets learners practice and review concepts as often and as long as they need to gain mastery.

 ## Educational Games

Educational games present and review instructional content in a game format. Content is repackaged so that it is furnished within the framework of a sequence of game rules and graphics (see Figure 6.7). Although educational games may present the same competencies that drill-and-practice or tutorial software presents, they are often better received by learners because the game component adds an element of interest and entertainment. Clearly, however, it is important to be sure the game elements do not overshadow the instructional elements.

FIGURE 6.7
Examples of Educational Game Software
Educational games present content in colorful and engaging formats.

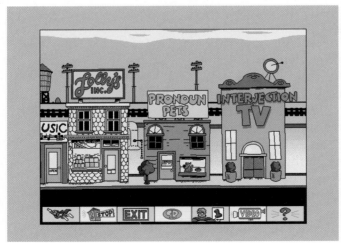

Screen capture of Reading Blaster by Knowledge Adventure, Inc. Reprinted by permission of Vivendi Universal Games, Inc.

Screen capture of Grammar Rock game by Creative Wonders. Courtesy of Riverdeep Interactive Learning.

Several broad categories of educational games are available to teachers who are interested in adding entertainment as an enhancement to the classroom, as shown in Table 6.4. Adventure games provide students the opportunity to solve mysteries and participate in educational adventures. An example of this type of game is the Carmen Sandiego adventure series. In this game series, students must have knowledge of a region or country to find the game's heroine. This educational game thus exercises social studies knowledge and critical-thinking skills while presenting the experience in an adventure game format.

TABLE 6.4 Spotlight on Academic Games

TYPES OF GAMES	POTENTIAL BENEFITS	EXAMPLES OF GAMES	POTENTIAL CLASSROOM APPLICATIONS
ACTION	Exercises hand–eye coordination, reasoning, content practice	• Blaster series (Math, Reading, etc.) *Davidson* • Jump Start Series *Vivendi*	Content practice in a shoot-'em-up format
ADVENTURE	Promotes problem-solving skills through adventure scenarios and role playing	• Carmen Sandiego series *Broderbund* • Magic School Bus series *Scholastic*	Geography/social studies in mystery format Math, reading, science, and art skills
STRATEGY/SIMULATION	Exercises problem solving, decision making, critical thinking, and content	• SimCity *Maxis* • Biology Explorer *Riverdeep*	Civics/architecture/urban studies/ social studies Anatomy, science
PUZZLES AND GAME CLASSIC	Reinforces and builds memory, logic, verbal, and planning skills	• Scrabble *Hasbro Interactive* • Zillions of Games *Zillions Development Corp.*	English and vocabulary review General knowledge

YOU Decide!

The role of educational games in the classroom is controversial. Some educators see value in the excitement and active learning a gaming environment presents. Others believe that the games detract from the implicit personal excitement and joy of learning. Still others object to educational games because they believe that students become so involved in the games themselves that they lose focus on the content. Some believe that game experiences are unnecessarily cumbersome ways to review content. Do you think educational games are valid learning tools?

YES! Just because software is fun for the students doesn't mean that it isn't meaningful. Educational games require students to solve math problems, spell correctly, or answer content-oriented questions to advance and win the game. Students are therefore practicing the content while playing and are more motivated to do so than if they were doing yet another review worksheet. Educational games have a very valid place in the classroom to both motivate and review.

NO! Games may have some use as a reward for good classroom behavior for brief amounts of time, but that's about all. Nothing takes the place of direct teaching and good old-fashioned practice. Students need to learn to accept and find self-motivation for the work that they are required to do. Sugarcoating the work in a game format detracts from it and is a detriment to teaching students to get the job done. When they get into the workplace, they will be expected to learn without playing any games. Teachers are not doing them any favors including games in instruction.

Which view do you agree with? YOU DECIDE!

Educational Games

A second category of educational games simulates traditional board or card games. These games typically require that the student respond with correct answers before advancing a game piece on a graphic of a board or playing a card in a virtual hand. This type of game superimposes content material on the traditional real-world game. Students must know how to play the traditional game to participate in the educational version.

Educational adaptations of television and popular video games can also add an element of "edutainment" to the classroom. Games that let students shoot down the right answer or race their virtual cars to the finish line by driving over the correct responses in the road are examples of video-game adaptations. Students enjoy the stimulating visuals and sound, practice eye–hand coordination, and review content simultaneously. Familiar and popular TV quiz shows have been adapted to software and can be used to review material preformatted into the software or added by the teacher. This category of educational games can add excitement and interest to content review.

Whether in the use of software games or a classroom game of hangman, gaming has been a widely accepted instructional strategy that has value in a classroom. As a reward for completing class assignments or as a replacement for other review strategies, playing educational games is a popular alternative for many educators. Clearly, it is important for you to carefully evaluate game activities in general and educational game software in particular for its suitability as a strategy to achieve your instructional objectives. Using the Academic Software Evaluation Rubric (Table 6.3) before incorporating educational game software into the classroom can help to ensure classroom time is well spent.

Simulations

Simulations are software packages that present the user with a model or situation in a computerized or virtual format. When using the software, learners interact with the simulation, and it responds to their actions. For example, flight simulator software mimics the conditions of flying various types of planes. As you move the mouse or press different keys assigned to represent speed, altitude, or various other aspects of the plane's conditions in its virtual sky, the screen displays a graphic of what one would see from the plane's cockpit. Conditions are thus simulated in response to user input.

In a more academic context, simulations are available that duplicate the conditions and appearance of a chemistry lab so that students can mix and heat virtual chemicals and see the results without having to deal with the real substances. Or students can dissect a virtual frog or examine parts of the human body and be able to see how each individual component works. Social science simulations might allow students to make decisions for virtual civilizations and then watch their impact on the social order and on the individuals within that society.

Simulations allow students to virtually manipulate models and situations safely in the classroom.

Whereas tutorials and drill-and-practice software provide very structured content environments, simulations offer the student opportunities to interact with the content and to participate in discovery learning. Simulations can time-shift models by slowing processes down or by speeding up the impact of student-directed changes. They can also provide safe versions of what would be dangerous experiments in the real world.

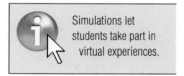

Simulations let students take part in virtual experiences.

Special Needs Software

Some educational software is specifically designed to address the requirements of learners with special needs as the result of a variety of physical or learning impairments. The category of **special needs software** includes software that reads words or letters aloud as they are displayed on the screen and software that enlarges text on the screen. These types of software address different levels of sight impairments in students. Special needs software also includes speech-synthesizing software, which converts spoken sounds and words into their graphic equivalent or into the text the sounds represent. Sounds are thus displayed on the computer screen to assist students who are hearing impaired and students who need additional perceptual feedback in reading. Specially prepared multimedia software targeting specific learning skills, such as listening skills, helps students with learning disabilities who require content presentation via additional modalities for accurate perceptual processing. Often, the assistive devices discussed in

E-Learning

www.mylabschool.com
video
View *Word Processing*

Special needs hardware and software assist physically challenged and special needs students to complete their academic tasks.

Assistive Software

Chapter 4 are sold with customized special needs software that takes advantage of the full range of features incorporated into the device.

Assistive software and hardware can address the special needs of exceptional students not only by facilitating their interaction with computers but also by presenting content in diverse formats. Learners with special needs may require that materials be presented in multisensory formats to be understood. Assistive software provides such diverse formats and may also include features that provide note-taking support and reading support. Assistive hardware and software may also facilitate communication so that a child can participate in academic interaction and assessment. The software also helps the special needs child participate in social communication and recreational activities.

A new technology support for special needs children is universal design. This type of support software automatically offers materials in a format that addresses the strongest learning mode for the individual student. For example, an E-book that uses universal design may be able to read a passage aloud for a sight-impaired student and offer that same passage in large print and vibrant colors for a student with a reading disability. This new approach to special needs software holds great promise in meeting the unique and diverse needs of exceptional students.

For those interested in additional information on the implications of technology for special needs students, the web offers abundant resources. Perhaps the best place to start is at the web site of the Council for Exceptional Children (**www.cec.sped.org**). First founded in 1922 at Teachers College, Columbia University, this organization has been a significant voice in advocating for exceptional students in all areas, including assistive technologies.

Integrated Learning Systems

Integrated learning systems (ILS) are online or hardware–software combinations of equipment and programs designed to assist students in learning targeted objectives. An ILS typically includes tutorial and drill-and-practice software as well as a comprehensive classroom management support system that records and can report on each student's progress after completion of every software lesson. Such systems address very detailed and specific objectives and can be used in whole or in part as reinforcement to an entire course or for a specific competency within a course. Often, ILS software is written to cover several consecutive grade levels and can therefore be easily adapted to address the different levels of skill found in the typical classroom.

Network-based integrated learning systems tend to be a more expensive solution to the need for technological support of instruction. They are often

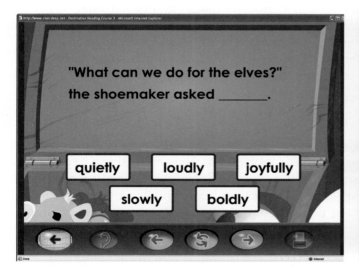

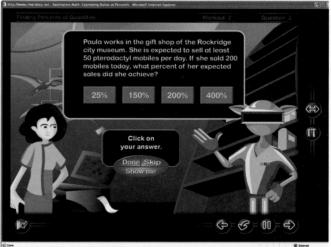

State	Product	State Standard / Inventory / Assessment	File Size	Grades
AL	Destination Math	Alabama Math Correlation	256.78 KB	1,2,3,4,5,6,7,8,K
AZ	Destination Math	Arizona Math Correlation	410.85 KB	1,10,11,12,2,3,4,5,6,7,8,9,K
CA	Destination Math	California Math Correlation	248.74 KB	10,11,12
CA	Destination Math	California Math Correlation	112.43 KB	3
CA	Destination Math	California Math Correlation	330.09 KB	4
CA	Destination Math	California Math Correlation	248.74 KB	4,5
CA	Destination Math	California Math Correlation	330.38 KB	5
CA	Destination Math	California Math Correlation	248.74 KB	6
CA	Destination Math	California Math Correlation	254.17 KB	6
CA	Destination Math	California Math Correlation	248.74 KB	7
CA	Destination Math	California Math Correlation	290.92 KB	7
CA	Destination Math	California Math Correlation	248.74 KB	8,9

Integrated Learning Systems, whether network based or online, correlate their products with each state's content area standards to ensure instruction is targeted to desired performance outcomes.

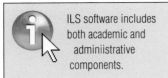

ILS software includes both academic and adminiistrative components.

bundled with their own hardware as well as software and are typically set up in a centralized location that allows all grade levels in a school to share the technology. Because of the cost and the shared implementation of these systems, a typical ILS may be sold to a district as a complete solution to the need for computers in schools and may take the place of individual computers in teachers' classrooms. This has led to some controversy over how computer dollars should be spent: by individual teachers addressing their students' needs or by a school district making decisions that try to address the needs of as many students as possible. Most schools and districts continue to have limited funding for the acquisition and implementation of computers, so this controversy is very likely to persist. Online subscriptions to ILS software are therefore fast becoming a preferred alternative.

Other Academic Software

Other types of software can be used for academic reinforcement, for building learning skills, and for enriching the teaching and learning environment. Some have been created with classroom use in mind; others have been creatively adapted to the classroom by innovative teachers. These software packages offer opportunities to add new dimensions to learning and to assist students in exercising critical-thinking skills.

Problem-Solving Software

Problem-solving software is written to help students acquire and practice problem-solving skills. Such skills include forming and testing a hypothesis; finding multiple-step strategies to solve problems such as math word problems; correctly applying theories, rules, and concepts to predict outcomes; and sequencing critical-thinking steps to come to targeted conclusions. Software of this type can be content oriented (such as math problem-solving software) or of a more general nature to help develop problem-solving skills that can be broadly applied and transferred to other areas.

Problem-solving software gives learners a platform on which they can learn by doing. Such software is designed to allow students to try to explain why a phenomenon occurs and then to run a series of tests to find out whether they are correct. Well-adapted to science experimentation, such software may let students develop an explanation of an aspect of the physical world, such as what friction is, and then test their concept to refine their assumptions. In math, the software may provide opportunities to test logical or mathematical relationships. The value for learners in using this type of software exceeds the content they experiment with. The greater

Students can use academic software to participate in problem-solving, critical-thinking, and creative experiences not otherwise available to them.

value may be the refining of their ability to see and solve problems independently. The ability to transfer such problem-solving skills to other content and activities may well be the greatest benefit.

For teachers who are interested in developing their students' problem-solving skills, such software offers a way to enhance the learning experience via a constructivist approach and a multimedia environment. Students can extend their knowledge by extending hypotheses based on what they already know, and they can do so in an environment that offers audio, visual, and text components. Problem-solving software can add dimension and depth to content while letting students extend and refine their problem-solving skills. For many teachers, problem-solving software offers learning opportunities for their students that would be difficult to construct and present any other way.

Brainstorming/Concept-Mapping Tools

Brainstorming tools provide a digital environment in which the learner can develop ideas and concepts and then create connections between them. Some of these software packages are primarily text based, while others allow for the creation of visual concept maps. Such **concept-mapping software** generates digital "maps" of concepts that represent a visual depiction of the brainstorming process and the interrelationships between ideas. In the classroom, this tool can be used to capture a cooperative learning group's diverse ideas and turn them into a cohesive whole; help individual learners to grasp large, complex ideas by enabling them to visualize the ideas on a computer screen; or help the class as a whole to develop a joint overview of a new instructional topic that is about to be explored.

Concept-mapping tools allow students to visually organize ideas and then link them to one another to show relationships. Such maps give students an opportunity to visually represent prior knowledge and then extend that knowledge base by linking it to new ideas. This constructivist approach offers students a chance to build and then test the connections between the ideas they have already assimilated and those they are just learning. As you can see in Figure 6.8, most concept maps (also called mind maps) are not highly structured but instead allow for a free-form summary of the relationships between ideas. This type of software tool offers individual learners and cooperative learning groups an opportunity to visually plan writing projects, see relationships between concepts they have learned, and brainstorm solutions in a highly visible and flexible format.

To better understand this unique academic software tool, you may wish to experience it for yourself. The material at mylabschool.com includes a demonstration version of Inspiration software and its companion software, Kidspiration. You may install this demonstration version on your own computer and use it for thirty days to experience concept mapping. To better help you see the instructional possibilities of this software, you may want to complete both the Inspiration and Kidspiration Skills Builder activities included on your CD.

Concept-mapping software incorporates the principles of visual learning into a single, easy-to-use software package. It offers opportunities for students to clarify thinking, understand relationships, and identify their own misconceptions. With this unique software tool, students will be encouraged toward creative thinking and deeper understanding. It can

E-Learning

www.mylabschool.com
Software Skills Builder
Inspiration Skills–Lesson Brainstorming

E-Learning

www.mylabschool.com
video
View *Using Concept Mapping Software*

E-Learning

www.mylabschool.com
Software Skills Builder
Kidspiration Skills–KWL Chart

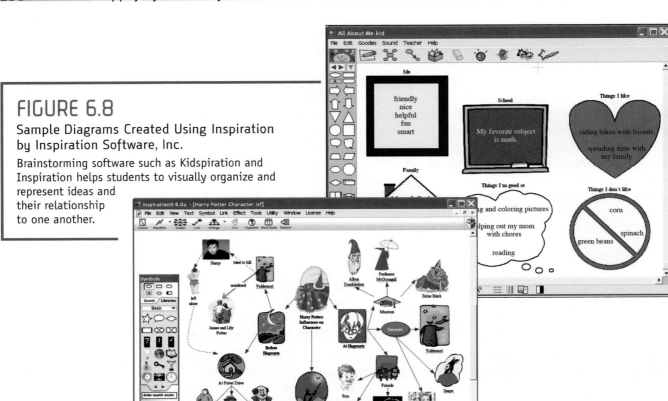

FIGURE 6.8

Sample Diagrams Created Using Inspiration by Inspiration Software, Inc.

Brainstorming software such as Kidspiration and Inspiration helps students to visually organize and represent ideas and their relationship to one another.

also be a powerful instructional tool for teachers wishing to visually present complex or multidimensional content to their students.

Academic Databases

When seeking information for researching a school project or activity, most students turn to online sources. They typically use a search engine on the Internet such as Google. What they do not realize is the search engine's list of returned web sites may or may not be reliable and authentic sources. A much more direct approach to finding research information would be to use a subscription database. As you learned in Chapter 5, a database is an organized and searchable collection of related information. Different academic databases are dedicated to particular types of information so that when selecting the one focused on the information you seek, you are ensured that the results of your search efforts will be on target. Most of these databases can be accessed only with paid subscriptions. These subscriptions are typically paid for by the district or schools. Once a subscription is purchased, students are provided log-ins and passwords and can then use the databases as much as desired. Online subscription databases, if available at your school, offer a unique academic reference that may well be a better option than a more general Internet search.

Tech Tips
for TEACHERS

Imagine having millions of articles from magazines, newspapers, and scholarly journals available to you at your fingertips. Subscription databases provide just that. Offered through your school or public library, subscription databases are an ideal technological tool for teaching and learning. While they are primarily used for research, features of these databases can be integrated into classroom instruction to enhance learning. Because these sources are 100 percent reliable, they usually make a better choice than a Google search on the Internet for doing research. There are many subscription databases out there. Below are a few of the best and most useful for educators.

- SIRS databases are useful to students in upper elementary grades and higher for research projects. They are easy to navigate with user-friendly interfaces and provide overviews of hot topics such as global issues, health, scientific developments, and more. Students can read pro and con arguments on topical issues and access many additional resources such as maps, profiles of notable people, and suggested research topics, among others. SIRS provides information through newspaper and magazine articles, as well as government documents, graphics, and many other resources.
- Grolier Online includes access to multimedia encyclopedia databases loaded with features, as well as magazines, web sites, dictionaries, and interactive atlases. With the Grolier Multimedia Encyclopedia, for example, students can find up-to-date news stories from wire and press services, historical timelines, suggestions for research topics, educational quizzes and games, and more. A useful feature for educators is the Teachers' Guide for news stories, providing questions and activities that can make current news stories come to life in the classroom. It's easily navigable for students, and teachers will find practically limitless ideas for classroom instruction. Grolier provides separate interfaces customized for elementary students and for secondary school students, making this database appropriate for most grade levels.
- NewsBank provides access to news articles from hundreds of local and national newspapers. Students in middle school through college can search for articles concerning social issues, economics, health, environment, sports, science, and government, going back over thirty years. NewsBank also offers many special features for students and teachers: current event hot topics for research papers, which even includes search terms to help guide students in the research process; news stories with accompanying activities; quick links to special reports; and access to political, physical, and black-and-white maps. Some especially useful tools for educators are the Teacher/Librarian Resources. These include the Big6 Resource Center for teaching research skills, a NewsBank training and support center, and links to state-by-state educational standards.
- Academic Search Premier, geared for high school and college students, is a collection of general academic, general science, business, social science, humanities, and education periodical sources. Included are some popular magazine titles, such as *People* and *Newsweek*, as well as thousands of peer-reviewed professional journals. Students and teachers can create an account and sign in to Academic Search Premier's EbscoHost and create a web page related to a classroom topic; save articles, images, and videos to their folder; save links to searches; and create search or journal alerts to be notified by email when a topic of interest becomes available. These EbscoHost features give this database the potential to be an essential teaching and learning tool.
- Biography Resource Center, suitable for middle school through college, is a database that can help students find that much-needed biography when doing a research report. Students can just type keywords into the search field and be presented with several encyclopedia biographical articles, thumbnail biographies, magazine articles, and links to web sites about the individual. As with all other databases, these articles can be printed or emailed to the student or teacher. Using the Biographical Facts Search feature, biographies can be searched for by occupation, nationality, ethnicity, gender, and more. Students will find that this database makes doing biographical research easy and efficient.

These databases, available to you and your students through your schools and public libraries, can help learners be successful in today's competitive, information-rich world. In teaching our students the critical thinking skills necessary to locate and manage information independently through databases, we can help them become information literate and more likely to be successful researchers and lifelong learners.

SOURCE: Contributed by Rita Mayer, MS, MLS, a former special education teacher and elementary school media specialist. She is currently a part-time reference librarian at Miami Dade College and can be reached at **rita.mayer@gmail.com.**

Content-Specific Academic Software

Some academic software is entirely unique to the content area that it supports. This type of software cannot easily be classified into typical academic software categories. Teachers should be aware of the availability of these content-specific applications so that they can call on them when needed to support instruction. Below is a sampling of this type of software.

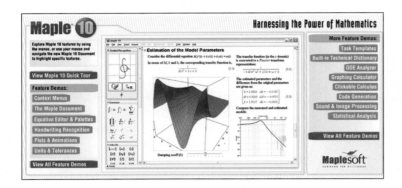

Math Software

Software programs written for math instruction are designed to support the instruction of abstract mathematical concepts and theory. This software includes software that displays virtual manipulatives that students can move, group, and arrange to visually see math operations. Other math software provides students with interactive graphing so that students can see the results of as well as solve algebraic formulas. Geometry software allows students to manipulate forms and examine their related mathematical theory. Dedicated mathematics software can also provide students in-depth, interactive exploration of statistical, trigonometric, and calculus concepts. This specialized group of software packages is available for every math discipline to introduce math concepts to any grade level.

Science

Software unique to the science classroom ranges from software to conduct a virtual dissection, to software that can be used with probes to measure science experiments accurately, to software that explores the stars. Almost any scientific topic has dedicated software that offers the student the opportunity for in-depth exploration of the topic. Virtual chemistry, biology, and physics labs can be created on computer so that students can conduct experiments safely and effectively. Modeling software allows students to examine the galaxy while Geographic Information Systems (GIS) software can provide the information needed to study wetlands that need protection or analyze other map-based data to solve real-world science concerns. Simulation software allows students to run long-term experiments that would otherwise have taken years and see the results instantly. Dedicated science software can provide students with an opportunity to explore concepts, problem-solve, practice scientific inquiry, and conduct experiments. This software is available for every discipline within the sciences and targets all grade levels.

E-Learning

www.mylabschool.com
video
View *Virtual Chemistry Labs*

Social Studies

Software for the social studies ranges from software that creates time lines, to CDs of famous speeches, to software that provides multimedia reenactments and information of specific historical events or ages. Social studies

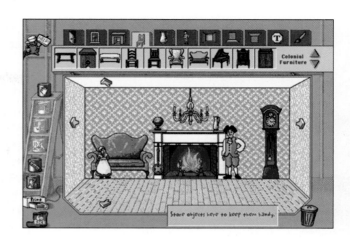

software includes packages targeted to specific disciplines including geography, ecology, economics, history, political science, and sociology and is adjusted for all grade levels. Examples of social studies cross-disciplinary software include searchable collections of historical photos, essays, and music. In our changing political world, map software offers teachers and students the most accurate possible world atlas on CD. Software is available to create virtual dioramas of historical periods, experience and practice the decision-making process related to current events, and examine the implications of population on Earth's resources. Social science software is one of the most abundant of all content-specific resources areas.

Language Arts

In addition to the many tutorials and drill-and-practice software packages for language arts, there are also a number of unique packages to practice language arts skills. Some packages help students step-by-step through essay construction by presenting a series of screens to help them think logically through the essay. Others help students practice spelling lists by reading words to them and allowing them to type in the correct spelling. Still other language arts software helps students develop literacy skills by exploring meanings of sounds, passages, and story lines. Reading software presents auditory stories and provides activities that practice comprehension, phonics skills, and sequencing, while other language arts software packages teach and practice the specific skills inherent in business writing or journalistic writing. Whether introducing and pronouncing the letters of the alphabet or constructing complex essays, language arts software dedicated to introducing and practicing these skills is available for your classroom.

Academic Software in Teaching and Learning

As you consider the methods and media you choose to employ to achieve your instructional objectives and best address the needs of all learners, academic software can be a most valuable asset. There is indeed a wide variety of types of academic software and, within each type, hundreds of choices. With so large a selection from which to choose, it is clear that the amount of effort necessary to review, evaluate, and select academic software and integrate it into teaching and learning is indeed high. However, the benefits derived from that effort are even greater.

E-Learning

www.mylabschool.com
video
View *Using GIS Software*

E-Learning

www.mylabschool.com
Listen to Podcast
Selecting Software

Integrating academic software into instruction adds excitement and innovation to the teaching and learning process.

Whether there is only one computer in a classroom or many, carefully selected and integrated academic software can patiently and tirelessly reinforce concepts for learners who need review, offer opportunities for exploration and discovery for learners who need additional opportunity, or provide creative experiences for cooperative learning groups working together to develop a multimedia report to share with peers. The possibilities are as vast as the number of academic software packages available to enrich the learning experience. It is true that exploration of academic software appropriate for your classroom does take time and effort, but for computer-using teachers and their students, inclusion of these packages in the teaching and learning environment will increasingly become a necessary and exciting part of teaching and learning in the twenty-first century.

KEY TERMS

academic software 209
authoring systems 209
clip art 218
concept-mapping software 235
desktop publishing (DTP) software 216
draw programs 220
drill-and-practice software 227
editing software 222
educational games 228
graphics software 217

hypermedia software 211
imaging software 221
integrated learning systems (ILS) 233
paint programs 219
problem-solving software 234
reference software 224
simulations 231
special needs software 231
tutorial software 224

STUDENT ACTIVITIES

CHAPTER REVIEW

1. What are authoring systems? How are they used for teaching and learning?
2. Describe the differences and applications of each type of graphics software that might be used in teaching and learning.
3. What is reference software? How has it changed the research process?
4. What is the difference between drill-and-practice software and tutorial software? When is it appropriate to use each in teaching and learning?
5. How do educational games and simulations differ?

6. What is an integrated learning system? What controversies surround the implementation of such systems in schools?
7. How is special needs software effective in meeting the unique needs of special education students? Give examples.
8. What is problem-solving software? Contrast it with brainstorming tools. How does each promote critical-thinking skills?
9. What is content-specific software? Give examples.

WHAT DO YOU THINK?

1. School budgets are typically limited in the amounts allocated for teachers to purchase materials and supplies for the classroom. With the additional expense of purchasing academic software packages, some teachers feel that even less money will be available for instructional basics. Do you think this may prove to be a problem as academic software continues to become a critical component in instruction? If so, how might it be resolved?

2. If an educator is given the time and training to author pedagogically sound multimedia teaching software for use in the classroom, how might this change his or her role in the classroom, if at all? Be specific in describing what might change, how it would change, and why; or explain why it would not change.

3. Some educators fear that academic software, especially game-oriented software, shifts the focus from the content to the delivery system. Do you think the entertainment aspect of academic software interferes with and detracts from the content? Why or why not? What are the benefits and disadvantages of using such software? What are the benefits and disadvantages of using more traditional instruction?

LEARNING TOGETHER!

1. With so many types of academic software available, it seems an overwhelming task to try to examine and evaluate enough software to make an informed decision about which packages to use. In a learning group of two or three participants, develop strategies for effectively selecting academic software for use in your classroom.

2. Assume that you are members of a grade or departmental team in a local school. Your grade or department has been given $2,000 to spend on educational software for this school year. Collect two to five educational software catalogs as sources and together decide how you plan to spend your funds. Be prepared to defend your decisions.

3. With your group, examine the objectives and contents of a unit of curriculum at the grade level you would like to teach. Consider how each type of academic software might be integrated to enhance the delivery of this unit. Which type of academic software packages would you use to achieve the objectives and how might you use them? Create a group consensus lesson plan using the software and strategies you have agreed on.

E-Learning

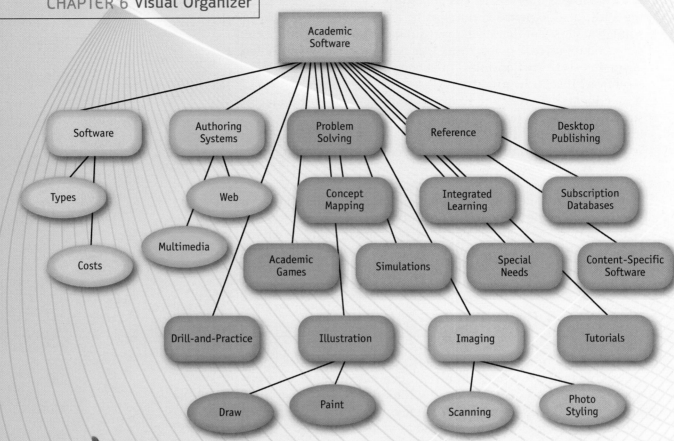

Academic Software

- Software
  - Types
  - Costs
- Authoring Systems
  - Web
    - Multimedia
- Problem Solving
  - Concept Mapping
    - Academic Games
      - Drill-and-Practice
    - Simulations
  - Illustration
    - Draw
    - Paint
- Reference
  - Integrated Learning
    - Special Needs
  - Imaging
    - Scanning
    - Photo Styling
- Desktop Publishing
  - Subscription Databases
    - Content-Specific Software
  - Tutorials

Podcasts www.mylabschool.com

Listen to a podcast relating to the use of administrative software in teaching and learning. Download the audio discussion to your iPod, computer, or MP3 player.

Software Skills Builder www.mylabschool.com

These step-by-step illustrated tutorials, accessible through mylabschool.com, teach you to use Microsoft Windows and Office on both PC and Mac by preparing documents that will be useful in your classroom.

Video Lab www.mylabschool.com

Accessible through the **mylabschool** web site are several video vignettes that offer you a look at software in teaching and learning. Learning guides for all videos can be found in the text's Learning Guide Supplement.

On the Web! Activities www.ablongman.com/lever-duffy3e
Noted in the margins of the chapter, these activities offer you

in-depth experiences in the topics and content presented in the chapter.

Online Practice Test www.ablongman.com/lever-duffy3e
Practice tests offer you an opportunity to test your knowledge and then review the results and send them to your teacher.

Outliner www.ablongman.com/lever-duffy3e
Chapter Outliners are fill-in-the-blank outlines of the main ideas presented in the chapter. Download the outliner and fill it in for an effective chapter study guide.

Power Practices www.ablongman.com/lever-duffy3e
Power Practices are animated tutorials made using Microsoft's presentation software, PowerPoint. This flash card tutorial will help you practice key concepts in the chapter.

Puzzler www.ablongman.com/lever-duffy3e
Puzzlers include content in crossword, word search, and other puzzle formats to help you master chapter content.

Useful Links www.ablongman.com/lever-duffy3e
These links offer you suggestions for expanded online research in the topics presented in the chapter.

INTEGRATION *Ideas*

The use of academic software has been an accepted and effective means of enriching curricula and supporting the achievement of learning objectives. There are many software packages to choose from, both commercial and as freeware or shareware. Careful review and evaluation of software should be done prior to purchase. Below is a sampling of software in each major content area.

Integrating Technology into Social Studies

"Africa Trail" is another one of the "Oregon Trail" series that follows the successful and ever-popular design of the original game-plus-learning formula of its predecessors. This CD takes students on a biking expedition across 12,000 miles of the African continent. As they travel, the team members learn about African history and culture, meet Africans and learn their customs, and encounter the topography of this huge and diverse land. As with the original version, decision-making skills and problem solving are called for. Visit **www.thelearningcompany.com** to learn more.

Integrating Technology into Language Arts

"Reading for Meaning," a Tom Snyder Productions product, teaches the five main skills associated with reading for comprehension: main idea, inferences, sequence, compare and contrast, and cause and effect. A model lesson is included, along with literature-based lessons written for different levels of competency. This is a cartoon-animated software that introduces a "Kid Cam" for teaching each of the five skills. For the literature-based passages, omit the animated clips and allow students to both read and listen to passages from literary works to illustrate the five skills in authentic writing. Learn more at **www.tomsnyder.com.**

Integrating Technology into the Sciences

A comprehensive aid to teaching science is "PLATO Life Science." This software gives visual images of scientific concepts to enable students to use the audio-narrated multimedia content as a means of tying new concepts into prior knowledge. The program has seven units, each with a read-along text, glossary, a scientific calculator, and unit converter. For teachers, there are Teachlinks so they can add to the program's content and materials, a test bank, and objectives for each unit. See **www.plato.com** for more information.

Integrating Technology into Math

"I Love Math" is a Dorling Kindersley (DK) publication that puts a positive spin on learning math skills. This software is designed as a time-travel adventure that engages children in learning measurement, basic geometry, problem solving, and fractions—all while taking part in six games that have animation and sound. An example of the creativity embedded in this program is the approach to teaching fractions: saving an underwater kingdom by laying pipes. Go to **www.learnatglobal.com** for more details

For these and many more Integration Ideas for using academic software in teaching and learning, visit the text web site at **www.ablongman.com/lever-duffy3e.**

There are never enough funds to purchase all the software and technology you would like to have for your classroom. Often, teachers will dip into their own pockets to supplement the limited software funds available in most schools. However, there is another option. Grant writing may sound ominous, but actually it is a straightforward process in which you state an innovative idea you have and your need for funds to carry it out. You must describe in detail your objectives, the idea, and how funds will be used. You create a budget to identify how much each of the items you need will cost. And you complete all forms required by the granting agency and your school. Since granting agencies often have a requirement to annually disburse all of their grant funds, the fact is that agencies are looking for innovative ideas to fund. A creative idea shaped into a well-written grant may be all that is needed to supplement your classroom technology.

Granting agencies may be public or private. Public agencies include such organizations as the U.S. Department of Education. Private agencies may be corporations such as Microsoft or foundations such as the George Lucas Foundation. Each type of agency has very specific requirements as to what they are willing to fund and the procedures for applying for the funds. Governmental agencies are often very rigorous in their requirements, while foundation requirements may range from requiring multipage forms to simple letters of request.

When an agency has monies available, it may publicize an RFP or Request for Proposals. These can be found in professional journals and on the Web. The RFP lets interested individuals know that monies are available, what they are for, and what process must be completed to apply. An example of a list of K–12 grants can be found at TechLearning's grant resources web site at http://techlearning.com/resources/grants.jhtml.

Agencies do not disburse funds to individuals but instead to institutions such as a school or your district. So while you may write the proposal for a grant, once it is accepted, the funds go to your institution and not to you. However, since you took the initiative to get the funds, you will typically be appointed the grant director or team leader and be responsible for spending the money, ensuring the terms of the grant are fulfilled, and reporting the grant outcomes when it is completed.

Grants are highly competitive. Depending on the grant, many may be applying for the same funds. Simple need for technology is not the primary criteria. Instead you must have a creative idea that is consistent with the objectives of the agency, and you have to be willing to make the effort to write the grant in accordance with the RFP criteria. While competition will be stiff, funds are ultimately awarded to someone. It could be you.

Below are some helpful hints for grant writing. Many web sites offer you more detailed advice, and the granting agency will provide you with everything you need to know for their particular grant, including, in some cases, an online or telephone support line to answer your questions. While it is an effort to write a grant, if you are funded it is well worth it for you and, most importantly, for your students.

Top Ten Helpful Hints for Grant Writing

1. Be sure your idea matches the granting agency's mission. You may have an innovative technology solution for teaching science, but if the agency grants are for ESL students only, you will not be funded.

2. Follow the RFP requirements exactly. There is no flexibility in grant writing. A ten-page limit means no more than ten pages exactly.

3. Be innovative and creative. Grants are most often awarded to fund a new idea or way to solve a teaching problem. They are not to supplement your day-to-day operating budget.

4. Build partnerships. Many granting agencies want to see partnerships between grade levels, schools, and community agencies. The more "bang for the buck" that you can demonstrate through partnerships, the greater your investment worth.

5. Be sure you have a well-researched budget. You need to state how the money will be spent precisely and accurately. Guesstimates will not get you a grant.

6. Have a clear evaluation plan. If you state that you are adding this software to improve reading scores, you will need to explain how you will know that has happened. You need to state how you will assess whether the grant objectives were met.

7. Cite applicable research. If your idea has a basis in previous research, do your homework and mention the studies that support why you believe this will be a successful project.

8. Proofread your grant carefully. If you want an agency to fund you, make a good impression.

9. Let someone unrelated to your project review it. Your writing must clearly convey your project to someone unfamiliar with the idea. Have someone else review it for clarity.

10. Don't get discouraged. You may get several rejection letters, but you only need one acceptance letter from one agency to achieve your goal.

chapter 7

The Internet and the World Wide Web

This chapter addresses these ISTE *National Educational Technology Standards* for Teachers:

I. TECHNOLOGY OPERATIONS AND CONCEPTS

Teachers demonstrate a sound understanding of technology operations and concepts. Teachers

A. demonstrate introductory knowledge, skills, and understanding of concepts related to technology (as described in the ISTE *National Education Technology Standards* for Students).

B. demonstrate continual growth in technology knowledge and skills to stay abreast of current and emerging technologies.

II. PLANNING AND DESIGNING LEARNING ENVIRONMENTS AND EXPERIENCES

Teachers plan and design effective learning environments and experiences supported by technology. Teachers

A. design developmentally appropriate learning opportunities that apply technology-enhanced instructional strategies to support the diverse needs of learners.

B. apply current research on teaching and learning with technology when planning learning environments and experiences.

C. identify and locate technology resources and evaluate them for accuracy and suitability.

D. plan for the management of technology resources within the context of learning activities.

E. plan strategies to manage student learning in a technology-enhanced environment.

P eople are inherently social creatures. Being alone and without other human contact, although pleasant for a while, usually turns into a longing to interact. People like—perhaps need—to communicate with each other. It is logical, then, that computers, being a tool in the hands of such social creatures, would also be made to interact. Enabling individual, stand-alone computers and their users to interact with each other is what computer networks are all about. Enabling networks and their users across the globe to interact is what the Internet is all about.

You have learned so far that the teaching and learning process is essentially one of communication. Networked computers are an efficient and effective communication tool. It is not surprising, therefore, that networking would prove to be a remarkable and useful educational resource to enable a new format for communication. Networking on its largest scale, across the Internet, empowers every teacher and learner who is able to connect to the network with expanded communication capabilities. The Internet makes it possible to seek, find, and communicate information that might otherwise have been impossibly out of reach. These tools make such communication as simple as pointing and clicking a mouse. The Internet makes it possible for teachers and learners to interact with each other globally to discover new perspectives and broaden personal horizons. It is no wonder that so many educators are awed by possibilities presented by Internet access in their classroom or the media center.

CHAPTER OUTLINE

- Real People, Real Stories
- Connecting to the Internet
- Telecommunication Technologies
- Internet Tools and Services
- Internet Service Providers
- The Internet: Connecting Networks to Networks across the Globe
- Internet-Based Communications
- Other Internet Services
- Using the Internet and Web in Teaching and Learning

For educators, the Internet is an amazing instructional tool. The Internet offers the potential to add a dimension to instruction that was previously unimagined. In the hands of innovative educators, the Internet becomes a powerful digital tool that can help them build exciting new instructional environments.

This chapter explores the Internet, the World Wide Web, and the role of these powerful digital tools in teaching and learning. In Chapter 7, you will

- Review the history and current structure of the Internet
- Explore the most frequently used Internet resources
- Survey the World Wide Web and its features

Real People Real Stories

Meet Karen Brown. Karen Brown is Assistant Professor of Instructional Technology in the Teacher Licensure Program at the University of Richmond, Virginia. Prior to her work in higher education, she has had 20 rewarding years in K–12 education. Her professional experience has culminated in her serving as the first director of the innovative Blue Ridge Virtual Governor's School.

The Blue Ridge Virtual Governor's School (BRVGS) is one of sixteen programs established by the Virginia Board of Education. These programs are charged with creating a regional "community of learners" and typically require students to leave their local high school for part or all of the school day. However, for many rural Virginia school districts, this is geographically impossible.

The division superintendents and school board members, who created BRVGS in the Central Virginia area, wanted a way for their students to enjoy the benefits of a governor's school while keeping the benefits of their home campuses. Many districts could not transport students to a central location—the geographical distances were just too great. These educators realized the point that David Thornburg makes—the challenge of today's schools is to provide schooling as an "activity" and not a "place."

How could the governor's school opportunity be made available to students in rural areas? How could the burden of asking students to choose between community and curriculum be avoided? The answer could be found in using the Internet.

Over a three-year period, a planning group listened to experts and the school gradually took shape as one that could exist physically in the high schools of all the counties involved and virtually, using the Internet. However, there was concern that the students needed to be involved in face-to-face activities. Most of the six schools involved had little experience with the Internet communication tools that would be needed. The planning group agreed to incorporate face-to-face field trips with online communication technology. The next question then was which Internet tools could best help with this huge task.

As teachers from all the involved schools began to cooperatively plan instruction, they needed a means for sharing resources, dividing responsibilities, and sharing common materials with students. Blackboard, an Internet-based learning management system, had served as a useful virtual classroom for higher education so members of the BRVGS considered its use for this high school program.

In a pilot of the system, an online discussion area for the tenth-grade biotechnology class was created. The initial goal was to have students become more familiar and comfortable with Internet-based electronic discussions centering around academic topics while learning to communicate responsibly and with a scholarly attitude. The second goal was to have students begin to have a dialog outside of class using the online discussion area as a way to bridge the geographical distance between them. This dialog could serve to keep students interacting for a greater period of time than videoconferencing and field trips were able to do.

As students became aware of and used the established discussion area, they requested the addition of a "general topic" forum—a place where they could exchange casual conversation with their peers from the other schools. To promote community and interaction, it was decided that this would be tried, but with some ground rules. They were, after all, teenagers! First, the discussion forums would center on common readings and classroom activities—they would be academic in nature and not for casual socializing. Secondly, since there was concern over some students' limited access to the Internet, it was determined that students would be given time during the school day to participate in the online discussion. Further, they would be required to participate only twice within a month's time. Finally, students would be assigned into small discussion groups of about ten students, each of which could be mixed up each time a new discussion topic was posted to ensure that students were conversing with peers from other schools.

This Internet-based discussion strategy successfully created a true learning community. Notable were the number of messages posted outside of the school day, despite the concern over limited access. In one group, the majority of messages were posted between 3:30 and 5:00 P.M. while in the two other groups messages posted outside of the school day were on the weekend. Students were choosing to go online and continue their academic discussion during otherwise social times of their lives. These students were learning together via the Internet.

In a summative evaluation of the experience, when the students were asked to compare their original thoughts about the assignment to how they felt at the end, most agreed that the use of the online discussion area allowed them to benefit from their diverse community of learners. One student summed it up by saying, "At first, I thought it would be boring. Actually, I now think this is a great idea for students. It's a great way to communicate with people from other schools."

The Internet had proven to be a successful and meaningful tool to build community and promote interactive learning.

For more information about this project, contact Dr. Karen Faison Brown, University of Richmond, at kbrown3@richmond.edu.

The Internet: Connecting Networks to Networks across the Globe

You learned in Chapter 3 of the value of connecting the stand-alone computers in your classroom to the resources available through a network. Now what if you could connect those same stand-alone computers to the resources available on millions of networks across the globe? If those networks allowed you to connect to them and provided you with guest rights to all or some of their resources, you could access huge amounts of information! That is the scope of the international network of networks known collectively as the **Internet** or simply the Net (see Figure 7.1).

Millions of interconnected networks form the Internet.

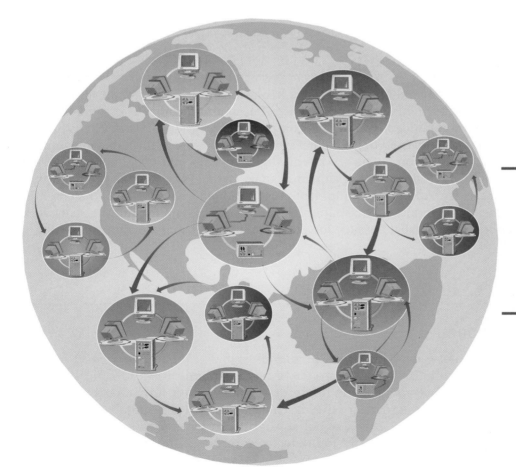

FIGURE 7.1
The Internet
The Internet is a global network of networks connecting hundreds of millions of users to each other and to worldwide resources.

The Internet is actually made up of millions of individual machines and networks that have agreed to connect, provide resources to each other, and share data. Initially, just a few select military and university networks connected, primarily for the purposes of research and national security. Since its early beginnings of just a handful of connected sites, however, the Internet has grown to an estimated 450 million host computers distributing information across the globe, and it is still growing! A common protocol called **TCP/IP** (transmission control protocol/Internet protocol) is used so that communications between these diverse computers can be understood. Internet users, whose numbers are, at the time of this writing, estimated to exceed over one billion around the world and still growing each month, can connect, via their school or business networks or from home via modem to the computers within this vast network of networks. Any single computer can, by connecting to the Internet, access an almost unimaginable wealth of information. For educators, the potential to share our world's collective knowledge base with our students is staggering.

But how does such an immense array of information become manageable and usable for a busy teacher? Even if you can access the Internet, how can you put it to work to enhance teaching and learning? How can we empower our students to use the Internet for their own academic and personal growth? To answer these questions, educators must first become familiar with the Internet and the tools and applications available to make its content accessible and responsive to users.

E-Learning
ON THE WEB! 7.1
The Evolution of the Internet

Connecting to the Internet

To connect stand-alone computers in one location to the Internet, telecommunication technologies are necessary. **Telecommunication** is essentially electronic communication between computers over distance. Carrier lines (phone and cable) are used in lieu of network wiring to interconnect distant computers. Because computers work with digital signals, and telephone wires were originally designed to transmit only analog (voice) signals, some adaptation is necessary. Additional equipment must be added to both ends of the communication circuit—that is, to both the home computer and the network server—to make it possible for a telecommunication connection to take place.

Telecommunication Technologies

Modems

Computers send and receive digital signals. Telephone lines transmit analog signals. For a computer to use telephone lines to send information, it must alter, or modulate, its signals into a form that is transmittable by these carrier lines. The computer peripheral designed to MOdulate a computer's signal so that it can be transmitted across a carrier line and then to DEModulate a responding computer signal received via a carrier line is called a MODEM. **Modems** are essentially translating

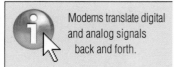

Modems translate digital and analog signals back and forth.

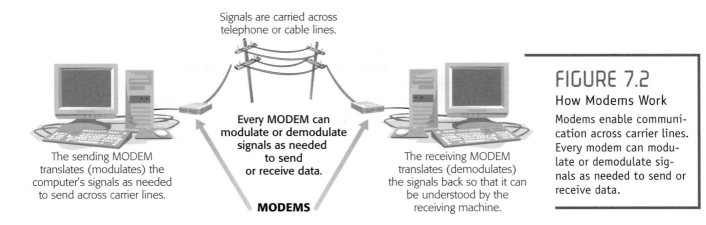

Signals are carried across telephone or cable lines.

Every MODEM can modulate or demodulate signals as needed to send or receive data.

The sending MODEM translates (modulates) the computer's signals as needed to send across carrier lines.

The receiving MODEM translates (demodulates) the signals back so that it can be understood by the receiving machine.

MODEMS

FIGURE 7.2
How Modems Work
Modems enable communication across carrier lines. Every modem can modulate or demodulate signals as needed to send or receive data.

devices. They translate computer output into a format that is transmittable across carrier lines and then translate signals that come across these lines back into a format that the computer can understand, as illustrated in Figure 7.2.

Modems provide only the hardware solution that makes the communication possible. Telecommunications software is also necessary to give the hardware the instructions necessary to make the computer and modem work together to establish a telecommunications link. Typically, such software is packaged with the modem for which it was programmed or provided by telecommunications services you subscribe to.

Home-to-Network Connections

If a classroom workstation can connect to other computers relatively easily via the school network, is it also possible to connect a home computer with a modem to the school network and beyond? Can you connect to your school's network to check your email from your house after school or on weekends? The answer is yes but with some limitations.

If you have a home computer, modem, phone line, and telecommunications software, your home computer can call your network modem's phone number. If your network accepts incoming calls, it will respond and establish a link to your machine. Once a connection is established, the network software will ask that you enter your log-in name and

SATELLITE EQUIPMENT

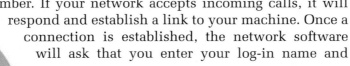

EXTERNAL MODEM

Modems and other connectivity hardware make it possible for computers to communicate.

DSL MODEM

your password. When it is recognized as valid, you will be able to work with your network just as you would when logging in from your classroom workstation.

Even so, you might find that the network responds sluggishly and that your requests take excessive amounts of time to fulfill. This is often the case in working with a network via phone lines. Network wiring usually has sufficient bandwidth and speed to accommodate workstation requests with responsiveness. However, analog phone lines do not have broad bandwidth, nor are they fast, so transmissions may bog down, resulting in slow responses to user requests.

DSL lines offer faster transmission speeds.

Phone companies, aware of consumers' desire for better responses via phone lines, have made higher-speed digital phone lines available in many areas. **Digital subscriber lines (DSLs)**, a high-speed option for home users, provide speeds up to thirty times faster than a standard phone line. DSLs offer both voice and digital communications on a single line, thus eliminating the need for two phone lines at your home, one for voice and another for data.

Another type of high-speed connection uses cable television lines. Some cable TV companies provide digital access via the lines that have already been installed for television. With the addition of a specialized modem known as a **cable modem,** home users can get access speeds potentially faster than a DSL. Although not available in all areas of the country, this alternative is fast becoming a powerful option for home users.

A final connectivity alternative that is becoming more widely available is wireless satellite access. Companies offering TV via satellite, such as Direct TV, also have the bandwidth and capability to offer access to networks that in turn connect to the Internet. Just as cable TV wiring provides faster transmission and greater capacity than phone lines, so too does the technology by which companies provide satellite television transmissions. Of course, to use this technology, you must first have the necessary dish to receive the transmission and subscribe to the service that sends the transmission via satellite.

Internet Tools and Services

As the Internet has developed, a variety of tools and services have become available for our use. Some services are provided free to all Internet users. Others are offered as a part of a membership package when you subscribe to an Internet service. Still others are available for a subscription fee. To use the Internet effectively, it is important to be aware of the many types of tools and services available and how best to evaluate and select those you might want to use.

Internet Service Providers

The first step in using the Internet is accessing and connecting to it. If you are using your school network, the network itself has been connected to the Internet, and you can use that connection as an authorized network user. However, if you are connecting to the Internet from a home computer, you need first to connect your home computer to a network that is connected to the Internet to access the Net's resources. Special networks that have been created to provide home and business computers a way to connect to the Internet are called **Internet service providers,** or **ISPs.**

ISPs are companies that provide home users with access to the Internet through their own network connections and communications software. Every ISP provides a series of phone numbers that home computers can dial via modem to attach to the ISP's computer. Most ISPs charge a service fee (typically around $10 to $20 per month) for providing Internet access, but if connecting to an ISP requires a long-distance call, those long-distance charges will cost the user extra money that is typically paid to the user's long-distance phone service provider. A few half-hour-long "surfs" on the Internet across a long-distance line can end up being an expensive experience.

For the monthly ISP service fee, some large providers include a variety of services beyond simple access (see Table 7.1). Most offer email, and some offer extensive phone support. Some of the largest providers, sometimes called online services, include exclusive member services as a part of the subscription package. Different providers vary as much in the services they provide as they do in monthly charges.

An ISP is necessary to connect to the Internet from a home computer.

Internet-Based Communications

Email

In addition to accessing a worldwide bank of information, the Internet offers some remarkable communication tools. These tools can offer both **synchronous** (same-time) and **asynchronous** (time-shifted) **communications** over the Internet. Because of their ability to link students to other students in classrooms across the globe, most of these tools offer fascinating educational applications. By far the most popular asynchronous communication tool is electronic mail.

Email is the primary communications tool on networks and on the Internet.

Communicating via Email

Electronic mail (**email**) is the key communication tool provided in a networked environment. Email works similarly to post office boxes in the physical world. When a log-in name is assigned to a network user, that same log-in name is used to create an electronic mailbox. This is similar to assigning a post office box to an individual post office customer. Just as mail can be delivered to your post office box at any time, to be picked up by you at your convenience, so too can electronic mail be delivered to your electronic mailbox. Email addressed to your log-in name may be received by the server from one of the network users and then directed to your electronic mailbox, where it will be stored until you pick it up. Once you review your stored email, you can choose to delete it or save it, just as you might throw away or keep mail that has been delivered to

TABLE 7.1   Common Services Provided by Internet Service Providers

ISP SERVICE	EXPLANATION
INTERNET ACCESS	An ISP offers you a way to connect your home or classroom computer to the Internet through its Internet server.
COMMUNICATIONS PROGRAM	ISPs provide a customized communications program that works with your modem and connects to the ISP's network. This program provides a list of local phone numbers that you can call to connect to the ISP.
BROWSER	ISP software packages may include a browser (usually Netscape Navigator or Microsoft Internet Explorer) to use on the Internet. Some ISPs (such as America Online) offer customized browsers adapted for their service.
EMAIL	Most ISPs provide email services to users. However, the size of a user's mailbox may differ from ISP to ISP. Small electronic mailboxes may fill quickly, especially when receiving attachments, and cause your email to bounce back to the sender.
TECHNICAL SUPPORT	All ISPs provide technical support when you have problems on their networks; however, you may experience long telephone wait times. User satisfaction surveys may give you an idea of the level of support from an ISP.
CHAT ROOMS	Some ISPs provide chat programs as a part of their service packages. Chats may be public or private and may include only those within the ISP network, so investigating chat options of an ISP is important if this is a critical tool.
INSTANT MESSAGING	Instant messaging services allow you to create a one-to-one chat with Internet users outside the ISP network. Nonnetwork users may need to download and install the free ISP chat software to communicate with you.
DISCUSSIONS	Some ISPs provide conferencing software that allows you to create and moderate an ongoing discussion group via the ISP services.
NEWSREADER	Most ISPs provide a newsreader, software that lets you read and send data to public groups dedicated to a single topic.
PERSONAL WEB SPACE	Some ISPs offer web space, web tutorials, and web authoring tools as a part of their service. As with electronic mailboxes, web space size varies with ISP; so if you plan to create a robust web site, you will want to determine if the ISP offers sufficient space.
OTHER SERVICES	ISPs offer a variety of services, from online malls to custom search engines to personalized, responsive home pages. It is a good idea to investigate these services to determine if they will be useful for you.

your real-world post office box. You may even decide to forward email to other network users or to leave it in your mailbox for later disposition. Figure 7.3 summarizes some of the key features most email systems provide.

E-mail is sent to your electronic mailbox on your network server, and it remains there until you retrieve it. E-mail you send is sent via the server to users within the network or on the Internet.

You can receive or send mail from networked computers at your convenience anytime, day or night.

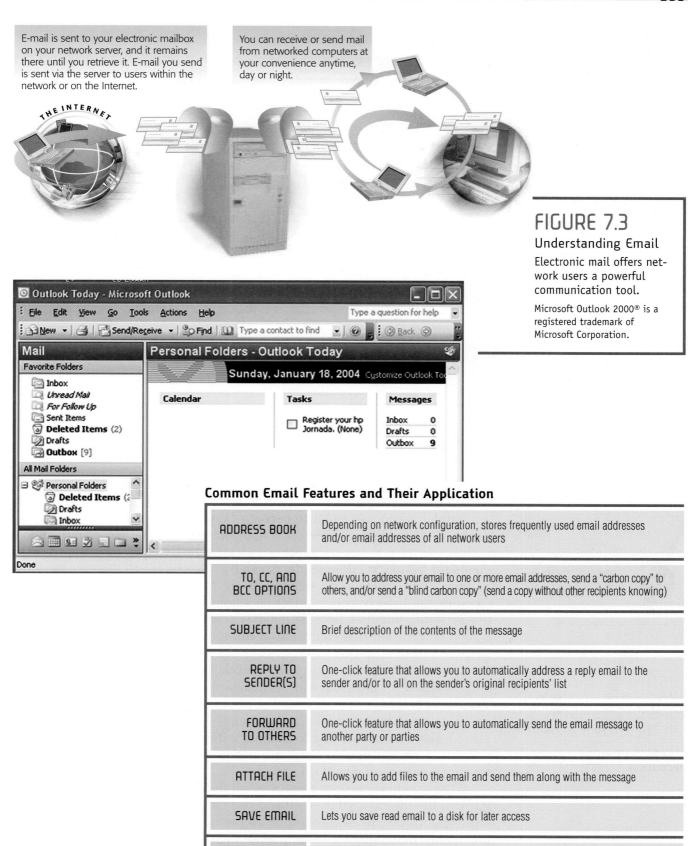

FIGURE 7.3
Understanding Email
Electronic mail offers network users a powerful communication tool.

Microsoft Outlook 2000® is a registered trademark of Microsoft Corporation.

Common Email Features and Their Application

ADDRESS BOOK	Depending on network configuration, stores frequently used email addresses and/or email addresses of all network users
TO, CC, AND BCC OPTIONS	Allow you to address your email to one or more email addresses, send a "carbon copy" to others, and/or send a "blind carbon copy" (send a copy without other recipients knowing)
SUBJECT LINE	Brief description of the contents of the message
REPLY TO SENDER(S)	One-click feature that allows you to automatically address a reply email to the sender and/or to all on the sender's original recipients' list
FORWARD TO OTHERS	One-click feature that allows you to automatically send the email message to another party or parties
ATTACH FILE	Allows you to add files to the email and send them along with the message
SAVE EMAIL	Lets you save read email to a disk for later access
PRINT EMAIL	Lets you print email you have received

TABLE 7.2   Using Electronic Mail in Teaching and Learning

APPLICATION	USE	BENEFITS
ASSIGNMENT TRANSMISSION	Assigned activities are emailed to teacher, may be corrected and emailed back for revision.	Activities remain soft copy until final revision; absent students can keep up with assignments; copies can be sent to parents.
CLASS DISCUSSIONS	Discussion question is asked by teacher and mailed to the discussion group list; responses are sent to all group members.	Responses can be thoughtful and delivered at students' own pace; allows shy students to respond; student responses are more carefully prepared when shared; responses can be tracked for review and grading.
ELECTRONIC KEYPALS	Students are assigned pals in other classes (at the same school or other schools in the district, state, or country) to communicate with for a given assignment.	Communication with others provides for social learning opportunities and multicultural exchange; information exchanged broadens data as compared to what individuals may have gathered; student responses are more carefully prepared when shared.
COMMUNICATION: Student–Student Student–Teacher Teacher–Parent	Students can email among group members to complete group activities; teacher and students can exchange information or ask questions outside of class time; teacher and parent can communicate outside school hours about student progress.	Email participants can communicate privately or publicly with other concerned parties regarding student progress or with questions or concerns about classroom activities or homework.

Email operates like a virtual post office box.

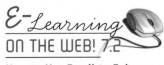

How to Use Email to Enhance Instruction

Schoolwide and districtwide email offers exciting communication possibilities for students and for teachers, some of which are shown in Table 7.2. Students can use email to become "keypals" or "e-buddies" with students in other classes within a school or with students at other schools within a district. Keypals can communicate socially or share written assignments for feedback. Older students can be "e-mentors" to younger students to help with grade-level transitions or to help on specific activities. Opening the lines of communication among students makes many innovative activities possible. Because email is asynchronous communication, that is, communication that can occur at different times convenient to the participants, student schedules do not impede communications.

Teacher use of email makes it possible to share ideas and lesson plans and to discuss concerns with colleagues across the school or district. Teachers often have very different schedules. If they do not have the same planning periods, it can be difficult to meet face-to-face with peers. Email provides an alternative way to interact with colleagues, share information, and get quick responses. Once accustomed to using email, few teachers would be willing to give it up.

If the school server can receive email from outside the network, such as through the Internet, your email account can also provide you with a powerful opportunity to establish links to parents. Many parents work outside the home, and communicating with them during your work hours by phone may be difficult. Printed notices carried by students might or might not make it home to parents. Even so, if you provide your email address to parents and if they too have email accounts, either personally through their Internet provider or through another source, you can establish a direct and personal communication link with them. This gives both you and your students' parents a convenient way to establish a partnership and open lines of communication for the benefit of the students in your charge. Email can be an important bridge to many homes.

Like network email, Internet email provides users with a way to establish one-to-one communications; but with Internet email, electronic messages are not bound to a single network. Internet email can be sent and received across the many networks attached to the Internet. With Internet email, each Internet user is given a log-in name and password. That same log-in name is thereafter used to designate the user's email account, including the email storage space assigned to that user. You can send and receive email via your ISP or school email account. Because Internet email can be sent to any email server available on any network that is attached to the Net, you need to add some information to your assigned email name to give it more specificity. For example, if your user name is bsmith and your

COOL TOOLS

Microsoft Outlook is the most popular mail package on the market. But Outlook not only provides the software needed to use email, it also offers you a calendar, task list, contacts address book, notes, and journal option. The calendar not only lets you schedule your own appointments and reminders, it can also be shared to easily coordinate meetings with other teachers on your team. The task feature allows you to create task reminders for yourself or assign tasks with due dates to others. The contacts folder is an email address book that not only tracks the information about your contacts but can even call them and open a journal page so you can take notes on the conversation. The notes option allows you to create electronic sticky notes to keep reminders visible while the journal option lets you make notes of ideas or conversations with contacts automatically.

Below are some ideas from Microsoft's Outlook web site for using each of these features. More tips and information on Outlook can be found at **www.microsoft.com**.

Mail Tip

No time to answer a message right now? No problem! Set a reminder to reply to a message! To do so, right-click the message you want to set the reminder for, point to Follow Up, and then click Add Reminder. In the Due By list, click the date when you have to complete the reply. In the second list, click a time. In the Flag color list, click the flag color you want and then click OK.

Calendar Tip

Want to remember those holidays? Automatically add holidays to your Calendar! On the Tools menu, click Options, click Calendar Options, and then click Add Holidays.

Contacts Tip

Want to add a new contact directly from an email message? Open the message. In the From field, right-click the name you want to make into a contact. On the shortcut menu, click Add to Outlook Contacts.

Task Tip

Working with a group on a task? Quickly send a new message about the task. Drag the task to the Mail button in the Navigation Pane. This creates a new message with the task name as the subject and the task details in the body of the message.

ISP account is with a company called bignet.com, your email address would be bsmith@bignet.com. The @ symbol that connects your user name to the name of the web server on which your email account is located enables email that is addressed to you to travel to its intended location. Similarly, to send email to colleagues via the Internet, you will need to know their full email addresses.

Some may confuse Internet email addresses with uniform resource locators (URLs). **URLs** are designations for specific locations on the World Wide Web. Email addresses designate individual users' electronic mailboxes on the Internet. Email addresses always consist of the user name, the @ symbol, and the location where the electronic mailbox is stored.

To read and send email, you will need email software, which is typically provided by your school network or ISP. Email software features typically include an address book to store frequently used email addresses and a location at the top of each email screen in which you can enter the email address of the person to whom you wish to send the email. Another area at the top of each email screen allows you to enter the email address of others to whom you wish to send a "carbon copy" of that email. Attachments, that is, separate files or even programs, can be attached to and sent along with the message. Most email programs also provide you with some sort of filing system that allows you to systematically store incoming and read messages that you have received and messages that you have sent (see Figure 7.3).

E-Learning ON THE WEB! 7.3

Building a Global Learning Community via Email

Discussions

Another asynchronous communications tool is the computer **discussion** (see Figure 7.4). Sometimes called a bulletin board, club, conference, or forum, this tool provides users with a way to communicate one-to-many.

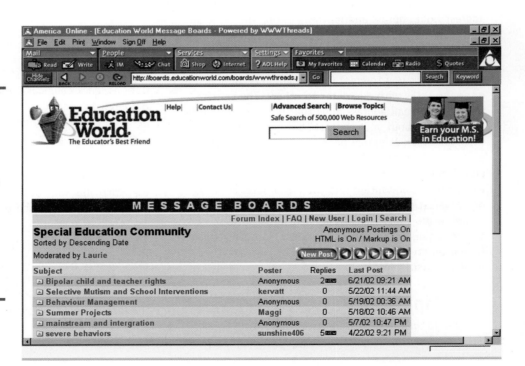

FIGURE 7.4

Online Teacher Discussions

Discussion software lets you view and participate in online conversations.

Screen capture © copyright Education World (**www.education-world.com**). Reprinted by permission. AOL browser window © 2002 America Online, Inc. Used with permission.

Just as you might post a message for anyone to read on a real-world bulletin board in a public area, so too can you post a message in an Internet discussion. Further, in a discussion, those reading your message can post either a public or private response. As various people post responses, and responses to responses, a "threaded" discussion evolves. Others accessing the discussion can follow the thread by reading through each original message and its responses.

Discussions offer electronic "threaded" conversations.

Discussions can be designated either public or private. Private discussions are created by emailing an invitation to participants and then setting up the discussion so that only invited members can read and respond. For teachers, discussions offer a way to open communication lines among students and educators. Teachers can interact with colleagues across the globe to share ideas. And their own students and students connected to the Internet anywhere in the world can join together to work collaboratively. Using a private discussion, students in your class can ask a question about the culture or community of students anywhere in the nation or world. Students from multiple locations can be invited to participate and respond, resulting in a lively cultural exchange. And because discussions provide asynchronous interaction, differing time zones or constraining classroom time schedules do not interfere. Students can check the messages posted whenever class time allows.

E-Learning ON THE WEB! 7.4

How Conferencing Can Enhance Learning

E-Learning ON THE WEB! 7.5

Using Educator Mailing Lists

Mailing Lists

An electronic **mailing list** (sometimes known as a "Listserv") is another asynchronous communications tool. This tool automatically delivers email to those who subscribe to the list. Messages are sent to an umbrella email address of the list itself and appear in email inboxes of all subscribers; in format, they are like any other personal email message. Mailing lists can be set up so that all members can post a message that will be automatically mailed or so that only the list administrator can broadcast messages. When a list administrator monitors and broadcasts messages, the potential for junk mail is greatly reduced, and the value of the list for members is improved.

Many excellent educational lists are available for educators. Each offers teaching ideas, lesson plans, and/or links to Internet sites that are very useful. You should, however, check to see whether you are subscribing to a monitored list; even then, subscribe only to those that you find particularly useful. Subscribing to a lot of lists, especially unmonitored ones, can result in your getting many more pieces of email than you can read in a day.

Tech Tips for TEACHERS

Unsubscribing to a Mailing List

When you have oversubscribed to mailing lists, you may find your email inbox inundated with mail. If you find yourself in this situation, you need to unsubscribe to some of the lists you are on. Since mailing lists are usually run by automated programs, sending an email asking to be taken off this list will usually not get your name removed. Instead, look at the bottom of one of the unwanted pieces of mail. Often directions and even a link will be provided to tell you how to have your email name removed from the mailing list. However, even if no directions are provided, most mailing list software will check the subject line of incoming email. If "unsubscribe" is found in that space, very often that will be enough of a command to the mailing list software to remove your name.

If the problem is severe enough to cause problems getting your desired mail, another option while you are waiting to be removed from the list is to identify the email from that list as spam. Spam is unwanted email, and most email programs will provide a spam filter. With the spam filtering feature, you can identify email you want to be blocked from entering your in-box. Blocked mail will be diverted to a spam folder from which it can be deleted. While not a long-term solution, blocking mail from a mailing list may be a useful option in the short run.

Chats

So far we have discussed only asynchronous communication tools. These are especially useful because they can fit easily into a busy instructional schedule, but sometimes asynchronous tools simply are not the right tools for the activity you have planned. In some cases, it is important to the activity to provide real-time interaction. In that case, an Internet chat is a good option. A **chat** is a service offered by some ISPs and some Internet sites that set aside a space in which two or more Internet users can meet in real time. A virtual space, called a "chat room," is established, which participants can enter. Those in the chat room communicate by typing their messages and then sending them for public display in the chat room. Individuals thus respond to each other in real time in this Internet space. Internet chats require that both you and the other chat participants have the same chat software available. Chat software can be downloaded, but it is most often offered as a part of an ISP's services.

Public and private chat rooms can have multiple participants. Another form of chat, called **instant messaging (IM),** is a one-to-one chat that can be

Electronic chats offer an opportunity for real-time interaction across the Internet.

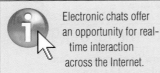

in the Classroom

IN THE SPECIAL EDUCATION AND SECONDARY CLASSROOM

Joan Thormann and **Dina Loebl** share how chatting, when carefully structured, is a means to teach communication skills and is especially helpful for special education students. They cite K–12 schools in Israel where computers are used to help these children verbally communicate. "Students," they write, "have also learned how to communicate using email and how to carry on meaningful virtual conversations." While the main focus of technology-implemented instruction for the special needs students is "developing literacy and research skills, using technology that is integrated in the curriculum," the students engage in online conversations, both email and chats, to experience communicating with people of different ages and backgrounds—seniors in a retirement community, peer mentoring for sixth graders "with eighth graders who served as mentors in a regular school setting using a combination of online and face-to-face meetings," and special projects such as the Internet project the Center for Educational Technology (CET) in Tel Aviv began that "addresses socialization issues for teenagers with special needs through contact with peers," a two-part program that is made up of "Virtual Friendship, where a student with special needs is paired with a non-handicapped student. These students communicate about their interests, build a friendship, and then

meet at the end of the year." Virtual Tutoring is the other segment of the program. Adult tutors work with the special needs students to "provide support to mainstreamed students as they learn and adapt to the regular school setting."

Aaron Joseph and **Jason Meistrich,** seniors at Torrey Pines High School in Carmel Valley, California, developed "a software program, Assignments2Go, that allows students to view their homework assignments for each class online." This service has a "chat room on academic topics selected by teachers. It will allow students to ask classmates and teachers for help on homework." From the perspective of a student, Meistrich said, "I like the idea of students and teachers working together this way. Normally if students have questions, they can't really contact a teacher unless they go to class. This site will allow for a more immediate response."

Parmet, S. (2004, January 2). They've done their homework: Two Torrey Pines High seniors create online student helper. Retrieved January 15, 2004, from **http:// signonsandiego. Printthis.clickability.com/pt/ cpt?action=cpt&title=SignOnSanDie. . .**

Thormann, J., & Loebl, D. (2005, March). Centralizing support: Technology for Israeli students with special needs. *Learning and Leading with Technology, 32*(6), 34–36.

YOU Decide!

Chats and instant messaging offer students a way to communicate with peers online. However, since the conversations are in real time, it is possible for interaction to become inappropriate before the teacher can intervene. Even with network monitoring software, it can be difficult for a teacher to oversee multiple live conversations and to ensure that nothing inappropriate is posted. Teachers must balance the risk of using synchronous chats with the value in encouraging online interaction. But is this tool worth it?

YES! Students can always say something inappropriate in a classroom. Just because the comments may be written rather than spoken, the risk of something inappropriate being expressed is no different. As long as the chat interaction is private and the general public does not have access, it is no different than the confined interaction of a classroom. It is definitely worth the effort to encourage student interaction, especially since that interaction could be with peers across the globe.

NO! Once an inappropriate comment is on the screen for all to see, it cannot be taken back. In a classroom a comment can be ignored or perhaps might have been heard by only a few students. In a chat room or on an instant message, everyone is sure to see everything everyone else says. Chats and similar live online communication are not worth the risk. It is better to use discussions that can be monitored and censored as needed before the damage is done.

Which view do you agree with? YOU DECIDE!

started whenever another user is simultaneously online. With IM, you typically configure the IM software to notify you when specific individuals go online. Once you are notified that one of those people is online, you can IM that individual, that is, open a two-person temporary message room in which to communicate. Like a chat, the two parties communicate by typing messages back and forth to one another. This more informal and spontaneous communication can offer teachers and students opportunities to communicate with online peers whenever they become available.

Like discussions, chats can be public or private. Public chats are very difficult to control and monitor for content and the use of profanity. They are therefore not particularly good tools for classroom use. However, private chats allow only designated individuals to participate. Using a private chat room, you can have your students exchange data for a common science project with experts in the field or with other classes participating in the project. You can also establish national and international dialog with colleagues across the globe. A chat room can be a powerful and useful tool, one that is often a free Internet resource. Of course, because chats are synchronous, all parties must be prepared to participate at a common time. This can take a bit more advance work than emailing or discussions, but if live interaction is desired, this is an ideal tool.

Videoconferencing

If all types of files, from text to graphics to video and audio, can be transmitted over the Internet, then why not live voice and video images as well? That, too, is very doable using current Internet tools. **Videoconferencing** software allows users at either end of a synchronous connection not only

Videoconferencing software lets you communicate via voice and visual images across a network.

to hear each other, but to see video images of each other as well. To add video to live conferencing on the Net, you must attach a video camera to your computer. Small, inexpensive monitor-top cameras are often used for this purpose. Thus, as you sit before the monitor looking at the screen, just by looking up and into the camera, you can make "eye contact" with the other participants in the video conference. Your image will display on their monitor, and theirs will display on your monitor.

In a classroom equipped with a multimedia computer, a monitor-top camera, video-conferencing software (such as the freeware program CUSeeMe), and Internet access, students can see, hear, and interact with their counterparts in similarly equipped classrooms around the world. Web sites such as the Global Schoolhouse (www.globalschoolnet.org/gsh) offer pages to help educators find and connect to other classrooms interested in video-conferencing. Students engaged in videoconferencing-based interaction can participate in real-time interactive learning experiences with their peers in classrooms anywhere in the world.

Classroom-based videoconferencing might look somewhat choppy, and there may be delays in transmission, but this system does add visual images to Internet-based communications. Of course, many dedicated video-conferencing systems are much more sophisticated and provide broadcast-quality images at much higher costs. As Internet bandwidth and speed continue to increase, even classroom-based videoconferencing will be able to approach the quality we have all come to expect from video images.

Exploring Videoconferencing Projects

Other Internet Services

The Internet provides a wide variety of other services that may be of interest to you as you expand your use of this network of networks. Each of the following services is described briefly so that you will be aware of its potential and use (see also Table 7.3).

FTP

File transfer protocol (FTP) programs transfer files across the Internet.

File transfer protocol (FTP) is the method used for transferring files among computers on the Internet. FTP programs are usually included in your Internet software. Typically, you are using this protocol whenever you download (bring files from the Net to your computer) or upload a file (send files from your computer to the Internet), even if you are not aware that you have activated an FTP program.

There are FTP sites on the Internet, many of which are maintained by the government or a university, that contain available text, graphic, sound, and video files for your use. Although some restricted sites require a password,

TABLE 7.3	Internet Services for Educators
INTERNET SERVICE PROVIDERS (ISPs)	Companies that provide access to the Internet and various services for a monthly fee
ELECTRONIC MAIL (EMAIL)	Asynchronous one-to-one communications tool available to everyone on a network connected to the Internet
DISCUSSIONS	Internet-based electronic discussion groups that allow those interested to read or post comments on a topic
MAILING LISTS	Automated lists of subscribers interested in a topic; subscribers automatically receive a copy of emails sent to the list
CHAT ROOMS	Virtual spaces in which individuals can meet virtually to hold real-time conversations via text and sometimes voice
VIDEO-CONFERENCING	Live video with audio across the Internet that lets individuals communicate in real time by seeing and hearing each other speak
FILE TRANSFER PROTOCOL (FTP)	Program that uploads and downloads files; FTP sites provide libraries of downloadable freeware and shareware software and files
NEWSGROUPS	Discussion groups dedicated to a specific topic and open to anyone interested in that topic

many are "anonymous" sites that allow you open access. Some of these require that you type in "guest" or "anonymous" at the welcome screen. Such requirements are usually clearly written on the screen.

When you upload and download files to and from FTP sites—and, indeed, most Internet sites—such files are often sent in a compressed format. Compressed files, sometimes called zipped files, have been temporarily reduced in size so that they will transfer faster and occupy less storage space on the FTP site. After they are downloaded to your computer, they must be decompressed to be usable again. Some files automatically expand after being downloaded. Others require the appropriate **decompression program.** If a decompression program is needed for an FTP site's files, it too is usually available from the FTP site and should be the first thing you download. A variety of decompression programs are also available from the Internet.

FTP sites can offer a wealth of freeware and shareware. All you need to do is know that this resource exists, visit the FTP site, and download files that are of interest to you. On many FTP sites, the files are listed by name alone, although you may find them organized by category. To be sure that you are getting the type of file you want, you should note the file's extension, the three letters following the dot in the file name. Different extensions represent different types of files. Table 7.4 summarizes the most common extensions.

TABLE 7.4   File Types Available at FTP Sites

File extensions (the last three characters following the dot [.] in a file name) can help you determine the type of file you are dealing with. Common file extensions and their descriptions are summarized here.

EXTENSIONS	DESCRIPTION
.doc, .htm, .html, .txt	**Text files:** Word-processed files (.doc), files readable with a browser (.htm or .html), and those readable with any text reader
.bmp, .jpg, .pict, .dig, .eps, .png	**Graphics files:** Graphic data ranging from clip art to high-resolution photographs; most files are readable by better art and draw programs
.avi, .mov, .mpg	**Video files:** Motion video clip files that typically require software and adequate hardware for viewing; software is freeware on the web
.au, .wav	**Audio files:** Audio clips of music, speech, or sound effects; usually require hardware and software
.exe, .com, .bat	**Program files:** Files that are programs of some type, usually found on FTP sites in application categories (for example, utilities, word processors)
.z, .zip, .sit	**Decompression files:** Large files of any of the above types that have been compressed for faster upload and download; require a decompression program (usually freeware on the Web) to decompress them

Newsgroups

Using electronic conferencing, a large number of topic-oriented newsgroups are continuously running on the Internet. A **newsgroup** is a public conference dedicated to a specific topic. To participate in a newsgroup, you use a newsreader (see Figure 7.5), a program that is included with your Internet software. The newsreader lets you read all the previously posted messages and follow the threads of the discussion. You can also post your own responses or start discussion of a new topic. Most newsgroups are open discussions on specific subject areas such as education, computers, news, music, and many more. Newsgroup names often indicate their topic areas. For example, biz.jobs.computers would be a discussion group about computer employment in business, and ed.middle.science would be a discussion about teaching middle school science. A newsgroup with a name such as alt.education.disabled would be an "alternative" newsgroup for discussion of issues related to educating individuals with disabilities.

Newsgroups offer a wide variety of Internet discussion groups on every possible subject of interest.

The World Wide Web

People are often confused by the difference between the Internet and the **World Wide Web** (the Web). Actually, the Web is the most popular of the many services available on the Internet. It is not a separate network, nor is *the Web* synonymous with *the Internet*.

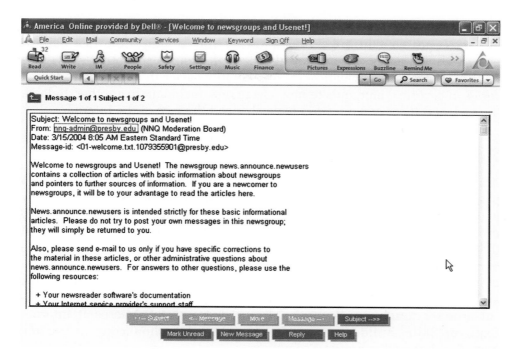

FIGURE 7.5

Using a Newsreader to Read a Usenet Group

Newsreader software lets you view and participate in newsgroup discussions.

Moderators of News.Announce .Newsusers. AOL browser window © 2002 America Online, Inc. Used with permission.

In its early days, the Internet was not particularly easy to use. Typically, commands to move about on or retrieve something from the Internet were text commands that required very exact syntax. To use Internet resources, you had to know the precise sequence of commands and be able to use them in a very specific order. The complexity involved in using and navigating the Internet and the increasing demands by non-technical users for access led to the creation of a user-friendly graphics interface in 1991. Tim Berners-Lee, working at the European particle physics lab (CERN) in Geneva, Switzerland, wrote a program for use on the Internet that fundamentally changed how users and the Net interacted. His program allowed users to move between linked web pages located on the Internet. Simply by clicking on a link, Internet surfers could jump from one document on the Net to another, without knowing a single complex command. These links, called **hyperlinks,** made Internet navigation as easy as pointing and clicking. The vast collection of hyperlink documents available on the Internet is known as the World Wide Web, W3, or simply the Web.

The World Wide Web is the user-friendly graphical side of the Internet that uses hyperlinks to move from one location to the next.

Web Sites: Linked Web Pages

A document that provides information and contains a series of hyperlinks to other resources is called a **web page,** and a collection of related web pages is called a **web site.** Web sites can contain multiple pages, and each page can contain text, graphics, animation, audio, and video data. Typically, web sites have a welcome or **home page** that provides basic information about the site and one or more connections to additional information pages. These connections, or links, are usually represented by colored and underlined words or **navigation button** graphics. Each of these is "hot-linked"; that is, it contains a hyperlink to another document at that web site or at another web site.

Activating a link causes a jump to that connected page or web site. Almost all web pages contain links, thus allowing you to jump from that page to other web site pages, which may also contain links to still other sites. This method of Internet navigation is considerably easier than having to type a series of cryptic commands to move from one document to another. Indeed, the web and its easy navigation have changed the face of the Internet.

Web Browsers

Web browsers display HTML code as web pages.

www.mylabschool.com
Software Skills Builder
Using Microsoft Internet Explorer

A special program is necessary to translate the language with which a web page is written into an image on your screen. Web pages are written by using a language called **hypertext markup language (HTML).** Your web browser is actually a type of translation software that reads HTML and then displays it as the web page you are familiar with. Browser software also enables you to easily locate a web page by typing in its web address, move to and display the target web page graphically, and even move back and forward between pages you have viewed. Figure 7.6 summarizes typical browser functions. You may also wish to try the Microsoft Internet Explorer Skills Builder, accessible at www.mylabschool.com, to become more familiar with a browser's features.

Locating Web Pages

Networks that are connected to the Internet usually have a dedicated server, called a web server, that stores web pages and responds to requests from web users. Each one of those web servers is given a very specific web address so that it can be located from among the millions of computers on the Internet. Web addresses can be easily recognized because they all start

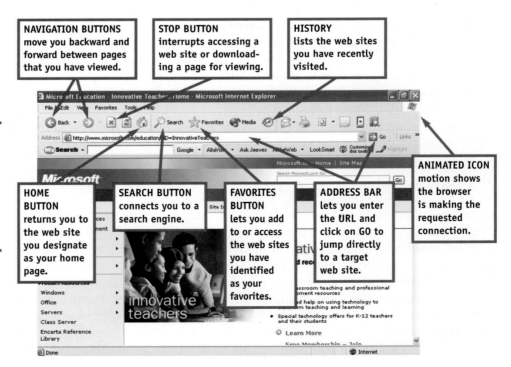

NAVIGATION BUTTONS move you backward and forward between pages that you have viewed.

STOP BUTTON interrupts accessing a web site or downloading a page for viewing.

HISTORY lists the web sites you have recently visited.

HOME BUTTON returns you to the web site you designate as your home page.

SEARCH BUTTON connects you to a search engine.

FAVORITES BUTTON lets you add to or access the web sites you have identified as your favorites.

ADDRESS BAR lets you enter the URL and click on GO to jump directly to a target web site.

ANIMATED ICON motion shows the browser is making the requested connection.

FIGURE 7.6
Key Browser Features
Browsers offer you a variety of features and commands via menus and buttons to make it easy to access and use the Web.

with a hypertext transfer protocol designation, written http://. This designation indicates that the document to be sought and transferred is using the web page protocol for transmission. A complete web address is written in a very specific format that can direct a browser to an exact location on a web server. This format is called a **uniform resource locator (URL).** URLs include precise components indicating a web location. At minimum they include the name of a type of web server on which the home page of the web site is found. A URL may also identify the specific directory, or folder and file name for the information you are looking for. Figure 7.7 summarizes the components of a URL to help you understand how it connects you precisely to a specific document.

URLs identify where a web page can be found.

Creating and Evaluating Web Sites

As you review various web sites, it might seem like a very complex task to create a web page. That is not necessarily the case. As you learned in Chapter 6, a wide variety of easy-to-use web page authoring software packages are available, many of which are provided as a component on common applications such as word-processing software. The fact that web page authoring can easily be accomplished is evidenced by the many teacher- and student-made web pages on the web today.

However, not all web sites created by and for educators are well made. Whether you are creating your own web site or you are reviewing another educational site for use in your classroom, it is important that you carefully examine the site for quality.

A web site's design should be well organized and logical; the site should also be easy to navigate to find the information sought. Furthermore, and of critical importance for educational sites, the creator of a site should have the appropriate authority and expertise necessary to present correct

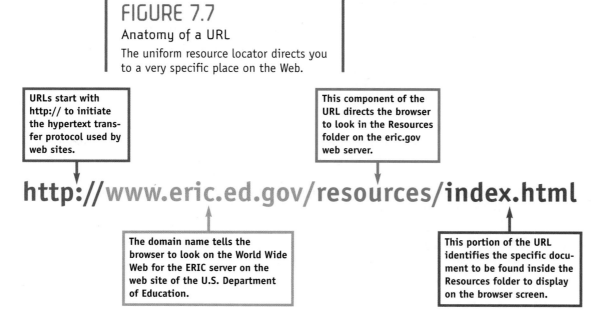

FIGURE 7.7
Anatomy of a URL
The uniform resource locator directs you to a very specific place on the Web.

URLs start with http:// to initiate the hypertext transfer protocol used by web sites.

This component of the URL directs the browser to look in the Resources folder on the eric.gov web server.

http://www.eric.ed.gov/resources/index.html

The domain name tells the browser to look on the World Wide Web for the ERIC server on the web site of the U.S. Department of Education.

This portion of the URL identifies the specific document to be found inside the Resources folder to display on the browser screen.

and meaningful information in the area on which the site is focused. Unfortunately, many web sites can be found that should not be considered authoritative but are too often assumed to be so just because they are available on the Internet. Equally important for educators and their students, educational sites should be free of any type of bias in their presentation of information and should not be trying to sell a product or their creators' views. Finally, high-quality educational web sites should clearly cite the sources that were used in the preparation of the information presented.

Before you use a web site in your classroom, be sure to examine it carefully and evaluate it using these criteria. Although many web sites are obviously inappropriate for classroom use, others may turn out to be so only after your careful evaluation. It is the teacher's responsibility to fully preview instructional materials, whether in print or on the web, before sharing them with students. Table 7.5 provides a rubric that will help you to evaluate web site quality.

Multimedia on the Web

Classrooms on the Web

Because educators want to appeal to a variety of learning styles, the need to make a web page more than an "electronic textbook" is critical when using it for instructional support. Fortunately, web pages support the multimedia components that are so useful in addressing diverse learning styles. Creating multimedia features for use on an educational web site is not difficult. Web page authoring programs typically enable you to include multimedia files when creating your web pages. The main disadvantage to using multimedia on a site is the fact that multimedia files can be quite large and therefore may take additional time to access and download. Furthermore, the user's browser may or may not include the program components that are needed to display multimedia. Some browsers may require an additional program, called a **plug-in,** to expand the browsers' capabilities in this area. Most plug-ins are offered free to those Internet users who wish to download them. This makes it possible for the users to easily upgrade their browser's capabilities via plug-ins so that they, too, can use web multimedia. Whenever you decide to use multimedia on a web page, you should also include the URL of the plug-in's web site. Adding this address to your web page makes it easy for those who wish to view your multimedia to upgrade their browsers if they need and want to.

Plug-ins add multimedia capabilities to browsers.

Graphics

Graphics files are the most frequent multimedia addition to web pages. The use of pictures and visual images adds significantly to the excitement of a teaching page. To use graphics on the web, you need to be aware of the various types of graphic formats that are compatible for this purpose. Graphics may be created in these formats through the use of most of the popular draw or paint programs. It is simply a matter of creating the graphic and then saving it in the desired format. Art software provides the translation necessary to save from one format to another.

The most frequently used formats for web graphics are GIF and JPEG. **GIF** stands for graphic interchange format, a graphics format that is used

TABLE 7.5   Web Site Evaluation Rubric

SITE NAME:

URL:

AREA/CONTENT OF SITE:

COMMENTS:

Using each of the criteria below, evaluate the usefulness of this web site for teaching and learning. For each dimension in the rubric, check the box that best reflects your opinion. Select web sites that score 4 or higher in the most dimensions.

DIMENSION	EVALUATION CRITERIA				
	2 Poor	3 Below Average	4 Average	5 Above Average	Excellent
DESIGN	Poorly organized; contains obvious errors; loads slowly	Organization somewhat confusing; some errors; loads slowly	Organization acceptable; no obvious errors; loads adequately	Good organization; no errors; loads quickly	Excellent organization; clear and free of errors; loads quickly and completely
NAVIGABILITY	Difficult to find and follow site navigation links	Navigation links visible but somewhat confusing	Navigation links clear and readily available	Navigation links clear and logical; site map included	Navigation logical and clear; site map and search engine available
AUTHORITY	Unclear who authored the site	Author name and contact information included; but credentials lacking	Author name, contact information, and some credential information included	Author name, contact information, full credentials included	Well-regarded author provides all necessary information; site is linked to by others
BIAS	Site attempts to persuade or sell views	Site presents facts, but some bias is evident	Site is mostly neutral; selling pages are segregated	Site contains no attempts to sell or persuade	Site presents multiple viewpoints with no bias
CITATIONS	No citations are evident	Citations are included on some sources but not all	All sources include brief citations, but site lacks bibliography	All sources are properly cited with site bibliography	All sources properly cited, full bibliography, with active links
DATES	No dates evident	Site contains creation date but no dates for update information	Site contains both creation and dates for update information	Site contains dates for creation and update information and some dates relating to data collection	Site contains creation, update, and data collection dates for all key information
CONTENT	Data quality is questionable, and quantity is limited	Data quality appears adequate, limited quantity	Data is adequate in quality and quantity	Data quality is established, and quantity is sufficient for coverage	Data quality is unquestioned, and quantity provides excellent coverage
LINKS	Few relevant working links included	Adequate number of links, but many no longer functional	Sufficient number of links, and all are functional	A good variety of useful, active links	Active links to wide variety of excellent sites
HANDICAPPED ACCESS	No options available for handicapped	Some pages on site offer text-only option	Site offers text-only option on all pages	Site offers clear options for handicapped	Site includes handicapped options on all pages and links to support software
RELEVANCE	Site does not meet instructional objectives	Site meets some aspects of instructional objectives	Instructional objectives are adequately met	Site exceeds most objectives' requirements	Site exceeds all instructional objectives

This and other downloadable forms and templates can be found on the Companion Website at www.ablongman.com/lever-duffy3e.

GIF and JPEG are common web graphics formats.

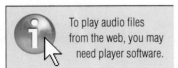

To play audio files from the web, you may need player software.

primarily for clip art and line art. GIFs are best for images that have large areas of solid color, sharp edges, and no gradients. Animated GIFs are sequences of images that, displayed in quick succession, give the appearance of movement. No doubt you have seen these popular animations on web pages. Because they are essentially a sequence of GIFs, they too are relatively quick for a browser to download and display. **JPEG** (pronounced "jay-peg") stands for Joint Photographic Expert Group, the agreed-upon standard for photographic images. JPEG graphics are used for high-quality images. This much higher-resolution image is needed to accurately reproduce scanned photos; however, JPEG files are typically large and require more time to display.

When displaying graphics, browsers typically load and display text first and then begin the graphics transfers. The graphics often appear to the user as partial or blurred images that gradually resolve into clear, complete, full-color images. The smaller the file and simpler the format, the faster a graphic becomes viewable.

The Web contains millions of images that are available for you to use. Many of them are copyright free; that is, you can use them without having to reimburse the owner of the image. Chapter 11 will help you better understand copyright and its impact on you as a teacher. However, at this point, it is sufficient to be aware that copyrighted images cannot be used or reproduced without the express permission of their owners. For most educators who create web sites or use images from web sites, this is not a problem, because so many free resources are available.

Audio

Audio on a web site can add another multimedia dimension in using the web for teaching and learning. Audio files that are stored in WAV and MP3 formats require that you first download an entire file before playing it. Because such audio files can be quite large, long delays result from incorporating audio into web pages using these formats.

A more sophisticated audio technology for the web, called **streaming audio,** sends audio in a continuous stream or flow. Streaming audio players such as the one shown in Figure 7.8 allow you to listen to the audio as it is received by your browser. There may be some short delays, but for the most part, you are able to listen as you download. Live Internet concerts and Internet radio stations use this technology. One of the most widely used formats for this type of audio is RealOne Player, developed by RealNetworks. If you decide to listen to an audio clip that is in the RealAudio (RA) format, you may first need to download the RealPlayer or RealOne Player plug-in to enhance your browser (see Figure 7.8).

Video

Just as audio clips can be added to a web site, so too can video clips be included. Video clips are typically brief because they take considerable amounts of time to transfer. **Streaming video** has improved that situation by allowing the user to view the video clip as it is downloaded. Given the current bandwidth and speed of most connections via modem, movement in many video images appears to be somewhat choppy and fuzzy. No doubt

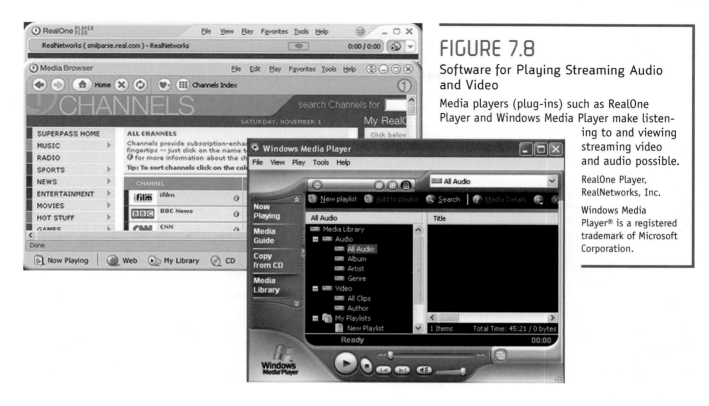

FIGURE 7.8

Software for Playing Streaming Audio and Video

Media players (plug-ins) such as RealOne Player and Windows Media Player make listening to and viewing streaming video and audio possible.

RealOne Player, RealNetworks, Inc.

Windows Media Player® is a registered trademark of Microsoft Corporation.

the constantly increasing bandwidth of available lines to homes and schools will quickly improve the quality of video on the Web. For educators, being able to access and show video clips from around the world with just a click of a mouse button offers many exciting educational opportunities. Current and emerging web-based video resources will be explored in detail in Chapter 9.

Virtual Reality

Virtual reality (VR) provides a three-dimensional graphic environment that can be accessed on the Web. A web site that is a VR world is one that is rendered in three dimensions and allows the user to manipulate that three-dimensional environment. When you visit a VR world museum, for example, it seems on your screen as if you can move down hallways, turn corners, and go up stairs to see the museum's displays. You can even manipulate objects of interest by coming close to them, picking them up with your mouse button, and turning them around to get a view of all sides. Once again, at the moment, low bandwidth can cause such environments to move slowly and even appear choppy; however, the promise of VR worlds for education is enormous. Imagine the possibilities of a student being able to enter a VR world at the molecular level and move electrons around to alter elements or being able to take a field trip to see the inside of the pyramids from a computer connected to the Web. Clearly, firsthand experiences are the best, but for experiences that are too far away or impossible to attain, the use of VR holds great potential.

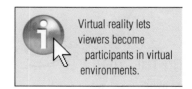

Virtual reality lets viewers become participants in virtual environments.

E-Learning
ON THE WEB! 7.8
Virtual Worlds

Search Engines

If an educator is interested in using any of the web resources described so far in this chapter, how can they be located from among the millions of web sites out there? The Web does not contain a central index or directory. Remember, it is, at its core, thousands of independent, interconnected networks and servers with no one single organization running it. With data spread so widely and no central index, the only way to find very specific data on the Web is to use a tool that searches the Web for you. This tool is called a search engine.

Search engines are programs that are designed to find web sites and pages based on key words that you enter. The key word can be a single word, a phrase, or a series of words. The search engine matches the search word against databases of web sites and their respective key words. When a match occurs, the search engine provides you with a hyperlink to the page or site related to the search term. These matches, sometimes called hits, provide you with a direct connection to relevant web pages.

Search engines use different techniques to generate their databases. Some store and read key words that web site authors provide when they register the site. Others use automated web robot programs, sometimes called spiders, to search for new sites. Because thousands of new web sites are being added to the web daily and different engines use different techniques to build their databases, it is very possible for searches using different search engines to have very different results. You will need to experiment with different search engines to determine which ones seem to bring you the hits that are closest to what you are looking for.

When using a search engine, it is important to structure your request for information so that you do not get an unmanageable number of hits. If you were to request an engine to search on the word *education,* millions of hits would be returned to you, making it essentially impossible for you to find the few that pertain to the topic within education in which you are interested. Although there may be some variation in the techniques used by any given search engine, all provide methods to narrow the search, typically using terms such as AND, OR, or NOT to control the scope of the search. By carefully constructing your search request, you will be able to get very precise results. You should always review the search instructions provided at a search engine site before using that search engine. Each engine differs somewhat, and a brief review will help you optimize your searches and may save you considerable time. Try the Software Skills Builder Using a Search Engine to fine-tune your search skills.

Portals

Various web sites, particularly those that began primarily as search engines, have begun to offer more and more services. Such sites, which include an assortment of services such as a search engine, news, email, discussions, electronic shopping, and chat rooms, are called portals. A **portal** is a doorway to the Internet and its many resources. The portal pro-

E-Learning

www.mylabschool.com
Software Skills Builder
Using a Search Engine

HANDS-ON LEARNING

Use a search engine to find an educational electronic discussion group and a mailing list for teachers. Join both. Monitor the discussions posted and post at least one comment of your own. Read the emails distributed through the mailing list. After using each for a week, respond to the following questions:

- What are the advantages and disadvantages of using each type of Internet communications tool?
- What type of information was shared on each?
- Would you recommend these tools to new teachers? Why or why not?

E-Learning
ON THE WEB! 7.9

Searching the Web

vides you with access and services that facilitate your use of the Internet. Creators of sites that have become portals hope that you will set your browser to open to their sites and then proceed with your Internet activity from there. To support their services, portals sell space on their sites to advertisers that are interested in marketing to you. Some of the most popular portals include Yahoo!, Lycos, and Excite. Portals such as Education World are dedicated to educational topics and services. Exploring portals may well be worth the expenditure of a busy educator's time.

Using the Internet and Web in Teaching and Learning

The Internet has, without doubt, great potential in teaching and learning. You have learned throughout this chapter of its many tools and services, as well as some of their innovative applications to teaching and learning. This global interconnection of thousands of networks has changed the way we communicate, much as the printing press revolutionized communication hundreds of years ago. We are all just beginning to grasp the social implications of this revolution as we have moved from the Industrial to the Information Age.

In Chapter 8, we will further explore how the World Wide Web can be used in teaching and learning. We will also review some of the key issues relating to the use of the Internet about which a prudent teacher should be aware. The Internet itself and the manner in which it is used by some offer potential for abuse. Educators who use the Internet in their classrooms must be aware of these issues and see to it that their own implementation of the Internet in teaching and learning is consistent with our highest professional standards and our responsibilities to our most important charges: our students.

E-Learning

www.mylabschool.com
video
View *A Dinosaur WebQuest*

The Internet is a powerful learning tool.

KEY TERMS

asynchronous communications 253
cable modem 252
chat 260
decompression program 263
digital subscriber line (DSL) 252
discussion 258
email 253
file transfer protocol (FTP) 262
GIF 268
home page 265
hyperlinks 265
hypertext markup language (HTML) 266

instant messaging (IM) 260
Internet service providers (ISPs) 253
Internet 249
JPEG 270
mailing list 259
modem 250
navigation button 265
newsgroup 264
plug-in 268
portal 272
search engine 272
streaming audio 270

streaming video 270
synchronous communications 253
TCP/IP 250
telecommunication 250
URL 267
videoconferencing 261
virtual reality (VR) 271
web page 265
web site 265
World Wide Web 264

STUDENT ACTIVITIES

CHAPTER REVIEW

1. What is telecommunication? What hardware and software are necessary to make it possible?
2. What is the Internet? What value does it hold for educators?
3. What is an ISP? Why is an ISP necessary for access to the Internet?
4. What is the difference between asynchronous and synchronous communication? Name and describe the Internet communication tools that fall into each category.
5. What is a web site? What role does a browser play when you are working on the Web?

6. What is HTML? Does a teacher need to know HTML to have a class web site? Why or why not?
7. What is a URL and how is it used? Why is a URL important when using the Web?
8. What are streaming audio and streaming video? How have they altered the use of audio and video on the Internet?
9. How do search engines help you find specific information on the Internet?
10. What is a portal? How can it be useful for busy teachers?

WHAT DO YOU THINK?

1. The Internet offers an almost overwhelming wealth of information and is growing daily. It is becoming clear that it will be increasingly difficult to fully define a content area or discipline without incorporating this resource's expanding knowledge base. This may radically change the skills children will need for lifelong learning. How has the Internet changed our concept of information? What computer and Internet skills do you think children should learn so that they will be prepared for life in the Information Age?
2. Internet communication tools open broad new opportunities for interaction among students across the globe. Of the communication tools you have learned about, which do you think holds the most promise? How might you use this type of tool when you teach?

3. The Internet is a public communication area that many believe is protected by the First Amendment. Others believe that the contents of the Internet ought to be moderated and the public protected from inappropriate content. What is your view on this controversial issue?

LEARNING TOGETHER!

These activities are best done in groups of three to five.

1. Each group member should interview at least three teachers who use the Internet in instruction. Be sure to ask the objectives of the Internet-based activity used in their teaching and precisely how it is carried out. Share interview findings with your peers and together develop an Internet Best Practices summary that details the best Internet activities you discovered. Be prepared to share your best practices with other groups in your class.
2. Create a private chat or conference using one of the Internet portals. Use the communication tool you have created to develop a Top Ten list of ways you might use this tool in a classroom.
3. Assume that all members of your group have decided to connect to the Internet from home. Each member should select one of the available ISPs in your area and research the features and services it provides and the costs for providing those services. Share your findings and select the best way for you to connect to the Internet from the choices your group has researched.

E-Learning

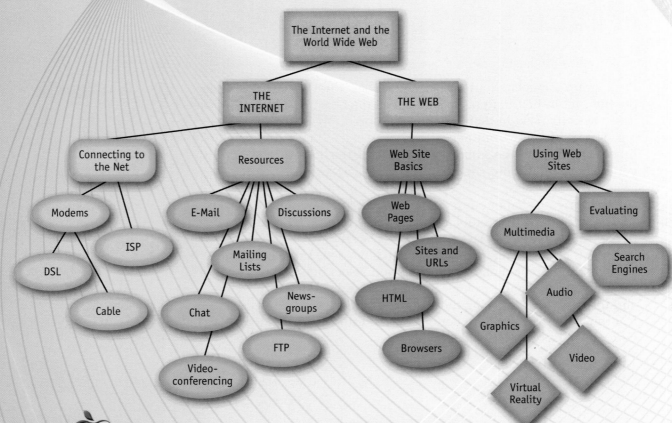

Podcasts www.mylabschool.com

Listen to a podcast relating to the use of administrative software in teaching and learning. Download the audio discussion to your iPod, computer, or MP3 player.

Software Skills Builder www.mylabschool.com

These step-by-step illustrated tutorials teach you to use Microsoft Windows and Office on both PC and Mac by preparing documents that will be useful in your classroom.

Video Lab www.mylabschool.com

Accessible through the **mylabschool** web site are several video vignettes that offer you a look at software in teaching and learning. Learning guides for all videos can be found in the text's Learning Guide Supplement.

On the Web! Activities www.ablongman.com/lever-duffy3e

Noted in the margins of the chapter, these activities offer you in-depth experiences in the topics and content presented in the chapter.

Online Practice Test www.ablongman.com/lever-duffy3e

Practice tests offer you an opportunity to test your knowledge and then review the results and send them to your teacher.

Outliner www.ablongman.com/lever-duffy3e

Chapter Outliners are fill-in-the-blank outlines of the main ideas presented in the chapter. Download the outliner and fill it in for an effective chapter study guide.

Power Practices www.ablongman.com/lever-duffy3e

Power Practices are animated tutorials made using Microsoft's presentation software, PowerPoint. This flash card tutorial will help you practice key concepts in the chapter.

Puzzler www.ablongman.com/lever-duffy3e

Puzzlers include content in crossword, word search, and other puzzle formats to help you master chapter content.

Useful Links www.ablongman.com/lever-duffy3e

These links offer you suggestions for expanded online research in the topics presented in the chapter.

INTEGRATION *Ideas*

The Internet has changed education, just as it has changed society. The world's knowledge base is essentially at everyone's fingertips. Regardless of the content area of interest, an unprecedented amount of information is now available in every classroom. Consider the following ideas for integrating the Internet and the World Wide Web. These will help to give you ideas of some of the innovative ways to integrate this powerful technology into your classroom. More ideas can be found on the text's companion web site.

Integrating Technology into Social Studies

"An Online History of the United States" is a program organized by chapters. The program has a narrative base expanded by links to Internet resources. These resources encompass an amount of content that is suitable as a replacement for textbooks or as an enhancement to them. A lesson plan for The Age of Imperialism is representative of lessons for the other chapters. It includes Objectives, Setting the Context, Online History, Enrichment Activities, Unit Wrap-Up, and a Unit Test. The objectives target all levels of Bloom's *Taxonomy*. The topics under "Setting the Context" review material already presented and tie it into the topics to be addressed in the chapter. "Enrichment Activities" are suitable for gifted and talented students who are placed in the regular or advanced placement classrooms. Check this out at **www.smplanet.com/ imperialism/teacher.html.**

Integrating Technology into Language Arts

For writing instruction, ePals is a tool students can use as part of their English class curricula to correspond online, telling each other about their culture online. As observed by Tim Discipio, ePals' cofounder, "Teachers say literacy is improving among students because when a child sends a message to another student, they spend a lot of time crafting it, wanting it to be right." This Internet tool, which brings communication to life and encourages a wide assortment of language arts skills, can be found at **www.epals.com.**

Integrating Technology into the Sciences

Following the lessons found in the NASA CORE (Central Operation of Research for Educators) site and the official NASA site, teachers can use "How Big Are We?" to tackle in the classroom a recognizably difficult scientific problem—finding a number that expresses the size of the universe. The NASA site has a search engine that brings up data to help students estimate numerically not only the size of the universe but also the number of stars in galaxies and the average mass of a star. The Procedure with Activities shows students how to design a rubric for assessment of their work. Extensions of this lesson can be found at "Astronomy Village," NASA's Classroom of the Future. The NASA sites are updated monthly. Science Standards and NETS Performance Indicators are given. Learn more at **http://education.nasa.gov/edprograms/core/home/index .html.** and **www.nasa.gov.**

Integrating Technology into Math

Online integration activities for math classes are found on Laura Candler's File Cabinet: Math Activities. General math activities, geometry activities, decimal activities, time and measurement activities, fraction activities, weekly math challenge activities (real-world math applications), and individual or cooperative problem-solving practice are the topics covered with multiple activities in each area accessible with a click of the mouse at **http://home.att.net/~clnetwork/math.htm.**

For these and many more Integration Ideas for using the Internet in teaching and learning visit the text web site at **www.ablongman.com/lever-duffy3e.**

The Internet and Education

The Internet offers educators a storehouse of targeted information to help them teach, help their students learn, and grow as a professional. Educational web sites, web portals, and online databases provide teachers with the ideas, tools, and research they need to answer essentially every professional question they might pose. This annotated summary of some of the most popular of these educational Internet resources offers you a sampling of the extensive educational resources on the Internet. Since the Internet is dynamic and changes continually, check the text companion web site at www.ablongman.com/lever-duffy3e for the most current list of educational Internet resources.

Teaching and Classroom Resources

The Gateway to Educational Materials (GEM)

This web site is the result of a consortium effort with organization and individual memberships. At GEM you will find Gateway access to quality instructional resources and tools available on the Web. Go to **www.thegateway.org** to learn more.

Education World

Education World is a portal for educators. You will find information and links on everything an educator might be interested in, from professional development to lesson plans, at **www.educationworld.com.**

Kathy Schrock's Guide for Educators

This extensive web site offers ideas, links, and resources to expand and enhance curriculum and to augment professional growth. It offers lessons, ideas, and practical tools for your classroom at **http://school.discovery.com/schrockguide/.**

EduHound

This site offers a directory of educational links for K–12 educators, students, and parents. In addition to excellent resources, the site offers a mailing list service for a free weekly newsletter, EduHound Weekly, at **www.eduhound.com.**

Learning Page

The Learning Page web site provides teachers with a wide variety of professionally produced instructional materials that can be downloaded and printed for use in your classroom. Find it at **www.learningpage.com.**

Busy Teacher's Website K–12

This site provides teachers with direct source materials, lesson plans, and classroom activities with a minimum of site-to-site linking while providing an enjoyable and rewarding experience for the teacher who is learning to use the Internet. Check it out at **www.ceismc.gatech.edu/busyt.**

Federal Resources for Educational Excellence (FREE)

Developed by a working group in 1997, this site makes hundreds of federally supported teaching and learning resources easier to find. Go to **www.ed.gov/free/index.html** to learn more.

Sites for Teachers

A free compendium of links, this web site offers teachers a collection of sites that contain teacher's resource and educational material ranked by popularity at **www.sitesforteachers.com/.**

Blue Web'N

This web site offers an online library of outstanding Internet sites categorized by subject, grade level, and instructional format at **www.kn.pacbell.com/wired/bluewebn/.**

Scholastic

This portal for educators, students, and parents offers instructional resources, productivity and communication tools, and links. Featuring K–12 online interactive activities, this site is an engaging tool in the classroom. It can be found at **www.scholastic.com/.**

The Teachers Corner

A web site for primary and elementary teachers, this site offers lesson plans, thematic units, links, tips, and educational news for teachers at **www.theteacherscorner.net/.**

Professional Resources

Education Resources Information Center (ERIC)

Sponsored by the Institute of Education Sciences (IES) of the U.S. Department of Education, ERIC is the world's premier database of journal and nonjournal education literature. ERIC provides a public web site for searching nearly 1.2 million citations going back to 1966 and, with contributor permission, accessing more than 110,000 full-text materials at no charge. Find it at **www.eric.ed.gov.**

The Educator's Reference Desk

This web site, developed and maintained by the Information Institute of Syracuse, offers teachers' resource guides, thousands of lesson plans, links to online education information, and an extensive archive of responses to AskERIC questions at **www.eduref.org/.**

Education Index

This web site offers teachers, parents, and learners resources and links on a wide variety of subjects organized by topic and lifestage. It also provides a virtual "coffee shop" where individuals can meet and discuss educational concerns at **www.educationindex.com.**

Tapped In

This web site brings educators together both locally and worldwide to cultivate a community that supports each teacher as a professional. The web site also provides educators professional support through peer networks supported by the Tapped In community. Check it out at **http://tappedin.org/tappedin/.**

chapter 8

Using the Web for Teaching and Learning

This chapter addresses these ISTE *National Educational Technology Standards* for Teachers:

I. TECHNOLOGY OPERATIONS AND CONCEPTS

Teachers demonstrate a sound understanding of technology operations and concepts. Teachers

A. demonstrate introductory knowledge, skills, and understanding of concepts related to technology (as described in the ISTE *National Education Technology Standards* for Students).

B. demonstrate continual growth in technology knowledge and skills to stay abreast of current and emerging technologies.

III. TEACHING, LEARNING, AND THE CURRICULUM

Teachers implement curriculum plans that include methods and strategies for applying technology to maximize student learning. Teachers

A. facilitate technology-enhanced experiences that address content standards and student technology standards.

B. use technology to support learner-centered strategies that address the diverse needs of students.

C. apply technology to develop students' higher-order skills and creativity.

D. manage student learning activities in a technology-enhanced environment.

V. PRODUCTIVITY AND PROFESSIONAL PRACTICE

Teachers use technology resources to enhance their productivity and professional practice. Teachers

A. use technology resources to engage in ongoing professional development and lifelong learning.

B. continually evaluate and reflect on professional practice to make informed decisions regarding the use of technology in support of student learning.

C. apply technology to increase productivity.

D. use technology to communicate and collaborate with peers, parents, and the larger community in order to nurture student learning.

VI. SOCIAL, ETHICAL, LEGAL, AND HUMAN ISSUES

Teachers understand the social, ethical, legal, and human issues surrounding the use of technology in PK–12 schools and apply that understanding in practice. Teachers

A. model and teach legal and ethical practice related to technology use.

B. apply technology resources to enable and empower learners with diverse backgrounds, characteristics, and abilities.

C. identify and use technology resources that affirm diversity.

D. promote safe and healthy use of technology resources.

E. facilitate equitable access to technology resources for all students.

ow that you have learned about network basics, the Internet, and a sampling of the services available on the Net, it is time to explore more fully its application to teaching and learning. Using the Internet, as it was configured in its earliest years, would have been a somewhat daunting task for most teachers. With complex text-based commands and no user-friendly screen displays, the early Internet challenged its most experienced users. Today much of the Net has evolved into the easy-to-use graphic format known as the World Wide Web. This new, more intuitive Internet with its simple point-and-click interface and convenient links has become a powerful tool in the hands of teachers and learners. This chapter examines the World Wide Web and the resources it makes available to teachers and learners. It explores the components of an instructional web site and reviews what such a web site should include if you decide to use or create one when you teach. The chapter concludes with a review of the steps necessary to incorporate web-based instruction in your classroom.

In Chapter 8, you will

- Explore sample classroom management and academic tools available on the Web

- Examine instructional support web sites and the resources they provide to you and your students

- Investigate how to use the Web to enhance communication and instruction

- Explore the steps necessary to create a classroom web site and make it available on the Web

Real People
Real Stories

Meet Rob Schwartz. If you're not familiar with Technology Education (TE), I'd like to give you a quick summary of some of the challenges faced by TE teachers. Generally speaking, the course is in your old "shop" classroom—the woodworking tools have been moved out, and the computers have been moved in. Most labs have a "modular" setup, meaning that there are workstations where two students work together on a particular project to learn a specific technological concept. In the same lab, you'll have students working on programming, robotics, biotechnology, desktop publishing, video editing, manufacturing, aerospace and rocketry, research and design, and a myriad of other topics—usually ten to fifteen different modules.

The first problem is that the students are learning all of these concepts at once. Joe and Suzy are learning robotics, while Jim and Carol are working on a computer-controlled lathe. At the same time Bob and Nancy can't figure out how to edit a video, and Lou and Gina are stuck trying to figure out how to edit a hyperlink in Web design. The problem is obvious. There are literally fifteen different lessons all going on at the same time in the same room, and you're only one teacher. When you stop to answer a question for a student, it doesn't benefit any other student, and you'll probably encounter the same question next week when the students rotate modules. And who is a master of *every* technology known to humankind? Even if such a person existed, tomorrow he or she would be obsolete with all the discoveries and enhancements made to technology today. You don't have all the answers, and you can't be in fifteen places at once answering fifteen different questions to fifteen completely unrelated topics.

The other problem is that many labs use a "canned" curriculum approach that uses videos to instruct the students. This is a fine way to begin, but it's very expensive and also goes obsolete as soon as the software is updated. The instructions in the videos or books are so specific that many of the projects cannot be done on new software using the old curriculum.

My solution to the problem is simple but has its own set of challenges. I decided not to use "curriculum" at all. I made the decision early on to treat my classroom like the workplace. "On the job learning" is the way that most of us learn the skills we use every day. The boss does not hand us a big book with instructions for each day so we know what to do. We're supposed to solve problems and develop creative solutions to the challenges we face. If we want to prepare students for real life, why should we teach them to learn in a way that's completely different from how they will have to learn for the rest of their lives? We need to learn to find resources to answer our questions; then we have to find the answers in those resources. We need to teach our students to learn on their own. But how will we ever find enough resources with broad enough coverage and enough depth to learn a new skill that doesn't get outdated with the technology we are currently using? Even if I found a library of books to buy, when the new software comes out my library would be as obsolete as my software.

If there were only a magic box with access to a global library that was updated millions of times every single day, easily searched, and had instant delivery of all materials to my classroom on demand . . .

And one more little thing . . . make it *free*.

Enter the Internet.

Instead of spending money on expensive curriculum that spoon-fed the answers to my students in step-by-step instructions, I simply wrote a set of memos that explained what the students had to do, the specifications they had to meet, and where to look for information. The memos started out as printed pages that mimicked interoffice memos or faxes from the "head office." I placed my students in a virtual workplace and gave them real-world projects to do. I didn't give them the answers ahead of time, I only gave them the problem. Finding the answers, as in the real world, was up to them.

After the first round of projects, all the students had obviously learned a few things. They typed these tips up and created CHEAT sheets (Concise Help, Explanations, And Tips) for the next group who would do the project. Web pages they found that were helpful were collected and placed on the Favorites menus. The interoffice memos were updated and modified (with student input) and placed on the computer hard drives so they could always be easily accessed and updated. CHEAT sheets were printed out and kept near the computer used for that project. I had just created a totally student-centric curriculum that the students loved, was very challenging, was true-to-life, and was *free*.

Ninety percent of our information came from the Internet. Online tutorials, "how-to" web sites, and even email to industry experts were used to build our knowledge base. We had taken a lot from the Internet community, and now, like that change dish next to the register at the gas station, we wanted to give a little back for the next guy.

I developed an Internet web site that was initially just Microsoft Word documents converted to HTML with a simple index page that linked to the data. Later, I used Netscape Composer (it's free!) to create a more complex web site in HTML. Eventually, I stumbled upon Dreamweaver Studio and began to develop the site using professional tools and finally achieved a professional look. The site won a few awards and began to get some regular traffic. I even found that some teachers in other states were actually using my curriculum in their classrooms! The problem was that I had to keep updating the site with new information as we found it.

Then I discovered content management software (CMS) for developing Internet web pages. This type of software (most of it is free) allows you to update your web page from any computer in the world with Internet access! Even better, others can register to your site and submit materials directly to your site as well! For example, students can submit web links to the site that I check out and instantly add to my web site with a single click. Now the students enter all the data, and I just check it for acceptability and accuracy and post it live! Create downloads, post a poll that students and visitors can vote on—your site can be completely dynamic with a ton of user input.

Today, my program has developed into a completely web-based curriculum. Nearly all project-related resources and information is available on the web page. The curriculum has gained local, state, and even national attention. The web site is an incredible tool for increasing parent and community awareness and involvement with the curriculum.

Feel free to visit my web site, www.brainbuffet.com. From the web site you can get more background information about the program and how the site came about and find links related to almost every academic subject. And feel free to email me at rob@brainbuffet.com for more information.

 ## Educational Resources on the Web

Just as the Internet and the World Wide Web have had a dramatic impact on society, so too have they had an impact on education. Schools no longer have to be isolated without access to information and resources. Instead, the world's knowledge base can be placed at the tips of the fingers of every learner. Communications, once limited to paper, pen, and post, are now instantaneous and international, opening new horizons for the development of learning communities. Crossing national boundaries and creating global connections, the Internet joined the peoples of the world as no other technological revolution has. But harnessing this powerful resource and implementing it in the classroom requires a knowledgeable teacher. With so vast and uncensored an information reserve and communications tool, the academic leadership of the teacher has become critical in order to ensure the Internet is used appropriately and wisely. For this reason, it is necessary for teachers to become familiar with the Internet, its academic resources, and the issues associated with implementing them in the classroom. Helping you to gain this familiarity then, is the goal of this chapter.

On the Web, a number of broad categories of resources are available for teaching and learning. These resources range from online professional publications and organizations to blogs to videoconferencing to podcasts and every imaginable capability in between. To use these resources, you must first be aware of them and then have some idea of their potential application to teaching and learning. Below you will find an introduction to a wide variety of resources available today.

E-Learning

www.mylabschool.com
video
View *WebQuest and Cooperative Learning*

Online Publications

Many educational journals now have an online version available via the Internet (see Figure 8.1). Most of these **online publications** include current and archived articles of interest to educators. Most also have local site-based search engines that allow you to type in key words to look for on the site. Electronic publications also typically offer a page of related links that may prove useful in your quest for information.

Once found, electronic articles can be saved or printed for your use. Many articles that you can view on the Web have been converted from their

E-Learning

ON THE WEB! 8.1

Online Publications

FIGURE 8.1
Popular Online Publications

These publications are not rank-ordered, because their usefulness depends on the reader's purpose. The annotations list only a few of the features offered.

techLEARNING   www.techlearning.com *(Technology & Learning* magazine*)*
Anecdotal classroom applications supplied by teachers in the "What Works" section are creative and practical. Contributors' email addresses are given for questions and commentary.

AERA.net   www.aera.net *(Educational Researcher)*
ER Online from the American Educational Research Association is a downloadable publication of articles primarily on statistical research.

ASCD   www.ascd.org
The Association for Supervision and Curriculum Development site includes *Educational Leadership* and the *Journal of Curriculum and Supervision*. Bulletins, updates, book reviews, and software evaluations, as well as other ASCD publications, are built into this site. Articles must be purchased.

T.H.E. Journal Online   www.thejournal.com
Technological Horizons in Education's online version of *T.H.E. Journal* has product features, Internet information, conference listings, and suggestions.

Learning and Leading with Technology   www.iste.org/L&L
The International Society for Technology in Education provides *Learning and Leading with Technology* online with articles on issues and ideas encompassing all levels of instruction and all content areas.

FNO.org   www.fno.org
From Now On: The Educational Technology Journal is a multipurpose site with editorials by Jamie McKenzie, assessment techniques, curriculum notes, grants information, and Internet policies.

JILR   www.aace.org/pubs/jilr/default.htm
The *Journal of Interactive Learning Research* is a scholarly site noted for research findings on interactive learning environments focused on technology-based instruction.

Scholastic—Teachers   www.teacher.scholastic.com
Standards-designed, thematic lesson plans and reproducibles, web projects, research reports, and online activities from *Instructor* magazine are available here.

JIME   www-jime.open.ac.uk
The *Journal of Interactive Media in Education* is an online professional journal with screen and multiple-screen interfaces of articles on the latest technological developments in education.

With Acrobat Reader, your PDF files will look just like the original printed page.

original word-processed format to HTML. Your browser displays the documents you select (click on), and your browser interprets their HTML code and displays the articles on your screen. The articles can then be saved or printed from the screen using your browser's Save or Print function.

Other web sites may save their articles as **PDF files,** which are files that have been saved in Adobe Acrobat format. Acrobat is a conversion software package that lets the user save a publication exactly as it looked on the printed page, including custom layouts, photos, and other graphics. PDF files are frequently used to share published information, since they maintain the formatting and detail that is lost when presented in HTML. To read an Acrobat file, you need Adobe Reader, a free download available from the Adobe web site. Usually, publication web sites that use Adobe Acrobat include a hot link to enable you to connect directly to Adobe's download page. Once you have downloaded and installed Reader, you are ready to use files saved in PDF format. All you will need to do is click on the files of interest to you, and your browser and Reader will then take over the process. The files will be downloaded, and Reader will be launched to

FIGURE 8.2
Adobe Reader

With Adobe Reader, Acrobat-created files display pages just the way they look in hard copy publications.

Microsoft Explorer® is a registered trademark of Microsoft Corporation.

Copyright © 2001 Adobe Systems Incorporated. Used with express permission. All rights reserved. Adobe and Acrobat Reader are either trademarks or registered trademarks of Adobe Systems Incorporated in the United States and/or other countries.

display the fully formatted article (see Figure 8.2). You can then read an exact reproduction of the original published article and even print it out.

Whether you read and print via your browser or via Adobe Reader, be aware that many journals copyright the information presented on their web pages. You should check the specific copyright policies for the e-publications you use. Further discussion of copyright is presented later in this chapter and in Chapter 11.

Some online publications also offer a service that will automatically send email to you regarding upcoming highlights or news in brief. Most send weekly or monthly updates and may include special offers. Such emails often come with imbedded hot links to the full-text articles they summarize. This type of service is an easy and convenient way to keep up with the latest news from e-publications of interest to you. Publication mailing lists can be valuable aids, but subscribe only to those in which you have sincere interest. Subscribing to too many of these services can easily result in a great number of email messages. On some school and ISP servers, you might not have unlimited space to handle all of your email. Mailing list messages may inadvertently fill up your mailbox, causing your personal email to bounce back to the sender. Typically, should you need to discontinue receiving email from a mailing list, you need only respond with an email message that includes "unsubscribe" in either the subject line or body of the email. Details on how to unsubscribe are usually sent when you first subscribe to a mailing list, and some lists include them in every mailing list email sent. You should save these "unsubscribe" instructions for each mailing list or newsletter that you sign up for.

Online Professional Organizations

Most major professional organizations now have a web presence. Teachers' unions, professional associations, content-area groups, technology groups, and many others have web sites that range from modest to robust. Organization web sites typically provide calendars of events, current and archived publications, online stores, and current news about issues critical to that organization. Some even include conferences, chats, and live audio or video Internet broadcasts featuring key people in the field.

Professional organizations offer a wide variety of services keyed to their missions. For educators, such organization web sites can offer a central repository of relevant and useful resources related to the organizational focus as well as links to other pertinent web sites. On the Web! Activity 8.2 summarizes some of the most popular organization sites. Others, especially those related to very specific content areas, can be easily discovered by using a search engine.

Online Organizations

Weblogs

Weblogs, or **blogs,** are virtual online spaces that support the posting of personal commentary on the Web. Blogs provide primarily one-way communication, but with the inclusion of comments and links, blogs become powerful interactive writing tools. Bloggers post their ideas, and others respond to these ideas, either in comments to the posting or in other blogs with a link back to the original posting. Bloggers can add links in their own commentaries to connect to other web resources or "backtrack" to other blogs. Since weblogs are powered by software that allows the writer and the audience to engage in an online communication cycle via the Web, blogs have unique educational applications.

Unlike a structured discussion group, a blog provides each individual with his or her own web space in which to post personal views and comments on any topic rather than to comment within the confines of a discussion group topic. Whether entered daily or less frequently, blog postings can be read by anyone wishing to view them and can be responded to instantaneously. If the blogging software supports it, blog postings can be responded to with comments added to the original posting. Or an individual can post comments about various other blogs on his or her own blog site. The ultimate effect is a lively group discussion, with readers able to jump from blog to blog via connecting links to see what others have to say. In much the same way that our attention turns from one person to another in a classroom discussion as each expresses a view, blog readers jump from one online blog to another to read comments in a posting thread. With these capabilities, educational blogging sites (edblogs) have evolved that have given online space to students from elementary age through college (see Figure 8.3). Edblogs have been successfully used to give students an opportunity to publicly post daily journal entries; to comment on peer postings; to collaborate on a group project even if participants are a world apart; to research what other bloggers have said on a topic; and to connect to resources they have found. Educational blogs have provided a unique

Edblogs

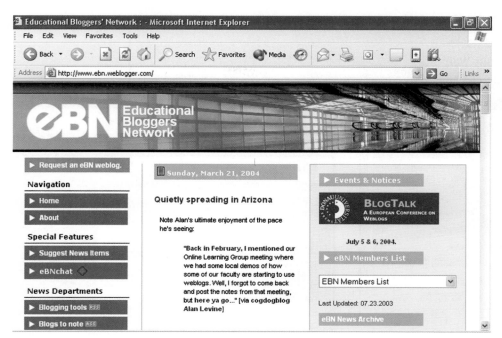

FIGURE 8.3
Educational Weblog Web Site

Educational weblog sites offer teachers and students unique opportunities for self-expression and interaction via the Web.

SOURCE: Educational Bloggers Network. Retrieved November 2003 from **http://www.ebn.weblogger.com.**

forum for the expression of ideas and for the thoughtful consideration of other viewpoints. In the hands of a skillful technology-using educator, this tool can empower students to write and communicate and teachers to facilitate that expression. With an estimated 50 million weblogs of all sorts on the Web at this writing, this easy publish-to-the-Web phenomenon is likely to become, in time, as common as the home page is today.

Governmental Sites

The U.S. Department of Education and most state departments of education have very comprehensive web sites with abundant resources for educators (see Figure 8.4). The U.S. Department of Education site (**www.ed.gov**) includes information about current education news, national standards, programs, grants, research, links to other federal agencies, and a wide variety of publications and reports available by mail or download. State department of education web sites offer similar services, but their emphasis is on educational issues within a given state.

The U.S. Department of Education (ed.gov) web site also provides some of the most useful and comprehensive education links available, including access to **ERIC,** the Educational Resources Information Center. ERIC is the world's largest database of education information, with more than one million abstracts of documents and journal articles, many available through the Internet.

Education Portals

A number of portals include an area focused on education. Educational resources found at portals may include teachers' guides to the Internet, lesson plans, Net events, audio and video clips, web hosting opportunities,

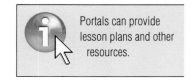

Portals can provide lesson plans and other resources.

FIGURE 8.4
Government Web Sites
Government education sites present critical and current educational resources.

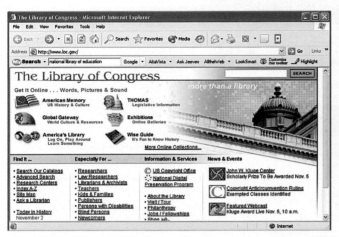

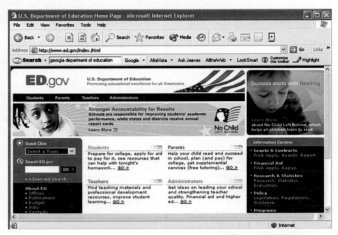

SOURCE: U.S. Department of Education. Microsoft Internet Explorer® is a registered trademark of Microsoft Corporation.

SOURCE: U.S. Library of Congress. Microsoft Internet Explorer® is a registered trademark of Microsoft Corporation.

Accessing the Internet

clip art libraries, educational games, information about schools and colleges, and a variety of instructional resources accessible by grade level and content area. Each portal offers differing services, so it is valuable to investigate what specific educational resources each offers. All portals and most web sites provide you with a wide variety of current links to other resources on the Net.

Favorite Links

Some of the best online resources are discovered through hot links from one site to another. Web sites often link to other sites consistent with the content of their own site. Some sites are a collection of links created for the sole purpose of providing connections to those seeking information on a given topic. When you find a useful web site, it is a good idea to check its links page and explore related sites.

But given that there are so many links and so many useful sites, how can a busy teacher possibly remember where they are? Browsers have a built-in function that assists you in creating your own collection of URLs called **bookmarks** or **favorites.** Bookmarking or adding to your favorites list allows you to store web site URLs that are of interest to you. When you decide to revisit a web site you have stored, you need only click on its name in your list, and the browser will immediately connect you to that site. Web sites can be added to or deleted from your list as you require. The use of bookmarks or favorites makes it easy to store and access the useful links that you discover as you search the Internet for valuable resources.

Use "bookmarks" or "favorites" to store your favorite URLs.

Classroom Management Tools

Classroom management tools on the Web include downloadable or online tools that assist you in the tasks required for your classroom. Several sites offer software that creates online or paper tests and, if they are online, grades them for you and sends you the results. These **test generators** can create tests by randomly selecting questions within their databases of questions, or you can select the questions to be included. Some allow you to add your own questions to the database. Others let you create multimedia tests. Many textbooks (including this one) have added these types of resources to their faculty web sites.

Other Internet-based management tools include formal and informal diagnostic tests to assess learning preferences, tools that generate class rolls with seating charts, and **electronic gradebooks** that let you store and easily average student grades. Many of these tools can be used online or downloaded to your machine. If they are used online, some security and privacy issues may be involved. Student information is private and must be closely guarded. Making information accessible by using a nonsecure online resource may be an issue. A later section of this chapter will deal more fully with your responsibilities in this regard.

Academic Tools

There is an abundance of Internet tools that support instruction. Many of these can be either used online or downloaded to your computer as freeware or shareware. Some of the most popular **academic tools** include worksheet generators of many types that help you make interesting student activity sheets. These tools help you create content-specific crossword puzzles, word searches, cryptograms, math exercises, and multimedia flash cards. Most of these tools allow you to input the key content and then generate the activity sheet of your choice, which can then be either printed or saved to a file. These creative and time-saving tools help you add interest and variety to your instructional plan.

One of the key academic resources available on the Internet is lesson plans. Some lesson plan sites offer subject-specific plans, others offer lesson plans submitted by colleagues across the nation, and still others offer lesson plans tied to national or state standards. In addition to sites dedicated to lesson plans, links on many educational sites offer lesson plans related to the content of that site. A related resource is lesson plan software programs that generate lesson plans for you and even relate them to specific standards. The

Tech Tips for TEACHERS

Managing Your Favorite Links

Over time, you will find that you have saved numerous favorite web sites. These links can be organized into folders for easy access. To save a favorite web site in Windows Internet Explorer, click on Favorites on the toolbar and then click Add. To create a folder, click on Organize in the Favorites window. The pop-up window will allow you to add and name a new folder. Once a folder is created, you can drag and drop your favorite links into it for easy access.

Folders and links within the folders are saved in a file on your hard drive or network space and can be backed up (saved on a jump drive, floppy disk, or other external device). It is a good idea to back up your favorites. It takes a significant amount of time and effort collecting links, and you will not want to lose them. To back up favorites in Windows, go to My Computer, click on the C: Drive and then select a folder called Documents and Settings. Within that folder you will find a folder with either your name on it or the default name, Main User. Double click to open that folder and you will see a file called Favorites. Copy that file to your external storage device to back up your favorites.

Online Classroom Tools

Academic Tools Online

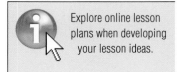

Explore online lesson plans when developing your lesson ideas.

COOL TOOLS

Online Teaching Tools

Many academic resources can be found on the Web. Web sites such as www.4teachers.org, sponsored by the Advanced Learning Technologies project at the University of Kansas Center for Research on Learning, provide a wide range of cool tools for teachers. Among many other tools you will find worksheet makers, puzzle makers, rubric templates, problem-based learning checklists, quiz- and test-making tools, standards checklists, lesson plans, awards templates, calendars, and more. These tools make it easy to create whatever you need to support your classroom and implement your lessons . . . all for free. A quick Google search on free online teaching tools will net you a long list of resources that will provide you with many handy tools for your classroom.

Bridging Theory to Practice

abundance of lesson plan sites and tools, from those sponsored by the U.S. Department of Education to those supported by individual teachers, is one of the most remarkable educational Internet resources available to busy educators. Browsing through these many lesson plans can offer you valuable ideas for use in your classroom.

Reference tools and resources, including dictionaries in all languages, thesauri, grammar and spelling tools, and world atlases, are also available on the Internet. These reference tools also include translation references that translate from one language to another, specialty dictionaries and glossaries that relate to specific professions or hobbies, and other vocabulary aids to provide you with a wealth of information about acronyms, anagrams, and homonyms. These reference tools bring the reference section of a large library to every classroom via the Internet.

CD-ROM-based multimedia encyclopedias are fairly common software for school media centers. It is often too costly, however, to buy one encyclopedia for each classroom or to buy the network hardware and site licensing that allow sharing. An alternative is to access these same tools on the Internet. Many of the most popular multimedia encyclopedias and research resources are available on the Internet. These tools work similarly to those on CD-ROM, including the ability to download and save or print entries. With a classroom Internet connection, it may no longer be necessary to purchase multiple CDs or reconfigure the network. Furthermore, because students are working on the Internet, online research resources can add hot links to related information. This allows for instant hyperjumps to follow up on information, a feature that most CD-ROMs cannot offer.

In addition to the more formal academic tools and resources mentioned thus far, the Internet provides teachers with a storehouse of innovation and great teaching ideas at every grade level and for every content area. Teachers from around the globe contribute to a variety of web sites ideas that have worked well in their own classrooms. Each site then categorizes and files these innovations to make them accessible via the site's search engines. Such sites are continually being updated and contributed to by creative educators. These sites are a storehouse of best practices that can be easily accessed with a few clicks and a few keystrokes.

Connection gateways are web sites that offer users the opportunity to communicate with each other. For educators there are a number of web sites that offer discussions and chats on specific topics related to teaching, on topics related to teaching a grade level, or on content areas across all grade levels. These sites offer educators a chance to engage in an interactive exchange with colleagues across the globe. Dialog such as this expands every participant's professional perspective and is likely to be the source of many useful insights and creative ideas.

Online chats and discussions can expand your professional horizons.

Whether Internet academic tools and resources are used by you to prepare to teach or by your students as they engage in learning, these educational resources add a dimension to your classroom that was an impossibility just a decade ago. The Internet has brought teaching and learning tools to every classroom that connects to it. But like all tools, they are only as useful as the hands that wield them. It is up to you as the leader and facilitator of the teaching and learning process to become sufficiently aware of these resources to make the best use of them in your instructional environment.

Web-Enhanced Instruction

E-Learning

www.mylabschool.com
video
View *Using Technology to Teach Reading*

Whether you choose to use the Internet in your classroom daily or only occasionally, an easy-to-use web site of your own can enhance the learning environment. The ways to integrate the Internet into instruction, particularly via your own web site, are limited only by your own imagination. This section will explore a few of the possibilities.

YOU **Decide!**

The Internet and, in particular, the easy-to-navigate World Wide Web are potentially powerful teaching and learning tools. But not all educators embrace and use this resource in their classrooms. Regardless of how ubiquitous the Internet and Web have become in our society, many teachers are slow to integrate them into their lessons. However, since schools are indeed a reflection of and extension of the society they serve, many educators feel the full integration of the Web and its resources are a mandate for all educators. Do you agree?

YES! Today computers and the Internet are as common as telephones. These technology skills are now life skills. Teachers need to help their students learn what they need to know to be successful adults, and that includes using the Internet. When we incorporate the Web into classroom activities, we are not taking time away from required curriculum but instead we are teaching our students that the Internet is a tool for them to complete their tasks at hand. Students need these skills and mastery of these tools to succeed. Our job is to give them an opportunity to learn how to use them, and when we integrate Internet skills, we don't even lose any curriculum time.

NO! Everyone is placing too much emphasis on computers and on the Internet. Students need to know the traditional ways to research and discover the information they need for their activities. What happens when the power goes off? Students need to appreciate books, journals, and the printed word. Traditional resources are more accurate anyway. Much of the information of the Web is not authenticated and can mislead students. Our kids will learn about computers and the Web at home and with their friends. We don't need to be taking academic time away from more important curriculum.

Which view on learning theories do you agree with? YOU DECIDE!

Enhancing Classroom Communication

As you have learned throughout this text, it is important to address the individual needs and learning styles of your students. Typically, a teacher will communicate instructional content and activities by telling students about them. However, for students who are primarily visual learners, this communication method can be difficult to follow. A classroom web site can help to support and enhance communication. For teacher-to-student communication, a classroom web site can contain daily, weekly, or unit assignments and thorough directions on how to complete them. It can also answer anticipated student questions on a linked **FAQ** (frequently asked questions) page. It can contain information about grading or tips for working on an assignment as well as links to relevant related pages such as the school's honesty or computer use policies. Finally, it can use web-based multimedia with voice, animation, or motion video to present key points in formats that address multiple learning preferences. This type of web page adds reinforcing dimensions to teacher-to-student communications as well as reiteration of key instructions.

When teachers work cooperatively by grade level or content-area department to create a shared web site, the impact is even more pronounced. Coordinated classroom web sites provide a common ground that is familiar and therefore easy for students to use. Such sites also provide common links to school resources as well as to each other, improving communications among all of the administrators, teachers, and students involved. Teacher-to-student communication is thus clarified, consistent, and open among all those involved.

Student-to-teacher communication can be enhanced via a classroom web site as well. Whether the student is in class but too shy to voice his or

A web site for your class can be a valuable tool for learning as well as communicating.

E-Learning
ON THE WEB! 8.8
Grade-Level Web Sites

TECHNOLOGY
SOLUTIONS
for All Learners

In August 1998, the Workforce Investment Act expanded the requirement that federal departments and agencies develop and maintain electronic information in a format usable by all, including those with disabilities. In response, the World Wide Web Consortium (W3C), which is responsible for developing standards for the Web, established the Web Accessibility Initiative (WAI). This initiative has set standards and provides resources to ensure web sites are accessible to all.

Several free and commercial online web site evaluators can be used to determine the accessibility of a web site. These evaluation tools compare the web site to the standards developed by the WAI and provide a report to the user as to how accessible the site is for disabled users. One of the classic tools for evaluating

access, Bobby (renamed WebXACT), is one of the many such tools available. It can examine a web page and provide a report as to quality, accessibility, and privacy issues. Other tools can be used to check screen reader accessibility and the appropriate use of text to describe graphical images. Some tools can even assist in correcting problems.

These online tools can be used to check a web site used in a lesson or to evaluate a teacher-made site before making it available. For teachers with disabled students, online accessibility checkers can provide valuable information to ensure that all children can use the resources needed to learn.

her questions or the student is at home and struggling with an assignment, email or a teacher–student electronic chat can provide an opportunity for direct, private, and meaningful communication. Additionally, for students who can't seem to carry hard copy successfully from one location to another, attaching homework to an email message can be a very effective tool for ensuring that work is turned in on time. Electronic conferencing can also support and enhance student-to-teacher communications if the teacher moderates posted public questions on activities or content. Adding some or all of these features to a classroom web site enhances student-to-teacher communications.

For student-to-student communication, a web site with email or chat options or with weblogs or electronic conferencing can encourage communication and build teamwork and communication skills. An activity in which students email the draft of a written assignment to each other for editing before completing the final version provides an opportunity for students to exercise proofreading and grammar skills. A group project that requires participation in a chat or conference helps students develop communication skills while building technology skills. For shy students who would otherwise be reluctant to contribute verbally in class, this opportunity for thoughtful communication at a pace that is comfortable for them may open new avenues of communication and build confidence in their own interaction skills. Creating such an adaptable and personal learning community within a classroom, grade level, or school is facilitated by the integration of a classroom web site.

E-Learning

www.mylabschool.com
video
View *The GLOBE Project*

Linking Your Students to Their World

Student-to-student communication within a classroom, grade level, or school is just the beginning of what the Internet has to offer to your students. One of the most imaginative ways of utilizing your classroom web site as a communication tool is to connect your classroom to others across the globe, thereby building a **global learning community** for your students. Keypals, e-pals, and cyberpals are some of the terms used to refer to the other people with whom your students may correspond. Whatever term you prefer, the idea is to use Internet-based communications to extend interaction beyond the walls of your classroom or school.

Use the web to form a global learning community.

Keypal assignments can help students practice communication skills while enhancing cultural awareness. Whole sites are dedicated to establishing this type of learning community. Some provide teachers' guides, keypal lesson plans and projects, opportunities to request and make connections with global members, world maps, and even translation services. Communicating with keypals can be an invaluable personal growth experience as well as a directed learning activity.

However you decide to develop Internet-based links between your own students and their peers across the globe, the cultural awareness, communication skills, and content-area enrichment that the Web makes possible can be a significant enhancement to classroom instruction. Connecting students to other students for the purpose of learning about each other and exchanging ideas offers an opportunity for personal growth and enrichment that would not be possible otherwise.

E-Learning
ON THE WEB! 8.9
Internet Pals

E-Learning
ON THE WEB! 8.10
Getting Connected Globally

in the Classroom

USING THE WEB IN THE SOCIAL STUDIES AND SCIENCE CLASSROOMS

Eileen Deveny, who teaches at Dover Elementary School in Dover, Massachusetts, helps her students learn research techniques in an activity guaranteed to capture the interest of young children, as well as introduce them to basic research practices. She submitted "Baking Cornbread Then and Now" as a lesson that gives the children a look at the early colonial period of United States history through the means colonists and Native Americans used to prepare and bake a household staple, cornbread. By going online and viewing digital photos, the class views a primary document, *The Pocumtuc Housewife: A Guide to Domestic Cookery,* from the American Centuries web site, http://memorialhall.mass.edu.html. They find the recipe for johnnycake in the cookbook and learn it was another name for cornbread. Ms. Deveney has assembled the tools for making cornbread then and now (a box of cornbread mix). In class the children "read (or listen as the teacher reads) the directions and ingredients on the cornbread mix package. They will discuss these and will prepare the mix in groups of 8–10. The teacher will keep a time sheet from start to finish, recording the amount of time spent gathering ingredients, mixing, and baking." For a next-day activity, again going to the digital collection at the American Centuries web site, the children return to the colonial cookbook. Ms. Deveney talks about the way women baked johnnycake in the seventeenth century. She shows the children a bake kettle, butter churn, milk pan, pothook/adjustable trammel, mill stone, mortar, and pestle—all through links on the web site. Under her supervision, the children "will imagine the process entailed in making the johnnycake recipe without the modern conveniences." She also explains to them "how

the ingredients were obtained: buttermilk is the milk left over from churning butter; corn was grown and taken to the mill for grinding; flour was obtained at a mill; saleratus, sugar, and salt needed to be purchased or bartered." A web site link is pulled up, and the students and teacher discuss the millstone shown. The time it took to prepare cornbread for these early settlers and how long it takes to prepare it now is shown on the time sheets the teacher has kept. Finally, the children get to use a mortar and pestle to "get an idea of grinding by hand as Native Americans did." They "grind some parched corn using a wooden mortar and pestle (or similar improvised setup if needed)."

Mike Calhoun, a middle-school science teacher, developed "a series of web-based activities that teach the importance of scientific reproducibility, the acceptance of different opinions." He found Cyberlab to be an important source for researching "the science protocol research reproducibility." As an added benefit, Cyberlab's assignments offer a variety of topics: "one to verify the reproducibility of a middle school student's procedure for making a 'plastic' like substance from milk; another to analyze a genetic karyotype to diagnose Down's syndrome; and a third to investigate data concerning the discovery of a new element by British high school students."

Calhoun, M. (2004, June 1). Cyberlab: An ally for teaching scientific collaboration. Retrieved August 25, 2005, from **www.techlearning.com/shared/printableArticle.jhtml?articleID=20900596**.

Deveney, E. (2004, May 13). Baking cornbread then and now. Retrieved August 1, 2004, from **memorialhall.mass.edu/activity/view.do?activityID=645**.

Building Bridges to Parents and the Community

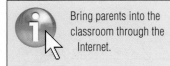
Bring parents into the classroom through the Internet.

However, communication among students locally or globally is not the only possibility provided by the integration of communication tools into the learning environment. Building bridges to parents and community is another opportunity created through implementation of the Web in instruction.

Parents and teachers share the common goal of helping students meet their personal potential. By working together in partnership, you and your students' parents have the best chance of helping the children. Undeniably, life circumstances often make communications difficult. Many parents work outside the home and are available only after school hours. Time-shifted (asynchronous) interaction can help to open lines of communication that might otherwise not be possible. A classroom web page offers many opportunities for such communications.

By posting classroom rules, schedules, and homework on a classroom web page, a teacher can directly communicate expectations to the parents of all students in a class. By adding communications tools, including email, chat, and conferencing, a means for private and public dialog can be established. When you are seeking parent volunteers for classroom activities, posting such requests on a classroom web site makes more partnerships and support possible.

Equally important, the ability to inform parents in a timely manner about student progress is a particularly powerful Internet-based communications tool. If you post grades via a secured web site or a secure service linked to a web site, parents can track how students are doing and even monitor their attendance. Such daily or weekly feedback to parents gives them a chance to join you in resolving performance issues before they permanently affect a student's grades. This creates a powerful home–school partnership to support learners and keep them on the right track.

Linking your classroom to the greater community is another potential opportunity provided through the Internet and a class web site. Community involvement can mean partnerships that enhance your learning environment through community members' participation as mentors or guest speakers or through community contributions to class projects. Your students might become the hub of a virtual community learning center that links generations in dialog and support. Senior citizens might share oral history with your students, or your students might mentor younger peers on a project. Parents, community members, and students can join together to explore and share views on issues of significance to the local community. In whatever way you choose to provide communications opportunities to parents and the community, the bridges you create can only enhance the learning environment you provide for your students and open doors to their world.

E-Learning ON THE WEB! 8.11
Using the Web to Create a Virtual Classroom

E-Learning
www.mylabschool.com
Listen to Podcast
Classroom Websites

Class Web Sites

As you have read through this chapter, you have discovered a wide variety of resources on the Web to assist you in teaching and in helping your students to learn. Today, many teachers have created their own classroom web sites so that the resources they select are readily available from a single convenient location. A classroom web site can offer class information as well as links to any useful sites on the web, from weblog sites to e-pal sites to content-related sites that might help your students find out more about a topic under study (see Figure 8.5). Just as every teacher has his or her own teaching style, a classroom web site offers a teacher the opportunity to customize what his or her students will do and see on the Web via a unique class site.

While a teacher might feel that creating a web site is too difficult, as you have learned in Chapter 6, **web authoring tools** are available to make the job easy to do. These tools range from very easy to more challenging,

E-Learning
www.mylabschool.com
video
View Using a Class Web Page for Learning

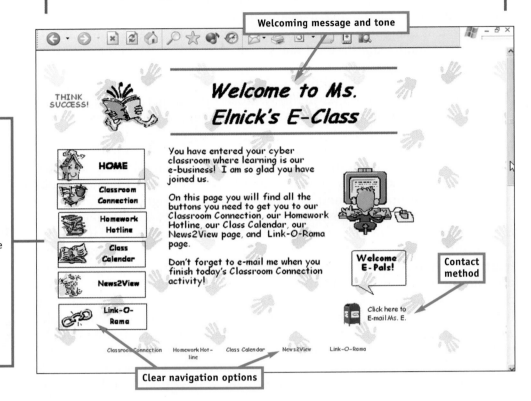

FIGURE 8.5

Elements of an Effective Classroom Web Site

Classroom web sites let teachers reflect their own style while communicating information and instructional content and while providing links to other web resources.

Screen shot reprinted by permission from Microsoft Corporation.

SITE PAGES

Classroom Connection page shares classroom information and current day's activities.

Homework Hotline page lets students and parents know what is required for homework this week.

Class Calendar tracks important due dates and holidays for students and parents.

News2View shares newsworthy events and class and student news.

Link-O-Rama offers students and parents links related to study units and school information.

but for every teacher who wants a class web site, an authoring tool at his or her level of comfort and computer skills is available. The next section will review these authoring tools and help you to decide which is best for you.

Before authoring a web site, a first critical step is to design it. Designing a web site involves a series of structured and organized steps to ensure that the final product is as professional and useful as you intended. Following this chapter, you will find a special feature section (Interchapter 8) that will take you through all of the steps to design a successful class web site. Once you complete each step and have designed the web site that best reflects your teaching style and your students' needs, then it is a simple matter to use the authoring tool to make it a reality.

Web Authoring Tools

Authoring tools make creating your own web site something you can do.

How exactly do you go about making a class web site? Fortunately, so many web authoring tools are available today that you no longer need a working knowledge of HTML. All you need is a well-planned idea for a site, a good storyboard, and some basic computer skills. A variety of tools

in the Classroom

USING THE WEB IN THE ELEMENTARY CLASSROOM AND ACROSS THE SCHOOL DISTRICT

Fred Roemer, a fifth-grade teacher at Pinellas Park Elementary School in Pinellas Park, Florida, recognized that although we generally think of blogging as student-to-student, blogs could be used to keep parents in touch with what's going on in his classroom. In conjunction with the class web site, parents can learn how their children scored on tests shortly after the tests are taken and what assignment deadlines are and also check in on the classroom blog the children maintain. One parent, Mrs. Schubert said, "I liked knowing what was going on in class, seeing what they were doing, what they were learning, just knowing my daughter was in a safe place." To create an environment that encourages parent–teacher communication, "blogs and web sites like Roemer's have begun to emerge as one possible solution." Students express enthusiasm about student-maintained blogging on the subjects they are studying in their classes. In his classroom, blogging is a daily activity. Roemer reflected that

> Some entries clearly bear the stamp of a fifth-grade imagination, describing giant snakes or evil chickens in the classroom. But often they are about the day's activities. One day last February, the class studied cells in science and the Civil War in social studies. They watched a Civil War movie, did math problems about money, and discussed a long-term writing assignment, according to a student blog.

The blogs have other advantages. Mr. Roemer pointed out that the students can communicate with him after school hours to get help with their homework, parents have advance notice about the homework to be done and can do some advance planning to be able to help with the assignments, and students can learn "the appropriate use of web logs," as noted by Will Richardson, an expert on educational blogs.

The safety measures observed when teachers enable students to blog in and about their classrooms are commonsense precautions: students are identified "only by their first and last initials. Though anyone can read the blog, only students and parents who register can post to it or access its other features, such as grade postings." Even though some parents do not have home Internet access, those who don't can go to public libraries to see the blogs. Mr. Roemer admits, however, there will be some parents who don't avail themselves of the opportunity to look inside the classroom to see the communication lines educational blogging opens up by establishing close links between teachers and parents.

Julia Taylor, Rolling Green Elementary School principal in Urbandale, Iowa, points out that classroom and school district web sites present avenues of contact with parents that were never before possible. No longer depending on notes being duly delivered by students to parents or mail arriving intact or at all, schools can post teacher-to-parent notes, school delays, how to contact school personnel, newsletters, and email links, among other services on their web sites. A web site with separate pages for each school was established in 2004 for the Urbandale, Iowa, school district (**www.urbandaleschools.com**) and is maintained by student webmasters for each school. Updates are the province of school administrators, teachers, and staff. Saving money on expenditures for paper is another plus for the web sites. Before the Urbandale School District activated the web site, Dr. Taylor said, "Rolling Green staffers made 350 copies every time they needed to send a message home to parents. With the new web site, they only need to make 53 copies for parents without Internet access."

Anthes, E. (2005, August 9). Blogging connects to parents. Retrieved August 9, 2005, from **www.sptimes.com/ 2005/08/09/News_pf/Tampabay/Blogging_classroom_ co.shtml.**

Glenn, C. (2004, February 3). Schools ditch paper for the web. Retrieved February 15, 2004, from **http:desmoinesregister.com/news/stories/ c4780927/23219264.html.**

are available; which one you choose to use depends on your skill level and your expectations for the final product.

Word Processors

One of the easiest ways to create a web page is to use a word processor with which you are already familiar. Word processors let you create files as you would any other file, laying them out with graphics and text, but then

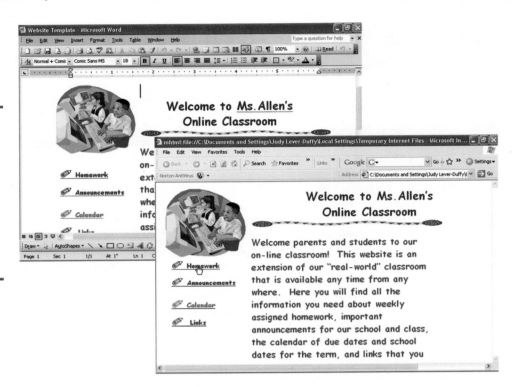

FIGURE 8.6

Using Microsoft Word for Web Authoring Capabilities

MS Word makes creating a web site an easy process.

Microsoft Word is a registered trademark of Microsoft Corporation.

save them in HTML format for uploading to the Web. Although this technique is reasonably simple to use, it creates only very straightforward and basic types of web pages.

The more sophisticated word processors also include **templates,** design **wizards,** and web authoring features for creating web pages (see Figure 8.6). Templates are predefined formats and wizards are interactive tools that not only use predesigned formats but also ask you customization questions in the process of creating them. These tools allow you to use web pages that are already fully designed and even an entire web site with hot links between pages already in place. Using these tools, you need only enter the data you want to display, save your new web page, and upload it to a web server.

The advantage of using the word-processing software with which you may already be familiar could be canceled out by its inflexibility. You might want more sophisticated layout capabilities or more features than the web component of a word processor can provide. The best way to decide is to try word-processing web authoring. Materials accessible at www.mylabschool.com include an activity that gives you hands-on experience with Microsoft Word's web authoring capabilities. If Word is insufficient for your needs, there are alternative software packages to consider.

Desktop Publishing Software

As you learned in earlier chapters, desktop publishing software gives you much greater control of the look of a printed page than is possible with a word processor. Objects can be moved about, and new elements can be easily added and rearranged. Just as desktop publishing allows you to manipulate a printed page more easily, so too can the desktop publisher that is

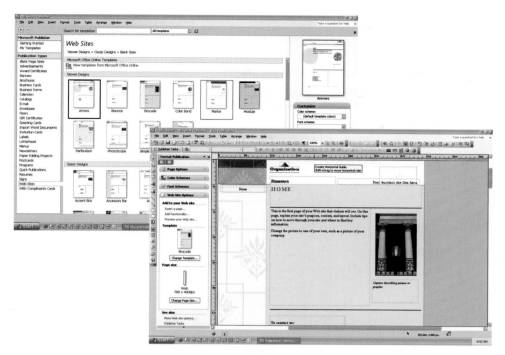

FIGURE 8.7
Microsoft Publisher Web Wizard

Word-processing and desktop publishing software may contain easy-to-use web authoring components.

Microsoft Publisher Web Wizard® is a registered trademark of Microsoft Corporation.

equipped with web production components give you more flexibility in manipulating a web site's page layouts. Additionally, like word processors, the more sophisticated desktop publishing programs include web wizards, allowing you to quickly create very dramatic web pages (see Figure 8.7). Because publishing software allows more flexibility and design features, the web pages produced by its wizards are typically a bit more sophisticated. Although this type of software will not allow you to include all of the bells and whistles you see on many commercial web sites, it will help you to create a very attractive, automatically linked web site.

Accessible at www.mylabschool.com is a hands-on activity using Microsoft Publisher's Web Wizard. The Web Wizard will help you to build a colorful and powerful web site using Publisher's familiar and easy-to-use tools. It can then be easily saved in HTML format and uploaded to the Web.

E-Learning

www.mylabschool.com
Software Skills Builder
Class Web Site with Publisher's Web Wizard

Dedicated Web Development Software

For those who are interested in developing a more sophisticated site, web development software programs are readily available (see Figure 8.8 on page 300). These programs range from fairly easy to very complex, depending on the sophistication you are trying to achieve in the finished web site. Most packages within this software category will help you author a web site that will do all of the tasks you see on commercial sites. Some will provide you with very advanced graphics and multimedia tools to add your own special effects to your site. You will have to decide what level of sophistication you want to achieve in your web site and decide for yourself how much time and how many resources you are willing to invest. Although dedicated web authoring tools are easy to use once you have

Web authoring tools can help you create web pages.

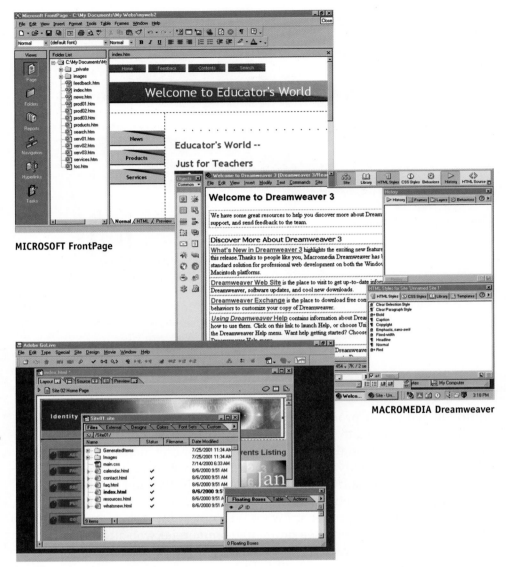

FIGURE 8.8

Web Development Software

Web development software gives you the potential to add every level of sophistication to your site.

Microsoft FrontPage Explorer® is a registered trademark of Microsoft Corporation.

Copyright © 2001 Adobe Systems Incorporated. Used with express permission. All rights reserved. Adobe and GoLive are either trademarks or registered trademarks of Adobe Systems Incorporated in the United States and/or other countries.

MICROSOFT FrontPage

MACROMEDIA Dreamweaver

ADOBE GoLive

Portals to the Web

mastered the skills, they are typically not as easy as using a web component of an alternative software package with which you are already familiar.

A final dedicated web authoring tool may be available through the ISP or portal that you use. Some ISPs allocate web space for their customers' web pages. Typically, those that do also provide a web creation tool. Usually, such tools do not have a great number of options, but they will allow you to create a web page with relative ease. Some portals also offer web space and tools with which you can create web pages. These range from simple tools such as those provided by an ISP, to downloadable shareware or freeware web authoring programs. Different portals provide different levels of service, so it is important to shop around if you decide to use them. Remember too that most ISPs and portals that provide you with web space will also let you upload a site you have created using your own software of choice. They usually do not require you to use their specific tools.

Moving Your Site to the Internet

Adding Your Site to the School or District Site

Once you have completed your web site authoring, how do you move it to the Internet? Your web site is actually a series of HTML and multimedia files stored on your hard drive or a CD. To put them up on the Web, you will need to move your collection of web site files to a web server. The web server, as you learned in Chapter 7, connects a network to the Web and stores web files for others to access. So to move your site to the Web, you must upload it to a web server.

Many schools and districts are now providing space on their web servers for teachers' classroom web sites. If that is the case, to add your site to the school's or district's server, you will need to give all of the related web site files, via CD or email, to the webmaster for your school. A webmaster's job is to create and maintain a site and to integrate new elements. Your school or district webmaster will take your classroom web site files and integrate them appropriately into the school or district site.

It is important to keep in mind that many webmasters have additional jobs as technical-support staff or have their hands full already maintaining complex institutional web sites. In either case, it may take a bit of time to see your web site come up on the Web, a problem that may repeat itself every time you want to update the site. More importantly, if you want to use your site for posting current activities and you cannot adjust the data yourself because of your limited network rights, you might find it very difficult to alter the site daily or weekly. This may interfere with your instructional intentions for the site. For that reason, some educators choose instead to use one of the many types of web site hosting services available on the Web.

Uploading to a Web Host

Free or inexpensive **web hosting** is a service offered by a number of ISPs, web sites, and portals (see Figure 8.9 on page 302). To use this type of service, you need only **upload** your pages to the host, usually via an **FTP** program. The service will take care of creating the web access for you. Links to very detailed instructions on how to upload files are usually displayed prominently on the service's web development page.

Hosting services allow you a given number of megabytes of space on the service's web server; some services offer an unlimited amount of space. In exchange, those who visit your site may be asked to fill in some personal information to "join" the service in order to access your page. At the very least, they will be exposed to ads on the service's home page as they navigate to your page. Other hosting services may add a banner ad to the top of your page or require you to allow pop-up ads. Collecting data from service "members" generates a potential customer list for the service's advertisers. Getting more visitors to a web site to navigate to sites hosted there improves the salability of ad space on the service's home page. This is essentially how services can offer to host your site for free or a reduced cost.

You should carefully investigate sites that offer these services, including reading the fine print in the online agreements. Because you will be

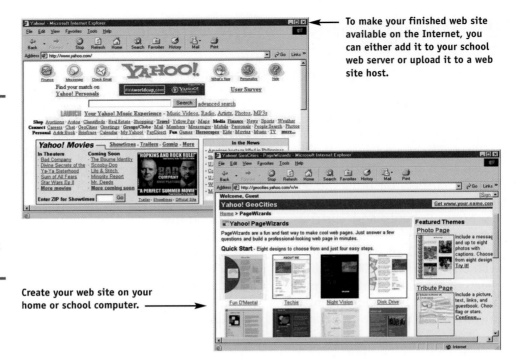

To make your finished web site available on the Internet, you can either add it to your school web server or upload it to a web site host.

FIGURE 8.9
Web Site Hosting

A web hosting service allows you to upload your web site to its web server to make it accessible on the Web.

Reproduced with permission of Yahoo! Inc. Copyright © 2000 by Yahoo! Inc. YAHOO! and the YAHOO! logo are trademarks of Yahoo! Inc.

Create your web site on your home or school computer.

asking your students to use the site, if the advertisements on a service's home page or the elements added to your home page seem inappropriate or too overbearing for young visitors, you might decide that it is best not to use that service. You need to make your best professional judgment about the value of a free or inexpensive web hosting service and the nonmonetary costs it entails. Your first responsibility is to ensure that your students are not exposed to excessive or inappropriate advertising within the requirements of your course. Before you use a free web hosting service, you might want to check with your school or district policies and procedures to determine whether any of these issues have already been formally addressed.

Uploading to a Private Host

If you have an ISP that provides web space as well as Internet access, or if you select to subscribe to a web host, you might want to upload your classroom web site to that server instead. Private hosts do not advertise on customer web sites, and they will give you a very direct URL so that your students can bypass the host's home page. Like their public counterparts, private web hosts typically include detailed instructions on their site on how to transfer your HTML files and step-by-step procedures on how to implement the upload process.

You want to shop around when you select an ISP to see whether the available ISPs do indeed provide web hosting and how much space they will give your account. Comparison shopping is equally necessary if you are considering subscribing to a private web-hosting service. If you plan to use a number of graphics and multimedia files, web site file size can increase dramatically. You will need to compare the space you need for the type of site you want with the amount of web space various private hosts offer.

Uploading to Academic Web Services

A final type of web hosting service is one that is incorporated within broader academic services. Some private and publicly funded web sites offer schools and teachers a variety of free educational services, including web hosting. These services refrain from advertising on your web pages and strictly control advertising on their broader sites. They are designed to provide an appropriate Internet environment for your students and your site. The only disadvantage to this type of site is that it often provides only a relatively small amount of storage space, which may make it inadequate for larger web sites. On the Web! Activity 8.13 summarizes some of the most popular academic sites, and Table 8.1 provides you with a rubric for their evaluation.

E-Learning
ON THE WEB! 8.13

Academic Web Hosts

Internet Issues and Concerns

With any resource that is used in the learning environment, professional judgment must be used in determining the appropriateness of the resource and ensuring that the resource is used within the ethical and legal parameters of the profession. Using the Internet in your teaching and learning environment is no different. A number of significant concerns are frequently voiced relating to the use of the Internet in schools. Three of these issues—acceptable use, privacy, and filtering—are introduced in this section. An expanded discussion of these issues can be found in Chapter 11.

Acceptable Use

Like any technology, the Internet can be abused. In a school setting, it is therefore necessary to identify and enforce the acceptable use of a school's network and Internet access. This is usually done through a district's or school's acceptable use policy (AUP). This policy articulates the ways in which the Internet can be used by students. Typically, parents are asked to confirm their understanding of the policy and the consequences for violating it through a signature acknowledgment. Teachers who use the Internet and who provide links to resources via their own class web sites should be familiar with the AUP that governs their students' use of the Internet.

Privacy

When sharing your students' work or including their images or names on a web site, a teacher must be sure to carefully guard a child's privacy. To include any student's information or work, it is best to first have the parent's or guardian's permission. Further, no specific details about the child should be divulged, including his or her name. Those who might harm children might use a class web site as a way to target them. The problem has become so significant that districts and schools typically have developed very specific policies regarding the content of a class web site. It is up to each teacher to be sure his or her site is consistent with district and school guidelines.

TABLE 8.1 Academic Web Site Evaluation Rubric

DEVELOPER'S NAME:

URL:

AREA/CONTENT OF SITE:

PURPOSE:

Using each of the criteria below, evaluate the usefulness of this web site for teaching and learning. For each dimension in the rubric, check the box that best reflects your opinion. Select web sites that score 4 or higher in most of the dimensions.

DIMENSION	EVALUATION CRITERIA				
	1 Poor	2 Below Average	3 Average	4 Above Average	5 Excellent
GOAL	Goal of this web site unclear and confusing	Conflicting themes make site's goal uncertain	Goal is clear, but site contains some unrelated or distracting elements	Clear purpose and goal; some elements seem unnecessary	Goal and purpose of site clear with no distracting elements
USER FRIENDLINESS	Unwelcoming to users	Does not evoke a welcoming message	Welcomes visitors but does not appear friendly	Welcoming and appears friendly	Exciting, welcoming, and very user-friendly
DESIGN	Poorly organized; contains obvious errors; loads slowly; difficult to read	Organization some what confusing; some errors; loads slowly	Organization acceptable; no obvious errors; loads adequately; easy to read	Good organization; no errors; loads quickly; easy to read	Excellent organization; free of errors; loads quickly and clearly; all elements easy to read
NAVIGABILITY	Difficult to find and follow site navigation links	Navigation links visible but some-what confusing	Navigation links clear and readily available	Navigation links clear and logical; site map included	Navigation logical and clear; site map and search engine available
AUTHORITY	Unclear who the teacher is and what class the site relates to	Teacher name and contact included, but sufficient class infor-mation lacking	Teacher name, contact information, and some class information included	Teacher name, contact information, full class information included	Teacher provides all necessary information to student, parent, and community visitors
DATES	No dates evident	Site contains some dates	Site contains both creation and update information but no dates related to class activities	Site contains creation and update information and some dates relat-ing to class activities	Site contains dates for creation, update, and all class activities
CONTENT	Content limited and lacks relevance to students and parents	Content appears relevant, but quantity limited in student needs	Content is adequate in relevance and quan-tity to meet student needs	Content is relevant and quantity is suffi-cient for student needs	Content is on target and provides excellent coverage to meet stu-dent needs
LINKS	Few relevant working links	Adequate number of links, but many no longer functional	Sufficient number of links, all functional	A good variety of useful, active links	Links offer connection to a wide variety of excellent sites
HANDICAPPED ACCESS	No options available for handicapped	Some pages on site offer text-only	Site offers text-only on all pages	Site offers clear options for handi-capped	Site includes handi-capped options on all pages and links to support software

This and other downloadable forms and templates can be found on the Companion Website at www.ablongman.com/lever-duffy3e.

Filtering

As you know, the Internet is not owned or controlled by any agency. Therefore, the Internet includes web sites and information inappropriate for children. A school has a responsibility to limit access to such web sites just as a parent would limit access at home. Schools use filtering software that checks the content of a site before allowing it to be displayed on the screen. Students are denied access to sites that contain or display inappropriate materials. Claims of freedom of speech are sometimes invoked when filtering software is used. Such controversy is more fully addressed in Chapter 11, but most would agree that it is appropriate to keep children safe from harmful Internet content just as they are kept safe from other harm while at school.

Using the Web in Teaching and Learning: Final Thoughts

As anyone knows who has used the Internet to discover something new or find an answer to a question, there can be little doubt that this resource holds enormous potential for education. No matter how many millions of sources are available on the Web or how exciting the interactive multimedia sites may be, without the thoughtful integration of these marvelous resources into instruction by trained and knowledgeable teachers, learners will miss the potential of the Internet. As with all technology tools, it is not the tool itself that enhances teaching and learning, it is how the tool is used by the creative professional educator who is wielding it. The Web is a marvel of limitless resources available at the touch of a key or click of the mouse. But your students need you, their teacher, to help make the Web truly meaningful in their attempt to achieve their academic potential. Just as you master your content area before you teach it, so too must you master Internet skills before you can use them effectively. This chapter, along with Chapter 7, has attempted to give you a foundation for this mastery. We hope that the potential of the Internet has been made abundantly clear and your enthusiasm for using this technology amply kindled.

KEY TERMS

academic tools 289
blogs 286
bookmarks 288
classroom management tools 289
connection gateways 291
electronic gradebooks 289
ERIC 287

FAQ 292
favorites 288
FTP 301
global learning community 293
online publications 283
PDF files 284
templates 298

test generators 289
upload 301
web authoring tools 295
web hosting 301
wizards 298

STUDENT ACTIVITIES

CHAPTER REVIEW

1. What online resources are available to assist educators in researching areas of interest? Describe each.
2. What is a PDF file? What advantage does it offer over files in HTML format?
3. What is a weblog? How might it be used for teaching and learning?
4. How are government educational sites of value in terms of resources? How do they differ from commercial and organizational sites?
5. What types of classroom management and academic tools are available via the Internet? Briefly explain how each tool might help you in your classroom.

6. How can a classroom web site improve communications with students, parents, and community?
7. What are web authoring tools? What types are available to educators?
8. How are new web sites added to the Web? What resources do teachers have to do so?
9. What is an acceptable use policy? What impact does it have on the use of the Web in the classroom?
10. Contrast the issues of privacy and filtering when using the Web in the classroom. What are the responsibilities of a teacher in each of these areas?

WHAT DO YOU THINK?

1. Your class has created a useful and interesting web site, but your school's technical-support staff is very overworked, so you might have to wait until the next grading period to have the site put on the web server. You decide to use a free web hosting service instead. What issues will you need to face in using a free web hosting service? How can you control unacceptable banner ads or pop-up ads that may be added to your site?
2. You have installed a filter on your stand-alone classroom computer that is connected to the Internet. You block all sites that you think might be pornographic, and then you decide to block all sites that may include what you feel might be communist propaganda. This might be a violation of your students' First Amendment rights. Why?
3. You decide that you want to create an electronic learning community for your students this semester. You would like to be sure they can converse with other students in the district, the state, and even around the globe. You have decided that you want to center the community on a multicultural theme in which they compare holiday customs and celebrations. How will you go about creating such a community? What kinds of activities will you include?

LEARNING TOGETHER!

These activities are best done in groups of three to five:

1. Search the Internet for outstanding educational sites. Each group member should find at least five sites. Prepare an annotated list of your group's top ten finds. Word-process your list, and distribute it to all members of your class. You are also invited to send it to one of this textbook's authors so that it may be considered for inclusion on the web site that accompanies this text.

2. Assume that you are a grade-level team that has been asked by your school to create a grade-level web site. Storyboard the web site you want to create. You should provide enough detail so that the text to be included and the types of graphics are evident.

3. Each group member should observe a classroom in which the Internet is used. Interview the teacher to discover the successes and experiences he or she has had using the Internet in teaching and learning. Compare the information gathered through observations and interviews. Word-process a summary of your discoveries. You are also invited to email your paper to one of the text authors for inclusion on the text web site.

E-Learning

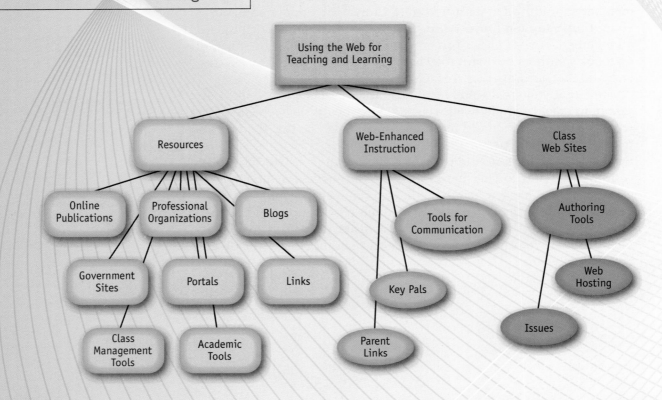

Podcasts ![apple] **www.mylabschool.com**

Listen to a podcast relating to the use of administrative software in teaching and learning. Download the audio discussion to your iPod, computer, or MP3 player.

Software Skills Builder ![apple] **www.mylabschool.com**

These step-by-step illustrated tutorials, accessible through mylabschool.com, teach you to use Microsoft Windows and Office on both PC and Mac by preparing documents that will be useful in your classroom.

Video Lab ![apple] **www.mylabschool.com**

Accessible through the **mylabschool** web site are several video vignettes that offer you a look at software in teaching and learning. Learning guides for all videos can be found in the text's Learning Guide Supplement.

On the Web! Activities **www.ablongman.com/lever-duffy3e**

Noted in the margins of the chapter, these activities offer you in-depth experiences in the topics and content presented in the chapter.

Online Practice Test **www.ablongman.com/lever-duffy3e**

Practice tests offer you an opportunity to test your knowledge and then review the results and send them to your teacher.

Outliner **www.ablongman.com/lever-duffy3e**

Chapter Outliners are fill-in-the-blank outlines of the main ideas presented in the chapter. Download the outliner and fill it in for an effective chapter study guide.

Power Practices **www.ablongman.com/lever-duffy3e**

Power Practices are animated tutorials made using Microsoft's presentation software, PowerPoint. This flash card tutorial will help you practice key concepts in the chapter.

Puzzler **www.ablongman.com/lever-duffy3e**

Puzzlers include content in crossword, word search, and other puzzle formats to help you master chapter content.

Useful Links **www.ablongman.com/lever-duffy3e**

These links offer you suggestions for expanded online research in the topics presented in the chapter.

INTEGRATION *Ideas*

Effectively using the World Wide Web in teaching and learning is an essential skill for educators. From classroom web sites to engaging webquests, teachers can use the Web to communicate, inform, and add excitement to instruction.

Integrating Technology into Social Studies

"Alpha Team leader, can you read me? You have successfully traveled back in time to the year 1250 B.C., ancient Egypt!" This is one of the opening statements in the "Ancient Egypt WebQuest." It is preceded by a tersely realistic, "Alpha Te . . . (crack, hiss, sizzle . . .)" from the home base, guaranteed to make even the most desultory sit up and take notice. The quest tells students, "Your mission is of the utmost importance! You must locate the burial mask of the Ancient Egyptian Pharaoh, Tutankhamen (King Tut). On the inside of the mask is written a message. If you successfully decode the message, you could solve our earth's environmental crisis. Your quest is to decode the ancient Egyptian message and return to our time. To be successful, you must utilize all your available resources (books, experts, and your computer). Your quest will be completed when each mission is finished successfully."

The Tasks assign a travel log and provide links to information on aspects of life in ancient Egypt: market days, mummification, mancala, a cartouche written in hieroglyphics, and a research books on ancient Egypt. There are six missions from which students must choose one. Mission 1 is representative of the other five in the way it builds solid learning into an intriguing format. "Our sources have learned that the ancient Egyptians will soon hold a festival to honor one of their gods, Osiris. You must plan and host a party during this celebration. Your mission will be to gather the clues we will need to find the tomb of King Tut. In order to be successful, you will need to work in teams to learn all that you can about the daily life of ancient Egyptians. Since King Tut was a boy king (10 years old), we suggest that you focus your investigation on Egyptian children."

Other links from the homepage are Ancient Egyptian Hotlists, Great Egyptian Books, Fun Egyptian Activities, Glossary, Search, Great Graphics, the six missions, and an Ancient Egyptian Annotated Bibliography. Check it out: Durant, M., Ancient Egypt WebQuest, **www.iwebquest.com/egypt/ancientegypt.htm.**

Integrating Technology into Language Arts

To wear school uniforms or not to wear school uniforms: That is the question students in Lori Reitano's ninth-grade English class are confronted with in the webquest, "A Uniform Decision." They will work for one of several consulting firms to research the topic before making a recommendation at an upcoming meeting of the Your Town, USA, School Board, who will decide whether or not to make wearing school uniforms mandatory throughout the district. After researching the stance the Consulting Firm is to defend, the students who are members of the firm assume roles as a lawyer, a teacher, a parent, or a student and write a persuasive essay defending their position from the point of view of the identity they have assumed. The webquest gives step-by-step instructions in the Process section. A modified rubric is included to evaluate the PowerPoint presentation students make as a part of the defense

they structure, written materials, participation, and the essay. This webquest can be found at: Reitano, L., A Uniform Decision, **http://education.iupui.edu/webquests/information/index.htm.**

Integrating Technology into the Sciences

Keeping in touch with his eighth- and ninth-grade science students, their parents, administrators, and interested others, Kent Franklin's web site welcomes visitors with a quotation from Einstein, "Imagination is more important than knowledge." The four courses Mr. Franklin teaches at St. James Senior High School, St. James, Minnesota—earth science, physical science, exploring Earth and space systems, and meteorology—are hyperlinked to make information for each course readily reached. Under Earth Science 8, for example, humorous clip art serves as icons to open up the Syllabus, Presentation Outline, Grade Status, Supplemental Activities, Supplemental Readings, Practice Quizzes, Related Sites, Audio Broadcasts, PowerPoint Notes, and Internet Tests. The Supplemental Activities include ten topics, each of which asks a question such as "How Are the Earth's Spheres Interacting?" By clicking on the question, students find information to answer the question. Class notes are posted as PowerPoints and appear on the web page the day they are given in class. All this is accessible at: Franklin, K., Mr. Franklin's Website, **http://hs-staffserver.stjames.k12.mn.us/fraken.**

Integrating Technology into Math

"Circles, Stars, and Candy Bars: Multiplication with Second and Third Graders" is a lesson plan from Julie Cox, South Topsail Elementary School, Pender County School District, North Carolina, which she has designed, in her words, "to create varied opportunities for my students to discover the patterns of multiplication through the use of pictorial representations and manipulatives." She integrated technology with "guided use of calculators, web sites, and mathematical software." The game, Circles and Stars, calls for multiplication skills. Candy Bars Research is an activity in which students undertake to design three rectangular candy boxes with each holding a designated number of different sizes of candy. Students do web-based research as part of the assignments. Ms. Cox cautions that she previews all web sites before sending her students to them and frequently uses "The Optima Projector" in the computer lab to avert any unfortunate visits. For appropriate sites to be used in the instructional process, Ms. Cox adds that she can help guide the students through the online instruction by working with them and being a troubleshooter should any problems occur. Her web site can be found at: Cox, J., Circles, Stars, and Candy Bars: Multiplication with Second and Third Graders, **http://ali.apple.com/ali_sites/ali/exhibits/1000568/Technology.html.**

For these and many more Integration Ideas for using the Internet in teaching and learning, visit the text web site at **www.ablongman.com/lever-duffy3e.**

Designing a Classroom Web Site

As you explore the Web, you will find that many teachers have their own class web sites. It may seem that creating a classroom or grade-level web site is far too difficult for you. Surprisingly, that is not the case. Given the abundant web authoring tools available, it is reasonably easy for any computer-using educator to create a web site. In fact, the greatest challenge for teachers wishing to create their own sites is in planning a pedagogically sound and useful educational site. This section will introduce you to the concerns you need to address to plan an educationally useful site. Once you have considered and responded to each of them, if you have not already done so, you may wish to complete the Software Skills Builder using Microsoft Publisher's Web Wizard to practice creating a site. The skills you gain from that activity will assist you in making your planned classroom web site a reality.

STEP 1 Storyboard

The first step to creating a classroom web site is to decide on the components you would like to include. Since a web site is typically intensely visual, the easiest way to plan and arrange all of the components is to storyboard it. Storyboarding is the process of sketching out each page of a web site and indicating where each textual, visual, and multimedia component will be placed. A storyboard may include a summary of the text to be included and a drawing of the intended visuals. A storyboard also indicates how each page is linked to the other pages.

Storyboarding may be done in a variety of ways. The traditional method is to write on several sheets of paper, but a more effective method is to use large index cards with each card representing a single web page. Since links can be adjusted as the web site is planned, using separate index cards allows you to rearrange your pages during the planning process. Another way to storyboard is to use your computer to help you. You may wish to use the Inspiration software included on your student CD to easily create boxes or circles as graphic representations of each of the "cards" in your storyboard. You can then add links between the pages to show relationships (see Figure I8.1).

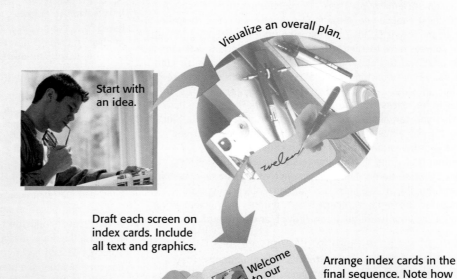

Visualize an overall plan.

Start with an idea.

Draft each screen on index cards. Include all text and graphics.

Arrange index cards in the final sequence. Note how cards will link to each other.

ACTIVITIES

Welcome to our site

FIGURE I8.1

Traditional and Digital Storyboarding

Whether using traditional pencil and paper or brainstorming software such as Inspiration, storyboarding helps you plan and design the most effective web site possible.

Create web pages from cards.

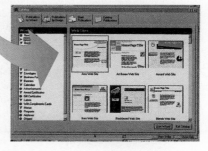

interchapter 8

STEP 2 Determine Your Content

As you plan the content for your classroom web site, you should have a goal in mind. Perhaps your web site is designed to showcase your students' work or to establish your class on the school's web site. However, if your goal is to use your web site instructionally to enhance teaching and learning in the classroom, there are a few key components to consider including. Each of these components emulates what you do in your classroom as you conduct your courses. Your web site is a communications support to your "live" classroom communication, so it makes sense that it should contain much of the same information.

Think of your web site visitor as a new student and ask yourself what that new student needs to know to be comfortable and functional in your classroom. That question will give you a good idea of what a well-rounded classroom web site should include. Regardless of the goal of your site, it should include the following basic components.

- Teacher Information

  The web site should clearly indicate whose classroom it relates to. Therefore, your name and the classes or grade level you teach should be prominent on the home page. Additional information about you can appear either on the home page or as an "About Me" link to another page. Such additional information might include degree(s) earned, certification area(s), school activities, and civic involvement. If you feel it is appropriate, you might also include awards earned, publications, and personal hobbies. The objective in sharing such information is to establish your credentials and to add a personal touch to the site for visitors, especially parents and community visitors.

- Class/Course Information

  Your home page should clearly identify the grade level or course(s) included on the page. If you teach multiple courses, you may wish to list them as hot links with a linked page for each class or course. On the linked page relating to each class or course you teach, it is useful to give the visitor an overview of the course, your objectives, relevant standards, materials requirements, and assessment and grading criteria. For parents, this type of information provides an orientation to your course and an idea of how you will proceed instructionally.

  Your course page should also list additional resources that you may be planning to use. If you have a reading or research list students are expected to use, it should be included with the course information. Your students, by accessing your course page, can then check their required resources from home, and parents can make themselves aware of the resources their children are expected to use.

  Your course page should also provide an overview of the term's activities. This summary may be presented as a link on the course page with additional information on a course activity page. The overview should present the major units of study and a general timetable for their implementation.

- Daily/Weekly Information and Homework

  If you intend to share homework or class activity information, it is best to use a separate page for current information, to make it easier to update. A "This Week" or "Today" link on the home page or the course page that connects to a page containing this information is your best bet. Your daily or weekly information page might include announcements, assignments, and any other information that you might have mentioned to your classes to orient your students to the week's or day's activities.

If you decide to use web pages as the basis for activities themselves, each activity page should be linked to your daily or weekly page. Web pages with hot links can be excellent teaching and learning pages that add excitement and interest to classroom assignments. You might pose an inquiry to the students and let them discover answers on the Internet, or you might create an interactive lesson using a conference, or you might center a writing assignment around a keypad activity. Whatever the activity you select, using web activity pages adds another dimension to learning. Additionally, students who are absent from class and have Internet access at home can look at the posted activities to gain access to the current day's work so they do not fall behind.

- Information for Parents
Your web site opens channels of communication with parents. Although your site will contain information on every page that will probably be of interest to parents, a parents' page offers you a chance to establish an explicit communications link with them. On an "Information to Parents" page, you might include school information (or links to the appropriate location on the school's site) such as the school calendar, dress code, students' rights and responsibilities, and safety procedures. You can also include a class newsletter, announcement flyers, and requests for volunteers. In fact, any document you may have otherwise handed out in class for students to take home to their parents is a good candidate for this type of page. It is easier to update, saves paper and copying costs, and is accessible at any time. You should also include your email address so that parents who have questions can email you on the spot rather than try to remember to call you (or play telephone tag with you) during your and their busy workday. A parents' page opens almost endless opportunities to enter into an effective partnership with parents.

- Information for the Community
The addition of a community page provides you with an opportunity to build partnerships with the community your school serves. In addition to school information (or links to it), your community page can inform the community of current and upcoming projects and activities and can solicit volunteers and even donations. Many retired community members have time and valuable experience to share with your school or your class. An explanation of how to become a school volunteer or guest speaker may be just the impetus needed to establish a new and fruitful partnership. Engaging and informing the community about what you are doing in your school and in your classroom can open new doors for community members and new resources for you.

Once you have your content planned, you can use any web authoring tool to create your web pages. Microsoft Publisher and Microsoft Word both offer wizards to assist you in turning your content into HTML. Publisher offers greater flexibility in design, but both will do an adequate job in helping you create your site. More sophisticated web authoring tools, such as Microsoft Front Page and Adobe GoLive, can add more sophisticated features. Regardless of the authoring tool you select, once content is planned and web pages are created, one last step is necessary.

STEP 3 Check Guidelines

The final step to creating an effective classroom web site is to ensure that the site meets some basic guidelines for educational web sites. These are summarized in Table I8.2. As you complete each page, review it to see if it meets the criteria identified. As you review, add a check to indicate you have conformed to each guideline. When all items are checked, you can be assured your web site is ready to upload and share with your students and their parents.

TABLE 18.2 Guidelines For Educational Web Sites

✓	GUIDELINE	EXPLANATION
○	**SITE CONSISTENCY**	• Keep each page consistent in look and feel and the entire site consistent with commonly used web Conventions. • Use consistent styles and names for navigation buttons, and keep the key navigation buttons in a consistent place on every page.
○	**MEDIUM VS. MESSAGE**	• Do not use too many fonts and colors that might detract from the message you are trying to communicate. • Animation and graphics should add interest but not overwhelm the text messages. • High-resolution pictures should be used sparingly. • Balance should be maintained on all pages, avoiding a cluttered look and providing plenty of "white space" to separate visual displays.
○	**BIAS-FREE CONTENT**	• Information presented should be presentations of fact rather than attempts to persuade. • All aspects of the site should be free from any cultural, ethnic, or gender bias.
○	**DATE NOTIFICATIONS**	• Date for creation of the web site and the last update date should be included. • Time-sensitive materials should be monitored and updated as necessary.
○	**SITE MAP OR SEARCH ENGINE**	• Either an outline of all the pages and the information located on each or a way to search the site should be provided.
○	**MULTIMEDIA ELEMENTS**	• Include alternatives to text (audio, animation, video clips) for communicating your message to meet alternative learning styles. • As necessary, include links to plug-ins needed for the multimedia you include.
○	**CURRENT LINKS**	• Add links to other web sites to enhance a lesson or broaden its scope. • Check to be sure that links are appropriate to the content of your site and that they are current and fully functional.
○	**CONTACT INFORMATION**	• Include your name, grade or department, school address, and school phone number. • Include a hot-link pop-up to your email address so that a visitor can send you an email message simply by clicking on that link.
○	**COPYRIGHT INFORMATION**	• Clearly display copyright information throughout the site. • Provide contact information for permission to use copyrighted information or provide permission for limited use right on your site. • Be sure you include all necessary links and citations for materials on your site.
○	**STUDENT PRIVACY**	• The site should include no student information unless expressed parental permission is obtained. • The site should ensure that shared student information does not violate a student's privacy or compromise safety.
○	**DISABILITY SENSITIVITY**	• Check your site with the Bobby online portal (**http://bobby.watchfire.com/bobby/html/en/index.jsp**) to test the usability of your site for those with disabilities.

chapter 9

Audiovisual Technologies

This chapter addresses these ISTE *National Educational Technology Standards* for Teachers:

II. **PLANNING AND DESIGNING LEARNING ENVIRONMENTS AND EXPERIENCES**
Teachers plan and design effective learning environments and experiences supported by technology. Teachers
   A. design developmentally appropriate learning opportunities that apply technology-enhanced instructional strategies to support the diverse needs of learners.
   B. apply current research on teaching and learning with technology when planning learning environments and experiences.
   C. identify and locate technology resources and evaluate them for accuracy and suitability.
   D. plan for the management of technology resources within the context of learning activities.
   E. plan strategies to manage student learning in a technology-enhanced environment.

III. **TEACHING, LEARNING, AND THE CURRICULUM**
Teachers implement curriculum plans that include methods and strategies for applying technology to maximize student learning. Teachers
   A. facilitate technology-enhanced experiences that address content standards and student technology standards.
   B. use technology to support learner-centered strategies that address the diverse needs of students.
   C. apply technology to develop students' higher-order skills and creativity.
   D. manage student learning activities in a technology-enhanced environment.

In the preceding chapters, you learned much about the computer technologies you are likely to find in instructional environments. However, if you were to visit any classroom today to examine the technologies in place, you would also find other types of technologies used on a daily basis. In Chapter 1, we defined educational technology in its broadest sense, that is, any technology that is used to support or enhance teaching and learning. To fully acquaint you with the types of technologies you are most likely to find in the schools you work in, it is important to become familiar with all of the types of technologies you are likely to encounter. Clearly, your classroom is likely to include a variety of computer technologies. This chapter will help you to explore some of the noncomputer technologies you will find as well.

Before the digital age, technologies that supported teaching and learning were often called audiovisual, or AV, media. Such technologies typically included overhead projectors, slide projectors, filmstrip projectors, movie projectors, tape recorders, and televisions. Today, as you have seen in this text, digital technologies have added significantly to the instructional tools educators have available to them.

This chapter will introduce you to audio and visual media of all types, from the more traditional visual, audio, and video technologies to their leading-edge digital counterparts. It will help you explore how each of these traditional and digital technologies can be used to address learning styles to support the instructional event, and to help you plan how to integrate these technologies into your classroom.

You will then be ready to explore how they have been used to change the face of education in many areas and the issues these changes have generated.

In Chapter 9, you will

- Examine the relationship and educational application of traditional and digital audio, visual, and video media
- Investigate the use of audio and video media in support of teaching and learning
- Review the application of visual media in support of teaching and learning
- Explore the use of projected and nonprojected visual media
- Examine the role of the Internet in providing audio, visual, and video support for teaching and learning

Real People Real Stories

Meet Wendi Takemoto. As chief information officer of Punahou School in Honolulu, Hawaii, Wendi Takemoto realized that to further engage the students, she needed to enhance the learning environment through the use of technology. Research supports her view that multiple modalities in an environment enhance learning. Experience shows that technology has the ability to affect a student, enhance a relationship with a teacher, and cause deep and meaningful reflection in learning. Her efforts have resulted in the integration of audio and visual technology into the learning environment and have deepened learning as a result.

Punahou School in Honolulu, Hawaii, is an independent, co-educational day school with a student body of 3,700 from kindergarten to grade 12. Students exhibit a wide range of abilities, interests, and talents, all contributing to the enrichment of the school community. Each student is recognized as an individual, encouraged to realize his or her potential, and challenged to strive for excellence.

The school is the largest single-campus independent school in the United States and, as a large school, we have a diverse population of learners. To achieve the school's mission of affirming the worth and dignity of each individual by teaching to the students' different learning styles, we have turned to technology.

At our school, we wanted to find a way to maintain a "small school" feeling in a large school environment. Team teaching is the primary approach in our middle school, where students share teachers in a team of four classes. Our high school operates in a collegiate model in which students are on modular schedules, and classroom facilities are shared. We wanted to:

- Enhance the opportunities for students to have a shared experience
- Create greater multisensory richness in the curriculum
- Support spontaneous inquiry both in and out of the classroom

We felt that the use of technology would enable us to allow each student to receive and reflect learning, individually, in the way that is best for him or her.

We decided to equip each of the classrooms in the high school with a standardized audiovisual console, complete with a projector, computer inputs, DVD/CD and VHS player, and document camera. The consoles are standardized to allow system mastery by faculty, no matter which classroom they are teaching in. Standardization also helped the technical support team to be able to provide the high level of support needed. Above all, we needed to ensure that the equipment would work when a faculty member wanted it to work and that the system would be so easy to use it would become a seamless part of teaching and the student learning.

For example, word processing tools, such as Word, have facilitated the notion of writing as a process. Revisions are easier to do via this technology. We have found that digital inking and sound comments have also facilitated the notion of writing as a process. Before, teachers made their comments in the $1/2$-inch margins on the hard copies submitted, and they tried to provide as much feedback and guidance as the space allowed. The ability to digitally ink directly on the student's file provides familiarity for our teachers and our students. Inking in the file allows feedback to be saved and reflected upon, all without the risk of losing that precious piece of paper.

Some of our teachers have now added sound comments in responding to students' work. Using the "insert voice comment" tool in Microsoft Word, teachers have found that they are able to say more to the student than they would have written. They can more easily convey the human side of their feedback, such that students feel encouraged on the affective level, while at the same time receiving specific guidance for their learning.

Our middle school has also ventured into the world of podcasting. Students study a period in Hawaiian history, write a script, and create a newscast. With the use of digital audio recording technology, such as Garage Band, students are able to record their newscast, enhance it with sound effects, and package it into a podcast. With the assistance of teachers, students are able to publish their podcast and share this with their peers and family. This creates an authentic audience for them and a true sense of engagement. The bottom line is that the students are making their learning real and are having fun.

We have found that, through the use of audio and video technologies, the reliability, the availability, and the flexibility in the system have indeed moved us toward the desired learning environments. Teachers are able to play videos, switch back to their computers, and look up topics on the Internet, all with the ease and fluidity they need in teaching.

Students agree that the use of technology has enhanced their learning. They have been almost unanimously pleased with the addition of voice comments to their work. We think this has worked well because engaging the affective part of the brain is so important to learning, and the voice is clearly more engaging on that level than the written comments.

Invariably, students have asked that the comments continue and have said things like, "I really understand better what I should do to revise," or "I feel like I'm having a conference with the teacher," or "I like being able to listen over and over again until I understand," or "I get a lot more feedback from my teacher this way."

Evidenced through the level of effort and care that students put into their work, be it a paper or a podcast, students are enjoying their learning experience—it is engaging.

These kinds of reactions have been made across the board about our increased use of technology. However, the technology, the visual and audio components, are not the focus of the class—the teaching and learning are.

For further information, contact:
Wendi Takemoto
Chief Information Officer
Punahou School
1601 Punahou Street
Honolulu, HI 96822
(808) 944-5701
wtakemoto@punahou.edu

Audiovisual Technologies

Teachers know instinctively that the more interactive and multisensory they make their teaching, the more likely it is that learning will occur. Common sense and instructional experiences have taught us that a lesson delivered through lecture alone is less engaging than a lesson delivered with audio and visual support. Few would disagree that giving a talk about native birds in North America becomes more meaningful when combined with presentation of the recordings of songs of such birds and either beautifully colored still images or motion images. During an instructional event, adding the appropriate audio and visual components can engage more of the learner's senses and help to build multiple cognitive connections to the content presented. And because learning styles vary, the addition of audio and visual images can make learning easier for many students by addressing their auditory or visual strength.

To be able to use all of the available technological tools at hand, educators need to be familiar with the full range of tools that will support the learner's efforts to make meaningful contact with, and build mastery of, the content presented. Audio and visual tools of all types, whether traditional technologies or those that have emerged from the digital age, can be valuable in supporting the teaching and learning process. For this reason, it is important for those who work with learners to be aware of the types of audio and visual technologies available and their application in teaching and learning.

Traditional and Digital Technologies in Instruction

In the first half of the twentieth century, education was enhanced through the introduction of sound and video technologies. The record player, tape recorder, and movie projector all came into being, became a part of society, and ultimately were introduced into the classroom. These traditional technologies have not disappeared yet, although many have altered their form. Figure 9.1 shows a timeline of audiovisual technology use in education. Movie projectors have given way to VCRs and then DVD players; reel-to-reel tape recorders have been replaced by cassette recorders and now iPods and MP3 players; and the record players that were designed to play sound stored on vinyl platters have been superseded by electronic equipment designed to play sound stored on optical discs. Although the storage and playback technology has changed, the intent remains constant. Audio and visual technologies help you teach and your students learn.

In essence, audio and visual enhancements to text and the spoken word are just as important in the digital age as they were in the beginning of the twentieth century. As technology advances, the format of audio and visual media may change, but its significance to teaching and learning will not. Given that many schools have many functional traditional audiovisual technologies still in service, it is important for educators to be aware of the potential of these traditional technologies. Digital versions of AV technologies will no doubt continue to replace more traditional media, but as long as these older technologies are still available, they remain useful to creative educators. And the instructional effort spent to use these more traditional technologies will easily transfer when they are eventually replaced by those that are emerging. The key to integrating both traditional and emerging technologies into teaching and learning is, as with all educational technology, not a question of their technical format but instead a question of the educator's creativity and familiarity with instructional design. Awareness of all the types of audio, visual, and digital technological tools available to you will give you more choices when you design instruction. See Table 9.1 for an overview of these technologies.

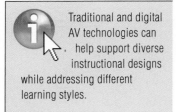

Traditional and digital AV technologies can help support diverse instructional designs while addressing different learning styles.

Audio in Teaching and Learning

Every teacher uses auditory delivery to teach students; the source of the audio is most typically the teacher's voice. Whether the teacher is verbally introducing a concept briefly to third graders or lecturing on a complex theory to college students, audio is a dominant delivery system in every educational environment. As you no doubt know from your own learning experiences, sometimes teacher-based audio is very effective, and sometimes it is not. To discover the differences between effective and ineffective audio instruction, it is critical to first take a closer look at the audio communications process.

Understanding Listening and Learning

Listening—that is, being able to hear and comprehend—involves several steps. The first step in the process of listening is to actually hear the auditory stimulus. Next, the brain needs to turn that stimulus into neural pulses and process it. Finally, the appropriate cognitive connections need

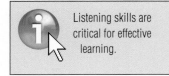

Listening skills are critical for effective learning.

TABLE 9.1 Audio and Video Technology Overview

FUNCTION	TRADITIONAL AV TECHNOLOGIES	DIGITAL AND OTHER EMERGING TECHNOLOGIES
DISPLAY INDIVIDUAL NONMOVING IMAGES	Overhead projector	Document camera, computer display, clip art, photo galleries on CD or the Internet
DISPLAY PHOTOGRAPHIC IMAGES	Slide projector, bulletin board, posters	Document camera, computer display, photo galleries on CD or the Internet
DISPLAY MOVING IMAGES	Movie projector, VCR	Computer display, DVD player, computer CD-ROM, Internet video
PLAY BACK MUSIC OR SPEECH	Tape recorder, record player	CD player, MP3 player, iPod, DVD player, Internet audio
PLAY TV PROGRAMS	TV monitor	Computer display, Internet webcast
RESEARCH SUPPORT	Books	Multimedia CD-ROMs, E-books, Internet searches

to be made to relate this new information to memories of real events or previously learned content. This entire process is as complex as it is intuitive. Listening is really a very critical prerequisite skill for effective auditory learning. For the many teachers who wish to use audio technologies for instruction, assisting learners in acquiring, improving, and applying listening skills may be a necessary first step. If you choose to use audio delivery, it is a good idea to help your students develop and practice these skills as a component of instruction.

Effective listening requires the hearing process to be accurately achieved. Consider **hearing** as the physical process that includes the generation of clear, audible sounds that are ultimately received correctly by others. In the classroom, this means that you need to ensure that the audio source is producing a clear signal and that other noises are controlled so that they do not interfere with or detract from the intended audio. Effective listening begins with being able to hear accurately.

The second step in effective listening is focused listening. To listen, you must give your full attention to the auditory stimulus. **Focused listening** is a skill that schools do not often teach directly as a part of curriculum. To encourage the development of focused listening in your students, you might want to structure listening games or activities into your instruction. You might also want to incorporate specific teaching techniques into your strategies that help students refocus their attention during active instruction.

Focused listening to help our students succeed academically.

It is in such instances that audio media can help. Capturing auditory information, storing it, and playing it back can be a very useful tool to support learning and encourage focused listening. A student can listen to a presentation multiple times at the pace necessary for full comprehension. For students who have difficulty listening effectively, being able to manage

FIGURE 9.1
Audiovisual Technology in Education
The twentieth century was a century of dramatic technological enhancements to education.

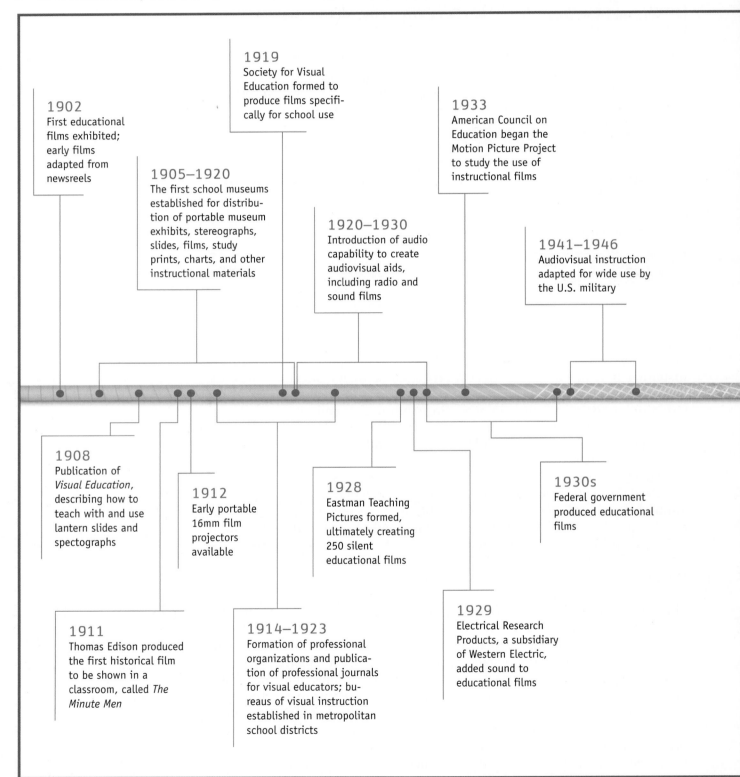

1902
First educational films exhibited; early films adapted from newsreels

1905–1920
The first school museums established for distribution of portable museum exhibits, stereographs, slides, films, study prints, charts, and other instructional materials

1919
Society for Visual Education formed to produce films specifically for school use

1920–1930
Introduction of audio capability to create audiovisual aids, including radio and sound films

1933
American Council on Education began the Motion Picture Project to study the use of instructional films

1941–1946
Audiovisual instruction adapted for wide use by the U.S. military

1908
Publication of *Visual Education*, describing how to teach with and use lantern slides and spectographs

1912
Early portable 16mm film projectors available

1928
Eastman Teaching Pictures formed, ultimately creating 250 silent educational films

1930s
Federal government produced educational films

1911
Thomas Edison produced the first historical film to be shown in a classroom, called *The Minute Men*

1914–1923
Formation of professional organizations and publication of professional journals for visual educators; bureaus of visual instruction established in metropolitan school districts

1929
Electrical Research Products, a subsidiary of Western Electric, added sound to educational films

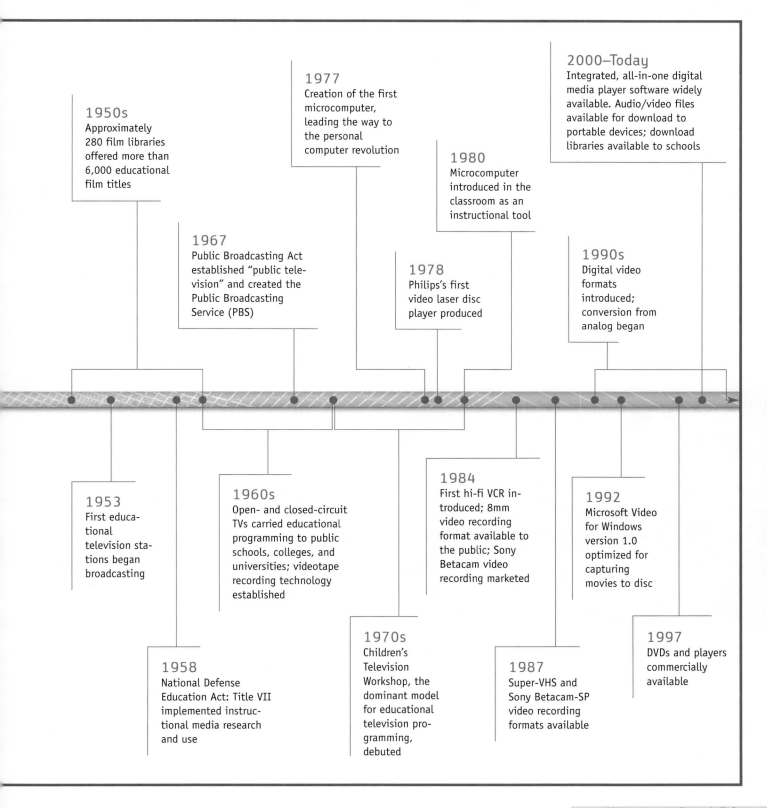

1950s
Approximately 280 film libraries offered more than 6,000 educational film titles

1967
Public Broadcasting Act established "public television" and created the Public Broadcasting Service (PBS)

1977
Creation of the first microcomputer, leading the way to the personal computer revolution

1978
Philips's first video laser disc player produced

1980
Microcomputer introduced in the classroom as an instructional tool

1990s
Digital video formats introduced; conversion from analog began

2000–Today
Integrated, all-in-one digital media player software widely available. Audio/video files available for download to portable devices; download libraries available to schools

1953
First educational television stations began broadcasting

1958
National Defense Education Act: Title VII implemented instructional media research and use

1960s
Open- and closed-circuit TVs carried educational programming to public schools, colleges, and universities; videotape recording technology established

1970s
Children's Television Workshop, the dominant model for educational television programming, debuted

1984
First hi-fi VCR introduced; 8mm video recording format available to the public; Sony Betacam video recording marketed

1987
Super-VHS and Sony Betacam-SP video recording formats available

1992
Microsoft Video for Windows version 1.0 optimized for capturing movies to disc

1997
DVDs and players commercially available

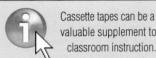
Recorded verbal information lets students control the pace at which they listen.

the pace of audio communication may be enough to turn a frustrating learning scenario into one that they are able to master. Audio technologies offer educators the tools needed to be able to support learners in this manner.

Traditional Audio Media

Audiocassettes

Cassette tapes can be a valuable supplement to classroom instruction.

Audiocassettes are an economical, durable, and easy-to-use magnetic medium that lets you record voice, music, or other sounds. Cassette tape players are inexpensive additions to the learning environment, although some units need additional speakers so they can be heard clearly throughout the classroom. Cassette players are compact and simple to operate for even the youngest learners. As a supplement to class instruction, playing audiotapes can enrich the learning experience and add audio sensory elements. For small-group instruction, creating and playing back an audiotape can enhance active learning. When coupled with earphones, cassette players can make a valuable addition as a classroom aid for individualized learning and review (see Table 9.2).

Talking books are a great way for students to practice their listening skills.

One of the most popular uses of audiotapes is the **talking book.** Whether for primary students who are learning to read or high school students who enjoy the dramatization of a play, recorded readings of books, plays, or short stories can add an auditory dimension to such texts. Students can either read along with a talking book or listen and respond to questions as the audio book or story progresses. This type of activity provides listening skills practice while reinforcing printed material.

Another popular use of audiotapes is the creation or acquisition of multimedia kits. Whether made by the teacher or commercially produced, **multimedia kits** usually include visual elements (texts and graphics) and supplemental audio enhancements on cassette tape. Such kits also usually include student activity sheets and suggested lesson plans. Although they may also include motion video or even real objects, text, graphics, and audiotapes are most common.

Listening centers with talking books help learners improve both listening and reading skills.

Oral histories and journals reinforce communication and listening skills.

An additional effective classroom application of audiotapes is their use for oral history and oral journal assignments. **Oral histories** are typically interviews captured on audiotape related to a single significant event. Students might interview parents or grandparents and ask questions related to their memories of a specific historical event, such as the first moon landing. Or they might ask interview

TABLE 9.2	Components of a Listening Center		
EQUIPMENT	PURPOSE	EQUIPMENT	PURPOSE
CASSETTE RECORDER AND PLAYER AND CD PLAYER 	Play back student-made, teacher-made, and commercially prepared audiotapes; record student reports, stories, read-aloud practice; record lesson instructions and reviews	**PRERECORDED AND BLANK CASSETTES AND CDs** 	Cassettes and CDs available alone, with texts, and in ultimedia kits provide tutorials, music, talking books, and lessons Variable-length, reusable blank cassettes and CD-Rs have a wide variety of student and teacher uses
EARPHONES 	Provide private listening; may require splitting device to plug in multiple sets of earphones	**TABLE AND CHAIRS** 	Table for listening center equipment; comfortable chairs contribute to a relaxed, nurturing learning environment

questions about a significant local event, such as a hurricane or the dedication of an important local monument. Interviews building an oral history of a significant event that have been captured on audiotape can be edited, and clips from multiple tapes can be condensed into a single audio collage of interviews. The edited oral history tape can be duplicated and distributed to all participants, creating an irreplaceable treasure that captures the voice and emotion of those who participated in history.

Likewise, **oral journals** provide learners with the opportunity to make unrestricted observations and reflections on their own experiences. Whether making oral notes of their observations during a field trip or reflecting on a classroom experience, oral journals give learners the chance to capture their own voices and emotions while giving them the opportunity to practice and listen to their own oral communication skills. Oral journals can later be listened to, reflected on, and synthesized by individual learners or shared with groups or the entire class.

Commercially prepared tapes or blank audiocassettes can also be valuable instructional tools. Furthermore, because both tapes and player/recorder equipment are reasonably priced, they offer an economical way to bring audio media into your classroom. Tapes can be reused or saved as desired. They can be copied quickly and in large quantity by using tape-duplicating equipment. Applied creatively, cassette tapes can provide auditory enhancement, teach listening skills, and reinforce content. Because the audio experience is stored on the tape, it can be played back whenever appropriate to meet learners' needs.

E-Learning
ON THE WEB! 9.1
Talking Books and Other Tapes

Broadcast Audio

Audiocassette tapes are not the only traditional audio medium available in the learning environment. **Broadcast audio,** that is, audio received via radio, can also provide valuable enhancement to content. The popularity of radio talk shows testifies to the potential of broadcast audio. For the classroom, National Public Radio offers a variety of listening opportunities in terms of both music and discussion. For those whose geographic location allows for reception of broadcasts from other countries, radio can provide valuable social studies and language opportunities. The National Oceanic and Atmospheric Administration (NOAA) weather service broadcasts provide opportunities for real-world science and math applications. Awareness of the potential of these types of audio broadcasts for instruction will help you to stay mindful of the possibilities of incorporating radio programs into teaching and learning.

 ## Digital Audio Media

Optical Media

Optical digital media are rapidly replacing analog audiotapes.

The more traditional analog storage media (audiotapes) are giving way to their digital counterparts, the most common of which is the **compact disc (CD).** CDs and DVDs have some distinct advantages over audiotapes. These advantages include clarity, storage format, and information access.

Digitized sound is sound recorded in distinct bits of data rather than analog waves. This results in a much crisper, clearer audio recording. Furthermore, because CDs and DVDs are highly durable media, the sounds recorded on them do not deteriorate with frequent use. Unlike magnetic tapes, which can become stretched or distorted, CDs maintain their shape and thus their clarity over time.

Additionally, CDs, with their capacity of approximately 75 minutes of audio, offer a capacity roughly equal to that of cassette tapes. Their digital storage format, further, provides for random access of the data stored, which means you can directly go to and play any segment on a CD. Tapes use a process called sequential access; that is, you must move through the taped information in the sequence in which it was stored to reach the content you want. CDs save the time and effort necessary to sort through the entire sequence of stored data. This ability to access randomly is a useful advantage during instruction. Figure 9.2 summarizes the advantages of using CDs.

CDs in the Classroom

FIGURE 9.2

Optical Media for Teaching and Learning

CDs offer unique advantages in teaching and learning.

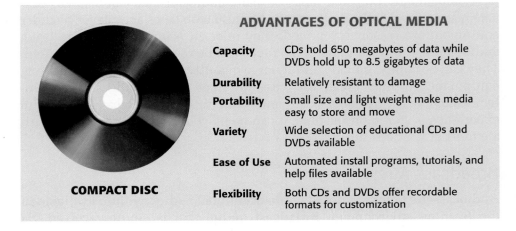

ADVANTAGES OF OPTICAL MEDIA

Capacity	CDs hold 650 megabytes of data while DVDs hold up to 8.5 gigabytes of data
Durability	Relatively resistant to damage
Portability	Small size and light weight make media easy to store and move
Variety	Wide selection of educational CDs and DVDs available
Ease of Use	Automated install programs, tutorials, and help files available
Flexibility	Both CDs and DVDs offer recordable formats for customization

COMPACT DISC

Internet Audio

Once digitized, audio can be delivered through the Internet as well as on digital storage media such as CDs. The Internet lets you find and download very specific audio clips for use in your classroom. Using **Internet audio,** you can download and store only what you need rather than having to buy a full CD that may have only a few portions that are useful as supplements to your lesson. The increasing availability of Internet audio has resulted in its becoming an emerging audio technology in today's classrooms.

To use Internet audio, it is necessary to be aware of its various formats and the hardware and/or software necessary for its playback. The two most common formats of audio files available on the Internet are WAV files and MP3 files. **WAV files** are the digital version of analog audio. This means that a sound or music clip has been converted directly into its digital counterpart. This can be done by recording voice or sound through a computer's microphone, converting it to its digital counterpart via the computer's sound card and software, and then storing it on disk. WAV files maintain the quality of the original sound but often result in very large digital files. A CD-quality recording in WAV format would take up approximately 2 to 3 megabytes of space for every minute of sound recording. Obviously, a long song or story would take an enormous amount of time to upload or download and a substantial amount of disk space for storage. For this reason, WAV files found on the Internet are often short. As a result of the size of audio files and the need for faster download times, a newer audio file format has been developed and is becoming widely used on the Internet. This format is called **MP3,** which stands for Motion Picture Experts Group, audio layer 3.

Audio recordings on the Internet are usually stored as WAV or MP3 files.

MP3 is an audio compression technology that has gained in popularity because it provides high-quality sound in a fraction of the space required for the same clip in older audio file formats. This compression significantly reduces upload and download times as well as necessary storage space. To play MP3 files, you must have MP3 playback software installed on your computer or a dedicated MP3 player device. MP3 player programs are available for free download online, as are many MP3 audio files.

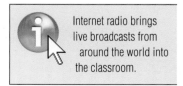

Internet Audio

Although most MP3 files available on the Web are music audio, MP3 has the capacity for other kinds of sound recordings and will no doubt experience greater applications in education. WAV files, the staple format for digital audio files used in instruction, may well be superseded by the compact MP3 format. Regardless of the digital audio format you select to use, educational applications are similar to those associated with traditional audio technologies and may even exceed them.

Internet Radio

Using digital formats combined with streaming audio technology, the Internet offers a broadcast service called **Internet radio.** Internet radio uses the Internet to offer online radio stations consisting of a wide variety of programming including music, sports, science, and local, national, and world news. Live and recorded programming from around the world can enhance language, social studies, science, and current events curricula. Typically, Internet radio sites offer a brief text summary with graphics in conjunction with the audio broadcast. For educators who wish to expand

Internet radio brings live broadcasts from around the world into the classroom.

COOL TOOLS

Digital Media Players

Windows Media player, RealNetworks' RealAudio, and Apple QuickTime are digital media players, all of which are available free on the Internet. These software players collect audio and video data in a special storage location called a buffer and then begin playing back the sound and images as soon as enough is collected. They continue to play while collecting the multimedia data so that, once started, the stream is not interrupted.

All of these players manage streaming audio from the Internet. Streaming audio is usually compressed so that unessential components such as very high and very low sounds are omitted. This makes the file smaller and faster to transmit across the Internet. Each streaming audio player has a slightly different compression scheme with some players offering advantages across different bandwidths. Generally, however, these players all provide excellent playback of WAV and MP3 files for most classrooms.

Some of the unique features provided with media players include the ability to play back digital audio and video from the Internet, from CDs, or from DVDs. Some players also have copying capabilities, the ability to organize files into playlists for easy playback, and the ability to change "skins." Skins are the alternative player interfaces that can change how the player looks and which features are accessed via convenient on-screen controls.

To download these popular media players go to these web sites:

- For Windows Media Player go to **www.microsoft.com**
- For Quick-Time Player go to **www.apple.com**
- For Real-Player go to **www.real.com**

ON THE WEB! 9.4

Internet Radio

their students' horizons, access to up-to-the-minute international radio broadcasts is just a mouse click away. And because visual, text, and audio information may be provided, different learning styles are addressed simultaneously. Whether used with a data projection unit for a whole class activity or with a single computer for an individual or small-group project, Internet radio broadcasts offer fascinating possibilities to creative teachers.

Visual Technologies in Teaching and Learning

Audio technologies directly address the needs of the auditory learner but also add dimension to instruction for all learners. Including audio in teaching and learning makes the instruction richer. However, for most learners, audio alone will not be sufficient to communicate content. Visuals are, for most learners, a necessity.

Whenever you visit an effective instructional environment, the most noticeable elements are the many eye-catching educational displays. Visual support for content can be seen throughout the teaching and learning space. Whether through posters, student work on bulletin boards, models, or dioramas, the content is articulated, clarified, and enhanced visually. Few educators would deny the necessity and effectiveness of visuals in teaching and learning. Learning style research, brain-based instruction, and common

Internet radio broadcasts like those provided by National Public Radio can offer audio resources on a wide variety of instructional content.

SOURCE: National Public Radio.

sense support the use of visuals in instruction. The question that remains for educators is how to determine and select the most effective and appropriate visual technologies for the content under study. To answer this question, it is important first to understand the nature of visual communication.

Visual Communication and Learning

Consider the visual displays shown in Figure 9.3. Are you able to answer the questions beneath each? No doubt you can. Because, over the years,

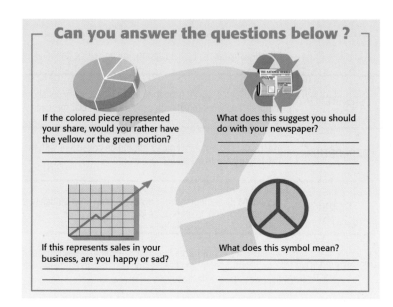

FIGURE 9.3
What Is Visual Literacy?
Visual literacy is necessary to understand and interpret displays.

Visual literacy is an important educational goal.

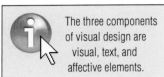

The three components of visual design are visual, text, and affective elements.

Visual Design

you have developed **visual literacy** just as you are in the process of developing technological literacy through this course. The visual literacy you have acquired was developed through the many teaching and learning processes you have experienced. Some were more visually intensive than others, but by the time most people reach adulthood, they have managed to acquire the visual literacy that enables them to accurately interpret the visuals necessary for functioning effectively in our society.

Children acquire visual literacy skills throughout their educational experiences. Regardless of what you teach, you will have an impact on the visual skills your students attain. No matter the content or grade level you teach, how you design, arrange, and present visual information to learners will affect their visual literacy skill set, positively or negatively. Clear, consistent visual information will help them to build skills.

Every **visual** consists of a number of elements presented in a deliberate arrangement. There are three primary categories of design elements: visual, text, and affective elements. Visual elements may include graphics, symbols, real objects, and organizational visuals. Text elements include all aspects of textual presentation, ranging from the words chosen to the font styles, colors, and sizes used. Affective elements are those components of a visual that can elicit a response from the viewer, such as pleasure, surprise, or humor. Selecting and arranging these elements appropriately results in effective displays. Following the guidelines summarized in Table 9.3 will assist you in creating clear and effective visuals.

TABLE 9.3	Guidelines for Effective Visual Design
DESIGN ELEMENT	**GUIDELINE**
RELEVANCE	All elements of the design add to the clarity of the overall visual; no elements detract from the message.
COHERENCE	Include only elements that support, enhance, or extend the message.
CONSISTENCY	While elements do not need to be uniform, all elements should be in harmony and work together to send a single, clear message.
PROPORTION	The relative size of all elements should be consistent with their respective importance to the visual's message.
CONTRAST	Key elements, including white space, should draw sufficient distinction between elements to emphasize key message points.
UNITY AND DIRECTION	All elements should work together to focus the viewer's attention on the visual starting point of the message and then to guide the viewer through the message's visual sequence.

Nonprojected Visuals in Teaching and Learning

The most common type of visuals found in today's classrooms are nonprojected visuals. These visual supports do not require projection for display and include real objects, models, exhibits, printed materials, graphics, and photographs. Although these visuals might not be high-tech, they may well be the best choice to support the content under study. Table 9.4 summarizes popular nonprojected visuals and examples of how they can be used in the teaching and learning process.

Real Objects

Real objects, as the name implies, are any objects that can safely and reasonably be brought into the classroom for examination. Abstract verbal descriptions of a real object do not have the same impact as sensory input resulting

E-Learning

www.mylabschool.com
video
View *Using Visuals in Learning*

Real objects address kinesthetic learning.

TABLE 9.4 **Nonprojected Visuals and Their Application**

NONPROJECTED VISUAL	EXAMPLES	APPLICATIONS
REAL OBJECTS	Rocks, stamps, fish, ants, plants, eggs, leaves	Scientific experiments, history projects, geology units, solar graphics, weather studies
MODELS	Globes; scale models; gear box circuit kits; timing devices; teaching clocks; teaching torsos; ear, eye, and nose models; hands-on heart models; solar system simulators	Teach and reinforce basic geographic locations; design and structure of bridges, boats, skyscrapers; human anatomy; astronomy
EXHIBITS	Dioramas, artifact collections, book displays, dinosaur mountain display, interactive dinosaur sound station, student craft projects	Show historical, geographic, or other wide-view, three-dimensional landscapes; showcase books to be read for a class or new publications; teach animal sounds through touching electronic soundspots on a vinyl playmat; feature traveling artifact collections from local museums
PRINT MATERIALS	Books, worksheets, posters, charts, bulletin boards, games, maps, puzzles, cards, handwriting desk tapes	Required and elective books for study and recreational reading; worksheets with learning activities for all subjects; charts showing pictorial representations of a topic with activity ideas and further study suggestions; bulletin boards showing classroom rules, star students, birthdays, computer care, content-area facts and details; games to teach skills; crossword puzzles for vocabulary study; flash cards for memorization of facts; desk tapes for teaching cursive writing
GRAPHICS AND PHOTOGRAPHS	Drawings, cartoons, diagrams, photographs, graphic organizers, graphing mats, graphs, Venn diagrams, glyphs	Student drawings to illustrate stories read, holidays, portraits; relevant cartoons to add humor to an assignment; photos students take of field trips, their vacations, their families and friends; graphic organizers to help students visualize and organize schoolwork; graphing mats, graphs, Venn diagrams, and glyphs to teach concepts that connect math to other subjects

Tech Tips
for TEACHERS

The appropriate application of visual design principles can make the difference between a visual that is effective and clear and one that is confusing. Examine the two visuals below. Both display information on the same topic. Which is more effective in communicating that information to you? Compare the two, then review the design principles below that will help you create effective visuals for your students.

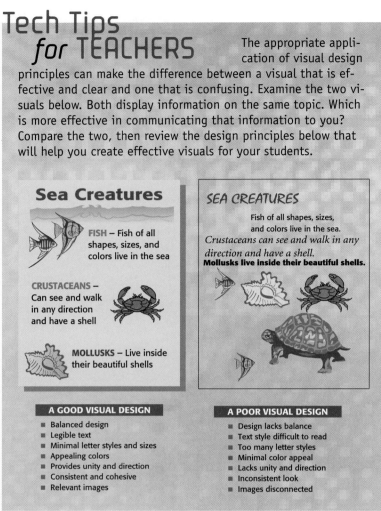

A GOOD VISUAL DESIGN

- Balanced design
- Legible text
- Minimal letter styles and sizes
- Appealing colors
- Provides unity and direction
- Consistent and cohesive
- Relevant images

A POOR VISUAL DESIGN

- Design lacks balance
- Text style difficult to read
- Too many letter styles
- Minimal color appeal
- Lacks unity and direction
- Inconsistent look
- Images disconnected

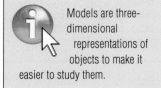 Models are three-dimensional representations of objects to make it easier to study them.

from looking at, touching, and feeling the real thing. Whenever possible, it is useful to support content with real objects that learners can examine and explore.

Models

Models include three-dimensional representations of concepts or real objects that cannot reasonably be brought into the classroom. Typically, models are representations that are scaled up or down to provide a three-dimensional visual, such as a scale model of a tooth (scaled up) or a globe (scaled down). Models can bring kinesthetic versions of concepts into the learning environment, and they can be manipulated and handled to provide tactile sensory support for abstract ideas.

Exhibits

Exhibits include dioramas and classroom displays that are created and/or arranged to illustrate instructional content. **Dioramas** are usually displays that represent a scene, often created from a cut cardboard box. The diorama background is painted on the back inside of the box, with objects or models situated in the foreground of the box to finish the scene. Making a diorama can be an effective activity in which students create a visual that is representative of natural habitats, geographical features, or historical events.

Classroom displays are exhibits of arranged visual objects that accentuate or enhance an instructional concept. Displays might include annotated rock collections, thematic book displays in libraries, and history displays that include antiques and photographs.

Regardless of the type of exhibit selected, such visual displays, especially if they are touchable, add both visual and concrete dimensions to concepts presented in instruction.

Print Materials

Whether created by teachers or students, **print materials** as visual displays remain a centerpiece in most learning spaces. Individual print materials may include books and worksheets, and group-oriented printed visuals may include posters and charts. Teacher-made, student-made, or commercially printed visuals, though a staple in most classrooms, vary in quality. Awareness of visual design principles and use of a design rubric will assist you in selecting high-quality print visuals for display in your classroom.

Graphics and Photographs

A pictorial image can be created (graphics) or captured photographically (photographs). These images can be used in their original size for individual or group instruction or can be blown up for whole-class instruction. **Graphics,** including drawings, cartoons, and diagrams, can represent and clarify concepts and relationships. **Photographs** can capture real-world images and transport them into the classroom. Both graphics and photographs illustrate, clarify, and enhance abstract concepts; however, to be effective, their presentation and use in the teaching and learning environment also need to conform to the principles of effective visual design.

Display Technologies for Nonprojected Visuals

Once nonprojected visuals are planned in accordance with visual design principles, the next step is to select the appropriate technology for the creation and/or display of the visuals.

To display print or graphic visuals, most classrooms offer a variety of display surfaces. The most common is the bulletin board. **Bulletin boards** offer a flexible surface that provides an easy-to-change venue for a variety of print and graphic elements.

Other surfaces for nonprojected visual display often found in classrooms include flip charts, magnetic boards, felt boards, and chalkboards or whiteboards. Availability varies by school and grade level, but familiarity with each will serve you well as you decide how best to share visuals with your students.

Magnetic and felt boards are alternative display surfaces.

Flip charts can be used to write text or graphic messages that can be either saved on the pad or torn off and displayed around the classroom. Flip charts are useful for capturing key points of group discussion and for creating impromptu illustrations of concepts. A recent enhancement to flip charts is the giant Post-it note. The size of a flip chart sheet, this type of padded paper comes with its own cardboard easel and self-sticking sheets that can be hung on almost any surface without the need for tape and without damage to the surface.

FLIP CHART

Electronic whiteboards expand on traditional whiteboard capabilities.

Magnetic boards and **felt boards** are usually small surfaces that display visual elements through magnets or friction. Both magnetic and felt boards are inexpensive and easy to manipulate by even the youngest students. For this reason, they are most frequently found in elementary classrooms.

Black or green **chalkboards,** also called blackboards, are found in many classrooms. A variety of chalk colors can be used to create impromptu text and visual displays. Chalkboards are rapidly being replaced by whiteboards. **Whiteboards** offer a slick white surface on which a variety of specially formulated dry-erasable colored markers can be used. Additionally, some whiteboards have a metal backing that will support magnetic displays. And, as you

MAGNETIC BOARD

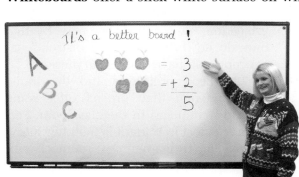

WHITEBOARD

learned in Chapter 6, when you combine the traditional whiteboard with digital technology, you get the electronic whiteboard, making this nonprojected display media doubly useful.

Projected Visuals in Teaching and Learning

Visuals that require projection to be seen are a critical component of many classrooms. This type of visual and the technology that supports it requires, in addition to the visual itself, specialized equipment and a projection screen for classroom display. As a rule, the visual is enlarged from its original format so that all students can see it. Because the visual and the technology necessary to project it cannot be separated, each will be considered with its projection technologies in the following sections.

Overhead Projectors

The **overhead projector** still remains a standard tool in many classrooms. Visuals are created on thin sheets of clear acetate, typically called **transparencies.** A powerful lamp inside the overhead projector shines through the plastic and then through a series of mirrors and lenses, so that the visual is magnified onto a projection screen. An enlarged image of the transparency is projected there for all to see.

Visuals for overhead projection can be created by using black or color inks and can be hand drawn, printed via computer and printer, or photocopied from a printed page. To draw on a transparency, special transparency markers must be used, or the ink will blotch and smear. Such markers can be either permanent or washable. Computer-generated transparencies offer more professional-looking, permanent visuals.

Commercial overhead transparencies are also very popular options for use in the classroom. These visuals are created and sold in booklets or sets and are sometimes offered as supplements to a textbook. The obvious advantage of commercial transparencies is that they are high-quality, ready-to-use visuals designed for overhead projection. A disadvantage may be that they do not fully target the instructional concepts you have selected to present.

Overhead projectors and the transparencies that they project offer some unique advantages in the classroom. Perhaps the most important is that they allow the teacher to maintain eye contact with

Learning with Visuals

- Offer visual literacy activities
- Provide practice interpreting visual messages
- Encourage students to create visuals that communicate

Use COLOR CONTRAST to add interest.

Include GRAPHICS that add interest, but keep them simple and avoid very complex diagrams.

Include MINIMAL TEXT on each transparency. A good rule is the Rule of Seven: no more than seven lines with seven words per line.

ELIMINATE unnecessary detail to keep the message concise and clear.

FIGURE 9.4

Elements of a Good Transparency
Guidelines for creating effective transparencies include limiting content, including graphics, and maintaining eye appeal through color and contrast.

learners during group instruction. Instead of having to turn to write on a whiteboard, using an overhead projector allows you to face the classroom while creating impromptu visual images. Another advantage is the longevity of the visual images. Transparencies also allow you to build a concept; this can be done by adding successive transparency layers, called overlays. Each overlay contains a bit of additional information that, when placed on top of the previous display, creates a more complex and detailed visual.

Transparencies offer an easy-to-create and easy-to-use option for educators. You should apply the same visual design principles when creating transparencies as you would when creating any other visual. Figure 9.4 offers some additional useful hints for effectively creating and using this visual technology.

Overhead projectors are common useful projection technologies.

E-Learning
ON THE WEB! 9.6
Overhead Transparencies

Digital Projectors

With the advent of digital imaging, **digital projectors** have taken a firm hold in schools. As you learned in Chapter 4, these computer output devices project digital images onto a projection screen, large monitor, or whiteboard so that they can be shared with a large group. (Features of digital projectors, as well as overhead projectors, are summarized in Figure 9.5.) Images can be captured with a digital still camera, with a digital video camera, from an analog videotape using a video capture card, or even from an electronic white board.

Regardless of the method used for capturing digital images, the use of digital projectors in education will no doubt continue to expand. As teachers become more familiar with the technology and schools increase their acquisition of digital imaging hardware and software, teaching and learning will continue to be visually enhanced through their application. Digital images are already being creatively applied and incorporated into innovative instruction. Digital projectors are becoming more powerful and full-featured as their cost continues to drop. More and more educators are discovering and using this versatile technology for sharing visual images with learners.

Transparencies should be created following standard visual design guidelines.

FIGURE 9.5
Comparing Display Technologies
Various types of displays can be found in schools.

OVERHEAD PROJECTOR
Features
- Versatile and inexpensive
- Displays commercial or teacher-made transparencies against a screen, classroom wall, or whiteboard
- In combination with computer-generated images and a color printer, transparencies can be created that specifically target instructional objectives

DOCUMENT CAMERA
Features
- Displays real-time still images
- Displays real-time 3-D objects
- Shows photographic slides
- Shows transparencies
- Captures video images

DIGITAL PROJECTOR

Features
- Attached to a computer, projector displays real-time computer images
- Displays software or Internet activities for large group
- Varies from inexpensive to costly along with the quality of the display and the features available

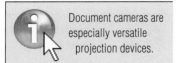

Document cameras are especially versatile projection devices.

Document Cameras

A projection device that combines the applications of several other types of visual projectors into one has begun to gain popularity. The **document camera** is actually a video camera, mounted on a stand, that captures and projects an image of whatever is placed on the stand's document table. The camera, pointed down toward the document table, captures a live video image of the document or object placed on its table and plays that image back through a video monitor or an LCD display. By using both top and back lighting on the table and the video camera's zoom features, overhead transparencies, slides, documents, and three-dimensional objects can all be projected to a large group.

This technology offers some practical projection advantages. Science experiments, demonstrations of small real objects, and procedural presentations can be easily shared. As the teacher proceeds with a live demonstration on the document camera table, the zoom feature built into the camera can be used to share minute detail with all students simultaneously. A teacher no longer needs to have students crowd around a demonstration to share it or walk around the classroom to show small objects. The document camera's live video makes sharing simple and readily viewable by all.

YOU Decide!

Projection tools such as a digital projector or a document camera can offer teachers a unique way to share images in a large group setting. Document cameras help teachers display visuals or a text page without first having to create a transparency from them. Further, document cameras let students see live images of a science experiment or a hands-on demonstration. Digital projectors allow teachers to share any digital image from a photograph, to a map, to a live demonstration of research on the Web. These technologies enrich teacher presentations and demonstrations so that they are as exciting as they are engaging. They are well worth the time and dollar investment when adding them to the classroom. Do you agree?

YES! For too long teachers have used the board or, at best, the overhead projector as visual aids to their instruction. These older technologies, while useful at times, don't have the same impact on students. And the images from the board or overhead transparency can be difficult to read and can't be used for real-time demonstrations. But add a digital display device or use a document camera and the content becomes exciting, interactive, and engaging. Both teachers and students can use these devices to share ideas, make reports, demonstrate projects, or for discovery learning. These devices make the difference between limited and boring presentations and those that keep everyone interested.

NO! Too much emphasis on audiovisual support misses the point of teaching. Good teachers make content interesting by the way they present it and by the types of activities they have their students do. It really doesn't matter whether the teacher uses the blackboard, overhead projector, or a document camera as support. The real core of great instruction is the instruction. Besides, those technologies are complex, hard to learn, and expensive. It is better to pay for other things needed in the school and in the classroom rather than invest in presentation equipment that doesn't really contribute to effective teaching or student learning.

Which view do you agree with? YOU DECIDE!

Video in Teaching and Learning

Video technologies have undergone a dramatic evolution from early silent movies to today's compressed video over the Internet. During each stage of this evolution, educators have used the most current video technology in support of teaching and learning. As each new video technology replaced the last, over time equipment and video media were also slowly replaced in schools. Still, because funds for technology and media are always in short supply, you may find some older video technologies still available and still useful in educational settings.

Deciding how best to incorporate motion video in teaching and learning can be a challenge for educators. Too often, watching motion video is an inactive, even boring experience for the learner. The medium tends to be passive and therefore can be unengaging. Because the experience is too often limited to viewing without participation, focus is easily lost. This is the challenge of motion video.

Early movies and then television were the first major forms of motion video to affect classrooms significantly. Following these, a new method for capturing video, videotape (initially reel-to-reel, later in a cassette, and now in DVD), changed the way video was recorded and played back. Easy-to-use and compact video cameras that stored images on videocassettes

Analog video camcorders are giving way to digital video cameras.

VCR and MONITOR

CAMCORDER

DVD PLAYER

Video technologies have evolved, but many older technologies can still be found in schools.

Discovering Digital Video

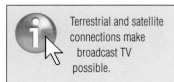

Terrestrial and satellite connections make broadcast TV possible.

opened new opportunities to capture sound and motion. Although many older video technologies can be found in schools, most have given way to digital video technologies that have emerged more recently.

Like older types of video, digital video technologies record and play back data, but the format in which the data are recorded also allows for full manipulation and editing. The recorded videos can be as easily manipulated in terms of images and sound as a word-processing document can be manipulated in terms of text. This capability opens up even more possibilities for the use of motion video in teaching and learning. Still, both traditional and digital video offer teachers a powerful tool in the classroom.

Traditional Video Technologies

Broadcast Video

Broadcast video is what is commonly thought of as television. Television images can be broadcast using **terrestrial** (land-based) equipment, or, for longer distances, a combination configuration of both terrestrial and satellite equipment is required. In **satellite transmission,** signals are sent to a satellite (**uplinked**) and then sent back down (**downlinked**) to a terrestrial system at another location on the globe (see Figure 9.6). The positioning of a string of such satellites around the globe allows television transmissions to be bounced by means of a series of uplinks and downlinks to positions anywhere on Earth.

Broadcast video can be in either a commercial format such as the programming broadcast by the major networks (such as ABC, NBC, and CBS) or an educational format such as programming on the **Public Broadcasting Service (PBS)** or a local learning channel. Public television, created by an

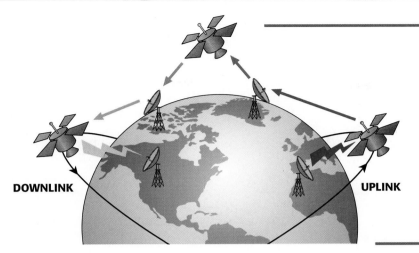

FIGURE 9.6

Television Uplinks and Downlinks

Television signals can be globally transmitted using terrestrial and satellite links. Signals are bounced across the globe via a system of satellites in geosynchronous orbit and dishes located strategically around the globe.

DOWNLINK

UPLINK

act of Congress expressly to provide high-quality educational programs, includes at its core the **Corporation for Public Broadcasting (CPB).** The CPB manages the acquisition and production of educational programming, and PBS disseminates the programming through local TV channels. Local learning channels, sometimes referred to as **instructional television (ITV),** use broadcast airwaves to distribute video signals of instructional programs throughout a school district that can also be viewed by anyone who tunes in to that channel. Video images sent by broadcast can be either live or prerecorded, depending on the nature of the program. Typically, both commercial and educational broadcast television programs have high-quality production values, making them quite expensive to produce but very entertaining to watch.

For educators, broadcast video offers high-impact, high-quality video production that can dramatically demonstrate content. In particular, the educational programming offered by local PBS stations can add a wide array of video support to instruction. News commentaries, documentaries, docudramas, plays, musical productions, and educational programs such as *Sesame Street* are typically available through public television stations. However, because broadcast video is synchronous (real-time) in delivery, it is often difficult to use in a classroom setting. The time a program is broadcast might be inconsistent with scheduled lessons unless video recording technology is used to capture it for more convenient playback.

Narrowcast Video

The alternative to broadcast video is a video transmission format that targets educational audiences. This type of video transmission is sometimes referred to as **narrowcast video.** Types of narrowcast transmissions are summarized in Figure 9.7.

Narrowcast video includes systems of video transmission that is sent to a specific audience. The most common system for this type of transmission is the **Instructional Television Fixed Service (ITFS).** ITFS is a terrestrial system that sends signals via microwave transmission from studios and ITFS broadcast locations to reception locations (usually schools) within a fixed area. Microwave signals require that the sender and receiver be

Instructional Television Fixed Service broadcasts to a specific, limited audience.

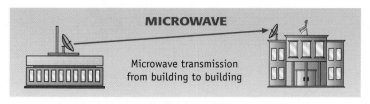

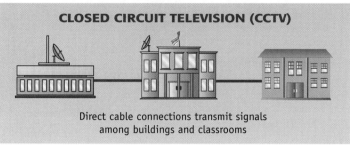

FIGURE 9.7

Narrowcast Systems

Narrowcast systems provide video to local areas.

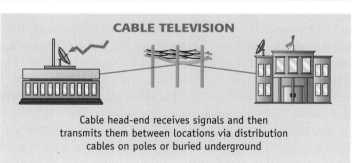

located in a line-of-sight formation. This means that the receiving equipment must have a direct and unobstructed "view" of the microwave tower that is transmitting the signal. This can be a drawback in some physical locations, but for many school districts, ITFS is a relatively inexpensive method of setting up a broadcast system. ITFS creates a dedicated video network for instructional programs that can be offered multiple times throughout the day to accommodate school schedules. Furthermore, programming can be designed to meet specific local instructional needs. This dedicated television network, if available in your school, can provide valuable districtwide instructional video resources.

Once an ITFS signal is received by a school, it is typically distributed to all classrooms by using a **closed-circuit TV (CCTV)** system. A CCTV system is a network of television monitors connected by coaxial cables running throughout a school building that can distribute television signals to all the connected classrooms. Thus, once an ITV or ITFS transmission is received at one central point in a school, it can be distributed via CCTV to all connected classrooms within the school. As with other forms of broadcast TV, there may be some difficulty arranging instruction around transmission times; but ITFS programming is much more often arranged to accommodate school schedules. Additionally, ITFS programming can be recorded and distributed through CCTV or videocassette distribution for later replay in classrooms.

The school's CCTV system is also often used for other narrowcast transmissions. In-school TV production classes typically create video programs of daily announcements and school information. These in-school "morning shows" use the CCTV system to reach all classrooms.

Cablecast Video

The same coaxial cables that connect classrooms to an ITFS receiver location or a CCTV system together can also transmit cable television stations; this is often called **cablecast video.** Schools that are hooked to their local cable TV company are able to use their classroom television monitors to tune in to cable channels just as you use your home television to tune in to cable channels there. The types of programming that are available to schools through their local cable companies range from standard commercial and educational television to premium stations supplied free to schools by the cable companies. Arrangements vary widely with each local area, but if cablecast video is available at your school, you would do well to explore the instructional possibilities it presents. Many high-quality cable stations, including the Cable News Network (CNN) and the Discovery Channel, offer instructional programming that can enhance your instruction.

Recorded Video Technologies

To overcome the scheduling problems inherent in broadcast, narrowcast, and cablecast systems in schools, recorded video has become the traditional video format of choice. **Videocassette recorders (VCRs)** can record video as it is transmitted, and the recording can be used for later playback. VCRs use a magnetic **VHS format tape** for recording moving images. VHS tapes are relatively inexpensive and can contain up to 120 minutes of recording at the standard playing speed or up to six or eight hours at slower speeds. Prerecorded tapes of movies can be purchased or rented, or you can tape a broadcast television program for later viewing. VHS tapes and their playback technology, the VCR, have replaced movie projectors in schools. They are compact, durable, inexpensive, and easy to use. Furthermore, teacher control over the screening of the video allows you to stop the tape at appropriate moments for clarification and discussion.

Videocassette recorders and monitors are available for use in most classrooms. They are usually either permanently assigned to the classroom or available on a rolling cart for checkout through the school media center. Large monitors can make it easy for a large class to view the videotape. If a larger image is desired, the VCR can be connected to a digital projector to project the image onto a large screen or light-colored wall. A broad selection of videotapes is often a part of the media center's holdings or is available through a district media distribution system. Although methods of distribution vary by locality, this video technology can usually be counted on as a useful support for your instruction. It is often wise to begin the school year by visiting the media center to review the video library. As with movies, it is important to preview any tape you might choose and to carefully plan for its use in the curriculum.

The broad availability of VCRs and monitors has made another video application readily available to most teachers. Compact **video camera/ recorders,** called **camcorders,** record sound and images that can be played back by using a VCR. These relatively inexpensive and easy-to-use units

Your local school media center is usually your handiest source for videos.

Educational Videocassettes

in the Classroom

IN THE VIDEO PRODUCTION CLASSROOM

Frank Bluestein, executive producer and teacher at Germantown High School, Germantown, Tennessee, offers an elective class, "Wake Up, Germantown," the national award-winning television news production show planned and aired by his students. The community access station for Germantown, GHS-TV, Channel 17, is the vehicle for airing the programs produced by these students. Instead of the usual PA announcements every morning at the school, the news is aired "like a CNN news report on classroom TV monitors, which include local, national, and international news." The award given the production team, the National Student Television Award for Excellence, was given by the National Television Academy to GHS-TV for its coverage of sports.

Although the daily programs started at only five minutes, they are "seamless and sophisticated, with graphics and musical introductions" and have been expanded to 15 minutes for the daily morning program. The early morning regimen for the students and their faculty advisers goes like this: At 5:30 A.M., the students and faculty advisers beat the sun to school. Writers scan newspapers and wires for the top headlines, hammering out scripts at breakneck speed. The anchors put on their suits and make-up. The director formats the script. At a quarter-to-seven, they're rolling. There's time for one retake if something goes wrong.

If they flub that one, the news goes live. Bluestein said, "You'd be surprised how smoothly things go when we're live."

The versatility of the training the students receive is apparent when looking at the responsibilities Waheed AlQawasmi, 17, assumed. This year alone, he was the station's promotions director, designed the web site, and was technical director for "Wake Up, Germantown!" among a number of other extracurriculars—including winning an independent filmmaking award and being copresident of the school's Modern Film Club.

Eight students—anchorman Jake DeFur, Bobby Ramsay, Waheed Al Qawasmi, Adam Winfrey, Blake Brewer, Jeffrey Ingram, Anthony White, and Nathan Babian—were the recipients of the National Academy Award for their work on the sports broadcasts. The tape the students entered in the contest was a three-piece composite, featuring the rapid pace of live sports coverages: "A quick cutaway to a Hail Mary pass . . . Cut back to the anchor . . . Cut to final scores . . . Cut back to anchor, etc." Summing up the work they do, which has brought GHS-TV five regional awards in addition to the national award, AlQawasmi said, "Bobby [Ramsay] and I have to go take inventory of the lights in the theater. It's like a family here. Your life starts to depend on this place."

Blank, C. (2004, May 28). Good show: G'town High broadcasters win national honor. *The Commercial Appeal,* pp. E1, 4.

make it possible to capture video images of your students, field trips, or your own instruction for later playback. You or your students can use camcorders to capture images of athletic events or debates for immediate feedback and review; to record student reports, documentaries, or dramatizations; and even to create a video historical or cultural archive of the school or community. These small recording units make it possible to produce videos economically and easily to support teaching and learning.

Digital Video Technologies

Traditional analog video accurately captures and displays high-quality sound and images. However, this video format is relatively inflexible. To edit or change taped analog images, cumbersome and somewhat expensive editing equipment is necessary. Additionally, to duplicate taped images, you need multiple interconnected video recorders and perhaps a signal amplifier to ensure that image quality is maintained. Clearly, for most educators, the processes and equipment necessary to edit or duplicate taped video require more time and resources than the product may be worth.

The same video images captured and stored in a digital format offer limitless editing possibilities. Video saved in a digital format, like other digital data, can be changed, edited, displayed, shared, or sent from one computer to another. Regardless of the technology used to capture and record it (including the conversion of analog video to digital), digital video provides a flexible and easy-to-alter format for video images. Digital video technologies offer a powerful teaching and learning resource that you can customize to support a specific lesson or to meet unique student needs.

Traditional video captures and plays back images and sound at approximately thirty frames per second. At this playback speed, the captured video looks just like real-time motion. To turn this true-to-life image into a digital form, each frame must be converted to its digital counterpart. The sequence of digitized frames, called a digital video clip, results in a very large file. In fact, a three-minute high-quality digital video clip can require as much as a gigabyte of storage space.

Because of the large file sizes resulting from digitized video, video **compression technologies** were developed. As you may recall from Chapters 7 and 8, video compression is often used to transmit digital video across the Internet. Compression software and hardware work by capturing the initial video image in full but then ignoring the nonchanging components of the image. Rather than redigitizing and storing every bit of every image, subsequent frames store only those bits that have changed since the last frame (see Figure 9.8). Thus, the total storage requirements for the video clip are reduced.

Several popular compression formats are used for digital video. Each format requires software that can decompress and play back the compressed file, but the software is readily available. Playback software either is included with the operating system of the computer or is available for download from the Internet. The most popular digital video compression formats are Audio Video Interleaved (**AVI**), Motion Picture Experts Group (**MPEG**), and QuickTime (**MOV**). Table 9.5 lists the advantages of each.

As compression technologies continue to advance, the large size of digital video files will become less and less significant. Each year, digital

E-Learning

www.mylabschool.com
Listen to Podcast
Cool Tools

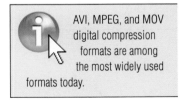

AVI, MPEG, and MOV digital compression formats are among the most widely used formats today.

TABLE 9.5 Digital Video Compression Formats

FORMAT	DESCRIPTION	ADVANTAGES
AVI	Audio Video Interleaved	Lower resolution, smaller video files; good for animation
MPEG	Motion Pictures Experts Group	Reduces video files up to 95 percent yet retains near television quality
MOV	QuickTime	Apple Computer's early nonbroadcast-quality format; easy to use and create

A *reference frame* is captured video that contains background and foreground images.

Subsequent frames omit the static, nonchanging background and include only the parts of the foreground that are moving.

Video compression (smaller digital video files) is achieved because all parts of every video image are recorded only in the reference frame. Thereafter, only changed images are saved resulting in significantly less video data saved for subsequent frames. The result...compressed video files.

FIGURE 9.8
How Digital Video Compression Works
Digital video compression reduces overwhelming video file sizes.

E-Learning
ON THE WEB! 9.9
Digital Video Resources

DVDs offer large storage capacity.

FIGURE 9.9
Digital Video Discs for Teaching and Learning
Video discs offer advantages over videotape. DVDs can store video that can be directly accessed at any point in the video. Desired frames can then be played back as motion video or frame by frame.

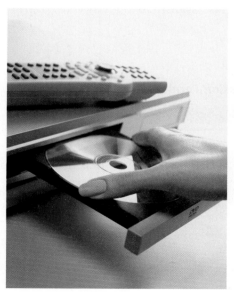

video technologies improve dramatically in their capacity and usability. Becoming familiar with the current digital video technologies is just a beginning.

DVDs

Although CDs offer excellent storage capacity, given the current sizes of compressed video files, even CDs cannot store a full movie. To remedy this storage limitation, a new storage technology was developed. The **digital video disc** (**DVD;** see Figure 9.9) can store 4.7 gigabytes of data on a standard disk and up to 10.5 gigabytes per side of a dual-layer DVD-ROM. This means that hours of full-motion, high-resolution video and sound can be stored in a durable and compact format. Furthermore, once stored, all of the data is directly accessible and easy to manipulate for display. For teachers, this means that you are able to access any segment of clear, high-quality video, frame by frame or in clips, simply by pressing the appropriate buttons. In the classroom, a digital video image can be instantly accessed, replayed, and discussed as a part of a lesson.

Additionally, DVD recorders offer the opportunity to record video digitally and save to a DVD for playback at a later time. This allows teachers expanded opportunity to capture video sequences for use in subsequent lessons. DVD recorders and playback units are quickly becoming the preferred video equipment for the classroom.

Digital Video Cameras

The most common option for creating digital video is to record it using a digital video camera (DVcam). **Digital video cameras,** like digital still cameras, capture and store the target images in a digital format that can then be downloaded to a personal computer. The resultant digital video files can then be manipulated, edited, and enhanced using **digital video editing** software.

The flexibility of digital video recording and editing has caused digital video cameras to largely replace analog camcorders. The many features included in even modest DV cams exceed the capabilities of previous camcorders, and their instant playback makes them popular favorites. These features include the ability to record digital images to mini DV tape for later transfer to a computer or for playback on a television; real-time editing and built-in special effects that can be recorded while taking the video; compatibility with popular digital video editing software; and the ability to record digital audio and still digital pictures as well as video. The compact size and ease of use have made DV cams popular, particularly as classroom tools in the hands of children. These features and many more have made digital video cameras the preferred choice for video.

Apple computers equipped with iMovie and iDVD software make a digital video camera in the classroom a powerful and simple-to-use tool for instruction.

Digital Video Editing

Once a digital video file has been recorded, it can be manipulated in a number of ways. However, just as you need word-processing software to edit a word-processed document, you need digital video software to edit video files.

E-Learning ON THE WEB! 9.10

Video Camcorders

iMovie courtesy of Apple Computer, Inc.

iDVD courtesy of Apple Computer, Inc.

Digital video editing software like iMovie lets you and your students create powerful instructional videos, while recording software like iDVD lets you store them in a convenient DVD format.

School TV production studios such as those that record the school's morning news might have specialized hardware for video editing. However, with the increased computing power of newer computers and the advent of desktop editing software, digital video editing is no longer confined to studios. For typical classroom or home use, video editing software that will run on a personal computer can easily be installed on the typical multimedia-capable computers that are available today. Such software allows you to select, edit, and manipulate digital video clips, add text, and even add special effects. Although not as powerful and capable as dedicated video editing hardware, this software can do a more than adequate job in customizing a digital video clip to meet your needs. For a teacher who is interested in creating and using digital video for teaching and learning, it can be a powerful software tool.

Compressed Video Teleconferencing Systems

All of the digital video explored thus far has been for use in a single classroom. It would seem possible to easily transmit digitized video from one classroom to the next, just as you might send a text file to be shared between classes. Although this is indeed possible, for full-motion, broadcast-quality video, there are currently some challenges. When you consider the size of compressed video and compare it to the bandwidth that is typically available for educational use, it is clear that transmission of compressed video has some specific requirements. For this reason, schools and districts that require the capability to transmit high-quality compressed video often invest in dedicated **compressed video teleconferencing systems.**

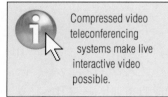

Compressed video teleconferencing systems make live interactive video possible.

Perhaps you have seen digital video displays that seemed choppy or fuzzy or had delayed movement. With a dedicated compressed video system, digitized video can be transmitted with image and sound as clear as broadcast video. These systems also allow you to record and display using traditional video technology.

Schools that are equipped with teleconferencing systems can bring live, fully interactive instruction from one location to the next or have distant guest speakers visit the classroom without having to travel (see Figure 9.10). The only requirement is to have the appropriate equipment at both locations. Such systems are particularly useful for distance learning, the subject of Chapter 10.

Internet Video

Digital video on the Internet has taken multiple forms. As compression software reduces file sizes, bandwidth increases, and computers become more powerful, new formats will continue to arise. Already, a number of Internet video formats offer great promise to education.

Internet Broadcasts

Many web sites are offering live **Internet broadcasts** of events and performances. These broadcasts use **streaming video** technology that compresses

E-Learning
ON THE WEB! 9.11
Internet Broadcasts

FIGURE 9.10
A Compressed Video Teleconferencing System
Compressed video systems create real-time digital communication networks.

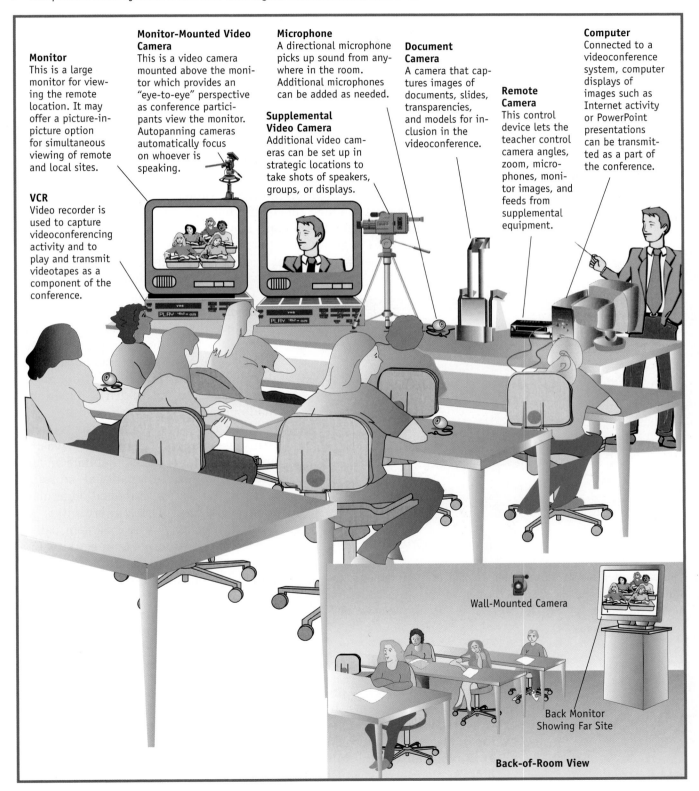

Monitor
This is a large monitor for viewing the remote location. It may offer a picture-in-picture option for simultaneous viewing of remote and local sites.

VCR
Video recorder is used to capture videoconferencing activity and to play and transmit videotapes as a component of the conference.

Monitor-Mounted Video Camera
This is a video camera mounted above the monitor which provides an "eye-to-eye" perspective as conference participants view the monitor. Autopanning cameras automatically focus on whoever is speaking.

Microphone
A directional microphone picks up sound from anywhere in the room. Additional microphones can be added as needed.

Supplemental Video Camera
Additional video cameras can be set up in strategic locations to take shots of speakers, groups, or displays.

Document Camera
A camera that captures images of documents, slides, transparencies, and models for inclusion in the videoconference.

Remote Camera
This control device lets the teacher control camera angles, zoom, microphones, monitor images, and feeds from supplemental equipment.

Computer
Connected to a videoconference system, computer displays of images such as Internet activity or PowerPoint presentations can be transmitted as a part of the conference.

Wall-Mounted Camera

Back Monitor Showing Far Site

Back-of-Room View

Streaming video makes motion video over the Internet practical.

and plays back digital video while it is being received. Streaming video requires that a player be installed on your computer. Such video players are typically available free for download on the Internet. Web sites that are sponsoring an event may add links to their sites that allow viewers to see and hear what the live audience sees. Others broadcast on the site alone, keeping the entire audience virtual. Internet broadcasts range from musical events to scientific events and from pop entertainment talk shows to interviews with archeologists who have just made dramatic new discoveries. The capability of sharing events and interviews without having to purchase costly television time has made Internet broadcasting an exciting opportunity for the education and entertainment industries.

Live Cams

Live Cams

An interesting application of Internet communication is the use of **live cams** (cameras) connected to the Internet. Live cams are cameras that are connected to a computer, which in turn is connected to the Internet. A live cam shares a digitized video image of whatever it is pointed at. For example, EarthCam (**www.earthcam.com**) is a gateway to a wide variety of live cams, such as the Penguin Cam at New York City's Central Park Zoo and the American Museum of Natural History's Butterfly Cam. By connecting to sites such as these, you can see live video images of whatever is in range of the camera. Because the camera is connected to an online computer, you can view the digital video feed by accessing the web site sharing the camera's images. You and your students can monitor the live behavior of wildlife, an extraordinary virtual field trip experience made possible by this technology.

Live cams are available for viewing many geographic regions, the weather around the globe, animal habitats on land and in the sea, international museums and historical sites, and even other classrooms globally. The opportunities are limited only by places a camera can be carried and by Internet connectivity. Live cam sites have increased rapidly and will no doubt continue to do so. The educational possibilities for this technology will increase with their proliferation into fascinating educational locations.

Live cams offer live streaming video feeds over the Internet so that students can view animals, science experiments, and locations from around the world.

SOURCE: Indianapolis Zoo.

Internet Meetings

Compressed video has produced another range of opportunities for educators and their students. **Internet meetings** are Internet-based "face-to-face" conversations with people around the world. With the addition of a monitor-top or classroom video camera and video compression software, individuals or groups can use the Internet to connect to each other and communicate live. As you learned in Chapter 7, several worldwide educational projects use meetings across the Internet to engage in collaborative projects. Compressed video transmitted across the Internet makes it possible for students around the world to work together and share educational experiences.

A recent addition to Internet meetings is the development of dedicated Internet meeting software such as Microsoft's NetMeeting. This type of software adds more capabilities to better simulate in-person meetings. For example, such software might add a virtual whiteboard that lets all Internet meeting participants collaborate in real time on a document or graphic, and a chat feature that lets them share notes that they key in as they meet. With the expansion of the capabilities of Internet meetings software and the increased bandwidth capacities in the future, net meetings are likely to become a logical alternative for collaboration.

For educators, such Internet meeting software can let classes around the globe meet together in a single virtual classroom to share ideas, experience instruction, and communicate with each other. For teachers who are willing to work with colleagues globally to set up and implement worldwide instructional experiences, Internet meetings can offer students a chance to see and interact with their peers around the world.

Internet meeting software like Microsoft's NetMeeting let you and your students communicate live with other classrooms anywhere in the world.

Microsoft NetMeeting® is a registered trademark of Microsoft Corporation.

Using Motion Video in Teaching and Learning

Whether you use traditional or digital video technology to support teaching and learning, the key to using motion video in instruction is to fully engage the learner in the sensory experience that motion video offers. Once you have established your instructional design and created your lesson plans, if motion video is the support technology of choice, you should carefully consider this specific medium and how it will be implemented to maximize its effectiveness. Your preview, evaluation, and appropriate implementation will help you to engage your learners in this potentially powerful technology.

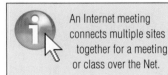

An Internet meeting connects multiple sites together for a meeting or class over the Net.

Slow-motion and time-lapse videos provide unique perspectives.

Using Video Media

Video offers some exceptional qualities that make it particularly useful in education. Video can appear to alter both time and space as it captures events. Video captured in real time can be played back in slow motion so that the eye can see events that occurred too fast to register through normal vision. Speeding up video playback (**time-lapse video**) may equally alter time for educational purposes. What might have taken days to occur can be viewed in the space of a few minutes. A time-lapse video of a seedling emerging from its shell and breaking through the soil into sunlight can offer students a science lesson that is not possible in the real world.

Of course, video has the potential to shift the viewers' location as well as the time frame they experience. Video travelogues, documentaries, and docudramas can seem to shift where viewers are located, from the classroom to the location they are viewing. Furthermore, regardless of the location, the viewing angle is always excellent and completely safe. Such location shifting is one of the key assets provided by videos in instruction.

To be sure, not all videos are of the same quality. Some offer breathtaking, well-narrated views of events, whereas others display little more than "talking heads." For this reason, before you use a video in support of your instructional design, it is critical that you preview and evaluate it. Any video that is used in support of your lesson plan should be thoroughly previewed and evaluated to be sure it is appropriate to the content and of the quality necessary to engage the learners. Table 9.6 presents a rubric that you may find helpful in previewing and evaluating video media.

TABLE 9.6   Video Evaluation Rubric

VIDEO TITLE:

DESCRIPTION:

SUBJECT AREA APPLICABILITY:

LENGTH: **COST:**   **VENDOR:**

COMMENTS:

Using each of the following criteria, evaluate the effectiveness of the video for teaching and learning. For each dimension in the rubric, check the box that best reflects your opinion. Select videos that score 4 or higher in the most dimensions.

	EVALUATION CRITERIA				
DIMENSION	1 Poor	2 Below Average	3 Average	4 Above Average	5 Excellent
RELEVANCE TO CURRICULUM	Video does not address significant aspects of the curriculum; addresses few targeted objectives.	Video includes both relevant and irrelevant elements; minimum objectives are met.	Some video elements add to and clarify the curriculum concepts; others are extraneous; some objectives addressed.	Most video elements add to and clarify key curriculum concepts and address targeted objectives.	All aspects of the video significantly add to and/or clarify key curriculum concepts; meets objectives.
CURRENCY AND ACCURACY	Video is not current and has a significant number of factual inaccuracies.	Video is somewhat current in images and content; mostly accurate.	Video is current and accurate overall, but there is sufficient dated content to be distracting.	Video is mostly current and accurate; occasional images are dated, and some facts are less than accurate.	Video includes current images and presents accurate content.
ENGAGEMENT	Video components do not provide sufficient interest and variety to engage the learner.	Video includes a number of elements that are likely to negatively affect the learner's attention.	Some video elements are interesting, while others are lacking; somewhat motivating and engaging.	Most elements of the video are interesting and motivating; some elements may not keep the learner's interest.	Video is interesting and provides motivation; fully engages the learner's attention.
SUPPORT MATERIALS	No additional support materials are available with this video.	Few additional materials are available; those included are of average quality and provide limited support.	Some additional materials are available; quality of additional materials is good; some target key objectives.	Key materials of good quality are available to accompany the video; most are of high quality and target objectives.	Ample additional materials are of high quality, are easy to use, and target key objectives.
TECHNICAL QUALITY	Video has poor video and audio quality overall; production values are minimal.	The video is of moderate technical quality, ranging from poor elements to average production elements.	Aspects of the video range from average to good quality in terms of production.	Most aspects of the video are well done in terms of audio and video production.	All aspects of the video are excellent in terms of production quality.

This and other downloadable forms and templates can be found on the companion web site at www.ablongman.com/lever-duffy3e.

Creating Videos for Teaching and Learning

You may prefer to create your own instructional videos to precisely support the lesson you are teaching. Such teacher- or student-made videos may be necessary if appropriate support video is not commercially available or if a lesson calls for students to capture images and record them themselves.

Today's camcorders, whether traditional or digital in format, offer a relatively easy-to-use technology even for those who have never used a video camera before. In fact, creating a video is more complex in the planning stages than in the recording stage. Video production requires careful consideration of the images and sounds that will be captured.

Once you have planned your video and storyboarded its content, then you are ready to record. One note of caution should be sounded with reference to student- and teacher-made videos. Some parents prefer not to have their child videotaped. Some believe that it is a violation of their child's privacy, or they may have justifiable concerns about when and how their child's picture will be distributed. Whenever a student's image is to be captured on videotape, permission must be obtained from the student's parent or guardian before taping. When you decide to begin a video production project that contains images of students, it is best to precede it with a notification to parents of what the project entails and how the video images will be displayed. Additionally, many districts require that you obtain written permission from the parents of all the children who are participating in the taping (whether they appear in the video or not) to authorize your creating a videotape that includes the child. Taking the time to research your school's or district's requirements on videotaping students and completing the necessary paperwork before taping are vital first steps whenever you plan classroom video productions that will include your students' images.

E-Learning ON THE WEB! 9.13
Classroom Video Production

Parental permission is required before including children in videos.

Implementing Video in Instruction

Because video tends to be a passive experience and we know that the more engaged the learner is, the more effective learning will be, it is important to take steps to ensure that viewing the video will be a compelling experience. To begin, even though it might have been previewed, the video should be tested in the environment in which it will be shown. Sound volume and quality should be tested, seating should be arranged appropriately, and lighting should be adjusted to avoid a washed-out image. Addressing these initial environmental variables before students arrive will reduce potential disruptions and distractions once the instructional event has begun.

The next, and perhaps most important, challenge is to fully involve the learner. It is a good idea to prepare your students for viewing by reviewing the concepts the video presents and discussing the objectives of the video and the key ideas it will present. Then, even though you have prepared your learners, it might be necessary to keep them engaged throughout the video screening. To create a more active video viewing experience, it is a good idea to provide a **video study guide.** Such a study guide may accompany commercial videos or could be created by you as you preview the video. For younger children or those with special needs, you might even choose to pause the video periodically to give learners time to respond orally or in writing. Video study guides can add significantly to the learning

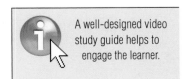

A well-designed video study guide helps to engage the learner.

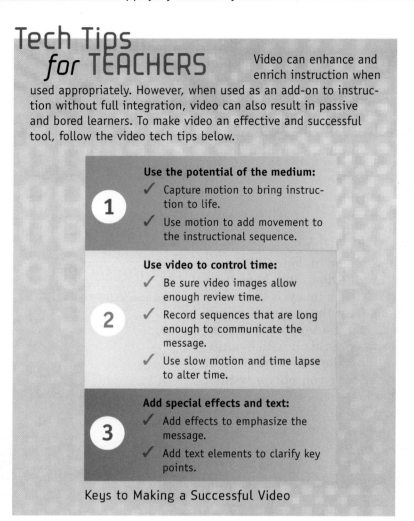

Tech Tips
for TEACHERS

Video can enhance and enrich instruction when used appropriately. However, when used as an add-on to instruction without full integration, video can also result in passive and bored learners. To make video an effective and successful tool, follow the video tech tips below.

1

Use the potential of the medium:
- ✓ Capture motion to bring instruction to life.
- ✓ Use motion to add movement to the instructional sequence.

2

Use video to control time:
- ✓ Be sure video images allow enough review time.
- ✓ Record sequences that are long enough to communicate the message.
- ✓ Use slow motion and time lapse to alter time.

3

Add special effects and text:
- ✓ Add effects to emphasize the message.
- ✓ Add text elements to clarify key points.

Keys to Making a Successful Video

experience by helping to build connections to prior knowledge, focusing attention, and reinforcing learning.

Other methods for engaging the learners in videos are to structure a discussion group after the video or at key stopping points during the video, to have students complete a kinesthetic project based on the video, or to create a sequel to the video they just watched. The possibilities are limited only by your own creativity. The key is to develop, as a component of video-enhanced instruction, some way to fully engage the learners in the concepts being presented by the video they are viewing.

The indispensability of video as an instructional tool is unarguable, but it requires a committment to its responsible use. As an educator, you are responsible for ensuring that the motion video you display is as appropriate for your students as it is in direct support of your lesson. Motion video can have significant emotional as well as factual content. As an adult, as you view a video, you are able to react to content and discriminate facts from emotion because of your maturity and experience. Your learners might not be able to do this. Some video may include content that is emotionally powerful or that offers ideas that may be in conflict with the student's personal beliefs. Your responsibility when screening videos includes anticipating potential student reactions to the emotional content of a video as well as to its instructional content.

A final consideration in using videos in instruction relates to the issues of fair use of copyrighted materials. Copyright issues are fully explored in Chapter 12 and introduced in the interchapter following this chapter. It is important to be aware of copyrights when using video in your classroom. Commercial video, like other media, is typically copyrighted. Fair use guidelines provide educators with a prescription for how copyrighted material may be used in an educational setting.

KEY TERMS

audiocassette 322
AVI 341
broadcast audio 323
broadcast video 336
bulletin board 331
cablecast video 339
camcorders 339
chalkboard 331
closed-circuit TV (CCTV) 338
compact disc (CD) 324
compressed video teleconference
  systems 344
compression technologies 341
Corporation for Public Broadcasting
  (CPB) 337
digital projector 333
digital video disc (DVD) 342
digital video cameras 343
digital video editing 343
diorama 330
document camera 334
downlinked 336

exhibit 330
flip chart 331
focused listening 319
graphics 331
hearing 319
instructional television (ITV) 337
Instructional Television Fixed Service
  (ITFS) 337
Internet audio 325
Internet broadcasts 344
Internet meetings 346
Internet radio 325
listening 318
live cams 346
model 330
MOV 341
MPEG 341
MP3 325
multimedia 350
multimedia kit 322
narrowcast video 337
oral history 322

oral journal 323
overhead projector 332
photograph 331
print material 330
Public Broadcasting Service (PBS) 336
real object 329
satellite transmission 336
streaming video 344
talking book 322
terrestrial 336
time-lapse video 347
transparencies 332
uplinked 336
VHS format tape 339
video camera/recorders 339
video study guide 349
videocassette recorders (VCRs) 339
visual 328
visual literacy 328
WAV files 325
whiteboard 331

STUDENT ACTIVITIES

CHAPTER REVIEW

1. Compare the four types of video found in schools.
2. What are the advantages and disadvantages of each of the following audio technologies in teaching and learning: Audiocassettes? Broadcast audio? Optical media? Internet audio?
3. What is visual literacy? Where and when is it learned? Why is it important?
4. Name and describe three types of nonprojected media. Explain how each is important in teaching and learning.
5. Name the five most common technologies for nonprojected media display. How do they differ?
6. What are projected visuals? When compared to nonprojected visuals, when are they most appropriate in the classroom?

7. What is a digital projector? How is it used? How might a document camera be used with a digital projector to enhance learning in the classroom?
8. How has recorded video improved video's usefulness to education? Name and describe the media used to record video.
9. What is a compressed video system? How can it assist in communications across a school district?
10. Contrast Internet broadcasts, live cams, and Net meetings. How can each of these Internet-based video technologies be used in teaching and learning?
11. Why is it important to preview and evaluate videos? What tools should you use to be sure a video is communicating the intended message to your students?

WHAT DO YOU THINK?

1. There is much discussion today about the role of computers in the classroom, often to the point at which this technology overshadows all other instructional technologies, many of which are described in this chapter. What do you believe is the appropriate balance among the various technologies you have learned about thus far? Will digital technologies and computers indeed replace all others? What will your classroom be like twenty years from now in terms of the technologies you will be using?

2. Imagine that you have moved into a new classroom, and no audio or visual technology or media have yet been ordered. You have been asked to prepare a wish list of your audio and visual needs to submit to the media center. What will you order? Justify your requests by explaining how you would use each technology or medium in instruction.

3. Visual literacy and audio delivery are inherent components of instruction. What can you do to help build skills in visual literacy and in effective listening in the grade or content area in which you teach or wish to teach?

4. Student-made videos are an effective and interactive teaching and learning tool. However, there is concern over student privacy when the images of students are included on tape. Research this issue and talk to a local teacher or administrator to gain a better understanding of the issue. Then describe the key concerns and how a teacher might best address them when filming students.

5. The great advantage of video in teaching and learning is its ability to represent a shift in time and space. Explain what this means and how you might use it in teaching a unit of your choice.

LEARNING TOGETHER!

These activities are best done in groups of three to five.

1. Visit the media center of a local school and ask the media specialist to show you the audio and visual technologies that are available. Make a list of these technologies and ask the media specialist how each is most often used. Compare your media inventory and applications list with those of the other members of your group. Create a list of the media that are most often found in schools and their most popular teaching and learning applications. Be prepared to share your list with other groups.

2. Listening centers are popular individual and group activity centers in classrooms today. As a group, design a listening center for the grade level you would prefer to teach. Describe the technologies and media you would include in the listening center and explain how each would be used to support teaching and learning.

3. Create a fully articulated lesson plan with supporting nonprojected media that would be useful in teaching and learning. Be prepared to exhibit the media and present the lesson plan to other groups.

4. Each group member should locate five Internet live cams that could be useful for educators and create an annotated list of them. Summarize your lists, eliminate duplicates, and prepare a "Top Ten" live cam resource list to share with the class.

5. Interview five teachers who use traditional or digital video in their classrooms and ask each for tips on using video effectively. Create a list of the helpful hints that are gathered as a result of all interviews. Share the list with your classmates.

E-Learning

CHAPTER 9 Visual Organizer

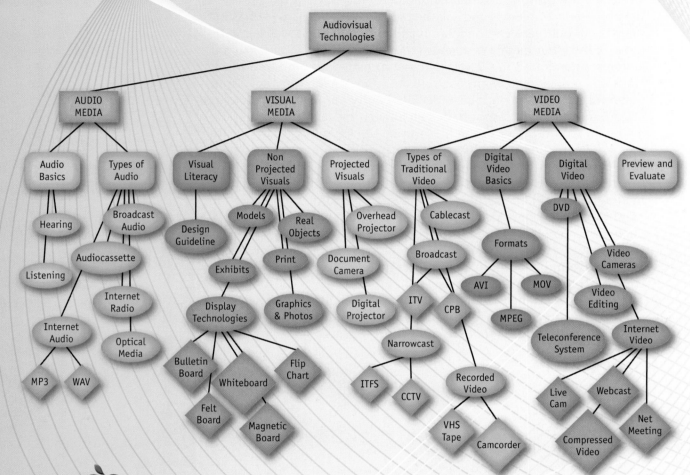

Audiovisual Technologies

- AUDIO MEDIA
  - Audio Basics
    - Hearing
    - Listening
    - Internet Audio
      - MP3
      - WAV
  - Types of Audio
    - Broadcast Audio
    - Audiocassette
      - Internet Radio
      - Optical Media

- VISUAL MEDIA
  - Visual Literacy
    - Design Guideline
  - Non Projected Visuals
    - Models
    - Real Objects
    - Print
    - Exhibits
    - Graphics & Photos
    - Display Technologies
      - Bulletin Board
      - Whiteboard
      - Felt Board
      - Magnetic Board
      - Flip Chart
  - Projected Visuals
    - Overhead Projector
    - Document Camera
    - Digital Projector

- VIDEO MEDIA
  - Types of Traditional Video
    - Cablecast
    - Broadcast
    - ITV
    - CPB
    - Narrowcast
    - AVI
    - MOV
    - MPEG
    - ITFS
    - CCTV
    - Recorded Video
    - VHS Tape
    - Camcorder
  - Digital Video Basics
    - DVD
    - Formats
    - Teleconference System
  - Digital Video
    - Video Cameras
    - Video Editing
    - Internet Video
      - Live Cam
      - Webcast
      - Compressed Video
      - Net Meeting
  - Preview and Evaluate

Podcasts www.mylabschool.com

Listen to a podcast relating to the use of administrative software in teaching and learning. Download the audio discussion to your iPod, computer, or MP3 player.

Video Lab www.mylabschool.com

Accessible through the **mylabschool** web site are several video vignettes that offer you a look at software in teaching and learning. Learning guides for all videos can be found in the text's Learning Guide Supplement.

On the Web! Activities www.ablongman.com/lever-duffy3e

Noted in the margins of the chapter, these activities offer you in-depth experiences in the topics and content presented in the chapter.

Online Practice Test www.ablongman.com/lever-duffy3e

Practice tests offer you an opportunity to test your knowledge and then review the results and send them to your teacher.

Outliner www.ablongman.com/lever-duffy3e

Chapter Outliners are fill-in-the-blank outlines of the main ideas presented in the chapter. Download the outliner and fill it in for an effective chapter study guide.

Power Practices www.ablongman.com/lever-duffy3e

Power Practices are animated tutorials made using Microsoft's presentation software, PowerPoint. This flash card tutorial will help you practice key concepts in the chapter.

Puzzler www.ablongman.com/lever-duffy3e

Puzzlers include content in crossword, word search, and other puzzle formats to help you master chapter content.

Useful Links www.ablongman.com/lever-duffy3e

These links offer you suggestions for expanded online research in the topics presented in the chapter.

INTEGRATION *Ideas*

Audio and visual technologies continue to enhance teaching and learning just as they have since their introduction in the early 1900s. Whether leading edge digital technologies or the more traditional versions, media that provide a multisensory experience for learners will never lose their place in the classroom. Below are a few examples of the integration of audiovisual technologies in content areas. More can be found on the text web site at **www.ablongman.com/lever-duffy3e.**

Integrating Audiovisual Technologies into Social Studies

"American Rhetoric: Top 100 Speeches" is described as giving social studies teachers "a chance to make history come alive for their students. This web site is an audio database with full text of these speeches, which cover great oratory from as early as Clarence Darrow and William Jennings Bryan up to the present day. The audio is MP3 Stream and Real Audio Stream. The site's URL is **www.americanrhetoric.com/top100speechesall.html** and is updated regularly (2006, June 30).

American rhetoric: Top 100 speeches. **www.techlearning.com/shared/printableArticle.jhtml?articleID=21100263.**

Integrating Audiovisual Technologies into Language Arts

Glenn English, formerly a reading teacher at Hubbard Elementary School in Hubbard, Texas, found a surefire way to interest his fifth graders in reading—videotape them as they read selections in front of the class. Video editing was the next step. He now heads the Tech Team at Hubbard Middle School, where the middle school students have produced a promotional video for the school and a travel series, which consists of "video brochure-style commercials." Mr. English is convinced that "Nothing else can teach students the essence of storytelling as powerfully as video."

English, G. (2006, February 1). Adventures in video storytelling, **www.techlearning.com/story/showArticle.jhtml?articleID=175804117.**

Integrating Audiovisual Technologies into the Sciences

Learning about forces of nature takes on an added dimension for fourth-grade students at the Learning Center Lab, Tremont Grade School, Tremont, Illinois. The "Tech & Text" research project the school is working on has four groups of students, each assigned a historical natural disaster. The students view "film and photographic archives on each of these events.

The students learn about primary sources, and source material obtained from the Internet is viewed critically to determine its reliability. Taking what they have learned researching, students role-play a mock panel of 'distinguished guests' commenting on the disaster. These different perspectives provide for even more understanding of the event and its impact on people, communities, and even our nation as a whole." Citation of sources, both traditional and electronic, is taught.

Bishop, S. (2006, May 1). Tech & Text Teaching Techniques. **www.techlearning.com/shared/printableArticle.jhtml?articleID=185303854.**

Integrating Audiovisual Technologies into Math

Watching VideoStream or listening to RealAudio Interview of the Rovers on Mars while learning calculus is definitely twenty-first century. Steve Crandall, mathematics and physical science teacher at Park City High School, Park City, Utah, uses Spirit and Opportunity, the Mars rovers, for mathematics lessons, as well as objectives for science lessons. The students listen to the RealAudio and watch the VideoStream from the Online NewsHour, January 26, 2004. In Lesson One, two overall questions are asked regarding the transmission times. Then they answer "Online Investigation Questions."

Crandall, S. Rovers on Mars. **www.pbs.org/newshour/extra/teachers/lessonplans/science/marsrovers_4-15.html.**

For these and many more Integration Ideas for using the Internet in teaching and learning visit the text web site at **www.ablongman.com/lever-duffy3e.**

Copyright

Copyright refers to the laws that protect the interests of those who own creative works, whether text, music, artwork, software, or any other creative product. Under U.S. copyright law, the copyright owner is granted exclusive rights to the product and to the financial gain resulting from the product that he or she creates, owns, or distributes for a specified length of time. Others cannot copy the product without the copyright owner's permission. Violation of the copyright owner's rights can lead to legal action.

Whether you copy pages from a text, music from a CD, or multimedia clips from the Internet, you may be in violation of the copyright laws. Someone put time, energy, and creative talent into the product and has the complete right to decide how it is to be used and to profit from his or her work. Copying data that you did not create, or allowing your students to do so, and then using that data in your lessons or class publications may place you, your school, and your district in a position to be sued by the owner of the data. Technology makes it easy to copy from a variety of digital sources, but such action may be as illegal as it is convenient. Whether the data is text, music, art, video, or audio files, the rights of the copyright owner must be observed.

It is generally accepted that any material placed on the Internet is automatically copyrighted even if a copyright notice does not appear on the site. Most publications include clear copyright notices within them, as indicated by the inclusion of a copyright symbol (©). Even if you do not notice any copyright indicators at all, however, as a prudent educator, you must assume that unless express permission to use materials you find freely is stated clearly on those materials, they are the property of their creator and cannot be used without permission.

Fair Use Guidelines

So how can teachers use a clever graphic, a map, or an educational photograph to enhance instruction if these elements are clearly or implicitly copyrighted? The answer is found in a special section of the copyright laws that is called "fair use." The fair use section (Section 107) of the law identifies four criteria under which you may be allowed to copy another's creative work. This section has enabled educators and students to temporarily use copyrighted materials if they meet the stated criteria. The fair use section has been interpreted for educators through a series of guidelines that have attempted to clarify it. In 1976, the first set of guidelines, the Agreement on Guidelines for Classroom Copying in Not-For-Profit Educational Institutions with Respect to Books and Periodicals, offered educators more specific information as to making copies for class handouts and other instructional materials. For example, students may use small portions of copyrighted works in academic projects if they properly credit and cite the owner of the work. Teachers may use reproductions of a copyrighted work in face-to-face classrooms as long as such reproductions are for only one course in the school and they will not be used over a long term. It is your responsibility to be familiar with these guidelines when you select and use copyrighted materials.

The situation became even more complex as technology advanced. As educational technologies came to include not only print but also audio, film, multimedia, and digital technologies, fair use guidelines began to be developed to address these new media as well. Debate over guidelines expanded and became more intense throughout the 1990s with many efforts made to establish voluntary guidelines for fair use. These debates led to the establishment of the Conference on Fair Use (CONFU) in 1994. After four years of effort, CONFU's final report in 1998 recommended guidelines for educators in the fair use of a variety of media (**www.uspto.gov/web/offices/dcom/olia/confu/**). While not a legal document, these guidelines offered educators a consensus view of the application of fair use.

These guidelines help teachers to determine if their actions and those of their students fall within the framework of fair use. For example, you may ask your class to create a project web site. During this project your students may wish to use a popular song as background audio for their home page. Or, you may want to copy several pictures of African animals from a virtual museum you found on the Web to add to a PowerPoint presentation to support your lesson. Can you and your students borrow these sound clips and images for your classroom activities? According to the guidelines, the answer is no unless the use of the audio and images falls within the guidelines limits for use of an audio and images. These limits suggest that only 10 percent of the musical composition, but not more than 30 seconds can be used. Further, once copied, the clip cannot contain any alterations that change the basic melody or character of the work. As to your desire to use pictures from a virtual museum, if the museum is displaying a single artist's work, guidelines mandate that you cannot use more than five images without violating fair use. However, if the museum is displaying a collection of assorted artists, you can use no more than 10 percent of that collection or no more than fifteen images, whichever is less.

As you can see, the Fair Use Guidelines are very specific and can be somewhat complex. Table I9.1 summarizes some of the areas of the guidelines of frequent concern to classroom teachers. It should be noted that, as copyright laws are tested in the courts and as educators and legal experts continue to explore the limits of fair use, these guidelines may change. As a professional, you have a responsibility to be aware of and adhere to the guidelines set forth by your school or district when you or your students use copyrighted works. It will be your responsibility to seek out your school's or district's copyright guidelines in order to be sure you follow them. In many schools, the media specialist will be your logical first source when seeking to discover the guidelines you need to follow. Or your school administrator may be the most knowledgeable person in that area. Regardless of whom you have to seek out to find the copyright guidelines for your school, it is your responsibility to do so before including copyrighted material in your classroom. In the area of copyrights, ignorance of the law will prove to be no excuse should your actions cause you or your school system to be sued for violation of copyright.

TABLE I9.1 Fair Use

AREAS OF USE	SAMPLE GUIDELINES FOR FAIR USE OF MULTIMEDIA
STUDENTS	Students can incorporate copyrighted work into their own multimedia creations when it is part of an academic assignment as long as the time, copies, and portion limitations (below) are met.
TEACHERS	Faculty can incorporate others' work into multimedia to create multimedia curriculum and to demonstrate that curriculum at professional symposia as long as the time, copies, and portion limitations (below) are met.
	LIMITATIONS
TIME	The time limit for fair use of others' multimedia work is two years after the first instructional use.
COPIES	Only a limited number of copies, including the original, may be made of an educator's educational multimedia project. There may be no more than two use copies, only one of which may be placed on reserve. An additional copy may be made for preservation purposes but may be used or copied only to replace a use copy that has been lost, stolen, or damaged.
PORTION	For copyright-protected works, you can use ● Up to 10 percent or three minutes, whichever is less, for motion media ● Up to 10 percent or 1,000 words, whichever is less, for text ● Up to 10 percent, but in no event more than 30 seconds, for audio ● No more than five images by an artist or photographer or, if collected works, no more than 10 percent or fifteen images, whichever is less ● Up to 10 percent or 2,500 fields or cell entries, whichever is less, of the numerical data sets

SOURCE: Adapted from CCMC guidelines as summarized in Georgia Harper's University of Texas System crash course in copyright; Retrieved from **www.utsystem.edu/ogc/intellectualproperty/ccmcguid.htm#3** February 2004.
These guidelines do not include adjustments for changes resulting from the TEACH Act.

The TEACH Act

Before 2002, fair use guidelines applied primarily to traditional classroom instruction. Under these guidelines, educators enjoyed a fairly liberal right to use copyrighted works. However, that was not the case if the work was to be broadcast. Use of copyright-protected works was much more restricted if the work was to be shared electronically. This caused inconsistencies in the educational use of materials through traditional versus computer-mediated instruction or distance education. As a result, in 2002, the Technology, Education, and Copyright Harmonization (TEACH) Act was passed to begin to resolve these inconsistencies. The TEACH Act provides for expansion of the range of works allowed, the number of locations receiving the works, and the right to digitize works from other formats provided they meet the act's very specific requirements.

Although the terms for use of copyright-protected materials under the TEACH Act are not quite as liberal under fair use as they are for traditional instruction, this act did begin to resolve some of the issues associated with applying copyright law and fair use to education in the digital age.

Some Final Thoughts on Copyright

As you can see from the above, much controversy has surrounded fair use and many guidelines have been created to help teachers better interpret and apply its principles. While not a legal discussion or interpretation of these complex issues, this interchapter should raise your awareness of the issues and concerns associated with using copyrighted materials when you teach.

When dealing with copyright-protected works, perhaps a safer, although more time-consuming, solution is to simply ask the owner of a copyright for permission to use the image, product, or text. Very often, when the use is for educational purposes, the owner is willing to grant permission. Although it is not necessary to write for permission if the educational use clearly conforms with the guidelines provided by your school district, it may be a good idea to take steps to obtain permission if there is any doubt. Writing for permission requires that you compose a letter on school letterhead that requests permission to use the work in question. You would need to include information as to when you would use the work, how often, how you would use it, and why. It is best to include an example of how the work will be incorporated. Permission, once requested, must be received from the copyright holder before using the work. Be sure to give your school administrator a copy of the letter granting you permission as well. You should keep your permissions letter filed and available for as long as you use the copyrighted work.

As educators, it is important to model the behaviors expected of our students. Ignoring copyright laws or taking them lightly when it is convenient sets a bad example for students and suggests to them that it is acceptable to occasionally ignore or break the law. This is an unfortunate precedent to set, and it is an unprofessional and illegal activity to engage in, one for which you and your school may pay serious consequences. Teaching students about the copyright laws, on the other hand, is an opportunity to instill the values of the legal system and respect for others' property. Demonstrating adherence to and enforcement of copyright laws in your classroom can be a lasting and meaningful lesson for your students, and it remains a legal and professional responsibility for you.

For more information, the following resources are suggested:

- U.S. Copyright Office
  www.copyright.gov/
- Copyright Clearance Center
  www.copyright.com/
- Crash Course in Copyright
  **www.utsystem/edu/ogc/intellectualproperty/
  cprtidx.htm**
- American Library Association—the TEACH Act
  **www.ala.org/Template.dfm?Section=Distance_Education_and_the_TEACH_Act&Template=/
  Contentmanagement/ContentDisplay.cfm&ContentID=25939**

PART THREE

Technology in Schools: Changing Teaching and Learning

Thus far, you have explored the teaching and learning process, examined how effective instruction can be designed and planned, and investigated the many technologies that can be used in support of instruction. Now it is time to take a look at how technology is changing education in today's schools and in the schools of the future.

We begin by looking at how technology helps creative teachers reinvent their classrooms. Just as you go into your classroom each year and arrange it to provide the best possible space for teaching and learning, so too you will use technology to create new spaces, even virtual ones, in which teaching and learning can occur. Some of these technology-enhanced instructional environments make it possible for the teacher and student to be at a physical distance from each other yet still allow for the teaching and learning process to occur. This type of instruction is often called distance education or distance delivery of education. These environments add a new dimension to the more traditional teaching and learning methodologies and are sometimes referred to as the alternative delivery of instruction.

This part begins with an exploration of both distance and alternative learning and how they are implemented in today's schools. Chapter 10 will help you understand the transformations that creative application of technology in education make possible. Chapter 11 will take you further into the transformation we are experiencing as technology is implemented in schools. You will explore the process through which technology is implemented and inquire into the social, ethical, and legal issues associated with the implementation of technology. Finally, Chapter 12 will investigate how technology is likely to change in the next decade and how those changes will further transform the schools in which you will be teaching.

The three chapters in Part Three will help you to see the important role you will play as our schools continue to evolve to better serve our society. As educators, we will continue to have the goal of helping our students prepare for the world in which they will work and live. That world, rich in technology and altered integrally by its existence, will make for a fascinating and exciting learning environment.

chapter 10

Distance Education: Using Technology to Redefine the Classroom

This chapter addresses these ISTE *National Educational Technology Standards* for Teachers:

I. TECHNOLOGY OPERATIONS AND CONCEPTS

Teachers demonstrate a sound understanding of technology operations and concepts. Teachers

A. demonstrate introductory knowledge, skills, and understanding of concepts related to technology (as described in the ISTE *National Education Technology Standards* for Students).

B. demonstrate continual growth in technology knowledge and skills to stay abreast of current and emerging technologies.

II. PLANNING AND DESIGNING LEARNING ENVIRONMENTS AND EXPERIENCES

Teachers plan and design effective learning environments and experiences supported by technology. Teachers

A. design developmentally appropriate learning opportunities that apply technology-enhanced instructional strategies to support the diverse needs of learners.

B. apply current research on teaching and learning with technology when planning learning environments and experiences.

C. identify and locate technology resources and evaluate them for accuracy and suitability.

D. plan for the management of technology resources within the context of learning activities.

E. plan strategies to manage student learning in a technology-enhanced environment.

III. TEACHING, LEARNING, AND THE CURRICULUM

Teachers implement curriculum plans that include methods and strategies for applying technology to maximize student learning. Teachers

A. facilitate technology-enhanced experiences that address content standards and student technology standards.

B. use technology to support learner-centered strategies that address the diverse needs of students.

C. apply technology to develop students' higher-order skills and creativity.

D. manage student learning activities in a technology-enhanced environment.

V. PRODUCTIVITY AND PROFESSIONAL PRACTICE

Teachers use technology resources to enhance their productivity and professional practice. Teachers

A. use technology resources to engage in ongoing professional development and lifelong learning.

B. continually evaluate and reflect on professional practice to make informed decisions regarding the use of technology in support of student learning.

C. apply technology to increase productivity.

D. use technology to communicate and collaborate with peers, parents, and the larger community in order to nurture student learning.

In your educational technology course, you have learned much about teaching and learning, designing instruction, and selecting the appropriate technologies to support instructional events, but all from the point of view of using technology to enhance what some refer to as traditional modes of instruction. As educators across the nation expand the use of technology in teaching and learning, it is becoming evident that technology might well end up doing more than just enhancing instruction; it might prove to be a serious force in changing the nature and form of instruction.

Consider for a moment how one technology—the cell phone—has changed the nature of personal and business communication. Being out of touch with family or business has become a thing of the past. The need for pay phones has been so significantly reduced that their numbers are steadily decreasing. Just think for a moment of the scene in one of our nation's major airports. Banks of pay phones once lined the walls in gate areas. Now passengers use their own cell phones to make local and long-distance calls. In this scene, we can see for ourselves the decline of one technology and the rise of another.

Like this cellular technology, educational technologies are essentially communication tools. As you have learned, teaching is, at its core, communication. It may, therefore, be reasonable to anticipate that advances in educational technologies will fundamentally alter the way in which we communicate educationally, just as such advances have already fundamentally changed personal and business communications. Some say we are at the threshold of just such a change. So far, the predominant mode of educational communication has been the traditional classroom format, that is, a teacher and a given number of students working together in a predefined instructional space. But we are now beginning to see technology broaden this concept. Indeed, implementation of current and emerging technologies may well redefine the classroom itself.

Such changes are already beginning to occur. You have no doubt noticed an abundance of college courses offered as *distance education* courses. Such courses may be delivered online or through various combinations of digital and other distance-delivery technologies. But have you ever explored exactly what these courses entail? Have you considered their implications in changing the way teaching and learning are defined? Have you thought about how these new delivery systems might affect you and your students? These considerations are the topic of this chapter. And although distance education implementations are at the moment most frequently found in higher education, the instructional innovations reflected by these new delivery systems are likely to have far-reaching repercussions throughout all levels of education. It is important to be aware of their potential impact on you, on your students, and on your professional career.

In Chapter 10, you will

- Explore distance and other technology-enhanced instructional delivery systems
- Examine the relationship and educational implications of traditional and alternative delivery systems
- Review the role various technologies play in the alternative delivery of instruction
- Explore the application of and issues associated with alternative delivery systems in teaching and learning
- Examine the role of the Internet in alternative delivery
- Explore ways to evaluate distance and alternative delivery systems

Real People
Real Stories

Meet Darlene Haught. Delivering curriculum from a distance, whether synchronously via two-way audio/video television, or online asynchronously via the Internet, requires innovative strategies that not only grab the attention of the students but also allow the students to break through the barriers to communication. Let's see how Darlene Haught handled this problem.

My name is Darlene Haught. I am the Dean of Distance Learning Technologies, and I work closely with the North Carolina School of Science and Mathematics (NCSSM) staff and faculty, as well as with those around the state, to coordinate the development and delivery of instructional programs that serve its outreach mission. NCSSM is located in Durham, North Carolina. It has a dual mission to provide a rigorous education to the 615 students who residentially attend the school, and equally important is its mandated mission to provide educational opportunities to students and educators throughout the state.

North Carolina is a state of 119 school districts, 42 percent of which are in rural settings. Getting upper-level curriculum to much of the state is a critical need. NCSSM created a Distance Learning Department to meet its mission and address this need. Since 1995, this department has provided curriculum via interactive videoconferencing (IVC), and more recently it is developing and delivering online curriculum. The need for this to be highly interactive and engaging is critical in the K–12 environment.

Being the major provider of IVC K–12 curriculum statewide, we have much experience in using multimedia and cutting-edge technologies to bridge the distance to the students, get and retain their attention, and foster their active participation. Additionally, with the emergence of asynchronous delivery, we frequently use these technologies to make our online courses equally engaging and interactive.

The NCSSM distance learning staff works closely with the instructional staff to use audiovisual technology effectively. In distance learning, this means more than simply pointing a video camera at a "talking head."

Our computer graphics illustrators will take a concept described by the instructor and develop a custom graphic image or animation to support or illustrate it. Other graphics support includes web graphics and HTML authoring that enhance instructors' web sites and courses. Diagrams, charts, maps, scanned images, and logos are developed frequently for printed materials to support courses, professional development workshops, and the like.

A high-end nonlinear video editing system gives us the capability to produce video segments and demonstrations for instructors to use. Instructors can prepare and present a host of videos, such as sophisticated science experiments, field observations, or mathematical problem solving. The capability to produce streaming media from video supports online courses; in addition, we stream and archive all IVC classes for students to access for review outside of class.

Four studios serve as the IVC distance learning instructor's "classroom." A computer is the hub providing access to the Internet and the school's network, as well as to specialized and application software. Classroom management software, such as Blackboard or Moodle, is used to electronically convey and collect assignments and communicate with students. A graphics tablet connected to the computer allows the teacher to write and draw diagrams with an "electronic" blackboard on the TV screen, just as if it were a blackboard on a classroom wall. The "flexcam," a small color video camera mounted on a jointed flexible arm, allows an instructor to show images from a textbook, zoom in on a science

demonstration, or display three-dimensional objects for the class. Students can use one to show homework or work out a problem visually for the rest of the class. One tool most enjoyed by students is the chromakey. This is the same technology that is used by TV stations when they put the weatherman in front of a map. This visual technology uses a "green screen" onto which an image is overlaid and then combined with the image of the instructor.

The studio managers are encouraged to employ audio and visual techniques in the broadcast. For example, when slides are being displayed to the class, the studio manager will create a picture-in-picture, with the instructor's image in the corner of the screen. Maintaining visual contact with the teacher as much as possible facilitates keeping the student engaged. "POTS"—plain old telephone service—bridges communication among technical staff and privately between instructor and student. The fax machine is used to transmit tests or quizzes and assignments.

Calculators and CBL technology that are commonplace in high school math and science courses are not unique to distance learning, either. Data from the calculator's LCD display can be transmitted via IVC through a TI Presenter that connects directly to the calculator. CBLs are used to collect data through different types of probes with sensors. These are used most effectively in science and math distance learning classes.

In my job as the dean of this department, I encourage my staff to explore and implement new technologies that support our efforts. Distance learning protocols are changing, as well as the technologies associated with it. As we continue to move into more asynchronous online learning, we will continue to explore innovative and effective ways to use visual and audio technologies to keep the learner engaged in the learning process.

For more information and a virtual tour, please visit the distance learning web site at **www.dlt.ncssm.edu.** Please contact the writer at haught@ncssm.edu; phone: 919-416-2877.

 # What Do I Need to Know about Distance Education?

Most would agree that technology has had a significant impact on our society and our schools. Regardless of whether any given teacher makes use of technology in the classroom, because technology is changing our world, its impact will ultimately be felt in all social institutions, including schools. One of the most dramatic changes enabled by technology is the potential for alternative delivery of instruction that has been created through the adaptation of communications technologies to education. Businesses are already using communications technologies to conduct virtual meetings and to hold virtual training sessions for employees who are spread out across the nation or the world. Many schools and institutions of higher education have adopted this idea of moving information rather than people and have

Technology enables us to move information instead of people.

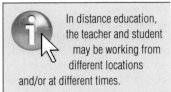

In distance education, the teacher and student may be working from different locations and/or at different times.

applied it to the delivery of instruction. Such technology-enhanced delivery approaches are typically referred to as **distance education.**

Distance education can be broadly defined as the delivery of instruction to students who are separated from their teacher by time and/or location. The teacher may be located at a school site, but the student may be "attending" the class at home, using technology to bridge the gap. Or both teacher and student may be at either the same or different locations but available to work on the course only at differing hours. Once again, technology serves as a bridge across this time gap. In such cases, instructional events and interactions occur just as they do in traditional settings, but their form may be radically different from that found in the traditional classroom. Consider the following possibilities.

If you were taking a college course in a distance education format, you probably wouldn't see your teacher on a regular basis, as you would if you were taking a class that met every Monday evening. From an instructional viewpoint, how could teaching and learning occur? For example, you might have a critical question that arose while you were reviewing your text or related assignment. How would you get clarification? How is a student's interaction with an instructor and among peers possible in such a situation?

In a distance education scenario, technology is the key to providing a format for academic communication and exchange. For example, a student might choose to email a question from his or her home computer to the teacher, asking for clarification or explanation. The student and the teacher are at different locations; the student is at home, and the instructor is at school. Or a student might choose to email a question at night when doing an assignment. The instructor might not respond to that question until the next morning. Thus, student and instructor are separated by time as well as distance. The student is engaged in the learning process at night, and the teacher is engaged in the teaching process in the morning. Still, with the help of technology, the student is able to communicate with the instructor and the instructor with the student. An instructional event has occurred. The student has asked a question, and the teacher has clarified and expanded on the content. Without the two parties being in the same location or even working in the same time frame, teaching and learning have occurred. This type of nontraditional interaction is at the core of distance education (see Figure 10.1).

Distance education was originally developed to deliver instruction to students in remote rural locations. For many years, distance education was accomplished primarily via correspondence courses or by sending an instructor out to remote locations to deliver instruction to groups of students. With the advent of technologies that make instructional delivery possible in ways never envisioned in previous years, distance education has come to have a much broader meaning. In fact, some educators have sought to broaden the term itself to better represent these new delivery systems. Thus, you will find terminology such as *distributed learning* or *virtual classrooms* used interchangeably with *distance education*. Regardless of the terminology, the idea behind them all is the delivery of instruction in nontraditional ways via technologies. Although the original term, *distance education*, remains dominant, it might not fully reflect the multitude of innovations and systems that make it possible for teachers and students to

Distance education technologies enable interaction among all participants.

Instructor interacts with students from any place and at any time.

THE INTERNET

Students interact with instructors from any place and at any time.

FIGURE 10.1
Distance Education Technologies Enable Communication

Distance education uses technology to connect teacher and learner across time and space.

connect instructionally. Still, for consistency and clarity, we will use this terminology throughout this chapter but ask you to think of it in its broadest possible meaning.

Distance education is likely to have a direct impact on you on at least two significant professional levels. First, because teacher licensing requires continual renewal, you may participate as a student in a distance-delivered course to remain current professionally, to pursue an advanced degree, or to renew your professional credentials. Distance delivery of instruction to educators means that you are no longer bound by the colleges in your immediate vicinity. Through distance delivery, you have the opportunity to enroll in courses offered by any organization or institution in the nation—or indeed the world. This gives you timely access to the latest developments in the field and provides you with the widest possible professional development options.

The second impact of distance education is more subtle, though perhaps more significant. Distance-delivery systems, especially those that emphasize delivery by the Internet, have become both more refined and more

E-Learning

www.mylabschool.com
video
View *Virtual School*

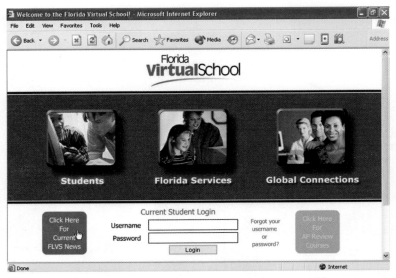

Many states have added online schools to their school systems to supplement those in traditional school districts.

SOURCE: State of Florida Virtual School.

robust. Advances in communication technologies and increases in available bandwidth are driving these continual improvements in distance-delivery systems. The instructional potential offered by these systems has, in turn, caused a rethinking of the nature of instruction. Which elements of the physical instructional environment must truly be fixed? Which ones can simply be redefined by using technology? Must a teacher and student be in the same physical space for teaching and learning to occur? The answers to these types of academic questions will ultimately affect every classroom. Instruction is already being redefined in many higher education environments, and this trend is now becoming evident in state and local school systems as well.

A number of states have created highly successful virtual high school programs that offer high school credit courses statewide. These programs expand the instructional opportunities for high school students across the state. Students are no longer limited to the courses that can be offered at the local high school they are assigned to attend. In some districts that have implemented distance education, low-enrollment courses that would not be offered in a single school may be offered by means of a distance-delivery system that can combine students from multiple schools into a single districtwide virtual classroom. Or instruction that is not otherwise available at a school, owing to a shortage of qualified teachers in a given content area, may be offered by a districtwide master teacher to all district schools through distance delivery. These innovative programs expand the concept of the traditional classroom. Such delivery models are likely to be just a forerunner of more dramatic changes to come. As a technologically literate professional educator, you need to have an awareness of distance education and its potential application for you and your students.

E-Learning

www.mylabschool.com
video
View *Options for Virtual Students*

Distance Education: A Brief History

As we noted earlier, the earliest distance-delivery systems were **correspondence courses,** consisting of books and assignments delivered to students via the postal system. As students did their readings and then completed assignments, they would mail their work back to the teacher. Tests were often given by local proctors, who mailed the completed exams to the teacher. Teaching was confined to the selection of books and the development of written learning activities. Learning was independent, with no interaction with peers and little interaction with the teacher. Of course, a student could mail a question to the instructor, but the time delay between question and response was critical, making meaningful exchange difficult.

As various other technologies were developed, they were added to enrich the correspondence course format (see Figure 10.2). The development of radio, and later television, resulted in instructional programming delivered via these two technologies. Distance students could listen to or watch a program featuring their teacher offering them direct instruction through audio and/or video. Distance students were also able to contact their instructor personally via telephone technology to ask a question or clarify

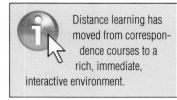
Distance learning has moved from correspondence courses to a rich, immediate, interactive environment.

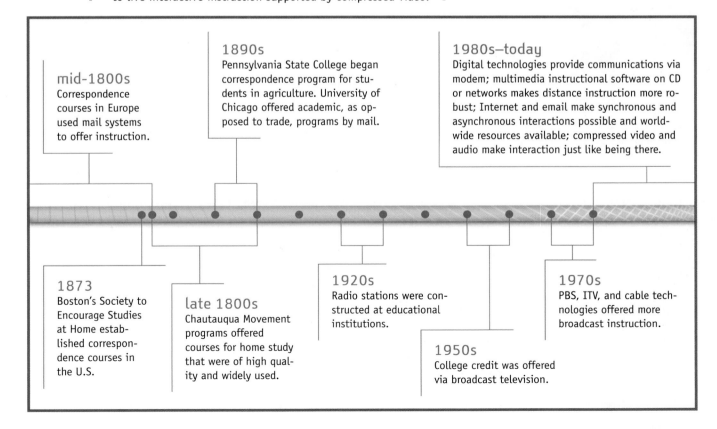

FIGURE 10.2
Distance Education Timeline
Distance education has evolved from correspondence courses to live interactive instruction supported by compressed video.

mid-1800s
Correspondence courses in Europe used mail systems to offer instruction.

1890s
Pennsylvania State College began correspondence program for students in agriculture. University of Chicago offered academic, as opposed to trade, programs by mail.

1980s–today
Digital technologies provide communications via modem; multimedia instructional software on CD or networks makes distance instruction more robust; Internet and email make synchronous and asynchronous interactions possible and worldwide resources available; compressed video and audio make interaction just like being there.

1873
Boston's Society to Encourage Studies at Home established correspondence courses in the U.S.

late 1800s
Chautauqua Movement programs offered courses for home study that were of high quality and widely used.

1920s
Radio stations were constructed at educational institutions.

1950s
College credit was offered via broadcast television.

1970s
PBS, ITV, and cable technologies offered more broadcast instruction.

content. Although these technologies did much to improve teacher-to-student communication when compared to a course delivered by the postal system, they did relatively little to enable student-to-student communication. Learners who were engaged in a distance course still missed the student discussion and interaction that can lead to a broadening of ideas. Learning still took place in relative isolation.

As other technologies emerged, a solution to learner isolation became possible. Phone bridges, a sophisticated telephone conferencing system, allowed a large group of students to dial in together and connect with each other and their teacher. Students could then interact and discuss content via the phone. Then, with the advent of the personal computer and later the Internet, live and time-delayed communication via modem became possible. Today, with the addition of streaming audio and video to distance-delivery technologies, live video and audio interaction between teacher and student or among students is a viable alternative.

Each of the technologies mentioned above will be discussed in more detail later in this chapter, but it is clear that the nature of distance education is changing and is coming to emulate more closely the interaction that occurs in the traditional classroom. The impact of distance delivery may

E-Learning
ON THE WEB! 10.1
Exploring Distance Education

in the Classroom

IN THE LEARNING ENRICHMENT CLASSROOM

Shirley Donovan, a learning enrichment teacher and advisor to the Technology Experienced and Creative Students (TECS) Club, helps the students who are members of the club at State College Area High School, State College, Pennsylvania, place high school courses online. While many schools are hard-pressed to find technologists who have the time to convert traditional classes to online delivery, State High has come up with a solution to the problem. How "the cyberschool project" began was "when Lu Xiao, a graduate student in Penn State's School of Information Sciences and Technology, approached the district about observing students working on technology projects," Shirley Donovan, learning enrichment teacher, said. Although the club has been in existence for some time, its focus on the cyberschool project began recently. Their first project, Health 9, was put online. The club has now moved on and has put English 12 online and recently English 15, a "suitcase curriculum class," a name that comes from it being a "curriculum the teacher can take to the students. The class is primarily taught to students in the district's Reclaiming Individual Talent program, an alternative education program for high school students," said John Sheridan, director of learning enrichment and student services.

Ben Pollard, a freshman, has been working on a quiz in his after-school time—"but in this case, he was typing in the questions, not just the answers." He commented, "It's fun to learn how these things work," while he gets "first-hand experience in providing education via the Internet." The students use Moodle, an open-source software program, and work in both a small lab at the school and in their homes. The thoroughness with which they approach their projects is seen in the testing to which they subject all the components of each course placed online, even "to see if they could hack into the system," Ms. Donovan reported. With the popularity of the online offerings evident in the number of courses lined up to be transformed into an alternative delivery format, the school district has taken measures to assure that only students with legitimate reasons such as a scheduling conflict can take their high school course work as distance learning. A fee is also charged "to make the cyber class self-sustaining," Mr. Sheridan said.

Ms. Donovan added, "It [the project] is basically student-driven. I am an adviser, but I'm not a technology teacher."

Danahy, A. (2004, May 10). Online learning. Retrieved May 15, 2004, from **www.centredaily.com/mld/centredaily/8631317.htm.**

therefore have significant repercussions in education and may eventually blur the line between traditional and distance education. This potential for educational evolution offers fascinating academic possibilities, not only for distance education but also for education in traditional settings. Such alternatives to current delivery formats warrant further exploration.

Designing Instruction for Distance Delivery

You have already learned about the importance of a well-conceived design and a carefully planned lesson to ensure the quality of your instruction. In a distance-delivery environment, planning is even more crucial. Unlike the traditional classroom, in which the teacher is present and can make adjustments to the teaching and learning process while it is being carried out, distance delivery requires that all aspects of the process be fully established before the teacher and learners engage in it. The distance education curriculum and fully articulated activities are typically prepared well in advance of the instructional event. Distance educators must anticipate learner responses and prepare a curriculum that answers questions and concerns before they are asked. Once the curriculum has been disseminated to students working in different locations or in different time frames, it can be difficult to make and disburse changes to it for other than Internet-based courses. For these reasons, every aspect of instructional planning is a critical component of distance delivery.

Distance Education in K–12

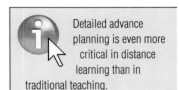

Detailed advance planning is even more critical in distance learning than in traditional teaching.

Beyond the Lesson Plan

The instructional design process, when applied to distance education, requires a strategic approach. The design must respond to both the instruction itself and the benefits and/or impediments of the distance-delivery technologies that will be used. Table 10.1 provides a summary of the process of preparing a distance-delivery course. Often, district or school distance education programs begin by determining which technologies are available or will be acquired to deliver instruction across spatial or temporal barriers. This may be a less-than-ideal, though necessary, approach. A better scenario would be identical to the process used for traditional instruction; that is, start with the instructional design and then determine which distance-delivery technologies are necessary and appropriate to support instruction. Unfortunately, because of the significant cost of distance-delivery technologies and their integral role in the process, a district might have little choice but to begin by determining which existing technologies can be repurposed for distance education. These determinations will not define the instructional event, but they do place parameters around it. When preparing an instructional design for distance education, you must implement the design process with full awareness of the technologies that will be made available to you for delivery. Your design itself may suggest changes to the planned delivery technologies that will be necessary to ensure effective delivery and meaningful interaction.

TABLE 10.1	Getting Ready for Distance Delivery

STEP	PROCESS
1	Review research and similar courses for your grade level.
2	Examine existing distance learning materials and presentation ideas for your subject.
3	Analyze the available delivery technologies and consider their strengths and weaknesses relative to your students and your subject area.
4	Complete available hands-on training in the delivery technology you plan to use.
5	Discuss your needs and student needs with technical and academic support staff.
6	In your plan: • Begin with instruction to students in how to use the delivery system. • Plan modular instruction, with content divided into manageable units of material. • Offer activities and experiences that address diverse learners to the extent the delivery system allows. • Include interaction and scheduled, frequent feedback. • Determine how you will assess students, both academically and logistically.
7	Plan for contingencies should technologies fail.

The steps of the DID process you have already learned do not change in distance education. In fact, they become even more fundamental when you are conceptualizing instruction that will be difficult to alter once it has begun. The environment in which your design will be implemented is likely to be very different from the traditional classroom and therefore must be fully considered and adapted in the initial design. Because distance education teachers are not in frequent face-to-face contact with their students, impromptu changes in the instructional plan are typically not practical. Developing a fully articulated design is the only way to create an instructional sequence that is precise enough to flow unerringly without requiring it to be frequently changed and adjusted.

Although instructional design for distance education takes on a strategic and situational perspective, the most significant change to the instructional planning process occurs in the lesson plan phase. Lesson plans for the traditional classroom are typically written by the teacher for the teacher. The teacher is in the classroom throughout the lesson and can modify the lesson plan at any time. Students rarely see the lesson plan itself; they simply experience it being carried out. In distance education, however, the teacher is not present and cannot make instant modifications. It is the student who works independently through a fully articulated lesson plan that was carefully prepared by the teacher to respond to anticipated needs. The instructional support and prompting that would

TABLE 10.2   Comparing Traditional and Distance Lesson Planning

OPTICAL MEDIA	TRADITIONAL CLASS	DISTANCE LEARNING CLASS
STEP 1: READY THE LEARNER.	*In your classroom, you would* • Ask questions to determine whether content needs to be reviewed • Review content as needed	*In your distance education materials, you should* • Prepare a pretest so students can self-assess whether they have the necessary previous content • Make review materials available
STEP 2: TARGET SPECIFIC OBJECTIVES.	*In your classroom, you would* • Select the target objective for the lesson • Prepare your students by explaining what they will be able to do as a result of the lesson • Respond to your students' questions about the lesson	*In your distance education materials, you should* • Post the target objective in a location students will notice • Explain the objective in detail, since there may be a time delay should students have a question • Articulate how questions should be asked and will be responded to
STEP 3: PREPARE THE LESSON.	*In your classroom, you would* • Decide how your classroom needs to be arranged for this particular lesson • Write notes for yourself as to how you will accomplish each step of the pedagogical cycle • Select and set up the materials, media, and technologies needed and decide how will they be used by you and your students • Decide upon assessments for the lesson and select materials and means for implementation	*In your distance education materials, you should* • Create content modules so that students have manageable materials to work with • For each module, sequence each step of the pedagogical cycle and provide a detailed explanation to the student as to how to proceed through each step • Prepare all materials with detailed instructions for their use and include them in the students' modules • Arrange for all media to be made available to students • Arrange for technologies to be available to students who do not have access • Provide students with detailed procedures for accessing and using media and technologies • Prepare assessments well in advance • Make arrangements for proctoring, and communicate procedures for assessments to students

normally take place in the classroom are included within the plan itself, with clear and precise instructions as to how each aspect of the plan should be carried out. Table 10.2 illustrates the relationship between the steps in a traditional lesson plan and those same steps as integrated into distance education curriculum.

Preparing Students

Because students must work through their lessons without benefit of the immediate presence of the teacher, they must first be prepared for the differences this type of experience will present. From the earliest grades, student behavior and expectations are shaped so that the students will be comfortable in a traditional classroom, but few learners have been similarly prepared to work in a distance environment. Therefore, in addition to preparing the learners for the content, you must prepare them to work differently than they would in a traditional classroom. Typically, that means that you must prepare them to work much more independently. This, then, is the next major consideration in designing instruction for alternative delivery.

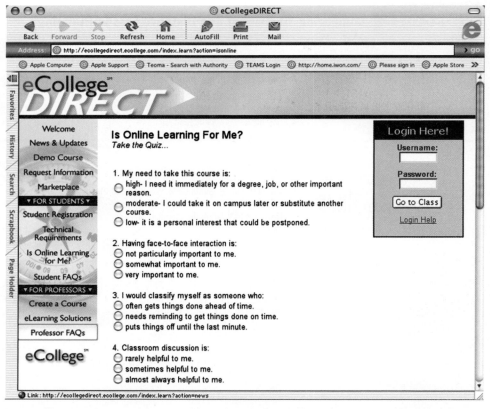

In an effort to ensure student readiness for distance education, many programs ask students to complete online self-assessments.

SOURCE: eCollege Direct.

In the traditional classroom, students listen to directions or instruction and then proceed to complete assigned work. If they have a question, they need only raise a hand, and their teacher responds to them. In a distance education environment, the process is different. Students may view, listen to, or read content and directions in the materials provided or by technology-based communications. They then begin to work on their reinforcing activities. If they have questions, the teacher might not be immediately available to respond. In some distance education situations, there might not even be other students in the same location to ask a question of or to discuss a concern with. Students working in this type of environment need to be trained to find the information they need from their materials and to use the systems in place to get answers to unresolved questions. This is a more independent learning format than the one that is typical of a traditional classroom.

Many distance education programs use a combination of screening and orienting students to prepare them to be successful in a distance education environment. Screening students, that is, determining whether or not their learning styles and study habits are consistent with the distance education format, is a frequently used first step. Each distance education program uses specific technologies and methods to deliver instruction. Matching students who have the potential to work well with these methods can increase learner success and decrease frustration. A second commonly used step is to prepare students for the distance education environment by providing a very specific orientation to and training in the methods and technologies they will be expected to work with. This step helps students become as comfortable with the experiences and tools of the distance teaching and learning environment as they would be if they were participating in a traditional environment. One or both of these preparatory steps will assist learners in maximizing their potential for success.

E-Learning
ON THE WEB! 10.3

Getting Ready for Distance Education

Planning Ahead for Murphy's Law

Murphy's Law says that anything that can go wrong will go wrong. Admittedly, Murphy's Law is an excessively pessimistic viewpoint. It does, nevertheless, offer those engaged in distance education an important warning. In traditional environments, the teacher is present to respond to any difficulties that arise. If you are planning to show a videotape and the VCR does not work, you adjust your lesson to adapt to the circumstance with relatively little effort. But if you are teaching a distance education class to students located in neighboring schools and the communications equipment does not work, how can the lesson go on? What provision have you made for this eventuality?

Because distance delivery is heavily dependent on events and technologies outside of the teacher's immediate control, it is important to anticipate possible points of failure and to have a contingency plan. In the case of technology problems, having a redundant delivery technology available as a **backup system** can resolve crises caused by technology glitches. For example, making a speakerphone available in a compressed video classroom provides a backup communication system if the primary video system fails. Planning potential solutions for possible technological problems and communicating such backup systems with students reduces the potential for interrupted instruction. Not all failures, however, are technological. Students might not get materials on time, or books might not be available. Such events as these and other nontechnical ones are unavoidable; yet you can still plan for how such possibilities will be handled. You might want to give a fellow teacher or the students a phone number they can call or an email address where they can send mail should such problems occur. How the event will be handled will be determined by the various circumstances of the school or distance education program. But anticipating that such events may happen and articulating appropriate responses are key responsibilities for the teacher planning for distance delivery. Table 10.3 lists some areas to consider in such planning.

Like teachers, students must be prepared to function in a distance learning environment.

Providing Feedback

One of the greatest challenges in teaching at a distance is how to provide **feedback** to your students. In the traditional classroom, you use body language and comments as well as written feedback to provide your students with an idea of how well they are mastering the content. In a distance environment, the technology you use often determines the types of feedback formats that are available to you. If you use a speakerphone in a classroom, you can ask questions and give voice feedback to individuals or groups. If you use the Internet, email feedback may be appropriate. Regardless of the

TABLE 10.3   Contingency Planning for Distance Delivery

PROBLEM	SOLUTIONS
Student Selection Is a distance education format right for the student?	Provide self-assessments of readiness for distance learning; offer online counseling and advising.
Interactivity Will interaction between student and teacher and among students be sufficient?	Establish technology and procedures for regularly scheduled electronic and/or telephone connections; train teachers to respond to students with alacrity, thoroughness, and compassion; schedule group interaction, such as group problem solving, study sessions, and online discussions; ensure that feedback is consistently and positively reinforced.
Student Support and Services Will students have available the academic advising and mentoring, as well as the on-site technological assistance, that they need?	Tutors, academic advisers, and technology paraprofessionals must be provided to allow the student to focus on the product, not the process; support staff should be available to help both synchronously and asynchronously with advising and non-subject-area matters, such as stress, time management, and study skills.
Alienation and Isolation Will social contact be sufficient?	Provide online discussions and chats, email, digitized photos, videoconferencing, and collaborative assignments to overcome isolation.
Technology Skills Will skills be sufficient to carry out the technological processes?	Prerequisite and in-progress technology training must be available; on-screen help, telephone access to technical experts, and hard-copy how-to manuals need to be easy to use.
Design of Instructional Materials Will the materials work at a distance?	Offer training sessions for teachers to help them modify materials to accommodate the delivery differences needed; include technology training and integration techniques as well as methods for interactively engaging students at a distance.

feedback mechanism you use, it is critical to plan for adequate and frequent feedback within the instructional design itself. Just as with any instruction, students need confirmation that their understanding of concepts is correct. Continual feedback, in any form, is no less valuable in distance instruction. For those who teach in a distance environment, determining how and when to provide feedback can be a challenge met through creative teaching.

Evaluating Progress

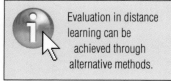

Evaluation in distance learning can be achieved through alternative methods.

Evaluation of students in a distance education course is one of the key issues for distance educators. How can students be fairly and accurately evaluated if they are not in a traditional testing situation? The answer to these justifiable concerns involves a creative and flexible approach to assessment. One of the most common approaches is to provide performance assessment alternatives that can be used in addition to testing. Such alternatives may be group projects conducted in Internet chat rooms, individual research projects with PowerPoint presentations that can be shared via computer, or even oral reports given by telephone. Distance educators must carefully consider the intended objectives and then creatively develop assessment alternatives that take advantage of the technologies in place.

TECHNOLOGY SOLUTIONS
for All Learners

Web Accessibility

Distance education offers learners flexibility in accessing education in terms of time and place. However, for learners with special needs, that access may be limited. The World Wide Web Consortium has therefore created a focus group called the Web Accessibility Initiative (WAI) to study and recommend how the web sites can be made accessible to all. Consistent with the work of the WAI, the University of Washington was awarded a grant from the U.S. Department of Education to "share guidance and resources on making distance learning courses accessible to students and instructors with disabilities" via the National Center on Accessible Distance Learning (AccessDL). This center offers educators resources to help ensure that all learners, regardless of any disabilities, can use distance education as a viable option to their personal growth.

AccessDL is a component of the DO-IT program at the University of Washington. As stated on their web site at

www.washington.edu/doit/, "DO-IT serves to increase the participation of individuals with disabilities in challenging academic programs and careers. It promotes the use of computer and networking technologies to increase independence, productivity, and participation in education and employment."

AccessDL offers specific resources to educators of learners with special needs in order to ensure that distance learning programs are fully accessible to them. These resources include a discussion list featuring a dialog on the best ways to make distance learning accessible, a list and explanation of ten indicators for distance learning accessibility, and a rich list of resource links to online training, research, streaming video presentations, and publications. These resources offer educators opportunities to investigate and decide how best to make their distance learning programs fully accessible to all learners. For more information on accessibility on the Web and, in particular, for distance learners visit:

AccessDL at **www.washington.edu/doit/Resources/ accessdl.html.**

W3C Web Accessibility Initiative at **www.w3.org/WAI/intro/ wai-overview-slides.**

Such assessments may challenge students to demonstrate competencies even more effectively than those commonly found in traditional classrooms.

Even so, traditional tests still have a place in distance delivery. Proctored examinations remain appropriate and expected as a part of a class taught via distance education. How the proctoring takes place may vary, however. In classes that are set up with a single teacher, with facilitators at each receiving site, proctored testing is easily accomplished. The facilitators take responsibility for the testing environment, proctor the tests, and then collect and return them to the teacher for grading. Even at sites without facilitators, proctors can be arranged for and tests given in secure environments, such as media centers or administrative offices. The combination of performance assessment and testing can ultimately provide as valid an assessment of student progress in a distance instructional environment as is available in a traditional instructional environment.

Assessing Learning at a Distance

 ## Support Technologies for Distance Teaching and Learning

Once the initial planning issues have been considered, just as in traditional instructional design, the next step is to examine the supporting technologies that are available or that need to be acquired to implement the instructional design. In distance education, such technologies fall into two broad categories, technologies that support synchronous distance education and those that support asynchronous distance education. **Synchronous** distance

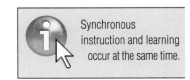

Synchronous instruction and learning occur at the same time.

TABLE 10.4 Delivery Technologies Summary

SYNCHRONOUS TECHNOLOGIES	ASYNCHRONOUS TECHNOLOGIES
TELEPHONE	VOICE MAIL/FAX
BROADCAST VIDEO	VIDEOCASSETTE
RADIO BROADCAST	AUDIOCASSETTE
INTERNET CHAT	INTERNET CONFERENCING
VIDEOCONFERENCING	EMAIL
NET MEETING	PRINT MATERIALS

education is instruction that occurs at the same time, although typically not in the same place. An example of synchronous instruction is a districtwide distance education foreign language class that is offered on "A" days in a block schedule, from 1:00 to 2:15. Students participating in such a class meet at the same time but at different locations across the district. In a web-based class, synchronous distance education might require that all students log on to a class chat room at the same time, although the locations from which they are working may vary. Synchronous technologies, then, are those that allow students to participate in the same time frame but in different locations. Table 10.4 lists synchronous and asynchronous technologies that can be used in distance education.

In contrast, **asynchronous** distance education is time shifted; that is, teacher and students can participate at differing times from the same or different locations. An example of an asynchronous distance education class is one that is conducted via the Internet. In such a course, materials may be available on a web site, with students and teachers interacting by email or class conference. Students and teacher may be located at the same school, at different schools, or even at home, but they have the option of interacting at different times.

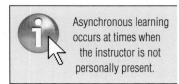

Asynchronous learning occurs at times when the instructor is not personally present.

The nature of the distance education program that a district or school chooses to implement will depend on whether the distance-delivery approach will be synchronous, asynchronous, or a combination of both. Arguments for and against each approach can be logically made. Synchronous delivery most closely emulates traditional instruction and is the easiest for teachers and students to adjust to. However, synchronous approaches do not offer flexible time frames, a lack that can cause significant resource and scheduling problems. Asynchronous delivery is more flexible, making it easier to allocate and schedule resources while also making instruction more convenient and accessible for learners. Asynchronous instruction is more complex to plan for and requires new teaching and learning formats that may require some accommodation for both teacher and learners. Still, both formats have their place in distance- and alternative delivery programs. Which format is best can be answered only in response to the diverse needs of the learners, the district's needs, and the content to be delivered. Whichever approach is chosen, several specific technologies can be enlisted to support instruction.

Support Technologies for Synchronous Instruction

You are already familiar with a variety of technologies that can be used to support synchronous instruction. Some, like the telephone, are relatively low-tech, while others, such as Internet-based compressed videoconferencing, are emerging high-tech options. The variety of technologies that can be adapted by creative educators to assist in communicating synchronously cover the full range of technological options. The key to selecting technologies for this purpose is to look for those technologies that provide same-time communication formats and explore them for their adaptability to distance education.

Telephone Technologies

The **telephone** and its by-product, telephone conferencing, are among the staple technologies for synchronous delivery. Whether as a primary medium or a backup technology, the telephone offers an easy-to-use, inexpensive, and readily accessible technology for communications. Like all synchronous technologies, the phone requires that all parties participate in the same time frame. Telephone exchanges, whether direct instruction or questions and answers, can be one-to-one or, through conferencing, group communication.

The most basic type of conference system is the use of a **speakerphone** that allows participants to communicate using a single, specially equipped phone. Speakerphones offer a simple, though potentially unwieldy, conferencing system. Speakerphones are equipped with an omnidirectional microphone that is designed to pick up voices from anywhere in the room.

They also have a speaker that is powerful enough to be heard across a room. Typically, this equipment has only a volume control to adjust sound levels. Although this makes for a very easy-to-use and economical system, the microphones and speakers imbedded in the phone might not accurately reflect voices on the other end of the line or in a larger room. Extended use of a speakerphone can be frustrating when critical content is being communicated. Furthermore, the phones pick up all sound, not just intended discussion, so extraneous room noise can be irritating.

A second audio option is the **conference call.** Conference calling can be done with personal phone services or school phone systems. Such systems typically allow three to eight participants to connect together. This type of conferencing is excellent for small-group instruction or discussion. Because all participants are speaking into their own telephone handsets, the clarity of exchange is better than that with a speakerphone. Extraneous noise is also easily filtered out. Finally, because all participants use their own phones, unlike the use of a speakerphone, which must be located in a single central place, every member of the conference can conceivably be calling from a different location. This technology bridges the location gap for every participant. Diversity of location can, however, be a disadvantage. Gathering together for a speakerphone conference offers opportunities for social learning that conference calling does not. Furthermore, the cost may be greater in these circumstances as a result of long-distance charges that may add up throughout the instructional activity.

E-Learning
ON THE WEB! 10.5
Telephone Conferencing

TEACHING AT A DISTANCE

Problem-Based Learning

Imagine that your success and talent for teaching character education has been recognized by your district. You have been asked to design a distance education program using your particular teaching methods and ideas to teach character education to students across your district. Your know what has worked so successfully for you in the classroom. Your lectures, written activities, personal journal, small-group discussions, and peer-to-peer values clarification and problem-solving groups have served you well. You have communicated the content and have provided students with the opportunity to thoughtfully examine their values. However, translating this successful program into one that could be run using the countywide compressed video system will be a challenge.

The county has offered you the job of designer and lead teacher. You now need to consider which distance education technologies can best be employed to deliver the methods you have tested and know work well. You will have teachers at all participating schools to work with you at their end to implement the program. What would the program look like? What activities would you keep, and how would you deliver them? Which technologies would you need? What would the role of your partner teachers be? Develop a one- to two-page proposal describing how you would make your character education accessible across the district.

A final and more sophisticated telephone-based method for synchronous interaction is the use of a **phone bridge.** This equipment, which is usually installed at the district level or subscribed to from phone service companies, provides the capabilities for large-group instruction via telephone. This technology allows from two to fifty callers to call a single central number and join in a conference call. The moderator or teacher has to establish ground rules so that two or more participants don't try to talk at the same time. Each speaker is also asked to identify himself or herself each time that person has something to say. The technology bridges all callers together and lets each individual caller join or leave the conference without affecting the conference itself. It is possible to arrange for a toll-free number as the bridge number, thus solving the problem of long-distance charges for participants.

Each of these telephone-based technologies adapts a common medium to distance education. Although such solutions are clever, the real challenge in using such technologies is in the design of effective instruction that takes advantage of the technology's strengths and overcomes its weaknesses. Like all instruction, effective telephone-based instruction is the result of innovative teachers being aware of this technology and able to adapt it to their purposes.

Videoconferencing

You have already learned about the ability to communicate via computer using a compressed **videoconferencing** system. Clearly, such a system is an ideal technology for synchronous distance education. Video and audio images are compressed and transmitted in different ways. Two of the most common methods are computer-based TCP/IP systems connected over the Internet and the use of broad-bandwidth digital telephone lines. International standards have been established for the compression of these signals, making it possible for different brands of compressed video equipment to communicate with each other.

Videoconferencing over the Internet can make distance learning come alive.

Compressed videoconferencing systems can be configured as individual systems on home or office PCs or as a classroom system. An individual system, as you will recall from previous chapters, uses the computer's speakers, a microphone, and a small monitor-top video camera for communication. Software enables the digital pictures and audio to be sent via modem to one or more similarly equipped machines on the Internet. Videoconferencing systems allow individual users to connect in a virtual meeting and exchange text, graphics, sound, and visual images. This combination of hardware and software is easily adapted for instruction at a distance. Teacher and learners connect to the Internet, create their virtual space using their meeting software, and communicate just as they would face-to-face.

Videoconferencing systems help to create interactive classrooms across a school district or a state.

Tech Tips
for TEACHERS

Using videoconferencing to teach can be a rewarding and exciting experience. Like any instruction, it does take careful planning and some practice with the equipment, but as you and your students become used to the environment, the technology "disappears," and you become comfortable with your expanded classroom. When teaching or participating in a videoconference, it is important to become aware of how the equipment changes some aspects of the instructional environment. Some general guidelines include the following.

The Room

If you are teaching via video conferencing, be sure that you can see all seats in the room and that any permanent camera angle is focused so that the students are at the center of the image.

Your Appearance

Be aware of the colors and patterns of the clothes you are wearing. Keep colors neutral or muted and avoid checks, as they tend to "swim" on camera. Keep jewelry simple, and avoid anything that jingles as the noise will be amplified by the microphones.

Visual Displays

A whiteboard can be difficult to see at remote sites. Shadows appear that blur the written content. Use PowerPoint or display prepared and previewed notes via a document camera. Black print on pastel paper displays best. When adding handwritten notes, be sure to use a thick pen, as regular ballpoint does not display well.

Audio

Instruct the students to use the mute button on microphones until they are ready to speak. The mics are sensitive, and a tapping pencil or too much paper movement can be distracting. Pause frequently to avoid speaking over each other as there is a few-second delay.

Other Movement

Movement can be exaggerated by the camera, so avoid nervous tics and keep body movements minimal. Rocking in a chair or tapping a foot can become a major distraction.

Adapted from Penn State's Etiquette and Tips for Successful Video Conferencing. Retrieved August 22, 2006, at **www.hbg.psu.edu/iit/ mw2/etiquette.htm.**

This type of videoconferencing system offers individuals with the required hardware and software an excellent opportunity to participate fully in instruction. Students can be at diverse locations with the only parameter for participation being that they all go online at the same time. Students can interact in a virtual face-to-face instructional event with their teacher and/or with their peers. Despite its potential, this delivery technology does currently have some disadvantages. The typical home or school computer system might not include all of the necessary hardware. Furthermore, as you have learned, video and audio files require significant bandwidth to avoid frustrating communication delays. Many home and school systems are not connected to the Internet at the bandwidth necessary to allow this technology to offer smooth communications. Finally, for students whose learning is augmented through social interaction, this technology might not offer sufficient social contact. Unless small groups meet informally—virtually or in person—outside of the instructional time, social interaction and the broadening of learning that often results may be lacking.

Another option for configuring compressed video for distance education is to connect compressed video classrooms across a district. In this application of compressed video, the personal equipment is scaled up to create an interactive classroom that can be connected by high-speed phone service to similarly equipped classrooms at other locations. Typically, such classrooms include one or more large monitors positioned so that all participants can see them; multiple microphones in strategic locations across the room to pick up individual and multiple voices; video cameras mounted on the monitors or in positions that allow for "eye-to-eye" contact when participants are looking at the monitors; supplementary video cameras for special shots; and the hardware and software to enable communication.

The compressed video classroom most closely emulates the traditional classroom for both teachers and learners. Because students gather in each of the classrooms that are connected by compressed video, the potential for social learning is returned to the instructional environment in this configuration.

E-Learning
ON THE WEB! 10.6

**Compressed Video
Communications**

Moreover, facilitators are often hired for the distant sites, so the teacher (located at the near site) has either team teachers or aides to help meet student needs. This allows for greater flexibility and more responsiveness at each far site. For most who have participated in this type of compressed video classroom, the technology quickly seems to disappear as participants become engaged in the instructional process. The fact that most participants are comfortable in the familiar surroundings of a classroom likely contributes to their ease in using this type of distance education technology.

Internet Chats

Another technology that is used for synchronous distance delivery is the **Internet chat.** Chat programs allow multiple Internet users to log on to and communicate within the same virtual space. This technology allows the teacher to conduct live interactive sessions or groups of students to communicate in real time with each other. Chats offer a way to hold an instructional session or a small-group discussion regardless of the participants' locations. Even though all must enter the chat room at the same time, distance barriers become irrelevant. For a large, physically spread-out school district or for a school that hires a distant expert teacher, this delivery technology provides a very effective solution to the need for interaction.

Using chats, students and the teacher can key messages to each other online in real time.

Chats can offer some marked advantages. Many who use chats for instructional interaction find that the quality of the exchange is quite high. Perhaps because participants have more time to consider and respond to questions or comments, the interaction is often more thoughtful than in the classroom. Also, unlike a classroom in which shy students may never raise their hands and contribute, chats allow the teacher to call on every student; in this way, everyone interacts. In addition, seeing that chat technology typically allows participants time to key in, reread, and correct their responses before sharing them, the delay gives reticent students a greater comfort level when participating. Figure 10.3 presents a segment of a class chat.

Internet Chats

CHATROOM MSB01	
MSB:>	Ok, class, let's see who can answer the next question. What were some of the social conditions that changed after the Civil War? *Becky, can you think of one?-o-*
BSMITH:>	Slavery was stopped.-o-
MSB:>	*Good, Becky. That is correct. Did that change the way former slaves lived? Alan, can you answer that one?-o-*
ACHAMPS:>	I'm not sure, but I don't think it made a whole lotta difference since people who were slaves didn't have anything and being free didn't give them anything but freedom. Heck, they didn't know how to not be slaves!-o-
MSB:>	*Right, Alan. It was hard for the former slaves to adjust to their new status since they had no opportunity to learn the skills they needed to function as full citizens. And, of course, the situation in the South was desperate for everyone from former plantation owners to city dwellers to former slaves. It was a very difficult time. Does anyone know what a "carpetbagger" was and what these folks did in the South after the war? Gina, do you want to take a stab at this one?-o-*
GVERRICIO:>	Sorry, Ms. B. you got me. I know they were from the North, but I don't know what they did.-o-
MSB:>	*Well, that was a good start, Gina, they were indeed from the North. Tom, can you share any type of activity a carpetbagger might have been engaged in?-o-*

FIGURE 10.3
Class Discussion via an Online Chat

Online instructional chats offer students and teacher exchanges similar to those that would occur in a traditional classroom.

Internet Classroom Sites

A final communication technology that can be used to create a virtual classroom is Internet-based meeting space. Whether in the form of software created primarily for business use (for example, Microsoft NetMeeting) or an educational site (such as Blackboard), this technology offers a variety of tools for both synchronous and asynchronous exchange. Teachers can conduct a class via the Internet in which they can engage in a group discussion in real time, show a PowerPoint presentation, or share an electronic work space. Together, these technologies, in the hands of a creative teacher, can offer a very solid learning environment.

Many sites offer authoring tools with which teachers can create and present site-based lessons. Such tools range from fill-in-the-blank virtual classroom authoring to test generators to syllabus makers. Different sites and meeting programs offer different capabilities. Some charge a school system a per-student fee to host a virtual classroom; others give the school system the software to run on its own network servers. In either case, preparing a distance education class using any of these resources requires a substantial up-front investment in a teacher's time and creativity. To be sure the investment is well spent, it is important to try and to compare these sites or programs and their tools before committing to using them.

E-Learning
ON THE WEB! 10.8
Virtual Classroom Web Sites

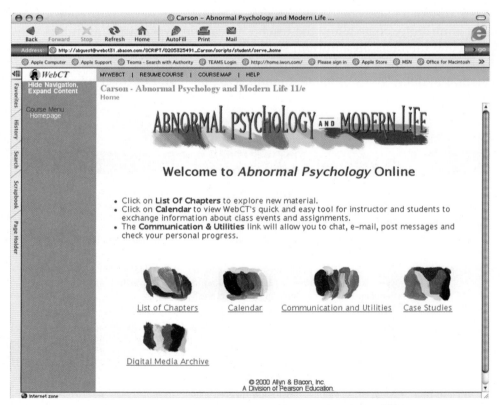

Students and teachers can participate in virtual classrooms with software such as Blackboard.

SOURCE: Allyn & Bacon, Inc. A Division of Pearson Education.

Support Technologies for Asynchronous Instruction

Asynchronous (time-shifted) instruction is also supported by a wide variety of analog and digital technologies. Because the term *asynchronous* suggests that teacher and students need not be connected at the same time, even the most basic classroom technologies can be considered a part of this category. Printed materials, televised broadcasts on educational channels, videotaped instruction, and audiotapes are all potentially asynchronous delivery technologies. Teacher and students do not need to be in contact at the same time or at the same place for instruction to occur. However, in using these types of technologies, interaction is typically one-way. The teacher delivers instructional content with these technologies, but there is little or no opportunity for teacher-to-student or peer-to-peer interaction. In view of the fact that most teachers build interactive experiences into their instruction, it is important for distance educators to identify and repurpose available technologies to support asynchronous interaction as well as delivery.

Telephone Technologies

The telephone is ordinarily a synchronous technology, but when you add an answering machine or voice mail service, you also add asynchronous capability. Because these technologies allow teachers and students to leave each other **voice mail** messages, voice communication becomes possible even when none of the participants communicates via phone at the same time. For districts with more sophisticated voice mail systems, it is possible to create a virtual verbal space for a class. A phone mailbox can be created in which a teacher can request oral responses to a question. Students can then call in to the mailbox and leave their verbal answers for their teacher to listen to later. Oral responses are crucial for a foreign language class, for example, and phone mail technology can make it possible to give them asynchronously.

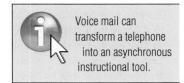
Voice mail can transform a telephone into an asynchronous instructional tool.

Another common telephone technology that can be adapted for asynchronous delivery is the **fax.** For instantaneous delivery of text or graphics, the fax machine provides simple yet effective communication. Teachers can fax questions, visuals, or replies to student inquiries directly to the students. Students can fax back responses, assignments, or questions. This common technology offers an instant and reasonably inexpensive communication tool, yet does not require that sender and receiver be working in the same time frame. Even if you do not have a dedicated fax machine, most computer operating systems offer at least a rudimentary fax program as an accessory to the system. Thus, whoever has a PC and a modem available typically also has fax capability. This simple tool has great potential for communication in the hands of a creative teacher.

Electronic Mail

The most significant digital asynchronous technology to support distance delivery is **electronic mail,** or email. Just as email has changed the nature of the way many individuals, businesses, and organizations communicate, so too has it revolutionized asynchronous instructional communication. This powerful tool makes possible easy yet thoughtful communications between teacher and student and among students. Unlike a voice mail message, email messages can include attachments to an original message. These attachments can even include animated graphics, audio, and compressed video clips.

Email messages are a private and thoughtful form of communication.

in the Classroom

IN THE SCIENCE CLASSROOM

Meredith Blanche is a project teacher and the coordinator of a distance education program carried out by Evergreen Elementary School in Fort Lewis, Washington, and Wesleyan Academy on St. Thomas, the U.S. Virgin Islands. Although the schools are separated by thousands of miles, students know their counterparts are just a mouse click away. Sixth-grade students at Wesleyan Academy on St. Thomas are working with the sixth graders at Evergreen Elementary in Fort Lewis, Washington, using My eCoach Online. They "share information, post ideas and findings, and develop inquiry projects on 10 topics about water." Combining project-based learning with technology has proven to be a rich opportunity for using the higher cognition levels (Bloom's *Taxonomy*) and encouraging constructivist theory to be placed into classroom practice. Projects were developed by "10 teams of two-to-three students from their schools [with a lead teacher] to guide them as they conducted research and engaged in hands-on research." Coordinators from each school trained with the virtual coaching offered by My eCoach to design the project and then passed their knowledge on to their lead teachers.

James L. Smith, Enhancing Education through Technology program supervisor for the Washington State Office of Superintendent of Public Instruction, said, "Not only did the students in the Virgin Islands get to learn about the cold water of the Puget Sound salmon habitat as they made their way from local streams to the ocean, but the students in Washington learned what a conch was." His praise for the project called attention to the avenues it opened for students from widely diverse backgrounds to come together to work as a team on topics that "included natural disasters and the effects on water, animals in our watershed, and pollution and its effects on sea life."

How did the students feel about such an approach to school assignments so different from just reading in textbooks about the topics? "The students' overall response to the program was extremely positive. They truly learned much more about their topics and enjoyed sharing their understanding through their hands-on projects and demonstrations," Ms. Blanche claimed.

Online tools allow distant students to collaborate on research projects (May, 2005). *T.H.E. Journal*, 14, 16.

Messages can be very brief or long, formal or informal. Because the sender has time to carefully compose a message and proofread it before sending, email messages tend to be a more thoughtful form of communication than speech. Finally, email messages can be composed, sent, and read whenever it is most convenient for the individuals involved. Email's attributes, harnessed together in support of the distance teaching and learning process, create a powerful and elegant tool for interactivity.

Email can be used to communicate one-to-one or one-to-many. A distance education teacher can communicate privately with each student or can choose to send a group email message to all, via a group mailing option or a formal mailing list. Students can respond to progress inquiries or content questions, or they can ask further questions. Additionally, because teachers can establish email processes and procedures, email interaction can be offered in private (email) or public (mailing list) formats. When private email is available to students, many feel more comfortable asking questions or requesting clarification without fear of their concerns and questions being seen as "dumb." Mailing lists, on the other hand, offer an email format in which questions and concerns can be automatically sent to all participants. Both public and private email offer channels that support the diversity of communication that might be found in a traditional classroom.

But email also offers an advantage over the typical interaction in a traditional classroom. The teacher's ability to address every student individually via email tends to increase participation. In an email–supported discussion on a topic of concern, a teacher can require that all students participate and respond via email. In this scenario, unlike the classroom, shy and thoughtful students are not overwhelmed by the enthusiastic responses of their more outgoing peers. There is also time for everyone to respond. The pressure to be the first student who has a hand up disappears. Students have enough time to respond within the framework of their own learning characteristics. Email can, in these ways, provide equity of response opportunities for all students and can fully engage everyone in an academic discussion.

In an email–supported discussion, student participation tends to be greater than in the traditional classroom setting.

E-Learning
ON THE WEB! 10.9

Academic Email

Electronic Discussions

Electronic discussions, or electronic forums, offer a platform for one-to-many communications. These virtual bulletin boards let individuals post messages for all participants to read. Others can then post responses, resulting in a threaded discussion. For distance education, a class electronic discussion is usually moderated by the teacher, with all students participating at a convenient time and from any location that offers access to the local network or the Internet. The teacher might post a question or an announcement and ask all students to respond. Students then post their responses or ask additional questions. All students can read all responses and can even save them or print them out. This formalized electronic discussion provides an opportunity for thoughtful interaction

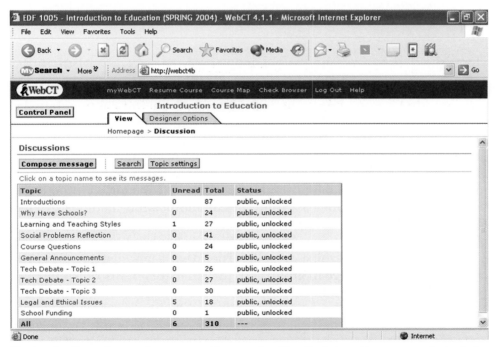

Electronic discussions or forums provide opportunities for interaction among students in a distance learning environent.

SOURCE: WebCT, Inc.

and the potential for complete note taking because all discussion can be captured and reviewed.

Students can also use electronic discussions to support distance cooperative learning groups and study groups. With one student acting as moderator, a small group of students can meet asynchronously in an electronic discussion to work on a task or share content. Students can thus assemble at a time that is convenient to each of them and from any location and still participate in class activities. Electronic discussions make it possible for students to interact with each other on group projects even if they are located in different schools across a district or are homebound. This tool makes it possible for the distance teacher to engage students in social learning as well as with the content.

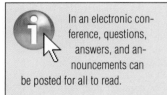

In an electronic conference, questions, answers, and announcements can be posted for all to read.

E-Learning ON THE WEB! 10.10

Classrooms on the Web

Class Web Sites

Many asynchronous technologies and even some synchronous technologies can be combined together in a class **web site** hosted on a school or district network or an Internet hosting service. The class web site can offer a distance student a single virtual place to go, at any time and from any place, to find all of the resources and tools needed to participate in a class. For district distance education classes, the class web site can offer an easy-to-access repository of all materials, a place where all students from any location can interact, and an efficacious communication tool for the teacher. Even if students meet synchronously via compressed video, a supporting class web site can become an important resource that will help to meet both anticipated and unanticipated needs.

Providing Interactivity via Distance Support Technologies

Both synchronous and asynchronous technologies support distance delivery not only by providing a channel for transmission of content, but also by providing a platform for interactivity. Unlike early distance education programs, in which instruction emanated from the teacher and learners remained essentially passive, today's technology-enhanced distance programs provide many opportunities for student-to-teacher and peer-to-peer interaction. Just as in the traditional classroom, the distance virtual learning environment can offer a variety of communication methods to meet learners' needs and preferences. A master teacher in a school district can present content to students across multiple schools or to those who are homebound by video, voice, or data. Then that same distance educator can have students engage in group activities that are not restricted by their particular location. Last, because school schedules may differ across a district, asynchronous technologies can offer a solution to scheduling problems. With these new tools at a teacher's disposal, it is no wonder that distance education programs are expanding at an amazing rate. Given its potential to emulate classroom experiences fairly accurately, distance education's early promises may soon be realized.

Issues in Implementing Distance and Alternative Delivery Systems

Teacher and Student Readiness

Distance learning systems require that teachers and students be ready to work within a new environment. There are two key aspects to their necessary **readiness:** readiness to accept new roles and readiness to work with new technologies. First, teachers and students must be prepared for new roles. In distance learning, teachers become guides and architects of complex learning environments. Less time is spent in direct instruction, and more is spent in creating a rich instructional environment and then guiding students through it. Students become less passive and more responsible learners. They must be ready to think through options rather than passively follow instructions. They must take more responsibility for their learning. These new roles may require some very specific orientation and training for both teacher and students for them to be ready to work in the new environments of these delivery systems.

A second type of readiness relates to being prepared to use the technologies selected to support these new environments. Both teachers and students may be expected to frequently use technologies they do not know or have not yet become comfortable with. When learners are expected to take more responsibility in these delivery formats, it can be frustrating if the technologies they need to use turn out to be a barrier to their tasks. When a teacher creates instruction to be delivered by a particular technology, it is essential for that teacher to fully understand the technology's capabilities and limitations. For teachers and students, it may be necessary to participate in very specific training sessions before being able to fully use a distance or alternative learning environment.

Are We Ready for Distance Education?

Distance education participants may need additional training.

Preparation and Classroom Management Time

Teachers who use distance and alternative learning techniques might find themselves surprised by an increase in the demands on their time. Distance learning and alternative learning often require a greater allocation of available planning time because the learning environment must be carefully mapped out in advance of its implementation. Furthermore, because distance education methods can sharply increase interactivity and because every student may now respond, teachers might find the number of responses overwhelming. Planning for instruction and responding to students will require that you carefully think through your time management strategies. Few would disagree that comprehensive planning and full interaction are both highly desirable, but for many teachers, finding adequate time to do both may be a problem. Districts that are interested in supporting distance and alternative instruction need to consider the requirements inherent in these alternative instructional systems and make adequate arrangements to meet them.

Distance delivery via compressed video can make classes available across a district. The technology, while it takes some time to learn to use, can effectively teach an advanced placement course or low-enrollment language course to just a few students at several schools. Offerings can thus be expanded to everyone, no matter how rural or how small the school may be. To be successful, districtwide distance education has some prerequisites. An investment in equipment and good technical support is a must. And, it is important to have a teacher partner at every location. Teachers need to be trained as well, but once everything is in place, with compressed video and Internet support, a district can meet student needs everywhere.

YES! Making more classes available to students is important to them, especially for seniors. Very often colleges want students to have taken a specific class, but a school is just too small to offer it, or no teacher is available. Districtwide compressed video distance delivery makes it possible to offer each student everything he or she needs! The compressed video is best since it is most like classroom instruction, but even the statewide online distance education programs will do to help students. Distance-delivery technology can help schools provide the instruction that students need to have.

NO! While these distance education programs may help support instruction, they are not the same as having the teacher in each classroom. K–12 students are not mature enough to handle instruction unless they are under the direct supervision of a teacher. Distance-delivered classes just don't work. The students have not learned to be independent enough learners to really understand the content. They need a teacher's direct guidance. For adults, distance education is fine if they like that format, but it has no place in K–12 schools.

Which view do you agree with? YOU DECIDE!

Technical Support

In implementing distance and alternative delivery systems that are supported by technology, it is critical to be sure that adequate **technical support** is in place. If instruction is dependent on a class web site and the district web server hosting that site goes down, how will instruction continue? If a class interacts by compressed video, what happens if one of the components does not function? Although technical problems are often unavoidable, adequate and readily available technicians, backup systems, and clear direction as to how to proceed if systems fail are critical for success. Too often, support personnel and related support costs are not fully considered in determining whether or not to engage in distance- or alternative delivery systems. Even if technical support is not the central consideration, nevertheless it is one of the critical components for successful implementation.

> Sufficient technical support is necessary for distance education to operate smoothly.

Instructional Support

Learners in traditional classrooms have a variety of **instructional supports** readily available. In addition to the teacher being present for clarification and questions, a media center offering a wide variety of resources is also typically present. Some schools may also provide tutoring programs for students who need additional help. Together, these resources provide a comprehensive instructional support system for students. However, in a distance environment, some of these supports may be missing. In a cross-district distance course, the local media centers might not have the resources available to supplement and support the instruction. It may also be too costly to replicate resources at all participating schools. How, then, can distance learning students access the resources they need? If the students need extra help, where can they find the tutoring support they need? These questions must be addressed in determining how distance education systems will be implemented. Solutions may be as new and divergent as the programs they support. Such solutions may include providing tutor telephone hotlines and homework help chat rooms. Whatever the solutions that are finally chosen, it is important to address the issue of academic support as a critical component of a distance education program before that program is implemented.

Copyright

As you learned in Interchapter 9, respecting copyright is a critical issue for teachers. The use of copyrighted materials in distance learning and on the Internet brought concerns over fair use in the digital age to the forefront. In 1998, Congress asked the U.S. Copyright Office to address the issue. The Technology Education and Copyright Harmonization (TEACH) Act was introduced in the legislature in 2001 as a result of the report produced by the Copyright Office. With the passage of the TEACH Act in 2002, many guidelines related to fair use for distance education were clarified, yet many issues still remain. For example, the TEACH Act conditions for the use of copyrighted materials are somewhat complex and often more restrictive than the fair use guidelines operating in traditional face-to-face classrooms. Further, restrictions under the TEACH Act limit the circumstances for use, which may in turn have an impact on the broader copyright policies adopted by the institution offering the distance education program.

Clearly, copyright will remain an issue for all teachers but particularly those teaching in a distance environment. However, as distance education becomes even more commonplace and instructional needs become more evident, policy decisions and law will no doubt evolve to better address these concerns. Indeed, the TEACH Act is likely to be just the first step in the resolution of copyright issues in distance education.

Reinventing the Classroom: The Future of Distance and Alternative Delivery

Technology is changing our society, and that changing society is putting new demands upon our schools. In response, our schools are changing. One aspect of the change is our perception of a classroom. Must the teaching and learning environment be a physical space? Can we offer effective instruction and help our students engage in meaningful learning without time and location constraints?

Whatever your views and experiences at this point, it is clear that many schools are currently attempting to create and implement high-quality distance programs. The number of schools, organizations, and even businesses that offer instruction at a distance increases each year. You may be asked to

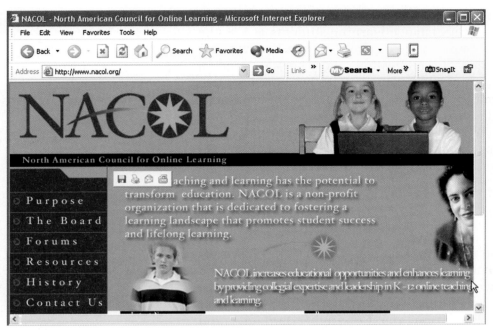

Distance learning organizations are helping to define standards, promote quality, and support dialog among distance educators.

SOURCE: North American Council for Online Learning.

participate in such programs sometime during your professional career. To adequately address such a possibility, your awareness of the methods and technologies that are currently being used and that may be used in the future to reinvent classrooms is a good start. How will classrooms evolve as the Information Age unfolds? That is difficult to predict with any precision. What is clear is that both traditional and nontraditional classrooms will evolve and may be completely reinvented to better address our changing world. Eventually, perhaps, there will be no distinctions among traditional education, alternative education, and distance education. Perhaps, instead, they will all be facets of the same complex and diverse educational system, offering options to meet every learner's unique situation and needs. As the future of instructional delivery unfolds, you can be sure that your classroom will be affected. Learning about and preparing for such potential change may be your best strategy for successfully changing with it.

KEY TERMS

asynchronous 377	evaluation 374	speakerphone 377
backup system 373	fax 383	synchronous 375
conference call 378	feedback 373	technical support 388
correspondence courses 367	instructional supports 388	telephone 377
distance education 364	Internet chat 381	videoconferencing 379
electronic discussion 385	phone bridge 379	voice mail 383
electronic mail 383	readiness 387	web site 386

STUDENT ACTIVITIES

CHAPTER REVIEW

1. What is distance education? How does it overcome temporal and spatial barriers?
2. Describe the two major impacts of distance education on K–12 teachers.

3. What early technologies enhanced distance education via correspondence? What impact did these have on student isolation?

4. What are alternative learning systems? How might they enhance traditional education?
5. Why is planning even more critical for distance delivery than for traditional instruction? How does planning differ between traditional and distance delivery?
6. Why is giving feedback a challenge in distance environments? How can this challenge be met?
7. What issues surround student evaluation in a distance environment? How might they be resolved?
8. What is the difference between synchronous and asynchronous delivery? What technologies support synchronous delivery? What technologies support asynchronous delivery?
9. How do synchronous and asynchronous technologies support interaction?
10. What types of support are critical to the success of distance education? Why?

WHAT DO YOU THINK?

1. There has been much discussion about whether distance education can provide students with instruction that is equal in quality to what they have received from traditional education. Do you think an equivalent experience is possible via distance delivery? Why or why not?
2. Distance learning and alternative learning require a significant use of technology to support instructional delivery. How does the inclusion of the technology affect the instructional experience for better and for worse?
3. One of the primary issues associated with implementation of distance education revolves around the teacher's ability to adequately and appropriately evaluate student progress and competencies. Do you believe that this is an issue? Why or why not?
4. Synchronous and asynchronous delivery both enhance and potentially impede instruction in different ways. What are your key issues and concerns related to each of these systems?
5. What role do you think distance education will play in education as the Information Age unfolds and technologies improve? What advantages and disadvantages for teachers and students do you foresee?

LEARNING TOGETHER!

These activities are best done in groups of three to five.

1. Research and examine your state's initiatives in distance education at the K–12 and postsecondary levels. On the basis of your research, prepare a summary of the programs that are available or under way and the pros and cons of each.
2. Each group member should locate and create an annotated list of three web sites offering access to technologies appropriate for distance or alternative delivery. Compare your finds and select your top five sites. Summarize these to share with your class.
3. Imagine that your group has been asked to develop a districtwide unit about your local ecology. You have decided to teach it by using distance delivery. Describe how you will deliver your unit across your district via synchronous and asynchronous systems.

E-Learning

CHAPTER 10 Visual Organizer

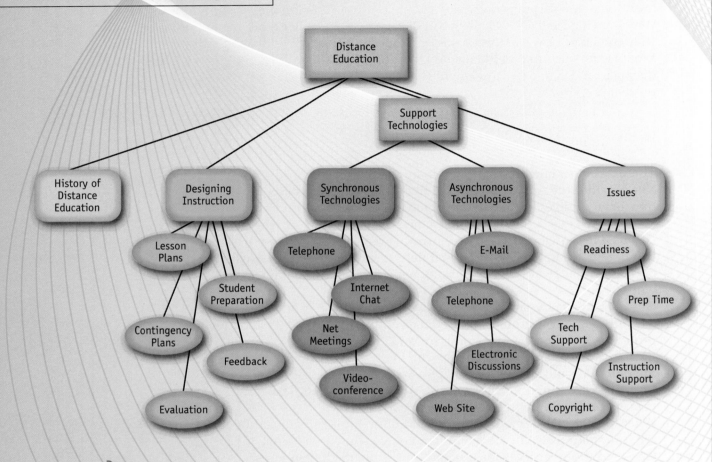

Podcasts www.mylabschool.com

Listen to a podcast relating to distance delivery in teaching and learning. Download the audio discussion to your iPod, computer, or MP3 player.

Video Lab www.mylabschool.com

Accessible through the **mylabschool** web site are several video vignettes that offer you a look at distance delivery. Learning guides for all videos can be found in the text's Learning Guide Supplement.

On the Web! Activities **www.ablongman.com/lever-duffy3e**
Noted in the margins of the chapter, these activities offer you in-depth experiences in the topics and content presented in the chapter.

Online Practice Test **www.ablongman.com/lever-duffy3e**
Practice tests offer you an opportunity to test your knowl-

edge and then review the results and send them to your teacher.

Outliner **www.ablongman.com/lever-duffy3e**
Chapter Outliners are fill-in-the-blank outlines of the main ideas presented in the chapter. Download the outliner and fill it in for an effective chapter study guide.

Power Practices **www.ablongman.com/lever-duffy3e**
Power Practices are animated tutorials made using Microsoft's presentation software, PowerPoint. This flash card tutorial will help you practice key concepts in the chapter.

Puzzler **www.ablongman.com/lever-duffy3e**
Puzzlers include content in crossword, word search, and other puzzle formats to help you master chapter content.

Useful Links **www.ablongman.com/lever-duffy3e**
These links offer you suggestions for expanded online research in the topics presented in the chapter.

INTEGRATION *Ideas*

Distance learning has seen huge gains in the numbers of students enrolling in courses for online education credits. The variety of courses offered has increased accordingly. Although universities still dominate the distance education format, high schools and middle schools, both state and private, are appearing frequently and in widespread locations. For each of the core content areas, English/language arts, mathematics, science, and social science, examples follow that give an overview of the types of courses offered and the experiences these courses disseminate

Integrating Distance Education into Social Studies

Casey Burton, who teaches elementary school social studies for the Denver Public Schools and designs distance learning projects for the Distance Learning Network, hosts "The Social Hour with Casey Burton" to arrange virtual field trips on a 30-minute television-based class that features one grade level each week of the month. Mr. Burton has 151 virtual field trips waiting to be taken.

Burton, C. The social hour with Casey Burton. **http://dln.denver.k12.co.us/elemed/elclasses/social.asp.**

Integrating Distance Education into Language Arts

Distance learning was used for a project in which students in English and music classes at the University School of Nashville, Nashville, Tennessee, discovered how to write an opera. Robbie McKay's literature and music classes took part in an in-depth dialogue via videoconferencing with Amy Tate Williams, chorus master and accompanist for the Nashville Opera Association. The class discussion began with the kinds of stories that would adapt well into operatic form. It proceeds to a look at characterization that led to consideration of the monologue as it appears in operas as arias or solo pieces. The students then decided on a story to put to music and what kind of accompaniment would be suitable for the story, as well as the ways opera music can be written. All of this learning time took place during videoconferences.

Merrick, S. (2004, June 1). Videoconferencing at its best: Nashville Opera brings "How to Write an Opera" to UNN students. **www.techlearning.com/shared/printableArticle.jhtml?articleID=20900611.**

Integrating Distance Education into the Sciences

Students at Briscoe Junior High School in Richmond, Texas, were able to take advantage of reaching out interactively to learn from locations and people far away from their school. Devoni Wardlow, the PLATO learning lab and manager, helps teachers learn to use the distance-learning lab and schedules class into it. Science teachers at Briscoe received acceptance to a NASA distance learning program and chose to work with the topic of robotics. Joy Sloan's sixth grade class created a robotic arm using Popsicle sticks, which performed for Erika Guillory, a NASA scientist, 50 miles away from the school at the Johnson Space Center in Houston, during a videoconference..

Adams, D. (2004, January 7). Reaching for the stars through distance learning. **www.herald-coaster.com/articles/2004/01/07/news/top_story.**

Integrating Distance Education into Math

An advanced placement calculus class is not always a part of a school's curriculum, especially if the school is small. For the gifted and talented who need the credits and who need the challenge of work that doesn't fall within those courses offered at their high schools, Polytech High School in Woodside, Delaware, offers the opportunity to take a school-sanctioned class as distance learning. Because of the critical shortage of math teachers, school officials had not been able to staff an advanced placement calculus class. The school found that Apex Learning, located in Seattle, Washington, had a two-semester advanced placement calculus course in place. Apex is approved by Carnegie Learning of Pittsburgh, a company formed by Carnegie Mellon University researchers, teachers, and scholars. Students used the Web to take the course from Apex to improve their chance at acceptance into the university of their choice.

Merriweather, J. (2005, January 14). Students take calculus via Web. **http://cgi.delawareonline.com/cgi-bin/advprint/print.cgi.**

For these and many more Integration Ideas for using the distance education in teaching and learning visit the text web site at **www.ablongman.com/lever-duffy3e.**

Alternative Delivery Systems

You have already learned how distance education was originally developed to deliver instruction across distances. But what if the same instructional designs, pedagogical methods, and technologies that make it possible to deliver across distance were adapted for the traditional classroom? How might these adaptations evolve into innovative classroom methodologies and alternatives? How might they affect instruction inside and outside of the classroom? How would they alter the traditional instructional delivery that is found in most classrooms? The answers to these questions are beginning to emerge as the influence of distance education techniques and technology expands.

Many educators who have taken or taught a course via distance education have found that they could adapt the innovative methods used for distance education to enrich and enhance their traditional teaching. Hybrid instructional delivery systems that use the best of both traditional and distance instruction are being adapted for and implemented in both types of programs. These alternative delivery systems, offered on a college campus, at a school, or across a district, may offer the first glimpse of how teaching and learning will ultimately change under the pressures of our current technological social evolution.

Using Distance Education Methods to Enhance Traditional Classrooms

Many of the techniques and support technologies that were originally introduced for distance education have proved to be useful in traditional classrooms. These alternative learning delivery options, when added to traditional delivery, offer more dynamic and diverse teaching and learning opportunities. Synchronous and asynchronous technologies and methods can add a new and distinctive teaching and learning dimension to classroom instruction when implemented by creative teachers. Adapting distance education lessons to the traditional classroom creates an alternative learning format that offers teachers and learners interesting and productive new tools. These can make instruction more engaging and can better meet learners' individual needs.

Using Distance Education Tools for Alternative Learning

Although the typical use of textbooks for independent reading assignments is asynchronous, most classrooms are by definition synchronous. Most synchronous technologies and methods that are used in a distance education classroom would therefore be redundant in the traditional classroom. But when you begin to use asynchronous techniques from distance education in your classroom, you may find surprising results. Table I10.1 lists alternative learning strategies that can be used in traditional classrooms. These techniques are discussed in the following sections in the context of how they might enhance different aspects of the teaching and learning process.

Individualizing Instruction

The first application of asynchronous tools is in the area of individualized instruction. Traditional classrooms are designed to provide group instruction and to supplement that instruction with individual activities. Because children do not all learn in the same way or at the same pace, group instruction might not be as effective as intended. Distance education programs require an individualized approach because groups might or might not actually meet. Some of the techniques that are used for individualizing distance education can become important tools for traditional teachers who are seeking a supplement to group instruction. Posting classroom announcements and reminders on an electronic conference can provide students with an additional resource to refer to when questions arise. Emailing class assignment calendars to parents can open lines of communication. Creating a class web site that houses content, activities, and review exercises can offer students an opportunity to revisit classroom instruction at the time and pace that works best for them. These methods and support technologies can supplement classroom group instruction and further individualize it to better meet student needs.

Promoting Interaction

The traditional classroom's large-group format might not be conducive to providing equal opportunity for interaction. In our often overcrowded classrooms and for students who are naturally reserved, this format is not optimal. The same distance education strategies that make it possible for all students to interact in the virtual classroom can also provide the opportunity for all students to interact in a traditional classroom. An electronic conference on an important aspect of content can offer an opportunity for every

TABLE 110.1 — Distance Education Tools for Alternative Learning in Traditional Classes

ALTERNATIVE LEARNING STRATEGY	APPLICATION IN THE TRADITIONAL SETTING
Online Lectures Make PowerPoint lecture or lecture notes available on network or web site.	• Provides opportunities for self-paced review of class lectures • Provides access to missed lectures for absent students • Offers review opportunities before exams
Course Calendars Post announcements and calendar on class web site or school network.	• Makes due dates available outside of class • Provides access to announcements and dates for parents • Allows for easy updating over weekends and vacations
Online Activities Post activities on class web site or school network.	• Makes activities accessible outside of class • Allows for making corrections or adjustments to activities • Provides students an opportunity to explore coming activities to better budget time

Online Interactivity
Conduct online conferences and chats; offer one-to-one interaction via email.
	• Conferences and chats provide opportunities outside of class to
	  • share concerns and exchange ideas
	  • work on group activities
	  • form study groups
	  • review materials prior to tests
	• Email provides for
	  • private teacher-to-student interaction after class hours
	  • student-to-student exchange of ideas
	  • clarification of content or procedures after class hours

Web-Based Assessments Offer online practice tests.	• Provides opportunities to practice content outside of class hours • Provides readiness feedback prior to exams

student to express a view, or it can provide a place for a group's consensus opinion to be posted. Email can provide a way for students to ask private questions of their teacher or to submit homework even when they are absent. Voice mail can give parents a way to communicate with their child's teacher without having to play telephone tag. All of these communication technologies, when implemented by creative teachers, provide new avenues for interactivity between and among the teacher, students, and their parents.

Enhancing Independent Learning

The final area in which distance methodologies and tools can enhance and provide alternatives for traditional classrooms is in their emphasis on independent learning. In traditional classroom processes, students are often expected to rigorously follow specific instructions. This approach facilitates the smooth functioning of a large group, but it tends to make individuals dependent. The obvious message of this type of instruction is to act only in accordance with specific instructions. The implicit message may be to not act if instructions are not specifically given—that is, to be passive in a new situation. This promotes dependency when, in fact, we actually want our learners to be self-initiating and responsible for their own learning. Because the distance environment cannot, by its very nature, provide continual instruction and redirection, its strategies must rely on a more independent and responsible approach to learning. The parameters of the virtual instructional environment thus foster independence. Using some distance education techniques as a supplement to traditional delivery can have the same effect. Placing student activities on a web page rather than handing out copies in class requires students to seek out the work they need. Emailing a class calendar of due dates or adding it to your web site helps students take responsibility for paying attention to the posted due dates. Making copies of your PowerPoint lecture available electronically offers students the chance to be responsible for content missed due to absence. These strategies, while integral to a distance education class, can become powerful tools in helping students gain independence in traditional classes as well.

chapter 11

Issues in Implementing Technology in Schools

This chapter addresses these ISTE *National Educational Technology Standards* for Teachers:

II. PLANNING AND DESIGNING LEARNING ENVIRONMENTS AND EXPERIENCES

Teachers plan and design effective learning environments and experiences supported by technology. Teachers

A. design developmentally appropriate learning opportunities that apply technology-enhanced instructional strategies to support the diverse needs of learners.

B. apply current research on teaching and learning with technology when planning learning environments and experiences.

C. identify and locate technology resources and evaluate them for accuracy and suitability.

D. plan for the management of technology resources within the context of learning activities.

E. plan strategies to manage student learning in a technology-enhanced environment.

IV. ASSESSMENT AND EVALUATION

Teachers apply technology in a variety of effective assessment and evaluation strategies. Teachers

A. apply technology in assessing student learning of subject matter using a variety of assessment techniques.

B. use technology resources to collect and analyze data, interpret results, and communicate findings to improve instructional practice and maximize student learning.

C. apply multiple methods of evaluation to determine students' appropriate use of technology resources for learning, communication, and productivity.

V. PRODUCTIVITY AND PROFESSIONAL PRACTICE

Teachers use technology resources to enhance their productivity and professional practice. Teachers

A. use technology resources to engage in ongoing professional development and lifelong learning.

B. continually evaluate and reflect on professional practice to make informed decisions regarding the use of technology in support of student learning.

C. apply technology to increase productivity.

D. use technology to communicate and collaborate with peers, parents, and the larger community in order to nurture student learning.

VI. SOCIAL, ETHICAL, LEGAL, AND HUMAN ISSUES

Teachers understand the social, ethical, legal, and human issues surrounding the use of technology in PK–12 schools and apply that understanding in practice. Teachers

A. model and teach legal and ethical practice related to technology use.

B. apply technology resources to enable and empower learners with diverse backgrounds, characteristics, and abilities.

C. identify and use technology resources that affirm diversity.

D. promote safe and healthy use of technology resources.

E. facilitate equitable access to technology resources for all students.

You have learned much about the many types of technologies that are available for teachers and their students. You have also learned about the theories related to teaching and learning and the process of designing effective instruction. As a result of the competencies you have gained so far in this course, you have already taken the first significant steps in using educational technology effectively in your classroom. But understanding the broader process inherent in implementing technology in schools and in districts requires that you expand your technological perspective even further. Indeed, the process of acquiring and implementing educational technologies in a school has its own set of challenges, both academic and administrative, of which you must become aware. Once a teacher has decided which technologies would be best for use in the classroom, these greater implementation issues can directly affect those initial decisions. Implementation issues, the concerns that arise in working through the details of acquiring and setting up a school's technology, may even alter the choices that have already been made. The implementation concerns that arise can be so significant that they can even change the direction and nature of a school's technology initiative. Will the preferred technology work with other types of technologies already in place? Must a school or district ensure that the technology decision making be strategic, that is, made within a larger school planning framework? Are there any legal, social, or ethical issues to attend to in implementing a technology initiative? How will technology selections fit into the future and with the technologies that are on the horizon?

Will the desired technology be outdated in just a few years? Questions like these must be answered to ensure a successful technology initiative and implementation. These broad implementation issues and concerns are the focus of this chapter.

As a teacher, you might think that such concerns have little to do with you. That is not the case. You will find that teachers have a unique and significant role in addressing many of the issues associated with implementing technology in schools. You might be asked to serve on the technology strategic planning team, you might serve as the chair of your grade-level technology committee, or you might want to become your school's technology coordinator. Regardless of the role you choose, you will find that you will be more prepared to understand and successfully address technology implementation issues after you have fully examined them.

In Chapter 11, you will

- Examine legal, ethical, and social issues that arise when a school implements technology
- Explore the technological trends that affect schools
- Examine the ways in which schools are likely to change as they progress in the Digital Age

Real People Real Stories

Meet Judy Kaplan. To most effectively teach research skills in a high school, students need initial instruction followed by a hands-on research experience for themselves. That experience is most effective if it is guided by a research specialist librarian and the subject specialist teacher. In planning with teachers, it became evident to librarian Judy Kaplan that a solution had to be found for the lack of access to her high school's two computer labs. She found that solution in wireless technology that allowed her to turn classrooms into computer labs when needed.

Peekskill High School, a small city high school fifty miles north of New York City, sits atop a hill overlooking the Hudson River and its old downtown, which is undergoing revitalization. Just as old buildings are taking on new businesses and new facades, the same is happening in the school. Traditional classrooms with student desks facing the blackboard and looking to the teacher for information have been altered. Now these rooms use technology to help students learn through individualized information searches.

As the library media specialist of Peekskill High School, Judy Kaplan is in charge of ensuring the best possible research instruction for students in her school. She plans with teachers to select the most suitable research sources for a particular topic, then aids teachers in instruction of the students. She has another role in the school as computer network administrator. In that role, she keeps up with technology issues such as this lack of access as she oversees the computers in the high school, ensuring that they're fulfilling student needs for research, word processing, and specific program instruction in reading, math, science, foreign language, and social studies. As such, she has often looked to new and emerging technologies to overcome existing limitations.

The most pressing technological problem in her high school was the limitation of computer lab access. There are two labs that are in use most of the day by business classes. The few periods a day that they are available are quickly booked by teachers who want

their students to do research, word process stories or term papers, format research into a Publisher newsletter or PowerPoint presentation, or even email in foreign languages with students in other parts of the country. As a result, there are always several classes unable to get access during the available periods and even more classes that have no chance at all. There was clearly a need for more computer labs; however, there was no classroom space in the school to create one.

To accommodate class needs for computer lab access, Judy investigated ways that computers could be brought into classrooms as needed. She wanted the new computers to connect to the school's existing network, and they had to be portable, which meant using laptops.

She spoke to her principal, who liked the idea but didn't have the money in his budget. Then she spoke to the administrators of the "Gear Up" grant in her building for improving student learning opportunities, and they agreed. On calling Dell for options, Judy learned that wireless laptops could easily connect to her school network. What she would need is a laptop cart that has a series of shelves for each computer and internal electrical outlets for recharging. It was even possible to have a printer on the cart to print wirelessly from each of the laptops.

When the laptops arrived, technicians had to prepare them to be compatible with the existing network. Once that was in place, the cart began rolling into classrooms. It did require that an access point in the cart, which transmits the network signal to the laptops, connect either by Ethernet or fiber optic wire into the classroom's network wall connection and also that the cart plug into an electrical outlet. But once all that was in place, the magic of turning any classroom into a computer research lab began.

Students were enthralled with the presence of a laptop on their desk and immediately focused on its screen. Students with usually short attention spans focused more easily on the screen on their desk than they ever did on the blackboard. And whereas taking students to the different setting of a computer lab caused some students to lose focus on the subject at hand, keeping them where they were accustomed to working in a particular subject area made it easier to get the intended instruction and task accomplished. Also, as another side benefit, students looked forward to research on the laptops and would ask when they could research with them again.

The actual research instruction within the classroom also worked better than within the typical lab. Students were physically further apart than in the labs and were less easily distracted by each other. Also, the delivery of instruction was easily accomplished by projecting the live research database from a laptop computer onto a screen while students followed along trying it for themselves. And the librarian and teacher were able to move around to students more easily and quickly without having to squeeze themselves within narrow rows of computers and thereby were able to offer more help.

The wireless computer lab was and is the perfect solution for Peekskill High School's inadequate availability of computer labs. Judy has now purchased another portable cart of wireless laptops and would like to get a few more.

For further information, email Judy at jkaplan@peekskillcsd.org.

Planning for and Implementing Technology

Because of the cost and complexity of acquiring and implementing the many educational technologies you have explored in this text, districts and schools typically begin the process with the creation of a formal technology plan. The technology plan is strategic in nature. This means it is a long-range plan and follows a series of defined steps common to **strategic planning.** Interchapter 11, following this chapter, articulates the process of strategic planning for technology. As you review this Interchapter, you will begin to understand why school districts spend so much time and energy preparing for technology acquisition.

Once technology is planned for and implementation has begun, many issues and concerns beyond those that are technical arise. A variety of legal, social, and ethical issues result from the use of technologies in schools. Teachers must be aware of these issues to ensure that they create a climate in their classroom that fosters respect for ethics, fairness, and the law as they relate to the implementation of technology. These issues are the subjects of the next section of this chapter.

Legal Issues in the Digital Age

Implementation of technology, whether in the classroom, school, or district, involves a number of legal issues (see Figure 11.1). Some of these issues, such as copyright violations, were of concern in education before the advent of technology. Technology implementation and the ease of accessing and incorporating digital data, including copyrighted text, graphics, video, and audio, exacerbated the problem. Other issues, such as the inequity of

FIGURE 11.1

Issues in the Digital Age

The Digital Age has enhanced education while giving rise to significant issues.

LEGAL

SOCIAL

ETHICAL

- Copyright and fair use
- Privacy
- Acceptable use
- Software piracy

The digital divide

- Freedom of speech
- Privacy
- Academic dishonesty

E-Learning
ON THE WEB! 11.1

Legal Issues in the Digital Age

Copyright protects the rights of the owner of intellectual property.

E-Learning
ON THE WEB! 11.2

Fair Use Guidelines

access to technology, sometimes called the **digital divide,** have arisen as a result of technology. Another set of issues involves ethical questions. Each of these issues affects how technology is ultimately implemented at all levels of an educational institution, from the classroom to the entire district. As a professional, you are responsible for becoming aware of these implementation issues and acting in accordance with professional ethics.

Copyright and Fair Use

You have already been introduced to many of the issues related to **copyright.** In Interchapter 9, you discovered that although materials protected by the copyright laws should generally not be used without the owner's permission, there are some occasions when such use is allowed. **Fair use** guidelines describe circumstances under which a teacher can use copyrighted materials in face-to-face instruction. The TEACH Act offers similar guidelines for the use of copyrighted materials in distance learning. Perhaps the easiest way for educators to use such materials is to ask themselves four basic questions related to the use of a copyrighted work. These questions, summarized in Table 11.1 are focused on the instructional intent of the use and the potential impact on the owner of the work. Asking yourself these questions before using copyrighted materials in your classroom will help you to avoid copyright infringement, an illegal act. As copyright law evolves in the Digital Age, new guidelines will emerge. The use of multimedia clips and information from the Internet has developed into an entirely new and complex area of the law. Regardless of the ultimate rulings by legislators or courts, it will continue to be an educator's professional and legal responsibility to stay aware of changes to the law and to model its application in his or her classroom.

Privacy

Every child in your charge, like every citizen in the United States, has a right to **privacy.** For minors, their parents must give permission to share any information about them to which you might be privy as a result of your position as their teacher. Technology has made the sharing of information simple and convenient. Nevertheless, this same convenience can lead to

TABLE 11.1   Fair Use Guidelines Self-Test

When concerned about whether or not to use copyrighted materials, answer this self-test to help you decide.

FAIR USE CONSIDERATION	ASK YOURSELF
PURPOSE AND CHARACTER OF USE	What is the intended use? • Are you using it for educational purposes? • Is the use noncommercial in nature?
NATURE OF THE COPYRIGHTED WORK	What type of work is it? • Is the work primarily factual in nature? • Does the work contain relatively little creative or imaginative substance?
AMOUNT AND SUSTAINABILITY OF THE PORTION USED	How much of the work do you intend to use?
EFFECT OF THE USE ON THE WORK'S MARKETABILITY	What impact does this kind of use have on the market for the work? • Would the use substitute for purchasing the original? • Would the use negatively affect the market potential of the original?

If your intended classroom use of copyrighted materials falls within fair use, then observe the following guidelines:

- Use the work only in face-to-face teaching. For distance learning, follow the guidelines in the TEACH Act.
- Limit copied materials to small amounts of the copyrighted work.
- Avoid making unnecessary copies.
- Be sure to include copyright notice and to attribute the work.
- Limit use to a single class and only one year. You need permission to use the work repeatedly.

For more detailed information, see Circular 21, "Reproduction of Copyrighted Works by Educators and Librarians," and other related materials at **www.loc.gov/copyright.**

inadvertent or intentional abuse. The right to privacy is one of the most significant issues in the Digital Age, both in society and in education.

Violations of privacy when using technology can take many forms. One of the most significant relates to online privacy. Internet sites that serve children have not been reluctant to gather and share personal information about these children, including their names, addresses, phone numbers, and photographs and even information about their families, all without asking parents' permission to gather the information or to share it. At one time, this was often done simply by asking children to complete a form to gain access to a tempting game or entertainment site. However, the problem became serious enough to lead to a congressional investigation that ultimately resulted in the passage of the Children's Online Privacy Protection Act (COPPA) in October 1998. Given the climate of concern and the passage of this law, how might the law affect you as you protect your students' privacy?

Although the legal landscape dealing with the Internet is continually changing, as a prudent teacher, you should be aware of the steps you should take to protect the privacy of your students. For example, if you want to

Protecting student privacy in the Digital Age is a critical technology implementation issue.

show a picture of your class or a sample of your students' work on your web site, you need to be sure that you are acting within the stated policies and procedures of your school and district. Typically, schools and districts require that you get written permission from a child's parent or guardian before you post anything regarding that child that would otherwise have been private. When a child turns in work to you, there is usually an assumption that only you will read it. Although it is customary to hang children's work in a classroom, that is different in scope from posting it on the Internet. You typically do not have the right to share a child's work publicly without parental permission. Most importantly, above and beyond the legal issue, indicating on the Internet that a child is in a particular class at a particular school and perhaps even including that child's name can jeopardize the safety of that child. Unsavory individuals can use such information to stalk a child or target the child for crime. Your primary responsibility, above all else, is to protect the safety of the children in your charge. Inadvertently exposing a child to risk by posting information about him or her on the Internet is a violation of your prime responsibility. A prudent teacher will become fully aware of the school and district policies related to posting students' names, pictures, or work on the Internet. The school and/or district policy will guide you in determining how student images or work can be used, as well as when and how parental permissions must be obtained.

Another area of concern is the collection of information about students at web sites they might visit. COPPA addressed this issue as well. Beginning April 21, 2000, operators of web sites directed at children under 13 had to conform to a series of rules and regulations regarding the request for and handling of personal information about their child visitors. One of the most significant regulations in this rigorous component of COPPA requires that these web site operators obtain verifiable parental permission before collecting personal data from children. Given that children may visit such sites in the course of a school day, what is the teacher's responsibility relative to such permission? COPPA allows teachers to act on behalf of parents during online school activities but does not require them to do so. However, district or school acceptable use policies may interpret this requirement differently. Each teacher should be fully aware of the school or district's acceptable use policy and act in accordance with it.

Because there is so much concern over children's privacy, particularly while online, the Federal Trade Commission has set up an informational web site that provides information to children, parents, and teachers (**www.ftc.gov/kidzprivacy;** see Figure 11.2). This site is a source of significant information and resources and should be explored fully by every educator.

Privacy when not online must also be protected. Software that allows you to manage grades and personal data relating to your students must be protected so that no others can gain access to information about them. If the school is networked, such grading software is installed on the network with specific rights for each account. That means that your account, as a teacher, has associated with it the rights to see and use software and data about all of your students. Student accounts have rights that may allow them to see only their own work. To protect student privacy, then, it is important for you to protect your own log-in and password because they allow access to private student data. Irresponsible sharing of your network account can result in a serious violation of a student's privacy. Even inattentiveness

Online Privacy

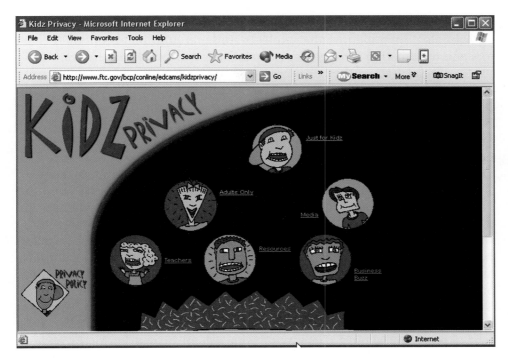

FIGURE 11.2

The Federal Trade Commission's Kidz Privacy Web Site

Web sites such as Kidz Privacy offer educators current and relevant information on how to protect their students' privacy.

SOURCE: Federal Trade Commission.

might be damaging. Leaving your computer logged in to the network when you are not using it can make the areas you are privy to available to others. On stand-alone machines that are available for student use, it is best to be sure that no files that may be considered private are stored on a drive that is available for all to use. It is your responsibility to guard the privacy of your students whether you are using the Internet, a network, or a public-access machine in your classroom.

Acceptable Use

Once technology is made available to students, it is the obligation of educators to ensure that it is used appropriately. Just as teachers oversee how students utilize textbooks and other media, they have a responsibility, to the extent possible, to ensure that access to and use of technology are consistent with the appropriate academic behaviors expected in the classroom. Just as educators would not allow questionable or inappropriate printed materials into the classroom, so too must they ensure that such materials available

Tech Tips *for* TEACHERS

Protecting Privacy

Just as you wouldn't post students' grades on your classroom door or tack letters to individual parents about student performance on your bulletin board, so too you must protect privacy in the Digital Age. Review this checklist for ways in which you can protect your students' privacy:

- Don't place confidential data or commentary on any unsecured electronic equipment.
- Guard your log-in names and passwords.
- Secure storage devices (floppies, CD-RWs, and USB drives) in places where they are not obtainable by people unauthorized to view their contents.
- Don't leave hard copy of assessments, evaluations, and reports of student behavior and achievement on printer trays in common areas.
- Once used, file privileged information, whether on storage devices or on hard copy, in secured spaces or, if no longer needed, shred it (preferably with a crosscut shredder).
- Follow school district policies and procedures in place to guard students' privacy.
- Guard photographs of students as well as text.
- Become aware of classroom and district software that offers parents access to their children's progress by password in read-only format.

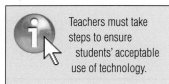

Teachers must take steps to ensure students' acceptable use of technology.

via technology be kept out of the classroom. The issues surrounding the use of technology in a manner that protects students from inappropriate behaviors and information are together referred to as **acceptable use** issues.

The most frequently voiced concern involving the acceptable use of technology relates to the Internet. The Internet contains salacious and inappropriate materials that do not belong in the classroom. You can do little to change the nature of the Internet, but a prudent teacher can help to ensure that the Internet is used appropriately in the classroom. Although your actions might not be able to guarantee that your students will never access an inappropriate web site, you can take every step possible to protect them.

The first important action you should take is to be sure that your students understand what constitutes appropriate use. Just as you might begin the school year explaining your expectations of classroom behavior, so too should you explain your expectations of how the Internet should be used in your classroom. Often, this is done through a **code of ethics** for computer use, a set of written expectations and definitions of what is considered appropriate or acceptable use. Codes of ethics should be signed by both students and their parents or guardians to ensure that they too are aware of these expectations. Signed codes should be stored for the duration of the school year. You should check with your school or district for its code of ethics or acceptable use policy. Most districts have established formal acceptable use policies, and schools within those districts are expected to follow them. After you check the details of the policy, it is wise to duplicate it and be sure to have your students and their parents sign it before your students are given Internet access or Internet assignments. If no such formal code has been established in your school or district, you should discuss these concerns with your school administrator. You might also want to review examples of various codes of ethics to determine what you might expect (see Figure 11.3).

Acceptable Use

FIGURE 11.3

Acceptable Use Policy Web Sites

You can learn about other organizations' acceptable use policies online.

Courtesy of the Virginia Department of Education. Microsoft Internet Explorer® is a registered trademark of Microsoft Corporation.

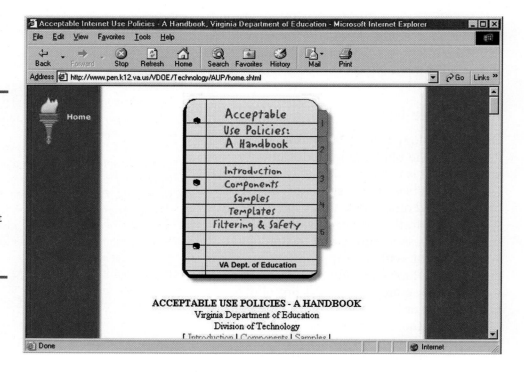

Many networked school systems have implemented **filtering software,** that is, software that filters out unacceptable Internet sites so students cannot access them (see Figure 11.4). Although not always successful in catching unacceptable sites, such filters do improve the chances of intervening if a child accidentally or deliberately attempts to access an inappropriate site.

Typically, filtering software will not allow access to off-limit sites, and many packages also gather the names of the users who are attempting to access such sites. Because users might innocently mis-key a URL or click on a link that inadvertently brings them to an unacceptable site, network administrators typically take minimal action, if any, for an occasional attempted access. However, if a user repeatedly and purposefully tries to access inappropriate sites using a school network, the administrator does typically track such activity and records it. For students and teachers alike, such activity is grounds for disciplinary action.

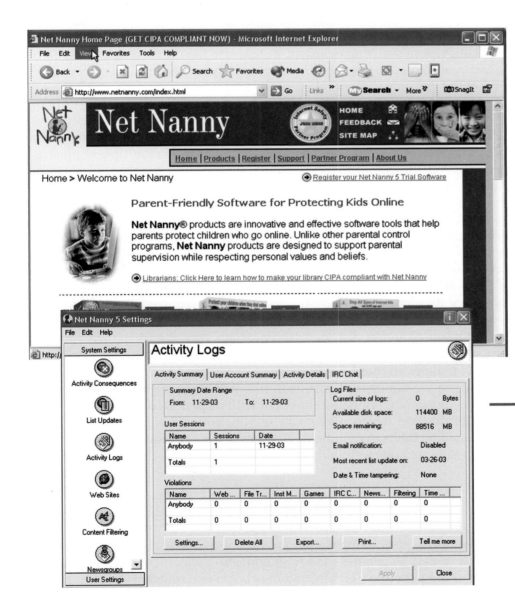

FIGURE 11.4

Filtering Software Web Sites

Software and web sites help to prevent unwanted materials from being downloaded to your computer.

Screen capture from NetNanny.com. Reprinted by permission. Microsoft Internet Explorer® is a registered trademark of Microsoft Corporation.

Software Piracy

Copying software to share with others or installing software on multiple machines when only one copy was purchased is software **piracy.** It is a violation of copyright laws to make and distribute copies of software or to install illegal copies of software on the machines in your classroom. Just as it is a violation to make copies of a music CD or a movie on videotape, it is illegal to copy and distribute software packages. The owners of the software have invested considerable resources in creating the software, and they have the right to sell and distribute their creation. Just because you purchased one copy does not mean that you have the right to make and use multiple copies.

Teachers who pirate software by making duplicate copies of a software package or by installing one software package on multiple machines in a classroom are in violation of the copyright laws. Teachers who know of and allow students to pirate software in their classrooms are condoning and allowing illegal activities. It is important to model appropriate behavior and ethical conduct and to proactively discourage software piracy whenever it is noticed. When a student offers you a copy of the new software he or she just got from a friend, you have a chance to model the correct behavior by refusing to accept it. You also have a teachable moment in which you have the opportunity to inform your student about copyright and his or her potential violation of the law.

Network administrators are charged with ensuring that all software on a network is appropriately licensed (the legal right to use the software). Every software package on a network must either be custom-made for that network or have a site license (a purchased right to use multiple copies) associated with it. Some network administrators also monitor all software that has been installed on the hard drives of any machine that is on the network to ensure that no pirated software is present on or attached to the network. It is therefore important for teachers to keep the software packages and documentation for any nonnetworked software that they install on the machines in a classroom. The network administrator who finds software on a classroom machine typically has the right and responsibility to ask to see the license. If the documentation and license are not available, the school or district network administrator may be required to erase any software that the teacher cannot prove was purchased.

Your school and/or district is likely to have very specific policies that address software piracy. A prudent teacher should research and become aware of such policies so that he or she does not personally violate them or allow students to violate them. Remember, like violating copyright laws with respect to multimedia, violating copyright with respect to software is also a violation of the law, which may result in you, your school, and your district being sued by the copyright holder. It is your responsibility as a professional and a public servant to uphold and support the laws relating to copyright.

Software Piracy

Social Issues in the Digital Age

The Digital Age has brought up a number of new issues that have more to do with society in general than with education specifically. These societal concerns are nevertheless reflected in schools and relevant to them. Equity and accessibility of technology are the most pressing and critical of these issues. Inequities in access to technology can result in some children leaping ahead in technological skills and knowledge through their readily available technological resources and others falling behind because of their lack of access to technology. This gap between digital haves and have-nots is often referred to as the digital divide.

For households in which parents are sufficiently affluent to afford a home computer and modem, computers and Internet access are often present and readily available for the children in the home to use. A recent report by the National Telecommunications and Information Administration, *Falling through the Net* (2000), indicates that approximately 46 percent of households earning $35,000 to $49,000 have Internet access, while 66 percent of households earning more than $50,000 have access. This level of accessibility gives children in wealthier households a head start in gaining computer skills and in developing the cognitive skills necessary to use hardware and software and to explore the Internet. For households that cannot afford a home computer, the child's use is limited to school time or perhaps time that is available through the local library. This type of relatively limited access may well cause such children to fall behind in the skills they need to use computers and the Internet in school. Other factors may also limit access. Not all schools and libraries are equally equipped with computers and Internet connections. The ones with less technology are often in poorer areas, causing limited access for people who cannot afford computers at home.

The digital divide does not occur along socioeconomic lines alone. Research in *Falling through the Net* shows that the divide also occurs along ethnic, gender, and education lines. Despite the increased presence of technology in our society, minorities and people with disabilities still have less access than others (see Figure 11.5). Furthermore, 60 percent of people with college degrees use the Internet, whereas Internet use is limited to only 7 percent of those whose education stopped at elementary school. Finally, gender differences exist as well. Although the numbers of men and women using the Internet are approximately equal, fewer women have computer-related degrees or work in computer-related fields. This reflects the continued math/science gender gap that has been present in schools for decades. This gap has now transferred to technology. According to many studies, boys are more encouraged to engage in technology-related activities than girls are, which may ultimately lead to the gender difference within the digital divide.

The digital divide cannot help affecting technology literacy at every level of education. Awareness of the gap in access and the possible inequities along ethnic, economic, gender, and education lines can help teachers to become sensitive to their students' needs (see Figure 11.6). Once aware that the digital divide does indeed exist, a teacher can choose to design technology and other content-area lessons to help bridge technological inequities. You might also decide to research and share information about community resources that provide access for those who do not have computers at home. You might decide to advocate in your school and your community for more and equitable opportunities for all of your students. The issue of the digital divide is so pressing and pervasive that many others are taking steps to close the gap as well.

The digital divide is the separation between those who have access to technology and those who do not.

E-Learning ON THE WEB! 11.6

The Digital Divide

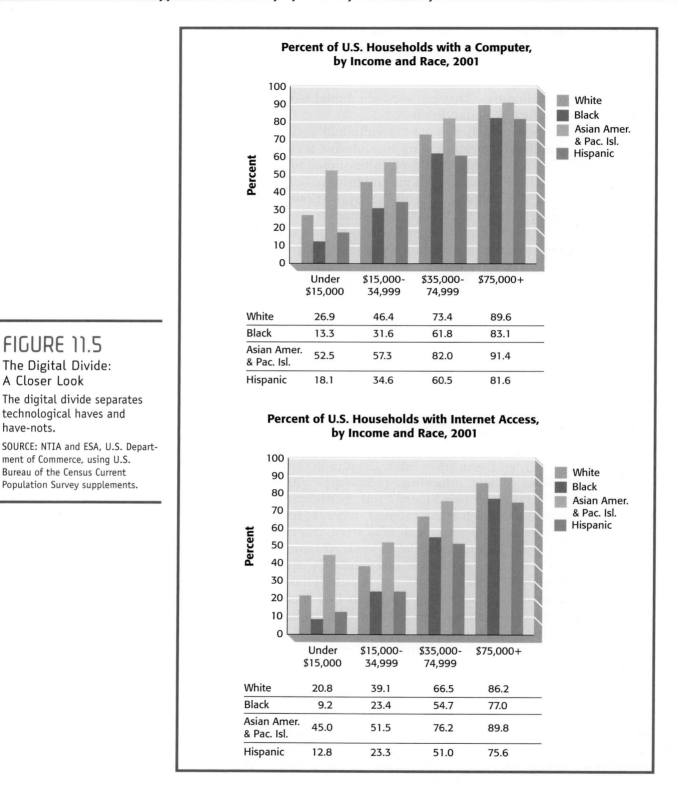

FIGURE 11.5

The Digital Divide:
A Closer Look

The digital divide separates
technological haves and
have-nots.

SOURCE: NTIA and ESA, U.S. Depart-
ment of Commerce, using U.S.
Bureau of the Census Current
Population Survey supplements.

**Percent of U.S. Households with a Computer,
by Income and Race, 2001**

	Under $15,000	$15,000–34,999	$35,000–74,999	$75,000+
White	26.9	46.4	73.4	89.6
Black	13.3	31.6	61.8	83.1
Asian Amer. & Pac. Isl.	52.5	57.3	82.0	91.4
Hispanic	18.1	34.6	60.5	81.6

**Percent of U.S. Households with Internet Access,
by Income and Race, 2001**

	Under $15,000	$15,000–34,999	$35,000–74,999	$75,000+
White	20.8	39.1	66.5	86.2
Black	9.2	23.4	54.7	77.0
Asian Amer. & Pac. Isl.	45.0	51.5	76.2	89.8
Hispanic	12.8	23.3	51.0	75.6

To make technology broadly available to all citizens, the Federal
Commerce Commission has established an education rate (**e-rate**), a discounted cost for telecommunications service for community access centers (such as schools and libraries). The e-rate has enabled schools and

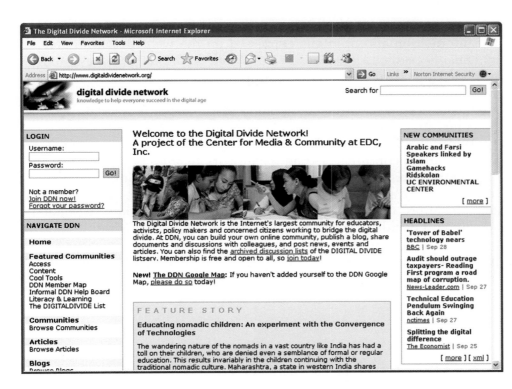

libraries to connect to the Internet at a significantly accelerated pace. Private foundations, such as the Bill and Melinda Gates Foundation, have donated computers to libraries in rural areas to help make technology more available to all. Schools across the nation are piloting programs that provide notebook computers to students to help equalize access. These and many similar initiatives are working in combination to help bridge the digital divide and ensure that all citizens have equal access to the tools of our Digital Age.

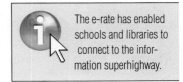

The e-rate has enabled schools and libraries to connect to the information superhighway.

Ethical Issues in the Digital Age

Freedom of Speech

In addition to social issues, the Digital Age has also engendered ethical concerns. One of the most significant of these is **freedom of speech** and the Internet. The content on the Internet is not regulated and, as a result, does contain materials that are objectionable and inappropriate for children. However, an issue that arises whenever regulation of Internet content is discussed is the constitutional right to free speech. The Internet is essentially a forum for sharing information and opinions. Some of the information and opinions expressed are grounded in scientific fact and academic research. Others are simply personal viewpoints that may be offensive to some. The question then arises whether society should censor some views expressed on the Internet. Is the right to express a viewpoint digitally as protected by the Constitution as the right to free speech

Free Speech

is? Is it the responsibility of an ISP or portal to monitor the content of the information and opinions expressed on the web sites, conferences, and emails available from its service? When do the actions of a few cross over into the legal domains that address fraud, libel, and hate crimes? The conflict between freedom on the Internet and the rights of individuals is a serious and far-reaching one that will have long-term ramifications for our society.

While this controversy continues to rage, it remains a school's responsibility to control access on its network to areas of the Internet that are inappropriate for an academic setting. Through monitoring and filtering software and through teacher observation, schools can make a reasonable effort to curb access to objectionable materials. Ultimately, society will decide whether objectionable materials are within the realm protected by free speech. Until then, teachers need to be aware of their professional responsibilities to guarantee students' "digital safety" while using technology.

Free speech and privacy are two of the critical ethical issues related to Internet use.

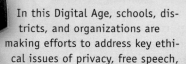 in the **Classroom**

ETHICS AND THE INTERNET

In this Digital Age, schools, districts, and organizations are making efforts to address key ethical issues of privacy, free speech, and academic dishonesty. An abundance of resources are available to help teachers deal with these issues. The Computer Ethics Institute (**www.brook.edu/its/cei/cei_hp.htm**) has developed the Ten Commandments for Computer Ethics:

1. Thou shalt not use a computer to harm other people.
2. Thou shalt not interfere with other people's computer work.
3. Thou shalt not snoop around in other people's files.
4. Thou shalt not use a computer to steal.
5. Thou shalt not use a computer to bear false witness.
6. Thou shalt not use or copy software for which you have not paid.
7. Thou shalt not use other people's computer resources without authorization.
8. Thou shalt not appropriate other people's intellectual output.
9. Thou shalt think about the social consequences of the program you write.
10. Thou shalt use a computer in ways that show consideration and respect.

Sharing these commandments with your students is an excellent first step for dealing with these ethical issues.

Other resources include the U.S. Department of Justice online guide to using the Internet written exclusively for kids. This guide helps students become aware of the issues they will face when using the Internet.

Another excellent resource is the TRUSTe organization's "Parent's and Teachers' Guide to Online Privacy," available for download at **www.truste.org/education/users_parents_teacher_guide.html.** This guide offers advice for dealing with privacy and other ethical issues related to student Internet use. A second valuable resource, *Technology & Learning* magazine's "The Concerned Educator's Guide to Safety and Cyber-Ethics" by Jerry Crystal, Cherie A. Geide, and Judy Salpeter (November 2000, vol. 21, no. 4), suggests a variety of strategies and resources teachers can use to address "cyber-ethics."

Although no solutions for ethical issues will fit all school or district situations, you will find that many expert online and print resources are available for your use in determining the best policies and responses to the issues facing you.

SOURCE: The Computer Ethics Institute. The Ten Commandments for Computer Ethics. Retrieved August 27, 2002, from **www.brook. edu/its/cei/cei_hp.htm.**

Privacy

A second ethical issue arising in the Digital Age relates to privacy versus control and monitoring. Individual rights and privacy are significant values in our society. In using any network or the Internet, it is technologically possible to monitor what an individual is doing and which sites he or she is visiting while connected. The controversy arises as to the rights of any agency, whether governmental or commercial, to closely monitor and record an individual's personal information or online activities. Is that not a violation of privacy? Should the government be allowed to monitor people who engage in illegal or dangerous activities? Who is responsible if activities are not monitored and someone gets hurt?

These complex social questions and the legal issues associated with them are evolving as the Digital Age unfolds. For educators, however, the situation is a bit less murky. In schools, the primary responsibility is the safety of the students. Because schools and their technologies are public entities, usually with clearly defined acceptable use policies, monitoring activities is both appropriate and expected. Students and public employees alike agree to use the school facilities to engage in appropriate activities. It is typically understood that monitoring to assure appropriate use and the safety of students will be done. Network administrators can monitor activity, and software can track what is said and what is sent by network users. Personal activities on the Internet, though monitored, are thus no more curtailed than they would be in the classroom.

Academic Dishonesty

The ease of manipulating and sharing digital data has led to numerous problems relating to **academic dishonesty.** Some web sites offer "services" to students so that they can hire someone to write papers for them. Others let students post assignments they have written or retrieve assignments written by others. Even web sites that do not intend to encourage dishonesty may support it as students copy and paste information from such sites into their assignments without giving the true authors credit. Cheating and plagiarizing are clearly not products of the Digital Age, but technology has made them easier to do and harder to detect.

To address potential digital dishonesty, teachers and schools should have clearly stated and enforced policies to deal with digital academic dishonesty just as they do for dishonesty of the more traditional sort. If academic dishonesty is widespread, a school can even install, or use online, **antiplagiarism software** that compares student's work with well-known authors' work and with work posted on the Web. Whether the approach is to enforce policy or to monitor student work via software, it is a teacher's responsibility to ensure, to the extent possible, that checks are in place to promote and enforce academic honesty.

E-Learning ON THE WEB! 11.8

Academic Dishonesty

Resources for Teachers

The legal, ethical, and social issues presented in this chapter are far-reaching and critically important. But a teacher is not alone in addressing and dealing with these issues. Typically, a school has a media specialist

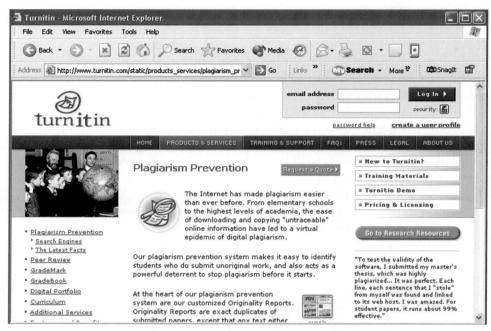

Software and web sites are available to educators to help reduce plagiarism.

SOURCE: From **www.turnitin.com.**

and/or a technology specialist available to assist teachers in addressing these issues. Both media and technology specialists have typically undergone special training sessions or have taken in-depth courses dealing with the issues related to technology implementation. A prudent teacher, when faced with questions regarding technology and its use in the classroom, would be wise first to contact the school media specialist, technology coordinator, or a school administrator for guidance. You will likely be surprised at the wealth of information and enthusiastic support you will be provided.

Emerging Technologies

New Technologies for Schools

E-Learning

www.mylabschool.com
Listen to Podcast
Emerging Technologies

A final consideration in implementing technology in today's schools relates to how technologies are likely to change and emerge in the coming years. Today's purchases are most wisely made when they are likely to be compatible with the technologies that will be available tomorrow. Although they are not always possible to predict, some emerging technologies are clearly on the horizon and should be considered even now in planning for and implementing technology in schools. The specifics of an emerging technology as it is finally formulated may be unclear in the present, but its potential to change education in the future must be taken into account today. Following are some of the most significant emerging trends that need to be kept in mind in considering technology in today's schools.

Wireless Connectivity

Many schools have spent a great deal of money retrofitting buildings for network cabling or creating new facilities to be network ready. The rapid improvement in wireless connectivity has begun to change this scenario. **Wireless networking** connects computers to a server and to each other just as wireless cell phones are connected to a phone company network, although the technology that is used to connect them differs. Wireless connectivity is likely to make all aspects of computing as commonplace as making a call on a cell phone.

Several new technologies are supporting the wireless revolution. WiFi (wireless fidelity) is a wireless networking technology that is based on the common 802.11 standard, a standard set for wireless LAN technology. Using radio frequencies set aside for consumer use, WiFi technology packages wireless networking that can offer connectivity across a school campus in hardware barely larger than a textbook. Then, using computers, notebooks, tablet PCs, or PDAs equipped with inexpensive WiFi networking cards, broadband Internet access is readily available everywhere within the WiFi range. Further, public WiFi networks are being created across the country in stores, airports, neighborhoods, city parks, and even across metropolitan areas. Simply by being located within a public WiFi network's range and using your WiFi-equipped device, you can use free broadband access to the Internet.

For schools, WiFi offers a reasonably simple and reliable technology that can make retrofitting schools for networking a thing of the past. However, because of their open access, some security issues arise. For districts and schools that must protect the privacy of student information, these issues will need to be resolved for wide implementation. Still, WiFi has the potential to change the way we access the Internet and all digital resources at home, at work, and at school. This emerging technology is one about which every educator should stay aware.

For connectivity within a classroom among various computing devices, other standards are evolving. Bluetooth technology, named after Harald Bluetooth, a tenth-century Danish king who unified Denmark and Norway, allows diverse types of electronic equipment to communicate with each other. Using Bluetooth-compliant devices, different kinds of equipment communicate with each other, and a personal area network (PAN) is automatically created. Within the PAN, devices can share data or interconnect so that one device can be controlled by another. With Bluetooth-ready devices, when you place the devices within the range of a PAN, your computer sends data to your printer; your PDA synchronizes with your computer; the phone book in your mobile phone exchanges new data with your notebook's Microsoft Outlook address book; and your television and DVD player operate together to play your favorite movie . . . all without wires.

In the classroom, Bluetooth technology makes it possible to arrange the learning environment without the limitations dictated by the length of cables. It allows you to create classroom PANs so that all your classroom computers can use your single printer even if the school network is not working at the moment. Your students can gather and record data on their PDAs or take digital pictures, all of which can be transferred to the computers without need of cabling. As Bluetooth technology becomes more

Notebook computers connected via a wireless network add high-tech flexibility to any classroom.

in the Classroom

GOING WIRELESS IN MIDDLE SCHOOL CLASSROOMS

Mike Smith, Superintendent of the Forney Independent School District in Forney, Texas, has had to deal with a shortage of textbooks. His school district is rapidly growing, and the time lapse between the number of textbooks that can be ordered based on the previous year's enrollment and current enrollments has caused a significant period of time to elapse with a percentage of students left without textbooks. To solve this dilemma, Smith's school district is combining the advantages of the wireless laptop with the adoption of e-books. The first groups to benefit from this approach to the problem were the fifth and sixth graders at Johnson Elementary School. Each one received "an IBM ThinkPad loaded with digital versions of textbooks and other works of literature." Superintendent Smith said, "If a delivery system such as the ThinkPad makes learning more exciting for the students and also solves the lack of textbooks, it's a system we need to explore. These are digital kids, accustomed to multitasking and accustomed to the electronic world."

Sue Cooper, a former middle school teacher at Rucker Stewart Middle School in Gallatin, Tennessee, remarked about the school's adoption of a package offered by Palm Digital Media that contains 500 e-books, as do other wireless technology suppliers. "It's fun. It's a lot easier than carrying around extra books," a student, Chris Kennedy, 13, at Rucker Stewart Middle School commented of his new e-book assignments. The e-books can be downloaded from the school's web site to either a computer or a PDA. Perhaps the strongest point in favor of reading from e-books is that students have a different attitude when it comes to reading by way of technology. Ms. Cooper said, "I see you hooking students you would not get with a normal book. The ultimate goal is to hook kids on reading any way you can."

Garton, N. (2003, July 13). Students turn on their computers to read classics. Retrieved October 26, 2004, from **www.tennessean.com/education/archives/03/07/35886253.shtml.**

Laptops replace textbooks at Johnson Elementary School. (2004, May 5). Retrieved May 15, 2004, from **http://forney. ednet10.net//prod_site/announcement_announcementelectronictext.**

widespread and more and more devices are Bluetooth-enabled, this wireless technology may make setting up and using a technology-rich classroom as simple as turning the technology on.

In many schools, students already have access to their school network and the Internet from any location on the campus by using one of these wireless technologies. For these students, a laptop computer or PDA connects to network resources and the Internet at the click of a button, regardless of whether the student happens to be in class, in the library, or sitting outside on the school grounds. In schools that already have wireless networking, the promise of classrooms without walls is beginning to come to fruition. As wireless connectivity emerges as a dominant technology, that same promise has the potential to expand to any location anywhere, making everyone capable of connecting whenever they wish to.

For education, these emerging trends in connectivity will bring about a significant change in the way networks are implemented. The potential for limitless connections in every classroom and the capability of arranging the instructional environment without regard for power or network nodes will be possible. Emerging connectivity capabilities combined with portable computing make computers in instruction truly powerful and flexible instructional tools.

Virtual Environments

As the speed and capacity of computers and communications increase, **virtual environments** will become possible. As you have learned, virtual reality (VR) refers to three-dimensional representations of real or imagined places. Virtual environments are fully rendered environments in which the user becomes immersed. Such immersion might mean that the individual participating in a virtual environment will feel, smell, taste, see, and hear aspects of the environment. VR systems today are the most rudimentary examples of the virtual environments on the horizon. Teachers and learners will someday be able to take full-immersion field trips in which they will be able to fully interact with the virtual world they are visiting. Virtual models will be able to be constructed and manipulated to determine how their real-world counterparts would work. People with physical disabilities will be free to "move" about and fully experience the virtual world without impediments.

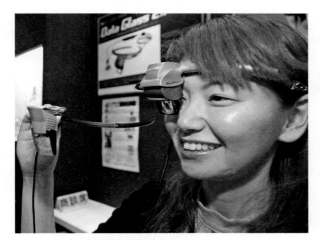

Emerging technologies such as virtual reality equipment, multifunction cellular devices, PDAs, and tablet PCs will soon impact education as they do society.

For education, improvements to VR offer the potential for full sensory experiences in learning scenarios constructed to teach. This technology also offers the possibility of altering virtual instructional environments to present and respond to unique differences in learners. Although this technology is still only on the horizon, its applications hold amazing promise for teaching and learning. For implementation of technology now, it is important simply to stay aware of the current VR resources and the emergence of VR environments and to explore how they might be used in teaching and learning.

Artificial Intelligence

Artificial intelligence programs provide intelligent assistants to help with computing tasks.

Artificial intelligence (AI) refers to programs that work in manners that are similar to the way the human brain works. In AI circles, software that learns and adjusts its responses on the basis of previous interactions is called a **neural network. Fuzzy logic software** is an AI program that resembles human decision making. **Expert systems** are AI programs that offer suggestions and advice on the basis of a database of expertise. Some AI systems use **intelligent agents** that are called on to help with specific tasks. Intelligent agents may ask questions, monitor work to determine patterns of action, and perform requested tasks. All of these types of AI programs are in existence now but have not yet sufficiently evolved to become significant tools in current teaching and learning environments.

Yet when applied to education, AI has the potential to improve and adapt software to a student's individual learning patterns and needs. An agent might be created for each individual student that would automatically customize learning software and instructional experiences in a manner that is responsive to the learner's learning style and needs. For education, AI holds the promise of programs that could become virtual teacher aides.

Communications and Collaboration

At the core of communications capabilities is available bandwidth. As bandwidth increases, so does the potential of the Internet and local networks. With improved bandwidth, communications could become almost instantaneous without regard to the size or type of files. Video files would be available on demand and of the highest quality via a broad-bandwidth Internet connection. Teachers would be able to access instructional videos or live broadcasts from a source anywhere in the world at the time most appropriate to their lesson. Instruction in a single classroom could be broadcast simultaneously to homebound students or to other schools via their Internet connection. Audio conferencing and videoconferencing would link experts across the world to be available for a guest lecture in your class. Regardless of the technology used to increase bandwidth, its implementation will make the Internet, local-area networks, and wide-area networks significantly more powerful tools.

E-Learning
ON THE WEB! 11.9
New Connections

Wiki

Another aspect of communication that is emerging is the phenomenon known as a **wiki.** Wiki is an adaptation of the Hawaiian term for *fast.* Originally created for fast collaboration and communication via the Web among programmers, a wiki site is a web site in which content is written collaboratively so that anyone with a computer and Internet access can edit and add to the information provided. A wiki results in a free and dynamic collection of information that anyone can edit.

One of the largest wikis, the Wikipedia, is published by the Wikimedia Foundation along with its sister wiki web sites, with Wikitionary, Wikibooks, Wikinews, and Wikiquote among the most popular. Wikipedia is not a forum for personal opinion, as is a blog, but is instead a collaboratively developed encyclopedia of information. Wikipedia articles offer links, cross-references, and citations contributed by those interested in that topic. While vandalism (misinformation and deliberate deletions) may occur, the many individuals interested in maintaining wiki integrity typically correct such problems quickly. Vandals are banned from future contributions, thus weeding out disruptive elements. The potential vandalism and inadvertent misinformation that is the disadvantage of a wiki is balanced by the unique opportunity to offer and maintain very up-to-date topical information in this collaborative community.

In education , wikis can provide a space for brainstorming and collaborative writing. They can offer an online, easily accessible area for debates, group projects, and shared resources. A teacher can have students author and edit articles on assigned topics or provide space for the creation of a collaborative booklet on a topic of interest. Using MediaWiki (**www.mediawiki.org**), a free public-use software for servers with which to create wiki spaces, schools can create private or public wiki web sites for use in the classroom. This unique software and its resultant online collaborative space offer infinite possibilities in the hands of a creative teacher.

SOURCE: From http://en.wikipedia.org/wiki/Main_Page.

Grid Computing

Communication via networking, whether local or across the Internet, has begun a new phase that some suggest may be as significant as the creation of the Internet itself. You will recall that the Internet began as a few networks experimentally connected together for research purposes. In a similar vein, some experimental networks, the purpose of which is to maximize computing power, are now being connected together. These computers are joined together on a "grid" to share resources and to communicate data so that the available computing power is a factor of the number of computers on the grid. The more computers connected to the grid, the more CPU power is available for the targeted task. One of the first major breakthroughs using grid computing has been the SETI@home project. In this experiment, individuals volunteer their personal computers' idle computing power to help to analyze radio telescope data for the SETI (Search for Extraterrestrial Intelligence) project. This popular and continuously growing grid uses the idle computing power of approximately 900,000 personal computers, resulting in the fastest dedicated computer in the world (Newport, 2005).

Today grid computing standards and tools are being refined, and more and more scientific computer grids are being created. Considering the cost and limited time available for the use of supercomputers, grid computing offers a viable alternative. For education, this may someday mean that everyday educators can have access to data and power previously reserved to only the most advanced research universities. Further, the power needed for intensive and complex multimedia instruction may become readily available to all despite any potential limitations of the computers located in any one classroom. The availability of seamless and powerful computing resources on every computer connected to the grid may revolutionize educational computing. For our society, grid computing may become a ubiquitous virtual master-computer available on demand to anyone requiring its use. Indeed, it may well be the next evolution in worldwide computing and communications.

Today, on a smaller scale, the basic operating principle of the grid, resource sharing, is already in place in the form of **peer-to-peer networking.** This type of networking differs from the more conventional networking structure in several significant ways. In a traditional network, we typically store the files we want to share on a network server's hard drive, which in turn is made accessible to others on the network or the Internet. We must go through the server to reach one another. Peer-to-peer networking offers another communication alternative. Instead of connecting through a server, in this networking structure, computers connect together directly. Each "peer" computer in the network then makes a portion of its hard drive public or shares its drives. This "public" drive acts like a type of virtual mini-server in that it allows others to use the resources we store there and gives us space to store resources we borrow from others. The need for specific services that offer server space and function and to which we must pay a fee is eliminated.

Such a technology has been used extensively on the Internet to share music (MP3) files. Unfortunately, many of the files made available through this type of peer-to-peer network have violated copyright laws. Many of the MP3 files stored on this type of private-public network were created by turning copyrighted musical CDs into digital files shared with other peers in the network without compensation to the artists and record companies that owned the music. As you know, this type of violation of copyright law is illegal. As a result, many of the music sites using this type of technology have been forced to shut down.

Although some people chose to use peer-to-peer networking in an unethical and illegal manner, the core technology of sharing resources and data directly between computers remains a great potential for education. Whether ultimately adapted to become a worldwide computing grid or simply used to share resources on a smaller scale, this new communications technology holds great promise for teachers and their students. Using a similar peer-to-peer structure, learning communities working on an international science project could share data easily. Teachers interested in teaching a common subject could share their lesson plans and research without the need of an education portal. For educators, this quiet, ongoing evolution in networking may indeed offer every teacher in every classroom all of the resources necessary to help students learn.

Displays

Another area of emerging technologies that holds significance for education is in display devices. Flat-panel LCD monitors, although an advance over bulky CRT monitors, are primitive compared to displays currently under development. The new prototypes use flexible plastic film that can be rolled up or laid flat on a desktop to display computer data. Though still in prototype stage, two of these technologies bear mentioning.

Flexible organic light-emitting devices (**FOLEDs**) are computer displays on flexible plastic that have the potential to be made small enough to roll up into a pen or large enough to be used as a wall-size mural and will be able to be bent or folded without harm. These capabilities give them the potential to expand well beyond the limits of current monitors and ultimately to become wearable computer displays, folded electronic newspapers, or displays that can be embedded in other devices, such as car windshields. These devices also offer better viewing, are less expensive to make, and are less power-hungry than LCD screens, in addition to being flexible. For the classroom, paper-size FOLEDs may become portable monitors that can be opened and laid flat on a student's desk or moved easily about the classroom and the school while staying connected to a CPU via wireless technology. Wall-size FOLEDs could potentially replace costly projection devices. Educational uses and applications for this emerging display technology have only begun to be projected. Clearly, as this technology evolves, educators will embrace its flexibility and potential to unclutter the technology-rich learning space.

A second, related display is **electronic paper**. Electronic paper is a sheet of transparent film containing millions of black-and-white beads of ink. When a current is applied, the beads rotate, showing either their black or white sides, thus creating an image on the film. The image can remain or be repeatedly refreshed with new data, depending on the current applied. The data can be text, graphics, or even video. Both writable and erasable, a single sheet of electronic paper is capable of displaying an electronic newspaper or the pages of a multimedia textbook. With information stored on a chip or other portable device and a sheet of electronic

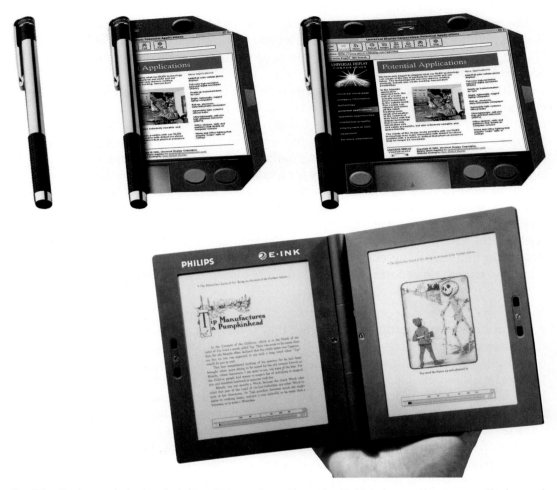

Flexible display and electronic ink prototypes have the potential to change the way we display and interact with computer data in the classroom.

paper powered by a battery, an entire library could be carried and viewed anywhere. Although thus far they have been marketed primarily as refreshable displays in stores, newer prototypes of electronic paper hold the promise for education of changing how and when the printed page might be used in the classroom. With the potential of providing all of a student's class textbooks while at the same time making the contents of the entire school library available to the student via a single sheet of electronic paper, the possibilities for the application of this technology to education are almost limitless.

Wearable Computers

An emerging technology still in its infancy is wearable computers. The future vision for such devices includes computing power built into clothing or devices small enough to pin to clothing or hang around the neck. Such devices would offer users enhanced information about the environment, reminders, and data on demand that might be useful within the context of activities. In education, wearable computers are

TECHNOLOGY SOLUTIONS
for All Learners

Wearable Computers

The Coventry Local Schools (Akron, Ohio), as part of a consortium project on wearable computers, provided a fully functioning scaled-down computer to disabled learners. These computers, weighing less than 2 pounds, are small enough to attach to a belt and come complete with keyboards and handheld monitors. They are capable of running academic software that helped students via "word prediction and speech synthesized word processors, Web-based learning through wireless connectivity to the Internet, computer-generated voice output

communication, speech output programs that provide verbal reminders to students, text-to-speech software for listening to text, visual schedules and organizational planners, enhancing competency in written expression, and enhancing or supplementing study and organizational skills." The computers offered learners a level of instantaneous support previously unknown. The outcomes of the initial project demonstrated that students using the wearable computers enjoyed more effective communication, functional independence, improved social and employability skills, and increased time on task. These portable devices, as their implementation is refined and expanded, may well revolutionize interventions for students with special needs.

Gides, Jeanne, and Gides, James, The Wearable Computer—Technology without Boundaries. Retrieved August 29, 2006, from **www.csun.edu/cod/conf/2003/proceedings/187.htm**.

being introduced for special simulation projects. One such project, sponsored by the Massachusetts Institute for Technology, has students study the spread of viruses by having them interact while wearing small computers that can communicate both data and a hypothetical virus. Thus, interacting students can simulate how viruses are spread within a healthy system. While wearable computers so small they can be integrated into clothing are not yet possible, early applications of the concept include advanced heads-up displays built into helmets for use in the military and, in education, miniaturized computers used to assist special needs students. This earliest phase of this emerging technology may seem like science fiction now; but with the rate of current advancements in computing, wearable computers may well be reality before the next generation of teachers retires from service.

Convergence

Convergence refers to the blending of technologies into a single multipurpose technology. Imagine a world in which the functions of television, radio, telephone, cell phone, beeper, and computer have blended into a single pocket device. Convergence of the many technologies already available is happening now. Cell phones can send and receive email across the Internet. PDAs have calling and email capabilities. This trend is likely to continue until the lines between all these technologies have blurred to the point of invisibility.

For schools, convergence will mean being able to pull limited resources away from acquiring many types of technologies and to focus instead on buying more of the multipurpose convergent technologies for teachers and learners. It will also mean less time and fewer resources spent training to use diverse equipment and more time for mastering the skills necessary to make the most of convergent equipment. As technologies continue to converge, educational planning and implementation are likely to become less complex and more coordinated in scope and purpose.

Converging technologies are blending into a single multipurpose technology.

E-Learning
ON THE WEB! 11.10

Converging Technology

Emerging Issues: The Changing Face of Instruction in the Digital Age

With so much technological change occurring each day, the future look and feel of technology are difficult to predict. Clearly, some emerging trends, such as those we have discussed, are evident, but others have yet to become visible even to the most astute observer. In fact, the only thing that is constant about technology is that it is in a constant state of change. How do all of these changes affect education in planning for technology today, and how are they likely to affect education in looking ahead?

Computers as Appliances

As you learned earlier in this chapter, the digital divide does exist; but as a result of many initiatives, it will ultimately close. Eventually, the computer, regardless of the shape into which it evolves, will be as commonplace in households as the television or the telephone is today. Over time, it will become an essential appliance that future generations will not be able to imagine living without. As this change occurs, schools will no longer be able to lag behind societal change. Classrooms will no longer be acceptable if they include primarily the instructional tools of fifty years ago. Instead, societal pressure will ultimately force change and demand that schools reflect the realities of the Digital Age.

In the emerging Digital Age schools, tablet PCs will be as common as backpacks, with every student responsible for bringing his or her own to every class. They may well replace books and paper and pencil. Students

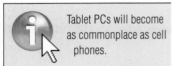

Tablet PCs will become as commonplace as cell phones.

Tablet or pocket PCs with portable keyboards make computing power accessible everywhere students need it.

might simply download the text components they need to read to their tablet PCs, complete their work on their digital devices using voice or handwriting recognition software, and then send it to their teacher's email account.

In a scenario in which computers become commonplace and indispensable educational appliances, students will need training in how to use future technologies for academic pursuits. Teachers will need to learn how to design lessons using such tools, just as they now plan lessons using rulers and calculators. Privacy and security issues will continue to challenge the technical staff as these new technologies proliferate. Schools and districts will need to determine appropriate policy and add staff to support both technologies and procedures.

In such an environment, instruction will be able to be highly individualized as teachers will be able to download intelligent agents to guide students through lessons developed to meet their particular learning needs. Assessment and evaluation of student progress will be able to be gathered electronically and shared appropriately to determine performance. The teaching and learning process will be able to be customized and then evaluated for effectiveness. When computer technology reaches the societal saturation point of the telephone, teachers will have the ultimate teaching tool at their fingertips.

Computer Literacy

Each year, more and more children become computer literate in the elementary grades. Indeed, the NETS for Students (see Appendix A) already identify levels of technology literacy expected today. For people who have already completed school, lifelong learning opportunities via higher education and community schools will make it possible for more and more adults to achieve **computer literacy.** As the Digital Age unfolds, using a computer will become as essential a skill as reading.

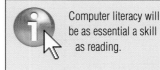

Computer literacy will be as essential a skill as reading.

For educators, this change will mean that it will no longer be necessary to spend time or resources catching up those who missed learning about computers in their public school years. In years to come, teachers will be able to expect computer literacy just as they expect students to read and write. This will make it easier for teachers to more easily integrate computer-enhanced instruction into the instructional design of their courses. At the same time, it will challenge teachers to maintain and improve their own levels of educational technology literacy to effectively use these powerful tools.

Teachers will have become computer literate either through preservice training or, eventually, through their own K–12 school experience. Expanded educational technology and computer literacy will allow courses like this one and in-service workshops to focus on integration skills rather than introductory skills. With teachers working at higher levels of technology integration competencies, the quality of technology-enhanced teaching and learning will no doubt improve.

Decentralizing Instruction

Perhaps the greatest change that may occur will not be in the equipment or the skill level of those who use technology. The most significant change

The definition of schools may change as the Digital Age unfolds.

may well be in the nature of instruction itself. As you have learned, distance delivery and alternative delivery already have the potential to redefine instruction. Classrooms that are now set within the framework of a given time and located in a particular place may expand to include virtual communities of learners located anywhere in the world. Virtual learning communities and environments may take students anywhere they wish to learn and at any time they wish to learn. Master teachers may join together from anywhere in the world to team-teach in their particular areas of expertise. Powerful communities of learners may assemble anytime, anyplace, and engage learners from anywhere.

Under such altered circumstances, will schools as we know them today survive? The answer is most likely yes, although schools must be prepared to fully evolve into institutions that prepare children for lives that will be

Computers in the classroom will continue to be a ubiquitous tool for both teachers and learners.

lived in the Digital Age. Classrooms may ultimately look quite different from their twentieth-century counterparts, but they will no doubt provide enriched learning environments where children can share and grow into their potential. Schools may no longer be so isolated from one another. Like stand-alone computers that are networked together and become more powerful because of it, the term *school* may come to refer to a network of educational opportunities, both physical and virtual, for learners. And teachers, like their classrooms, will need to change to embrace the Digital Age and use its resources to help students learn.

The Classroom of Tomorrow

The Changing Role of the Teacher

Some people believe that with so many coming changes, teachers will become obsolete. That is not the case. The technologies of the Digital Age can support instruction, but teachers will continue to have the central role in designing it, just as they do today. Of course, a Digital Age instructional design with so much capacity for individualization might look quite different from contemporary curriculum, but the educator behind it will never be obsolete.

Teachers may find themselves in a new, more challenging role. Rather than directing instruction in a single classroom setting, teachers will facilitate learning by creating optimal instructional experiences and then assisting their students through these. Furthermore, the same technology that supports worldwide student interaction will support professional interaction among educators. Teachers will not be isolated in their classrooms but will instead become part of a collegial network that is focused on high-quality educational practices. With the help of virtual teaching communities and with the ever-expanding resources available through technology, students will be better served than was ever before thought possible.

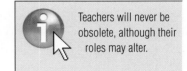

Teachers will never be obsolete, although their roles may alter.

Your role in teaching will most likely change over the course of your professional career. Technology will play a large role in instigating the changes in both our society in general and education in particular. Knowledge of educational technology will enable you to anticipate and easily adjust to the changes to come in this Digital Age. It will also help you to become an educational professional who is empowered by extraordinary technological tools that you can harness to help your students succeed. The tools are there for you, and your students are waiting. You need only pick up the tools and use them to build the powerful, technology-rich learning environments your students need and deserve.

KEY TERMS

STUDENT ACTIVITIES

CHAPTER REVIEW

1. What are the legal, social, and ethical issues arising in the Digital Age? Summarize each.
2. What four questions related to the fair use guidelines should teachers ask before using copyrighted materials?
3. What does the right to privacy entail for students in your class?
4. How do acceptable use policies help protect students and schools?
5. What is software piracy?
6. What is the e-rate? How has it helped schools and libraries connect to the Internet?
7. How might virtual environments enhance teaching and learning?
8. What is artificial intelligence? How might intelligent agents assist teachers and learners?
9. What advantages can broad bandwidth and wireless networking offer schools? Describe the current technologies available for wireless connectivity.
10. What display devices are emerging that may have significant impact on the classroom? Briefly describe each.

WHAT DO YOU THINK?

1. As emerging technologies continue to affect education, there is little question that the role of the teacher will change. Imagine yourself teaching a class in the technological future. How do you think your role would be different from the typical teacher's role today?
2. There is much controversy over issues of privacy in the Digital Age. Schools have an obligation to ensure student safety, both physical and virtual. When using the Internet or the network, this requires keeping close tabs on students' activity when they are using computers. Do you think this is a violation of privacy? Justify your opinion. Include in your justification your consideration of both points of view.
3. Of the emerging technology trends presented in the chapter or those you discovered through your research on the Web, which emerging technology or trend do you think will have the most significant impact on education? Be prepared to share your views with your peers.

LEARNING TOGETHER!

These activities are best done in groups of three to five.

1. Strategic planning is a complex, formal process that results in more effective and efficient technology implementation. After reviewing Interchapter 11 on strategic planning for technology, ask each member of the group to interview a teacher or administrator from a different school or district office to determine whether strategic planning for technology took place in that school or district. If strategic planning occurred, ask the interviewee to describe the process. If you discover that it did not occur, ask the interviewee how technology is acquired and implemented. Compare your interviews. Be prepared to share them with the class.

2. Examine your institution's acceptable use policy and compare it with two others you find on the Web. Discuss how well the policies you reviewed address the ethical issues described in the chapter. On the basis of your discussions, together create an acceptable use policy that you agree would be useful for your own classrooms.
3. The digital divide is a serious inequity that may well affect the children whom members of your group will eventually teach. Together, review the issues of inequity and access. Then identify ten strategies that you might use to mitigate the impact of the digital divide on the children you will teach.

E-Learning

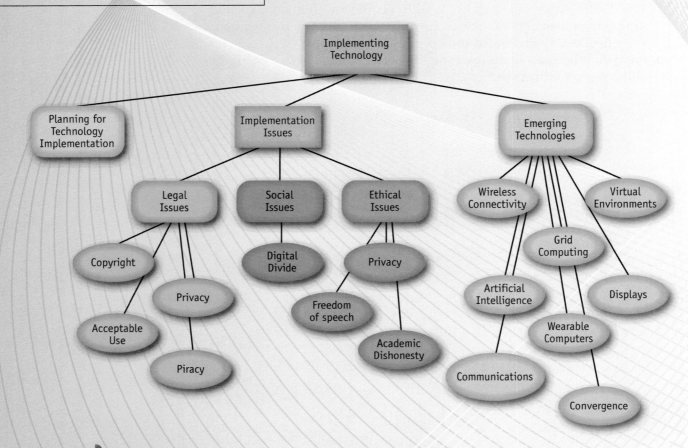

Podcasts www.mylabschool.com

Listen to a podcast relating to the use of administrative software in teaching and learning. Download the audio discussion to your iPod, computer, or MP3 player.

Video Lab www.mylabschool.com

Accessible through the **mylabschool** web site are several video vignettes that offer you a look at software in teaching and learning. Learning guides for all videos can be found in the text's Learning Guide Supplement.

On the Web! Activities www.ablongman.com/lever-duffy3e
Noted in the margins of the chapter, these activities offer you in-depth experiences in the topics and content presented in the chapter.

Online Practice Test www.ablongman.com/lever-duffy3e
Practice tests offer you an opportunity to test your knowledge and then review the results and send them to your teacher.

Outliner www.ablongman.com/lever-duffy3e
Chapter Outliners are fill-in-the-blank outlines of the main ideas presented in the chapter. Download the outliner and fill it in for an effective chapter study guide.

Power Practices www.ablongman.com/lever-duffy3e
Power Practices are animated tutorials made using Microsoft's presentation software, PowerPoint. This flash card tutorial will help you practice key concepts in the chapter.

Puzzler www.ablongman.com/lever-duffy3e
Puzzlers include content in crossword, word search, and other puzzle formats to help you master chapter content.

Useful Links www.ablongman.com/lever-duffy3e
These links offer you suggestions for expanded online research in the topics presented in the chapter.

Strategic Planning for Technology

Before any technology decisions are made, it is critical that careful, "big picture" planning occurs. Such planning is called strategic planning because it takes into account long-range goals as well as short-term objectives. Because a strategic plan will ultimately affect those inside an organization and those interacting with the organization, planning facilitators often create a plan through a formal group process that includes representatives of all concerned parties. Representatives from all groups that will be affected by the plan are selected and actively participate together in the strategic planning process. These individuals, called stakeholders, bring to the table their distinct sets of interests and perspectives. By including all stakeholders, the final strategic plan is more likely to fully address everyone's needs and is more likely to be accepted because everyone has equal ownership of the development process.

The strategic planning process typically has several distinct steps, each of which contributes toward focusing the stakeholders and the district or school they represent in a single, clearly articulated direction. Figure I11.1 shows the steps in the strategic planning process and the questions to be answered at each step.

Strategic Planning Steps

Setting
The strategic planning process usually begins with a description of the setting (district or school) in which the plan will be implemented. Although it might seem an extraneous exercise, articulating a complete description of the school or district setting helps the planning participants to become fully aware of the conditions of the setting for the plan they will create. Often, participants are aware of only the part of the school or district with which they interact. A full description of the school and/or district and the setting in which it operates makes everyone in the process much more aware of all aspects of the institutional setting.

SWOT Analysis
SWOT is an acronym for "strengths, weaknesses, opportunities, threats." In SWOT analysis, participants brainstorm all of the factors, both positive and negative, that will affect the potential success of the plan they are developing. Through this process, the circumstances that are likely to help or hinder implementation come to light and can subsequently be addressed.

Mission
The planning participants then develop a mission statement that broadly describes the overall intent of the plan. Typically, the technology plan mission statement emanates from the school or district mission statement but refocuses the institutional mission in terms of technology. The mission statement sets the direction for the rest of the planning process.

Describing the Setting
What are the significant features in the setting in which the plan will be implemented?

Conduct SWOT Analysis
What are the strengths and weaknesses within the setting? What opportunities and threats are related to implementation?

Determine Mission and Goals
What are the technological mission and the significant technology goals of the institution formulating the plan?

State Objectives
What are the specific technology objectives that must be met to achieve the goals?

Develop Strategies
What strategies must be implemented to successfully achieve the stated objectives?

Determine Evaluation
What methods must be in place and implemented to determine whether objectives were met successfully?

Disseminate Plan
How will the plan be shared with all stakeholders, and how will it be adjusted based on input?

FIGURE I11.1
The Strategic Planning Process
Strategic planning follows a set sequence of steps.

FIGURE I11.2

Strategic Plan Excerpts

Strategic plans include goals, objectives, and the strategies necessary to achieve them.

Goals

Once a mission statement has been articulated, the group then brainstorms the overarching goals for the technology that it intends to consider. Such goals can be either administrative or academic. These goals set the plan on a distinct path for technology implementation. Figure I11.2 provides some examples of strategic technology goals.

Objectives with Criteria

Once goals have been established, specific objectives are articulated that describe what must happen to achieve the goals. Much like lesson objectives, which focus on teaching and describe intended outcomes, strategic planning objectives focus on the implementation efforts and describe the desired outcome. Also, like lesson objectives, planning objectives describe the criteria that will be used to determine whether the objectives were successfully met. Because strategic plans often cover a period of more than one year, objectives are often organized sequentially by year. Subsequent years' objectives are typically built on the assumption that the previous years' objectives will have been met.

Strategies

Given the objectives articulated in the plan, the group then addresses precisely how the objectives can be achieved. The planning participants brainstorm possible strategies that will achieve the objectives. These strategies are often quite specific and are typically arranged by the year when they will be achieved. In this component of the process, it is particularly valuable that the planning team consists of diverse participants, each with a different perspective and expertise.

The description of strategies, like a lesson plan's description of methods and media, provides the formal guidelines for implementation of technology in the school or district.

Evaluation

The final component of a strategic plan is evaluation. How will the strategies be evaluated to determine their effectiveness? Using the criteria identified in the objectives, what process will demonstrate that the objective was met? In this final section, the participants plan the process that will inform them that the plan has been successfully carried out.

Dissemination

When all steps of the planning process are completed, the planning team disseminates the plan to all stakeholders. That wider group would include not only the constituencies that the planning team represents but all others who have an interest (stake) in the technology plan. Feedback from dissemination may validate the plan as presented, or it may suggest to the planning team that modifications to the plan need to be made before implementation.

The Action Plan

Once the planning team has disseminated the strategic plan and it is approved, the final step is implementation. The actual implementation often requires that an action plan be formulated that describes how each of the strategic plan's strategies will be accomplished. An action plan might include a description of which technologies need to be acquired and in what sequence. It might also include a description of services that need to be contracted from within or outside of the school or district. The action plan summarizes, in chronological order, each point of action that needs to be carried out for the plan to be fully implemented.

The action plan thus creates a blueprint for activities to be carried out, whereas the strategic plan articulates the overall direction and the necessary strategies to achieve the objectives that will move the school or district in the desired direction (see Figure I11.3).

The Teacher's Role in Technology Planning

The purpose of technology in schools is to improve either the teaching and learning process or the administrative processes that support schools. Because teachers play a significant role in both academic and administrative processes, teachers are major stakeholders in strategic planning for technology. Thus, teachers play a critical role in the planning processes that ultimately result in technology implementation.

School technology planning teams typically include a number of teachers from various departments or grade levels. District planning teams include teachers from various schools. As a professional educator, you will be asked to serve on committees that address the technology implementation issues that affect your colleagues and your students. Although some districts and schools plan less formally than the process we have just described depicts, all will expect and need your input when determining how best to acquire and implement technology.

Your role as a teacher in the school or district planning process requires that you maintain your awareness of current and emerging technologies and their usefulness in supporting teaching and learning. You do not need to be a technical expert, but you do need to be educational-technology literate to make a sound contribution to the planning process that will shape the way your school or district addresses technology.

STRATEGIC TECHNOLOGY PLAN

Sets the direction for technology implementation

ACTION PLAN

Details the tasks that must be completed in order to successfully complete the *strategic plan*

FIGURE I11.3
Technology Action Planning

An action plan completes the planning process.

chapter 12

Technology, Teaching, and You

This chapter addresses these ISTE *National Educational Technology Standards* for Teachers:

I. TECHNOLOGY OPERATIONS AND CONCEPTS

Teachers demonstrate a sound understanding of technology operations and concepts. Teachers:

A. demonstrate introductory knowledge, skills, and understanding of concepts related to technology (as described in the ISTE *National Education Technology Standards* for Students)

B. demonstrate continual growth in technology knowledge and skills to stay abreast of current and emerging technologies.

V. PRODUCTIVITY AND PROFESSIONAL PRACTICE

Teachers use technology to enhance their productivity and professional practice. Teachers:

A. use technology resources to engage in ongoing professional development and lifelong learning.

B. continually evaluate and reflect on professional practice to make informed decisions regarding the use of technology in support of student learning.

C. apply technology to increase productivity.

D. use technology to communicate and collaborate with peers, parents, and the larger community in order to nurture student learning.

Technology has become ubiquitous. It assists us in our personal life, our academic life, and our professional life. As a result, technology literacy has become an essential skill. From getting information through the Internet to purchasing public transportation tickets, listening to music, or communicating with others, technology surrounds us. Being conversant in all aspects of technology gives us the ability to function in the Information Age today and will be increasingly important in the future. Lacking technology literacy will soon be similar to being unable to read and write. As educators, the professionals charged with ensuring that our students are prepared for their place in a technology-intensive society, technological literacy becomes even more critical. We cannot imagine a teacher unable to read and write. We should no more be able to imagine a teacher unable to use technology. But how does one gain these skills and maintain them? That is the focus of this chapter.

In Chapter 12 you will

- Explore the role of educational technology literacy as a teacher or other educator

- Investigate licensure and certification requirements in terms of technology literacy

- Review the evolution and application of standards and the role of educational technology within them

- Explore how educational professionals achieve and maintain educational technology literacy

Real People Real Stories

Meet Dianne Gauthier. When the federal No Child Left Behind legislation mandated that teachers of core academic subject areas become Highly Qualified by the end of the 2005–2006 school year, Louisiana made the decision to use the Virtual School as a way to meet this challenge. Below, Dianne Gauthier, Algebra I Online Coordinator for the Louisiana Center for Educational Technology, describes how Algebra I Online is helping to meet these standards and the requirements of the profession.

Louisiana has an active Virtual School, and the school personnel thought they could help teachers meet the required standards. They decided to focus on the many uncertified teachers who were teaching Algebra I. The students' success has been measured for many years using the LEAP, the Iowa Tests, and Graduation Exit Exam. Now, requiring student achievement gains for all students is making meeting the achievement gap and teacher quality top priorities, and Louisiana is addressing the challenge of meeting those goals.

Research shows that teacher knowledge, skill, and ability greatly affect student achievement. Highly Qualified teachers of mathematics generally know how to actively engage students of diverse backgrounds and strengths to help them understand concepts and solve problems. Unfortunately, many middle school teachers are not Highly Qualified, especially in the area of mathematics. Louisiana has many small rural areas where middle school teachers are often faced with teaching multiple subjects, teaching out-of-field, and holding only K–8 certificates. Teachers in many isolated areas have limited access to quality professional development to help them become Highly Qualified.

The Louisiana Virtual School staff discussed ways that distance learning could possibly address raising student achievement by enhancing curriculum offerings and helping teachers become Highly Qualified. Many middle schools want to offer Algebra I to grade 8 students but do not have a certified mathematics teacher on the faculty. We decided that a hybrid course (part online and part face-to-face) would benefit students and teachers best, since students would have two teachers and the in-class teacher could be provided with a mathematics-certified mentor as well as high-quality professional development offerings during the year.

To help these mathematics teachers acquire the knowledge and skills to become high-quality Algebra I teachers and to create needed curriculum enhancements for the Algebra I course, the Algebra I Online Project was created. It is supported by the Louisiana Board of Elementary and Secondary Education (BESE) and funded by the state legislature. By combining a new Algebra I curriculum with online instruction by expert teachers, both the students and the teachers now have the opportunity to acquire the needed skills and knowledge.

The high-quality, standards-based online course was developed by a team of Louisiana mathematics teachers and offers a conceptual approach where students are engaged in higher-order thinking. Technology, an essential tool for teaching and learning mathematics, is used to enhance student learning. In the student-centered classroom, students of diverse backgrounds and strengths learn mathematics while using graphing calculators, digital tablets, and CBLs and probes. Administrators, as the schools' instructional leaders, observe the algebra students each week.

The in-class teacher is provided with ongoing, job-embedded professional development and a certified mathematics online teacher mentor. Professional development topics reflect the needs and requests of the teachers. During the summer, teams of online and in-class teachers meet face-to-face to begin establishing relationships and making decisions on roles, responsibilities, and grading policies. The in-class teacher participates in as many as four professional development workshops during the year that focus on technology and knowledge building of content, pedagogy, and capacity for strong mathematics instruction. Additionally, the teacher earns Continuing Learning Units (CLUs) that are required to be Highly Qualified. An evaluation is completed each year by external evaluators to study the program components and determine if revisions should be made to help ensure student success and high quality teaching and learning.

For more information, contact Dianne Gauthier at dianne.gauthier@la.gov.

Educational Technology Literacy

ISTE NETS are technology standards for teachers, students, and administrators.

Just as teachers need to be able to read and write, so too do they need to be technologically literate. However, as you have learned in this text, just being able to use technology is not enough. Teachers must also be able to apply the technologies they know to enrich their teaching and to enhance their student's learning. This unique technological literacy specific to education is **educational technology literacy.** It is an essential skill that must not only be acquired but must also be continually updated. The recognition of this necessity is demonstrated by the extent to which states have adopted the NETS standards. Figure 12.1 summarizes the extent of standards adoption.

In a continued response to the technological imperative created by the unfolding Information Age, additional educational standards reflecting the new emphasis on educational technology have become evident at every level. From the federal **No Child Left Behind (NCLB) Act** to national organizational standards to individual state professional preparation requirements, the thrust toward required educational technology literacy is evident. As educators, it has become necessary to understand and accept this expectation and to plan how, during your preservice and in-service years, to meet this escalating professional requirement.

STU	TCH	ADM	STATE	STU	TCH	ADM	STATE
(A=adopted, adapted, or aligned with; R=referenced)				(A=adopted, adapted, or aligned with; R=referenced)			
A	A	A	Alabama	A	A	A	Nebraska
R	R	R	Alaska		A		Nevada
A	A	A	Arizona	R	A	A	New Hampshire
A	A	A	Arkansas	A	A	A	New Jersey
		R	California		A		New Mexico
A	A		Colorado	A	A	A	New York
A	A	A	Connecticut	A	A		North Carolina
A	A	A	Delaware	A		A	North Dakota
	A		District of Columbia	A		A	Ohio
A	A		Florida	A			Oklahoma
	A	A	Georgia	A		A	Oregon
A			Hawaii			A	Pennsylvania
	A		Idaho	A			Rhode Island
A	A	A	Illinois	A	A		South Carolina
	R	R	Indiana		A	A	South Dakota
A	A	A	Kansas		A	R	Tennessee
A	A	A	Kentucky	R	A	R	Texas
A	A	A	Louisiana	A			Utah
		R	Maine	A	A	A	Vermont
R	A	A	Maryland	A	R	R	Virginia
A	A		Massachusetts	A	A	A	Washington
A	A	A	Michigan	A	A	A	West Virginia
A	A	A	Minnesota	A		A	Wisconsin
A	A	A	Mississippi			A	Wyoming
A	A	A	Missouri				

FIGURE 12.1

National Educational Technology Standards (NETS) and the States

The *NETS for Students* were released in June 1998, *NETS for Teachers* in June 2000, and *NETS for Administrators (TSSA)* in November 2001. At the state level, 49 of the 50 states have adopted, adapted, aligned with, or otherwise referenced at least one set of standards in their state technology plans, certification, licensure, curriculum plans, assessment plans, or other official state documents. States that have adopted, adapted, aligned with, or referenced the NETS in state department of education documents are shown here.

http://cnets.iste.org/docs/ states_using_nets.pdf

Professional Educational Technology Requirements

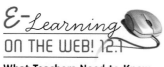

What Teachers Need to Know about NCLB

The current emphasis on technology literacy for teachers and students is grounded in the No Child Left Behind Act (NCLB). NCLB requires that by the time students finish the eighth grade they should be technology literate. This mandate has created a series of action steps for states, districts, and schools to use to evaluate their use of technology in improving student achievement. In response to NCLB, as of the 2004–2005 school year, forty-eight states had developed technology standards for students. Consequently, states have also developed associated technology standards for teachers and have included these, directly or indirectly, within their certification and licensing requirements.

State Certification and Licensure Technology Requirements

Certification Search

In all states, teachers must be licensed or certified by the state to be employed as educators. The requirements for **teacher licensure/certification** are set by each state's Department of Education. While the state licensing requirements differ among states, teachers must fulfill certain basic requirements. These state certification requirements typically include specific technology requirements, most often met through an undergraduate course in educational technology. For teachers who graduated prior to such specific technology requirements, courses in educational technology are often a recommendation for certificate renewal.

Awareness of licensure or certification requirements is every educator's individual responsibility. While districts and colleges may provide support, the ultimate resource is the agency that grants the license, the state Department of Education. Reviewing your state's requirements is strongly recommended to be sure you are meeting all licensure provisions for the area in which you plan to teach. Figure 12.2 offers you convenient access to those requirements through the University of Kentucky web site dedicated to certification.

National Certification and Educational Technology

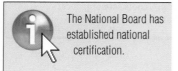

The National Board has established national certification.

In addition to state licensure, the National Board for Professional Teaching Standards (NBPTS at **www.nbpts.org**) offers **national certification** recognition. The NBPST is a nonprofit, nongovernmental agency governed by a sixty-three-member board of directors, the majority of whom are classroom teachers. This board was created in 1987, influenced by the release of *A Nation Prepared: Teachers for the 21st Century,* a report of the Carnegie Forum on Education and the Economy's Task Force on Teaching as a Profession. The purpose of NBPTS is to improve teaching and learning by encouraging teachers to become nationally certified through a voluntary system. This certification is awarded to teachers who can demonstrate that they have achieved high and rigorous standards in what they know and

Tech Tips
for TEACHERS

The College of Education at the University of Kentucky provides a web site that links to the teacher certification requirements for all fifty states. While this web site is a very rich resource, please be aware that states continually revise their teacher certification or licensure rules and requirements. To gain access to the web site and linked state certification requirements, go to **www.uky.edu/Education/TEP/usacert.html.**

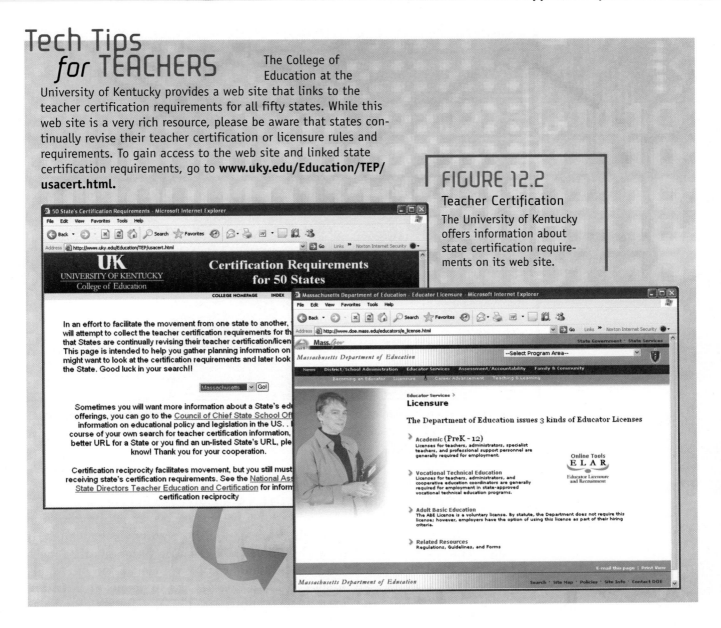

FIGURE 12.2

Teacher Certification

The University of Kentucky offers information about state certification requirements on its web site.

what they do. NBPTS also promotes educational reform by guiding this voluntary certification process, and it uses the expertise of already National Board–certified teachers to promote the process and assist others to attain certification.

While there are no directly stated technology requirements for national certification, diversity of teaching methodology is a requirement. Teachers who obtain National Board certification must use multiple methods and pathways in their approach to teaching. In addition, National Board–certified teachers employ multiple methods to measure student growth and the depth of understanding students have achieved in the subject matter. Educational technology literacy assists teachers in reaching the level of competence to be granted this prestigious national certification.

National certification is awarded to outstanding teachers able to demonstrate they meet the highest standards in their discipline.

Technology Standards

Discipline-specific and other education standards provide teachers and administrators with direction and guidance for creating programs that meet the needs of students. Well-written standards have measurable outcomes so that educators can assess student learning, the level of learning achieved, and how the learning is demonstrated. Typically state and national educational associations have created standards in their content area or discipline. Often, these standards address or incorporate educational technology requirements, particularly those set forth by ISTE. ISTE's NETS standards, then, have established their place at the core of national and state educational technology literacy requirements. For that reason, an in-depth examination of the history, organization, and implication of these standards is useful for educational professionals.

ISTE National Educational Technology Standards

As you have learned, ISTE is a national educational technology organization that has led to the development of the nationally recognized technology standards for both teachers (**NETS-T**) and students (**NETS-S**). In 1998, ISTE prepared and released a document called *Technology Foundation Standards for Students* from its new project called NETS (National Educational Technology Standards). The project was initiated to create a series of national standards that could be used to facilitate the use of educational technology by students, teachers, and administrators to promote school improvement in the United States. These standards as created by the NETS project are used to benchmark student achievement in specific technological areas proven to be critical for success in society and industry and to measure teacher technology preparedness.

Many school districts use the NETS standards to guide their efforts to ensure that their teachers (NETS-T) and students (NETS-S) achieve technology literacy. According to NETS, a technologically literate student is one who is deemed to be proficient in six broad areas or categories. Teachers can use these standards and profiles as guidelines for planning technology-based activities in which students achieve success in learning, communication, and life skills. Further, NETS teaching standards include not only the student standards but then extend beyond them to ensure that teachers can use technology appropriately and effectively in both academic and administrative tasks. The inside front cover of your text includes both NETS-T (on the left-hand side) and NETS-S (on the right-hand side) for your review.

In addition to NETS-T and NETS-S, ISTE has recently created Technology Standards for School Administrators (**NETS-A**). These new standards are based on a national consensus among educational stakeholders of what best indicates effective school leadership for comprehensive and appropriate use of technology in schools. An underlying assumption of these standards is that administrators should be competent users of information and technology tools common to Information Age professionals.

NETS standards for teachers, students, and administrators have become foundational in the development of technology standards for other professional entities. For example, the National Council for Accreditation

E-Learning
ON THE WEB! 12.3

NETS Comparison

YOU Decide!

Educational standards offer measurable outcomes for student achievement and for professional competency. Whether standards are discipline based or generic standards that cross multiple disciplines, they are important guideposts for educators. Without standards, there would be no consistency as to what is taught or what skills students should achieve in any given area. And in terms of technology literacy, standards are all the more important, as baseline technology competencies are often prerequisites for achieving content-area requirements. Standards are essential for education.

YES! Without standards, each state, each district and even each school could have different requirements for their students and for professional educators. A grade of A in one school might not be equivalent to the same grade in another school. Standards give everyone the same requirements to teach toward. Without them, required competencies could be very different in whatever school you happened to be in. That would make it impossible for students to be ready if they change schools or when they graduate and prepare for college.

NO! Standards are just more unnecessary and time-consuming paperwork for teachers. When lesson plans require that standards be addressed, it just takes too long to review and select which of the hundreds of standards should be addressed by a lesson. For teachers already buried in too much paperwork and with too little planning time, it is a waste of what little valuable time is available. Standards are fine to learn about in college, but once a teacher is working in the field, they are extraneous.

Which view do you agree with? YOU DECIDE!

of Teacher Education (**NCATE**), the official body for accrediting teacher preparation programs, changed their teacher preparation guidelines in response to NETS. These changes support the use of technology in teacher preparation programs. The result of the adoption of the NETS standards within NCATE has been that teacher preparation programs must now include courses and/or experiences to develop an understanding of the use of technology for the subjects those taking the program plan to teach, the impact of technological changes on schools, and the use of computer and other technologies in instruction, assessment, and professional productivity. This change has had a profound positive impact on educational technology literacy for preservice teachers.

NETS and Strategic Technology Planning

States use NETS in standards and in strategic planning.

E-Learning

www.mylabschool.com
video
View *State Technology Planning*

Many states have utilized NETS not only in adopting standards but also in strategic planning for technology. As of 2004, only Iowa and Montana had not made reference to NETS. And with the NCLB requirement that students be technologically literate by the end of their eighth grade, states have felt the pressure to find appropriate technological benchmarks for their students. Since NCLB requires technology literacy without specific mandates on how to achieve this or how to assess the level of success, states have taken a variety of approaches to achieving technology requirements. For example, Indiana's K–12 Plan for Technology requires that students have access to appropriate technologies, including hardware and connections, and teachers who are highly skilled in the uses of technology. It further recognizes the need for ongoing professional development for teachers. These two mandates within the Indiana Technology Plan affect

district decision making as to technology acquisition and implementation. Other states vary widely as to how NETS is incorporated, from designating additional certification requirements to identifying student technology competencies within the curriculum to inclusion of mandates within a strategic plan. Regardless of how the state addresses the standards, it is clear that technology literacy is now a critical component of education across all states. ISTE NETS can often be found at the heart of state solutions to achieving technology literacy.

Once a state adopts, adapts, or aligns with NETS, these technology standards typically become part of their "accomplished teacher" requirements. Also known as "accomplished practices," these requirements dictate the expectations for educational professionals. Once accomplished practices are determined, the local school districts within that state must demonstrate how they ensure that teachers meet these practices, thus eventually applying standards to the local schools and individual classroom.

Teacher Professional Preparation for Educational Technology Literacy

Ultimately, the national and state standards that are adopted have a direct impact on current and future teachers. These standards and requirements reverberate in colleges and universities where preservice teachers are educated. National Council for Accreditation of Teacher Education (NCATE) guidelines require that colleges of education include courses or experiences in the use of technology for instruction, assessment, and professional productivity. While some programs have added an educational technology course in the first two years of preservice teacher education programs, other programs require alternative technology-focused coursework. These required courses provide information about and practice in integrating technology into unit and lesson plans. This is also a mandate from NCLB (Title II, Part D—Enhancing Education through Technology) whose primary goal is to improve student academic achievement through the use of technology in elementary and secondary schools. As current and future preservice teachers complete their professional education requirements, educational technology literacy will play an increasingly significant role.

For in-service teachers, educational technology standards and requirements are often included directly or indirectly into annual professional evaluations. For teachers who need to ensure they are prepared to demonstrate required skills, two options are commonplace. Teachers can either return to a college or university to take credit courses in educational technology or other targeted technology skills, or they can participate in district workshops to achieve the same competency. For those who wish college credit, the additional value in doing so may include meeting requirements to add additional endorsement areas to their teaching certificate or meeting certificate renewal requirements.

NCATE guidelines have been adjusted for educational technology.

E-Learning

www.mylabschool.com **video**
View *QUEST Training for Teachers*

 HANDS-ON LEARNING

The International Society for Technology in Education, in conjunction with Learning Point Associates, a division of the North Central Regional Educational Laboratory (NCREL), has drafted an technology literacy achievement rubric. It is aligned with the NETS-T. Download this self-test for teachers, NETS for Teachers Achievement Rubric, from **www.ncrel.org/ tech/nets/nets-t-rubric.pdf.** Use the rubric as a self-test to determine how far you have come in meeting your NETS-T requirements.

E-Learning
ON THE WEB! 12.4

District Training Options

E-Learning

www.mylabschool.com
Listen to Podcast
*Professional Development
and Technology*

In any case, an expectation of educational technology literacy has come to be at the core of professional preparation and ongoing development.

States and districts often also provide ongoing professional development activities to support continuous improvement in technology skills and curriculum integration. The professional development ranges from individually attended or accessed opportunities to group or grade level options. School districts typically provide these training opportunities free of charge to in-service educators. Further, to meet the requirements of the federal NCLB legislation, many states provide valid third-party assessment of workshop outcomes to document the numbers of teachers who are meeting state standards in technology.

Many state education associations, under the auspices of the National Education Association (NEA), also give workshops for professional development in technology-related content at local locations and without charge. Technology curriculum integration is one of the most popular topics for these sessions. Collaborative agreements with local colleges, universities, and training companies also give rise to in-service workshops for PreK–12 teachers with technology skills updates and curriculum integration of technology being high on the lists of preferred topics. All of these options provide the in-service teacher an opportunity to achieve the skills necessary to meet NETS-T and NCLB requirements.

But perhaps one of the most convenient opportunities for achieving technology literacy results from the application of distance education methods to educational technology training. Online training opportunities are rich and varied. Many sites offer professional development courses and workshops, including some of the premier technology vendors. For example, Apple offers professional development at **www.apple.com/education/apd.** This rich

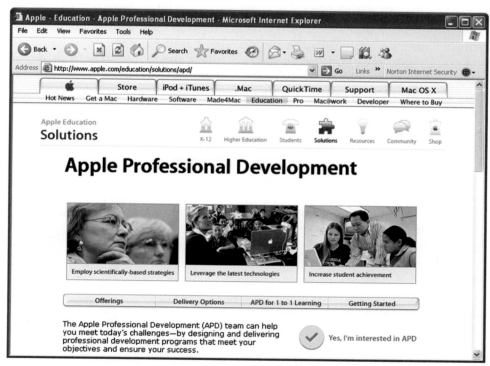

Technology vendors often offer rich technology training online to educational professionals.

site offers teachers many options for professional development, but two of the most engaging links to ensure you have the latest and some of the most interesting experiences in learning about enriching your lessons with technology are "Digital Literacy offerings provide new and experienced educators the opportunity to learn about new hardware and applications—all from an educational perspective" and the "Technology Infused Learning" strand that provides for educators who know "the basics of technology in the classroom . . . how to leverage digital tools to engage students, enhance learning and meet state content standards."

While many of the major technology vendors charge for their technology training, Annenberg Media's Learner.org offers free video-based online professional development training for K–12 teachers. This online resource offers training in a wide variety of discipline specific topics as well as educational technology training.

These online examples are just a few of the many training opportunities offered to teachers. Table 12.1 summarizes additional opportunities.

E-Learning

www.mylabschool.com
video
View *Staff Development for Online Learning*

Technology Training for Other Educators

Technology literacy is no less important for noninstructional educators. Each professional serves unique student needs and contributes to the school community. For technology to succeed in enriching the instructional environment, all educators need to achieve their own technology competencies. While these may vary from one noninstructional professional

TABLE 12.1	Sampling of Online Training Opportunities for Educators
VENDOR	**DESCRIPTION**
ADOBE	Self-paced courses, instructor-led courses, certification, professional development workshops, books, events and seminars, additional learning resources in text, audio, video, live and on-demand format. www.adobe.com/training/
APPLE	Instruction in technologies such as Mac OS X or the iLife applications iMovie, iPhoto, iTunes, and iDVD to understand how better to employ computers in education; technology integration opportunities for teachers to develop units or lessons for their classrooms. www.apple.com/education/services/training/
INSPIRATION SOFTWARE	There are Quick Tours of the software products, Quick Start Tutorials, Training CD, and Classroom Project Tours. www.inspiration.com/prodev/index.cfm?fuseaction=training
MICROSOFT	Product tutorials, lesson plans for K–12 educators, and how-to articles. www.microsoft.com/education/schools.mspx
WebCT	Just-in-time online training and workshops to be offered on-site. www.webct.com/products/viewpage?name= products_training

to another, all are critical to achieving successful technology implementation in the school.

Media Specialists

Media specialists must meet unique technology competencies.

Media specialists are the current evolution of librarians in the Information Age. As a result of the Internet, library information is no longer bounded by the four walls of the media center. Media specialists must be able to assist students with seeking information beyond the books on the shelf in order to complete a research assignment. Keeping up with the latest developments in student scholarly research is a part of the media specialist's responsibility. Professional publications for media specialists are dominated by the technology they must use to obtain information for students and teachers. *Library Journal* and *School Library Journal* feature in each issue articles largely devoted to technology literacy in the context of media centers. In addition, Google has introduced a librarian newsletter, *Newsletter for Librarians*. Media specialists, like teachers, have access to credit courses and workshops to hone their technology skills. Technology literacy is even more critical for the media specialist than for teachers, since this is the group of educators most often asked to schedule, organize, and provide technology training to their peers. Like all educators, for media specialists, current and comprehensive educational technology literacy is a necessity.

Administrators

For future **administrators,** the acquisition of technology literacy is a key skill not just for administrative use but also for effective decision making. *Technology Standards for School Administrators* (**TSSA**) were developed by a collaborative effort of several school administrators' professional organizations, the Departments of Education of Mississippi and Kentucky, several regional educational organizations, and ISTE. This group recognized that administrators are essential in how effectively technology will be used in schools. It took into consideration the varied responsibilities assumed by administrators in diverse school systems, such as the size of the school system, the type of governance the system employs, the prevailing culture of the community, and the characteristics of the administrators themselves. The TSAA further stressed that administrators have a professional obligation to further the potential for technology literacy from their position of leadership by pointing out the positive influence they can bring about for digital equity in the schools. The TSAA was the foundational document for the establishment of ISTE's NETS-A standards.

To achieve and maintain educational technology literacy, administrators participate in university or college credit courses and targeted leadership workshops. In particular, the American Association of School Administrators offers numerous publications as well as a comprehensive program of workshops through its Center for System Leadership and through professional development conferences. Many of these focus on technology.

E-Learning
ON THE WEB! 12.5

Educator Technology Standards

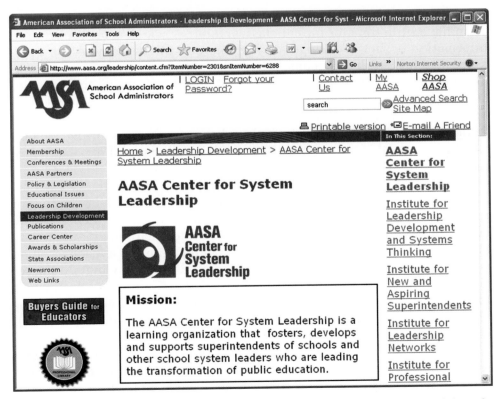

Administrators, like all educators, maintain currency in technology through training offered by their professional associations.

Other Educational Professionals

For future guidance counselors or instructional support fields, such as speech therapy and reading specialists, technology literacy is equally as important as for the classroom teacher. In addition to accomplishing the many administrative tasks associated with an education support role, technology literacy is required to make the most of available online resources for the benefit of students. Training opportunities to achieve appropriate technology literacy are typically offered through college credit courses, district technology workshops, and professional organizations and conferences. Like all other educators, educational support personnel must acquire and maintain their technology skills to perform professionally.

Maintaining and Expanding Your Technology Literacy

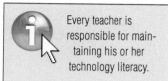

Every teacher is responsible for maintaining his or her technology literacy.

In your role as a professional, you will have the responsibility to continuously update your skills. With the advent of the NCLB legislation, it became apparent that the future of education rests on assuring that each child has teachers with a depth of content knowledge involving more than the key facts they learned while getting their professional degree. Teachers would need to be able to continually expand their knowledge base and that, in turn, would require technology literacy. Busy teachers often have little time for formal classes. Internet searches for background information or fact checking have become part of everyday lesson planning. Further, it has become clear that teachers would need ever-expanding technology skills to keep up with the emerging technologies available to them as professionals and to their students. Educational technology literacy is a dynamic and fluid requirement. Whether achieved through college courses, in-service workshops, vendor training, or personal research, this requirement is a core component and expectation of the educational professional.

E-Learning
ON THE WEB! 12.6

Meeting Standards

Fortunately, teachers as a group are typically intellectually curious. They seek out the knowledge they need to help their students learn. For success in this profession, you too must have the initiative and energy to be a **lifelong learner.** You too must embrace the technology our society has placed at the core of its twenty-first century life. As a teacher, when you address and support the learners in your classroom, you hold the society's future in your professional hands. You are bound to use the best instructional means to achieve the end of shaping the lives and actions of the young people who are entrusted to you. Without doubt, that will include technology.

Professionally you should expect that the course for which this text was used is just the foundation of your educational technology literacy. The knowledge gained gives you a basis from which you can expand your technological skills and your ability to use technology for teaching and learning. But it is just a beginning. As technologies emerge and the

Internet morphs into its next evolution, you will be expected to be on the forefront so that you can help your students bridge to their future. The Information Age is an exciting and dynamic time to be an educational professional. While the demands may be daunting, the outcomes in terms of our students' ability to succeed are without measure. Technology will help you achieve these professional goals and, further, will assist you in helping your students achieve theirs.

KEY TERMS

administrators 445
educational technology literacy 435
lifelong learner 446
media specialists 444

national certification 436
NCATE 440
NETS-A 439
NETS-S 438

NETS-T 438
No Child Left Behind (NCLB) Act 435
TSSA 445
teacher licensure/certification 436

STUDENT ACTIVITIES

CHAPTER REVIEW

1. What is educational technology literacy? Why is it important for educators?
2. What impact does NCLB have on educational technology standards?
3. What is certification? What role does technology literacy play in certification and licensure?
4. What is the difference between state and national certification? How is technology literacy incorporated in each?
5. How and for what purpose did ISTE establish NETS? What standards are currently in place?
6. How have states used NETS for furthering the advancement of educational technology?
7. What is NCATE? How have NETS standards changed college programs through NCATE adoption?
8. What options do preservice teachers have to achieve technology standards? How do they differ from options offered to inservice teachers?
9. How do corporations provide training resources for teachers? Give examples.
10. What unique technology training is required for noninstructional educators? Why are they different?

WHAT DO YOU THINK?

1. Standards have altered teacher preparation programs and the curriculum requirements in schools. The intention behind standardization is to ensure equivalent and consistent instruction and to provide measurable outcomes. Do you feel the implementation of standards by national, state, and curriculum organizations have accomplished their intent? Explain why or why not.
2. Lifelong learning is not just a preference of most teachers, it is a requirement to maintain state certification. Technology literacy courses and workshops are some of the most popular experiences for certificate extension and renewal. Do you feel that technology literacy is as important as taking additional courses in your content or discipline? Is too much emphasis being placed on developing and maintaining technology competency? Defend your view.
3. NCLB has altered education in innumerable ways. In particular, the call for high-stakes testing in every state, mandated standards in multiple areas, and the requirement of employing highly accomplished teachers have all changed state and district approaches to teacher preparation and training. Has the implementation of NCLB helped or hurt education? Do you feel it has had a positive or negative impact on technology literacy in particular? Research NCLB if necessary and be prepared to explain your views.

LEARNING TOGETHER!

The following activities should be done in small groups.

1. Join a group interested in teaching the same grade level or content area as your own preference. Research the standards on the Internet for your discipline or grade. Identify the specific standards that relate to educational technology. Prepare a summary to share with your class.

2. Brainstorm the technology training that you would find most useful during your first three years of teaching. Make an annotated list of the top ten technology-related workshops you would most like to attend. Be prepared to share your list with your peers.

3. Create a visual that represents the impact of the NETS-S, NETS-T, and NETS-A or other national and or state technology standards. Incorporate the visual into a PowerPoint presentation. Include specific examples of how NETS has altered technology planning and/ or training.

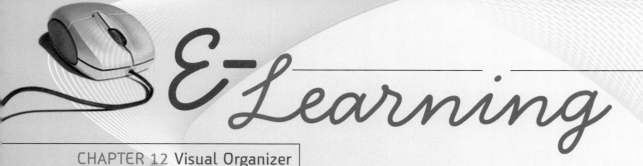

E-Learning

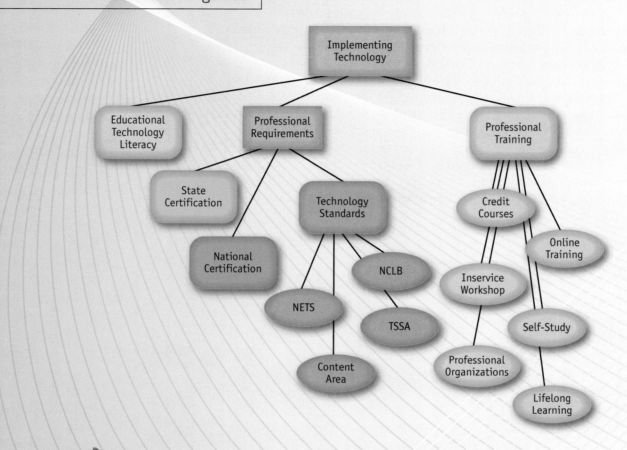

Implementing Technology

- Educational Technology Literacy
- Professional Requirements
  - State Certification
  - National Certification
  - Technology Standards
    - NETS
    - NCLB
    - TSSA
    - Content Area
- Professional Training
  - Credit Courses
  - Inservice Workshop
  - Online Training
  - Self-Study
  - Professional Organizations
  - Lifelong Learning

Podcasts www.mylabschool.com

Listen to a podcast relating to standards and technology training. Download the audio discussion to your iPod, computer, or MP3 player.

Video Lab www.mylabschool.com

Accessible through the **mylabschool** web site are several video vignettes that offer you a look at technology training. Learning guides for all videos can be found in the text's Learning Guide Supplement.

On the Web! Activities **www.ablongman.com/lever-duffy3e**
Noted in the margins of the chapter, these activities offer you in-depth experiences in the topics and content presented in the chapter.

Online Practice Test **www.ablongman.com/lever-duffy3e**
Practice tests offer you an opportunity to test your knowledge and then review the results and send them to your teacher.

Outliner **www.ablongman.com/lever-duffy3e**
Chapter Outliners are fill-in-the-blank outlines of the main ideas presented in the chapter. Download the outliner and fill it in for an effective chapter study guide.

Power Practices **www.ablongman.com/lever-duffy3e**
Power Practices are animated tutorials made using Microsoft's presentation software, PowerPoint. This flash card tutorial will help you practice key concepts in the chapter.

Puzzler **www.ablongman.com/lever-duffy3e**
Puzzlers include content in crossword, word search, and other puzzle formats to help you master chapter content.

Useful Links **www.ablongman.com/lever-duffy3e**
These links offer you suggestions for expanded online research in the topics presented in the chapter.

Rate Your Educational Technology Literacy

You have learned much about educational technology as you read through this text. Take the self-assessment below to determine your own technology literacy. Place a check in the Achieved/Not Achieved column that best represents your current status with regard to each competency. Note in the My Plan column when and how you will achieve any competencies you have not yet mastered.

COMPETENCY	NOT YET ACHIEVED	ACHIEVED	MY PLAN FOR ACHIEVING THIS COMPETENCY
I am aware of learning theories and their impact on implementation of educational technology.			
I can prepare a comprehensive instructional plan that uses technology effectively.			
I understand the basics of a computer system.			
I can use administrative software for my administrative tasks.			
I can use academic software to encourage student learning.			
I can use technology for communication and collaboration.			
I can use technology to improve my professional productivity.			
I can use and integrate technology for more effective lessons.			
I can use technology to create an effective learning environment.			
I can use technology for adding creativity to my lessons.			

Continues on next page ➤

interchapter 12

COMPETENCY	NOT YET ACHIEVED	ACHIEVED	MY PLAN FOR ACHIEVING THIS COMPETENCY
I can use technology for precise and clear presentation of ideas, including multimedia technology.			
I can use technology to help manage student learning activities.			
I can use the Internet for global communication and research.			
I can use technology to accurately assess student progress in a variety of ways.			
I can use technology to support learner-centered strategies and meet content standards.			
I can organize data via technology for reporting for both administrative and academic purposes.			
I am aware of emerging technologies that will impact education in the future.			
I am aware of social, ethical, and legal issues associated with technology.			
I can use technology to address special needs students' unique requirements.			

COMPETENCY	NOT YET ACHIEVED	ACHIEVED	MY PLAN FOR ACHIEVING THIS COMPETENCY
• I can use technology to address student diversity.			
• I am aware of how to use technology in a manner that ensures my students' safety.			
• I can use technology in a manner that ensures equity in my classroom.			
• I am aware of acceptable uses of technology and how to implement them in my classroom.			
• I can use technology to engage in lifelong learning and professional development.			

APPENDIX: EDUCATIONAL TECHNOLOGY RESOURCES AND ORGANIZATIONS

American Educational Research Association
http://www.aera.net

Apple Classrooms of Tomorrow
http://www.eworld.com/education/k12/leadership/acot

Association for Career and Technical Education
http://www.acteonline.org

Association for Educational Communications and Technology
http://www.aect.org

Association for Supervision and Curriculum Development
http://www.ascd.org

Association for the Advancement of Computing in Education
http://www.aace.org

Center for Children and Technology
http://www2.edc.org/CCT

Computer Learning Foundation
http://www.computerlearning.org

Computer-Using Educators
http://www.cue.org

Consortium for School Networking
http://www.cosn.org

Digital Divide Network
http://www.digitaldividenetwork.org

EDUCAUSE
http://www.educause.edu

Global SchoolNet Foundation
http://www.globalschoolnet.org

Intercultural E-Mail Classroom Connections
http://www.teaching.com/iecc

International Council for Educational Media
http://www.aect.org/Affiliates/National/icem.htm

International Society for Techology in Education
http://www.iste.org

International Technology Education Association
http://www.iteawww.org

National Center for Technology Planning
http://www.nctp.com

National Council for Accreditation of Teacher Education
http://www.ncate.org

National Educational Computing Conference
http://www.neccsite.org

National School Boards Association Education Technology Programs
http://www.nsba.org/itte

National Telecommunications and Information Administration
http://www.ntia.doc.gov

Regional Technology in Education Consortia
http://www.rtec.org

Society for Applied Learning Technology
http://www.salt.org

Society for Information Technology and Teacher Education
http://www.aace.org/site

Special Education Resource Center (SERC)
http://www.serc.org

TEAMS Distance Learning
http://www.teams.lacoe.edu

Technology in Education
http://www.tie-online.org

U.S. Department of Education, Office of Educational Technology
http://www.ed.gov/Technology

U.S. Department of Education, Technology State Contacts
http://www.ed.gov/about/contacts/state/technology.html

U.S. Distance Learning Association
http://www.usdla.org

www4teachers
http://www.4teachers.org

academic dishonesty Cheating and/or plagiarizing in academic work that may be facilitated by the ease of copying and pasting information from web sites or multimedia.

academic software Software designed to assist and support both educators and learners in teaching and learning.

academic tools On a computer network, academic software that provides the teacher with tools to help in the instructional process; for example, the ability to monitor student activities on each networked computer, including the ability to take control of individual computers to demonstrate a process.

acceptable use The school or district policies to help ensure that school technology made available to students is used appropriately and for academic purposes.

action plan The plan listing the specific action steps that describe how each of the plan's strategies will be accomplished.

administrative software Software that assists an educator in accomplishing the administrative, professional, and management tasks associated with the profession.

administrative tools Software programs that are shared by all network users and usually provide, at a minimum, a common calendar, address book, and facilities reservation list. Also called groupware.

Administrators Members of the teaching profession who maintain the day-to-day organizational, curricular, resource, and financial management of schools and other educational institutions.

alternative delivery system A hybrid instructional delivery system that uses the best of both traditional and distance strategies for the delivery of instruction.

analog video An electronic signal that varies continuously in strength and is generated by a camera or a videotape source.

antiplagiarism software Software that compares a student's work with well-known authors' work and with work posted on the web to detect plagiarism.

antivirus program Programs that detect and destroy computer viruses.

application program A set of instructions that tell a computer how to complete a unique task such as word processing, database management, or drawing.

artificial intelligence (AI) Programs that work in manners that are similar to the way the human brain works, allowing computers to adapt and respond beyond their initial programming.

AskERIC A personalized Internet-based service that provides education information to teachers, librarians, counselors, administrators, parents, and anyone else who is interested in education.

Association for Educational Communications and Technology (AECT) A professional association of thousands of educators and others whose activities are directed toward improving instruction through technology.

asynchronous A method of instructional delivery that is time shifted; that is, teacher and students can participate at differing times from the same or different locations.

asynchronous communications Online tools that do not require real-time interaction; examples are email and electronic bulletin boards.

attention Focusing on a specific object or thought sufficiently to become fully aware of it.

audiocassette An economical, durable, and easy-to-use magnetic tape medium that lets you record voice, music, or other sounds.

authoring system A category of software that allows the educator to easily create custom computer-enhanced lessons of all types, including multimedia lessons and web-based lessons.

AVI (Audio Video Interleaved) A popular digital video format that offers low resolution and smaller file sizes compared to other formats; good for animation.

back up To create a duplicate copy on another storage medium for use in case the original copy is lost.

backup system A system of redundant processes and technologies that provide for continuity of instructional delivery even when problems occur in the primary delivery system.

bandwidth The carrying capacity (size of the "roadway") of electronic transmission media for sending and receiving information.

behaviorists Those who view all behavior as a response to external stimuli; they believe that the learner acquires behaviors, skills, and knowledge in response to the rewards, punishments, or withheld responses associated with them.

Bloom's taxonomy A method for categorizing differences in thinking skills; it includes six levels of cognition ranging from recall of knowledge to evaluation of knowledge.

bookmarks A function that is built into internet browsers which allows the user to create a collection of URL favorites. Once a website is stored, it can be revisited later by simply locating it on the list of favorites and clicking on it.

Boolean logic A type of logic that uses operators, such as AND, OR, or NOT, to limit or expand the scope of a search such as one would do on the Internet using a search engine.

booting up The process of powering on a computer during which it reads the instructions stored in ROM to tell it how to start itself up.

broadcast audio Audio that is transmitted and received via radio.

broadcast video Video that is broadcast via terrestrial equipment or by a combination of terrestrial and satellite equipment; Commonly thought of as television.

bulletin board A surface usually made of cork that provides a flexible, easy-to-change display area for a variety of print and graphic elements.

byte Eight bits (on-off pulses) of data, roughly equal to one alphabetic (A) or numeric (1) character of information.

cable modem A specialized modem that provides high-speed connections for digital access via cable lines that are already installed for cable television. Users can use get speeds up to 100 to 1,000 times faster than is possible with a standard modem and a telephone line.

cablecast video Video that is transmitted by a cable company via coaxial cable to remote locations.

camcorder A compact video device that includes a camera and recorder; used to record sound and images that can be played back by using a VCR.

CD Compact Disk, also CD-ROM. An optical media that stores digital data via tiny holes burned into the disk surface with a laser.

CD-R (compact disc-recordable) A type of compact disc on which the user can record (write) data. Once recorded, the data cannot be changed. Each disc is capable of storing approximately 600 megabytes of data (text, sound, graphics, animation, or video).

CD-ROM (compact disc read-only memory) An optical storage device on which data is stored and read via optical technology. CD-ROM disks are written on when created, can be read many time, but the original data cannot be changed.

CD-RW (compact disc/rewritable) A type of compact disc that allows the user to record many times and to change the data stored on the CD. Each disc is capable of storing approximately 600 megabytes of data (text, sound, graphics, animation, and/or video).

chalkboard A hard-surfaced board that can be written on with a variety of chalk colors to create impromptu text and visual displays.

chat A network or online service that sets aside a virtual space in which two or more users can meet in real time by typing their messages and then sending them for display in the chat room.

chip A small square of highly refined silicon on which microscopic electronic components (such as transistors and resistors) have been embedded. Chips can be designed to serve many different purposes, from memory to CPU chips, such as Intel's Pentium IV microprocessor.

classroom management support software Off-the-shelf or customized software written for educators to help them manage school and classroom tasks, including the creation and maintenance of seating charts, class rolls, student records, and school budgets.

classroom management tools Downloadable or online tools such as test generators, diagnostic tests, and class roll generators that assist you in the tasks required for your classroom.

clip art A term that is carried over from the days of manual page layout but now refers to collections of prepared artwork that can be inserted into electronic documents.

closed-circuit TV (CCTV) A network of television monitors connected via coaxial cables running throughout a school building that can distribute television signals to all the connected classrooms.

code of ethics A set of written expectations and definitions of what is considered appropriate or acceptable use that is published by a school or district.

codec A compression/decompression algorithm that is used to digitize and compress video and audio signals for transmission and to reverse the process on reception.

cognitive style How one thinks. Each person has his or her own unique tendencies and preferences when it comes to cognition (thinking).

cognitivists Those who focus on learning as a mental operation that begins when information enters through the senses, undergoes mental manipulation, is stored, and finally used.

coherence An element of a good visual that suggests logical connection or integration of diverse elements, relationships, or values.

command An instruction that the user gives the computer or a program for the next operation to be performed.

communications cycle The interchange of information between two or more individuals, such as the teacher and a student. In the cycle, information is encoded by the sender and decoded by the receiver, with various filters affecting the clarity of the message.

compressed video system An integrated system that includes a video camera and microphone with a codec to compress the signals to transmit them over ISDN phone lines for two-way video and audio communication.

compression technologies Software and hardware that make video files smaller by capturing the initial video image in full but then ignoring the nonchanging components of the image in transmitting the images.

computer literacy The basic computer skills and knowledge necessary to ensure that individuals can effectively use computers.

computer system The combination of input devices, central processing unit, memory, output devices, and storage devices.

computer-assisted instruction (CAI) A term that was originally applied to drill-and-practice software but is now more broadly used to describe any software that uses the computer to tutor or review content and provide a platform for reasoning with reference to content.

computer-managed instruction (CMI) Software that instructs as well as manages instructional lessons; in addition to reviewing content, it keeps track of student progress with reference to the material.

computing cycle A processing cycle that includes the steps of taking data in, processing it, storing it as necessary, and outputting the finished information to the user.

concept-mapping software Software that generates visual, digital "maps" of concepts that depict the outcome of the brainstorming process and the interrelationships between ideas.

conference call A telephone call placed via personal phone services or the school phone system that allows three to eight participants to connect together to support small-group instruction or discussion.

conference A tool that provides users with a way to communicate one-to-many. Participants post a message for anyone to read; those reading the message can post either a public or a private response. Sometimes called bulletin boards, clubs, or forums.

connection gateway Node or web site that serves as an entrance point to another network.

consistency An element of a visual that suggests that diverse elements work together and build on each other to produce a single clear message.

constructivists Those who believe that knowledge is a constructed element resulting from the learning process and that knowledge is unique to the individual who constructs it.

contrast The communication power of a visual as determined by the arrangement and balance of the elements.

convergence The blending of diverse digital technologies into a single multipurpose technology such as a cell phone that can also access the Internet and provide the functions of a handheld computer.

copyright The laws that protect the interests of those who own creative works, whether text, music, artwork, software, or any other creative product.

Corporation for Public Broadcasting (CPB) A public corporation that manages the acquisition and production of educational programming while PBS (Public Broadcasting System) disseminates the programming via local TV channels.

correspondence course The earliest distance delivery system, consisting of books and assignments delivered to students via the postal system.

CPU (central processing unit) The "brain" of a computer, incorporated into a single microprocessor chip. Within it, calculations are performed; the flow of information between input, output, and memory is coordinated; and program instructions are transmitted.

data projection unit A projection device that plugs into a computer's monitor port and displays the computer image in an enlarged, room-size format.

data projector A computer projection unit that combines an LCD display unit and a light source in a single, relatively lightweight box.

database management software (DBMS) A software system that can be used to easily and quickly record, organize, access, and extract information electronically from stored data.

decision matrix A chart containing choices to help the individual determine which choice is the one that she or he believe is best.

decompression program A program that decompresses and makes usable files that have been compressed (or zipped).

Design-Plan-Act! (D-P-A) system A comprehensive three-part system that is designed to help maximize the quality of teaching plans. The Design-Plan-Act! (D-P-A) system includes three planning processes: designing the instruction, articulating specific lesson plans, and developing an instructional action plan.

desktop publishing (DTP) software Software that can not only perform typical word-processing tasks, but also make extensive and precise adjustments to page displays, such as creating an attractive arrangement of graphics and text on a page.

digital camera A camera that takes pictures and stores them digitally rather than on photographic film. Photos are stored in the camera's memory card or on a disk inside the camera and then transferred to a computer for processing or display.

digital divide A descriptive term referring to the gap between those who have ready access to and knowledge of digital technologies and those who do not.

digital projector A computer output device that projects digital images onto a projection screen, large monitor, or whiteboard so that they can be seen by a large group.

digital subscriber line (DSL) A special phone line that provides speeds up to 25 times faster than those possible with a standard phone line. Both voice and digital communications are provided on a single line, thus eliminating the need to subscribe to two phone lines.

digital video disc (DVD) A type of optical storage device that uses laser technology to store data. DVD discs store considerably more data than CD-ROMs because they store data on both sides of the disc (unlike the one-sided CD-ROM) and on up to two layers per side.

digital video Video signals that are recorded as discrete numerical values that represent the video images.

digital video camera A video camera that captures and stores the video in a digital format that can then be directly manipulated by using a personal computer.

digital video editing Integrated hardware and software that allow the user to edit images and audio frame by frame.

digitizer An electronic device that converts lines drawn on a special tablet into digital data that can be manipulated on a computer. Sometimes called a graphics tablet.

diorama A display that represents a scene with a foreground containing three-dimensional objects and a two-dimensional painted background.

direction Arrangement of visual elements to establish the initial focus and the appropriate direction for viewers' attention to follow when looking at a visual.

discussion An asynchronous internet tool that allows users to communicate with other students or educators in a forum or bulletin board format. Discussions link individuals across geographic boundaries, and provide users with the flexibility of participating in the discussion at a time that is convenient for each individual. For educational purposes, they are typically moderated by the teacher, with opportunities for everyone to ask questions and post responses.

dissemination The sharing of a strategic plan with all stakeholders when all steps of the planning process have been completed.

distance education The delivery of instruction to students who are separated from their teacher by time and/or location.

document camera A video camera mounted on a stand that takes and projects an image of whatever is placed on the stand's document table.

downlink A data link by which signals are transmitted from a satellite to a terrestrial system at another location on the globe.

dpi (dots per inch) A measure of resolution in printers and some other output devices.

draw programs Software that provides tools to create digital images; this software is known as object-oriented or vector graphic programs because the graphics are created by layering objects on top of one another.

drill-and-practice software Software that uses a behaviorist format that offers rewards following successful completion of routine exercises.

DVD (digital video disc) A laser disc that is similar to a CD-ROM but is designed and recorded to hold significantly more information than a CD. DVD discs can store data on both sides of the disc (unlike the one-sided CD-ROM) and on multiple layers per side.

DVD-ROM (digital video disc read-only memory) An optical storage device that is similar to a CD-ROM disc but can store considerably more data. DVD discs can store data on both sides of the disc (unlike the one-sided CD-ROM) and on multiple layers per side.

dynamic instructional design (DID) model An instructional design model that includes these six phases: know the learners, articulate your objectives, establish the learning environment, identify teaching and learning strategies, identify and select support technologies, and evaluate and revise the design.

e-book Electronic book. A computing device designed to download, store, and display electronic versions of books. These devices may include multimedia features as well as access to the Internet to enhance or expand on linked text within the book.

editing software Software that provides the user with the capabilities to alter, enhance, or add special effects to digital images.

educational games Software that presents and reviews instructional content in a game format.

educational technology Any technology used by educators in support of the teaching and learning process.

educational technology literacy The ability to employ technology to enrich teaching and to enhance student learning; because technology is perpetually changing, it is important that literacy skills be continually updated.

electronic conferences A method of one-to-many electronic communication much like a virtual bulletin board on which individuals post messages for all participants to read and then others post responses, resulting in an online discussion.

electronic discussion See "discussions"

electronic gradebooks Grading tools that let a teacher store and easily average students' grades.

electronic mail An asynchronous communication method in which a written message can be sent from one user to another; messages can include extended attachments enhancing the original message with animated graphics, audio, and compressed video clips in addition to text.

electronic spreadsheet Software that enables the user to organize, input, edit, chart, and produce accurate professional reports for task dealing extensively with numbers.

electronic whiteboard A combination of computer technology with a whiteboard display that not only displays information like any other whiteboard, but also captures the information written on it into a computer file. A digital projector can project the image on the computer screen onto the board, where it becomes a touch screen to which the computer will respond.

e-mail Electronic messages sent from one computer to another across the many networks attached to the Internet.

environmental factors aspects of the learning environment that are external to the learner or teacher, but have an effect on the learning process; physical environmental factors, such as the room temperature, external noise or lighting, can create obstacles for student-teacher communication.

e-rate Also called the Education Rate, a discounted cost for telecommunications service for community access centers (schools, libraries, etc.).

ERIC A national information system that is supported by the U.S. Department of Education, the U.S. Office of Educational Research and Improvement, and the National Library of Education; the world's largest database of education information, with more than one million abstracts of documents and journal articles, many available through the Internet.

evaluation The final component of strategic planning in which the participants plan the processes that will be used to determine whether the plan has been successfully carried out. It is also a method of assessing a student's achievement of stated objectives. In a distance environment, it may include alternative assessments and proctored testing.

exhibit A diorama or other classroom display created and/or arranged to illustrate instructional content.

expert systems Artificial intelligence programs that offer suggestions and advice based on a database of expertise.

fair use A section of the copyright law that identifies the criteria under which you may be allowed to copy another's creative work.

FAQ An abbreviation for the "frequently asked questions" that many web sites include to anticipate the questions that users will have.

favorites A collection of URLs that have been saved by using a function of the browser, allowing the user to go to a desired web page again without having to retype its URL; also known as bookmarks.

fax Technology that, with a combination of a scanner, a modem, and a printer, translates hard copy into digital signals, sends them across communications channels, and then prints them when they are received by another fax machine; fax technology is useful for communication of materials in a distance education environment.

feedback Providing another person with information on how well a task was performed or how successful an experience was in order to help improve future performance.

feedback loops Provisions within the instructional design plan to collect evaluative information for two main purposes: The information is used by the learners to see how they are doing so that they can change their approach, and the data is used so that immediate changes can be made to improve the plan.

felt board A cloth-covered board on which visual elements cut out of flannel or felt and backed with Velcro™ can be arranged to illustrate instructional content.

file A collection of related data, usually a product of a single task, that is saved on a storage device.

file transfer protocol (FTP) The application protocol that is used to facilitate the transferring of files between computers on the Internet.

filtering software Software that filters out and blocks unacceptable Internet sites so that students cannot access them.

firewall A combination of software and hardware that provides various levels of security measures designed to keep computer hackers out of networks and to keep data safe.

flat-bed scanner A scanner with a flat glass plate on which the original is placed (allowing the user to scan a page from a book); a cover can then be placed over the back of the original to block ambient light during the scan process.

flip chart A large (25" × 30") pad of paper usually mounted on an easel.

floppy disk A nonvolatile, portable magnetic storage device. The standard floppy disk can contain 1.44 megabytes (millions of bytes) of data.

focused listening Giving one's full attention to an auditory stimulus.

folder A digital organizer that is created by the user to hold related files on a disk; also known as a directory in non-Windows operating systems.

formative feedback Feedback that ensures a way to facilitate the continuous flow of information as a system is implemented so that corrections and adjustments can be made while the process unfolds.

freedom of speech The ethical issue that arises whenever Internet content is regulated such that it restricts the constitutionally guaranteed right to free speech.

freeware Software that is offered to users without charge.

FTP (file transfer protocol) A protocol used on the Internet for uploading and downloading files.

fuzzy logic software Artificial intelligence software that functions in a manner that resembles human decision making.

GIF (Graphic Interchange Format) A graphics format that is used primarily for color images, clip art, line art, and gray-scale images.

gigabyte Approximately one billion bytes of data or characters of data.

global learning community A community of learners built through the use of communication tools on a classroom web site to connect one classroom to others across the globe.

goals In strategic planning, the overarching direction and purpose for technology that set the plan on a distinct path of technology implementation.

graphic A pictorial image, such as a drawing, cartoon, or diagram, that can represent and clarify concepts and relationships.

graphics software Software that enables the user to create images from nonelectronic sources and to create, edit, alter, enhance, and add special effects to digital images; the three categories of graphics software are drawing, imaging, and editing.

graphics tablet An electronic device that converts lines sketched on a special tablet into their digital equivalent on the screen. Sometimes called a digitizer.

groupware Administrative software tools that are shared by all network users and usually include, at a minimum, a common calendar, address book, and facilities reservation list.

GUI (graphical user interface) The method of interaction in which the user enters commands by using a device such as a mouse or trackball to point to and click on icons displayed on the monitor.

H.320 Standard International standards established for the compression of video signals across ISDN lines so that diverse brands of compressed video equipment can communicate with each other.

H.323 Standard International standards established for the compression of video signals across networks and the Internet.

handheld computer Also Personal Digital Assistants (PDA). Palm size computer that offers a scaled-down version of PC operating system and applications programs. Most are also internet capable and offer wireless connectivity to networks.

handshaking The process that occurs when one computer calls another computer and the second computer answers the call and responds with a high-pitched sound known as a carrier signal.

hard copy The printed version of material generated by a computer. It is the most common output of a computer other than what appears of the monitor screen.

hard disk A disk storage area in which the operating system, applications programs, and most personal data are stored. The disk or platter is built into the hard disk drive and can hold gigabytes, or billions of bytes, of data.

hardware Computer hardware includes all of the computer components that are physical, touchable pieces of equipment.

headphones Miniature speakers that are placed directly over the ears. They allow individual students to listen to audio without disturbing anyone else.

hearing The physical process that includes the correct receiving of clear, audible sounds.

home page On a web site, a welcome page that orients the visitor to the site and provides a connection to additional information pages.

hub A series of centralized connections for workstations or peripherals so that they can be connected to the network.

hypertext markup language (HTML) The formatting language that is used to determine how the information presented on web pages will look.

hyperlink A graphic or segment of text on a web page that contains instructions to link to another web page or a different web site.

hypermedia software A type of multimedia software that not only uses multiple media but also organizes information such that the student can make "hyperjumps," student-driven connections in either linear or nonlinear sequences, from and to different components of the instructional content.

icon A small graphic image that represents one of a GUI's system options.

imaging software Software that creates a digital version or images from a nonelectronic source.

independent learning A type of learning strategy in which students must take greater responsibility for the processes and procedures necessary to master content.

individualized instruction An instructional approach in which the techniques used are focused more on the individual learner than on a class or larger group; often the approach used for distance learners.

input device A computer peripheral that the user might use to enter data into a computer system.

instant messaging (IM) A type of chat software that allows two users to spontaneously open a private two-person chat room when both are online.

instructional action plan (IAP) A template in which the teacher is prompted to list lesson requirements and to detail what he or she will need for successful implementation.

instructional design model A plan of instruction that results in a complete and precise blueprint of what should happen and how to arrange the key critical components necessary to designing effective instruction.

instructional event A learning experience that has been designed by a teacher from specific learning objectives to outcomes with the use of appropriate media to enhance the learner's achievement of the objective.

instructional support Systems to support learners, such as a teacher being present for clarification and questions or a media center or tutoring program for students who need additional help. Such systems are often absent in distance education; alternative support systems are required in their place.

instructional television (ITV) Local learning channels that use broadcast airwaves to distribute video signals of instructional programs throughout a school and/or district.

Instructional Television Fixed Service (ITFS) A terrestrial system that sends signals via microwave transmission from studios and ITFS broadcast locations to reception locations (usually schools) within a fixed area.

integrated learning systems (ILS) A network of computers, all running customized software designed to assist students in learning targeted objectives.

integrated productivity package A software package that includes the major applications (word processing, spreadsheet, database management, presentation) but not all of the features and capabilities of the stand-alone application packages.

Integrated Services Digital Network (ISDN) High-speed digital phone lines that can provide speeds up to five times that of regular analog phone lines and can offer both voice and digital communications on a single line.

integrated software package A collection of the main features of popular applications integrated into a single comprehensive application.

intelligence The inherent capability of a learner to understand and learn.

Intelligence Quotient (IQ) A quantitative measurement of the inherited capability of the learner to understand and learn. A commonly used measure is the Stanford-Binet, which is typically given to students several times during their academic careers.

intelligent agents Subprograms used by artificial intelligence systems to help with specific tasks such as asking questions, monitoring work to determining patterns of action, and performing requested tasks.

interaction Communications and discussion between teacher and student and among students that clarify and enhance their understanding of course content.

interface The component of an operating system that establishes the methods of interaction (via menus, text, and/or graphics) between the user and the machine.

International Society for Technology in Education (ISTE) A nonprofit professional organization dedicated to promoting appropriate uses of information technology to support and improve teaching and learning.

Internet An electronic communications network of networks that connects computers and organizational computer facilities around the world with a standardized means of communication called Internet protocols (IP).

Internet audio Audio, usually digitized as a WAV or MP3 file, that is delivered to the user over the Internet.

Internet broadcast The broadcasting of live events and performances over the Internet, using streaming video technology that compresses digital video and plays it back while it is being received.

Internet chat A synchronous communication in which two or more people online at the same time communicate, typically via typed messages in a virtual space.

Internet meeting An Internet-based "face-to-face" conversation with people around the world via compressed video.

Internet radio Online radio stations consisting of a wide variety of programming, including music, sports, science, and local, national, and world news broadcast over the Internet.

Internet service provider (ISP) A company that provides home and business computers with a way to temporarily connect to the Internet usually for a monthly, quarterly, or annual fee.

ISDN High-speed telephone lines that are often used to connect compressed videoconferencing systems.

JPEG (Joint Photographic Experts Group) The agreed-upon standard for high-resolution images; pronounced "jay-peg."

keyboard The primary input device for a computer. A typical computer keyboard is laid out much like the keys on the typewriter but with several additional keys, not typically found on a typewriter, that are used to control the computer or give software commands.

kilobyte Approximately 1000 bytes or 1000 characters of data.

laser disc Eight- or twelve-inch optical discs that are made and played by using laser technology similar to that used for CDs; a recording medium that was developed to provide a higher quality of image and sound than videotape provides.

LCD (liquid crystal display) A display screen made of two sheets of a flexible polarizing material with a layer of liquid crystal solution between the two.

learning environment The instructional climate in which the student is expected to learn. It includes all aspects of the environment from the physical to the nonphysical.

learning strategies The way in which instruction is presented to the learner determines how the learner can process the information. Providing for active learning activities is an example of the use of an effective learning strategy.

learning style Those conditions under which an individual best learns. The most common learning style theory identifies three primary modalities for learning: auditory, visual, and kinesthetic.

lesson planner A detailed guide to creating a daily or weekly lesson plan. It is the pragmatic product of the instructional design process.

lifelong learning The willingness to sustain intellectual curiosity across the life-cycle.

link A connection to another point on the web, either on the same document, on a different page of the site, or on another web site altogether.

liquid crystal display (LCD) projection panel A display device made up of a large glass panel in which the liquid crystals can be activated by an electrical current to form letters, numbers, and visual images. The panel is connected to the computer and placed on an overhead projector so that the projector's light shines through the panel's glass and projects the computer image onto a screen.

listening Being able to hear and comprehend auditory stimuli; it involves several steps: (1) actually hearing the auditory stimulus, (2) the brain turning that stimulus into neural pulses and processing them, and (3) making the appropriate cognitive connections to relate this new information to memories of real events or previously learned content.

live cam A digital video camera that is connected to a computer, which in turn is connected to the Internet so that the digital images from the camera can be see by those connecting to the live cam web site.

local area network (LAN) Small networks that connect machines in local areas, such as a classroom or school.

macro A prerecorded set of commands that automates a complex task such as formatting output to fit on labels.

magnetic board A metal display surface on which visual elements with magnets attached to them can be arranged to illustrate instructional content.

mailing list An electronic list of email addresses for individuals and/or companies that is equivalent to a printed phone list. Email can be sent electronically to everyone on the mailing list with one command.

media Aids to teaching that assist a teacher during instruction. They range from printed materials to audiovisual equipment to computers.

media specialists Librarians who assist in finding information beyond the library, especially information that is available electronically or on the internet. Media specialists are often responsible for training teachers and students in how to use technology as a tool to locate information.

megabyte One million bytes or 1,000,000 characters of data.

memory A series of RAM chips that provide temporary, volatile electronic storage that is used by the CPU to store short-term data.

menu A listing of command options. In the Windows and Mac operating systems, command menus appears across the top of open windows.

method A technique or strategy of teaching, such as lecture, demonstration, or discussion.

mission statement A statement that broadly describes the overall intent of a strategic plan; typically, a mission statement emanates from the school or district.

model A three-dimensional representation of a real object or concept that cannot reasonably be brought into the classroom.

modem A device that Modulates a computer's signal so that it can be transmitted across a phone line to a similar device that DEModulates the signal.

monitor The primary output device of a computer, displaying computer information on its screen. Monitor screens typically have higher resolution than TV screens.

motivators Objects or activities that get the learners' attention and encourage them to become engaged in the lesson.

mouse A pointing device that rolls about on the user's desk. It is often called a "work-alike" device because it moves the cursor on the computer screen in the same direction that the user moves the mouse on the desk.

MOV The file type of one of the most popular digital video formats; it is known as QuickTime, and the file type is abbreviated as MOV for "movie."

MP3 (Moving Picture Experts Group Audio Layer 3) An audio compression technology that provides high-quality sound in one twelfth of the space that the same sound would take in previous formats of audio files.

MPEG (Moving Picture Experts Group) A popular digital video format that reduces the size of video files up to 95 percent yet retains near-television quality.

multimedia Multiple types of media that are combined into an integrated whole that presents instructional content. Although not only digital media may be included, the term is often used to refer to a computer-based format that combines text, graphics, audio, and even video into a single, coherent, digital presentation.

multimedia kit An instructional kit that includes multiple media to present content; a kit may include visual elements (texts and graphics), cassette tapes, student activity sheets, suggested lesson plans, motion video, and even real objects.

multimedia software Software that uses multiple types of technology that typically address different learning modalities.

narrowcast video Video transmission that is targeted to a small (narrow) audience, particularly schools.

national certification A set of standards developed by the National Board for Professional Teaching Standards for the purpose of improving teaching and learning. The NTBPS awards certification to teachers who can demonstrate that they have achieved high standards for what they know and do as teachers.

navigation button Connections or links to other locations on the same or a different web site; they are usually colored or underlined words or graphics, and when they are passed over with a cursor, the cursor arrow turns into a pointing hand, indicating something that can be clicked on.

NCATE National Council for the Accreditation of Teacher Education; an official body for accrediting teacher education programs. NCATE has adopted their own NETS standards requiring teacher education programs to include courses or experiences to develop understanding of the use of technology.

NETS National Education Technology Standards; developed by the ISTE to create a series of national standards used to facilitate the use of educational technology by students, teachers and educators to promote school improvement in the United States.

NETS-A National Education Technology Standards for Administrators; requires administrators to enact effective school leadership for comprehensive and appropriate use of technology. These standards evolved from the Technology Standards for School Administrators (TSSA), a foundational document of the ISTE stressing administrators' obligation to use their leadership positions to promote technological literacy.

NETS-S National Education Technology Standards for Students; requires students to be proficient in using technological knowledge, to use technology in a responsible way, and to utilize technology as a tool to increase problem solving, creativity and productivity.

NETS-T National Education Technology Standards for Teachers; requires teachers to use technology to plan and design learning environments and experiences, increase assessment capabilities, more effectively design curriculum and increase productivity.

network A collection of computers and peripherals that are connected together so that they can communicate information and share resources.

network interface card (NIC) An expansion card with an electronic port with connectors that is placed in each computer that is to be connected to a computer network.

network modem A modem that is connected to a network server, allowing computers that are connected by the network to share a single Internet connection.

neural network Artificial intelligence software that learns and adjusts responses on the basis of previous interactions.

neuron A nerve cell that consists of three major components—the cell body, the axon, and the dendrites—and is part of a vast neural network.

newsgroup An electronic public discussion or conference, dedicated to a specific topic, that is continuously running on the Internet. It may be hosted privately on one server, or it may be hosted on many servers in a decentralized fashion.

No Child Left Behind Act (NCLB) A federal law to improve U.S. primary and secondary schools through increased standards of accountability as well as flexibility of school choice. The major provisions of the act focus on outcome-based measurements of student progress, as well as measuring teacher quality.

node Any workstation or peripheral that is connected to a network. All nodes are ultimately connected back, through one or more hubs, to a server.

objectives Carefully articulated statements that describe what must happen to achieve the goals of a strategic plan; strategic planning objectives focus the implementation efforts and describe the desired outcome.

OCR (optical character recognition) software Software that recognizes printed characters when they are scanned and then turns them into their electronic word-processing equivalent.

online publications Online, electronic versions of material that would traditionally be produced in hard copy. Also known as e-publications, these resources typically include current and archived articles of interest to educators.

operating system A program that tells the computer how to function and how to manage its own operation.

oral history Historical commentary that is made up of a series of interviews captured on audiotape.

oral journal The use of audio technology to record observations, reflect on personal experiences, or practice and listen to one's own oral communication skills.

output device The pieces of hardware that move information (data that has been processed) out of the computer.

overhead projector A projector that uses a powerful lamp and a series of mirrors and lenses to shine through a clear acetate sheet (i.e., a transparency) so that the images on the transparency can be seen by all.

packet Data that is broken into small units and sent through a network one unit or packet at a time.

paint programs Software that uses an electronic pen, brush, and other tools to create and manipulate digital pictures in a manner very similar to the way in which one paints a picture in the real world.

palmtop computer A palm-sized, hand-held computer that merges the digital organizer and the computer into a single powerful but small computing device.

password A combination of letters and numerals that a user must enter along with the login name as a second level of security.

PDF files Files that have been saved in Adobe Acrobat format so that the publication appears exactly as it would look on the printed page, including custom layouts, photos, and other graphics; these files require the use of Acrobat Reader to display them.

pedagogical cycle Teaching and learning strategies are components of a continuing cycle that is played out again and again as a lesson is implemented.

pedagogy The actual function of teaching or what teachers do when implementing their craft to assist their students' learning.

peer-to-peer networking A network configuration that allows users to share files, not by uploading them to a central site, but instead by making files available on their machine, which in turn is accessible to others on the network.

performance objectives Objectives that specify what the learner will be able to do when the instructional event concludes.

personal digital assistant (PDA) A hand-held computer that may vary in capabilities from simply functioning as a personal organizer to running scaled-down versions of productivity software.

personal filter Personal characteristic of the learner/receiver that can impact the communication process by shaping how the individual processes objective messages. Individual characteristics, such as personal values, cultural heritage and belief systems, can have the effect of distortion or misinterpretation of communication.

perspective The way in which people look at things and interpret them; different people can look at the same thing and see it in their own unique ways.

phone bridge Communications technology that allows multiple users to call in to a central phone number to participate in a phone conference.

photograph A pictorial image captured via camera, film, and a photochemical development process.

piracy Illegally copying software to share with others or installing software on multiple machines when only one copy was purchased.

pixel The smallest unit of information in an image. Each pixel represents a portion of the image in a specific color. The term pixel stands for "picture element."

plug-in A program that may be downloaded from the Internet, usually free, to expand a browser's capabilities, for example, to allow multimedia to be displayed.

port A connection on a computer into which peripheral devices can be plugged.

portal A site on the Internet that offers an assortment of services, such as a search engine, news, email, conferencing, electronic shopping, and chat rooms.

POST (power-on self-test) A self-diagnostic program that ensures that all of the computer's components are functioning as expected.

preorganizer An early warning system to let the learners know what knowledge they are responsible for acquiring.

presentation software Software that includes programs designed to create digital support materials for oral presentations.

print material Hard-copy printed pages that may include books and worksheets as well as posters and charts.

print server A dedicated computer that provides printing services to all local network workstations by attaching the printer to one of the workstations on the network or by directly connecting the printer to the network.

privacy An ethical issue that arises when an individual's right to privacy conflicts with the rights of any agency, whether governmental or commercial, to closely monitor and record an individual's personal information or online activities.

problem-solving software Programs that involve the learner by focusing on creative problem-solving situations rather than on routine drill-and-practice skills.

productivity software Generic business application software that educators can use and adapt for the administrative and professional tasks they must address.

program A set of computer instructions, written in a special computer language, that tells a computer how to accomplish a given task.

programmed instruction An instructional system in which material is presented in a series of small steps. Each step requires active learner response, to which there is immediate feedback to the learner as to the correctness of the response.

proportion The relative size of elements in a visual in comparison to their importance.

protocol A common, standardized set of conventions for the format for communication that governs the formatting of data and the way it is handled.

Public Broadcast System (PBS) A local nonprofit television channel that disseminates high-quality educational programs, especially to schools but also to the general public; part of a nationwide system of public stations.

public files Public storage areas on a network where files can be stored and read by all users; the files can be read-only, or they may be designated as read/write.

RAM (random-access memory) The series of chips that make up a computer system's temporary memory area. This area empties when the application is closed and fills up again when the user opens a new application.

readiness In distance and alternative learning, the capacity of teachers and students to work within the new environments; includes readiness to accept new roles and readiness to work with new technologies.

real object An object that can be safely and reasonably brought into the classroom for examination or demonstration.

reference software Digital versions of volumes of reference materials recorded in a linear fashion on a compact disc that contains an interface that enables hyperjumps to any point of information recorded on the CD.

removable hard disk A hard drive that can be removed from the computer. It can either be mounted in the computer or plugged into the back of the computer and run as an additional, external drive.

resolution The clarity and crispness of the images on the monitor screen or printer. Pixels are the measure of resolution in monitors; printer resolution is measured in dpi.

resource sharing A network function that allows programs that are installed on the network server to be available to all workstations.

retrofit To prepare and remodel existing facilities to accommodate computer networks.

ROM (read-only memory) A chip created to hold a stored program such as the BIOS (Basic Input/Output System) that provides instructions to the computer as to how to start itself up. ROM chips are read but are typically not written on.

router Connecting devices used to direct (route) network communications along the correct pathways to and from the appropriate network.

satellite transmission Signals transmitted to a satellite (uplinked) and then sent back down (downlinked) to a terrestrial communication system at another location on the globe; the satellites are in orbits that allow signals to be bounced via uplinks and downlinks to positions anywhere on the globe.

scaffolding The process of building bridges to prior knowledge at the beginning of a lesson.

scan converter A device that converts a computer's image into one that can be displayed through analog (video) technology by converting a digital (computer) signal to an analog (video) signal.

scanner An input device that captures and then translates printed copy or images into digital data.

school and classroom management support software See *classroom management support software*.

search engine A special program on the Internet that allows the user to type in keywords to look for online material that contains those words or topics.

server A powerful computer that provides services to other computers in the network, such as email, program sharing, and printer sharing.

shareware Software that is offered to users for a small fee, usually paid on the honor system after the user has had a chance to try out the software and determine whether it is indeed useful for the user's purposes.

sheet-fed scanner A scanner that allows the user to feed a series of pages into the scanner one after the other. Some sheet-fed scanners include a document feeder so that the user does not have to do this manually.

simulations Software packages that present to the user a model or situation in a computerized or virtual format.

site licenses Purchased rights to use a single copy of a program on any machine on the network at a defined site.

site map An outline of all the pages included on a web site, usually with a description of the type of information that can be located on each page.

slide A small photographic transparency made from pictures taken on slide film and then permanently mounted in a cardboard holder.

slide projector A projector that shines a bright light through a slide (usually 35mm) to display the image on a screen.

soft copy Data that is still in an electronic form within the computer. Soft copy is volatile; it will disappear when power to the machine is cut off.

software Computer programs created to accomplish specific tasks or perform specific functions.

speaker An audio output device to amplify the sound generated by a computer program, a CD, or other sound device.

speakerphone Telephone technology usually equipped with an omnidirectional microphone designed to pick up voices from anywhere in the room that allows all participants in a room to communicate using a single, specially equipped phone.

special needs software Software specifically designed to address the needs of learners with special needs as the result of a variety of physical or learning impairments.

stakeholders Representatives from all groups that will be affected by a strategic plan who, as a result, are selected and actively participate together in the strategic planning process.

stimulus-response A stimulus is the initial action directed to the organism, and the response is the organism's reaction to that action.

storage A nonvolatile, electronic space on a magnetic or optical disc that the computer can use to store instructions and data for use at a later time.

storyboarding A technique that is used to plan a video sequence by sketching each of the main planned image ideas (and script if desired), one per card, to allow the planner to consider the relationships of the video images, sound, and use and positioning (staging) of props and to revise as desired.

strategic planning A process that includes a series of several distinct steps, each of which helps to focus the stakeholders and institution participating in the process in a single, clearly articulated direction.

strategies As a component of the strategic plan, statements that describe how the plan's objectives can be accomplished.

streaming audio An audio technology for the web that sends audio in a continuous stream or flow to allow the user to listen to the audio as it is received by the browser.

streaming video A video technology that compresses and plays back digital video that is sent in a continuous stream, allowing the user to view the video clip while it is being downloaded over the Internet.

summative feedback Data that is returned at the end of a process.

SWOT analysis An acronym for "strengths, weaknesses, opportunities, threats"; during this component of a strategic plan, participants brainstorm all of the factors, both positive and negative, that will affect the potential success of the plan they are developing.

synchronous A method of instructional delivery that occurs at the same time, although typically not in the same place.

synchronous communication A method of communicating in which the participants interact at the same (or in real) time.

systems approach A model that specifies a methodical approach to the analysis and design of instruction, including a statement of observable learning objectives and the use of a systematic process that includes the specific evaluation techniques and instructional experiences.

Tablet PC A personal computer that is similar in size to a traditional laptop, but allows the user to write on the surface of the screen with a stylus "pen." The text is then converted into a word processing or graphics file.

talking book A dramatization of a play or the recorded reading of a book, play, or short stories usually recorded on cassette tape or CD-ROM.

TCP/IP The agreed-on transmission protocol that is used on the Internet and on networks so that communications between diverse computers can be understood.

Teacher Licensure/certification Professional standards requiring educators to demonstrate specific skill and knowledge proficiencies in teaching. Certification standards are determined by each state's Department of Education.

teaching strategies The techniques or methods a teacher uses to present information to students. The teaching strategies can take student learning styles into account by providing different approaches to the same topic.

teaching style Typically, a teacher's personal preferences as to how to teach, frequently influenced by the way the teacher previously found effective for his or her own learning.

technical support Support personnel for distance or alternative delivery systems who are available when systems fail and/or who provide technical assistance to users so that instructional delivery can continue.

technologists Those whose primary responsibilities relate to the management of equipment, or educational technology.

telecommunication Electronic communication between computers via telephone lines.

telephone Traditional synchronous voice technology that allows two people to communicate orally via phone lines.

telephony The transmission of sounds between widely removed points with or without connecting wires. Telephony with computers uses the speakers and microphone of two or more computers connected to the Internet to transmit audio conversation across the Internet.

template A document that has been preformatted for a specific use but contains no data.

terrestrial A land-based component of a video broadcast system.

test generator Software that creates tests by either randomly selecting questions within the database of questions or allowing the user to select the questions to be included.

theories Scientists' statements of their beliefs about an event or a cause usually supported by a large amount of experimental or observational evidence.

Theory of Multiple Intelligences Howard Gardner theorized that each individual has multiple types of intelligences, only a few of which can be measured by IQ tests. These intelligences (or talents) include the verbal-linguistic, mathematical-logical, musical, visual-spatial, bodily-kinesthetic, interpersonal, intrapersonal, naturalistic, and existential intelligences.

time-lapse video Video whose playback has been sped up to give the appearance of altering time so that what may have taken days to occur can be viewed in the space of a few minutes.

touch screen A monitor that has a light-sensitive screen and software that interprets an interruption to the light on a specific spot on the screen as a command to select the icon or option that is displayed on that spot.

transparency A visual created on a thin sheet of clear acetate for projection on an overhead projector.

tutorial software Software that presents new content with an opportunity to review and practice it; frequently, it also provides additional content or appropriate correction depending on student responses.

twisted-pair wire An inexpensive, flexible type of cable similar to telephone wire that is made up of a pair of copper wires twisted around each other.

uniform resource locator (URL) The address for a web page (the designation for a specific location) on the World Wide Web; the most common type of URL typically begins with "http://www" followed by a web site's domain name.

unity The elements of a visual in which the components work together to help focus the viewer's attention.

uplink A data link by which signals are transmitted from a terrestrial system to a satellite so that they can be bounced back down to another point on the globe.

upload To transfer data from a microcomputer to a remote computer, typically one that is connected to the Internet.

URL (uniform resource locator) The addresses for a web pages (designations for a specific location) on the World Wide Web. A URL typically begins with "http://www" and then a domain name.

usenet A collection of thousands of newsgroups.

utility program Specialized programs that manage, improve, or oversee computer operations.

VHS tape A relatively inexpensive type of magnetic recording tape that can contain up to 120 minutes of recording at the standard playing speed (SP) or up to six or eight hours at slower speeds.

video camera recorder A camera that records sound and images on magnetic tape that can be played back by using a VCR. Also called a camcorder (camera and recorder).

video capture card A component that can be added to a computer to allow for the conversion of traditional analog video into its digital equivalent.

video disc Eight- or twelve-inch optical discs that are made and played by using laser technology similar to that used for CDs; a recording medium that was developed to provide a higher quality of image and sound than videotape provides.

video study guide A study guide that accompanies a video and usually provides the viewer with a series of brief questions on key ideas presented in the same sequence as that in which they are presented in the video.

videocassette recorder (VCR) A type of recorder that uses a VHS magnetic tape for recording moving images and can also record video as it is being transmitted for delayed playback. Prerecorded tapes can be played in class and stopped for discussion when desired.

videoconferencing A combination of software and hardware that enables users at either end of a synchronous connection not only to hear each other, but to see video images of each other as well. The audio and video may be transmitted over the Internet via ISDN or regular phone lines by being compressed at the sending end and decompressed at the receiving end.

virtual environments Fully rendered three-dimensional representations of real or imagined environments that allow the user to become fully immersed in the system.

virtual reality (VR) A combination of hardware and/or software that together create a three-dimensional digital environment with which the user can interact.

virus A program written specifically to disrupt computer operation and/or destroy data.

visual Any combination of text or images, projected or not projected, that is used for illustration or demonstration.

visual communication Encoding and decoding information so that a message is communicated through visual elements.

visual literacy A type of literacy that enables the viewer to accurately interpret the visuals necessary for functioning effectively in our society.

voice mail Asynchronous voice recording technology that allows teachers and students to leave each other messages even when none of the participants are available to communicate via phone at the same time.

voice technology Technology that enables the computer to accept voice commands and dictation of data.

WAV file The digital version of analog audio. WAV files maintain the quality of the original sound, but the file size is often very large.

web authoring tools Software tools that automatically generate HTML code, making it reasonably easy to create a web site.

web hosting A service by which the user can upload the pages of a web site to the web host server, usually via an FTP program, which then makes the site available on the web; such services can be free or charge a monthly or annual fee.

web page A document written in HTML that displays information for use on the web and may contain a series of hyperlinks to other resources on the web.

web site A collection of related web pages.

what-if analysis A capability of spreadsheets that allows the user to ask a "what-if?" question and then change the value in one or more cells to see how those changes will affect the outcome.

whiteboard A slick, white surface on which a variety of specially formulated dry-erasable colored markers can be used. Whiteboards also provide a flat surface on which self-stick flip chart sheets can be hung. Additionally, some whiteboards have a metal backing that will support magnetic displays.

wide area network (WAN) Networks that connect machines across a wide area, such as all of the schools in a district or all of the districts in a state.

Windows The operating system software for some types of personal computers that tells the computer how to work. It is primarily a graphical user interface but also includes typed-in (text) commands, choices from preset menus, and icons.

wireless devices Devices that use wireless communications technology (e.g., microwave) to send and receive voice and digital data.

wireless network A network in which information is transmitted via infrared, radio wave, or microwave technology rather than through wires.

wireless networking Networking technologies and configurations that allow for connections between computer workstations and a server without cabling.

wizard A miniprogram that creates a customized template according to the user's instructions.

word-processing software Software that is used for text-oriented tasks such as creating, editing, and printing documents. It has all but replaced typewriters.

workstation An intelligent terminal or personal computer that is connected to a computer network.

World Wide Web The part of the Internet that uses a graphical user interface and hypertext links between different addresses to allow easier navigation from one site of interest to another.

WYSIWYG ("What You See Is What You Get") A feature of many word-processing and web-authoring programs that allows the user to preview a document and see exactly what it will look like before it is printed out or put on the web.

REFERENCES

Abaya, B. 2000. Brisbane. Retrieved September 2, 2000, from www.wested.org/tie/dlrn/k12de.html.

Abdullah, M. H. 1998. Guidelines for evaluating web sites. Eric Digest. Retrieved May 12, 2002, from www.ed.gov. databases/ERIC_Digests/ed426440.html.

Acceptable Use Policies: Bangor, Michigan Public Schools/ Bangor Computer Network. 2001. Retrieved July 31, 2001, from www.bangorvikings.org/BTS/aup.

Acceptable Use Policies—A handbook. 2001. Retrieved June 21, 2001, from www.pen.k12.va.us/go/VDOE/Technology/AUP/ home.shtml.

Acceptable Use Policy: Bellingham, Washington Schools. 2001. Retrieved July 31, 2001, from www.rice.edu/armadillo/ About/bellingham.html.

Accessing challenging math curriculum. 2003. Retrieved June 22, 2003, from http://www.ldonline.org/ld_indepth-technology/opening_the_door_mike.html.

AECT home page. Retrieved March 22, 1999, from www. aect.org.

AECT. 1994. Instructional Technology: The Definition and Domains of the Field. Bloomington, IN: AECT.

Alliance for Technology Access. 2002. Retrieved April 20, 2002 from http://ataccess.og/community/successes/ successes.html.

American Montessori Society. n.d. The Montessori method of education. Retrieved May 18, 2001, from www.amshq.org.

American Psychological Association. 1997. *Publication manual of the American Psychological Association,* 4th ed. Washington, DC: American Psychological Association.

Andrews, J. F., & Jordan, D. L. 1998. Multimedia stories for deaf children. *Teaching Exceptional Children* (May/June): 29.

Andrews, K., & Marshall, K. 2000. Making learning connections through telelearning. *Educational Leadership* 58(October): 53–56.

Archambault, R. D. ed. 1974. *John Dewey in education.* Chicago: University of Chicago.

Artificial intelligence (AI). 2001. Retrieved June 26, 2001, from www.britannica.com/original?content_id=1209.

ASPIN: Innovative K–12 Connectivity with CATV: Enhancing math and science through technology. 2001. Retrieved June 27, 2001, from http://aspin.asu.edu/projects/catv.

Association for Supervision and Curriculum Development. 1995. *Constructivism: Facilitator's guide.* Alexandria, VA: Association for Supervision and Curriculum Development.

Ausubel, D. P., J. D. Novak, & H. Hanesian. 1978. *Educational psychology: A cognitive view.* 2nd ed. New York: Holt, Rinehart & Winston.

Banathy, B. H. 1995. Developing a systems view of education. *Educational Technology* 35:55.

Bandura, A. 1971. Analysis of modeling processes. In *Psychological modeling: Conflicting theories* (pp. 1–62), edited by A. Bandura. Chicago: Aldine Atherton.

Bandura, A. 1976. *Social learning theory.* Englewood Cliffs, NJ: Prentice-Hall.

Barlow, J. A. 1963. Programmed instruction in perspective: Yesterday, today, and tomorrow. In *Prospectus in programming: Proceedings of the 1962 Center for Programmed Instruction,* edited by R. T. Filer. New York: Macmillan.

Barrios, B. 2002. The subtle knife: Blog*diss: Blogs in the classroom. Retrieved May 8, 2003, from http://www. barclaybarrios.com/tsk/blog/classroom.html.

Bates, A. W. 1995. Technology, open learning and distance education (London: Routledge). Retrieved December 27, 2000, from www.ed.gov/databases/ERIC_Digests/ed395214.html.

BBC Online. 2000. Audio/video: The best of BBC in sound and pictures. Retrieved July 6, 2000, from www.bbc.co.uk/ audiovideo.

Behrmann, M. M. 1998. Assistive technology for young children in special education. In *Learning with technology: ASCD yearbook 1998* (p. 90), edited by C. Dede. Alexandria, VA: Association for Supervision and Curriculum Development.

Berlo, D. K., & Reiser, R. A. 1987. Instructional technology: A history. In *Instructional technology: Foundations* (p. 16), edited by R. M. Gagné. Hillsdale, NJ: Erlbaum.

Bernard, J. Cotter High School's virtual school. Retrieved April 15, 2000, from www.rrr.net.

Bloom, B. 1956. *Taxonomy of educational objectives: The classification of educational goals,* 1st ed. New York: David McKay.

Bloom's taxonomy. Learning Skills Program. Retrieved May 8, 1999, from www.coun.vic.ca/learn/program/hndouts/ bloom.html.

Boerner, G. 1999. Videoconferencing skills to maximize student learning. *School Executive* (January/February): 6–7.

Boettcher, J.V. 2001. The spirit of invention: Edging our way to 21st century teaching. *Syllabus* (June): 14, 10–11.

Bogue, B. 2003. Spokane Public Schools. Retrieved October 3, 2003, from http://www.palmone.com/us/education/studies/ study53.html.

Bolton, T. Cognitive flexibility theory. Retrieved April 21, 1999, http://alcor.concordia.ca?~tbolton/edcomp/mod10b.html.

Bolze, S. 1998. Spin city. *Instructor* 108(November/December): 20.

Boyce, A. 2002. Using cars to build Internet search skills. Retrieved January 10, 2002, from http://www.nea.org/cet/ wired/index.html.

Brangwin, N. 1999. Carmen Sandiego: A fifth-grader discovers a special tutor. Retrieved December 4, 1999, from www.techlearning.com/db_area/archives/WCE/archives/ brangwin.htm.

Brewer, W. R., & Kallick, B. 1996. Technology's promise for reporting student learning. In *Communicating student learning: ASCD yearbook 1996* (pp. 181–182), edited by T. R. Guskey. Alexandria, VA: Association for Supervision and Curriculum Development.

Bruner, J. S. 1962. *On knowing.* Cambridge, MA: Harvard University Press.

Bruner, J. S. 1966. *Toward a theory of instruction.* Cambridge, MA: Harvard University Press.

Bruner, J. S. 1969. *The relevance of education.* New York: W. W. Norton.

Bump, K. 2000. Creating healthy classrooms. *Classroom Leadership* 3(6), 7.

Burton, Mrs. 2003. KinderKonnect web page. Retrieved November 2, 2003, from http://www.kinderkonnect.com.

Butler, M. 1994. *How to use the Internet.* Emeryville, CA: Ziff-Davis Press.

Butler, S. 2002. Project Groundhog. Retrieved January 5, 2003, from http://www.ciconline.com/Enrichment/Teaching/learningwithtechnology/expertadvice/default.htm.

Cain, C. 1999. Networking classroom workstations. *School Executive* (November/December): 8.

Caine, R., & Caine, G. 1994. *Making connections: Teaching and the human brain.* New York: Addison-Wesley.

Caine, R., & Caine, G. 2000. Brain/mind learning principles. Retrieved July 9, 2000, from www.cainelearning.com/bbl/bbl2.htm.

Campbell, R. 2000. Leadership: Getting it done. Retrieved July 4, 2000, from www.ssu.missouri.edu/faculty/Rcampbell/Leadership/chapter6.htm.

Campion, C., & Mizell, A. P. 1999. SAXophone events [and] SAXophone schools. Retrieved July 31, 1999, from www.mhrcc.org/sax/saxevent.html and www.mhrcc.org/sax/saxskool.html.

Cannings, T. & Finkel, L. 1993. *The technology age classroom.* Wilsonville, OR: Franklin, Beedle, and Associates.

Certification requirements for the 50 states. University of Kentucky College of Education. Retrieved August 30, 2006 http://www.uky.edu/Education/TEP/usacert.html.

Civello, C. 1999. "Move over, please": The decentralization of the teacher in the computer-based classroom. *English Journal* (March): 92–94.

Clark, S. 2002. #2556. Cars. Retrieved May 20, 2003, from http://www.teachers.net/lessons/posts/2566.html.

Collaborative for Technology Standards for School Administrators. Retrieved August 31, 2006 http://cnets.iste.org/tssa/pdf/tssa.pdf.

Compressed video for instruction: Operations and applications. Washington, DC: Association for Educational Communications and Technology.

The Computer Ethics Institute. The Ten Commandments for Computer Ethics. Retrieved August 27, 2002, from http://www.brook.edu/its/cei/cei_hp.htm.

Conley, E. 2003. Movie night. Retrieved June 2, 2003, from http://www.nea.org/helpfrom/growing/works4me/tech/equip.html.

Cronin, G. 1999. Running a business. Retrieved August 7, 1999, from www.teachers.net/lessons/posts/1004.html.

Cross, K. P., & Angelo, T. A. 1998. *Classroom assessment techniques: A handbook for faculty.* Ann Arbor, MI: The University of Michigan.

Crotty, T. 2000. Constructivist theory unites distance learning and teacher education. Retrieved August 11, 2000, from http://edie.cprost.sfu.ca/it/constructivistlearning and www.hseidensticker.de/476.htm.

Crowder, N. A. 1963. A theorem in number theory [Presentation]. Intrinsic programming: Facts, fallacies, and future. In *Prospectus in programming: Proceedings of the 1962 Center for Programmed Instruction* (pp. 90–92), edited by R. T. Filer. New York: Macmillan.

Cyrs, T. E. 1976. Modular approach in curriculum design using the systems approach. In *Instructional media and technology: A professional's resource* (pp. 115–121), edited by P. J. Sleeman & D. M. Rockwell. Stroudsburg, PA: Dowden, Hutchinson, & Ross.

Davidson, H. 1999. The educators' lean and mean no-fat guide to fair use. *Technology & Learning* 20(September): 58–60, 62, 66.

Davidson, K. 1998. Education on the Internet: Linking theory to reality. Retrieved January 5, 2000, from www.oise.ca/~kdavidson/cons.html. Also in Mergel, B. 1998. Instructional design & learning theory. Retrieved January 8, 2000, from www.usask.ca/education/coursework/802papers/mergel/brenda.htm.

Davis, A. 2003. Elementary writers learn to love their weblogs. Retrieved October 31, 2003, from http://www97.intel.com/education/odyssey/day_300/day_300.htm.

Davis, D. 2002. Using assistive technology to help students write. *Media & Methods* (September/October) 39 (1), 14.

Debate over copyright protection in the Digital Age. Retrieved May 10, 2002, from http://groton.k12.ct.us/mts/eg15.htm.

Dede, C. 1995. The evolution of learning devices: Smart objects, information infrastructures, and shared synthetic environments. The Future of Networking Technologies for Learning. Retrieved June 12, 2001, from www.ed.gov/Technology/Futures/index.html.

Dede, C. 1996. Emerging technologies in distance education for business. Retrieved December 27, 2000, from www.ed.gov/databases/ERIC_Digests/ed395214.html.

Dede, C. 2000. Emerging technologies and distributed learning in higher education. Retrieved December 27, 2000, from http://virtual.gmu.edu/SS_research/cdpapers/index.htm.

DeKorne, C., & T. Y. Chin. 2002. Links to the missing: Exploring how technology is used in locating missing persons. Retrieved May 4, 2002, from http://www.nytimes.com/learning/teachers/lessons/20020425thursday_print.html.

Delisio, E. R. 2002. Research at the river links two schools. Retrieved April 3, 2003, from http://www.education-world.com/a_tech/tech122.shtml.

Denofrio, S. 1999. Technology notebook. *Instructor* 108(April): n.p.

Dewey, J. 1944. *Democracy and education.* New York: Macmillan.

Dewey, J. 1998. My pedagogic creed. In *Kaleidoscope: Readings in education* (pp. 280–285), edited by K. Ryan & J. Cooper. Boston: Houghton Mifflin. [Original work published in 1899.]

Diamant, R., & Bearison, D. 1991. Development of formal reasoning during successive peer interactions. *Developmental Psychology* 27: 277–284.

Diamond, J. 1999. [Abuzz question]. Retrieved September 20, 1999, from http://questions.nytimes.com.

Diaz, C. J. 2001. [No title]. Retrieved January 9, 2001, from www.nea.org/cet/wired/index.html.

Dickman, J. 2000. A student perspective. *Curriculum/Technology Quarterly* 9(Spring): 1–2.

Dodd, J. 2000. Music & MP3. *PC Tricks* 6: 95–98.

Dodge, P. 2002. Fixing grammar with technology. Retrieved February 13, 2003, from http://www.teachers.net/lessons/posts/2584.html.

Dodson, J. 1999. Using electronic sketchbooks in the classroom. *Media & Methods* (March/April): 10.

Donahue, B. 2000. Brenda Donahue's class: Centennial Education Center, Santa Ana, CA. Retrieved December 27, 2000, from www.otan.dni.us/webfarm/emailproject/cec.htm.

Drucker, P. 1999. Beyond the information revolution. *Atlantic Monthly* 284(October): 54, 57.

Dudzik, J. 1999. A marriage made in heaven. *Instructor* (September): 16.

Dudzik, J. 1999. E-pals. *Instructor* 109(October): 73.

Dudzik, J. 1999. Technology notebook. *Instructor* 108(April): n.p.

Duffy, M. 1999, June. [Interview].

Dunn, R. 1999. How do we teach them if we don't know how they learn? *Teaching K–8* 29(7), 50–52.

Dunn, R., & Dunn, K. 1992. *Teaching elementary students through their individual learning styles.* Boston: Allyn & Bacon.

Dunn, R., & Greggs, S. A. 1988. *Learning styles: Quiet revolution in American secondary schools.* Reston, VA: National Association of Secondary School Principals.

Dunn, R., Krimsky, J. S., Murray, J. B., & Quinn, P. J. 1985. Light up their lives: A review of research on the effects of lighting in children's achievement and behavior. *The Reading Teacher* 38: 863–869.

Dwight, V. 1998. [no title]. *Family PC* (September): 60.

Eagle Eye News. 2002. Retrieved May 15, 2002, from http://www.sisd.k12.ak.us/content/schools/pa/news%20letter/webmake.html.

Edling, J. V., Hamreus, D. G., Schalock, H. D., Beaird, J. H., Paulson, C. F., & Crawford, J. (1972). *The cognitive domain.* Washington, DC: Gryphon House.

Educational computing: How are we doing? 1997. Retrieved February 17, 1999, from www.thejournal.com/magazine/97/jun/feature4.html.

Educational standards, what are they? Retrieved August 25, 2006 http://www.education-world.com/standards/national/index.shtml.

Fairhurst, A. M., & Fairhurst, L. L. 1995. *Effective teaching effective learning: Making the personality connection in your classroom.* Palo Alto, CA: Davies-Black.

Felder, R. M., & Soloman, B. A. Learning styles and strategies. Retrieved April 22, 1999, from www.crc4mse.org/ILS/ILS_explained.html.

Filipczak, B. 1995. Putting the learning in distance learning. Retrieved December 27, 2000, from www.ed.gov/databases/ERIC_Digests/ed395214.html.

FitzRoy, M. 2003, Sept. 6. Newest TV dateline: Landrum classroom. Retrieved September 8, 2003, from http://cgi.jacksonville.com.

Fry, E. 2003. Rural schools look to online courses. Juneau Express (June 25). Retrieved July 1, 2003, from http://www.juneauempire.com/stories/062503/loc_webschool.shtml.

Future technology. 1999. *PC Magazine* (June 22): 104, 113, 116, 119.

Gagné, R. M. 1985. *The conditions of learning.* 4th ed. New York: Holt, Rinehart & Winston.

Gagné, R. M., Briggs, L. J., & Wager, W. W. 1988. *Principles of instructional design,* 3rd ed. New York: Holt, Rinehart & Winston.

Garden State Pops Youth Orchestra. 1997. Learn and hear about different instruments. Retrieved July 6, 2000, from www.gspyo.com/education/html/instr-intro.html.

Gardner, H. 1988. Mobilizing resources for individual-centered education. In *Technology in education: Looking toward 2020,* edited by R. S. Nicerson & P. P. Zodihiates. Hillsdale, NJ: Erlbaum.

Gardner, H. 1993. *Multiple intelligences: The theory in practice (a reader).* New York: Basic Books.

Gardner, H. 1999. A multiplicity of intelligences. *Scientific American* 9(Winter): 23.

Gardner, H. 1999. *Intelligence reframed: Multiple intelligences for the 21st century.* New York: Basic Books.

Gardner, H. 1999. Who owns intelligence? *The Atlantic Monthly* 283(February): 67–76.

Gates, B., October 28, 1999, Microsoft Corporation, Speech at the New York Institute of Technology, New York, NY. Retrieved May 5, 2002, from www.microsoft.com/billgates/speeches/10-28genl.asp.

Gazin, A. 2000. Focus on autobiography. *Instructor* 109 (January/February): 49.

Gold Ridge Elementary School web site. Retrieved November 2, 2003, from http://www.sonic.net/kargo/parent.htm.

Goldberg, L. 2002. Web pages to the rescue. *Instructor* (August), 112 (1), 27–28, 78.

Gore, A. 1998. Speech to the 15th International ITU Conference, October 12.

Guenter, C. 2003. Student teaching electronic portfolio. Retrieved October 5, 2003, from http://www.csuchico.edu/educ/estport.htm.

Guerriero, A. 1999. [Abuzz question]. Retrieved September 22, 1999, http://questions.nytimes.com.

Guerriero, A. 1999. [Abuzz question]. Retrieved September 28, 1999, http://questions.nytimes.com.

Hackbarth, S. 1996. *The educational technology handbook: A comprehensive guide.* Englewood Cliffs, NJ: Educational Technology Publications.

Hakes, B. T., Cochenour, J. J., Rezabek, L. L., & Sachs, S. G. 1995.

Hardy, D. W. 2000. Algebra across the wire. Retrieved September 2, 2000, from http://wested.org/tie/dlrn/k12de.html.

Harper, G. 1998. Fair use guidelines for educational multimedia: The Copyright Act of 1976, as amended. Updated August 4, 1998. Retrieved July 19, 2000, from www.utsystem.edu/OGC/IntellectualProperty/ccmcquid.htm.

Harris, J. 1998. *Design tools for the Internet-supported classroom.* Alexandria, VA: Association for Supervision and Curriculum Development.

Harris, S. L. 1995. *The relationship between learning theory and curriculum development.* Unpublished manuscript, Florida International University at Miami, Florida.

Harrison, C. 2002. The WKEY Morning News. *Learning & Leading with Technology* (October), 30 (2), 40–43.

Harrison, J. L. 1999. [AT&T's virtual classroom]. Retrieved October 29, 1999, from www.nea.org/cet/wired/index.html.

Harrison, S. 2000. TEAMS distance learning. Retrieved August 9, 2000, from www.nea.org/cet/wired/index.html.

Heese, V. 1999. [No title]. Retrieved November 6, 1999, from www.techlearning.com/db_area_archives/WCE/archives/heese.htm.

Heese, V. 1999. Simple methods of integrating technology into primary classrooms. Retrieved November 5, 1999, from www.techlearning.com/db_area/archives/WCE/archives/heesepri.htm.

Heimdal, J. 2001. Rates on your life insurance go up last month? Retrieved January 10, 2002, from http://www.lesson-planspage.com/printables/PCIOMDDevFamilyBudgetOnSpreadsheet812.html.

Higgins, K. J. 1999. School system broadcasts video with ATM/LANE. *Network Computing* 10(7): 72.

Hill, B. 1998. Senior project. Retrieved December 22, 1998, from www.intel.com/education/technology/mec/case_studies.htm.

Hirsch, S. 1999. A comparative study: San Diego, California, and Biarritz, France. Retrieved July 26, 1999, from www.edweb.sdsu.edu/triton/SDBiarritz/SDBiarritzUnit.html.

Hirschbuhl, J. J. (Ed). 1998. *Computers in education.* Guilford, CT: Dushkin.

History of inventions. 2001. Retrieved June 26, 2001, from www.cbc4kids.ca/general/the-lab/history-of-invention/calendar.html.

History pen pals. 2002. Retrieved April 10, 2003, from http://www.nea.org/helpfrom/growing/works4me/tech/techclas.html.

Hoban, C. F., Sr., Hoban, C. F., Jr., & Zissman, S. B. 1937. *Visualizing the curriculum.* New York: The H. W. Wilson Co.

Hoffman, E. 1999. The dark side of the Internet: Controls of student access. *Syllabus: High School Edition* 1(1): 14–16.

Hofstetter, F. T., & Fox, P. 1997. *Multimedia literacy.* New York: McGraw-Hill.

Holloway, J. H. 2000. The digital divide. *Educational Leadership* 58(2): 90.

Holzberg, C. 2001. Yes, you can build a web site. *Instructor* 110(May/June): 62.

Hudson, M. & A. Cooley. 2003. Digital video camera use in classrooms. *Media & Methods* (February), 39 (4), 6.

Hughes, S. 2002. Cutting costs. Retrieved April 10, 2003, from http://www.nea.org/helpfrom/growing/works4me/tech/technclas.html.

Huitt, W. 1998. Bloom et al.'s taxonomy of the cognitive domain. Educational psychology interactive: The cognitive domain. Retrieved January 24, 2000, from www.valdosta.peachnet.edu/~whuitt/psy702/cogsys/bloom/html.

Hunt, M. 1993. *The story of psychology.* New York: Doubleday.

Huschak, I. H. 1999. Digital archaeology: Uncovering a city's past. Retrieved May 12, 2000, from http://techlearning.com/db_area/archives/WCE/archives/huschak.htm.

A Hypertext History of Instructional Design. Retrieved October 3, 2003, from http://www.coe.uh.edu/courses/cuin6373/idhistory/index.html.

Ideas for using video conferencing in the classroom. 2003. Retrieved June 13, 2003, from http://k-12.pisd.edu/distance_learning/uses.htm.

IDG. 1995. *Internet and the World Wide Web.* Foster City, CA: International Data Group Company.

Indiana's K-12 Plan for Technology. Retrieved August 30, 2006 http://www.doe.state.in.us/olr/techplan/.

Instructional event with lesson activity. Retrieved August 2, 1999, from www.seas/gwu.edu/sbraxton/ISD/GIFS/lesson_gagne.gif.

Integration via a browser-based intranet. 2002. Retrieved June 11, 2003, from http://www.nps.k12.va.us/infodiv/it/techconf/integbrw.htm.

The International Society for Technology in Education. 2000. *ISTE National Educational Technology Standards for Teachers.* Eugene, OR: ISTE.

The International Society for Technology in Education (ISTE). Retrieved August 25, 2006 from http://www.iste.org.

James, S. 2003. One digital future. Retrieved November 9, 2003, from http://www.ldresources.com/articles/one_digital_future.html.

Jarvinen, E. M. 1988. The Lego/logo learning environment in technology education: An experiment in a Finnish context. *Journal of Technology Education* 9. Retrieved June 5, 1999, from http://scholar.lib.ft.edu/ejournals/JTE/v9n2/jrvinen.html.

Johnson, E. 1998. Making geography come alive with technology. *Media & Methods* (March/April): 14–16.

Johnson, S. R., & Johnson, R. B. 1971. *Assuring learning with self-instructional packages, or up the up staircase.* Chapel Hill, NC: Self-Instructional Packages.

Jung, C. G. 1990. *Psychological types.* Rev. ed., translated by H. G. Baynes. Princeton, NJ: Princeton University Press.

Kekkonen-Moneta, S., & G. Moneta. 2001. E-learning in Hong Kong: Comparing learning outcomes in online multimedia and lecture versions of an introductory computing course. *British Journal of Educational Technology,* 33 (4), 2002, 423–433.

Kelly, E. J., & Partin, R. M. 1999. Mexico City earthquake. Retrieved August 17, 1999, from http://nardac.mip.berkeley.edu/tmp/browse_equis_res_14284.3html.

Kemp, J. E., & Smellie, D. C. 1989. *Planning, producing, and using instructional media.* New York: Harper & Row.

Kerka, S. 1996. Distance learning, the Internet, and the World Wide Web. ERIC Digest. Retrieved December 27, 2000, from www.ed.hov/databases/ERIC_Digests/ed395214.html.

Kinzie, M., Strauss, R., & Foss, J. 1994. Interactive frog dissection: An on-line tutorial. Retrieved December 26, 2000, from http://curry.edschool.virginia.edu/go/frog.

Knapps, K. J. 2000. Art and life in Africa project. Retrieved June 15, 2000, from www.uiowa.edu/~africart/teachers/lessons/036.html.

Kozma, R., & Schank, P. 1998. Connecting with the 21st century: Technology in support of educational reform. In *ASCD Yearbook 1998* (pp. 73–74), edited by C. Dede. Alexandria, VA: Association for Curriculum and Development.

Krech, B. 1999. Show, don't tell. *Instructor* (October): n.p.

Kriwox, J. 2003. Quilting and geometry-patterns for living. Retrieved October 5, 2003, from http://ali.apple.com/ali_sites/deli/exhibits/1000077.

Krug, C. 1999. Video editing techniques in schools. *Media & Methods* (May/June): 55–56.

Kultgen, S. 1999. Computer portfolios. *Arts and Activities* (May): 20–21.

Laird, L. (1999). NEA CET: Wired classroom. Retrieved January 5, 2000, from www.nea.org/cet/wired/index.html.

Landon, A. 2003. How do you measure up? Retrieved October 4, 2003, from http://pegasus.cc.ucf.edu/~ucfcasio/measure.htm.

Laurino, B. 1999. Using chunks from class readers. Retrieved July 5, 2000, from www.ncte.org/teach/Laurino14954.html.

Le, P. 2003, September 16. Online coursework appeals to teenagers. Retrieved September 18, 2003, from http://www.indystar.com/print/articles/9/074716-3989-P.html.

LEARN NC. 2003, March. Student teachers and high school seniors beam the Internet. Retrieved April 2, 2003, from http://www.learnnc.org/Index.nsf/printView.

Learning styles. 1998. Retrieved August 15, 1999, from www.funderstanding.com/learning_theory_how6.html.

Lee, J. 1998. Web-based instruction. Retrieved January 28, 2000, from http://www.dsmt.org/exlee.

Lee, P. 1999. Tech learning. Retrieved December 15, 1999, from www.techlearning.com/db_area_archives/WCE/archives/paulalee.htm.

Lehmann, K. 1998. Travel and tour guide unit. In Wired Classroom: Etools Weekly Tip. National Education Association. Retrieved December 30, 1998, from www.nea.org/cet/wired/.

Leo, L. 1999. Picture perfect lessons. *Instructor* (March): 80–81.

Lever-Duffy, J. (2000). The evolution of distance education (pp. 251–274). In *Taking a big picture look at technology, learning, and the community college,* edited by Mark Milliron & Cindy Miles. Mission Viejo, CA: League for Innovation in the Community College.

Lewis, A. 2001. Sell yourself. Retrieved May 15, 2001, from www.successlink.org/great/g163.html.

Lopez, A. M., Jr., & Donlon, J. 2001. Knowledge engineering and education. *Educational Technology* 41(2): 45–50.

Lopez, W. J. 2003, August. Content delivery for a virtual high school. *T.H.E. Journal,* 31 (1), 32.

Lutkenhaus, K. 2000. [E-mail]. Retrieved March 4, 2000, from www.nea.org/cet/wired/index.html.

Mahoney, M. J. 1994. *Human change processes.* New York: Basic Books.

Makled, C. 2002. Pilot program: Paddock project to aid in reading assessment. Retrieved May 21, 2003, from http://www.wirelessgeneration.com/web/print_milan.html (reprint from the *Milan News-Leader,* April 18, 2002).

Maple Lake School District: 1998. Acceptable use policy on district provided access to electronic information, services, and networks. Retrieved June 27, 2001, from http://www.maplelake.k12.mn.us/districtinfo/AUP.html.

Maran, R. 1998. *Computers Simplified,* 4th ed. Foster City, CA: IDG Books.

March, T. 2003. Eyes on art. Retrieved May 6, 2003, from http://www.kn.pacbell.com/wired/art2/guide/guide.html.

Martin, C. R. 2002. Looking at type: The fundamentals. Retrieved March 22, 2002, from www.knowyourtype.com/enfp.html.

Martin, S. 2000. Greece and Rome: A CBT project. Retrieved August 2, 2000, from www.techlearning.com/db_area/archives/WCE/archives.smartin.htm.

Maryland digital schools project: Field trips and interactives. 2003. Retrieved July 1, 2003, from http://www.thinkport.org/classroom/oftinteractive/default.tp.

Mater, J. A. 2001. My dream room. Retrieved May 25, 2001, from www.lessonplanspage.com/CILAPostersWithWord-FormattingGrammar4.8.htm.

Mattingly, L. 1999. Integrating technology in the classroom. Retrieved August 26, 1999, from www.siec.K12.in.us/~west/slides/integrate/sld024.htm.

Maze, B. 1999, May. [Interview].

McDonald, B. 1999, May. [Interview].

McDonald, E. J. B. 1973. The development and evaluation of a set of multi-media self-instructional learning activity packages for use in remedial English at an urban community college (Doctoral dissertation, University of Memphis, 1973). *Dissertation Abstracts International* 34:04A.

McDonald, J. 1996. The paperless composition: Computer-assisted writing. *Innovation Abstracts* XVIII(October 18): n.p.

McGoogan, G. 2002. Around the world in 24 hours. *Educational Leadership* (October), 60 (2), 44–46.

McGowan, K. 1999. [Beehive question]. Retrieved September 28, 1999, from http://questions.nytimes.com.

McKibben, B. 2000. The world streaming in. *The Atlantic Monthly* 286 (July): 78.

McLean, M., & Miller, S. 1997. Importing video stills into computer documents. *Media & Methods* (September/October): 12.

McLuhan, M. 1998. *Understanding media: The extensions of man.* Cambridge, MA: The Massachusetts Institute of Technology Press.

McLuhan, M., & Fiore, Q. 1967. *The medium is the message.* New York: Bantam Books.

McLuhan, M., & Fiore, Q. 1996. *The medium is the message: An inventory of effects,* renewed by J. Agel. San Francisco, CA: HardWired.

Meiers, V. 1999. Into the next millennium. Retrieved August 23, 1999, from http://cnets.iste.org/ss_68_1_done.html.

Mergel, B. 1998. Instructional design & learning theory. Retrieved January 8, 2000, from www.usask.ca/education/coursework/802papers/mergel/brenda.htm.

Merrimack Valley School District. 2001. Acceptable use policy. Retrieved June 27, 2001, from http://www.mv.k12.nh.us/schools/mvms/acceptable_use_ policy.htm.

Michigan's Educational Technology Plan. Retrieved on August 30, 2006 http://www.techplan.org/STP2006 ProposedMar032006.doc

Microsoft in Education: new Teachers Corner. 2000. Lifesavers: How to find your way on the web. Retrieved May 20, 2002, from www.microsoft.com/education.mctn/newteacher/lifesavers/52001saver.asp.

Milici, J. (2003). Foreign studies. Retrieved October 23, 2003, from http://www.nea.org.

Miller, E. B. 1996. *The Internet resource directory.* Englewood, CO: Libraries Unlimited.

Miller, S. 1999. Greece and Rome: A CBT project. Retrieved May 12, 1999, from www.techlearning.com/db_area/archives/WCE/archives/smiller.htm.

Millspaw, E. 1996–1997. Student team designs and maintains internet/intranet web sites. *The High School Magazine* (December/January): 58–59.

Milone, M. 1999. Enterprise computing. *Technology & Learning* 20(September): 31–32.

Milstein, M. 1999. The sound of dinosaurs. Retrieved July 5, 2000, from www.discovery.com/exp/fossilzone/sounds/dinosaurs.html.

Minsky, Marvin. 1988. Papert's principle. Retrieved September 28, 2001, from www.papert.org/articles/PapertsPrinciple.html.

Mir, S. 2002. Art exchange. Retrieved April 10, 2003, from http://www.nea.org/helpfrom/growing/works4me/tech/techclas.html.

Mitchell, L. 1999, April. [Interview]. South Elementary School, Pinson, TN.

Moore, J. Branksome Hall. Retrieved July 15, 1999, from www.branksome.on.ca/main.html.

Moore, K. 1999. *Volcanoes: A multi-media unit for cross-curricular instruction in the junior high school.* Henderson, TN: Chester County Junior High School.

Moore, K. April 1999. [Interview].

Moore, S. 2002. Creating tests with Microsoft Word. *Instructor* (September), 112 (3), 16.

Morgan, A. 1995. Research into student learning in distance education. Victoria, Australia: In Distance education at a glance: Guide #9: Strategies for distance learning, edited by B. Willis. Retrieved November 11, 2000, from http://www.uidaho.edu/evo/dist9.html.

Morris, P. (Developer). 21st century schoolhouse: Lesson plans. Retrieved February 27, 1999, from www.coedu.usf.edu/~morris/acsi_1p2.html.

"Mrs. Claus's Workshop," prepared by Mrs. Slaven's class at Elementary West in Loogootee, Indiana, http://www.siec.k12.in.us.

Multiple intelligences survey. Retrieved September 23, 1999, from http://familyeducation.com/article/print/0,1303, 4-3201.00html?obj_gra.

Murphy, M. 1999. Expanding your classroom. Retrieved July 15, 1999, from www.techlearning.com/db_area/archives/WCE/archives/muggs2.htm.

Murphy, M. 2000. Expanding your classroom. Retrieved February 25, 2000, from http://www.techlearning.com/db_area/archives/WCE/archives/muggs2.htm.

Naisbitt, J. 1982. Megatrends. New York: Warner Communications.

National Board for Professional Teaching Standards. Their mission. Retrieved August 30, 2006 from http://www.nbpts.org/about_us/background/mission

National Education Association. 1996. Technology and portfolio assessment. NEA: Technology Brief No. 4. Retrieved May 5, 2002, from www.nea.org/cet/BRIEFS/brief4.html.

National Educational Technology Standards for Teachers. Retrieved March 29, 2002, from http://cnets.iste.org/pdf/page24–25.pdf.

National Telecommunications and Information Administration. 2000. *Falling through the Net.* Washington, DC: Author.

NCATE and ISTE. Retrieved August 30, 2006. http://cnets.iste.org/ncate/n_unit.html

Negroponte, N. 1996. *Being digital.* New York: Vintage Books/Random House, p. 230.

Nellen, T. (2000). Cyber short stories. Retrieved August 21, 2000, from www.techlearning.com/db_area/archive/WCE/archives/tnellen.htm.

Newport, Stuart (ed). (2005) Largest Computation. *Guiness World Records.* Retrieved October 12, 2006.

Niess, M. 1999. Integrating technology into math instruction. *Media & Methods* (January/February): 26–27.

Nix, D., & Spiro, R. J. (Eds.). 1990. *Cognition, education, and multimedia: Exploring ideas in high technology.* Hillsdale, NJ: Erlbaum.

Norris, B. 2000. [Gaggle.net]. Retrieved January 14, 2000, from www.nea.org/cet/wired/index.html.

Notebloom, R. 2000. One teacher's view. *Curriculum/Technology Quarterly* 9(Spring): 1–2.

Novak, J. D. 2001. The theory underlying concept maps and how to construct them. Retrieved May 5, 2002, from http://cmap.coginst.uwf.edu/info.

Novelli, D., S. Edmunds, & D. Gurwicz. Screen-saver stories. *Instructor* (May/June 2001) 110 (8), 74.

NTTI video utilization strategies. 2002. Retrieved November 30, 2003, from http://www.thirteen.org/edonline/ntti/resources/video2.html.

Nunes-Turcotte, O. 1998, November/December. Electronic learning in your classroom [Project page]. *Instructor,* n.p.

Nunley, K. 2000. How to layer your curriculum. Retrieved July 9, 2000, from www.brains.org/layered.htm.

Ocean in view. 2002. Retrieved May 12, 2003, from http://www97.intel.com/education/odyssey/day_289/day_289.htm.

Office of Technology Assessment. U.S. Congress. 1995. *Teachers and technology: Making the connection.* Washington, DC: U.S. Government Printing Office.

Oh, P. 1999. Back to basics: No-frills, but super, drill-and-practice software. *Instructor* 108(March): 74–76.

Oros, L., Finger, A., & Morenegg, J. 1998, January/February. Creating digital portfolios. *Media & Methods,* 15.

Paivio, A. 2001. Dual coding theory. Retrieved October 4, 2001, from http://tip.psychology.org/paivio.html.

Papert, S. 1992. *The children's machine: Rethinking school in the age of the computer.* New York: Basic Books.

Papert, S. 1999. Papert on Piaget. Retrieved October 5, 2001, from www.papert.org/articles/Papertonpiaget.html.

Papert, S., & Harel, I. 1991. Situating constructionism. Retrieved September 28, 2001, from www.papert.org/articles/SituatingConstrutionism.html.

Parker, R. C. 1988. *Looking good in print.* Chapel Hill, NC: Ventana Press.

Pavlov, I. P. 1927. *Conditioned reflexes.* London: Oxford University Press.

Payton, T. Traveling buddies. Retrieved July 15, 1999, from www.techlearning.com/db_area/archives/WCE/archives/tpayton.html.

Pearson Education Development Group. (2003). Authentic assessment overview. Retrieved October 5, 2003, from http://teachervision.fen.com/lesson-plans/lesson-4911.html.

Peters, T. 1998. *Thriving on chaos: Handbook for management revolution.* New York: Alfred Knopf.

Piaget, J. 1952. *The origins of intelligence in children.* New York: International Universities.

Piaget, J. 1960. *Psychology of intelligence.* Paterson, NJ: Littlefield, Adams, & Co.

Piaget, J. 1970. *Science of education and the psychology of the child,* translated by D. Coltman. New York: Orion.

Piaget, J. 1976. *The grasp of consciousness: Action and concept in the young child,* translated by S. Wedgwood. Cambridge, MA: Harvard University Press.

Picture-perfect lessons. 1999. *Instructor* (March): 80–81.

Platt, P. Projects. Retrieved June 14, 2000, from http://gsh.lightspan.com/pr/_cfm/GetDetail.cfm?plD=593.

Popham, W. J., & Baker, E. L. 1970. *Establishing instructional goals*. Englewood Cliffs, NJ: Prentice-Hall.

Potter, B. 1999. *Parent power: Energizing home-school communication*. Portsmouth, NH: Heinemann.

Price, D. 1999, June. [Interview].

Price, S. D. 2001. Techie teacher takes prize/She gets Thinkquest Fellowship [Cathie Thomley]. *The Commercial Appeal* (February 13): n.p.

Prochelo, D., & Kmiec, B. 1998. Speech with advanced technology. Retrieved January 2, 1999, from www.ncrel.org/cw/availabl.htm.

Pruett, H. 2002. Having students learn basic grammar through technology. Retrieved May 23, 2003, from http://www.techlearning.com/db_area/archives/WCE/archives/hpruett.html.

Rahmani, L. 1973. *Soviet psychology: Philosophical, theoretical, and experiential issues*. New York: International Universities.

Railsback, K. 2001. Peering into the future. *InfoWorld* 22(42): 85–95.

Raskauskas, N. 2000. Interactive sports guides. Retrieved December 29, 2000, from http://henson.austin.apple.com/edres/shlessons/sports.shtml.

Rasmussen, K. 1999. Partners in education: How schools and homeschoolers work together. *Education Update* 41(June): 1–4, 5.

Re: Pido datos biográficos de Benjamin Bloom. I ask Benjamin Bloom's biography. Retrieved August 12, 1999, from www.funderstanding.com/messages/1138.htm.

Recipe for the classroom: 1 ideal computer learning station. 1998. *Children's Software Review* (September/October): 27.

Reed, J., & Woodruff, M. 1995. Videoconferencing: Using videoconferencing technology for teaching. Retrieved December 30, 2000, from http://www.pacbell.com/wired/vidconf/Using.html.

Rehak, M. 1999. Questions for John Ashbery: A child in time. *The New York Times Magazine,* April 4:15.

Reiser, R. A. 1987. Instructional technology. A history. In *Instructional technology: Foundations* (pp.12–20), edited by R. M. Gagné. Hillsdale, NJ: Erlbaum.

Renner-Smith, S. 2002. "Fontastic" idea! *Creative Classroom* (March/April), 26.

Richardson, W. 2003. High school journalists use weblogs to mentor young writers. Retrieved October 31, 2003, from http://www97.intel.com/education/odyssey/day_301/day_301.htm.

Rivera, J. 2002. School on a postcard. Retrieved May 29, 2003, from http://www.ciconline.com/Enrichment/Teaching/learningwithtechnology/expertadvice/default.htm.

Roche, E. 1998. #258. Cooperative learning, technology, science, language. Retrieved August 17, 1999, from www.teachers.net/lessons/posts/258.html.

Rohfield, R. W., & Hiemstra, R. 1995. Moderating discussions in the electronic classroom. Retrieved December 27, 2000, from http://www.ed.gov/databases/ERIC_Digests/ed395214.html.

Roth, M. K. 2003. Palm pilots beaming lessons. Retrieved October 3, 2003, from http://www.pdaed.com/vertical/features/Beaming.xml.

Rowling, D. 1999. Introducing the geometer's sketchpad to the classroom. Retrieved December 16, 1999, from www.techlearning.com/db_area/archives/WCE/archives/rowling.htm.

Royal, K. W. 1999. If you had computers in your classroom, what would you do with them? Retrieved May 12, 1999, from www.techlearning.com/db_area/archives/WCE/archives/royal.htm.

Russell Elementary School. 2001. Wade through the wondrous wetlands. Retrieved May 17, 2001, from http://applecom.

Saettler, P. 1968. A history of instructional technology. New York: McGraw-Hill.

Saettler, P. 1990. *The evolution of American educational technology*. Englewood, CO: Libraries Unlimited.

Sagan, C. 1998. *Billions and billions: Thoughts of life and death at the brink of the millennium*. New York: Ballantine.

Santo, C. 1998. An Internet day. *Family PC* (October): 54.

Santo, C. 1999. The Malverne method. *Family PC* (August): 101.

Santo, C. 1999. The way we were. *Family PC* (May): 119.

Schrock, K. 2000a. The ABCs of web site evaluation. Retrieved May 15, 2002, from www.kathyschrock.net/abcevol/index.htm.

Schrock, K. 2000b. Kathy Schrock's guide for educators. Retrieved May 20, 2002, from http://school.discovery.com/schrockguide/edtools.html.

Seavey, E. 2002. A team approach to oral history. Retrieved February 14, 2003, from http://www.col-ed.org/cur/sst/sst45.text.

Sharer, S. 2000. Videoconferencing and distance learning. *School Executive* (November/December): 6.

Sharp, W. 2001. Becoming a wireless campus: A student initiative. *T.H.E. Journal* 28(10): 60–66.

Shasha, D., & Lazere, C. 1998. *Out of their minds*. New York: Copernicus.

Shelly, G., Cashman, T., Waggoner, G., & Waggoner, W. 1998. *Discovering computers 98: A link to the future*. Cambridge, MA: Course Technologies.

Short, D. D. 1994. *Enhancing instructional effectiveness: A strategic approach*. Norwalk, CT: IBM Higher Education.

Skinner, B. F. 1953. *Science and human behavior*. New York: Macmillan.

Skinner, B. F. 1958. Teaching machines. *Science* 128: 969–977.

Skinner, B. F. 1971. *Beyond freedom and dignity*. New York: Alfred A. Knopf.

Skinner, B. F. 1974. *About behaviorism*. New York: Alfred A. Knopf.

Slaven, K. 1998. Mrs. Claus's workshop. Retrieved November 20, 1998, from www.siec.K12inu;.s./~west/proj/claus/facts1.htm.

Small wires, big learning: A Britannica online success story. 1999. *T.H.E. Journal* (January): 38.

SMART whiteboards. 2002. Retrieved April 20, 2002, from www.smarttech.com/profilees/charyk.asp.

Smith, S., Tyler, J. M., & Benacote, A. Internet supported teaching: Advice from the trenches. Retrieved January 9,

2001, from http://www.usdla.org/ED_magazine/illuniactive/JAN00_Issue/Internet.htm.

Solomon, G. 2000. A home (page) of your own. *Technology & Learning* 20(March): 46.

Sonoma County Department of Education. 2000. Twelve principles for brain-based learning. Retrieved July 9, 2000, from http://talkingpage.org/artic011.html.

Sorrentino, L. 1999. [Abuzz question]. Retrieved September 28, 1999, from http://questions.nytimes.com.

Sprenger, M. 1999. *Learning and memory: The brain in action.* Alexandria, VA: ASCD.

Stanford-Binet intelligence scale. Retrieved September 13, 1999, from www.richmond.edu/~capc/Binetmain.html.

Starr, L. 2000. Meet Bernie Dodge—the Frank Lloyd Wright of learning environments! Retrieved June 1, 2003, from http://www.education-world.com/a_tech/tech020.shtml.

Stein, C., & Driggs, L. 1999. Freedom of the press: Where should it end? Retrieved April 12, 1999, from www.nytimes.com/learning.

Stembor, E. 2000. University of Connecticut. Retrieved September 2, 2000, from http://www.wested.org/tie/dlrn/k12de.html.

Stephens, D. 2000. Timber Ridge Middle School travel brochures. Retrieved April 16, 2000, from www.timberridgemagnet.net/ad/tchpg.htm.

Sternberg, R. J. 1999. How intelligent is intelligence testing? *Scientific American* 9(Winter): 14.

Stetler, J. 2002. Internet exchange concert. Retrieved April 10, 2003, from http://www.nea.org/helpfrom/growing/works4me/tech/techclas.html.

Stowe, E. 1999. [Abuzz question]. Retrieved September 21, 1999, from http://questions.nytimes.com.

Sturgeon, K., & Lemen, D. 2001. Magnolia Elementary School: Policy and leadership. Retrieved June 27, 2001, from http://www.esc6.net/tiftrain.student/magnoliaelem/p1.html.

Suzanne. 2000. Farm sound. Retrieved July 4, 2000, from www.alfy.lycos.com/teachers/teach/lesson_bui/overView.asp?LessonId=95&saveVal=ye.

Submission process for NBPTS. Retrieved August 25, 2006 http://www.nbpts.org/for_candidates/the_portfolio

Sweaty palms, circa 1914. 1998. *The Wall Street Journal,* March 31, p. R8.

Sylvester, R. 1995. A celebration of neurons: *An educator's guide to the human brain.* Alexandria, VA: ASCD.

Tapia, S. T. 2000. Online classes moving into O. C. high schools. Retrieved November 30, 2000, from http://www.ocregister.com/education/online01130.cci.shtml.

Taverna, P., & Hongell, T. 2000. Meet Harriet Tubman: The story of a web site. *Learning and Leading with Technology* 27(March 20): 43–45, 62.

Teaching our youngest: A guide for preschool teachers and child care and family providers: Developing listening and speaking skills. 2002. Retrieved January 27, 2003, from http://www.ed.gov/offices/OESE/teachingouryoungest/developing.html.

Teaching with EPals. 2000. Retrieved May 17, 2002, from www.epals.com/curriculum_connections/index_en.html.

TEAMS distance learning: For all K–12 educators. Retrieved December 26, 2000, from http://teams.lacoe.edu.

Teleconferencing. 1999. Retrieved September 2, 2000, from http://www.wested.org/tie/dlrn/teleconferencing.html.

Tener, M. 2002. Learning with lyrics. *Creative Classroom* (November/December), 17 (3), 27.

The eight intelligences. Retrieved July 29, 1999, from http://familyeducation.com/article/print/0,1303,4-3201,00.html?obj_gra.

The Monster Exchange. 1998. *Family PC* (November): 194.

Thorndike, E. L., & Woodworth, R. S. 1901. Education as science. *Psychological Review* 8:247–261, 384–395, 553–564.

Thorndike, R. L. 1911. *Animal intelligence.* New York: Macmillan.

Tiene, D., & Ingram, A. 2001. *Exploring current issues in educational technology.* New York: McGraw Hill.

Tietz, H. 2002. Savoring expository writing through PowerPoint. Retrieved June 10, 2003, from http://www.techlearning.com/db_area/archives/WCE/archives/htietz.html.

TLC project showrooms: Networking. 2001. Retrieved June 27, 2001, from http://web.nysed.gov/technology/projects/oswegocs.html.

Turner, J. 2000. Cyberschool. Retrieved September 2, 2000, from http://www.wested.org/tie/dlrn/k12de.html.

Turner, M. A. 1999. [No title]. Retrieved April 23, 1999, from www.nea.org/cet/wired/index.html.

U.S. Department of Commerce. 2000. Digital divide. Retrieved June 27, 2001, from http://www.digitaldivide.gov.

U.S. Department of Education. 1994. *Strong families, strong schools: A research base for family involvement in learning from the United States Department of Education.* Washington, DC: U.S. Department of Education.

U.S. Department of Education Office of the Secretary *Benefits of Technology Use.* Retrieved August 25, 2006 http://www.ed.gov/about/offices/list/os/technology/plan/national/benefits.html

U.S. Department of Education Office of the Secretary *Educational Technology Fact Sheet.* Retrieved August 25, 2006 (www.ed.gov/about/offices/ list/os/ technology/facts.html).

Use of NETS by State, Retrieved August 25, 2006 http://cnets.iste.org/docs/States_using_NETS.pdf.

Vaughn, K. 1999. [TeleMath]. Retrieved November 20, 1999, from www.nea.org/cet/wired/index.html.

Velez, L. 2003. Postcards from abroad. Retrieved May 14, 2003, from http://teachersnetwork.org/teachnetnyc/lvelez/postcards.htm.

Video conferencing in Plano ISD. 2003. Retrieved June 13, 2003, from http://k-12.pisd.edu/distance_learning/vidconf.htm.

Vitaska, D. 2002. The new language classroom: Bringing French to the U.S. *Media and Methods* (September/October) 39 (1), 10.

VMSTV 2003. Retrieved August 12, 2003, from http://www.vmstv.com.

Vygotsky, L. S. 1978. *Mind in society: The development of higher psychological processes.* Cambridge, MA: Harvard University Press.

Vygotsky, L. S. 1981. *Thought and language,* translated by E. Hanfmann & G. Vakar. Cambridge, MA: The MIT Press.

Vygotsky, L. S. 1987. *The collected works of L. S. Vygotsky.* Vol. 1. New York: Plenum.

Vygotsky, L. S. 1987. *Thinking and speech,* translated by N. Minck. New York: Plenum.

Wallace, L. 2002. Using projection technology to enhance teaching. *Media & Methods* (September/October), 39 (1), 6.

Watson, J. B. 1962. *Behaviorism.* Chicago: University of Chicago Press.

Weiger, E. 1999. [No title]. Retrieved July 20, 1999, from www.nea.org/cet/wired/index.html.

Wenglinsky, H. 1999. Teacher classroom practices and student performance: How schools can make a difference. Retrieved May 5, 2002, from www.ets.org/research/dload/RIBRR-01-19.pdf.

Wertheimer, M. 1945. *Productive thinking.* New York: Harper.

What to do with digital cameras. 1997. *Media & Methods* (November): 2, 8.

White, R. 1993. *How computers work.* Emeryville, CA: Ziff-Davis Press.

Wilkes, D. 2001. Wireless laptops in the classroom. *Media & Methods* 37(February): 33.

Williams, P. 2000. In-school broadcasting: Capturing the excitement. *Media & Methods* (May/June): 6.

Willig, B. 2000. Schoolwide comprehensive courseware: An update. *Media & Methods* (January/February): 24, 26.

Willis, B. 1995. *Guide #2: Strategies for teaching at a difference and strategies for teaching at a glance; Guide #4: Evaluation for distance educators; Guide #6: Instructional audio; Guide #7; Computers in distance education: Guide #9: Strategies for distance learning; Guide #10: Distance education research; Guide #11: Interactive videoconferencing in distance education.* Retrieved November 11, 2000, from http://www.uidaho.edu/evo.html.

Windschitl, M. 1999. The challenges of sustaining constructivist classroom culture. *Phi Delta Kappan* 80: 751–755.

Wohlert, H. 2000. German by satellite. Retrieved June 17, 2000, from http://www.syllabus.com/casestudies/o.html.

Wolfe, B. 1999. Using technology as a tool for teaching across the curriculum. Retrieved July 15, 1999, from www.techlearning.com/db_area/archives/WCE/archives/bwolfe.htm.

Wood, J. M. 2001. Virtual art, real learning. *Instructor* 110(January/February): 80.

Wood, S. 1998–1999. *Computer projects.* Jackson, TN: Northeast Middle School.

Wrenn, E., S. Udell, & S. Sorensen. 2003. If I were president. Retrieved May 16, 2003, from http://www.apple.com.

Yam, P. 1999. Intelligence considered. *Scientific American* 9(Winter): 12–17.

Yarnell, K. 2002. Intranets: Repositories of school data. *School Executive* (September/October), 39 (1), 28.

Zimbalist, A., & Driggs, L. 1999. Fan(tom) of the opera: Applying the plots of famous operas to modern life: A music genre appreciation lesson. Retrieved September 10, 1999, from http://www.nytimes.com/learning.

Zimbalist, A., & Driggs, L. 1999. When Moore is less for microprocessors: Examining how computer chips work and the Moore's Law prediction: A technology lesson. Retrieved July 1, 1999, from www.nytimes.com/learning.

Zora, D.. 2003. A living alphabet. Retrieved May 16, 2003, from http://www.apple.com.